Linguistik Aktuell/Linguistics Today (LA)

Linguistik Aktuell/Linguistics Today (LA) provides a platform for original monograph studies into synchronic and diachronic linguistics. Studies in LA confront empirical and theoretical problems as these are currently discussed in syntax, semantics, morphology, phonology, and systematic pragmatics with the aim to establish robust empirical generalizations within a universalistic perspective.

General Editors

Volume 120

Syntax and Semantics of Spatial P
Edited by Anna Asbury, Jakub Dotlačil, Berit Gehrke and Rick Nouwen

Syntax and Semantics of Spatial P

Edited by

Anna Asbury

Jakub Dotlačil

Berit Gehrke

Rick Nouwen

Utrecht Institute of Linguistics OTS

John Benjamins Publishing Company

Amsterdam / Philadelphia

The paper used in this publication meets the minimum requirements of American National Standard for Information Sciences – Permanence of Paper for Printed Library Materials, ANSI z39.48-1984.

Library of Congress Cataloging-in-Publication Data

Syntax and semantics of spatial P / edited by Anna Asbury, Jakub Dotlačil, Berit Gehrke and Rick Nouwen.
    p. cm. (Linguistik Aktuell/Linguistics Today, ISSN 0166-0829 ; v. 120)
Includes bibliographical references and index.
1. Grammar, Comparative and general--Prepositional phrases. 2. Grammar, Comparative and general--Locative constructions. 3. Semantics. I. Asbury, Anna.

P285.S97   2008

415--dc22   2007052074
ISBN 978 90 272 5503 7 (Hb; alk. paper)

John Benjamins Publishing Co. · P.O. Box 36224 · 1020 ME Amsterdam · The Netherlands
John Benjamins North America · P.O. Box 27519 · Philadelphia PA 19118-0519 · USA

Table of contents

Introduction

Syntax and semantics of spatial P

Anna Asbury, Berit Gehrke, Henk van Riemsdijk & Joost Zwarts

1. Basic concepts

Approaches to spatial adpositions vary greatly across the different linguistic dis-
ciplines. This section outlines the different areas and introduces some of the basic
concepts that are common to syntactic and semantic research on the subject and
relevant to the articles in this volume. Research by Jackendoff (1973, 1983, 1990,
1996) on the conceptual structure of spatial relations has been particularly influential for recent approaches to adpositions.

Spatial adpositions are divided between those which denote the ontological
categories of *Path* (e.g., TO, FROM, VIA) and *Place* (e.g., IN, ON, UP). Jackendoff finds
that Path generally dominates Place in examples such as those in (1). (1a) shows
that Place dominates the noun, and (1b–c) show that Path dominates Place.

(1) Path and Place relations
   a. *in the room*: [$_{\text{PLACE}}$ IN ([$_{\text{THING}}$ ROOM])]
   b. *into the room*: [$_{\text{PATH}}$ TO ([$_{\text{PLACE}}$ IN ([$_{\text{THING}}$ ROOM])])]
   c. *through the cheese*: [$_{\text{PATH}}$ VIA ([$_{\text{PLACE}}$ IN ([$_{\text{THING}}$ CHEESE])])]

For example, with *into the room* a PLACE function IN takes a Thing as its argument, the *reference object*, to return a PLACE. The PLACE in turn is the argument
of the PATH function TO that returns a PATH. In a similar vein, Talmy (1975) and
subsequent work makes use of the concepts *Figure* and *Ground* to describe the
arguments of prepositions, where the Figure is an entity which is moved, or is
conceptually potentially moveable, with respect to a specific Ground (2).

(2) Figure and Ground relations
   a. John hung *the painting*$_{\text{Fig}}$ on *the wall*$_{\text{Gr}}$.
   b. *The children*$_{\text{Fig}}$ travelled to *school*$_{\text{Gr}}$.

These core semantic notions are widely used in research on adpositions and are
also employed in syntactic work on the category. Other terms for Figure and Ground
reference object are *Trajector* and *Landmark*, respectively, which are especially
common in the cognitive linguistic approaches of Lakoff (1987), Langacker (1987)
and related works.

In other respects, there is considerable variety in the treatment of adpositions. Clearly it goes beyond the scope of this study to handle the broader issues of adpositions and spatial cognition. We do not attempt here to touch on approaches from the perspective of cognitive semantics, radial networks or image schemas (Brugman 1981, Lakoff 1987), psycholinguistics (Bowerman 1996; Levinson 2003; Coventry & Garrod 2004; among others), or grammaticalisation (Heine et al. 1991; Svorou 1993). We also do not address the role of verbal prefixes and particles in much detail, even though these have been argued to belong to the category P as well (see section 2.1). For treatments of verbal particles we refer the reader to a recent collection of articles in Dehé et al. (2002).

Here we focus on the internal syntax and semantics of PPs and only occasionally address the external PP syntax and semantics. Spatial expressions can function as predicates, arguments and adjuncts (3).

(3) a. *predicate*: The bird is on the roof.
     b. *argument*:   The book lay on the table.
     c. *adjunct*:   Mary read a book on the plane.

These different functions are discussed in detail in Bierwisch (1988), Wunderlich & Herweg (1991), among others. In general, different positions on the syntactic and semantic integration of spatial PPs in its environment have been defended. For example, Cresswell (1978) assumes that PPs are generally predicate modifiers, and Wunderlich (1991) suggests that PPs are always predicates. Creary et al. (1989) argue in line with Jackendoff (1983) that spatial expressions are always arguments. Keenan & Faltz (1985) assume that a locative PP is an intersective modifier, and Nam (1995) carries their analysis over to directional locatives.

In the following sections, we provide an overview of relevant research on adpositions in syntax and semantics, introducing the works that have been particularly influential for the contributions in this volume. Where the details of specific analyses are treated, the section on syntax focuses on research in the Principles and Parameters framework, and the section on semantics on recent formal semantic approaches, though many of the empirical issues raised are of interest for any formal syntactic or semantic treatment of the category.

2.   The syntax of spatial P

There are many areas of controversy regarding the syntax of the category P. Even the defining characteristics of the category are uncertain, with the guiding intuition being that the category consists of relational markers that precede or follow the noun or its functional or modifying categories (such as articles or adjectives).

Chomsky (1970) claims that Ps have the feature matrix [-N,-V], thus predicting that they form distinct natural classes with nouns (being -V) and verbs (being -N), but not adjectives. Jackendoff (1975), however, provides a different matrix, defining Ps as being like verbs in having an object and like adjectives in having no subject. Van Riemsdijk (1978: 114–9) casts doubt on the usefulness of such a matrix, and indeed the discussion in the following sections will show that little has been clearly established even about the defining characteristics of the category. Section 2.1 examines the difficulties in drawing the boundary between P and the core lexical categories of V(erbs), N(ouns) and A(djectives). Section 2.2 looks at the lexical/functional distinction and whether the category can be defined as one or other. Section 2.3 outlines some of the proposals for mapping out the internal structure of spatial adpositions. Section 2.4 considers issues of case assignment within PP.

2.1   Boundaries of the category P

It is not always clear which linguistic elements should be considered members of the category P and which should be excluded. For example, one work aimed at comprehensively describing the range of senses for English, the Preposition Project (http://www.clres.com/prepositions.html), finds 847 preposition senses for 373 prepositions, including 'phrasal prepositions', such as the one in (4a) below. The range of English prepositions receiving attention in generative syntax is rather narrower, though the boundaries of the category are still controversial. The P-status of small spatial Ps such as *in, on, to* and *into* is generally accepted, whereas the classification of those words and phrases derived from other categories is not so obvious. (4) gives examples of some Ps which have nominal characteristics and appear to incorporate nouns.

(4)   Ps with nominal characteristics
    a.   on *top* of
    b.   be*side*

Stringer (2005) notes that such items as in (4a) behave unlike regular lexical nouns in being acceptable without a determiner (5a), and unable to combine with adjectives (5b).

(5)   Distinctions between nominal-looking Ps and lexical nouns
    a.   on top of   *vs.* *on roof of
    b.   *on snow-covered top of the hill   *vs.* on the snow-covered top of the hill

(6) gives examples of the likeness between certain Ps and verbs.

(6)   Ps with verbal characteristics
    a.   regarding your proposal / I regard the matter as closed.

b.   considering the circumstances / He considered the matter carefully.
c.   following the events of last week / They followed the red car home.

Here it is sometimes possible to make a distinction based on word order, with the words in question behaving more like verbs in one position and more like Ps in another, as shown for Dutch in (7).

(7)   Dutch P/V distinction by word order
a.   niet-tegen-staande   het   slechte   weer   (PP)
        not-against-standing   the   bad   weather
b.   het   slechte   weer   niet-tegen-staande   (VP)
        the   bad   weather   not-against-standing

Similarly, some Ps seem to relate to adjectives. For example, *near* is ambiguous between a preposition and an adjective, being P-like in being able to combine directly with a noun, but adjective-like in being able to form a comparative, as shown in (8) (see also Maling 1983).

(8)   P with adjectival characteristics
a.   *near* (to) the house
b.   *nearer* to the house

The identity of certain English prepositions and complementisers (9) also led Emonds (1985) to propose the conflation of the two categories.

(9)   Identical prepositions and complementisers
a.   They headed *for* the hills.
b.   It would be a good idea *for* John to do this.

It has also been debated whether particles (10) can be considered members of the same category as prepositions.

(10)   Particles
a.   John phoned Mary *up.*
b.   Mary turned *down* the job offer.

Emonds (1972) argues for treating them as intransitive prepositions, whereas van Riemsdijk (1978) argues that a distinction can be maintained, with true intransitive prepositions having a more literal meaning, and particles a more idiomatic interpretation, also finding syntactic differences based on Dutch data.

Similar controversies are reflected in work on adpositions in many different languages. Nominal elements such as those in (5) above are increasingly accepted as part of P-structure in syntax (cf. Stringer 2005 on English, French and Japanese; Terzi 2006, to appear, on Greek & Hebrew; Svenonius 2006). It is difficult to be sure where to draw the line with either the nominal or the verbal elements in some languages (cf. Aboh 2006 on Kwa spatial expressions). The ambiguous nature of such nominal and verbal Ps can in some cases be attributed to grammaticalisation processes. It has been observed for various languages that the apparently more open-class style adpositions are formed via a grammaticalisation process from nouns and also verbs (cf. É. Kiss 2002 on Hungarian), and in English complex prepositions such as *beside* and *on top of* clearly relate to nouns. Thus there are many cases where it is difficult to distinguish between the category P and the other syntactic categories.

2.2   The lexical vs. functional debate

The status of the category P as lexical or functional has been much debated. Many languages seem to exhibit a two-way split amongst adpositions, some appearing more lexical and some more functional. This is sometimes clearly linked to the relation with core lexical categories as discussed in Section 2.1. For example, some of the apparently more lexical Ps in English are those with the most likeness to verbs, nouns and adjectives. However, in some languages it is possible to identify splits in behaviour within the category of adpositions independent of the relation with other lexical or functional categories. This has led to some debate on whether such a split should be counted as a categorial divide itself. The controversy stems from the mixed behaviour of the category with respect to common diagnostics for functional or lexical status. Typical assumptions on the behaviour of lexical and functional categories are outlined in the following table (11), drawn from diagnostics in Corver & van Riemsdijk (2001).

(11)   Characteristics of lexical and functional categories

Lexical categories	Functional categories
relatively specific/detailed semantic content	non-conceptual meaning, grammatical function
open membership	closed membership
generally free-standing words	generally phonologically and morphologically dependent
variable c-selection (top-down)	strict c-selection (bottom-up)
theta-mark their complement	do not theta-mark their complement
can be moved away from complement	usually inseparable from complement
license empty categories	cannot license empty categories

Verbs, nouns and adjectives emerge as clearly lexical on the basis of such diagnostics, and tense and determiners as clearly functional. By contrast, it is not simple to give a consistent classification of the category P on this basis. On the one hand, Ps appear to form a very closed class in certain languages. Tzeltal (Levinson 1996: 185) and Oro Nao (Everett & Kern 1997: 5), for instance, are said to have only one preposition serving spatial and non-spatial functions. On the other hand many of the familiar Indo-European languages have much larger inventories of Ps, as is the case for English, albeit still considerably smaller than the inventories of nouns, verbs and adjectives in the same languages. Adpositions also vary enormously in terms of semantic content, from comparatively vacuous, morphologically simple Ps such as *of* to comparatively contentful, morphologically complex Ps such as *into, behind, beside.*

Following Emonds (1972) and Jackendoff (1973), it has been standard to treat the category P as a lexical category. The apparent status of case assigners (12) is seen as evidence for this, since the lexical verb assigns Case.

(12)　Case assignment in PP
　　a.　to me/him/her/them/*I/*he
　　b.　auf　dem　　　Berg　　　　　　　　　　　　(German)
　　　　on　the.DAT　mountain
　　　　'on the mountain'
　　c.　in　urbe　　　　　　　　　　　　　　　　　(Latin)
　　　　in　city.ABL
　　　　'in the city'

Further research such as Den Dikken (2006) draws more detailed parallels with the category V, proposing that P, as a lexical category, has its own functional structure mirroring that of the other lexical categories. These approaches receive further treatment below in the discussion on structure and VP parallels.

Other recent approaches argue that P should rather be considered a functional category, focusing on the differences between P and the other three lexical categories, N, V and A. Grimshaw (2000) draws full parallels between the verbal extended projection and that of the noun, proposing that P in the nominal extended projection corresponds to C in the verbal projection. Kayne (2001) argues that prepositions are probes, with their own ϕ-features. Baker (2003) dismisses P from the inventory of lexical categories based on incorporation facts. He further notes that the category P differs from N, V and A in not having clear derivational endings in any language. English nouns, for example can be formed with *-ation*, verbs with *-ise* and adjectives with *-able*, but P-forming suffixes of this kind seem not to exist. Maintaining the position that P is a uniformly functional category, Botwinik-Rotem (2004) accounts for the diversity in functions of P by defining three different types: P_R specifies a particular semantic relation of the noun, P_C has a case checking function, and P_{PRED} has predicate status.

Finally some researchers, faced with the diversity of the category P, opt for a mixed analysis. Van Riemsdijk (1990) proposes that there are both lexical and functional members of the category P, making use of the notion *little p*, by analogy with little v. Zwarts (1997a) proposes a more elaborate division, setting Dutch prepositions along a graded scale from the most lexical to the most functional.

Others invoke the notion of semi-lexicality, as outlined in Corver & van Riemsdijk (2001). Zeller (2001), for example, defines a semi-lexical head as a morphologically complex element consisting of a lexical node and a functional suffix. He claims that German and Dutch postpositions are semi-lexical elements, derived from lexical prepositions via suffixation of a zero-operator, which alters the thematic properties of the P-element.

Thus the different camps remain divided in their classification of Ps as functional or lexical, the different standpoints often reflecting the different languages or types of P studied and the implicit assumptions about the boundaries of the category. The question of lexical or functional status has further consequences for the structure of the category, as shown below.

2.3   Structure of P

Following the line of Jackendoff (1973), van Riemsdijk (1978), and Chomsky (1981, 1986, 1995) that P is a lexical category, the structures assumed for P have developed from relatively simple X-bar structures such as those in (13) to much more elaborate and diverse structures.

(13)   Simple P structure conforming to X-bar

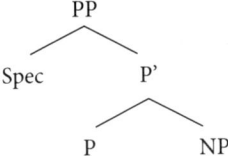

In order to account for Germanic circumpositional phrases such as (14), van Riemsdijk (1990) proposes a structure with a light p, drawing a loose parallel with light v. (See also Noonan 2005 for a more detailed perspective on German circumpositional phrases).

(14)   Light p structure for German circumpositional phrases
        auf   den   Berg   herauf
        on   the.ACC   mountain up
        'up on the mountain'

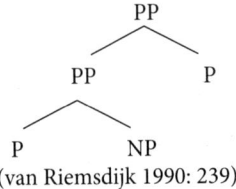
(van Riemsdijk 1990: 239)

In later research semantic labels have been incorporated into the proposed syntactic structures for P, in recognition of the fact that there seems to be a universal ordering of path-denoting Ps and PLACE-denoting Ps, with PLACE appearing closer to the noun than PATH (van Riemsdijk & Huijbregts 2007, Kracht 2002).

Koopman (2000) and den Dikken (2006) have been particularly influential in developing a rich functional structure associated with the category, finding parallels between the verbal and prepositional extended projections. Den Dikken (2006) thus proposes the following structures, recognising a division between PATH and PLACE, as shown in (15).

(15)   Schematic structure of PathP and PlaceP (den Dikken 2006:23)

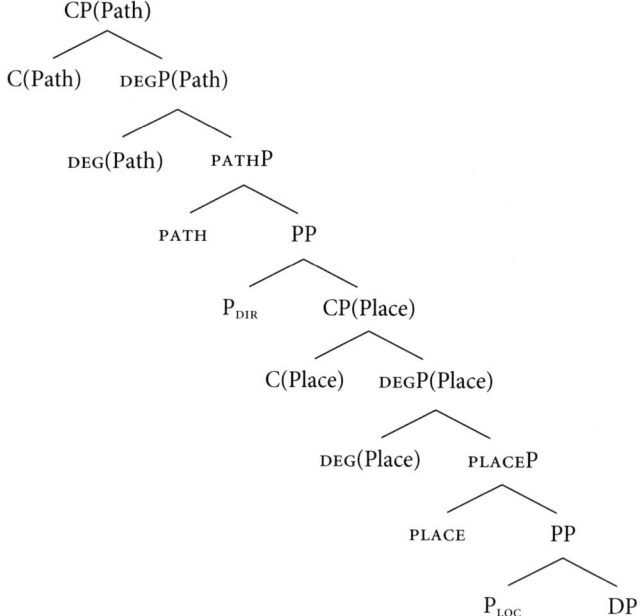

He argues that the elaborate functional structure is necessary in order to accommodate the complexity of possible modification of spatial Ps, as illustrated in (16).

(16)   Modification of spatial P in Dutch (Den Dikken 2006:22)
het vliegtuig vloog ⟨er⟩ tien meter lang ⟨er⟩ tien meter hoog ⟨er⟩
the aircraft   flew   there ten metre long there ten metre high there
boven(langs)
above along

Den Dikken (2006) draws explicit parallels between PP and both VP and NP, finding functional categories corresponding to Tense and Aspect in all three domains, as illustrated in (17).

(17)   Parallels between functional structure of P, V and N (from den Dikken 2006:24)
   a. $[_{CP}$ C$^{[FORCE]}$ $[_{DxP}$ Dx$^{[TENSE]}$ $[_{Asp}$P Asp$^{[EVENT]}$ $[_{VP}$ V ...]]]]
   b. $[_{CP}$ C$^{[DEF]}$ $[_{DxP}$ Dx$^{[PERSON]}$ $[_{Asp}$P Asp$^{[NUM]}$ $[_{NP}$ N ...]]]]
   c. $[_{CP}$ C$^{[SPACE]}$ $[_{DxP}$ Dx$^{[SPACE]}$ $[_{Asp}$P Asp$^{[SPACE]}$ $[_{PP}$ P ...]]]]

Svenonius (2004, 2006) assumes a rather simpler structure, proposing an additional s pace for a nominal element, termed Axial Part, low in the PP structure, along the lines of (18).

(18)   Structure of PP with Axial Part (Svenonius 2004, 2006)

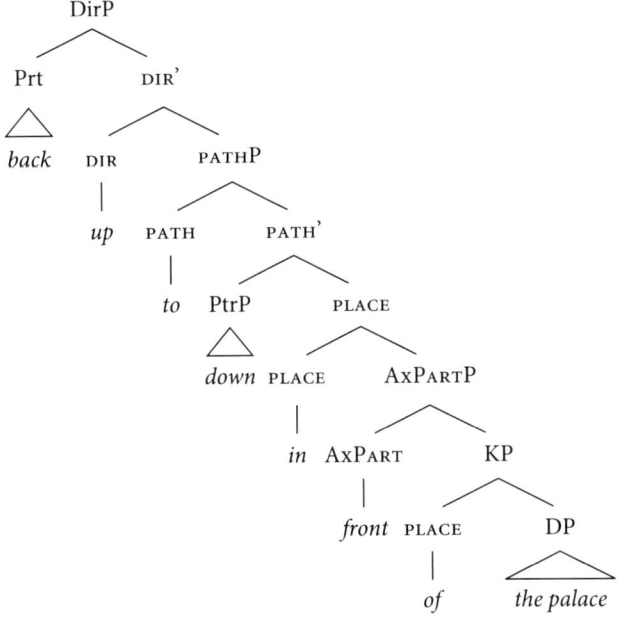

As discussed in section 2.1, nominal behaviour amongst adpositions is prevalent in many different languages. Such instances of nominal behaviour of P seem only recently to have received treatment in the mainstream literature on adpositions. In addition to the overt nominal phenomena accounted for in the structure in (18), the notion of an empty noun denoting PLACE in the P structure has also been proposed to account for some languages. For example, Terzi (2006, to appear) finds evidence for an empty noun in the Greek P projection. This empty noun PLACE was earlier proposed in Katz & Postal (1964), and later developed in Kayne (2004), as part of the structure of English adverbial phrases, such as *here* and *there*. It remains to be seen whether connections can be made between such empty noun structures and the Axial Part structure in (18).

Thus research on the syntactic structure of spatial P has made use of the semantic terms PATH and PLACE, integrating these labels into the syntactic structure
alongside more purely syntactic terms, such as DP and Axial Part.

2.4 Case in PP

In many languages, P appears to be a case assigner, as illustrated in (12), repeated
here as (19).

(19) Case assignment in PP
    a.   to me/him/her/them/*I/*he
    b.   auf   dem   Berg   (German)
        on   the.DAT mountain
        'on the mountain'
    c.   in   urbe   (Latin)
        in   city.ABL
        'in the city'

In other languages this is not so clear. For example most Hungarian postpositions combine with a bare noun, and only a few with a case-marked noun, as shown in (20).

(20) Hungarian PP: presence and absence of case
    a.   János-sal   szemben
        John-INSTR opposite
        'opposite John'
    b.   János   mögött
        John   behind
        'behind John'

Many recent approaches give relatively short shrift to the role of case in the PP,
assuming a case feature or a KP projection in the structure. Past analyses, however, have explored the idea that case itself involves a PP structure. This idea was
championed by Fillmore (1968), though similar ideas appear in Nikanne (1991)
for Finnish cases, and more restrictively in van Riemsdijk & Huijbregts (2007) for
Lezgian spatial cases.

The standard assumption has been that prepositions assign oblique case. There
have been a few attempts recently to account for the variety of different oblique
cases found on complements of P. As an example, we discuss briefly three treatments of case alternations in German PPs, Abraham (2003); Zwarts (2005b) and
van Riemsdijk (2007). A number of German prepositions can vary in the case they
assign, the P itself then covarying in meaning, as in (21).

(21) German case alternations in PP
    a.   Anna   stand   in   dem   Zimmer.
        Anna   stood   in   the.DAT room
        'Anna stood in the room.'

b. Otto trat   in   das   Zimmer.
    Otto stepped in   the.ACC   room
    'Otto stepped into the room.'

Zwarts (2005b) concludes that case on objects in PP differs from that in VP, being more related to historical development than syntactic assignment, and that the combination of P and case cannot be analysed as semantically compositional. Abraham (2003), on the other hand, argues that Ps in German exclusively govern dative case. Where the accusative case appears, Abraham argues that it is governed by a secondary predicate like *hin-* or *her-*, which are deictic particles exemplified in (22), by an (optional) verb particle, or by a complex adverb of direction together with the verb of movement.

(22)   in das   Wasser *hin*-ein
       in the.ACC   water   hither-in
       'into the water'

Similarly, van Riemsdijk (2007) assumes that dative case in German PPs represent the default case in oblique domains in general. Unlike Abraham, though, he argues that the structure of PPs involving goals and routes generally contain a route component in their structure (as opposed to sources and locative PPs in general, see section 3 and Jackendoff 1983, among others, for these distinctions), which is responsible for the accusative case emerging in the particular PPs. The object of this route component, in turn, is argued to act as a measure phrase, and van Riemsdijk assumes the function of measurement to be tied to accusative case in other domains as well.

This area seems to have received relatively little attention, by comparison with the detailed structure of P, and there are many more issues regarding the choice of case within PP which remain to be resolved.

3. The semantics of spatial P

The purpose of a locative PP in general is to describe the location of a particular entity, the Figure, which can be an object or an event, with respect to another entity, the Ground, or more precisely with respect to the location of another entity. A directional PP, in turn, usually describes a potential change of location of an entity with respect to (the location of) another entity. In line with Jackendoff's work and the syntactic literature on PPs, it is generally assumed that directional PPs are in some way related to locative PPs, e.g., there is some mechanism to derive directional PPs from locative ones or relate them to one another in a systematic way. Hence, any treatment of the semantics of directional PPs needs to rely on a particular account of the semantics of locative PPs.

3.1 Locative PPs

In this subsection, we discuss representatives of two main approaches to the semantics of locative PPs. The first is in terms of *regions* (Creary et al. 1989, Wunderlich 1991, Wunderlich & Herweg 1991; Nam 1995; among others), and the second in terms of *vectors* (O' Keefe 1996, Zwarts 1997b, Zwarts & Winter 2000, Zwarts 2005a). Since many authors in this volume refer directly to Zwarts (1997b) and subsequent work and often assume his semantic account of spatial expressions, we will outline this framework in more detail.

3.1.1 *Regions*

A representative of an analysis of locative PPs in terms of regions is found in Wunderlich (1991) and Wunderlich & Herweg (1991). To derive the location of the entity (the Ground, represented as v), with respect to which another entity (the Figure, represented as u) is located, Wunderlich (1991) defines a function p, the *eigenplace function*, which yields for each object or event the place it occupies, its *eigenplace*, which is some region. He furthermore assumes that there is a family of functions, which yield for each object or event a set of surrounding or neighbouring regions. For example, the function INT[v] yields a set of regions that are internal to v. Based on this, we can define the *in* location between Figure and Ground as in (23).

(23) $\langle u,v \rangle \in$ [[*in*]] iff $p[u] \subseteq$ INT[v]

To refer to such regions, English commonly uses *in*. Other functions are EXT[v] for regions external to v or PROX[v] for regions in the proximity of v. These regions can further be decomposed into subregions according to particular spatial axes in relation to v. For example, Wunderlich discusses the vertical axis ±VERT, which is relevant for prepositions such as *under* (24).

(24) $\langle u,v \rangle \in$ [[*under*]] iff $p[u] \subseteq$ EXT[v, -VERT]

The relevant region in (24) is the region below v which is properly included in EXT[v].

Wunderlich (1991) assumes that directional PPs refer to paths which are extended regions that unify the places of an object at different times, in case events are involved. However, he notes that there are uses of directional PPs independent of time. Similarly, Bierwisch (1988) argues for an analysis of paths not based on time but assumes instead that a path is a specifically structured place or location, i.e., nested locations. We will come back to the notion of path in section 3.2.1.

3.1.2 *Vectors*

Zwarts (1997b) and Zwarts & Winter (2000) argue that the vector space semantics approach to PPs opens up a way of looking at algebraic properties of spatial PPs that are familiar from and relevant to inferences in other semantic domains, most notably quantified expressions. In particular, they discuss properties in the prepositional domain such as point monotonicity, vector monotonicity, or preposition conservativity. For illustration, we will discuss the notion of vector monotonicity in the prepositional domain.

One of the reasons for Zwarts (1997b) and Zwarts & Winter (2000) to use vectors in their semantic analysis of locative PPs is that it allows a straightforward treatment of modification in the prepositional domain. The denotation of a locative PP is represented as a set of vectors, which are directed line segments between points in space. For example, *behind the house* is associated with the set of vectors that go from the house to points behind it. The modified PP *5 metres behind the house*, then, is a simple composition, namely the intersection of two sets of vectors, those that are five metres long and those that are behind the house.

Zwarts & Winter (2000) note that measure phrase modification is available only with a subset of the locative prepositions. Whereas locative PPs headed by *behind* or *outside* can be modified by measure phrases, locative PPs headed by *between* or *in(side)* cannot (25).

(25)   a.   two metres behind the car
              two kilometres outside the village
        b.   *two metres between the houses
              *two metres in / inside the house

They show that for a locative preposition to be modifiable by a measure phrase it has to be both upward and downward vector monotone (26).

(26)   *Modification Condition* (informally after Zwarts & Winter 2000)
        A set of located vectors satisfies the modification condition iff it is upward and downward vector monotone and non-empty.

For complete definitions of vector monotonicity the reader is referred to the work cited. What is useful to note here is that the intuition behind this definition is that of truth preservation when the located object gets further from / closer to the reference object.

Zwarts & Winter show that all simple locative Ps in natural language are downward monotone. Thus, to determine whether a locative PP can be modified by a measure phrase or not, it is enough to concentrate on upward monotonicity. English examples for upward monotone locative prepositions and those that are not upward monotone are given in (27).

(27)   VMON↑: in front of, behind; above, over, below, under; beside; outside not
        VMON↑: near, on, at; inside, in; between

For example, *behind the house* is upward monotone: when a vector that points to x is in the denotation of *behind the house*, i.e., a vector that leads from the house to some point x behind it, then also any lengthening of this vector is in the same denotation since the particular point would merely be further away from the house but still behind it. This does not hold for *inside*, though, because lengthening of vectors that go inside could eventually end up going outside again. Hence, *inside* is not upward monotone and does not meet the Modification Condition. (This is a bit of a simplification. See Zwarts & Winter for some further complications with non-projective reference objects, with which *in*-phrases can be modified again.)

3.2   Directional PPs

In this section, we discuss representatives of three ways to analyse the semantics of directional PPs, namely in terms of atemporal *paths* in space (Bierwisch 1988; Verkuyl & Zwarts 1992; Nam 1995; Zwarts 2005a; among others), *phase quantifiers* that are independent of time and space (Fong 1997, 2001), or as *combinations of paths and phase quantification* (Wunderlich 1991; Wunderlich & Herweg 1991; Kracht 2002).

3.2.1   *Paths*

Following Jackendoff (1983), Bierwisch (1988) notes that paths are related to places in a systematic way, namely that each path has a part which has the property of a PLACE. This can generally be illustrated by an example like the goal PATH *into the house*, one of the ending-points of which (the final location) has the same properties as the locative PP *in the house*. Wunderlich & Herweg (1991) characterise paths as a sequence of places through which an entity moves during an interval of time. Similarly, Nam (1995) argues that directional PPs are interpreted as denoting paths or orientations, which are sequences of regions that intuitively involve a movement of an object. To represent such movement, Nam introduces a predicate TRAV (for traverse), which is similar to Jackendoff's (1983) GO function.

However, both Bierwisch and Nam explicity argue that paths are strictly topological entities that are independent of time, and also Wunderlich (1991) notes that the interpretation of path structure in terms of temporal structure is only one possible way to relate paths to other linear orders. Hence, the particular interpretation of a path as time-dependent is merely a result of the embedding of a directional PP within a motion event and is thus due to its external semantics and syntax.

A comparable treatment of directional PPs in terms of paths is found in Verkuyl & Zwarts (1992), who interpret dimensionality and directionality features from Jackendoff's conceptual structure framework as sets of model-theoretic structures (28), (29).

(28)   Model-theoretic interpretation of [n-DIMENSIONAL]

(Verkuyl & Zwarts 1992: 496)

The dimensionality of an object is the number of spatial orderings that can be imposed on the material parts of that object.

(29)   Model-theoretic interpretation of [+DIRECTIONAL]

(Verkuyl & Zwarts 1992: 497f.)

A set is directional if it is linearly ordered in one direction, yielding one unique beginning point and a potential end point [...] directionality imposes a certain order on an unordered set [...] the linear order of a spatial path is not the result of an intrinsic ordering of space, but of something moving through space and yielding a particular order.

Also Verkuyl & Zwarts argue that a spatial path is atemporal. Reference to time is available, however. They assume that the movement to a goal, for example, involves a bounded sequence of moments in time $\langle t_1, ..., t_n \rangle$. The application of Jackendoff's GO function to the spatial PATH gives a mapping from the atemporal spatial PATH into the temporal PATH, creating a new spatio-temporal Path Π, which consists of pairs of points in space and points in time: $\langle (t_1, p_1) ..., (t_i, p_i), ... \rangle$ (see also Jackendoff 1991, 1996).

The treatment of directional PPs as paths is further developed in Zwarts (2005a), who assumes that directional prepositions map the location of the reference object (the Ground) to a set of sequences of vectors, paths, where each of these sequences determines a potential change in position of the located object (the Figure). One of the ideas in Zwarts (2005a) is to explore parallels between the prepositional domain, on the one hand, and the verbal and the nominal domains, on the other. Such parallels are also drawn in syntactic research, as discussed in section 2.

Zwarts assumes that locative prepositions can be compared to states in the verbal domain, whereas directional prepositions share properties with dynamic events. For example, a property like boundedness, which is relevant for distinguishing between atelic (unbounded) and telic (bounded) events in the verbal domain, or between mass (unbounded) and count (bounded) nouns in the nominal domain (e.g., Bach 1981, 1986), is also at play in the prepositional domain. This leads him to make a further subdivision of directional prepositions into atelic/unbounded and telic/bounded ones (30).

(30)   a.   *bounded, telic*:   to, into, onto, from, out of, off, away from, past, via
        b.   *unbounded, atelic*:   towards, along
        c.   *(un)bounded, (a)telic*: across, around, down, over, through, up

Zwarts argues that the distinguishing property between telic and atelic reference in the prepositional domain is cumulativity. Cumulativity in the verbal and nominal domain is exemplified in (31).

(31)   *drink water* (cumulative) vs. *drink a glass of water* (non-cumulative)

For example, if one adds water to water the result is still water, so *water* has cumulative reference. If one adds a glass of water to a glass of water, the result is not in the same denotation of *a glass of water* anymore, rather the result is *two glasses of water*. Thus, *a glass of water* is not cumulative. Similary, an event of drinking water is cumulative, whereas an event of drinking a glass of water is not.

A PP, then, is bounded (telic) iff it does not have cumulative reference, which is defined in the following way (with **p** and **q** as variables over paths) (32).

(32)   A set of paths X is **cumulative** iff
    i.   there are p and q ∈ X such that p+q exists and
    ii. for all p, q ∈ X, if p+q exists, then p+q ∈ X.   (Zwarts 2005a: 751)

The crucial operation involved here is concatenation of paths (closure under sums), which is a partial operation subject to the condition that the second path has to start where the first path ends. Atelic PPs are closed under sums whereas telic PPs are not.

For example, a *to*-path is not cumulative because there are no two paths in the denotation of *to* that can be concatenated: the final end-point of a *to*-path is always just outside the reference object whereas the initial end-point is not. On the same grounds, goal-paths involving *into* and *onto* are not cumulative. Furthermore, the denotations of the source prepositions *out of, from* and *off* do not involve any paths that can be concatenated, either, since they are defined as the mirror images of the goals. They are therefore non-cumulative as well.

To put things differently, prepositions with bounded reference have in common that they involve a two-stage structure, a negative and a positive phase. They have exactly one positive phase that overlaps either with the starting point or the ending point of the path. This is the perspective taken in Fong (1997), who treats the semantics of PPs in terms of phase quantification, which is outlined in the next section. However, Fong explicitly argues against using space as the domain for directional PPs.

3.2.2   *Phase quantifiers*

Fong (1997, 2001) points out the existence of directional locative predications (DLs) in non-motion contexts to argue against restricting them to spatial movement. First, noun phrases in both English and Finnish (as well as in other languages) can freely be modified by DLs, even though there is nothing in motion (33).

(33)   a bridge out of San Francisco

Second, verbs can demand a DL, even though nothing is moving. In particular, Finnish DLs appear as complements of aspectual verbs such as *begin, end* (34a), verbs that according to Fong presuppose properties of anterior or posterior phases such as *find, forget* (34b), and more generally, verbs that are inherently Achievements or Accomplishments (in the sense of Vendler 1957).

(34) a. Toini   rupeaa luke-   ma-   an.
          Toini begins read- inf- illative
          'Toini begins ('into') reading'   (Finnish, Fong 1997: 46)
      b. Unohdi-n kaku-n   uuni-in   kahde-ksi tunni-ksi.
          Forgot -1P cake-ACC oven-INTO two-TRA hours-TRA
          'I forgot the cake in the oven for two hours.'   (Finnish, Fong 1997: 41)

From data like these Fong concludes that directional locatives have a semantics that is more abstract than the PATH meaning, which she sees as intrinsically bound to (literal or hypothetical) movement in space. She argues instead that directional locatives (DLs) denote ordered structures, which are interpretable in domains that are diphasic. An analysis of the semantics of directional PPs with a reference to phases is also found in Wunderlich (1991) and Wunderlich & Herweg (1991). Fong mainly concentrates on Finnish and English data and assumes that English and Finnish differ in that Finnish DLs (expressed by case suffixes on the noun phrase) can operate on the aspectual (or temporal) structures of the verb, while English DLs (expressed by PPs) cannot. The lexical semantics of English and Finnish verbs, however, is treated as the same.

Fong follows Löbner's (1989) concept of phase quantifiers, according to which the truth of propositions is time dependent and phase quantifiers can be viewed as functions from the time line to the set of truth values $\{0, 1\}$. Given a proposition p, an interval I is *admissible* for p if the truth value changes in I and (the restriction of p to the interval I) is a nonconstant monotonic function from I to $\{0, 1\}$. So I is the disjoint union of two nonempty intervals J_0 and J_1 such that J_0 is entirely before (or entirely after) J_1, and p is false in J_0 and true in J_1.

Fong applies this idea to the analysis of DLs, extending the notion of phases and phase quantification to objects and events. Her definition of an admissible interval for locations such as *into San Francisco* (Fong 1997: 32) is given in (35).

(35) I is an admissible interval in terms of p (LOC-IN(san francisco)) and s iff
      i. $I = (s_i, s_e]$ for some $s_i < s_e$
      ii. I begins with a phase of not-p: $\exists s' \in I \, \forall s \in I(s < s' \rightarrow \sim p(s))$
      iii. the function p is monotone in the interval I:
           for all $s, s' \in I$, if p is defined for s, s' then if $s < s'$ then $p(s) \rightarrow p(s')$

This definition characterises an interval as admissible if there is a monotonic phase change from $\sim p$ to p and the truth of the particular DL predicate can be evaluated in the second phase. Example (33), then, is analysed as follows.

(36) Phase quantification analysis of *a bridge out of San Francisco* (Fong 1997: 33)
      $\exists a(bridge(a))$ and

    i.   *I* is an interval, which is an ordering of the range of σ(a), and contains one phase change (p < ~p) with respect to the location of some part of the bridge in San Francisco; and

    ii. ∃s∈ I ∀y∈ I(y<s → LOC-IN(y, san francisco)) ∧
        ∃s'∈ I ∀z∈ I(s'<z → ?LOC-IN(y, san francisco))

The spatial trace function σ(a) in condition i. in (36), which is defined in analogy to Krifka's (1998) temporal trace function τ, provides a one-dimensional ordering of (the locations of relevant parts of) particular objects, in this case *the bridge*. This condition assures that there is only one phase change involved. Condition ii. states that the location of one part of the bridge, *y*, should be in San Francisco if it is early enough in the ordering, whereas the location of another part of the bridge, *z*, if late enough in the ordering, is outside of San Francisco.

It is easy to see, then, that this account can straightforwardly be carried over to cases where the particular order is not a spatial but a temporal one as in (35) so that the ordering provided by the temporal instead of the spatial trace function becomes relevant. Thus, this analysis of DLs has wider applications than merely the spatial domain and allows for including non-spatial cases in the analysis as well, such as the Finnish essive and translative, which talk about an object having or acquiring a particular property. At the same time, it is possible to relate the relevant phases to other domains than the temporal one to account for time-independent uses of DLs. Finnish DLs can be properly interpreted in the temporal domain even if no spatial extension is involved. Fong argues that the reason why English DLs do not occur with this same class of verbs is due to the language restricting DL interpretation to only spatial or spatio-temporal domains.

Fong assumes that the interaction between the semantics of DLs and verbs of manner of motion, as in *dance into the room*, involves lexical aspect shift, where the verb gets associated with an accomplishment reading rather than with a process or activity reading. She states that this explanation also carries over to typological differences, discussed in Talmy (1975) and subsequent work, between languages like French, Mandarin Chinese, which do not allow the aspect shift with manner of motion verbs, on the one hand, and Finnish and English, which allow the aspect shift, on the other. This typological variation is discussed in more detail in section 4.

3.2.3   *Spatiotemporal event modifiers*

Kracht (2002) notes that Fong's definition of phase quantifiers is too inflexible, since it matches only goals (*into, onto, to*) and sources (*out of, off of, (away) from*). However, her analysis cannot directly be carried over to route expressions such as *through, along, past* since these do not necessarily involve transitions from one phase to another where *p* would necessarily be true on one and false in the other. He argues that the notion of path is still necessary at least to account for these latter cases.

Kracht mainly discusses spatial cases in languages with rich case systems such as Tsez, Finnish or Hungarian and assumes that there is no semantic or syntactic distinction between spatial cases in these languages and spatial adpositions in other languages like English or German. He treats this distinction as a mere morphological distinction and assumes that the semantic structure he proposes for spatial cases is also applicable to spatial adpositions. Kracht views directionals as event modifiers, where directionality is treated as a phase quantifier with a slightly more liberal definition of phase quantifier than Fong's (1997). He assumes that spatial cases with a spatial meaning are systematically organised along two orthogonal lines: one specifying the location and the other specifying a change with respect to time. Hence, directional PPs are spatiotemporal event modifiers.

Kracht furthermore argues that locative expressions universally consist of two layers, one for the configuration and one for the mode. This is more or less what Jackendoff terms PLACE and PATH, respectively. The *configuration* describes the way in which several objects are positioned with respect to each other. Configurations can be brought into correspondence with prepositions, which do not indicate a change of location. Examples are *at, in, on, between, in front of* etc. The *mode*, on the other hand, describes the way in which an object moves with respect to the named configuration. While there is no plausible bound on the number of configurations that a language distinguishes, the number of modes seems to be limited. Kracht addresses evidence for the static, the cofinal, the coinitial, the transitory and the approximative mode (37).

`(37)   a.   *static*: the object remains in that configuration during event time, e.g., *in the house*, Finnish and Hungarian inessive case
   b.   *cofinal*: the object moves into the configuration during event time, e.g., *into the house*, Finnish and Hungarian illative case
   c.   *coinitial*: the object moves from the configuration during event time, e.g., *out of the house*, Finnish and Hungarian elative case
   d.   *transitory*: the object moves in and again out of the configuration, e.g., *through the tunnel*
   e.   *approximative*: the object moves approaching a configuration, e.g., *towards the tunnel*

From a semantic and syntactic point of view, Kracht assumes that a locative expression is structured as in (38), where *M* is a *modaliser* (specifying the mode) and *L* is a *localiser* (specifying the configuration).

(38)   [M [L DP]]

This is generally in accordance with the literature on the syntax of PPs as outlined in section 2.

Kracht notes that only two of the directional modes, namely the transitory and the approximative, make reference to the PATH of an object, the others make reference only to the PLACE of the object at some points of the interval. Hence, he combines insights from treatments of directional PPs as paths with Fong's (1997) analysis in terms of phase quantification. In contrast to Fong, however, Kracht argues that a directional locative needs a moving entity, which is something which is by necessity moving in the specified event, including cases of fictive motion as discussed by Talmy (1983) and others.

4.   Verb-framed and satellite-framed languages

Another thread in the research on PPs is cross-linguistic variation in the realm of motion events and spatial PPs. In particular, Talmy's (1975, 1985, 1991, 2000) work became relevant not just for cognitive linguistic frameworks, but also for typology in general, most notably the typological distinction between verb-framed and satellite-framed languages, terminology issues such as the notions of Figure and Ground, or the idea of conflation, which is further developed in the l(exical)-syntactic framework of Hale & Keyser (1993) and subsequent work.

Talmy (1985, 2000) addresses the issue of which semantic elements (such as Motion, Path, Figure, Ground, Manner, or Cause) are expressed by which surface elements (such as verbs, adpositions, subordinate clauses, or satellites) and what kind of typological patterns and universal principles are at play in the realm of motion events. He assumes motion events to have four ingredients, Figure, Ground, PATH and Motion. An object, the Figure, moves or is located with respect to another object, the Ground. The PATH is the course followed or site occupied by the Figure with respect to the Ground; hence Talmy's notion of Path subsumes Jackendoff's Paths and Places. Finally, Talmy characterises Motion as to whether either motion (MOVE) or location (BEL) is present in the event. Manner and Cause are viewed as distinct external events that can be configured as Co-Events to a Motion event.

The question as to which surface elements express the PATH of a Motion Event leads Talmy (1991 / 2000) to the typological distinction between satellite-framed and verb-framed languages. Satellites are not of a particular syntactic category, but stand in a particular grammatical relation to the verb. Satellites are characterised as "immediate constituents of a verb root other than inflections, auxiliaries, or nominal arguments" and are assumed to be related to the verb root as periphery (or modifiers) to a head (sister to the verb). Since it is clearly not a syntactic category, we will only use this term as a description.

Satellite-framed languages are characterised as having a large collection of verbs of motion, which additionally convey Manner or other Co-Event meanings, but that do not encode Path. At the same time, these languages have a large collection of satellites. This type, which is represented by Indo-European (except Romance), Chinese, Finno-Ugric, Ojibwa, Warlpiri, typically conflates Motion and Co-Event on the verb root (39).

(39)　Satellite-framed languages, e.g., English
　　　a.　The bottle floated into the cave.
　　　b.　The bottle floated out of the cave.

Verb-framed languages, on the other hand, typically express PATH (but not Manner) on the verb and have a large collection of verbs of inherent motion such as *entrar* 'enter' or *salir* 'exit' in (40). These languages typically conflate Motion and Path on the verb, but a Co-Event such as Cause or Manner is expressed separately, e.g., by a subordinate clause, or not expressed at all. Languages and language families that belong to this type include Romance, Semitic, Polynesian, Nez Perce, Caddo, Japanese, Korean (40).

(40)　Verb-framed languages, e.g., Spanish
　　　a.　La　botella　entró　　　a　la　　cueva　(flotando).
　　　　　the　bottle　MOVED-in　to　the　cave　(floating)
　　　　　'The bottle floated into the cave.'
　　　b.　La　botella　salió　　　de　la　　cueva　(flotando).
　　　　　the　bottle　MOVED-out　of　the　cave　(floating)
　　　　　'The bottle floated out of the cave.'

In addition, manner of motion verbs in verb-framed languages cannot combine with path expressions but only with PPs denoting places (41).

(41)　a.　*La　botella　flotó　　a　la　　cueva.　　　　　　　(Spanish)
　　　　　the　bottle　floated　to　the　cave
　　　　　(intended meaning: 'The bottle floated to the cave.')
　　　b.　La　botella　flotó　　en　la　　cueva.
　　　　　the　bottle　floated　in　the　cave
　　　　　'The bottle floated inside (*into) the cave.'

There are indications that Talmy's typology needs to be refined. First, it has been argued that it is not a directional PP per se that cannot be combined with manner of motion verbs in verb-framed languages, rather only PPs referring to a path that reaches an end-point are excluded (Aske 1989, Stringer 2002) (42).

(42)　a.　La　fille　a　　dangé　*vers*　　la　　chambre.　　　(French)
　　　　　the　girl　has　danced　towards　the　room
　　　　　'The girl danced towards the room.'
　　　b.　La　fille　a　　dangé　*le*　　*long　de*　la　　rivière.
　　　　　the　girl　has　danced　the　　long　of　　the　river
　　　　　'The girl danced along the river.'

The example in (42a) contains an unbounded goal PP whereas the path in (42b) is expressed by an unbounded route PP under standard treatments of boundedness in the prepositional domain such as Jackendoff (1991, 1996) or Zwarts (2005a), outlined in section 3. Similar examples from French are found in Fong & Poulin (1998), who do not note the correlation with boundedness, though.

There is a general correlation between the possibility of PPs to obtain a directional telic reading with manner of motion verbs and the possibility of forming secondary resultative predicates. Languages that allow one usually also allow the other, whereas such resultative phrases are generally ungrammatical in languages that have been classified as verb-framed (for discussion see Aske 1989; Beck & Snyder 2001; Beck 2005; Folli 2002; Folli & Ramchand 2005; Mateu 2002; Mateu & Rigau 2002; Zubizarreta & Oh 2007; among others). For example, resultative constructions with adjectival phrases (AP) are grammatical in (satellite-framed) English (43a) but ungrammatical in (verb-framed) Spanish (43b).

(43) English vs. Spanish resultatives
    a. Mary beat the metal flat.
    b. *Mary golpéo el metal plano.   (Spanish)
        Mary beat the metal flat

Second, Jones (1983), Cummins (1996) as well as Fong & Poulin (1998) note that in French, a verb-framed language according to this typology, there are verbs which also refer to the manner of a motion but that can still combine with (mostly locative) PPs to refer to a telic directed motion event (44).

(44) a. La balle a roulé dans la boîte.   (French)
        the ball has rolled in the box
        'The ball rolled into the box.'   (Fong & Poulin 1998)
    b. Max a couru dans sa chambre / au magasin.
        Max has run in his room / to.the shop
        'Max ran into his room / to the shop.'   (Cummins 1996)
    c. L'alpiniste a glissé /#trébuché dans une crevasse.
        the mountaineer has slipped / #stumbled in a crevice
        'The mountaineer slipped (#stumbled) into a crevice.'
              (#: ungrammatical under the directional reading) (Jones 1983)

In examples of the type in (44), the three components Motion, PATH and Manner are expressed by the composition of one verb and one PP, and apparently it is this composition or the overall syntactic structure that brings about a PATH reading. Similar examples from Italian, another verb-framed language under Talmy's typology, are discussed in Folli (2002) and Folli & Ramchand (2005). Cases like these are not accounted for under Talmy's typology, because this is neither the verb-framing strategy (the verb without the PP only expresses Motion and Manner) nor the satellite-framing strategy (without the verb there is no PATH but only a location because the PP by itself denotes a PLACE).

Third, Folli (2002) and Folli & Ramchand (2005) show that the 'verb-framed' language Italian has complex PPs that are made up of a locative P and the P *a* 'at, to'. Such complex PPs systematically express Path even with manner of motion verbs that usually cannot bring about a directed motion reading such as *gallegiare* 'to float' (45).

(45) Italian complex PPs expressing PATH
   a. La   barca galleggió dentro la   grotta.
       the boat   floated   inside to.the cave
       'The boat floated into the cave.'
   b. La   barca galleggió dentro la   grotta.
       the boat   floated   inside the   cave
       'The boat floated inside (*into) the cave.'

The strategy of employing complex PPs, made up of a locative P and a cognate of *to*, to express PATH is typical for satellite-framed languages like English, exemplified by the translation in (45a), but not for a verb-framed language like Italian.

Data like these suggest that the difference between so-called verb-framing and satellite-framing might be sought not just in the inventory of verbs but also in the inventory of adpositions available in particular languages. It seems to be the case that languages that have been classified as verb-framed typically lack Path adpositions like English *to* that can freely combine with locative prepositions like *in* and *on* to derive more complex paths or other operations to derive PATHs from PLACES expressed by locative prepositions. French, for example, does not have complex PPs of the type in (45a):

(46) *La fille   dansait à   dans / dans à   la   chambre.
       the girl   danced   to in /   in   to the room
       (intended meaning: 'The girls danced into the room.')

Despite these criticisms, Talmy's typological distinction between verb-framed and satellite-framed languages has proven to be useful and has generated much research, from typological works providing additional data and evidence for this distinction (e.g., Jones 1983; Slobin 1996, 2004; Song 1997; Zlatev & Yangklang 2003; among others) to formal semantic or generative syntactic approaches already cited, and some papers in this volume are also concerned with this distinction. The following section summarises the main ideas of the papers in this volume.

5.   Paper summaries

In her paper *Why are they different? An exploration of Hebrew Locative PPs*, **Irena Botwinik-Rotem** aims to account for the observation that locative PPs, unlike other PPs, are able to function as full-fledged predicates, assigning an external semantic role. This aspect of locative PPs is unexpected if one assumes that P is a uniformly functional category. However, Botwinik-Rotem shows that such a functional classification of all Ps can be maintained, since the external role can be argued to originate in a phonetically null noun *Place* that heads the extended nominal projection of a locative PP. She discusses a variety of evidence from Hebrew that shows that locatives originate in the functional projection of NP-*Place*, distinct from the locative PP.

In their paper *Silent prepositions: evidence from free relatives*, **Ivano Caponigro and Lisa Pearl** provide evidence in favour of silent prepositions. The existence of silent prepositions has been previously argued for on the basis of the behaviour of expressions like *there, now*, and *that way*. Caponigro & Pearl present a detailed study for free relatives introduced by the *wh*-words *where, when*, and *how*, and show that once silent prepositions are assumed to select both for a *wh*-word and for a free relative as a whole, we can have a fully compositional syntactic/semantic analysis for these free relatives that accounts for their puzzling nominal/prepositional distributional and interpretative properties. Furthermore, they discuss how the proposal can be extended to interrogative clauses introduced by the same *wh*-words, as well as what the licensing conditions and semantic properties of silent prepositions are.

Bert Cappelle's paper *The microstructure of English particle phrases* provides a descriptive classification of the syntax of what Cappelle calls particle phrases (PrtPs). He discusses a range of data, focusing especially on particles being preceded by one or more other particles, particles being followed by a post-modifier (such as a PP), and particles being preceded by peripheral modifiers. He shows that strings of multiple particles are structurally indeterminate. That is, such strings suggest a multiplicity of valid structural analyses, without yielding obvious differences in meaning. A single structure, however, can be put to communicative use in a multiplicity of ways.

Raffaella Folli's paper *Complex PPs in Italian* addresses combinations of two prepositions in Italian, where one indicates the 'PATH of motion', associated with PathP, and the other the 'end point of motion', associated with PlaceP embedded under PathP. It is shown that such complex PPs can combine with any verb of motion to describe an event involving directed motion. Simple PPs, on the other hand, are argued to be locative only. Nevertheless, such locative PPs can still combine with one type of verbs like *run* (as opposed to *float*) to denote an event involving directed motion. Folli argues that the combination of such verbs with locative PPs involves telic pair formation in the sense of Higginbotham (2000). These verbs are argued to be lexically specified with an optional Rv feature (for resultativity), building on Folli (2002). Finally, it is argued, following recent work by Tortora, that the Place denoted by PlaceP can be bounded or unbounded.

In his paper *The fine structure of spatial expressions*, **Marcus Kracht** develops the meaning of spatial PPs based on the idea that the meaning is obtained in several stages. Following insights from Svenonius (this volume), Pantcheva (this volume), and Caponigro & Pearle (this volume), he assumes the structure for spatial PPs in (47).

(47) $[P_{DIR} [P_{STAT} [P_{AXPART} [P_{LOC} DP]]]]$

As Kracht shows, each of the layers can be independently motivated by their semantic contributions to the overall meaning of the PP. This has partly been done already in Kracht (2002), especially for the semantics of location and direction and their interaction. The main innovation of the paper in this volume consists in a more detailed approach to the semantics of location denoting PPs. As shown, location is established by inducing momentary coordinate frames into which the space is coded. This coding is further divided into three subtypes which make use of the inner structure of PPs, the axial part (P_{AXPART}) and the origin (P_{LOC}).

Sander Lestrade's paper *The correspondence between directionality and transitivity* looks at case marking within the PP, focusing on alternations between accusative and another case in several languages, including German, Polish, Russian, Latin and Ancient Greek. He argues for a parallel between the spatial meaning in the adposition phrase and the transitivity in the verb phrase in terms of the notion Proto-Patient. Direction goal and route meanings are argued to be more like transitive meaning than locative expressions. Lestrade draws a distinction between the structural and semantic use of the accusative case, claiming that accusative canonically expresses the Proto-Patient role, and is structurally associated with the object. The analysis is set in terms of Bi-Directional Optimality Theory, relying on the constraints *COMPLEXITY, ACC/PROTO-P, and OBJ/ACC. *COMPLEXITY militates against complexity of interpretation. The intrinsic relationship between accusative case and Proto-Patient interpretation is reflected in the constraint ACC/PROTO-P, and OBJ/ACC places the structural restriction on accusative in the object position.

Jaume Mateu's paper *On the l-syntax of directionality/resultativity: the case of Germanic preverbs* provides a l(exical)-syntactic account of Germanic preverb constructions. Specifically, Mateu sets out to show that such constructions are not as problematic to Hale & Keyser's (1998) syntactic approach to argument structure as they have been claimed to be. He uses two different l-syntactic analyses to explain the formation of complex verbs in German. Those where the Ground is conflated in the verb are analysed using Hale & Keyser's (2000) cognation analysis, where P is seen as a cognate complement. Other complex verbs receive a root-V compound analysis.

Tatiana Nikitina's paper *Pragmatic factors and variation in the expression of spatial goals: The case of into vs. in* explores different strategies to mark goals in American English corpus data. Even in a language like English, where directionality can be encoded lexically by means of a specialised preposition *into*, the same meaning need not be overtly expressed and can instead be inferred from the context, allowing speakers multiple options in describing the same event. Nikitina notes that the tendency to avoid the use of *in* in descriptions that focus on manner or path of motion suggests that the choice between available options is further constrained by pragmatic factors related to the conceptualisation of the event. She takes the variation in the expression of spatial goals found in languages other than English to suggest that the problem of choosing between *into* and *in* is related to a more general problem of co-existence of alternative strategies of expressing directed motion.

Marina Pantcheva's paper *The PLACE of PLACE in Persian* presents the prepositional system in Persian, focussing on the noun-like behaviour of one particular class of prepositions. Considering the silent PLACE hypotheses suggested for Greek and Hebrew locatives in Terzi (2006, to appear) and Botwinik-Rotem (this volume), she argues that a null PLACE element in the extended PP can account for several nominal properties of these Ps. At the same time these Ps are distinct from true nouns, their only nominal property being that they can modify nouns, including the silent PLACE element. Finally, she shows how the entire structure can capture various phenomena characterising this particular prepositional class. The structure she proposes makes it possible to maintain the distinction between Axial Parts, proposed in Svenonius (2006) and nouns, making Axial Parts less nominal by assuming that the only property they share with nouns is that they can be noun modifiers.

Peter Svenonius's paper *Projections of P* presents a cartographic approach to the structure of the adposition phrase. Arguing for a fine-grained syntactic structure for spatial adpositions, including separate projections for degree, he addresses the question of which of the functional projections postulated for the English PP are obligatory in the absence of overt phonological evidence in specific contexts, concluding that in this situation several of the syntactic functional projections are present and have a default setting. The paper examines data from various different languages, including English, Japanese, Yukatek and Zapotec, and draws parallels with debates on the licensing of empty categories elsewhere in syntax. It builds on Svenonius' previous work on Axial Part, a nominal category sometimes found in the extended projection of P, concluding that Axial Part is present as an independent projection in all locative PPs, and suggests that null path projections can be assumed where path is not overtly lexicalised, drawing an analogy with questions of lexicalisation of Tense in the verbal domain.

In her paper *The distribution and interpretation of adjunct locative PPs,* **Naoko Tomioka** notes that adjunct locative PPs in Japanese are more restricted in their interpretation possibilities than their English counterparts. Specifically, she argues that Japanese spatial PPs may express the location of events in the sense of Davidson (1967), but not the location of sub-events. She attributes this interpretive restriction to the claim that adjunct locative PPs in Japanese are subject to the same set of distributional restrictions as so-called "small" modifiers. The exploration of the distribution of these elements leads to the second goal of the paper, namely to couch the current investigation in a larger project concerning event modification. Using the spatial expressions as an example of an event modifier, Tomioka argues that the distribution of event modifiers correlates with the presence of the category that mediates event modification and she identifies this category as VoiceP.

Christina Tortora's paper *Aspect inside* PLACE *PPs* argues that certain PP data from Italian suggest that PLACE, like PATH, can be conceptualised as bounded or unbounded, and that this has a reflex in the grammar. This extension of the 'boundedness' feature to PLACE allows for the more general claim that space (the supercategory that subsumes PATH and PLACE; Jackendoff 1991) can be conceptualised as bounded or unbounded. This in turn reveals that boundedness is relevant not only to *events* and *entities*, but to *space* as well, suggesting that these three super-categories themselves are potentially treatable in a similar way. This is consistent with the tradition, initiated by Bach (1986) (among others), and expanded upon by Jackendoff (1991), of unifying major linguistic categories under one abstract semantic system. Tortora takes the data under discussion to support the claim (proposed by e.g., van Riemsdijk 1990) that Ps are syntactically like Vs and Ns in the sense that they project similar types of functional categories. This similarity across categories is further corroborated by a preliminary discussion that the nature of the argument (e.g., plural vs. singular) can affect the aspectual interpretation of the entire PP.

Chinedu Uchechukwu's paper *The Grammaticalization of prepositional markers in Igbo: The example of the verb root -nyé 'give'* addresses the claim that the Igbo language lacks the category prepositions, making use of other elements to express prepositional meanings. Arguing against this claim, Uchechukwu provides evidence for the presence of prepositions in the languages, examining the grammaticalisation of certain verbs with spatio-temporal meanings to take on prepositional functions. Over the years several researchers have identified certain elements as prepositions, the latest list containing four prepositions (Ụwalaka 1997: 69). Uchechukwu argues that the Igbo language does not suffer from a 'poverty of prepositions,' but instead that it expresses the category in a different manner, through a group of 'prepositional markers.' He focuses on the verb -*nyé* ('give') to illustrate the development of such markers, which occur in specific environments as the second component of compound verbs. Theses elements are sometimes also subject to the rule of vowel harmony in the identified compound verb environment.

Joost Zwarts' paper *Priorities in the production of prepositions* studies the semantic interaction between pairs of closely related prepositions in order to establish the priorities that determine the application of these prepositions to ambiguous situations. He proposes that the division of labour between prepositions is strongly determined by stereotypical regularities in the way notions like support, containment and superiority are related. He takes a production perspective on prepositions, using the theoretical framework of Optimality Theory. Thereby, the mapping from meanings (spatial relations) to forms (prepositions) is construed as an optimisation process. Given a particular spatial relation, different prepositions present themselves as candidates, competing with each other. The winner of the competition, the optimal preposition, is that candidate that best satisfies a ranked system of constraints. In the course of his paper, Zwarts goes through a range of simple two-way competitions between prepositions to derive several spatial priorities.

References

Aboh, E.O. 2006. Possession and predication in complex spatial phrases. Paper presented at the Conference on the syntax and Semantics of Spatial P, June 2nd–4th 2006, Utrecht Institute of Linguistics OTS, Utrecht University.

Abraham, W. 2003. The myth of doubly governing prepositions in German. In *Motion, Direction and Location in Languages. In Honor of Zygmunt Frajzyngier* [Typological Studies in Language 56], E. Shay & U. Seibert (eds), 19–38. Amsterdam: John Benjamins.

Aske, J. 1989. Path predicates in English and Spanish: A closer look. In *Proceedings of the Berkeley Linguistics Society* 15: 1–14.

Bach, E. 1981. On time, tense, and aspects: An essay in English metaphysics. In *Radical Pragmatics*, P. Cole (ed.), 63–81. New York NY: Academic Press.

Bach, E. 1986. The algebra of events. *Linguistics and Philosophy* 9: 5–16.

Baker, M. 2003. *Lexical Categories: Verbs, Nouns, and Adjectives*. Cambridge: CUP.

Beck, S. 2005. There and back again: A semantic analysis. *Journal of Semantics* 22: 3–51.

Beck, S. & Snyder, W. 2001. Complex predicates and goal PPs: Evidence for a semantic parameter. In *Proceedings of the 25th Annual Boston University Conference on Language*, A.H.-J. Do, L. Domínguez & A. Johansen (eds), 114–122. Somerville MA: Cascadilla.

Bierwisch, M. 1988. On the grammar of local prepositions. In *Syntax, Semantik und Lexikon* [Studia Grammatica XXIX], M. Bierwisch, W. Motsch & I. Zimmermann (eds), 1–65. Berlin: Akademie Verlag.

Botwinik-Rotem, I. 2004. The Category P: Features, Projections, Interpretation. PhD Dissertation, Tel-Aviv University.

Bowerman, M. 1996. Learning how to structure space for language: A cross-linguistic perspective. In *Language and Space*, P. Bloom, M.A. Peterson, L. Nadel & M.F. Garrett, (eds), 385–436. Cambridge MA: The MIT Press,

Brugman, C. 1981. *Story of Over*. Bloomington IN: Indiana University Linguistics Club.

Chomsky, N. 1970. Remarks on nominalization. In *Readings in English Transformational Grammar*, R. Jacobs & P. Rosenbaum (eds), 184–221. Waltham MA: Blaisdell Publishing.

Chomsky, N. 1981. *Lectures on Government and Binding: The Pisa Lectures*. Dordrecht: Foris.

Chomsky, N. 1986. *Knowledge of Language: Its Nature, Origin and Use*. New York NY: Praeger.

Chomsky, N. 1995. *The Minimalist Program*. Cambridge MA: The MIT Press.

Corver, N. & van Riemsdijk, H. (eds). 2001. *Semi-lexical Categories*. Berlin: Mouton de Gruyter.

Coventry, Kenny R. & Garrod, S. 2004. *Saying, Seeing and Acting: The Psychological Semantics of Spatial Prepositions*. Hove: Psychology Press.

Creary, L. J., Gawron, M. & Nerbonne, J. 1989. Reference to locations. In *Proceedings of the ASL 1989*.

Cresswell, M. J. 1978. Prepositions and points of view. *Linguistics and Philosophy* 2: 1–41.

Cummins, S. 1996. Movement and direction in French and English. *Toronto Working Papers in Linguistics* 17: 761–794.

Davidson, D. 1967. The logical form of action sentences. In *The Logic of Decision and Action*, N. Rescher (ed.), 81–95. Pittsburgh PA: University of Pittsbuurgh Press.

Dehé, N., Jackendoff, R., McIntyre, A. & Urban, S. (eds). 2002. *Verb-Particle Explorations*. Berlin: Mouton de Gruyter.

den Dikken, M. 2006. On the functional structure of locative and directional PPs. Ms. City University of New York.

Emonds, J. 1972. Evidence that indirect object movement is a structure preserving rule. *Foundations of Language* 8: 546–61.

Emonds, J. 1985. *A Unified Theory of Syntactic Categories*. Dordrecht: Foris.

Everett, D.L. & Kern B. 1997. *Wari': The Pacaas Novos Language of Western Brazil*. London: Routledge.

Fillmore, C. 1968. The case for case. In *Universals in Linguistic Theory*, E. Bach & R.T. Harms (eds). New York NY: Holt, Rinehart & Winston.

Folli, R. 2002. Constructing Telicity in English and Italian. PhD Dissertation, University of Oxford.

Folli, R. & Ramchand, G. 2005. Prepositions and results in Italian and English: An analysis from event decomposition. In *Perspectives on Aspect*, H. Verkuyl, H. de Swart & A. van Hout (eds), 81–105. Dordrecht: Springer.

Fong, V. 1997. The Order of Things: What Directional Locatives Denote. PhD Dissertation, Stanford University.

Fong, V. 2001. Into doing something: Where is the path in event predicates? Ms. National University of Singapore.

Fong, V. & Poulin, C. 1998. Locating linguistic variation in semantic templates. In *Discourse and Cognition*, J.-P. Koenig (ed.), 29–39. Stanford CA: CSLI.

Grimshaw, J. 2000. Extended projections and locality. In *Lexical Specification and Insertion*, P. Coopmans, M. Everaert & J. Grimshaw (eds), 115–133. Amsterdam: John Benjamins.

Hale, K. & Keyser, S.J. 1993. On argument structure and the lexical expression of syntactic relations. In *The View from Building 20: Essays in Linguistics in Honor of Sylvain Bromberger*, K. Hale & S.J. Keyser (eds), 53–109. Cambridge MA: The MIT Press.

Hale, K. & Keyser, S.J. 1998. The basic elements of argument structure. *MIT Working Papers in Linguistics* 32: 73–118.

Hale, K. & Keyser, S.J. 2000. Aspect and the syntax of argument structure. Ms. MIT.

Heine, B., Claudi, U. & Hünnemeyer, F. 1991. *Grammaticalization: A Conceptual Framework*. Chicago IL: University of Chicago Press.

Higginbotham, J. 2000. Accomplishments. Ms. USC and University of Oxford.

Jackendoff, R. 1973. The base rules for prepositional phrases. In *A Festschrift for Morris Halle*, S. Anderson & Paul Kiparsky (eds), 345–356. New York NY: Holt, Rinehart & Winston.

Jackendoff R. 1975. Morphological and semantic regularities in the lexicon. *Language* 51(3): 639–671.

Jackendoff, R. 1983. *Semantics and Cognition*. Cambridge MA: The MIT Press.

Jackendoff, R. 1990. *Semantic Structures*. Cambridge MA: The MIT Press.

Jackendoff, R. 1991. Parts and boundaries. *Cognition* 41(1): 9–45.

Jackendoff, R. 1996. The proper treatment of measuring out, telicity, and perhaps even quantification in English. *Natural Language and Linguistic Theory* 14: 305–354.

Jones, M.A. 1983. Speculations on the expression of movement in French. *A Festschrift for Peter Wexler* [Occasional Papers No. 27 of the Department of Language and Linguistics], J. Durand (ed.), 165–194. Colchester: University of Essex.

Katz, J.J. & Postal, P.M. 1964. *An Integrated Theory of Linguistic Descriptions*. Cambridge MA: The MIT Press.

Kayne, R.S. 2001. Prepositions as probes. Ms. New York University.

Kayne, R.S. 2004. Here and there. In *Lexique, Syntaxe et Lexique-Grammaire/Syntax, Lexis and Lexicon-Grammar: Papers in Honor of Maurice Gross*, C. Leclère, E. Laporte, M. Piot & M. Silberztein (eds), 253–275. Amsterdam: John Benjamins.

Keenan, E.L. & Faltz, L.M. 1985. *Boolean Semantics for Natural Language*. Dordrecht: Reidel.

Kiss, É.K. 2002. *The Syntax of Hungarian*. Cambridge: CUP.

Koopman, H. 2000. Prepositions, postpositions, circumpositions and particles. In *The Syntax of Specifiers and Heads*, H. Koopman (ed.), 204–260. London: Routledge.

Kracht, M. 2002. On the semantics of locatives. *Linguistics and Philosophy* 25: 157–232.

Krifka, M. 1998. The origins of telicity. In *Events and Grammar*, S. Rothstein (ed.), 197–235. Dordrecht: Kluwer.

Lakoff, G. 1987. *Women, Fire and Dangerous Things. What Categories Reveal about the Mind*. Chicago IL: University of Chicago Press.

Langacker, R.W. 1987. *Foundations of Cognitive Grammar I. Theoretical Prerequisites*. Stanford CA: Stanford University Press.

Levinson S. 1996. Relativity in spatial conception and description. In *Rethinking Linguistic Relativity*, J.J. Gumperz & S.C. Levinson (eds), 177–202. Cambridge: CUP.

Levinson, S. 2003. *Space in Language and Cognition: Explorations in Cognitive Diversity*. Cambridge: CUP.

Löbner, S. 1989. German *schon – erst – noch*: An integrated analysis. *Linguistics and Philosophy* 12: 167–212.

Maling, J. 1983. Transitive adjectives: A case of categorial reanalysis. In *Linguistic Categories: Auxiliaries and Related Puzzles*. Vol.1: *Categories*, F. Heny & B. Richards (eds), 253–89. Dordrecht: Reidel.

Mateu, J. 2001. Unselected objects. In *Structural Aspects of Semantically Complex Verbs*, N. Dehé & A. Wanner (eds), 83–104. Frankfurt: Peter Lang.

Mateu, J. 2002. Argument Structure. Relational Construal at the Syntax-Semantics Interface. UAB Dissertation, Bellaterra.

Mateu, J. & Rigau, G. 2002. A minimalist account of conflation processes: Parametric variation at the lexicon-syntax interface. In *Theoretical Approaches to Universals*, A. Alexiadou (ed.), 211–236. Amsterdam: John Benjamins.

Nam, S. 1995. The Semantics of Locative Prepositional Phrases in English. PhD Dissertation, UCLA.

Nikanne, U. 1991. Zones and Tiers: A Study of Thematic Structure. PhD Dissertation, University of Helsinki.

Noonan, M 2005. Spotlight on spatial PPs: Evidence from German shadows. Ms., McGill University.

O'Keefe, J. 1996. The spatial prepositions in English, vector grammar, and the cognitive map Theory. In *Language and Space*, P. Bloom, M.A. Peterson, L. Nadel & M.F. Garrett (eds), 277–316. Cambridge MA: The MIT Press.

van Riemsdijk, H. 1978. *A case study in syntactic markedness: The binding nature of prepositional phrases*. Lisse: The Peter de Ridder Press.

van Riemsdijk, H. 1990. Functional prepositions. In *Unity in Diversity: Papers Presented to Simon C. Dik on his 50th Birthday*, H. Pinkster & I. Genee (eds), 229–241. Dordrecht: Foris.

van Riemsdijk, H. & Huijbregts, R. 2007. Location and locality. In *Clausal and Phrasal Architecture: Syntactic Derivation and Interpretation: A Festschrift for Joseph E. Emonds*. S. Karimi, V. Samiian & W. Wilkins (eds). Amsterdam: John Benjamins.

van Riemsdijk, H. 2007. Case in spatial adpositional phrases: The dative-accusative alternation in German. In *Pitar Mos: A Building with A View. Papers in Honour of Alexandra Cornilescu*, G. Alboiu, A. Avram, L. Avram & D. Isac (eds). Bucharest: Bucharest University Press.

Slobin, D.I. 1996. Two ways to travel: Verbs of motion in English and Spanish. In *Grammatical Constructions: Their Form and Meaning*, M. Shibatani & S.A. Thompson (eds), 195–220. Oxford: Clarendon.

Slobin, D.I. 2004. The many ways to search a frog: Linguistic typology and the expression of motion events. In *Relating Events in Narratives: Vol. 2. Typological and Contextual Perspectives*, S. Strömquist & L. Verhoeven (eds), 219–257. Mahwah NJ: Lawrence Erlbaum Associates.

Song, G. 1997. Cross-linguistic Differences in the Expression of Motion Events and their Implications for Second Language Acquisition. PhD dissertation, Northwestern University.

Stringer, D. 2002. Predication of path in French and Japanese. *Durham Working Papers in Linguistics* 8: 153–166.

Stringer, D. 2005. Locative N in layered PP. Paper presented at the LAGB Annual Meeting 2005, Newcastle University.

Svenonius, P. 2004. Spatial P in English. Ms. Tromsø University.

Svenonius, P. 2006. The emergence of axial parts. *Tromsø Working Papers in Linguistics* 33(1): 50–71.

Svorou, S. 1993. *The Grammar of Space*. Amsterdam: John Benjamins.

Talmy, L. 1975. Semantics and syntax of motion. In *Syntax and Semantics*, Vol. 4, J.P. Kimball (ed.), 181–238. New York NY: Academic Press.

Talmy, L. 1983. How language structures space. In *Spatial Orientation: Theory, Research, and Application*, H. Pick & L. Acredolo (eds), 255–282. New York: Plenum Press.

Talmy, L. 1985. Lexicalization patterns: Semantic structures in lexical forms. In *Language Typology and Syntactic Description* III: *Grammatical Categories and the Lexicon*, T. Shopen (ed.), 57–149. Cambridge: CUP.

Talmy, L. 1991. Path to realization: A typology of event conflation. *Berkeley Lingusitics Society* 17: 480–519.

Talmy, L. 2000. *Towards a Cognitive Semantics*, Vol. 2: *Typology and Process in Concept Structuring*. Cambridge MA: The MIT Press.

Terzi, A. 2006. The misleading lexical status of locative prepositions. Ms. Technological Educational Institute of Patras.

Terzi, A. To appear. Locative prepositions, predicate inversion and full interpretation. Paper presented at 17th International Symposium on theoretical and applied linguistics, University of Thessaloniki.

Ụwalaka, M.A.A.N. 1997. *Igbo Grammar*. Ibadan: The Pen Services.

Verkuyl, H. & Zwarts, J. 1992. Time and space in conceptual and logical semantics: The notion of path. *Linguistics* 30: 483–511.

Wunderlich, D. 1991. How do prepositional phrases fit into compositional syntax and semantics? *Linguistics* 29: 591–621.

Wunderlich, D. & Herweg, M. 1991. Lokale und Direktionale. In *Handbuch der Semantik. Ein Internationales Handbuch der Zeitgenössischen Forschung* [HSK 6], A. von Stechow & D. Wunderlich (eds), 758–785. Berlin: de Gruyter.

Zeller, J. 2001. Lexical particles, semi-lexical postpositions. In *Semi-Lexical Categories*, N. Corver & H. van Riemsdijk (eds), 505–549. Berlin: Mouton.

Zlatev, J. & Yangklang, P. 2003. A third way to travel: The place of Thai in motion-event typology. In *Relating events in narratives: Typological and contextual perspectives*, S. Strömquist & L. Verhoeven (eds), 159–190. Mahwah NJ: Lawrence Erlbaum Associates.

Zubizarreta, M.L. & Oh, E. 2007. *On the Syntactic Composition of Manner and Motion*. Cambridge MA: The MIT Press.

Zwarts, J. 1997a. Lexical and functional properties of prepositions. In *Lexikalische und Grammatische Eigenschaften Präpositionaler Elemente*, D. Haumann & S.J. Schierholz (eds), 1–18. Tübingen: Niemeyer.

Zwarts, J. 1997b. Vectors as relative positions: A compositional semantics of modified PPs. *Journal of Semantics* 14: 57–86.

Zwarts, J. 2005a. Prepositional aspect and the algebra of paths. *Linguistics and Philosophy* 28(6): 739–779.

Zwarts, J. 2005b. The case of prepositions: Government and compositionality in German PPs. Ms. Radboud University Nijmegen and Utrecht University.

Zwarts, J. & Winter, Y. 2000. Vector space semantics: A model-theoretic analysis of locative prepositions. *Journal of Logic, Language and Information* 9: 169–211.

PART I

The general architecture of spatial PPs

The fine structure of spatial expressions

Marcus Kracht
Department of Linguistics, UCLA

In this paper I argue that the meaning of locative PPs is obtained in several stages, more than hitherto assumed. Each of these stages corresponds to a layer of the PP. This is in line with recent developments indicating that the PPs have more than just two heads (Svenonius, this volume). The main innovation of this paper consists in a new way in which the semantics of location denoting PPs is conceived. The idea is that these PPs induce a momentary coordinate frame into which the space is coded. This coding, called *aspect*, is also compositionally defined. Therefore, in order to understand this process properly one needs to look not only at the meaning of the elements but also at the accompanying aspect they induce on the space around us.

1. Introduction

This paper is a continuation of Kracht (2002).[1] Recently, new work has appeared or come to my awareness that has made it necessary to rethink large parts of the earlier work. I am referring here especially to O'Keefe (1996, 2003), Svenonius (this volume), and Zwarts (2003, 2005). The novelty of the present paper is that it uses in addition to the meaning of an expression also the *aspect*, which is an encoding of the space surrounding us.

My main interest is in finding the exact nature of meanings of the various parts involved in a locative expressions and how they work together to form the overall meaning. Much of what I am going to say is not all that new. However, it seems to me that there has been little interaction between – especially – semantic field work and linguistic theory, notably formal semantics. For example, there are studies on direction in language (see the collections van der Zee & Slack 2003; Senft 1997; Bennardo 2002, Levinson & Wilkins 2006; and the monograph Levinson 2003 among others), yet formal semantics seems to be untouched by it. I am trying to

---

1. I wish to thank Marcus Smith and Brook Lillehaugen and two anonymous referees for insightful discussions. Thanks also to the audience of "Syntax and Semantics of Spatial P" for their comments. Errors and omissions are my own responsibility.

rephrase what has been said in other work in terms of conventional (= Montague style) formal semantics in order to bridge this gap. In doing so, I also wish to get a tighter grip on the conceptual issues raised by expressions for location.

2.   The structure of Local PPs

The structure of locative PPs is traditionally thought to be as follows (see Jackendoff (1983)):

(1) $[P_{DIR} [P_{STAT} DP]]$

Here, P_{STAT} is a static preposition[2] and P_{DIR} is a preposition denoting a path or a movement pattern, depending on conceptualisation. An exemplification of this structure is

(2)   [from [under the bridge]]

'the bridge' denotes a particular object; 'under' selects a location on the basis of this object. Finally, 'from' describes a motion in space on the basis of the location. Recently, it has emerged that there is more structure to locative PPs. Based on data of Kham and other languages, Svenonius (this volume) concludes that inside P_{DIR} we also find a projection of P_{AxPart}, describing axial parts of an object (see also Pantcheva this volume). Caponigro & Pearl (this volume) argue for the existence of a silent location creating preposition, which I call here P_{LOC}. Taking this together we arrive at the following structure.

(3) $[P_{DIR} [P_{STAT} [P_{AXPART} [P_{LOC} DP]]]]$

An example, analysed in detail in Section 7, is

(4) $[_{DIR}$ to $[_{STAT}$ in $[_{AXPART}$ front of $[_{LOC} e [_{DP}$ Schumacher's car]]]]].

The present paper will fill this structure with semantic detail. It will be seen that each of these projections can independently be motivated and that they are type theoretically different. (For the notation on types see Appendix B.) This provides a convergence of purely semantic analysis on the one hand and syntactic/morphological analysis on the other, which is so often lacking. Part of the reason that the relationship is so tight is in my opinion the fact that the structure of PPs is less obscured due to movement than that of a clause.

---

2.   In this paper, I shall blur the distinction between pre-, post- and adpositions, as the exact nature of the form does not matter. Also, I am not interested in whether what is a preposition in one language is a case in another or something else.

3.   Aspects of space

This paper will be incomprehensible without getting clear about certain fundamental distinctions. To make this more accessible to a linguistic audience, I have
moved the technical discussion to the end (see Appendix A). Here I shall deal with
the conceptual issues. One important issue is the distinction between *points, vectors* and *coordinates*. On the one hand there is an ontological distinction between
them (see also Appendix A). On the other hand the same space can be looked
at essentially in three ways, using points, using vectors, and using coordinates.
These ways of looking at the same object (the space) I call an *aspect*. The space
consists of points (the aspect is the identity). Points are given to us as *locations* of
things. Based on some fixed givens we can name the locations (or points) via some
scheme. The first scheme is by means of *vectors*. These are sets of pairs of points
(see Appendix A). A vector indicates *motion*. (The name comes from Latin *vehere*
'to carry, to drive'.) Given a set of cardinal points we can set up a coordinate frame
and associate with each point a tuple of numbers, called the *coordinates*.

The distinction between these three notion is relevant even in the Euclidean
space $\mathbb{R}^3$, where points *are* triples of numbers, and vectors can be (and often are)
seen as members of the space itself. Even here the identification between points
and vectors is not as innocent as it appears because the coordinates of an object
change as we change the cardinal points of our coordinate frame. Thus, coordinates are not absolute; they are established with reference to some other points.
This makes them impractical in daily life. We shall return to this issue below.

However, the distinction is perhaps best seen by looking at the nature of physical spaces. Spaces are sets of points that have a particular topological structure.
They constitute what is called a *differentiable manifold*: if you have an object moving in it you can define the derivative of motion, the *motion vector*. The motion
vector, unfortunately, cannot always be identified with a vector of your manifold.
Consider living, as we do, on the surface of a ball. Then if some object, say a car, is
in motion along a street, the motion vector points straight ahead. If you follow that
vector you are actually moving away from the surface. The car, however, does not
actually follow that vector even if it appears to go straight; rather, it will constantly
readjust its motion vector so as to stay on the surface. (This is a consequence of
the earth's gravity. If that did not exist, the car would really leave the surface.) One
may check in fact that any motion vector for some object has the same property:
though it points in the direction of motion, it can only be followed for a small
distance until it needs readjustment. One would like to dismiss these facts as hair-
splitting since the curvature is so small. But I plead caution: we shall argue that
many Oceanic systems are exactly like our cardinal directions; but because the
singularity of the system is quite close to the speakers, the anomaly of such systems

is clearly felt. Also, when sailing with a ship, these problem really do matter. Vector fields arise naturally (cardinal directions are a case in point) and we shall look at them below.

Thus vectors arise as the directions of momentary motion. How can we actually represent them? The idea is this. Manifolds are subsets P of the Euclidean space $\mathbb{R}^n$ for some n. Vectors are not objects of P, they are equivalence classes of pairs of points. At each point $\underset{\sim}{x}$ of P there is a so-called *tangent space* of vectors tangential to the surface of P. (Intuitively, it is the space of all vectors from $\underset{\sim}{x}$ to $\underset{\sim}{z}$, where $\underset{\sim}{z}$ is infinitesimally close to $\underset{\sim}{x}$.) A *vector field* is a function f from P into the vectors of $\mathbb{R}^n$ such that for each $\underset{\sim}{x}$, $f(\underset{\sim}{x})$ is a member of the tangent space at $\underset{\sim}{x}$. Vectors can be added but points or pairs of points cannot (see Appendix A). Typically, sentences do not talk about vectors directly. Mostly, they qualify their length (by talking about speed). For example, the following does not talk about a motion vector, it only gives us begin and end points of a motion event.

(5)   Jack was driving from Paris to Bordeaux.

A further distinction to make is that between points and their coordinates. It is often taken for granted that points in space simply are triples of numbers. The fact that this identification is possible in theory does not mean, however, that it is practically speaking helpful. There is namely a difference between talking abstractly about coordinates and actually calculating with them. There are good arguments to reject the view that humans store locations of objects by assigning absolute coordinates to them (a view, that has to my knowledge never been explicitly proposed anyway):

1.   it is very difficult if not impossible to establish these coordinates in the first place, and
2.   since we are ourselves moving in space we would either have to constantly update our own position or else recalculate all coordinates of the objects.
3.   there are no agreed upon coordinates of universal validity.

Instead, we establish coordinates – when needed – relative to some objects. And so we express location relative to an object (the *landmark*) and all positions are calculated relative to this object. Thus whether or not an object is seen as 'moving' depends on its relative position with respect to the landmark, and not on its own movement.[3]

---

3.   The reader may be aware that there is actually no such thing as an absolute coordinate frame, so that even in physics it is pointless to ask which object is moving and which one is not. In fact, constant motion cannot be differentiated from rest; only the change of velocity can.

To see the difference, consider two racing cars, one steered by Schumacher and the other by Alonzo. Alonzo is staying exactly 50m behind Schumacher throughout the first lap. One way of saying this is as follows.

(6)   Alonzo stayed behind Schumacher during the first lap.

It is clearly not the case that Alonzo's car was at rest. It was, however, at rest relative to the other car. To express this simple fact in absolute coordinates – anchored, say in Greenwich – would be a painful exercise, and useless, too. Instead, we think of Schumacher's car as the origin of a coordinate frame relative to which the trajector's location is defined. Now, if there is anything we must take home from physics it is this: it does not matter where we choose the origin of our coordinate system. All that changes is the triple of numbers for each point.

The point ultimately is what actually is cognitively speaking the most convenient way to establish or find a location. We would expect on that basis that absolute coordinates are rarely used as opposed to positions relative to known landmarks (mountains, buildings etc). Moreover, we use polar coordinates, separating distance and orientation, rather than Cartesian coordinates. This has been established also experimentally (see Landau 2003 and O'Keefe 2003 for just two sources).

However, as much as the present paper is informed about the cognitive research on space, it is not the primary goal to go into any details of it. Rather, I want to take the opportunity to develop a framework inside formal semantics that takes as much advantage as it can from cognitive and foundational work in order to present a coherent picture. Again, Joost Zwarts in the work cited above has taken important steps in this direction. What is missing so far is a complete, bottom-up picture of how spatial meanings are being built.

4.   Orientation

We shall walk the reader through the three steps: from objects to axial parts, from there to locations, and finally to directions. (As will become apparent later, some of these steps are optional.) The reader should think about the example (4). At the bottom we have an object, from which we extract a location. Using the object we establish some target location using polar coordinates: they consist in a direction

---

Our earthly frame of coordinates, on which 'north' and 'west' and so on are defined looks perfectly absolute, but as the earth is revolving around the sun the 'absoluteness' of this frame only holds with respect to points on earth.

combined with a distance. While the distance is given by the metric of the space, the direction is established with reference to some cardinal axes. Here is an example.

(7)   We live 1/4 mile to the west of UCLA.

The reference point is (the location of) UCLA, the direction is 'west', and the distance is 1/4 mile. We occasionally draw attention to the fact that statements such as (7) must be understood with reference to some chosen 'centre' of the region under discussion. For it is evident that distance from a region is not well defined if that region is large, as in this case.

An example involving motion is this.

(8)   They sailed north for 1000 miles.

The reference point is (the location of) the ship, direction is 'north', and the distance covered is 1000 mile. There are significant differences between these examples, as we shall see.

4.1   Origin

The calculations begin at the bottom, with the element e of (4). It is usually empty. It derives a *location* ϱ from an object. Moreover, as it does so, it provides us with a new aspect to our space: from now on we may actually look at each of the space points as 2 vector. Namely we associate to x the vector $\overrightarrow{ox}$.

The DP provides us with the *landmark* (or *ground*, depending on usage). From this we derive a region as follows. We assume that there is a function loc', which, given an object x and a time point t returns the region that x (or more exactly the *solid* of x) occupies at t.

(9) $loc' : e \times \tau \to r$

To define the origin of the coordinate frame, we can make several choices, for example, we may choose the volumetric centre (see Appendix A for the function $c(\cdot)$):

(10) $origo' : e \times \tau \to p : (x, t) \mapsto c(loc'(x, t))$

4.2   Directions

Having established the origin, we now turn to coordinate frame. The coordinate frame is the basis for defining any directions. It needs three points that define what I call the *cardinal directions*, which we may, loosely speaking, identify as 'up', 'front' and 'left', in that order.

Definition 1. A **coordinatiser** *is a function from points of the space (and additional parameters) into the set of coordinate systems such that f(x) is a coordinate system anchored at x.*

Thus, coordinatisers are mappings from $P \times S$ into P^4, such that $f(\varrho, \overrightarrow{q}) = \langle \varrho(\overrightarrow{q}), p_1(\overrightarrow{q}), p_2(\overrightarrow{q}), p_3(\overrightarrow{q}) \rangle$ is a coordinate system (where $\overrightarrow{q} \in S$ is a possibly empty sequence of extra parameters). The intuitions behind this is that the coordinate system represents an ideal viewer positioned at ϱ, facing p_2, head directed towards p_1. Our definition therefore restricts the range of coordinatisers to right handed orthonormal systems. This can be relaxed; we may allow vectors of any length for the coordinate systems (applying some rescaling, so that the metrical structure is not affected) and we may even allow skew coordinates (where the axes are not orthogonal to each other). Nothing will affect the setup that I sketch here, so I shall remain with a more conservative choice. Once a coordinate frame has been set up, our aspect on the space changes again; now points are no longer assigned vectors, but rather triples of numbers, called *coordinates* (Cartesian or polar).

Alternatively, a coordinatiser is a triple of maps

(11) $(\underset{\sim}{x}, \cdots) \mapsto \langle u(\underset{\sim}{x}, \cdots), f(\underset{\sim}{x}, \cdots), \ell(\underset{\sim}{x}, \cdots) \rangle$

where, $u(\underset{\sim}{x}, \cdots), f(\underset{\sim}{x}, \cdots)$ and $\ell(\underset{\sim}{x}, \cdots)$ form a right handed system of vectors. Here the dots represent additional parameters on which the functions depend. This allows to reduce coordinatisers to maps from P to vectors, as we shall from now on assume. As Levinson (2003) explains, there are mainly three systems, *absolute*, *intrinsic* and *relative*. The key difference between them is the number of parameters that go into their definition.

4.2.1   *Absolute frames*
The easiest case is provided by functions needing no additional parameters. These are the absolute systems. The standard absolute system derives from a coordinatiser which returns for every point on earth three directions: up, north, and west. However, there is more flexibility. A *absolute system* creates a coordinate system based on only one input: the origin.[4] Given that we need three vectors, it is easy to see that an absolute coordinatiser is a triple of vector fields.

Recall that a vector field is a function that returns for every point a vector. Examples of vector fields are: the direction and string of wind on earth. There is a theorem known as the *Hairy Ball Theorem*, which says that for every continuous

---

4.   I ignore here some fascinating complications. Some local expressions can be used only within a certain range. For example, body parts may very often only be used if distances are small. This is true even for English: you normally don't say that Hamburg is to your left when standing somewhere in Berlin facing north. The islands of Polynesia have a coordinate system based on a seaward-landward axis as 'front'. Such systems tend to be local, they are confined to the (more or less) immediate surroundings of the island. For a specific example of dependence on distance see (Florey & Kelly 2002).

vector field over the earth there must be at least one point for which the value of the vector field is the zero vector. Thus, there must always be one point on earth where the wind is not blowing. There is an application for absolute systems: no matter how an absolute system is defined, it is either discontinuous or is undefined at certain points. Consider for example the vector field $\lambda x.\text{north}'(x)$ denoted by 'north', which returns for every point a unit vector pointing north. By the Hairy Ball Theorem this is impossible. Indeed, if you are standing on the north pole, there is no direction north any more, while if you are standing on the south pole, any direction could be called north. Similar systems are found in many Oceanic languages: these generally have two directional terms, one meaning 'seaward' and the other 'landward' (see part 4.2 in the survey (Palmer 2002)). The 'landward' vector points from the location towards some specific location ℓ_c on the island, say, the peak of some mountain. (Oceania consists basically of plenty of relatively small islands.) 'Seaward' points opposite to 'landward'. Obviously, when standing at that location ℓ_c, neither 'landward' nor 'seaward' are defined any more. If we were to extend the system over the entire surface of earth, there would be analogous point (the antipode of ℓ_c).[5]

The Oceanic systems work well on a small scale, while they become unusable on a large scale. Our cardinal directions are somewhat hard to use in general, and people vary in their ability to use them consistently. Levinson (2003) has argued that speakers of Guugu-Yimidhirr manage to keep track of the direction of north, and has argued that this is due to the lack of intrinsic or relative frames. Such language is certainly extreme. Moreover, more than just the influence of language seems to be needed. Ed Keenan (p.c.) tells me that conversations in Malagasy can only be successful if the participants know where north is. In contrast to speakers of Guugu-Yimidhirr, who seem to manage this orientational task with considerable ease, one does find Malagasy speakers enter in a conversation with people in a foreign village and, before starting the actual conversation, ask the other one "Tell me where north is!". Thus, setting up coordinate frames (and therefore coordinates) is a considerable task, one that has been somewhat neglected in the work in formal semantics of spatial expressions.

4.2.2   Intrinsic frames

Coordinatisers that are not absolute are *relative*. A subpart of the relative coordinatisers are the *intrinsic coordinatisers*. An *intrinsic* coordinatiser is one that uses the properties of the landmark alone. The additional parameters are thus the

---

5.   It was Ben Keil who brought it to my attention that the Oceanic system is analogous to our north-south system.

landmark plus its orientation and posture. One example is 'in front of', which defines an axis depending on the canonical front of the object. I will not go into much detail; the front is as much shape dependent as it depends on use, for example. Suffice it to say that 'in front of' is certainly not absolute since on the same spot objects can be oriented in different ways. A distinct version of intrinsic frames is exemplified by 'ahead' or 'behind'. The direction 'front' is here specified using the direction that the landmark is taking at reference time. This is one use of 'behind', which is distinct from another and which uses the canonical orientation rather than the direction. This can lead to ambiguities. Consider the following sentence

(12)   Alonzo is right behind Schumacher.

Imagine the situation where Schumacher is actually driving backwards. Then there is a conflict between an understanding of 'behind' as deriving from 'towards the rear of the car' and another understanding which is 'against the direction of movement'. Typically these are aligned: if someone is driving forward, in order to face the people behind him he has to turn his head, that is, look against the direction that he is driving. But when he is driving backwards, he is facing the people that are driving 'behind' him, in one sense of 'behind'; but in another he is not. This ambiguity is pervasive. 'Top' can mean among other: 'against gravitational force' (absolute), or 'in direction of its top' (intrinsic).

In Niikanne (2003) it is reported that Finnish has postpositions that can only be used when the landmark is in motion.

(13)   Buick on Volvon edellä.
       'The Buick is driving such that it stays in front of the Volvo.'

(14)   Buick on Volvon edessä.
       'The Buick is in front of the Volvo.'

I analyse this as follows. The postposition simply requires motion of the landmark. It is not clear to me whether this is because it establishes the coordinate frame on the basis of the movement direction (since this would require motion). That will have to be established.

4.2.3   Viewer oriented frames

There is a third kind of coordinatiser, called *relative* by Levinson; since the previous was also relative, let me call this one *viewer oriented*. This one involves yet another point, namely the point of a *viewer*. The latter is left undefined; under normal circumstances it will be 'speaker's eyes', but that is shiftable. One situation where this might occur is in indirect speech or speech or attitude report. The viewer contributes a canonical system in the following way. 'Up' is aligned with 'top' (so, if the viewer is standing upside down, that may be what other people call 'down'). 'Front' is aligned with the vector from viewer to landmark. (And here, as in all cases, directions are established from centre of the solid to centre of the solid, or, in the case of humans, using the 'third eye' in place of the volumetric centre as origo.) 'Top' presents this third kind: I can use it with viewer centred coordinates. When I am standing upside down then what I call top is what other people call bottom. Let me note that viewer centred directions are subject to the same dichotomy as tenses: we can imagine them to pick as viewer the one producing the utterance, or the one holding an attitude in an attitudinal report or issuing the utterance in a speech report. In Pima (Uto-Aztecan), verbs are obligatorily accompanied by particles that indicate whether the situation happens in front of the speaker or on the side or elsewhere.[6] These particles respond to the place of the person issuing the utterance; when used in reported speech, they respond to issuer of the utterance in which they occur. Thus, they are *relative* or *shiftable*.

I will briefly mention a subtlety concerning orientation. I am consistently speaking of vectors. This means that given a point as origin and a line through it, there are two unit vectors originating at this point, and they go in opposite directions. This matters, though not always to the same degree. There is a noticeable difference between 'up' and 'front' on the one hand and 'left' on the other. The first two typically are distinguished form their antipodes 'down' and 'back', while many languages do not differentiate 'left' and 'right'. This happens in some Oceanic languages (see Palmer 2002, or Hyslop 2002 for specific cases). Psychologically, confusion between 'left' and 'right' is not uncommon, while the other directions are never confused with their antipodes. This is important insofar as the idea that a preposition such as 'behind' needs an entire coordinate system to be defined will strike one as an overkill: it simply needs only one direction (direction of movement) and is otherwise rotationally symmetric. Yet, it makes a (psychological) difference whether that axis is the 'up' or 'front' axis as opposed to the 'left axis' (see work cited in Niikanne 2003), and so I opted for the more elaborate analysis.

Before closing this section, let me add some remarks on the life span of a coordinate frame. In principle, any preposition can use its own coordinate frame. Thus, when we say something is south of UCLA and to my right I am issuing descriptions based on two different coordinate systems. Furthermore, one is intrinsic and the other is absolute. Thus, whether at a given instance we apply our own coordinate system or an intrinsic one or an absolute one depends – in part – on the preposition. Thus part of the meaning of the preposition is contained in the coordinatiser. (This is why I have decided to gloss 'in front of' as containing the

---

6.   Thanks to Marcus Smith for bringing this to my attention.

parts 'in (direction)' and 'front of'. The second is the coordinatiser.) Not all prepositions need a coordinatiser; I mention 'in' as an example. True body part expressions are another case in point. In the latter case we talk about the close region projected from the volumetric centre through some specified region of the solid. This part – it seems to me – is specified independently of the coordinate frame. A case in point is provided by 'back' in Zapotec (see Lillehaugen 2006). It has two meanings: 'behind' and 'at or on the back of'. These are distinct in the case of a deer, for example. It seems, if only for historical reasons, beneficial not to force the true body part nominals through the process of coordinatisation, and have them establish the region directly through projection from the volumetric centre. This does throw up questions about the entire system of prepositional meanings in a language and its interconnections because we need to know when and how it is that a body part nominal is coerced into a purely spatial expression that functions by means of coordinatisation. The empirical side is well documented (see (Svorou 1993)). What I wish to provide here is a formal framework within which these questions can be raised to sufficient degree of precision.

Also, if a rocket is flying vertically upwards, then to fly behind the rocket is the same as to fly upwards. The 'front' axis then seems to be aligned with the 'up' axis. This, however, is a misunderstanding. Each spatial expressions projects its own coordinate system; sometimes some of the expressions are used with the same coordinatiser, for example, 'south' and 'west'; and similarly 'front' and 'left' in their intrinsic readings. Also, many coordinate frames that appear to be skewed result from a conflict between the definitions of the axes. Some axes are defined by the sun, others by the direction of winds (e.g., the Monsun), yet others by the shape of the environment (the coastline, rivers) (see Palmer 2002 for details). In all these cases, it is generally assured that different adpositions are based on the same coordinate frame and therefore do not constitute evidence for skew coordinate systems.

4.3   Summary

The origo is defined as above. The 'up' axis is typically defined to be 'against gravitational force'. (Exceptions exist.) So, it remains to specify 'front' and 'left'. Here, considerable variation occurs.

1. **Absolute type.** The directions are fixed by the origo o alone. Typical representatives: 'north', 'west'.
2. **Intrinsic type.** The directions are fixed by properties of the landmark x alone.
   a. 'front' is defined to be: 'in direction of x's motion'. This obviously requires x to be in motion. Typical example: Finnish 'edessä' (see Niikanne, 2003); English 'behind'.

b. x has an inherent axis of the required kind (people, animals, cars, chairs, buildings). Typical example: 'in front of'.

3. **Viewer oriented type.** The directions are fixed with reference to a second entity (typically the viewer). The front/back axis is determined by drawing a line from viewer to the origo. Typical examples: 'behind'. (In Hausa, 'in front of' is used in this situation just like English 'behind', as if the object faces the same way as the viewer rather than facing the opposite direction.)

It is noted that the Hausa preposition 'in front of' is classed as intrinsic, but from a type theoretic point of view it must be seen as involving the viewer; it is therefore viewer oriented.

Notice the qualifying phrase 'of the right kind' in ②(b). A flagpole, for example, has an axis, but is significantly less felicitous with 'in front of' since its canonical orientation is upward. It is interesting to note that if that same flagpole was lying on the ground, still the phrase 'in front of' is not felicitous simply because the flagpole has no intrinsic front-axis. One should bear in mind, though, that this is a convention of the phrase 'in front of' and the English language.

It thus emerges that the sentence 'the car turned left' can have various distinct meanings. If the car is moving we may consider ourselves aligned with its motion vector and determine the direction of 'left' using the direction of our left arm. This is independent of which way the car or the driver is facing. If you are sitting in the car facing opposite, 'left' then means exactly the other direction. Still different is the meaning of the sentence uttered by an outside observer, who may take his own perspective on the matter. Crucially, the distinctions have nothing to do with the direction of 'left' per se. They have to do with the way the coordinate frame is established.

5. Location

When we are done with setting up the coordinate frame, our space can be seen as fully coordinatised. Regions can be coded as subsets of $\mathbb{R}^3$, with the coordinates established using the origin and the axis system. We have therefore reached a third level of abstraction, where the spatial schema is now represented using triples of numbers.

The location of the figure is determined on the basis of the location of the landmark. This is typically done by giving a direction and a distance, both of which are optional.

(15)   The library is 100m to the west from here.

(16)   The squirrel is in front of the car.

(17)   Hamburg is less than 300 km away from Berlin.

The distance is determined by the metric and shall interest us no further; the direction however makes use of the coordinate frame just established. A preposition such as 'in front of' determines the direction where the figure is found by comparing it with the direction of the front axis. This is in turn the y-axis of the intrinsic landmark system.[7] This is the idea behind *templates* (from (Logan & Sadler 1996)). A template is a function from $\mathbb{R}^3$ to $[0, 1]$ (of type $\xi \to d$). It measures the degree to which a given point is in the described location (see also O'Keefe 1996, 2003). A point will fit the description to a certain degree and so there are not just two answers to the question 'is x in front of y' but rather a continuum; I shall refer to the elements of $[0, 1]$ as *truth degrees*.

5.1   Spatial templates

A spatial template tells us how well the trajector is located, based on its coordinates. It takes advantage of the coordinate frame. O'Keefe (2003) gives specific formulae to calculate the value. The formula correlates distance with aberration from the 'front' axis. For example, O'Keefe (2003) uses the formula for the so-called *boundary vector cells* (BVC), which predicts the strength of the stimulus in a cell (I have simplified the formula setting $d_i = \varphi_i = 0$; α means 'is proportional to').

(18) $g(r,\theta) \exp[-r^2/2\sigma_r^2]/\sqrt{2\pi\sigma_r^2} \times \exp[-\theta^2/2\sigma_a^2]/\sqrt{2\pi\sigma_a^2}$

These templates have the shape of a raindrop. The idea here is that there is a two way normal distribution across distance and aberration. From this we can get a template $\varphi(x)$ calculating the polar coordinates for x before submitting this to $g(r, \theta)$.[8] Therefore, the meaning of 'in front of' does not simply establish two sorts of regions, those that *are* in front of and those that are *not*. Rather, the judgement is graded. An object is not merely 'in front of' another object; it is 'in front of' that object to a certain *degree*. The degree of fit is added through a process that is governed by cognitive processes which are independent of the language in question.[9] An additional consequence of formulae like (18) is that the acceptability of

---

7.   More precisely, the way I'd like to think about it is to align 'front' with the x-axis, 'left' with the y-axis and 'up' with the z-axis. But this is a minor issue. Also notice that a language can use several coordinatisers, and Ps select for one or the other. The details of this are straightforward to implement.

8.   This is just a suggestion.

9.   It may depend on the number of oppositions the language provides, a point that I shall suppress here for simplicity.

'in front of' decreases with distance, which is desired. All directionals have the tendency to become less good at great distances.

If this template derives from the physiology of the visual apparatus, then from a linguistic perspective it is enough to know that 'in front of' denotes a certain axis. Linguistically, the meaning of 'in front of' resides entirely in the coordinatiser (rather, the second component thereof). This at least is language dependent. In Zapotec, for example, many objects have intrinsic parts (see Levinson 2003), and in Hausa trees have intrinsic fronts. We may learn that 'front' is determined by shape, use, direction to different degrees. However, once we know all this there still is a residue that is encoded in the template and seems to be quite independent of language, and more or less cognitively determined. However, it is important to point out that the fact that 'in front of' can be taught simply by saying which axis it establishes does not mean that the axis alone is its real meaning. The addition of templates definitely changes the extensional content of 'in front of' and must therefore be counted in. It is the fact that language is taught from humans to humans that allows us to omit certain details of meaning. Part of the meaning is simply 'subliminal'; but that does not mean it is not there.

In order to judge whether an object is 'above' or 'in front of' a landmark, several factors must be taken into account. These are: the aberration from the principal axis that the localiser is based on, the distance of the trajector, and the shape of both trajector and landmark. As O'Keefe (2003) points out, there is a correlation between distance and aberration. The larger the aberration, the closer the trajector must be in order to still be in the relation. All this is a matter of the precise formulation of the relation. What is however substantial is that the functions proposed in O'Keefe (2003) do not define precise regions. Rather, they are continuous functions from coordinates to [0, 1]. This affords us two interpretations: we consider a prototypical notion of 'in front': no aberration, and at a certain distance. We then assign all other points in space a goodness of fit value (from [0, 1]) which declares how well the location of that point fits the description 'in front of'. Or, we declare the function itself to be the meaning of 'in front of' (which we have to do in an extensional setting).

5.2   Graded neighbourhoods

A template assigns values to points. However, the location of an object is a region. Therefore, we need to see how that point based template can be upgraded to regions. This could be done in several ways. One is to reduce the region to a point, say, the volumetric centre; another is to average over the entire region; the third is to take the maximum value over the region. I am inclined to dismiss the last option. The reason is twofold. Consider a ring around the landmark. If we take the maximum value we would get that the ring is a perfect fit for 'in front of', but this is intuitively not right. I am unable to choose between the other two options. If we choose the first, we now have constructed the core meaning of 'in front of' as

(19) $\xi(r) := \lambda r.\varphi(c(r)): p \to d$

(Recall that ρ ranges over connected subset of $\mathbb{R}^3$, not to be confused with actual regions. As with ξ, a path connected set of triples may denote many regions; exactly which one it denotes depends on the coordinatisation.) More serious problems arise with the landmark itself. We have so far pretended that the landmark is a point at the origin. But how about expressions such as 'in front of the house'? Here, different proposals have been made, see (Carlson et al., 2003). Overall, the idea is to reduce region based relations to point based relations, the difference in the proposals are mainly with respect to the formula that is being employed.

Now take again the phrase

(20)   in front of the house

The meaning we have just arrived at for this expression is that of what I call a *graded neighbourhood*. It tells us for any region r to what degree it fits the description. The limiting case of such a neighbourhood is provided by a function that has only two values: true and false. For that function, a region either receives 1 (is in the neighbourhood) or 0 (is out of the neighbourhood). This is precisely the definition of neighbourhood in Kracht (2002). Here we use degrees of membership.

5.3   Parametrised neighbourhoods

Since both the landmark and the trajector may be in motion there is a complex interaction between the motion of the trajector and the actual description as its motion has to be coordinatised through the position of the landmark. To stay behind Schumacher is not to stand still; in fact, the spectators cannot be said to stay behind Schumacher. However, another pilot, say Alonzo, can stay behind Schumacher, though he in fact is also moving very fast. Thus, to uphold a stationary spatial relationship with respect to a moving landmark one has to move as well.

Fortunately, matters are not that complex. Since the landmark is the centre of the coordinate frame, the motion of landmark is already accounted for. Only the relative motion is visible. Let us see how this goes. The ingredients into the meaning of 'in front of' are – at least – twofold. First, we are given a coordinatiser $\kappa(x, t)$, which yields a coordinate frame based on the landmark x and time point t. The second ingredient is the template χ.

(21) $\sigma(x, t) := (\chi(\mathrm{loc}'(x, t)_{\kappa(x,t)}))^{\kappa(x,t)} : p \to d$

This function depends on the object and time point. To remove the time dependency we abstract:

(22) $\sigma := \lambda x.\lambda t.(\chi(\text{loc}'(x,t)_{\kappa(x,t)}))^{\kappa(x,t)} : e \to t \to p \to d$

So, the meaning is a function from objects to functions from time points to functions from points to values. It gives acceptability ratings for space points, given a landmark and a time point.

5.4   Distance

Distance to the landmark is given in terms of phrases like 'half a mile', '3mm' and so on. The reflex of a syntactician is to label these phrases as specifiers of the PP, which means they would semantically compose with the P'. The meaning of the P' as we have just indicated is a parametrised region. To apply the meaning 'half a mile' to the parametrised neighbourhood 'behind Schumacher' requires considerable sophistication, though. This is because it factually states the distance of the trajector from the landmark (the r in polar coordinates), and such information is only indirectly present in the parametrised neighbourhood, if at all. On the other hand, in and of itself it can be construed as a relation between regions, and so there is a natural interpretation of it as a modifier for P.

6.   Directionality

We have now finished the semantics of the inner layers: the meaning of PP_{Stat} is a function from time points to functions from space points to the unit interval. There is a time dependency, which monitors the position of the trajector relative to the landmark. The evaluation metric is determined by the spatial template, which is part of the meaning of P_{Stat}.

Now we shall look at the outer layer. Directionality specifies change of the trajector with respect to the landmark. Fong (1997) has analysed directionals as phase quantifiers. These are special functions from I to $\{0, 1\}$, the set of truth-values. By contrast, Zwarts (2005) claims that directionality is best described in terms of canonical paths. In Kracht (2002) directionals were classed as event modifiers, and directionality was taken to be a phase quantifier, though the definition of a phase quantifier was slightly more liberal. By generalising the idea of phase quantification even more, we obtain a synthesis of these views.

Let us call a *path* a function π from $[0, x] \rightarrow \mathbb{R}^3$, where $x \geq 0$.[10] The *velocity* is defined by the length of $\frac{d}{dt}\pi(t)$. (This requires that π is differentiable.) π is *canonical* if its velocity is 1.

Lemma 2. *Let* $\pi : J \rightarrow \mathbb{R}^3$ *be a differentiable path. Then there is a positive real number* x, *a monotone, bijective function* $\sigma : J \rightarrow [0, x]$ *and a canonical path* $\gamma : [0, x] \rightarrow \mathbb{R}^3$ *such that* $\pi = \gamma \circ \sigma$. *Both* x *and* σ *are unique.*

The number x is the length of the path π. Intuitively, γ represents the motion pattern. It shows us in what order the object visits the space points. σ grounds the abstract motion pattern in real time: it maps an interval of time points onto the unit interval and shows how fast the movement is. Since $\frac{d}{dt}\gamma = 1$ we have

$$(23) \quad \frac{d}{dt}\sigma = \left| \frac{d}{dt}\pi \right|$$

Since $\sigma(0)$ is given, this completely defines σ.

Zwarts (2005) observes that movement patterns can be characterised as certain sets of canonical paths. We shall be content with a brief list.

1. **stative:** the path stays inside the location;
2. **cofinal:** the path is moving into the location;
3. **coinitial:** the path is moving out of the location;
4. **approximative:** the path moves closer to the location (but not necessarily reaching it);
5. **recessive:** the path moves away from the location.

The motion can in fact be recoded as a change in goodness of fit. Recall that rather than giving us truth values, the spatial template actually supplies real numbers between 0 and 1. These numbers depend – holding aberration constant – directly on distance: the closer an object, the better the fit. It follows that a path is static if the goodness of fit remains constant and close to 1 throughout event time; cofinal if it improves (is upward monotone) during event time and reaches 1 (or some sufficiently close neighbourhood); coinitial if it decreases and approximative if it is monotone increasing. We can now attempt a synthesis of these views in the following way.

Definition 3. *A generalised phase quantifier is a function from* [0, 1] *to* [0, 1] *(of type* $\tau \rightarrow d$).

---

10. I refrain from discussing the possibility of open or half open intervals. They are only relevant in connection with aspect. Also, since we are now assuming that we have a coordinate system, we treat space points as triples of reals. In general, paths are functions into the point set.

The codomain is the domain of truth values, while the domain is actually a unit time interval. Thus a generalised phase quantifier describes a change in truth value. We expect this change to be continuous, but no such condition has been put in. Directionality of movement can now be described entirely by means of the (generalised) phase quantifier that it uses.

A movement is *approximative* if the phase quantifier is monotone increasing, *recessive* if it is decreasing. Movement is *cofinal* if the quantifier is monotone increasing and reaches 1, *coinitial* if it is monotone decreasing and starts at 1.

7.   The syntactic structure revisited

I shall now revisit the structure (3) and retrace the types associated with the phrases. Our target phrase is the somewhat stilted (4), repeated here as (24).

(24) $[_{DIR}$ to $[_{STAT}$ in $[_{AXPART}$ front of $[_{LOC}$ e $[_{DP}$ Schumacher's car]]]]].

As we walk up the structure, not only do we get different objects, but also our space gets structured differently; the aspect on it changes.

Definition 4. *An **aspect** on the space P is an injective function $\alpha : P \to Q$ for some Q. The type of Q is the type of the aspect α.*

We start with the identity aspect $\alpha : P \to P$. on the space P. P is a manifold embedded into some space $\mathbb{R}^n$. The constant s̲c̲ denotes Schumacher's car.

7.1 P_{LOC}

This element can be identified with loc′. Applied to an object (denoted by the DP) and a time point (to be supplied), it yields a *region*. Additionally, the region is compressed to a point, the gravitational centre. This point serves as the origin of the coordinate frame. The space becomes structured as a vector space (the tangent space to the manifold at the origin).[11] The empty preposition argued for in Caponigro & Pearl (2007) is of the kind P_{LOC}.

Spatial points can be given as vectors. These vectors code the points as follows: given $\vec{x}$ and the origin ọ, the space point denoted by $\vec{x}$ is the unique u such that (ọ, u) ∈ $\vec{x}$. If ọ depends on time, so does u. The aspect is the function x ↦ ọ, with ọ the origin. It is of *vector type* (v). Thus, the contribution of e is both in having a

---

[11].   See Kracht 2002 for a discussion as to why objects and locations are conceptually distinct in language.

meaning and giving us an aspect. The phrase $[_{\text{LOC}}e\ [_{\text{DP}}\text{Schumacher's car}]]$ denotes the location of Schumacher's car at t; its aspect is the function assigning to each space point the momentary vector from Schumacher's car to that point.

Assume an object x. Assuming a time point t, we get an origo $\varrho(t) := c(\text{loc}'(x, t))$ and an aspect. Let $[\![\cdot]\!]$ denote the meaning assignment. Thus we get three objects, the meaning, the origo, and the aspect:

(25) $[\![e]\!] := \lambda x.\lambda t.\text{loc}'(x, t)$
       $\varrho := \lambda t.c([\![e]\!](\underline{\text{sc}}, t))$
       $\alpha_e := \lambda t.\lambda\ \underline{x}.\overrightarrow{\varrho(t)\underline{x}}$

α_e is a parametrised aspect. The entire phrase PP_{LOC} is of type $\tau \to r$ (parametrised region).

(26) $[\![e\ \text{Schumacher's car}]\!] = \lambda t.\text{loc}'(\underline{\text{sc}}, t)$

The origo is the volumetric centre of Schumacher's car. This is a time dependent location, so of type $\tau \to p$.

7.2   P$_{\text{AXPART}}$

This element establishes a coordinate frame; more precisely, it returns the three unit vectors. After this step, the space (more precisely the tangent space) is fully coordinatised. We can now regard our space as isomorphic to $\mathbb{R}^3$. A triple $\langle x_1, x_2, x_3 \rangle$ codes the vector

(27) $\overrightarrow{x} = x_1 e_1 + x_2 e_2 + x_3 e_3$

Let $\gamma(\underline{x}) := \langle u(\underline{x}), f(\underline{x}), \ell(\underline{x}) \rangle$ be the canonical coordinatiser. (I am suppressing the additional parameters on which it depends.) We assume that 'front' is aligned with the y-axis, that is, with $f(\cdot)$. This is to say with more precision: we assume that 'front' uses the coordinatiser γ and projects the result onto the second component. In that case γ defines also the *aspect change* α_{front} contributed by the word 'front'. This aspect change is not an aspect; it merely takes us from vectors to triples, so it will be composed with α_e to yield the current aspect α_g given further below.

(28) $[\![\text{front}]\!] = \lambda\underline{x}.\lambda t.f(\underline{x}(t))$

$$\alpha_{\text{front}} = \lambda t.\lambda\underline{x}.\lambda\overrightarrow{y}. \begin{vmatrix} \langle \overrightarrow{y}, u(\underline{x}(t)) \rangle \\ \langle \overrightarrow{y}, f(\underline{x}(t)) \rangle \\ \langle \overrightarrow{y}, \ell(\underline{x}(t)) \rangle \end{vmatrix}$$

(Notice that $\underset{\sim}{x}$ ranges over parametrised locations: $\tau \to p$). The aspect is now a (time dependent) function from P to $\mathbb{R}^3$. In the present case the aspect is calculated using the origo, giving us a the contribution to the aspect by the new word:

$$(29) \quad \alpha_n = \lambda t.\lambda y.\lambda \vec{y} \; \alpha_{\text{front}} (t)(\varrho) = \lambda t.\lambda \vec{y}. \begin{vmatrix} \langle \vec{y}, u(\varrho\,(t)) \rangle \\ \langle \vec{y}, f(\varrho\,(t)) \rangle \\ \langle \vec{y}, \ell(\varrho\,(t)) \rangle \end{vmatrix}$$

The meaning of the entire phrase is obtained through the mediation of the aspect. Let

$$(30) \quad \text{red} := \lambda r.\lambda t.c(r(t))$$

This is a reduction from time dependent regions to time dependent points. It should not be confused with the origo.

$$
\begin{aligned}
(31) \quad & [\![\text{front } e \text{ Schumacher's car}]\!] \\
& = [\![\text{front}]\!](\text{red}([\![e \text{ Schumacher's car}]\!])) \\
& = [\![\text{front}]\!] ((\lambda r.\lambda t.c(r(t)))(\lambda t.\text{loc}(\underset{\sim}{sc}, t))) \\
& = (\lambda \underset{\sim}{x}.\lambda t.f(\underset{\sim}{x}(t)))(\lambda t.c(\text{loc}'(\underset{\sim}{sc}, t))) \\
& = \lambda t.f (\lambda t_0.c(\text{loc}'(\underset{\sim}{sc}, t_0))) \\
& = \lambda t.f (c(\text{loc}'(\underset{\sim}{sc}, t)))
\end{aligned}
$$

The type of this expression is $\tau \to v$, a time dependent vector. Turning to the aspects, we have $\alpha_e(t) : p \to v$ and $\alpha_n(t) : v \to \xi$. The overall aspect is the functional composition:

$$(32) \quad \alpha_g := \lambda t.\alpha_n (t) \circ \alpha_e (t) = \lambda t.\lambda \underset{\sim}{x}. \begin{vmatrix} \langle \overrightarrow{\varrho(t)\underset{\sim}{x}}, u(\varrho(t)) \rangle \\ \langle \overrightarrow{\varrho(t)\underset{\sim}{x}}, f(\varrho(t)) \rangle \\ \langle \overrightarrow{\varrho(t)\underset{\sim}{x}}, \ell(\varrho(t)) \rangle \end{vmatrix}$$

7.3 P_{stat}

This element picks out a location using a spatial template. This yields a goodness of fit function: a function $\eta : \mathbb{R}^3 \to [0, 1]$, telling us for each coordinate triple how well it fits.[12] Using the aspect, this can be translated into a goodness of fit for space points.

---

12.   In the discrete case the function becomes a subset of $\mathbb{R}^3$, which must be a region. This conflicts with the claim in (Kracht 2002) that we get a set of regions. However, to be accurate, we must lift the goodness of fit function to regions!

The phrase "front of Schumacher's car" has type $\tau \rightarrow \nu$ and aspect α of type $\tau \rightarrow p \rightarrow \xi$. This aspect is time dependent. It is used in establishing the meaning of the element "in" (in the sense of "in direction of"):

(33) $[\![\text{in}]\!] = \lambda y.\eta(y)$

However, we do not want 'in' to act on triples but rather to locations. The mediation is though the aspect. Thuse we want to get

(34) $\lambda\alpha.\lambda\underline{z}.\lambda t.\eta(\alpha(t)(\underline{z}))$

The way to get this is by definition 'aspectual encoding'. It returns for a template i a recoding of the template in terms of the parametrised aspect:

(35) $\text{enc} := \lambda i.\lambda\alpha.\lambda t.\lambda\underline{x}.i(\alpha(t)(\underline{x}))$

The aspect remains the same. Notice that this takes a space point (the location of the trajector), transforms it into a coordinate triple using the aspect and then measures its goodness of fit via η. The meaning of the entire phrase is obtained by "aspect driven application". The meaning of the head is applied to the aspect of its complement using aspectual encoding.

(36) $[\![\text{in front of } e \text{ Schumacher's car}]\!]$
       $= \text{enc}(\eta)(\alpha_g)$
       $= (\lambda\alpha.\lambda\underline{z}.\lambda t.\eta(\alpha(t)(\underline{z})))(\alpha_g)$
       $= \lambda\underline{z}.\lambda t.\eta(\alpha_g(t)(\underline{z}))$

which is of type $p \rightarrow \tau \rightarrow d$.

7.4 P_{Dir}

The element describes a change of goodness of fit through time. Its input is an interval (typically the event time) and an object (the trajector, the mover of the event, see Kracht 2002). Based on these two and the denotation δ of PP_{stat} we define the following generalised phase quantifier:

(37) $\pi(x, I) := \lambda t.(1/|I|)\delta(c(\text{LOC}(x, t)), t)$

$\pi(x, I)$ tells us how well the location of x fits the description within I. To minimise distraction we assume that $I = [0, 1]$. Otherwise, we would have to introduce a temporal aspect as well, in order to renormalise the time points. This reduces the previous to

(38) $\pi(x) := \lambda t.\delta(c(\text{LOC}(x, t)), t)$

The meaning of "to in front of Schumacher's car" is the claim that the goodness of fit is increasing and reaches a certain threshold. So, define

(39)   to $:= \lambda q.((\forall xy)(0 \le x < y \le 1 \to q(x) < q(y)) \wedge q(1) > \theta)$

where $\theta \in [0, 1]$, but closer to 1 than to 0. to is a property of generalised phase quantifiers saying that they are monotone increasing and reach some threshold.

Now, let e be an event. Then time(e) returns the interval of e, which we suppress, since it is $[0, 1]$) and mov(e) the trajector of e.

(40) $[\![$to$]\!] = \lambda\pi.\lambda e.to(\pi(\text{mov}(e)))$

Then, taking (24) to be an event modifier, we propose the semantics

(41) $[\![$to in front of e Schumacher's car$]\!]$
$= [\![$to$]\!]$ ($[\![$in front of e Schumacher's car$]\!]$)
$= (\lambda\pi.\lambda e.$to$(\pi(\text{mov}(e))))$ ($[\![$in front of e Schumacher's car$]\!]$)
$= \lambda e.$to$(\lambda t.[\![$in front of e Schumacher's car$]\!](c(\text{loc}(\text{mov}(e)(t),t))))$

This is of type $\varepsilon \to t$, a property of events. It says that the degree to which the mover of e is in the location of in front of Schumacher's car during event time increases and goes beyond θ.

8.   Resilient cases

There are some expressions that do not fit the scheme as outlined above. If the parallelism between syntax and semantics is perfect, as I believe it is, they raise the question whether the projections postulated in (3) are always present. A problematic case, already mentioned, is 'in'. There seems to be no need to establish coordinate systems in order to form an opinion whether an object is in another object. There is no contradiction in this; we may simply say that the semantics works without a coordinate system. A second case is provided by 'along' and 'around'. Here the decomposition into an inner, static part and an outer, directional part is called into question. For the static meaning of 'along' is the same as 'near', but the movement pattern is not described using a generalised phase quantifier. Similarly for 'around'. In this case, the movement must be described in different terms. We are led to say that the directional part describes a certain kind of path in the vicinity of the landmark.

9.   Conclusion

The present paper has given a more fine grained picture of how spatial meanings are built up from the basic meanings of words. In particular, the addition of the coordinatiser has led to considerable change in the way this process is seen. For we must note that when people issue or process spatial expressions there is no coordinate frame to begin with, or at least none that is readily available. Hence, in many cases the first step must be to define an origo and coordinate axes. The choice of axes turn's out to be subject to many factors, as research has shown, and provides a fascinating topic in itself. Once they are set, the meaning of axis direct- ed Ps is actually in the point case a single formula expressing a correlation between aberration from the axis and distance from the landmark. This formula is called a *template*. It takes values in [0, 1] and therefore allows to classify change in location using a change in value. This feeds the final element of the locative expression, the one that expresses movement with respect to the landmark.

The notion of aspect seems to be useful also for other areas of semantics. We found the need to recode time points. The mechanics seems to be analogous, but a rigorous formulation still needs to be worked out. This must be left to another occasion, though.

Appendix A. Mathematical preliminaries

I start with the following geometrical structure. $\mathbb{E}$ is a three-dimensional Euclid- ean metric space. This means the following. $\mathbb{E}$ consists of a set P or points, a set $G \subseteq \wp(P)$ of lines, and a set $H \subseteq \wp(P)$ of planes, and a function $d : P \times P \to \mathbb{R}_+$, the distance function. d must be invariant under translations and rotations. Points are henceforth denoted by a dot, like this: $\underset{.}{x}$. The postulates are the typical postu- lates for three dimensional geometry: for any two different points $\underset{.}{x}$ and $\underset{.}{z}$ there is exactly one line (denoted by $\underset{.}{x}\underset{.}{z}$) that contains them, for any three points $\underset{.}{w}$, $\underset{.}{x}$ and $\underset{.}{z}$ not on a line there is exactly one plane – denoted by $\underset{.}{w}\underset{.}{x}\underset{.}{z}$ – that contains them, and so on.

Before I continue, I need to briefly discuss the status of these primitives. It has been claimed repeatedly (see Gambarotto & Muller 2003 and references therein) that the Euclidean geometry is not basic from a cognitive point of view; and that it should be replaced by an approach based on regions. I am sympathetic to these claims; however, as Howard (2004) explains, vision is organised into several inter- acting layers of different degrees of abstraction, and that shape recognition is only one such layer. Given that we are perfectly able to recognise points within a region, I am not sure it is profitable to abandon the Euclidean space altogether. Ultimately, we can do something similar to what has been done in research on time: there is a duality between an ontology based on time points and an ontology based on intervals. One can be defined from the other. I should point out here one major difference between my terminology and the one employed in mereotopology.

A *region* is for me not an arbitrary open subset of the space but rather a path-connected set (like intervals on the real line). This is because I maintain that individuation of objects crucially employs a notion of path-connectedness.

Let me now continue and explain how we derive the necessary geometric concepts in $\mathbb{E}$. Angles are measured by the length of the corresponding segments on the unit circle. Distance moreover introduces a topology via the open balls. The open ball of radius δ around x is the set

(42) $K_\delta(x) := \{z : d(x, z) < \delta\}$

A set is *open* if and only if it is a union of finite intersections of unit balls. The topologies on the lines and planes are introduced in such a way as to make the map $(x, z) \mapsto xz$ (from pairs of different points to lines) and the intersection $(\ell_1, \ell_2) \mapsto \ell_1 \cap \ell_2$ (from pairs of nonparallel lines to points) continuous with respect to the topologies.

Given this, we can introduce the *half line* $\overrightarrow{xz}$ as the following set of points:

① $\overrightarrow{xz} \subset xz$; and $x, z \in \overrightarrow{xz}$;
②   for every δ there is exactly one point in $\overrightarrow{xz}$ that has distance δ from x;
③   if z and w are such that $d(x, z) > d(x, w)$, then $d(x, z) = d(x, w) + d(w, z)$

Having half lines, we can define the line segments by

(43) $\overline{xz} := \overrightarrow{xz} \cap \overrightarrow{zx}$

Given two points x and z, the ordered pair (x, z) defines a *vector* in the following way. We say $(x, z) \sim (y, w)$ if and only if (a) the lines xz and yw are parallel, and (b) the lines xy and zw are parallel. In this case, the four points form a parallelogram and opposing sides (the line segments) are of equal length. A *vector* is an equivalence class of $\sim$. Vectors are denoted by arrows, like this: $\overrightarrow{xz}$ (for the vector defined by the pair (x, z)). Given a point x and a vector $\overrightarrow{v}$, there is a unique point z such that $(x, z) \in \overrightarrow{v}$.

Having introduced vectors, we can also introduce the scalar product. To start, the *norm* of a vector $\overrightarrow{xz}$ is simply $d(x, z)$. This is simply the *length* of any of the line segments that are defined by pairs in the vector. Given two vectors x and y, we pick three points a, b and c such that $(a, b) \in \overrightarrow{x}$ and $(a, c) \in \overrightarrow{y}$. Let d be the point obtained by drawing a line through b perpendicular to ac. (This is the 'shadow projection'.) Then define

(44) $\langle \overrightarrow{x}, \overrightarrow{y} \rangle := \dfrac{d(a, d)}{d(a, c)}$

This number is independent of the representatives, and it also does not change when the roles of $\overrightarrow{x}$ and $\overrightarrow{y}$ are interchanged. The form $\langle -, - \rangle$ is symmetric, and linear in both components. Two vectors are *orthogonal* if $\langle \vec{x}, \vec{y} \rangle = 0$. That $\mathbb{E}$ is three dimensional means that every sequence of pairwise orthogonal vectors has length 3. Now fix any such sequence, $\langle \vec{e_1}, \vec{e_2}, \vec{e_3} \rangle$. We require that these vectors are of length 1. Given a vector x, we can now assign coordinates, x_1, x_2 and x_3, as follows

(45) $x_1 := \langle \vec{x}, \vec{e_1} \rangle, x_2 := \langle \vec{x}, \vec{e_2} \rangle, x_3 := \langle \vec{x}, \vec{e_3} \rangle$

It is important to stress two things: these definitions apply to vectors, not to points; and secondly, the coordinates are dependent on the coordinate vectors. Both facts need close attention. The resulting triple is called a *coordinate vector*.

First, three vectors alone do not allow to issue coordinates for points. In order to do this, we must choose an *origin*. Given an origin ǫ, a given point x is now assigned the (unique) vector $\vec{ox}$, and given the coordinate vectors this latter vector is finally assigned a set of three coordinates. Coordinates depend on the origin as follows. If we choose a different origin ṇ, the new vector is obtained by adding (ṇ, ǫ) to (ǫ, x), a vector that is independent of x. Coordinates also depend on the chosen vectors. First of all, the coordinate vectors themselves also have coordinates. These are

(46) $$\begin{pmatrix} 1 \\ 0 \\ 0 \end{pmatrix}, \begin{pmatrix} 0 \\ 1 \\ 0 \end{pmatrix}, \begin{pmatrix} 0 \\ 0 \\ 1 \end{pmatrix}$$

The coordinate vectors are written vertically. The coordinate vectors are obtained by

(47) $$\begin{pmatrix} x_1 \\ x_2 \\ x_3 \end{pmatrix} = \begin{pmatrix} \langle \vec{e_1}, \vec{x} \rangle \\ \langle \vec{e_2}, \vec{x} \rangle \\ \langle \vec{e_3}, \vec{x} \rangle \end{pmatrix}$$

Let me briefly mention the following fact about coordinates. We may arrange any three vectors $\vec{x}$, $\vec{y}$ and $\vec{z}$ into a matrix, by computing their coordinate triples and arranging them in a sequence. If we do this with the unit vectors we get

(48) $$\begin{pmatrix} 1 & 0 & 0 \\ 0 & 1 & 0 \\ 0 & 0 & 1 \end{pmatrix}$$

Now take three vectors $\vec{a_1}$, $\vec{a_2}$ and $\vec{a_3}$. These three vectors have three coordinates each, called a_{ij} for vector i, and so the sequence of these three vectors form a matrix

(49) $A = \begin{pmatrix} a_{11} & a_{12} & a_{13} \\ a_{21} & a_{22} & a_{23} \\ a_{31} & a_{32} & a_{33} \end{pmatrix}$

Now, the following evidently holds for any coordinate vector x (on condition that A is invertible):

(50) $x = AA^{-1}x$

This is standardly seen as follows: the matrix A gives us the new coordinate vectors, expressed in the old ones (so that we have numbers). Therefore, $A^{-1}x$ gives us the vector x *in the new coordinate system* . One says that coordinates are *contravariant*, since you find them by applying the inverse of A.

Generally, any invertible matrix can be used to recoordinatise the space. However, for our purposes we can restrict attention to the following. A matrix is said to be *special orthogonal* if $A^{-1} = A^T$, and A has determinant 1. The group of special orthogonal matrices of $\mathbb{E}$ is denoted by $SO(\mathbb{E})$. The matrices describe either coordinate sets or transformations, just as triples stand for points and vectors. We shall see how the ambiguity can be resolved. A special orthogonal matrix describes a rotation in space. Thus, new coordinate vectors A forming a special orthogonal matrix can be obtained by rotating the original vectors.

Definition 5. A **coordinate system** is a quadruple (o, e_1, e_2, e_3) such that

1.   *the vectors $\overrightarrow{oe_i}$ have length 1;*
2.   *$\overrightarrow{oe_i} \perp \overrightarrow{oe_j}$ if and only if $i \neq j$;*
3.   *the system $\overrightarrow{oe_1}, \overrightarrow{oe_2}, \overrightarrow{oe_3}$ is right handed.*

There are several definitions of right handedness. One is that the determinant must be positive (in whatever coordinates, since it is independent of them); the other is that we can align them with thumb, index finger and middle finger of the right hand. Given a coordinate system C, we write x_C for the triple of coordinates that identify x in the coordinate frame C. Given a triple $\overrightarrow{x}$ of numbers, let $\overrightarrow{x}^C$ denote the point that it defines in C.

A *path* is a continuous function $\pi : I \to P$, where I is an interval. A *region* is a path-connected subset of $\mathbb{R}^3$. Here, a set S is *path-connected* if for any $x, y \in S$ there is a path $\pi : [0, 1] \to S$ such that $\pi(0) = x$ and $\pi(1) = y$. Reg denotes the set of regions. Given a distance function for the space P, we define the distance for regions R and S by

(51) $d(R, S) := \inf\{d(x, z) : x \in R, z \in S\}$

The volume of a region is defined as follows. Let C be a coordinate frame, and $R_C := \{x_C : x \in R\}$.

(52) $V(R) := \int_{R_C} dx\,dy\,dz$

Notice that this is independent of C (for this we require that the distance function is invariant under translations and rotations). The *volumetric centre* is now defined by

$$(53) \quad c(R) := \left(\frac{1}{V(R)} \int_{R_c} d\bar{x} \right)^c$$

Notice that we have to first move to coordinates to do our calculations, and then return to the points. The definition is independent of the actual coordinates chosen.

Appendix B. Types

The semantics below makes use of type theory. Here are my conventions. e is the type of objects; p is the type of space points, v the type of vectors, ξ is the type of triples of reals; r the type of regions; τ is the type of time points, i is the type of time intervals. P ranges over P, our space, while v ranges over the set $P \times P/ \sim$ and ρ over the set of path connected subsets of $\mathbb{R}^3$. Finally, d is the type of truth degrees and t the type of truth values.

References

Bennardo, Giovanni (ed.). 2002. Representing Space in Oceania – Culture in Language and Mind. Pacific Linguistics. Canberra: Australian National University Press.

Carlson, L., Regier, T. & Covey, E. 2003. Defining spatial relations: Reconciling axis and vector representations. In *Representing Direction in Language and Space* [Explorations in Language and Space, vol. 1], E. van der Zee & J. Slack (eds), 111–131. Oxford: Oxford University Press.

Florey, M. & Kelly, B. 2002. Spatial Reference in Alune. In *Representing Space in Oceania*, G. Bennardo (ed.), 11–46. Canberra: ANU Press.

Fong, V. 1997. The Order of Things: What Directional Locatives Denote. PhD Dissertation, Stanford University.

Gambarotto, P. & Muller, P. 2003. Ontological Problems for the Semantics of Spatial Expressions in Natural Language. In *Representing Direction in Language and Space* [Explorations in Language and Space, vol. 1], E. van der Zee & J. Slack (eds), 144–165. Oxford: Oxford University Press.

Howard, H. 2004. *Neuromimetic Semantics*. Amsterdam: Elsevier.

Hyslop, C. 2002. Hiding behind trees on Ambae: Spatial reference in an Oceanic language of Vanuatu. In *Representing Space in Oceania*, G. Bennardo (ed.), 47–76. Canberra: ANU Press.

Jackendoff, R. 1983. *Semantics and Cognition*. Cambridge, Mass.: MIT Press.

Kracht, M. 2002. On the Semantics of Locatives. *Linguistics and Philosophy* 25: 157–232.

Landau, B. 2003. Axis and direction in spatial language and spatial cognition. In *Representing Direction in Language and Space* [Explorations in Language and Space, vol. 1], E. van der Zee & J. Slack (eds), 18–38. Oxford: Oxford University Press.

Levinson, S.C. 2003. *Space in Language and Cognition. Explorations in Cognitive Diversity* [Language, Culture and Cognition 5]. Cambridge: Cambridge University Press.

Levinson, S.C. & Wilkins, D.P. 2006. *Grammars of Space. Explorations in Cognitive Diversity* [Language, Culture and Cognition 6]. Cambridge: Cambridge University Press.

Lillehaugen, B.D. 2006. Expressing Location in Tlacolula Valley Zapotec, PhD Dissertation, UCLA.

Logan, G.D. & Sadler, D.D. 1996. A computational analysis of the apprehension of spatial relations. In *Language and Space*, P. Bloom, M.A. Peterson, L. Nadel & M.F. Garrett (eds), 493–529. Cambridge, Mass.: MIT Press.

Niikanne, U. 2003. How Finnish postpositions see the axis system. Representing Direction in Language and Space, edited by van der Zee, Emile and John Slack, no. 1 in Explorations in Language and Space, 191–208. Oxford: Oxford University Press.

O'Keefe, John. 1996. The Spatial Prepositions in English, Vector Grammar, and the Cognitive Map Theory. Language and Space, edited by P. Bloom, M.A. Peterson, L. Nadel & M.F. Garrett (eds), 277–316. Cambridge, Mass.: MIT Press.

O'Keefe, John. 2003. Vector Grammar, Places, and the Functional Role of the Spatial Prepositions in English. In *Representing Direction in Language and Space* [Explorations in Language and Space, vol. 1], E. van der Zee & J. Slack (eds), 69–85. Oxford: Oxford University Press.

Palmer, B. 2002. Absolute spatial reference and the grammaticalisation of perceptually salient phenomena. In *Representing Space in Oceania*, G. Bennardo (ed.), 107–157. Canberra: ANU Press.

Senft, G. 1997. *Referring to Space. Studies in Austronesian and Papuan Languages*. Oxford: Oxford University Press.

Svorou, S. 1993. *The Grammar of Space*. Amsterdam: John Benjamins.

van der Zee, E. & Slack, J. 2003. *Representing Direction in Language and Space* [Explorations in Language and Space 1]. Oxford: Oxford University Press.

Zwarts, J. 2003. Vectors across spatial domains: From place to size, orientation, shape and parts. In *Representing Direction in Language and Space* [Explorations in Language and Space, vol. 1], E. van der Zee & J. Slack (eds), 39–68. Oxford: Oxford University Press.

Zwarts, J. 2005. Prepositional Aspect and the Algebra of Paths. *Linguistics and Philosophy* 28: 739–779.

Projections of P

Peter Svenonius
CASTL, University of Tromsø

This paper examines the obligatoriness of projections which are not independently lexicalized, taking the extended projection of P as the empirical domain. The paper also makes an explicit proposal about certain aspects of the syntax-semantics mapping in spatial P. It is argued, on the basis of the distribution of measure phrases and relative frames of reference, that null projections are syntactically present. In fact, even when material from two projections appears to be lexicalized by a single morpheme, intermediate projections are syntactically present. This constrains theories of lexical insertion.

1. Introduction: The extended projection of P

This is a paper about extended projections and the obligatoriness of individual functional projections in a fine-grained tree structure. It follows the general cartographic project in mapping distinct functional projections associated with different morphemes or phrasal modifiers (for example Cinque 1994, 1999, 2004; Zamparelli 2000; Julien 2002, 2005; Svenonius 2007; to appear a; for P see in particular Koopman 2000; den Dikken to appear, Svenonius 2006; to appear b, and various of the papers in this volume).

In Svenonius (to appear b), I investigate the meaning contributions of the different projections, an investigation which I have called the 'Anatomy' of P. The anatomy of P includes a wealth of spatial and non-spatial meanings, starting with the distinction between Path and Place (Jackendoff 1983) and including such features as the frame of reference (Levinson 1996) and the Axial structure of the Ground object (Svenonius 2006).

The end result is a large number of projections, for example a structure like (1) for *from in front of the house*.[1]

---

1. In this paper I abstract away from the question of where the Figure argument (the theme of motion) is introduced; see Botwinik-Rotem (this volume) for discussion. I also abstract away from the more general question of how the PP is integrated into the structure that it modifies; see Tomioka (this volume) for discussion.

(1)

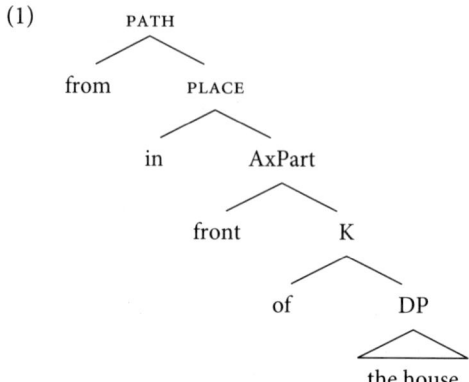

The question immediately arises whether such projections are present in every PP, or whether they are only present some of the time. For example, does the PP *from the house* have a structure more like that in (2a) or like that in (2b)?

(2)

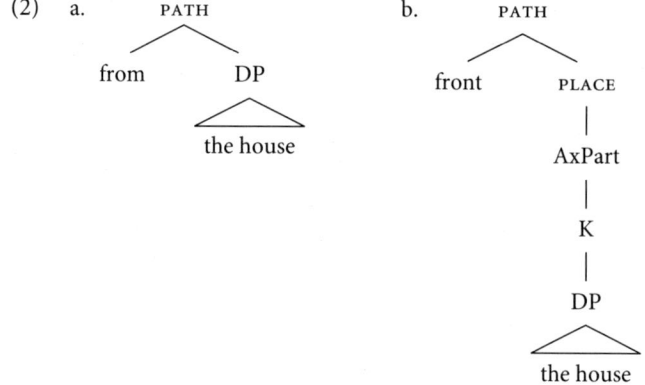

This is a much more general question, e.g., is there a T node in a sentence in which there is no overt morphology corresponding to tense, or is there a D node in a noun phrase with no overt morphology corresponding to a determiner? Ramchand & Svenonius (to appear) argue that there are T and D nodes in such cases, though we also suggest that there is room for cross-linguistic variation in the underlying presence of certain other features.

I will suggest here a model in which the elements which are not lexicalized necessarily make a "default" or maximally underspecified contribution. This has important consequences for various proposals concerning the lexicalization, government, and licensing of null elements.

2.   Null elements

Research into restrictions on the distribution of NP-trace, Ā-trace, *pro*, and PRO have led to various proposals invoking phonological emptiness as a syntactic property; for example the *Empty Category Principle* of Chomsky (1981: 250) is a condition meant to hold of this entire class of phonologically null elements (though not necessarily all phonologically null elements).

Emonds' (1985: 99) 'Limitation on Empty Nodes' and his (op cit p. 227) *Invisible Category Principle* go even further in connecting phonological non-overtness to specific conditions; the latter essentially states that a functional head may remain empty if its complement or specifier bears a morphological reflex of a feature of that head.

Similarly, Koopman (1996) suggests that a projection cannot have a silent head and a silent specifier, and Kayne (2006) proposes that all and only material in the specifier of a phase head fails to be spelled out.

However, a strict modular separation between syntax and phonology would entail that syntax is insensitive to phonological non-overtness. The fact that LF movement is subject to many of the same restrictions as overt movement (Huang 1982) suggests that the restrictions on the distribution of trace are not connected to phonological overtness. Also, restrictions on *pro* are not clearly different from restrictions on specific classes of overt pronouns (e.g., weak pronouns, or clitics, are also subject to cross-linguistic variation, as are the specific restrictions on *pro*). The conditions on PRO have never been satisfactorily reduced to the conditions on *pro* or trace anyway.

So it remains a viable alternative that there are no specific conditions on phonological non-overtness, apart from conditions of learnability and recoverability, and this is what I will assume below.

3.   Measure expressions and vector spaces

To establish some basic terminology, take the Figure to be the item located, and the Ground to be the reference object for the location of the Figure (Talmy 1978). Syntactically, the Ground-denoting DP is the complement of a preposition. Another useful notion in the formal analysis of locative expressions is that of REGION, which can be modeled as a contiguous set of points in space (Nam 1995; Kracht 2002; Kracht this volume). Wunderlich (1991) introduces the notion of EIGENPLACE, which we can take to be the region occupied by an object.[2]

---

2.   Compare Kracht's LOC', *this volume,* and see his formalization for a way to take the dimension of time into consideration.

A locative preposition like *behind* or *above*, at a first approximation, is a mapping from the eigenplace of the Ground to another region, hence a function from regions to regions, at first approximation. There are some important differences, however; as Kracht (this volume) points out, for example, the region which is the output of mapping is coordinated, in the sense that it is oriented in space, whereas the eigenplace is not; this will be discussed below.

Furthermore, the possibility of measure phrases (*ten inches under the desk*) and directional modifiers (*diagonally over the door*) shows that locative PPs have additional structure; Zwarts (1997) and Zwarts & Winter (2000) argue for a vector-based model for such PPs, since vectors have direction and length (see Kracht, this volume, for discussion).

They introduce a function from regions to vector spaces, which they call LOC, and another one from vector spaces to regions, which they call LOC⁻. In a tree representation, this would look something like the following, replacing their LOC⁻ with DEG for Degree (for typographical perspecuity and other reasons that will become clear below):

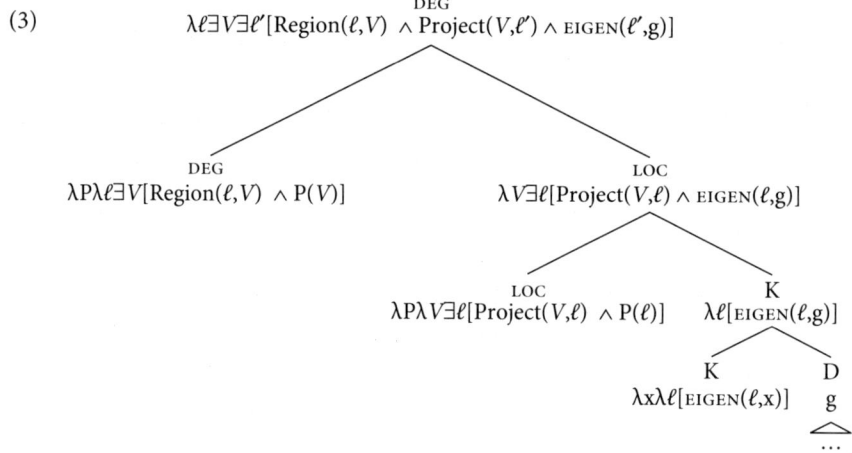

In the diagram in (3) I have dignified each type-shift with a label: K (for Kase) for the shift from objects to eigenplaces, and Zwarts & Winter's (2000) LOC for the shifts from regions to vector spaces, and Koopman's (2000) Deg for the one Zwarts & Winter proposed to shift vector spaces back into regions. The semantic notation is in a simple shorthand: ℓ is a variable over regions, and EIGEN is the relation of being the eigenplace of a thing; so if "g" is a house, then $\lambda\ell[\text{EIGEN}(\ell, g)]$ (the denotation of KP) is the region which is the eigenplace of the house, that is, the set of points that house occupies (the representations will be made more informative below, in a way that will also be more compatible with Kracht, this volume).

V is a variable over vector spaces, and PROJECT is the relation of being a vector space projected from a region in a way specified by a particular preposition. For example, if the "LOC" head here is *behind*, and the KP is *the house*, then $\lambda V \exists \ell [\text{Project}(V, \ell) \wedge \text{EIGEN}(\ell, g)]$ in the tree (the denotation of LOCP) is the set of vectors which are projected from the eigenplace of *the house* in the manner specified by *behind*; that is, backward-projecting vectors, or vectors projected from the back of the house.

Finally, DEG introduces the relation REGION, which simply gives the region which is picked out by the vector space denoted by its complement. In this case, the points which are pointed to by all the backward-pointing vectors coming off the eigenplace of the house.

A directional adverbial, then, can be a simple modifier of vector spaces, as suggested in the tree below (continuing to use 'Project' as a general label for whatever projective preposition is inserted).

(4) $\lambda \ell \exists V \exists \ell' [\text{Region}(\ell, V) \wedge \text{diagonal}(V) \wedge \text{Project}(V, \ell') \wedge \text{EIGEN}(\ell', g)]$

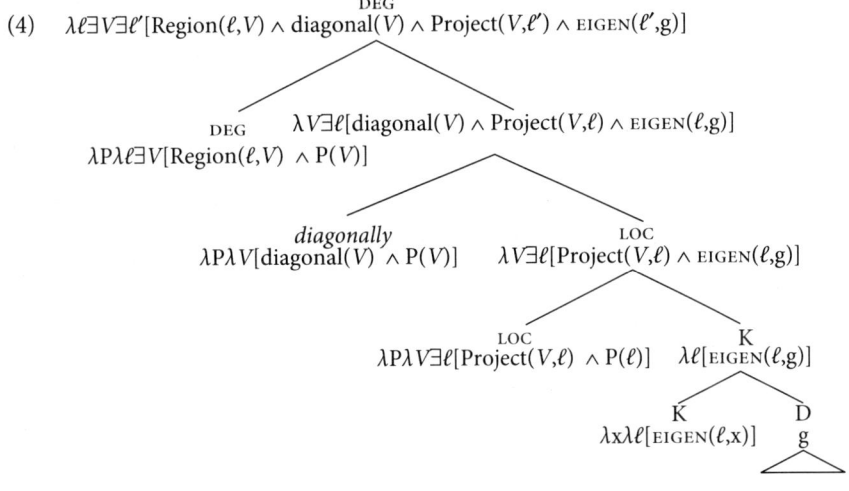

LOC introduces vectors at a range of angles, and a directional adverb like *straight* or *diagonally* restricts the range. Similarly, a measure expression like *thirty feet* or *ten centimeters* picks out vectors of a certain length.

The order of measure phrases and directional adverbs is rigid.

(5)   a.   The lamppost is three meters diagonally behind the house.
       b.   The crack is twenty centimeters straight below the window.

(6)   a.   *The lamppost is diagonally three meters behind the house.
       b.   *The crack is straight twenty centimeters below the window.

If measures and directional adverbs both modified vector spaces, then it would be unclear why they cannot be combined in either order. If, on the other hand, there is a functor which introduces measure expressions, and outputs a category different from the one with which directional adverbials combine, then the order would be rigid.[3] Suppose that functor is a variant of DEG; I will call the variant which introduces measure expressions DEG$_{MEAS}$.

DEG and DEG$_{MEAS}$ can be seen as two different versions of the same category, as they both take a vector-space denoting complement and project a region-denoting maximal projection. The logical type of DEG$_{MEAS}$ is given in (7), where m is a variable over measure expressions like *ten centimeters* and MEAS is a measurement function over vectors.

(7) $[\![\text{DEG}_{MEAS}]\!] = \lambda P \lambda m \lambda \ell \exists V[\text{Region}(\ell,V) \wedge \text{MEAS}(V) \succeq m \wedge P(V)]$

Thus, in the computation of the meaning of the expression *six meters behind the house*, only those vectors which are six meters in length are considered (or longer, subject to pragmatics). Each picks out a point which is *six meters behind the house*. In (8), I depict the LOC head as being filled by the preposition *behind*, and replace the general relation PROJECT with the specific instantiation of it, BEHIND. Here, h is a constant standing in for 'the house.'

(8)

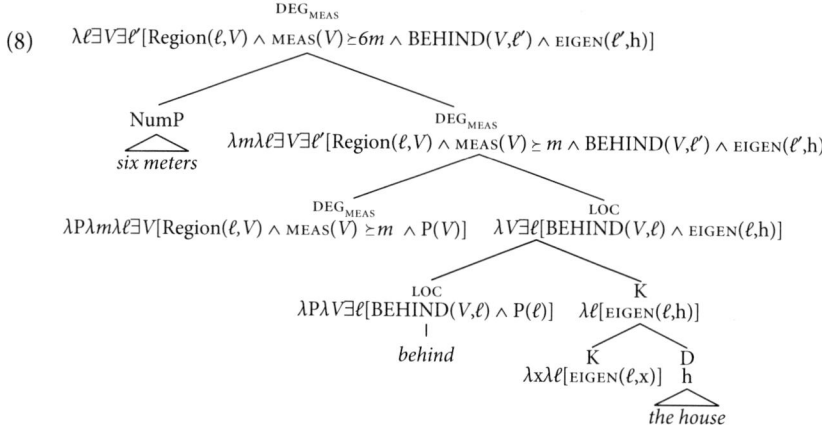

It can be seen that the semantics proposed so far correctly predicts the possibility of combining directional adverbs and measure expressions, in the observed order.

---

3.   Dominique Sportiche has pointed out to me that a vector space has certain mathematical properties, such as closure under addition, which may be relevant here. A set of diagonal vectors, or of straight vectors, could still have these properties; but a set of vectors of a certain length could not. So if directional adverbials are functions on vector spaces, then this would explain why they cannot combine outside a measure expression. On the model proposed here, this is formally encoded, if LOC is taken to consistently denote a vector space, and if that property is what both Deg and the directional adverbials seek to combine with.

Furthermore, it seems that the tree representations that I have provided work fairly well as syntactic representations; I take it as a working hypothesis that they are good approximations of the actual syntactic trees.

Thus, I will assume that there is a syntactic category LOC, which takes KP as a complement, and denotes a function from regions to vector spaces. LOC is the locus of the component of meaning that distinguishes different projective prepositions from each other (e.g., the difference between *behind* and *above*). There is another category DEG, which takes LOCP as a complement, and denotes a function from vector spaces to regions. DEG is where vector length is specified, if it is specified.

Cartographic studies suggest that certain aspects of meaning are consistently localized at particular heights in a functional sequence; thus, given that vector length is specified in DEG, it is not expected that vector length will also be specifiable at other heights in the extended projection of P.

4.   Immeasurable prepositions: *Beside* and *next to*

Measure phrases are incompatible with *beside* and *next to*. A ladder can be one meter from the house, and simultaneously be *beside the house* or *next to the house*, but one cannot grammatically utter (9b). Similarly for (10).

(9)   a.   The ladder is beside the house, one meter away.
     b.   *The ladder is one meter beside the house.

(10)   a.   The ladder is next to the house, just six inches away from it.
     b.   *The ladder is six inches next to the house.

It is clear that the badness of the measure phrase cannot be due to conceptual or world-knowledge factors, given that these distances are fully compatible with the notions expressed by these prepositions. Instead, it seems that a syntactic solution is called for.

One possibility would be that these prepositions simply do not denote vector spaces; this would make it impossible for DEG_{MEAS} to combine with them, on the assumptions outlined here. Instead, these prepositions could be functions from eigenplaces to 'beside' or 'next to' regions, without vector semantics.

However, for at least some speakers, direction-specifying adverbs like *diagonally* and *straight* are compatible with *beside* and *next to*.

(11)   a.   There is a tree diagonally beside the house.
     b.   The post office is diagonally next to the convenience store.

Some speakers reject these sentences. Therefore, I add a couple of examples found on the internet, long enough to provide some natural context.

(12) a. Always look to both sides, using mirrors & looking **straight beside** &
          over your shoulder, to where you intend to move & always indicate your
          intentions before you change lanes.
      b. There is no more corrosive an atmosphere than a fertiliser plant especially
          with our location **straight beside** the Brisbane River on one side and a
          creek on the other we are pretty well surrounded by water sea water and
          close to the mouth of the river also.
      c. in the three cases the runner arrived before the ball but was just unable
          to get around the third baseman due to the way 3rd was blocking the bag,
          he was crouched **diagonally beside** the bag on the baseline about 1 foot
          infront of the bag.
      d. I got a DIRECT view of the stage, minus the fact that there were 2 tall
          gentlemen in front of us, and **diagonally beside** me, which blocked me
          a little.

I have discounted numerous examples of the following sort:

(13) a. She lies still, her arms **straight beside** her.
      b. I heard that if you take 2 mirrors and place them **diagonally beside**
          eachother like this: /\ And then look into it, that is how people see you.

In these cases, straight or diagonal orientation might be being predicated of the Figure
argument (arms in (13a), mirrors in (13b)). This is not the same as picking out straight
or diagonal exemplars of a 'beside' space, which is what is happening in (12). It seems
that examples like those in (12) can best be modeled by assuming that *beside* does
project a vector space to the sides of the ground, normally consisting like other vector
spaces of vectors at a variety of angles. Then *straight beside* is restricted to the vectors
projecting perpendicular to the Ground, while *diagonally beside* is restricted to oblique
vectors, at least for those speakers who find the examples in (12) grammatical.

Similar examples can be found for *next to*.

(14) a. As soon as a track tile is placed horizontally or vertically (NOT diagonally)
          next to one of these buildings, then a stop sign is placed on top of that tile.
      b. Click each of the four corners, then each of the "off" lights diagonally next
          to each corner.
      c. Now the million dollar question, why did they put the key "Q" just
          diagonally next to "1" on the keyboard when they know how critical
          could it be when managing Unix servers remotely ;-)

I conclude, then, that *beside* projects a vector space, for some speakers (as does *next
to*, but I will illustrate with *beside* here).[4] For some reason, however, that vector
space cannot be overtly measured.

---

4. If some speakers have a non-vector-based lexical entry for *beside*, it is possible that speakers
may also differ with respect to *beside* and *next to*, for instance having a vector-based semantics
for the one but not for the other.

It does seem that *beside* implies proximity, or nearness. For example, if two houses are very far apart then the one is not *beside* the other. As already noted, if this were simply a conventional or encyclopedic association, there should be no incompatibility with measure phrases expressing short distances, such as *one meter* (which is short relative to houses).

I propose, therefore, that the closeness component of the meaning of *beside* is syntactically represented. In other words, *beside* spells out or lexicalizes both LOC (it specifies that vectors are projected from the sides of the Ground DP) and Deg (it specifies that the vectors are short). This prevents the head DEG$_{\text{MEAS}}$ from being inserted together with *beside*.

Directional adverbials like *diagonally* are compatible with closeness and are not dependent on the specific meaning of the Place head DEG$_{\text{MEAS}}$. Therefore, they are correctly predicted to be compatible with *beside*, as long as the LOC head projects a vector space. This is depicted in tree form in (15).

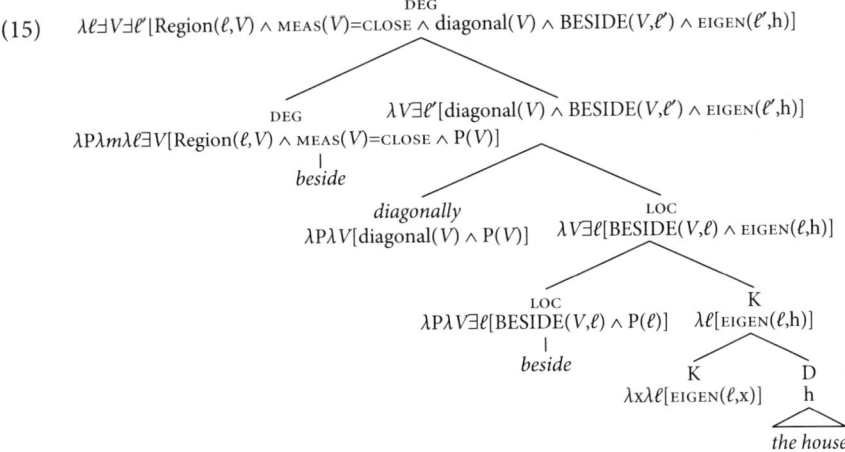

(15) $\lambda \ell \exists V \exists \ell'[\text{Region}(\ell,V) \wedge \text{MEAS}(V){=}\text{CLOSE} \wedge \text{diagonal}(V) \wedge \text{BESIDE}(V,\ell') \wedge \text{EIGEN}(\ell',h)]$

I have drawn the word *beside* under both the DEG node and the LOC node, because there are values under both nodes which are lexicalized by *beside*; thus, the lexical item *beside* must check features both in LOC and in DEG. The locality of such checking appears to be similar to that of head movement (cf. Svenonius 1994), though other implementations are of course possible. Since *beside* does not precede direction adverbs like *diagonally*, the head-movement in question is either covert or is obscured by other movement.

If the assumptions made above are on the right track, then they constitute an argument against 'bundling' DEG and LOC in the syntax, even when the two are lexicalized by a single preposition like *beside*. In order for an adverb like *diagonally* to attach, there must be a projection corresponding to the level of vector spaces, as depicted above.

5.   Comparison to decomposition in *v*P

There is a well-known argument for decomposition in the verb phrase which has a partly similar character to the one I have sketched for decomposition in the adpositional domain. Here I briefly sketch the argument for the sake of comparison to the current situation.

Von Stechow (1995, 1996) argues (following up on older arguments by McCawley 1971 and others) that the differences in interpretation between examples like (16a) and (16b) motivate a syntactic decomposition of the verb into component parts (of the sort articulated by Kratzer 1996).

(16)   a.   weil   Fritz   das   Fenster   wieder   öffnete
            because Fritz   the   window   again   opened
            'because Fritz opened the window again' (repetitive or restitutive)
       b.   weil   Fritz   wieder   das   Fenster   öffnete
            because Fritz   again   the   window   opened
            'because Fritz again opened the window' (repetitive only)

The definite DP in German leaves the verb phrase, so that when *wieder* precedes it as in (16b), it is clearly also external to the verb phrase, and scopes over both arguments. Hence, only the repetitive reading is available (the one which presupposes that Fritz has opened the window before). On the other hand, in (16a), the adverb could either be attached outside the verb phrase, as before, or to a subpart of it – in which case the reading is restitutive (which presupposes only that the window has been in a closed state before).

Alternatives have been proposed; for example Jäger & Blutner (2000) present various counterarguments to von Stechow's analysis, including notably the following sentence.

(17)   A Delaware settled in New Jersey again.

As they point out, this could be true in the following scenario: The Delaware Indians had always been in New Jersey until they were forced out, 200 years ago, and relocated to Oklahoma. Then, recently, a Delaware who grew up in Oklahoma settled in New Jersey. This is not a repetitive reading, because the Delaware in the scenario has never settled in New Jersey before; it is a restitutive reading, one in which the state restored is that of Delaware Indians living in New Jersey.

Jäger & Blutner provide an account in which *wieder* is lexically ambiguous, one variant being repetitive and the other restitutive. Both attach at the same height, but one asserts that there is a resultant state which is being restored.

As pointed out by von Stechow (2003), the account does not account for the sensitivity of the different readings to different word orders (cf. (16)). Furthermore, the account overgenerates, as it implies that the restitutive version of *wieder* should combine with any causative verb with an indefinite subject. For example, von Stechow suggests a scenario in which everyone is born with a disease (as in the film *The Omega Man*); the question is then whether a sentence like (18) has a restitutive reading, in which the state restored is that of there being a healthy person.

(18) Jetzt hat sich wieder jemand   geheilt.
     now has RFX again   somebody cured
     'Now someone has cured himself again.'

Apparently, sentences like this do not have restitutive readings, in English or in German, so there is something interestingly different about (17). Von Stechow suggests that (17) has a non-agentive use, in which case the indefinite can originate lower than the low attachment site of *wieder*, giving the right result, namely that the restitutive reading includes the existential quantifier; von Stechow sketches the essence of this solution as in (19).

(19)   BECOME$_e$ (again $\exists$x[Delaware(x) & x live in NJ])

See von Stechow (2003) for responses to Jäger & Blutner's other challenges. In sum, then, the argument from *wieder* seems to go through, and it seems that verb phrases consist of more syntactic projections than they have morphemes to head them – a verb like *öffnen* might consist of two or three syntactic parts (CAUSE-BECOME-OPEN) even apart from tense or an infinitival ending, and these parts are active for the attachment of adverbial modifiers.

Thus, the situation I outlined above for P should not be surprising: there are multiple parts to a preposition like *beside*, and these parts are available for adverbial modification. It is tempting to equate the two parts with the two morphemes *be-* and *-side*, especially given the prepositions *inside, outside*, and *alongside*. However, the restricted measurement meaning is not present in *between, behind*, or *beneath*, so it is not straightforward to identify *be-* with the specifics of the DEG component of the meaning of *beside*. Instead, I suggest below, there may be a different decomposition for *beside*.

6.   AxParts

I have elsewhere (Svenonius 2006) argued for a further decomposition of the projection called LOC in Section 3 into two subcomponents, which can be called Place and AxPart. AxPart, a formal adaptation of Jackendoff's (1996) term *axial part*, is a category manifested in very many languages by a set of about five to fifteen words with meanings like 'front,' 'back,' 'top,' 'bottom,' 'side,' 'interior,' 'vicinity,' and so on (for examples, see the Persian, Hebrew, Japanese, and Spanish locative expressions in the articles in this volume by Pantcheva, Botwinik-Rotem, Tomioka, and Tortora respectively).

Such parts can be identified either on the basis of intrinsic properties of the Ground object itself (for example people, houses, and cars have conventional fronts and backs and sides), or on the basis of what is known as 'relative' frame of reference (for example when the 'front' of an object is the part facing the observer, for English, or the part facing away from the observer, for Hausa, as described by Hill 1974; cf. also Herskovits 1986; Levinson 2003).

In the discussion in Section 3, I characterized LOC as a class of functions which projected vectors in particular ways with respect to an eigenplace (e.g., backward-projecting vectors for *behind*, upward-projecting vectors for *above*). In a decomposition of LOC, I suggest, AxPart is a function from eigenplaces to regions which are normally subparts of those eigenplaces such as front, back, top, side, interior, or exterior. Place, then, is a function which identifies spaces on the basis of those subparts. As discussed by Kracht (this volume), AxPart is the level at which a coordinate frame is fixed.

This means that Place (Kracht's P$_{stat}$, this volume) can simply project vectors 'away' from the denotation of the AxPart phrase, the coordinate system having been established at the AxPart level. Other spatial relations such as containment, attachment, and so on might be alternative expressions of Place (cf. the analyses in Pantcheva, this volume, Botwinik-Rotem, this volume); compare English *in front of* and *on top of*; see also Svenonius (2006).

The decomposition is sketched in (20), where 'Project' is retained from §3 as the label for the relation introducing vectors, and PART is introduced as the label for the axial part relation.

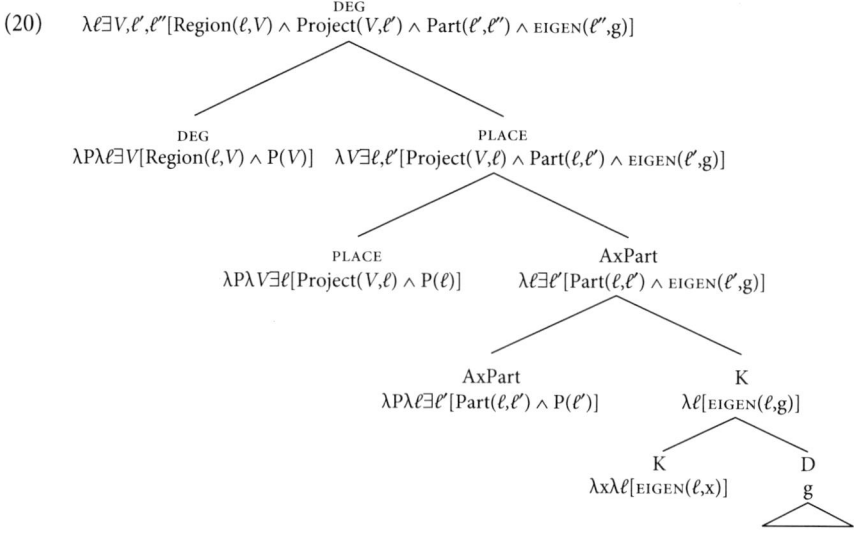

(20) $\lambda \ell \exists V, \ell', \ell''[\text{Region}(\ell,V) \wedge \text{Project}(V,\ell') \wedge \text{Part}(\ell',\ell'') \wedge \text{EIGEN}(\ell'',g)]$

Many languages which lexicalize AxPart using what are variously called relational words, relational nouns, component part terms, and so on, combine them with a generalized locative adposition or affix. This analysis provides an explicit semantics for each of the morphologically realized components. It may be directly compared to the highly compatible proposal of Botwinik-Rotem (this volume), where my Place corresponds approximately to her P_{LOC}, and my AxPart serves roughly the function of her X; an important difference is that I am abstracting away from the introduction of the Figure argument, which is the chief motivation for the nominal projection (her *Place*) which she postulates below X.[5]

6.1   Overt and covert Place

Languages vary concerning how many overt morphemes are involved in expressing projective space. An example of a language which lexicalizes both Place and AxPart is Japanese, in which the postposition/case suffix -*ni* can form a locative expression from an ordinary DP (Sadakane & Koizumi 1995), as illustrated in (21a); it also appears on AxPart words such as *mae* 'front,' *ushiro* 'behind,' *yoko* 'side,' and so on, as illustrated in (21b) (both examples from Takamine 2006).

(21) a. Taro-ga isu-ni   suwatta
          T-NOM *chair*-LOC *sat*
          'Taro sat on the chair.'
      b. Mary-ga Taro-no mae-ni   suwatteiru
          M-NOM *T*-GEN *front*-LOC *sit*
          'Mary is sitting in front of Taro.'

In both cases, -*ni* can be taken to occupy the Place node. If it is to have a consistent meaning in the two cases, then (21a) may be vague, with the specific part of the chair being sat on being contextually determined; I will suggest below that there is a null AxPart projection in similar cases (again compatible with Botwinik-Rotem's analysis of Hebrew in this volume).[6]

---

5. Also note that the analysis here is compatible with the proposal of Terzi (2004; to appear) that Greek locative expressions are phrases in the specifier of X, my AxPart (see also Botwinik-Rotem & Terzi 2008). Both Botwinik-Rotem and Terzi also argue that certain nominal characteristics of the AxPart constructions motivate the presence of an N node. The N node is also more extensively argued for in Pantcheva's (this volume) analysis of Persian, which is also interestingly different from the present proposal in that the node which I label AxPart here corresponds to a complex there, consisting of AxPart modifying the null N (PLACE). It remains to be seen to what extent all these analyses can be unified completely or whether they reflect differences among the different languages investigated (Botwinik-Rotem & Terzi 2008 explicitly explores the difference between Hebrew and Greek).

6. I am simplifying slightly here, in abstracting away from the question of how the PP combines the the larger structure in which it is embedded. In non-selected contexts, Japanese locative expressions may be marked with -*de* (Naoko Tomioka, personal communication).

(footnote continued)

In other constructions, the Place node is not overtly realized. For example, in the variety of Zapotec studied by Lillehaugen (2006), AxPart terms (which Lillehaugen terms Component Part Locatives) appear with no supporting locative adposition, as illustrated in (22) (from Lillehaugen 2006: 197–198).

(22)   a.   Mnnààà' zuu   dehts   co'ch.
            woman   stand   behind   car
            'The woman is standing behind the car.'
       b.   Mnnààà' zuu   cwe'eh   co'ch.
            woman   stand   beside   car
            'The woman is standing beside the car.'

Lillehaugen provides extensive argumentation that phrases like *dehts co'ch* and *cwe'eh co'ch* have the distribution of PPs. Thus, we can postulate a null Place head in Zapotec, corresponding to the overt *-ni* of the Japanese examples.

In most languages, AxPart terms may make use of either intrinsic or relative frames of reference, depending on various factors including the nature of the Ground. Lillehaugen reports that in Zapotec, relative reference is only possible if the ground is inanimate; thus, (22a), like its English translation, can either mean that the woman is in a space projected from the car's conventional back end, or that the woman is in a space projected from the side of the car which is away from the observer (or from the perspective chosen). In contrast, (23) is only natural with intrinsic reference, because the Ground is animate.

(23)   Bìinny zuu   dehts   mì'iny.
       person   stand   behind   child
       'The person is standing behind the child.'

In other languages, some AxParts may appear with overt Place heads while others might not. For example, Yukatek Maya as described by Bohnemeyer & Stolz (2006) employs a set of relational nouns to express spatial relations, and most of them require a locative preposition *ti'*, which I gloss here 'at'; it shows an agreement marker, here 3 for third person (parse and gloss otherwise simplified from Bohnemeyer & Stolz 2006: 286).

(i)   a.   Taro-ga beddo-de neta.
           *T-*NOM *bed-*LOC *slept*
           'Taro slept in the bed'
      b.   Taro-ga beddo-no ue-de   neta.
           *T-*NOM *bed-*GEN *top-*LOC *slept*
           'Taro slept in the bed'

This suggests that *-de* must function both as Place and also as a connector to the VP, as discussed in Tomioka (this volume).

(24) Te'l   kulukal   u   pèek'il   t-u   pàach   le   naho'
      there sits   3   dog   at-3 back   the house
      'There the dog is sitting outside the house.'

Bohnemeyer & Stolz (2006) observe that a small number of Yukatek spatial terms do not require *ti'*, namely *àanal* 'bottom, underside,' *iknal* 'proximity,' and *óok'ol* 'top.' The latter is illustrated in (25), from Bohnemeyer & Stolz (2006:285), again with simplified parse and gloss.

(25) Le   ch'iich'o'   túun   xíiknal   y-óok'ol   le   che'o'
      the bird   PROG fly   3-top   the tree
      'The bird is flying above the tree.' (e.g., circling, not directed motion)

Such expressions can be taken to lexicalize both AxPart and Place, as a lexical characteristic, just as English *behind* was found in Section 4 to lexicalize deg as well as loc (where loc is now decomposed into AxPart and Place).

This means that the American English expression *in back of* and the apparently monomorphemic Zapotec *dehts* 'behind' might have exactly the same structure, i.e., Place over AxPart over K. In the next subsection, I provide one additional argument that there is an AxPart projection present even with simple-looking spatial adpositions (and by extension this will imply that Place is present as a separate projection in PPs with AxParts, like the ones in Zapotec).

6.2   Binding

The argument is based on the analysis by Rooryck & Vanden Wyngaerd (2007) of the fact that locative expressions allow an alternation between anaphoric and pronominal complements, under certain conditions. Some examples are given in (26)–(28), based on similar examples in Rooryck & Vanden Wyngaerd (2007) (see also Botwinik-Rotem, this volume).

(26) a. Karen talked about herself/*her.
      b. Karen looked about herself/her.

(27) a. Miranda relies on herself/*her.
      b. Miranda pulled the blanket over herself/her.

(28) a. Samantha has confidence in herself/*her.
      b. Samantha has it in herself/her to become a great musician.

In each pair, the non-locative example requires an anaphor, while the locative example allows a pronominal complement, with coreference. It is often assumed that this is because locative PPs can be attached relatively high, and escape the binding domain, but there is no evidence that the locative PPs in (26)–(28) are attached outside the VP. For example, VP-fronting and VP-ellipsis tests suggest that these PPs are an integral part of the VP, as illustrated below.

(29) a. I said Karen would look about her, and look about her she did.
      b. *I said Karen would look about her, and look she did about her.

(30) a. Pull the blanket over her though she did, Miranda still felt cold.
      b. *Pull the blanket though she did over her, Miranda still felt cold.

(31) a. Samantha has it in her to become a great musician, and you might too.
      b. *Samantha has it in her to become a great musician, and you might in you
          to become a great mathematician.

Rooryck & Vanden Wyngaerd offer a novel explanation for the binding facts. They
note (citing earlier work) that the choice between anaphor and pronoun correlates
at least partly with perspective.

(32) a. They placed their guns, as they looked at it, in front of themselves/*them.
      b. They placed their guns, as I looked at it, in front of *themselves/them.

The contrast may not be as sharp as Rooryck & Vanden Wyngaerd indicate it, but
it certainly goes in this direction.

Rooryck & Vanden Wyngaerd adopt the AxPart analysis of locative PPs proposed in Svenonius (2006), and propose that the frame of reference is manifested
in the syntax by binding. A discourse-based perspective is achieved by coindexing
the AxPart with a deictic center, which Rooryck & Vanden Wyngaerd locate in
an Evidentiality projection at the top level of the clause. In the intrinsic frame of
reference, on the other hand, AxPart is coindexed with the Ground object, acquiring its orientation. This is sketched in (33), closely following Rooryck & Vanden
Wyngaerd (2007).

(33) a. $[_{\text{Evid}} \text{Sp The suitcase is } [_{\text{PLACE}} \text{be-} [_{\text{AxPart}} \text{hind}_i [_{\text{DP}} \text{the car}]_i]]]$
      b. $[_{\text{Evid}} \text{Sp}_i \text{The suitcase is } [_{\text{PLACE}} \text{be-} [_{\text{AxPart}} \text{hind}_i [_{\text{DP}} \text{the tree}]]]]$

For an object with an intrinsic front and back, such as a car, it is natural to coindex
AxPart with the Ground, in which case *behind the car* means in the space projected
from the car's back end. The other option is to bind AxPart with a higher, discourse-based perspective, which Rooryck and Vanden Wyngaerd represent as **Sp**,
for 'speaker'. This is the most natural option for an object without any intrinsic front
and back, such as a tree. In this case, *behind the tree* means in the space projected
from the part of the tree which is turned away from the perspective chosen.

The binding facts are then explained, if pronouns like *him* do not provide axes
suitable for establishing the intrinsic frame of reference, while complex anaphors
like *himself* do. In order for a pronoun to be used, a relative frame of reference has
to be chosen. This is sketched in (34).

(34) a. $[_{\text{Evid}} \text{Sp They}_i \text{placed the guns } [_{\text{PLACE}} \text{in } [_{\text{AxPart}} \text{front}_i \text{of } [_{\text{DP}} \text{themselves}]_i]]]$
      b. $[_{\text{Evid}} \text{Sp}_i \text{They}_j \text{placed the guns } [_{\text{PLACE}} \text{in } [_{\text{AxPart}} \text{front}_i \text{of } [_{\text{DP}} \text{them }]_j]]]$

The fact that the non-locative examples in (26)–(28) lack the additional binding possibility suggests that they lack AxParts.[7]

Possibly, the intrinsic reference should actually involve coindexation between AxPart and N, rather than between AxPart and DP; in any case, it has been argued that binding cannot involve subparts of words (cf. Williams 2007). Suppose that we interpret this to mean that coindexation can only be with syntactically represented constituents. This would mean that the binding in question could only occur when AxPart is present in the syntax as a distinct projection; since the two frames of reference are both available in locative PPs even when there are not two morphemes, as seen in (26)–(28) above, this suggests that AxPart projects in locative PPs in general, not just in explicit collocations like *in front of* and *on top of*.

Note that Rooryck & Vanden Wyngaerd's analysis neatly provides a place for the two parts of *beside*: *side* is clearly an AxPart, with a consistent meaning in *inside*, *outside*, and *alongside*, and *be-* has a consistently projective meaning in *beside*, *behind*, *beneath*, and perhaps also *between*. This is already implicit in their representations on which (33) is based.

7.   Conclusion

I have assumed a strict distinction between encyclopedic or conceptual-intentional information associated with lexical entries on the one hand, and syntactico-semantic information which bears on the well-formedness of syntactic structures on the other. This means that all prepositions with the same syntactic characteristics have the same syntactic representation. Given that *one meter beside the house* is plausible and coherent, but nonetheless ungrammatical, it must be ruled out by syntax. This leads to the postulation of a syntactically represented distance component in the meaning of the word *beside*, which precludes the attachment of a measure phrase. This entails that measure phrases are not simply freely adjoined to the category projected by Ps like *beside*, but rather are introduced syntactically by an instantiation of the syntactic category (which I called DEG) which represents the additional meaning component distinguishing *beside* from *behind*.

Since *behind* and *beside* otherwise show every sign of belonging to the same category, I concluded that there must be a null DEG head (or a set of them) which combines regularly with *behind*, and all other locative expressions that allow measure phrases. This is compatible with the position taken by Cinque (1999), that all

---

7. Botwinik-Rotem (this volume) notes other differences between locative and non-locative PPs in Hebrew, which indicate additional differences between the two types of PP, at least in that language.

functional heads which are present in a given language are always present in an extended projection, even if they are not overtly lexicalized by any phonologically pronounced material. Vague, default interpretations can be assumed to be available when no lexical material is inserted to specify otherwise.

Similarly, I presented an argument that AxPart is present as a distinct syntactic component in all locative PPs, building on the proposal of Rooryck & Vanden Wyngaerd (2007) to analyze frames of reference in terms of binding. If binding is a relation between syntactic constituents, as they assume, then even PPs headed by simple adpositions like *in* appear to have an AxPart component, like the one which is overt in *inside* or *in front of.*

It has been quite widely assumed that there is a T node in sentences like *John sat*, without the verb occupying T, and I pointed out some of the specific reasons for believing that verbs are even more complex than that. I believe that other null projections in the PP can also be motivated (I have assumed a K projection here, without discussing it in any detail). Arguments of this kind are not new; Bennett (1975: 21–25) presented arguments that Path (his d-exs, 'directional expressions') must be distinguished from Place (his l-ex, 'locative expression') in the syntax, and that both are present in directed motion sentences like *Trevor went behind the door* or *The bridegroom has arrived at the church*, even though there is no overt Path head in either.

I have not directly addressed the question of whether the same categories are present in all languages (see Sigurðsson 2004 for discussion of the difference between presence and overtness). There are plausible claims in the literature for differences among languages that might very well be characterizable in terms of the systematic absence of one category or another. The aspectual projection proposed by Tortora (this volume), for example, might conceivably be present in Italian and Spanish but absent from some other languages, though its semantic contribution is fairly subtle and it is difficult to be sure at this point whether it is an obligatory component of locative expressions cross-linguistically or not.

Pederson et al. (1998) and Levinson & Wilkins (2006) argue that there are languages in which the relative frame of reference is systematically absent.[8] In my terms, these languages might lack an AxPart projection, or lack any way to lexicalize it.

Munro (2000) and Lillehaugen & Munro (2006, 2007) argue that Chickasaw systematically lacks expressions with the external distribution of adjunct PPs, though there are expressions that look very much like projections of AxPart (for example as the complements of positional verbs, and in locative expressions introduced by applicatives). Possibly, then, Chickasaw would be a language in which there is no lexical expression of Place.

---

8.   See also the critique in Li & Gleitman (2002) and the response in Levinson et al. (2002).

The syntax of measurement has not been adequately investigated, but anectodal evidence suggests that there are languages with no way to add measure expressions to PPs. Possibly, some subset of such languages would lack the DEG projection altogether. Such languages would have to have other ways to introduce locative expressions, like Chickasaw does.

An important projection above DEG is Path. Ever since Talmy (1978) (see also Talmy 1985, 2000), there has been a great deal of work investigating the possibility that some languages lack Path heads. This is an intense area of ongoing research, but as of this moment it does seem plausible that the difference that Talmy observed between Spanish on the one hand and English on the other could be stated in terms of a functional head that Spanish lacks and English has.

Furthermore, it appears from comparing Hebrew as described by Botwinik-Rotem (this volume), or Japanese as described by Tomioka (this volume), or Persian as described by Pantcheva (this volume) to each other, or to English, that the possibilities for combining PPs with other categories varies from language to language. This might be due to differing properties of functional heads relatively high in the extended projection of P, or of heads in the extended projection of the categories modified.

If these suggestions turn out to be correct, then a substantial component of cross-linguistic variation might be in the presence or absence either of the functional heads themselves, or of the means to 'license' them (the distinction is a subtle one) – as has been suggested many times, in one form or another.

8.   Acknowledgments

Thanks to two anonymous reviewers for feedback and helpful suggestions on a previous draft. Thanks also to Gillian Ramchand and the other *Moving Right Along* seminar participants for discussion, and finally to the audience at the P conference in Utrecht.

References

Bennett, D.C. 1975. *Spatial and Temporal Uses of English Prepositions: An Essay in Stratificational Semantics*. Longman: London.
Bohnemeyer, J. & Stolz, C. 2006. Spatial reference in Yukatek Maya: A survey. In *Grammars of Space*, S.C. Levinson and D.P. Wilkins (eds), 273–310. Cambridge: CUP.
Botwinik-Rotem, I. & Terzi, A. 2008. Greek and Hebrew locative prepositional phrases: A unified case-driven account. *Lingua* 118(3): 399–424.
Chomsky, N. 1981. *Lectures on Government and Binding*. Dordrecht: Foris.

Cinque, G. 1994. On the evidence for partial N-movement in the Romance DP. In *Paths towards Universal Grammar: Studies in Honor of Richard,* S. Kayne, G. Cinque, J. Koster, J.-Y. Pollock, L. Rizzi & R. Zanuttini (eds), 85–110. Washington, DC: Georgetown University Press.

Cinque, G. 1999. *Adverbs and Functional Heads: A Cross-Linguistic Perspective.* New York: OUP.

Cinque, G. 2004. Restructuring and functional structure. In *Structures and Beyond: The Cartography of Syntactic Structures, vol. 3,* A. Belletti (ed.), 132–191. New York: Oxford.

den Dikken, M. to appear. On the functional structure of locative and directional PPs. In *Cartography of Syntactic Structures, vol. 6,* G. Cinque and L. Rizzi (eds). Oxford: OUP.

Emonds, J.E. 1985. *A Unified Theory of Syntactic Categories.* No. 19 in Studies in Generative Grammar. Dordrecht: Foris.

Herskovits, A. 1986. *Language and Spatial Cognition: An Interdisciplinary Study of the Prepositions in English.* Cambridge: CUP.

Hill, C.A. 1974. Spatial perception and linguistic encoding: A case study in Hausa and English. In *Papers from the Fifth Annual Conference on African Linguistics,* W.R. Leben (ed.), vol. Supplement 5 of *Studies in African Linguistics,* 135–148. Los Angeles: UCLA.

Huang, C.-T. J. 1982. Logical Relations in Chinese and the Theory of Grammar. PhD Dissertation, MIT.

Jackendoff, R. 1983. *Semantics and Cognition.* Cambridge, Ma.: MIT Press.

Jackendoff, R. 1996. The architecture of the linguistic-spatial interface. In *Language and Space,* P. Bloom, M.A. Peterson, L. Nadel, & M.F. Garrett (eds), 1–30. Cambridge, Ma.: MIT Press.

Jäger, G. & Blutner R. 2000. Against lexical decomposition in syntax. In *The Proceedings of the Fifteenth Annual IATL Conference,* A.Z. Wyner (ed.), 113–137. Haifa: The Israeli Association for Theoretical Linguistics.

Julien, M. 2002. *Syntactic Heads and Word Formation.* New York: OUP.

Julien, M. 2005. *Nominal Phrases from a Scandinavian Perspective.* Amsterdam: John Benjamins.

Kayne, R.S. 2006. On parameters and principles of pronunciation. In *Organizing Grammar. Linguistic Studies in Honor of Henk van Riemsdijk,* H. Broekhuis, N. Corver, R. Huybregts, U. Kleinhenz, & J. Koster(eds), 289–299. Berlin: Mouton de Gruyter.

Koopman, H. 1996. The spec head configuration. In *Syntax at Sunset,* E. Garrett & F. Lee (eds), 37–64. Los Angeles: Department of Linguistics, UCLA.

Koopman, H. 2000. Prepositions, postpositions, circumpositions, and particles. In *The Syntax of Specifiers and Heads,* H. Koopman (ed.), 204–260. London: Routledge.

Kracht, M. 2002. On the semantics of locatives. *Linguistics and Philosophy* 25: 157–232.

Kratzer, A. 1996. Severing the external argument from the verb. In *Phrase Structure and the Lexicon,* J. Rooryck and L. Zaring (eds), 109–137. Dordrecht: Kluwer.

Levinson, S.C. 1996. Frames of reference and Molyneux's questions: Cross-linguistic evidence. In *Language and Space,* P. Bloom, M.A. Peterson, L. Nadel, and M.F. Garrett (eds), 109–169. Cambridge, Ma.: MIT Press.

Levinson, S.C. 2003. *Space in Language and Cognition: Explorations in Cognitive Diversity.* Cambridge: CUP.

Levinson, S.C., Sotaro K., Haun, D.B.M., & Rasch, B.H. 2002. Returning the tables: language affects spatial reasoning. *Cognition* 84 (2): 155–188.

Levinson, S.C. & Wilkins, D.P. 2006. Patterns in the data: Towards a semantic typology of spatial description. In *Grammars of Space,* S. C. Levinson & D. P. Wilkins (eds), 512–569. Cambridge: CUP.

Li, P. & Gleitman, L. 2002. Turning the tables: Language and spatial reasoning. *Cognition* 83 (3): 265–294.

Lillehaugen, B.D. 2006. *Expressing Location in Tlacolula Valley Zapotec*. PhD Dissertation, UCLA.

Lillehaugen, B.D. & Munro, P. 2006. Relational nouns and prepositions in a typology of component part locatives. Presented at LSA Annual Meeting in Albuquerque; Ms., UNAM and UCLA.

Lillehaugen, B.D. & Munro, P. 2007. Component part locatives and frames of reference. Presented at SSILA Annual Meeting in Anaheim; Ms., UNAM and UCLA.

McCawley, J. D. 1971. Pre-lexical syntax. In *Report of the 22nd Roundtable Meeting on Linguistics and Language Studies*, S. J. O'Brien (ed.), 19–33. Washington, D.C.: Georgetown University Press.

Munro, P. 2000. The leaky grammar of the Chickasaw applicatives. In *The Proceedings from the Main Session of the Chicago Linguistic Society's Thirty-Sixth Meeting*, A. Okrent & J. P. Boyle (eds), 285–310. Chicago: Chicago Linguistic Society.

Nam, S. 1995. *The Semantics of Locative PPs in English*. PhD Dissertation, UCLA.

Pederson, E., Danziger, E., Wilkins, D., Levinson, S., Kita, S., & Senft, G. 1998. Semantic typology and spatial conceptualization. *Language* 74 (3): 557–589.

Ramchand, G. & Svenonius, P. to appear. Mapping a parochial lexicon onto a universal semantics. In *The Limits of Syntactic Variation*, T. Biberauer (ed.). Amsterdam: John Benjamins.

Rooryck, J. & Vanden Wyngaerd, G. 2007. The syntax of spatial anaphora: In *Nordlyd, Tromsø Working Papers in Language & Linguistics: 34.2, Space, Motion and Result*, M. Bašić, M. Pantcheva, M. Son & P. Svenonius (eds), 33–85. Tromsø: University of Tromsø.

Sadakane, K. & Koizumi, M. 1995. On the nature of the "dative" particle *ni* in Japanese. *Linguistics* 33 (1): 5–33.

Sigurðsson, H. 2004. Meaningful silence, meaningless sounds. *Linguistic Variation Yearbook* 4: 235–259.

von Stechow, A. 1995. Lexical decomposition in syntax. In *Lexical Knowledge in the Organisation of Language*, U. Egli, P.E. Pause, C. Schwarze, A. von Stechow & G. Wienold, (eds) 81–177. Amsterdam: Benjamins.

von Stechow, A. 1996. The different readings of *wieder* 'again': A structural account. *Journal of Semantics* 13 (2): 87–138.

von Stechow, A. 2003. How are results represented and modified? remarks on Jäger & Blutner's anti-decomposition. In *Modifying Adjuncts*, E. Lang, C. Maienborn & C. Fabricius-Hansen (eds), 417–554. Berlin: Mouton de Gruyter.

Svenonius, P. 1994. C-selection as feature-checking. *Studia Linguistica* 48 (2): 133–155.

Svenonius, P. 2006. The emergence of axial parts. In *Nordlyd, Tromsø Working Papers in Language & Linguistics: 33.1, Special Issue on Adpositions*, P. Svenonius & M. Pantcheva (eds), 49–77. Tromsø: University of Tromsø.

Svenonius, P. 2007. 1...3-2. In *Oxford Handbook of Linguistic Interfaces*, G. Ramchand & C. Reiss (eds), 239–288. Oxford: OUP.

Svenonius, P. to appear a. The position of adjectives and other phrasal modifiers in the decomposition of DP. In *Adjectives and Adverbs: Syntax, Semantics, and Discourse*, L. McNally & C. Kennedy. Oxford: OUP.

Svenonius, P. to appear b. Spatial prepositions in English. In *Cartography of Syntactic Structures, vol. 6*, G. Cinque and L. Rizzi (eds). Oxford: OUP.

Takamine, K. 2006. Categorical properties of space expressions in Japanese. In *Nordlyd, Tromsø Working Papers in Language & Linguistics: 33.1, Special Issue on Adpositions*, P. Svenonius & M. Pantcheva (eds), 78–97. Tromsø: University of Tromsø.

Talmy, L. 1978. Figure and ground in complex sentences. In *Universals of Human Language*, J.H. Greenberg (ed), vol. 4, 625–649. Stanford, Ca.: Stanford University Press.

Talmy, L. 1985. Lexicalization patterns: Semantic structure in lexical forms. In *Language Typology and Syntactic Description, III: Grammatical Categories and the Lexicon*, T. Shopen (ed.), 57–149. Cambridge: CUP.

Talmy, L. 2000. *Toward a Cognitive Semantics*. Cambridge, Ma.: MIT Press.

Terzi, A. 2004. Locative prepositions and possession. Ms., Technological Educational Institute of Patras.

Terzi, A. to appear. Locative prepositions and *Place*. In *Cartography of Syntactic Structures, vol. 6*, G. Cinque & L. Rizzi (eds). Oxford: OUP.

Williams, E. 2007. Dumping lexicalism. In *The Handbook of Linguistic Interfaces*, G. Ramchand & C. Reiss (eds). Oxford: OUP.

Wunderlich, D. 1991. How do prepositional phrases fit into compositional syntax and semantics? *Linguistics* 29: 591–621.

Zamparelli, R. 2000. *Layers in the Determiner Phrase*. New York: Garland.

Zwarts, J. 1997. Vectors as relative positions: A compositional semantics of modified PPs. *Journal of Semantics* 14: 57–86.

Zwarts, J. & Winter, Y. 2000. Vector space semantics: A model-theoretic analysis of locative prepositions. *Journal of Logic, Language, and Information* 9: 169–211.

Priorities in the production of prepositions*

Joost Zwarts
Utrecht University

This paper studies the semantic interaction between pairs of closely related prepositions, like *in*, *on*, *over*, and *around*, in order to determine the priorities that determine the application of these prepositions to ambiguous situations. It is proposed that the division of labour between prepositions in such situations is strongly determined by stereotypical regularities in the way spatial notions like support, containment and superiority are related.

1. Introduction

When a speaker wants to express a spatial relation between two objects, a Figure and a Ground, she has to make a choice from an inventory of expressions, typically prepositions. One way of studying the semantics and pragmatics of prepositions is to focus on such choices and to look for the spatial (and other) factors that determine them. At first sight, this may seem like a simple research enterprise. After all, are prepositions not ways of directly labeling spatial relations: *in* names the relation of containment, *on* that of support, and similarly for other prepositions? The research on prepositions in the last couple of decades has demonstrated that this is in fact a far from simple matter. The choice between two prepositions for a particular spatial scene is typically the outcome of the interaction between quite complicated perceptual, geometric, pragmatic and conventional factors, as shown in the studies of Talmy (1983), Herskovits (1986), Vandeloise (1991), Regier (1995), Feist (2000), and Conventry & Garrod (2004), for example.

---

* An early version of this paper was presented at the P-conference in Utrecht, June 4, 2006. I thank the audience for useful comments and questions. The research for this paper was financially supported by a grant from the Netherlands Organization for Scientific Research NWO to the PIONIER project 'Case Cross-Linguistically' (number 220-70-003), which is gratefully acknowledged. I thank Henriëtte de Swart for comments on an earlier paper and Moreno Coco for inspiring discussions about the issues discussed in this paper, as well as three anonymous reviewers who have helped me to make considerable improvements.

Consider, for example, a spatial trajectory that has the shape in Figure 1, partially enclosing a Ground.

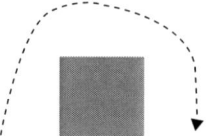

Figure 1. *Over* or *around?*

There are, prima facie, two prepositions competing for the description of this situation, *around* and *over*. The reason is that a path of this shape is among the usages of both of these prepositions (as shown in Schulze 1991, 1993 for *around* and Lakoff 1987 and others for *over*). Without any further spatial information about the spatial scene we would tend to say that the path goes *around* the Ground, but when we know that the picture offers us a side view, then it is more natural to say that the path goes *over* the Ground. Why is this? What are the principles behind the competition between prepositions like *around* and *over*? Why do we have to use *over* when vertical orientation becomes salient? I will argue that it is more important or useful to express the vertical orientation of a path with respect to the Ground than its curvature. This is one of the *priorities* in the system of prepositions: *over* takes precedence over *around* on the basis of a deeper semantic ordering of vertical orientation and curved shape.

In this paper I will study a number of situations where two prepositions compete with each other for a particular meaning, but only one of the two is appropriate. This will reveal important principles for the semantics of prepositions. I will use the theoretical framework of Optimality Theory. The mapping from meanings (spatial relations) to forms (prepositions) is construed as an optimization process. Given a particular spatial relation, different prepositions present themselves as candidates, competing with each other. The winner of the competition, the optimal preposition, is that candidate that best satisfies a system of ranked constraints. Formulating the problem in this way will help us to make explicit which factors play a role in the production of prepositions and how these factors interact.

The next section will spell out my (Optimality-Theoretic) assumptions in somewhat more detail. After that I will go through a range of simple two-way competitions between prepositions and derive several spatial priorities. At the end of the paper I will tie these case studies together to examine the origins of these priorities more closely and draw some general conclusions. I want to stress already at this point that we have to work here with a partial picture of preposition interactions, with very strong semantic idealizations and simplifications. But nevertheless, in this way we can hopefully see more clearly the semantic priorities that play a role in the production of prepositions and the implications that these priorities might have for the system and grammar of prepositions and other spatial markers.

2.   Optimality Theory, production and lexicon

Optimality Theory is a theory about input-output mappings in natural language. It was first applied in phonology, to the mapping from underlying lexical forms to surface pronunciations, and later also to the syntax-semantics interface, in the mapping between form and meaning (Prince & Smolensky 1997; Blutner, de Hoop, & Hendriks 2005). The following elements of OT are important for this paper. The input gives rise to a set of candidate outputs through some unrestricted generative mechanism (the generator GEN). These candidates compete with each other for being the output. There is a set of well-formedness constraints $C_1, \dots , C_n$ applying to the candidates. Each of the candidates will typically violate some of the constraints, and there is usually no candidate that is perfect. The reason is that constraints can be in conflict with each other, imposing demands on the output that work in opposite directions. This conflict is resolved by ranking constraints with respect to each other, with higher constraints being more important for the output than lower constraints. The output is then the candidate that is *optimal*, i.e., that produces less violations for higher ranked constraints, roughly speaking.

Here is a simple and well-known example from OT syntax, the component that maps meanings to sentential forms. The appearance of the expletive subject *it* in the sentence *It rains* in English is analyzed as arising from the interaction of two general constraints (following Grimshaw & Samek-Lodovici 1998). FULL INTERPRETATION requires every word to have an interpretation, a requirement that is violated by the non-referential (expletive) pronoun *it* here, which does not have an interpretation. SUBJECT states that a sentence always should have a subject, even if the verb does not project an external argument. In English, SUBJECT is ranked over FULL INTERPRETATION, which means that the output with an expletive pronoun wins the competition, as shown in the following table:

Table 1.   Inserting an expletive subject

'It rains'	SUBJECT	FULL INTERPRETATION
Rains	*!	
☞ It rains		*

In this table the semantic input is informally represented as 'It rains'. Below this input, two candidate outputs are given: *Rains* and *It rains*. The operation of the two constraints is given by two columns, with an asterisk indicating that an output is violated for a constraint. *It rains* is the optimal output: even though it violates the lower-ranked constraint FULL INTERPRETATION, it is still better than *Rains*, which violates the higher-ranked constraint SUBJECT. Switching the order of the constraints leads to an Italian-type language, in which subjects can be dropped.

In Optimality Theory faithfulness constraints play an important role. They require the output to reflect the input in certain respects. The more the output diverges from the input, the more faithfulness constraints are violated. In the above example, FULL INTERPRETATION is such a faithfulness constraint.

Most of the Optimality-Theoretic applications take a production perspective. The input of the optimization process is an underlying phonological form or a meaning, the output is a surface phonetic form or a syntactic structure, respectively. OT semantics, on the other hand, starts with a form or syntactic structure as an input and tries to define the optimal output interpretation for that (Hendriks & de Hoop 2001). Combinations of both perspectives are possible and lead to interesting enrichments of our views on linguistic well-formedness (Blutner 2000). However, in this paper, I am only concerned with the mapping from an input meaning to an output form, like in OT syntax. Nevertheless, while OT syntax is primarily concerned with morphosyntactic issues of word order and inflection, the OT system that I have in mind here involves the problem of choosing the best word for describing a particular input meaning, a process prior to OT syntax. There are different ways to formulate this optimization process, depending on the kind of semantic framework one adopts.[1] I will make the following assumptions here, concerning the input meanings, the output words, and the constraints that determine the mapping from meanings to words.

First, in order to keep things simple and accessible, I will assume that the input for the OT mapping is some bundle of semantic features $[F_1, \ldots, F_N]$ that characterizes what the input situation is like. What these features are like depends on the semantic domain; in the domain of prepositions we want to characterize a spatial relation and therefore we need features about direction, distance, reference frame, curvature of a path, force dynamics, etc. Alternatively (and ideally), we define a formal model of spatial meanings, on the basis of vector spaces, mereotopological regions or trajectories and draw spatial input meanings from such

---

1.   Not much work has been done about lexicalization or the mapping from meanings to words in Optimality Theory. Jones (2003) deals with kinship terminology from an OT perspective, while Solstad (2003) consider the use of prepositions from this perspective.

2.   In my own work I have tried to formalize these notions in terms of vectors (Zwarts 1997; Zwarts & Winter 2000), and curves (Zwarts 2004 & Zwarts 2005).

a model.[2] However, defining prepositional meanings in such models is not always straightforward, and providing and explaining the relevant definitions here would not be beneficial for the major focus of this paper. I will therefore work with very rough spatial features like SUPERIOR and SUPPORT, in spite of various sorts of justified criticism that could be raised against such features. I believe that the general points that I want to make about priorities and optimization in the prepositional domain are relatively independent of the issue of whether meanings are formulated in terms of primitive features, topological image-schemas or model-theoretic objects. So these capitalized features stand for the reader's favourite explicitation of spatial relations. The important thing is that we have some way to differentiate various spatial relations in the input in a sufficiently explicit way.

Second, the candidate outputs in a particular language are words from that language that express one or more of the input features. In this paper, we are only dealing with the English words *in*, *on*, *over*, *above*, and *around*. Each of these words is specified for at least one spatial feature. *On*, for instance, is specified as expressing the feature SUPPORT, while *over* carries the feature SUPERIOR.[3] Prepositions are often polysemous, and therefore they may have different feature specifications for their different senses, as we will see in section 5 for *over* and *around*. In addition to the prototypical *around*$_{CIRCLE}$, we also find *around*$_{HALF}$ and *around*$_{QUARTER}$. There might also be prepositions that combine different features, like *on top of*, which seems to be both SUPERIOR and SUPPORT at the same time, but I will not deal with such complex prepositions here. I am interested in the competition between prepositions for which one core meaning and maybe a few additional meanings can been identified.

Third, there is a faithfulness constraint FAITH(F_i) for every feature F_i, which is violated when F_i is part of the input but not reflected in the output. The output depends on the ranking between the various faithfulness constraints. Let us make more concrete what can happen with a simple abstract example, in which the input of the optimization process is the feature bundle [F, G]. In theory, there are three possible candidate words for this input: a word that expresses F (*word*$_F$), a word that expresses G (*word*$_G$) and a word that expresses both F and G (WORD$_{F, G}$), but in the concrete cases that I will discuss in this paper, there are only words with one feature. Then both *word*$_F$ and *word*$_G$ violate a constraint and their competition needs to be decided by ordering the faithfulness constraints. The following tableau shows the patterns of violations with the ordering FAITH(F) >> FAITH(G).

3.   By using only the feature SUPERIOR I am collapsing the place and path use of *over* here. In a fuller treatment we would want to make this distinction explicit, e.g., PLACE SUPERIOR versus PATH (or VIA) SUPERIOR. Here we concentrate on *over* as a preposition of spatial superiority, glossing over these more general spatial distinctions.

Table 2.   The optimally faithful word for [F, G]

	[F, G]	Faith(F)	Faith(G)
☞	word$_F$		*
	word$_G$	*!	

We will now go through a series of binary competitions between prepositions, starting with two very basic prepositions: *in* and *on*.

3.   *In* versus *on*

Even though *in* and *on* are very short and frequent prepositions in English, characterizing their semantics has turned out to be far from simple. One of the reasons for this is that, even though *in* and *on* are often characterized as topological prepositions, their semantics is actually not purely geometric, i.e., based on spatial inclusion or contact. There are many functional and force-dynamic factors in their use and interpretation that have to do with how the Ground object fulfills its role with respect to the Figure as a container or a means of support. For discussion about this, I refer the reader to Herskovits (1986), Vandeloise (1991), Feist (2000), Bowerman & Choi (2001), Conventry & Garrod (2004), Carlson & van der Zee (2005). There is also polysemy and vagueness in the way *in* and *on* and similar items in other languages apply to a variety of different situations (as shown, for instance, in Cuyckens 1991; Levinson & Meira 2003).

Despite the complexities that characterize the semantics of *in* and *on*, I am going to assume two semantic features CONT(AINMENT) and SUPP(ORT) that are relevant for the use of *in* and *on*. CONT is lexically associated with *in* and SUPP with *on*. These two features stand for complexes of spatial and force-dynamic properties of the relation between a Figure and a Ground. If a pen is in a box, it is included in the spatial region occupied by the box as a whole, but an apple in a bowl with apples might be outside the spatial region of the bowl, but still be part of what is contained by the bowl, as shown in Figure 2a.

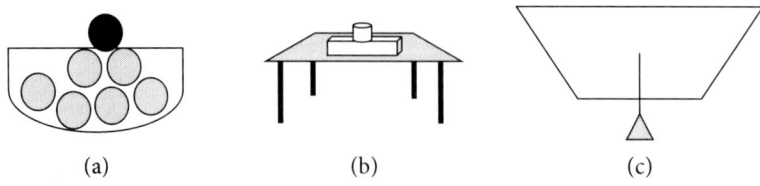

| (a) | (b) | (c) |

Figure 2.   (a) apple in bowl, (b) cup on table, (c) lamp on ceiling.

Similarly, the relation of SUPPORT will have a spatial ingredient of contact, e.g., when a book is lying on the table or a fly is on the ceiling, but this element of contact between Figure and Ground might be missing when there is still a prominent relation of force-dynamic support or attachment between them, as in Figure 2b and 2c. Even though there is no direct contact between Figure and Ground in these situations, we can talk about *the cup on the table* and *the lamp on the ceiling*.

What I am interested in now is what happens with a situation that has both containment *and* support. There are situations of pure containment, described by *in* PPs (*a fish in the water, a bird in the air*) and there are situations of pure support, described by *on* PPs (*a book on the table, a picture on the wall*). There are also situations that involve both containment and support, like a pen in a box or an apple in a bowl, in which the Ground object not only contains the Figure, but it also supports it from below. Another situation known from the literature is that of a light bulb in a socket: there is partial containment of the Figure in the Ground, but the socket is at the same time keeping the light bulb from falling. The important question is now: how is such an ambivalent situation described? Which preposition is used: *in* (the containment preposition) or *on* (the support preposition)?

It is clear that the preposition *in* is used for these situations. As was already obvious from the description in the previous paragraph, we talk about a pen *in* a box, an apple *in* a bowl and a light bulb *in* a socket and not about a pen *on* a box, an apple *on* a bowl or a light bulb *on* a socket. It is important to realize that this is not a trivial fact, but something important to be accounted for. Why is *in* used and not *on*? In the terminology of this paper, containment takes priority over support. We can express this now in Optimality-Theoretic terms, by a combination of two faithfulness constraints FAITH(CONT) and FAITH(SUPP), ranked as in (1).

(1)   FAITH(CONT) >> FAITH(SUPP)

When applied to the input [CONT, SUPP] (bowl-with-apple, socket-with-bulb), we get the optimization process that is worked out in the tableau in Table 3.

Table 3.   Optimal description of supporting containment

	[CONT, SUPP]	FAITH(CONT)	FAITH(SUPP)
☞	in$_{CONT}$		*
	on$_{SUPP}$	*!	

This process gives us as output the optimal description of 'supporting containment', given the way the two faithfulness constraints are ordered. Since there is no special-purpose preposition for this combination of features in English, we have to extend the use of one of the two relevant prepositions, and, because of the predominance of containment, it is *in* that takes care of this extension.

There is another way of representing this, through a small-scale *semantic space* (Gärdenfors 2000; Haspelmath 2003; Levinson & Meira 2003):

(2)   CONTAINMENT ------ CONTAINMENT + SUPPORT ------ SUPPORT
        <----------------------- in ----------------------->   <---------- on --------->

In this semantic space, there are only three semantic 'points': the extremes of pure support and pure containment and an area of overlap between containment and support, sharing a feature with both. As we can see, this area is covered by *in* and not by *on*, because of the higher ranked faithfulness for containment that we saw in the tableau of Table 3. Why would containment take priority over support? This is an important question to which we will return in section 6 after we have studied some other priorities in the production of prepositions.

4.   *On* versus *above/over*

We saw in the previous section that *on* can be used for different situations of support. In many cases of support the Ground object is below the Figure, e.g., *a book on the table*, but there are many other situations where this is not the case, like *a picture on the wall, a lamp on the ceiling*. So, some of the situations that are covered by *on* can be characterized as [SUPPORT], others are [SUPPORT, SUPERIOR], i.e., the Figure is supported by the Ground *and* superior to it, with respect to the vertical axis, as in example (3a). Like in the previous section, I assume that *on* is only specified for the feature [SUPPORT]. If we would associate it with the combination [SUPPORT, SUPERIOR], then many uses of *on* would not be covered (e.g., *a picture on the wall, a lamp on the ceiling*). [SUPPORT] is the defining feature of *on*. The use of *above* however, suggests a situation in which support is absent and there is only superior location. The same is true for the locative uses of *over* (but not for motion and extension uses, see Lakoff 1987, Tyler & Evans 2001 for the relevant distinctions). This is shown in example (3b), in which there is no contact or support between the table and the lamp.

(3)   a.   The lamp is on the table.
        b.   The lamp is above/over the table.

Just like in the previous section, we can construct a small semantic space from the features SUPPORT and SUPERIOR and show how *on* and *above/over* divide up this space.

(4)   SUPPORT ------ SUPPORT + SUPERIOR ------ SUPERIOR
        <---------------- on -------------------->   <- above/over ->

The preposition *on* covers the two meanings on the left, leaving the pure SUPERIOR sense to the prepositions *over* and *above*. An ambiguous situation, offering features for the application of different prepositions, shows again a clear priority for the faithful expression of only one spatial feature, SUPPORT in this case. The constraint ranking that corresponds to this priority is as follows:

(5)   FAITH(SUPPORT) >> FAITH(SUPERIOR)

The OT optimization process for different inputs is very similar to what we have seen in the previous section with CONTAINMENT and SUPPORT, assuming the lexical specifications $on_{SUPPORT}$ and $above_{SUPERIOR}$ and $over_{SUPERIOR}$:

Table 4.   Optimal description of superior support

	[SUPP, SUPER]	FAITH(SUPP)	FAITH(SUPER)
☞	on_{SUPP}		*
	$above_{SUPER}$	*!	
	$over_{SUPER}$	*!	

Notice that this time there are three competing prepositions, two of which, *above* and *over*, are identically specified in this case with SUPERIOR. Obviously, *above* and *over* are not semantically equivalent lexical items. There are many other uses of *over* that are not (or not exclusively) specified as SUPERIOR, but that require features for moving or extended figures or 'end-point focus' (see also the next section):

(6)   a.   Sam walked over the hill.
       b.   Mother put the tablecloth over the table.
       c.   Alex lives over the hill.

Also, there are differences between the superiority use of *above* and *over* in (3b) that are not accounted for by a simple feature SUPERIOR (Coventry & Garrod 2004), but for our purposes at this point, it is sufficient to characterize *above* and *over* as both SUPERIOR.

We can combine the two rankings that we have now seen in the following way:

(7)   FAITH(CONTAINMENT) >> FAITH(SUPPORT) >> FAITH(SUPERIOR)

This does not necessarily make sense, however, because containment and superiority might exclude each other. Strictly speaking, a Figure can only be above a Ground if it is not inside that Ground. Nevertheless, with more liberal interpretations of containment and support, we might think of examples in which all three spatial elements are present, e.g., *the flowers in the vase* (Vandeloise 1991). The flowers are partially in the vase, they are supported by it in various ways, but they are also largely above the vase. If this is really a situation that satisfies the three relations (and this of course depends on the way we define the spatial features SUPPORT, CONTAINMENT and SUPERIORITY), then it also confirms our predictions in an interesting way: the preposition used here is *in*, and not *on* or *above*. In other words: CONTAINMENT is stronger than both SUPPORT and SUPERIORITY. This analysis is shown in the tableau of Table 5.

Table 5.   Optimal description of flowers *in* a vase

[CONT, SUPP, SUPER]	FAITH(CONT)	FAITH(SUPP)	FAITH(SUPER)
☞ in$_{CONT}$		*	*
on$_{SUPP}$	*!		*
above$_{SUPER}$	*!	*	
over$_{SUPER}$	*!	*	

Interestingly, CONTAINMENT even takes priority in the well-known puzzle of Figure 2a, where an apple is not in the geometric interior of the bowl, but on top of a pile of apples. We can still say that this apple is *in* the bowl, because (as argued by Vandeloise 1991; Coventry & Garrod 2004, and many others), the notion of CONTAINMENT is not purely geometric, but it has an important functional or force-dynamic element, which extends its use beyond the narrow area of purely spatial inclusion.

5.   *Around* versus *over*

The preposition *over* is probably one of the most polysemous and intensively studied prepositions in English. We have already seen that it is used in a way quite similar to *above*, to indicate the location of ordinary objects. There is also a prominent use to describe how an object moves along a *path* that is located above the Ground object, as illustrated in the examples in (8), taken from Lakoff (1987).

(8)   a.   The bird flew over the yard.
       b.   Sam walked over the hill.

The path of *over* goes *via* the region that is above the Ground, which means that most of its points, except possibly the end points, are above the Ground. We can represent this for the purposes of this paper as a combination of two features: [PATH, SUPERIOR]. Whether the path follows a straight line (as in (8a)) or is curved around the Ground (in (8b)) is simply not specified as part of the meaning of *over*. The features also leave open whether or not there is contact between path and Ground or whether the Ground supports the moving object. All that we need is the specification SUPERIOR to indicate where the PATH is.

What I want to study in this section is the interaction of *over* with the preposition *around*. *Around* is one of the most complicated and polysemous prepositions of English (Schulze 1991, 1993; Zwarts 2004), so it is necessary to make idealizations to study its interaction with *over*. Let us assume that *around* refers to paths that curve outward with respect to the Ground, i.e., that are convex, as in the pictures in Figure 3.

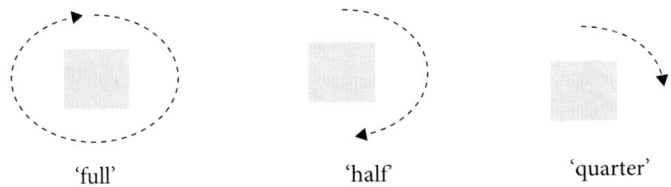

'full'   'half'   'quarter'

Figure 3. Three paths around an object.

Typical examples of such convex paths are given in (9):

(9) a. Alex ran around the house
b. Alex drove around the barrier
c. Alex came around the corner

To distinguish these different senses from each other, we would need to specify how much of the object is enclosed by the path: COMPLETE (for 9a), HALF (for 9b), QUARTER (for 9c). However, since this is not relevant for the comparison with *over*, I use the more general feature CONVEX that I take to apply to all three senses. I refer to Zwarts (2004) for more precise definitions of the various senses and shapes of *around*.

I assume that *around* does not specify *where* the path is relative to the Ground: above, below or beside it. This requires some justification. One might have the intuition that *around* is strictly a *horizontal* path preposition: it simply does not apply to paths that have a vertical orientation, let's say because it is lexically associated to the set [CONVEX, HORIZONTAL]. However, this analysis misses the point that there are situations in which *around* in fact *can* refer to paths with a vertical orientation, when the path completely encloses the Ground:

(10) a. The snake coiled around a branch.
b. The airplane made a looping around the bridge.

So horizontality can not be an inherent lexical feature of *around*, and I will show that it must be an *effect* of its competition with other items that have to take priority in expressing the location of a path above a Ground. There is also a more principled objection against including HORIZONTAL in the definition of *around*, because it is not clear what the semantic motivation would be of including this feature. Why would *around* have to be horizontal, and why only with partial enclosure?

So, assuming the specifications *over* [PATH, SUPERIOR] and *around* [PATH,CONVEX]' these two prepositions now have a theoretical overlap:

(11)   PATH   PATH   PATH
         SUPERIOR ------- SUPERIOR+CONVEX ------- CONVEX
         <-- over -->   ???   <-- around -->

In virtue of their definitions, *over* and *around* could in principle both apply to a spatial situation with a path that is *both* SUPERIOR and CONVEX. The question is: which preposition is actually used in that case? Let us consider the situation in Figure 4.

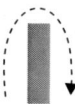

Figure 4. *Over the wall* or *around the wall*?

Which of the following two sentences is the correct way of describing this situation?

(12)   a.   Sam climbed around the wall.
        b.   Sam climbed over the wall.

The competition between *over* and *around* with respect to Figure 4 has *over* as a clear winner. Sentence (12a) could only be used if the climbing path of Sam is located more or less in a horizontal plane. We see a similar thing with paths that enclose only a corner or edge of an object, as in Figure 5.

Figure 5. (a) *around the edge* and (b) *over the edge*.

When the path is in the horizontal plane, we use the preposition *around* (example (13a) and Figure 5a) but when that same path has a vertical orientation, *over* (example (13b) and Figure 5b) is used.

(13)   a.   Sam climbed around the edge.
        b.   Sam climbed over the edge.

So, if there is a strong bias to a particular superior location of the path, then this bias needs to be reflected in the choice of the superior preposition *over*. If the path completely encloses the Ground, as the first path in Figure 3, then there is no such bias. All the directions are represented in the path and then *around* is the only appropriate preposition.

We get the picture that is by now familiar. There are two faithfulness constraints ordered in the following way:

(14)   FAITH(SUPERIOR) >> FAITH(CONVEX)

The expression of superior location of a path has priority over the expression of convexity of the path. If the input is [PATH, SUPERIOR, CONVEX], then the optimal output with these constraints is the output $over_{[PATH, SUPERIOR]}$. Notice that there is no lexical item (say $curver_{[PATH, SUPERIOR, CONVEX]}$ 'over with an arc') that specifically refers to paths that are both convex and superior to the Ground object, otherwise that preposition would have been chosen as the optimal output. Having such an item would be too expensive for the lexicon, which simply cannot provide specific words for every possible combination of features. In other words, a choice *has* to be made by giving priority to one of the features, by ordering the features as in (14).

Another conceivable but questionable way to make sure that *over* applies to the situation in Figure 4 and Figure 5b is to add another feature to *over*, namely CONVEX. This is in line with the proposal of Dewell (1994), for instance, who argues that the prototype of *over* involves paths that have an arc or curve. *Over* will then presumably take precedence over *around* because it is the more specific, richer item. But the problem with this approach is that we need to get rid of the feature CONVEX in the many cases where *over* simply refers to a straight path above the Ground object, like in (8a). The advantage of the approach that I sketched is that the lexical meanings of *over* and *around* have a wider coverage (because they are underspecified), but *around* gets limited in application through the priority of *over*.

An interesting question is how *around* interacts with other directions besides the superior one. Consider the path in Figure 6.

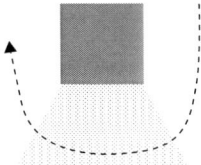

Figure 6. Passing *under* or *behind* an object.

When the curve of the path goes through the under region of the Ground object, we have a path that we would rather describe as going *under* the Ground than *around* the Ground, i.e., FAITH(INFERIOR) >> FAITH(CONVEX). However, if the indicated region is the backside of the Ground, then there might be a true choice between *around* and *behind*:

(15)   a.   We passed around the desk
       b.   We passed behind the desk

This suggests that there is no ordering between FAITH(BEHIND) and FAITH(CONVEX). We will come back to this in the next section when we consider the deeper motivations for constraint ranking in this domain.

6.   Motivating spatial priorities

The methodological approach of this paper was to make the meaning specifications of prepositions as simple and general as possible. In this way the potential areas of application of prepositions will inevitably *overlap* with each other and these situations of overlap force us to investigate why one preposition takes precedence over another preposition in such a situation.

The total set of priorities that we have seen adds up to the following ranking (omitting FAITH(INFERIOR), which is only partially ordered with respect to the others):

(16)   FAITH(CONTAINMENT) >> FAITH(SUPPORT) >> FAITH(SUPERIOR) >>
        FAITH(CONVEX)

In order to understand this hierarchy we need to take a closer look at the way the semantic features relate to each other, starting with CONTAINMENT and SUPPORT. These two notions are not completely independent of each other, but situations of containment will *typically* also be situations of support. So there is a kind of default inference from CONTAINMENT to SUPPORT, based on our knowledge of typical containers, gravitation, the mechanisms of support, and on what is statistically the most common way of using *in*. If I learn that the pen is *in* the box, then I will make the inference that it is lying *on* the bottom, kept from falling by the box. If a Figure is in a container Ground, it will usual not be floating freely in the hollow part of that container, but the gravitational pull will make sure that the inside of the container also fulfills a support role through contact with an internal surface. The reverse is not true. There are many situations of support (by tables, floors, etc.) that do not bring along containment or inclusion.

By ranking FAITH(CONTAINMENT) over FAITH(SUPPORT) the lexical system draws heavily on this regularity. Most situations that combine CONTAINMENT and SUPPORT can be analyzed as situations that first of all have the feature CONTAINMENT and *because of that* also the feature SUPPORT. Applying the preposition *in* to combined situations does not extend it very much beyond the range of application that we find anyway for this preposition on the basis of its association with the notion of containment. Seen from a slightly different, pragmatic perspective, the preposition *in* is stereotypically enriched with the notion of support, or, in other words, its prototypical use of *in* involves both containment and support.

A similar story can be told for the relation between SUPPORT and SUPERIOR. The typical, most common instance of support involves situations where the supporting Ground is *under* the supported Figure. That is the easiest way to avoid a Figure from falling. There is therefore a default implication from 'G supports F' to 'F is superior to G'. Of course, there are also other ways to defy gravitation: attaching something to the vertical surface of a wall or to a ceiling (*a painting on a wall*, *a lamp on a ceiling*), but these assume special assumptions about attachment or adhesion and the nature of Figure and Ground. The implicational relation between SUPPORT and SUPERIOR makes it natural to treat situations that combine both as special cases of SUPPORT and not of SUPERIOR. Such combined situations form in fact the prototypical core of the preposition *on*.

In the same way, *over* acquires a stereotypical curved path, often incorporating the feature of convexity (as suggested in Dewell 1994). Many cases where a Figure moves *over* a particular Ground object can be understood against a canonical background of spatial assumptions. When I go over a fence, I typically start on the ground level, then I have to move up to be on or above the fence and then down again on the other side of it, yielding the arced kind of path that is stereotypical for *over*. It is in fact natural to move over objects in this way, given that flying is unusual and objects are not flat. There is a default implication from SUPERIOR to CONVEX as far as paths are concerned and the faithfulness constraints for prepositions make use of this implication by making convexity less prominent than superiority. The conceptual and statistical bias is thus built into the priorities for lexical description.

There are two important conclusions to draw from this account. The first conclusion is that the ranking in (16) cannot be subject to cross-linguistic variation. The priorities discussed here are determined by what the spatial and physical world is like. This does not mean that there cannot be cross-linguistic variation in how these concepts can be lexicalized, but the priorities cannot be changed. What might vary between languages is how many prepositions are available and what kind of spatial features these prepositions carry.

The second conclusion is that it seems possible to have a system with relatively simple lexical meanings and still account for prototype effects and pragmatic enrichments. In my proposal these two are factored out between a system of lexical specifications (like *in*[CONTAINMENT]) on the one hand and a hierarchy of faithfulness constraints on the other hand. This is in line with the lexical-pragmatic approach of Blutner (2000). His bidirectional version of Optimality Theory can also account for how competing prepositions like *in* and *on* are understood by a hearer (see also Levinson 2000 for a very similar idea in Gricean terms). When we compare *the pear in the bowl* with *the pear on the bowl* we get the stereotypical interpretation for the first expression, but a marked interpretation for the second expression (with the bowl upside down and the pear balancing on top of it). This fits the well-known division of pragmatic labor of Horn (1984). The priority of *in* over *on* allows us to derive this division. When *on* is used with a typical container instead of *in*, the hearer will have to figure out a plausible non-stereotypical interpretation for that use of *on*, a process which can be modeled within Blutner's definition of optimality over form-meaning pairs.

7. Conclusion

In this paper, we have seen some basic priorities between prepositions at work. It is obvious that after this first exploration, it is important to go beyond unana-lyzed features like SUPPORT and CONVEX to a more principled and precise system of meaning distinctions. Then we can base our conclusions and hypotheses on a more solid foundation and extend them to other prepositions.

It would also be interesting to study further implications of the (partial) hier-archy that we worked out in this paper:

(17) CONTAINMENT >> SUPPORT >> SUPERIOR >> CONVEX
       in   on   over   around

The task for future research is to work out the hierarchy of spatial priorities, both theoretically and empirically and to study its implications for a much broader range of languages, morphosyntactic categories, and linguistic domains. In this way we can better understand to what extent the structure of the language of space is shaped by very basic properties of the spatial world around us.

References

Blutner, R. 2000. Some aspects of optimality in natural language interpretation. *Journal of Semantics* 17(3): 189–216.

Blutner, R., de Hoop, H. & Hendriks, P. (eds). 2005. *Optimal Communication*. Stanford CA: CSLI.

Bowerman, M. & Choi, S. 2001. Shaping meanings for language: Universal and language-specific in the acquisition of spatial semantic categories. In *Language Acquisition and Conceptual Development*, M. Bowerman & d S.C. Levinson (eds), 475–511. Cambridge: CUP.

Carlson, L.A. & van der Zee, E. (eds). 2005. *Functional Features in Language and Space: Insights from Perception, Categorization, and Development*. Oxford: OUP.

Coventry, K.R. & Garrod, S. 2004. *Saying, Seeing and Acting: The Psychological Semantics of Spatial Prepositions*. Hove: Psychology Press.

Cuyckens, H. 1991. The Semantics of Spatial Prepositions in Dutch: A Cognitive-Linguistic Exercise. PhD Dissertation, University of Anwerp.

Dewell, R.B. 1994. Over again: Image-schema transformations in semantic analysis. *Cognitive Linguistics* 5(4): 351–380.

Feist, M.I. 2000. On in and on: An investigation into the linguistic encoding of spatial scenes. PhD Dissertation, Northwestern University.

Gärdenfors, P. 2000. *Conceptual Spaces: The Geometry of Thought*. Cambridge MA: The MIT Press.

Grimshaw, J. & Samek-Lodovici, V. (1998). Optimal subjects and subject universals. In *Is the Best Good Enough? Optimality and Competition in Syntax*, P. Barbosa, D. Fox, P. Hagstrom, M. McGinnis & D. Pesetsky (eds), 193–219. Cambridge MA: The MIT Press.

Haspelmath, M. 2003. The geometry of grammatical meaning: Semantic maps and cross-linguistic comparison. In *The New Psychology of Language*, M. Tomasello (ed.), 211–242. Mahwah NJ: Lawrence Erlbaum.

Hendriks, P. & de Hoop, H. 2001. Optimality theoretic semantics, *Linguistics and Philosophy* 24: 1–32.

Herskovits, A. 1986. *Language and Spatial Cognition: An Interdisciplinary Study of the Prepositions in English*. Cambridge: CUP.

Horn, L. 1984. Towards a new taxonomy of pragmatic inference: Q-based and R-based implicature. In *Meaning, Form, and Use in Context: Linguistic Applications*, D. Schiffrin (ed.), 11–42. Washington DC: Georgetown University Press.

Jones, D.M. 2003. The generative psychology of kinship, Part II: Generating variation from universal building blocks with Optimality Theory. *Evolution and Human Behavior* 24(5): 320–350.

Lakoff, G. 1987. *Women, Fire, and Dangerous Things*. Chicago IL: University of Chicago Press.

Levinson, S.C. 2000. H.P. Grice on location on Rossel Island. In *Berkeley Linguistics Society* 25, S.S. Chang, L. Liaw & J. Ruppenhofer (eds), 210–224.

Levinson, S.C. & Meira, S. 2003. 'Natural concepts' in the spatial topological domain – adpositional meanings in cross-linguistic perspective: an exercise in semantic typology. *Language* 79(3): 485–516.

Prince, A. & Smolensky, P. 1997. Optimality: From neural networks to universal grammar. *Science* 275: 1604–1610.

Regier, T. 1995. A model of the human capacity for categorizing spatial relations. *Cognitive Linguistics* 6(1): 63–88.

Solstad, T. 2003. Towards the optimal lexicon. In *Proceedings of the Conference sub7 - Sinn und Bedeutung*, M. Weisgerber (ed.), 182–294. Konstanz: Universität Konstanz.

Schulze, R. 1991. Getting round to (a)round: Towards a description and analysis of a spatial predicate. In *Approaches to Prepositions*, G. Rauh (ed.), 251–274. Tübingen: Narr.

Schulze, R. 1993. The meaning of (a)round: A study of an English preposition. In *Conceptualizations and Mental Processing in Language*, R.A. Geiger & B. Rudzka-Ostyn, (eds), 299–431. Berlin: Mouton de Gruyter.

Talmy, L. 1983. How language structures space. In *Spatial orientation: Theory, research, and application*, H. Pick & L. Acredo (eds), 225–283. New York NY: Plenum.

Tyler, A. & Evans, V. 2001. Reconsidering prepositional polysemy networks: The case of over. *Language* 77(4): 724–765.

Vandeloise, C. 1991. *Spatial Prepositions: A Case Study from French*. Chicago IL: University of Chicago Press.

Zwarts, J. 1997. Vectors as relative positions: A compositional semantics of modified PPs. *Journal of Semantics* 14: 57–86.

Zwarts, J. & Winter, Y. 2000. Vector space semantics: a model theoretic analysis of locative prepositions. *Journal of Logic, Language and Information* 9: 171–213.

Zwarts, J. 2004. Competition between word meanings: The polysemy of (a)round. In *Proceedings of SuB8*, C. Meier & M. Weisgerber (eds), 349–360. Konstanz: University of Konstanz.

Zwarts, J. 2005. Prepositional aspect and the algebra of paths. *Linguistics and Philosophy* 28(6): 739–779.

The grammar of complex particle phrases in English

Bert Cappelle[1]
K.U. Leuven Campus Kortrijk

This paper provides a description of English particle phrases (PrtPs), which I define differently than in much generative work, where 'particle phrase' refers to the presumed constituent formed by the particle and the phrasal verb's direct object. Particles can be preceded by one or more other particles and/or peripheral modifiers and/or followed by a PP (e.g., *it fell several meters right back on down to the bottom*). A single such complex sequence can be structurally indeterminate, allowing multiple phrase-structure analyses depending, e.g., on whether the PP is parsed as part of the PrtP. Also, a single structure can have multiple uses–and thus have syntactic autonomy–depending on whether the modifier semantically targets the particle or the entire VP.

1. What sort of structure under what sort of study?

Particles in English (*back, down, in, off, out, up*, etc.) typically enter into a dependency relation, syntactically speaking, with verbs, yielding combinations like *come back, calm down, sneak in*, etc.[2] The particle is perceived as a subordinate element to the verb in such constructions, which are therefore popularly known as *phrasal verbs* rather than as *phrasal particles*. However, it is not always appreciated that particles may themselves also be the head of what can righteously be termed a *particle phrase*, that is, a phrasal structure clustering around a particle as head. While the particle literature has sufficiently often acknowledged that particles can, in certain structural configurations, be preceded by a modifier like *right*, only few authors (most notably

1. The author is a Postdoctoral Fellow of the Research Foundation – Flanders (FWO – Vlaanderen) and gratefully acknowledges financial support from this institution.

2. The use of the modification "syntactically speaking" is not superfluous, because it has often been pointed out that the particle is very often the primary *semantic* element in verb-particle combinations, English being a "satellite-framed" language, in Talmy's (1985, 1991) classification of languages.

Bolinger 1971: 132–133, Fraser 1976: 59–62, and Nicol 2002: 183–185) have pointed out that they can also combine among themselves, giving rise to multiple-particle sequences. In the next two subsections, I will give some simple examples of particle phrases and briefly discuss the framework I adopt to describe them.

1.1   Some preliminary examples

Consider the sentence in (1), with the unadorned particle *off* as a complement of the verb *rip*:

(1)   A violent gust of wind ripped the roof *off*.

The particle in this sentence is in fact the head of a phrasal category, which happens to consist of only one word here but which can be expanded into a multiword sequence. This is clear from sentences like the following, which illustrate that the particle can be preceded by an intensifying adjective like *right* or by another particle like *back*:

(2)   a.   A violent gust of wind ripped the roof *right off*.
      b.   I'd only just nailed the roof of the garden shed in place when a violent gust of wind ripped it *back off*.

Finally, observe that the particle can even be preceded by both *right* and *back*, in that order:

(3)   I'd only just nailed the roof of the garden shed in place when a violent gust of wind ripped it {*right back* / **back right*} *off*.

The italicized sequences in (2) and (3) are complex particle phrases. In this study, I will dissect the internal structure of such phrases.

1.2   The framework

The approach taken in this paper is, first and foremost, descriptive and data-oriented. The terminological and analytical apparatus is similar to that used in Huddleston and Pullum's (2002) reference grammar of English, and so is the main goal of this paper:

> wherever it is possible to make a factual point overshadow a general theoretical point, we attempt to do that; whenever a theoretical digression would fail to illuminate further facts about English, we curtail that digression; if ever the facts at hand can be presented in a way that is neutral between competing theoretical frameworks, we try to present them that way.
>
> (Huddleston & Pullum 2002: 19)

My paper makes use of a linguistic formalism which non-generativists would presumably brand as "Generative Grammar Lite" (cf. Tomasello 1998: x) and which generative grammar buffs themselves would call, and have called, "distinctly retro-grade" (cf. one of the reviewers of an earlier version of this paper). The former kind of linguists would probably praise the way the tree diagrams in this paper contain a minimum of inaudible material but might argue that I am too much concerned with the formal syntactic representation of the structures under discussion to the detriment of profound insights in the cognitive and functional mechanisms that account for their use and interpretation. The latter kind of linguists would feel I am giving purely descriptive concerns priority over insights in the formal mecha-nisms that explain the (un)grammaticality of the data and over attempts to move with the times by striving for maximal economy of representation and derivation and maximal cross-linguistic generalization.

Although it is undoubtedly true that my main aim is descriptive rather than explanatory, I would like to dismiss the impression that my paper might lack any theoretical foundation whatsoever. This foundation remains mostly implicit in the discussion of the data, but in the remainder of the present section, I will spell out some of the tenets and assumptions underlying this paper.

First of all, I adopt a monostratal view of grammar. That is, I hold the view that there is only one level of syntax that needs to be described, which is the level of what can be perceived in actual utterances. In other words, there is no such thing as a deep structure on which movement transformations operate to pro-duce surface forms. My occasional use of process terms like 'preposing', 'fronting', 'inversion', and the like might seem to imply that I do recognize the existence of reordering operations which derive surface structures from more basic underly-ing structures. However, in line with Huddleston & Pullum (2002: 48), I would like to stress that such terms are only meant to capture the structural relation of the sentence patterns they denote to their more canonical counterparts. This is different from assuming that the former is actually derived from the latter. Thus, for instance, although the syntactic representation of the preposing pattern con-tains a gap that is co-indexed with the preposed constituent ("___$_i$"), this gap must not be understood as a transformational *trace*. In other words, the two related structures are considered to be 'base-generated' (to use a generative term), that is, they can both be directly retrieved from the 'constructicon' (to use a constructionist term).

As we will see in Section 2.1.2 below, the essentially non-derivational na-ture of my descriptive framework has an important consequence for the analysis of the two post-verbal particle placements in English (*viz.*, pre-object and post-object). Since frequently encountered structural patterns can be (and are likely to be) stored in the mind, there is no need to adopt intricate movement operations to derive one structure from the other, Again, this does not mean that they are not felt to be related by speakers of English. In Cappelle (2006),

I have described them as 'allostructions', that is, as different formal realizations of a single more abstract transitive phrasal verb pattern which itself remains underspecified with respect to the order of the particle vis-à-vis the direct object NP.

A second theoretical assumption underlying this study is that a grammar need not be maximally parsimonious in the number of different grammatical categories it contains. While removing superfluous entities and distinctions is undeniably a scientific demand, one should also be careful not to commit the mistake of lumping diverse entities together for the sake of the elegance of the grammatical model, thereby potentially losing the means of making interesting observations about fine-grained categories. With regard to the topic of this study, there are good reasons not to share the now prevalent view that particles ought to be subsumed by the more general class of prepositions. This view has been embraced by generativists because it makes PPs accord with X-bar theory: if PPs can be headed by a particle, this means that they contain an optional complement, like all other phrasal categories. In fact, non-generativists like Langacker (1987: 243), too, have argued that particles are just a kind of prepositions which have an understood Ground (or 'landmark' in his terminology). As we will see in Section 2.2, there are sufficient arguments for claiming that particles ought to be considered as a class of their own. Since particles and prepositions unquestionably have much in common–most importantly, they both have the capacity to convey spatial information–it is very likely that speakers have a hyper-category that includes them both. However, this does not mean we should recognize only this hypercategory and not its subcategories.

As a third and final theoretical point, I generally uphold the idea that form is inseparable from meaning. However, and this is theoretically important to the present study, I leave room for the possibility that structures can become 'detached' from their semantic content (see Section 5), thus allowing for what might otherwise appear to be a mismatch between form and meaning. In a sense, even, there may be structures that are largely independent of their conceptual structure, and whose very existence seems to be to provide some familiar form to diverse chunks of semantic content, as Jackendoff (2002a) argues is the case for the transitive verb-particle template. In a sense, then, grammar does seem to be parsimonious in the number of different structures it has: rather than provide a different structure for every different sort of conceptual structure, it offers only a limited number of distinct structural patterns which speakers have no choice but to use for different semantic purposes. On the other hand, the grammar is redundant in other respects, in that it can also provide alternative ways of coding what is (truth-conditionally at least) a single meaning, the two particle placement structures being a case in point.

2. On the term 'particle phrase'

That particles can be expanded into a full-fledged phrasal category might seem a very uncontroversial claim. After all, recall from the previous section that particles have often been analyzed as 'intransitive prepositions' (e.g., Jespersen 1924: 88–89; Emonds 1970: 15; Jackendoff 1973: 345; Langacker 1987: 243; Lee 1999; Huddleston 2002: 272; Pullum & Huddleston 2002: 612–613). In the same way, now, that verbs which do not take an object NP can still be the head of a VP, particles can be the head of a phrasal category with an empty complement position. In keeping with the practice of naming a phrasal category after the lexical (X^0) category that heads it, we can then speak of a 'particle phrase' (PrtP). If the complement position of particles is always empty, since particles by definition do not take an NP, this merely means that PrtPs do not conform to the generalized structures of phrases as laid out in X-bar theory, which dictates that all phrases contain a complement position, even if that position is only optionally filled. In Section 3.3 below, however, we will investigate whether PrtPs, in spite of having no NP complements, might nonetheless still display normal X-bar properties.

In this section, which precedes the actual descriptive work, I want to make clear what exactly I mean by the term 'particle phrase', and how my understanding and use of this term diverges from the way other linguists have applied it.

2.1 PrtPs are not made up of a particle and the phrasal verb's object NP

My usage of the term 'particle phrase' differs markedly from another usage of this term that can often be found in the generative literature (e.g., Guéron 1990; Harley & Noyer 1998; Haegeman & Guéron 1999: 262–263; Ramchand and Svenonius 2002; den Dikken 2003), where particle phrases are typically taken to be constituents consisting of a particle and the direct object NP.[3] Thus, on this conception (from which I depart), there is a level of representation on which the particle phrase comprises the underlined part in either (4a)or (4b):

(4) a. The wind ripped <u>off the roof</u>.
     b. The wind ripped <u>the roof off</u>.

2.1.1 *Problems with the 'PrtP = Prt + Object NP' analysis*
I will not go in any detail into any of the analyses in which the PrtP extends to what I consider to be an immediate constituent of the verb phrase. Let me just point out

---

3. I use NP throughout even if the generative literature I refer to would label the phrasal constituent concerned as DP, 'determiner phrase'.

that analyzing the particle and the object NP as forming a single constituent raises some obvious problems that need to be dealt with. These problems might very well be easy to solve in generative accounts, but even so, I would like to point them out here, because the problematic facts I mention do not at all directly follow from a theory that does *not* contain sophisticated generative machinery. Claims as to constituenthood which can only be argued for within a particular theoretical framework should be treated with serious suspicion, since constituent structure is a basic and universal property of grammar and should therefore remain theory-independent.

A first immediate problem is that there are no syntactic environments, other than the one illustrated by (4a, b) in which the particle and the object NP (or a pro-form for it) can remain adjacent. Indeed, all of the sentences in (5) and (6) are ungrammatical:

(5) a. *Off {which roof / what} did the wind rip?
     b. *The roof off which the wind ripped was mine.
     c. *It was off the roof that the wind ripped.

(6) a. *The roof off was ripped by the wind.
     d. *What the wind ripped was the roof off.
     e. *It was the roof off that the wind ripped.

While the ungrammaticality of these sentences may perhaps fall out from certain well-established rules and principles in generative grammar, the point I want to make here is the following: if the particle and the object NP really formed a constituent (to the exclusion of the verb), there should at least be one construction in which they appear together in a non-canonical position. If, on the other hand, the NP is treated as a syntactic constituent distinct from the particle, as is done in this study, the ungrammaticality issues of (5) and (6) simply do not arise.

Secondly, proponents of the view that the object NP and the particle form a constituent together might refer to the possibility of coordinating NP + Prt sequences in a gapping construction (see, e.g., Svenonius 1992; den Dikken 1995):

(6) Turn the oxygen off with your elbow and [___ [the acetylene on]$_1$ [with your knee]$_2$].   (den Dikken 1995: 43)

The argument given by Svenonius (1992) and den Dikken (1995) for treating the object NP and the particle as a constituent is that the gapping construction can involve no more than two conjoined constituents, as observed by Stillings (1975) and Hudson (1982). Since it would not make sense to bracket the particle and the instrumental adjunct together, joining the particle with the object NP appears to be the only possible option. However, this conclusion is wrong because the argument it is based on does not hold water. According to Huddleston, Payne & Peterson (2002: 1339), gapping constructions in which the second conjunct contains three constituents are rare but not impossible:

(7) Ed had given me earrings for Christmas and [[Bob]$_1$ ___ [a necklace]$_2$ [for my birthday]$_3$].   (Huddleston, Payne & Peterson 2002: 1339)

Admittedly, if the object NP and the particle are not joined together in (6), we have three constituents after the gap, while in (7), we only have two constituents after the gap. One might therefore try to salvage Svenonius's and den Dikken's argument by invoking a restriction on gapping such that there can be no more than two *post-gap* constituents. However, even on the assumption that the maximum number of post-gap constituents is two, there is no reason to analyze the object NP and the particle as a single constituent given a (marginally acceptable) sentence like (8) below, which contains a similar kind of gapping as (7). (A question mark is added here because gapping with retention of a subject may be somewhat harder to accept if the post-gap constituents are an NP and a particle (Farrell 2005: 115, note 28).)[4]

---

4. Remarkably, den Dikken directly switches from his so-called extreme gapping case in (i) to the example in (6), repeated here as (ii):

(i)   John eats spaghetti, and [[Mary]$_1$ ___ [chop suey]$_2$].
(ii) Turn the oxygen off with your elbow and [___ [the acetylene on]$_1$ [with your knee]$_2$].

Surely, den Dikken must have realized that the sentence in (ii) displays a different kind of gapping than the sentence in (i) and that if (ii) contains (in his view) only two constituents left behind in gapping, this is due in part to the fact that the verb form is imperative and hence has no subject. If he had used a non-imperative sentence (as in (iii)), which I do not think would have resulted in a very significant degradation of acceptability (but see below), this would have immediately revealed the invalidity of the argument that gapping cannot involve more than two constituents, even if one accepts his idea (which is mistaken, I believe) that the object NP and the particle form a constituent together.

(iii) ?Ed turned the oxygen off with his elbow and [[Bob]$_1$ ___ [the acetylene off]$_2$ [with his knee]$_3$].

I am using a question mark in (iii) and in example (8) in the main text because gapping with more than two constituents may be somewhat more restricted if one of these constituents is a subject, as Farrell (2005: 115, fn. 28) notes. But Farrell observes that in subjectless gapping constructions, the number of constituents in the second conjunct is unlimited, as is illustrated by an example like (iv):

(iv) I want you to turn the oxygen off with your knee right now and [___ [the acetylene]$_1$ [on]$_2$ [with your elbow]$_3$ [right after that]$_4$].   (Farrell 2005: 115)

This disarms any argument for the joint constituency of the object NP and the particle hinging on the acceptability of an example like (6) and the apparently unjustified assumption that there is a maximum number of post-gap constituents in subjectless gapping.

(8)   ?Ed turned the oxygen off and [[Bob]$_1$ __ [the acetylene]$_2$ [on]$_3$].

Besides, gapping cannot be used at all as an argument for constituenthood of the object NP and the particle if the particle precedes the object (as in (4a)), because in that case, gapping is clearly ungrammatical:

(9)   *Ed turned off the oxygen and [Bob [__ on] [the acetylene]].

Here, gapping actually serves as a *counter*argument for constituenthood of the particle and the object NP. Indeed, if they formed a constituent together, they should be allowed to occur together after a gapped verb. Unfortunately, the ungrammaticality of (9) cannot be used as an argument supporting the claim that the particle and the object NP are distinct constituents either, for if they were, gapping the verb should also be possible (on the assumption that the second conjoint can contain one pre-gap and up to two post-gap constituents, as in (7)). We will see below that the impossibility of (9) is due to the fact that when a particle directly follows the verb and precedes the object NP, it is part of a V-Prt compound, as the bracketing in (9) indicates.

A third problem, finally, is that in (4a) the particle *off* cannot be accompanied by a modifier:

(10)   The wind ripped (*right) off the roof.

Under the hypothesis that the particle and the NP form a constituent (with the latter being a complement to the former), it is not at all obvious how to explain why there should be such a restriction without taking recourse to movement operations such as raising, by which the particle on its own (i.e., without the object NP) ends up as an unmodifiable clitic to the verb – a solution which then necessitates the further assumption that a modifier cannot be stranded in its base position (cf. Harley & Noyer 1998: 147), because, for instance, we cannot have *The wind ripped-off$_i$ [right __$_i$ the roof]. Also if *the roof* in (4a) is considered to belong to the PrtP without actually originating in the particle's complement position, one still needs to explain why moving the particle from end-postion to mid-position excludes the possibility of an intervening degree modifier. Although Ramchand and Svenonius (2002: 394–395) and den Dikken (2003: 4) provide a generative account, it should be clear that, given my own theoretical assumptions (cf. Section 1.2), treating the particle and the verb's object NP as a constituent is not a satisfactory analysis because there are no surface phenomena which clearly prove that they belong together as a phrase to which the verb does not also belong. (One might object that the string *the roof off* does have other surface realizations than right after the verb, for example *With the roof off, everything is exposed to rain* and *Try to imagine, right now, the roof off again*, but see Farrell (2005: 109–121) for an extensive critique that what we have in *The wind ripped the roof off* is the same kind of structure as in these examples with a true small clause.)

2.1.2   *The alternative: the NP is an immediate constituent of the VP*

Analyses in which the object NP makes up a constituent with the particle are riddled with problems, as we have just seen. What, then, is the alternative? Following Zeller (2002) and Farrell (2005), I assume that transitive verb-particle combinations can generally be directly realized in one of two structural manifestations or, to use the term coined in Cappelle (2006), 'allostructions': either as a complex lexical (X^0) category in which the verb forms a compound with the adjacent particle (see (11a)) or as a phrasal category containing the verb as head and the particle as a phrasal complement (see (11b)).[5]

In the former case, the particle is part of a lexical (word-level) category, and hence, it cannot within the boundaries of that lexical category be expanded into a phrasal category which hosts a modifier like *right*, on the standard assumption that words do not contain phrasal material.[6] In the latter case, the particle functions as

---

5.   As is well known, an unstressed object pronoun cannot follow the particle (e.g., *the wind {*ripped off it / ripped it off}*). This general rule is even observed with verb-particle combinations like *blow off* and *drum up* for which realization as a compound verb happens to be the only grammatical option (e.g., *{blow off steam / *blow steam off}; {drum up support / *drum support up}*):

(i)   a.   The "angry youth" were allowed to blow off steam. Well they *blew it off*, alright, and stabbed a visiting Australian yeshiva student named Yankel Rosenbaum to death. (www)

     b.   … *Well they blew off it, alright,…

(ii)   a.   Still, many people find that if they want support for coping with a rare disease, they have to *drum it up* themselves. (www)

     b.   … *they have to drum up it themselves.

Farrell (2005: 130–131) proposes a solution for this word order restriction on unstressed object pronouns. The essence of his analysis is that the pronoun object is always attached to the verb as a kind of affix, whether the verb-particle combination is realized as a lexical compound or as a phrasal category. This leaves one problem, namely that verb-particle compounds which normally do not have a phrasal variant (like *blow off, drum up, take up*) may occasionally be used with an expanded particle if the object is an unstressed pronoun, as (iiib) illustrates for *take up*. Compare:

(iii)   a.   As soon as I broke up with her, she {took up smoking / *took smoking up} again.

     b.   It's like the girlfriend I had who quit smoking for me (although she said over and over it was for her, not me) and then, as soon as I broke up with her, *took it right back up* again (and in later conversations admitted she gave it up for me). (www)

This seems to be evidence that (some?) V-Prt compounds do allow the phrasal variant if the object is pronominal.

6.   This assumption is basically correct but its formulation here is slightly simplified, as is witnessed by derivations like *nuclear physicist* and *transformational grammarian* and compounds

(11)   a. The wind ripped off the roof.

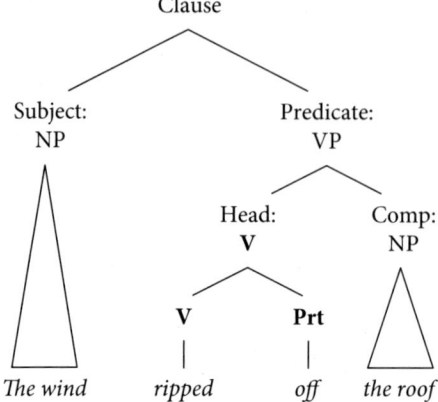

b. The wind ripped the roof off.

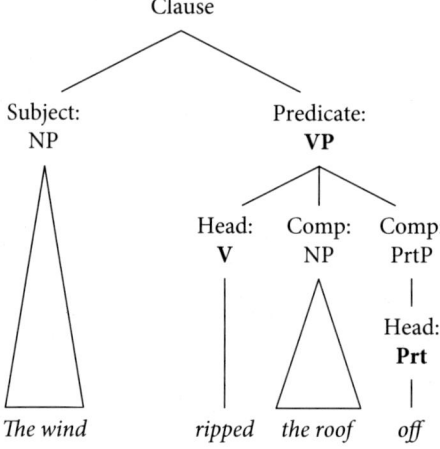

---

like *human rights organization* and *criminal justice authorities*, all of which are words containing syntactic phrases (*nuclear physics; transformational grammar; human rights; criminal justice*). However, on closer inspection, these syntactic phrases are fully lexicalized items and therefore qualify as lexemes, a term which covers clichéd linguistic units, whether these units are words or phrases. A more precise formulation of the 'no phrases within words' assumption is then that words cannot contain *unlexicalized* phrasal material.

This formulation is still not completely adequate, since it would allow *bad grammarian* to be interpreted as someone who studies – or even merely as someone who is prone to–*bad grammar*. While *bad grammar* is a lexicalized phrase, the word *grammarian* is based on a different sense of *grammar* than the sense used in *bad grammar*: a grammarian is an expert in the 'system of rules and principles governing the form and meaning of linguistic units' rather than an a real complement to the verb and can therefore be expanded into a full phrase. The object noun phrase and the particle phrase are then sisters to the verb within a flat, ternary-branching VP. In short, the dual realizability of verb-particle combinations (as words or as phrases) naturally explains the distribution of particle phrases.

A possible objection to this analysis is that one cannot just claim that the two structures illustrated in (11a,b) are available side by side and leave it at that, without discussing what this entails, for instance, for the status of the NP. That is, one might argue that the NP is in a different structural relationship to the lexical verb and to the particle in (11a) than it is in (11b) and that this should have particular consequences for its interpretation. Such an objection implies that there is a stable semantic relationship between the object NP and the other constituent(s) in the VP across instances of the *same* syntactic structure. This is not the case, as is clear from Jackendoff's (2002a) analysis of the transitive verb-particle construction. For example, the following examples (taken from or based on Jackendoff 2002a) all display the same ordering – hence, they all pattern like (11b), at least on my account – but there is not at all a similar kind of relation, semantically speaking, between the object NP and its sister constituents:

---

expert in the 'way an individual conforms in speech or writing to a set of stylistic choices that are socially accepted'. Thus, a phrase is allowed inside a word as long as (1) this phrase is lexicalized and (2) the syntactic head of that phrase is used in the same sense as the morphological head of the morphologically derived word. These two conditions have been described by Spencer (1988) as the '*Lexicalization Requirement*' and the '*Same Lexical Source Requirement*'.

In the case of compounding, too, it is possible to have phrasal material to the left of the head, but then condition (2) should read: "(as long as) the syntactic head of the phrase included in the compound is used in a sense which meets the selection restriction, if any, of the head of that compound". Thus, while *American history teacher* can mean 'teacher of American history', *glorious history teacher* can only mean 'history teacher who is glorious', not 'teacher of glorious history' (cf. Carstairs-McCarthy 2005: 37), since the word *history* in *glorious history* is not used in its sense of 'subject that is part of the course curriculum in schools, colleges and universities and that deals with events which happened in the past'. The first part of this sense is an essential part of the selection restriction of the word *teacher* when this word is used as the head of a compound. Likewise, while *local television* is a lexicalized phrase, the word *television* is used here in the sense of 'organized television broadcasting', a sense we also find in the most salient interpretation of phrases like *commercial television, British television, Soviet television, popular television, nationwide television*, etc. This sense is different from the sense of *television* in the compound *television repairer*, where the first part refers to the actual television set in one's home, since this sense of *television* is the only sense that can be fixed by a *repairer*. A *local television repairer* could therefore only refer to a 'television repairer in one's neighborhood'.

(12) a. Beth carried the food in. (the food was actually carried and it also moved 'in' as a result of the carrying Beth did)

b. Bill ate his cereal up. (the cereal was actually eaten but it did not move 'up' as a result of the eating Bill did)

c. I've knitted myself out. (something has happened to myself, but it's not having been knitted nor having been literally moved 'out' of something as a result of the knitting I did)

d. Sue really grossed my mom out. (something happened to my mom, but it was certainly not being *grossed nor being literally moved 'out' of something as a result of Sue's *grossing, which is not even an acceptable verb form without the particle out)

e. Frank drank the night away. (nothing happened to the night: it was neither drunk nor did it move 'away' as a result of the drinking; the NP just indicates the stretch of time during which the activity of drinking was done heedlessly)

f. Richard programmed his head off. (nothing literally happened to Richard's head: the idea that it moved (e.g., fell or got severed) 'off' as a result of all the programming Richard did is meant as a hyperbole)

Rather than posit a different kind of syntactic structure to account for all the semantic differences in the relation between the verb and the object NP, it makes more sense to propose a single structure for this word order, which then must have some autonomy over semantics. It cannot be denied, now, that the semantic status of the NP in (11b) is more similar to the semantic status it has in (11a) than to the semantic status the object NPs have in (12b–f), although its syntactic status (i.e., its position in the tree) is different in (11a) and identical to the syntactic status of the object NPs in (12b–f).

If there are any differences in interpretation between the two structures shown in (11a,b) then these have something to do with information structure, which does not only relate to the discourse-familiarity of the object NP but also, for instance, to the focal status of the verb, the particle, and/or the object NP (see Cappelle to appear). Thus, if the speaker wants to stress the idea that the wind did not just *blow* or *lift* the roof off, but actually *ripped* it off, then the structure shown in (11b) is highly preferred. For a similar, authentic example, consider (13):

(13) a. He did not *wash any of the dust off*. He brushed it off and patted everything real hard with his hands. (www)

b. ??He did not *wash off any of the dust*. He brushed it off . . .

2.1.3 Interim conclusion

To conclude Section 2.1, we have seen that generative analyses in which 'PrtP' is taken to comprise the particle and the object NP are not viable because the existence of such a constituent cannot be argued for on theory-independent grounds. We have then proposed to treat the NP as an immediate constituent of the VP, which in addition to the NP comprises either just a compound V-Prt verb (cf. (11a)) or a verb and, on the right side of the NP, a particle phrase (cf. (11b)).

2.2 The class of PrtPs does not include PPs.

As pointed out above, particles are often considered to be prepositions that happen to have no complement. Indeed, the particles in the a-examples below do not seem to differ semantically from their prepositional homophones in the b-examples:

(14)   a.   I was just strolling [$_{Prt}$ around].
       b.   I was just strolling [$_{PP}$ around the downtown area].

(15)   a.   He placed his hands on the fence and jumped [$_{Prt}$ over].
       b.   He placed his hands on the fence and jumped [$_{PP}$ over it].

(16)   a.   The magma burst [$_{Prt}$ through].
       b.   The magma burst [$_{PP}$ through the crust].

One might be tempted to capture this similarity between particles and PPs by allowing particles to take either a null complement or an NP complement. In that case, both the a-sentences and the b-sentences in (14)–(16) would contain a PrtP. However, such a move would be equally problematic as calling all the bracketed constituents in these examples PPs. Although many linguists have proposed that treating particles as intransitive prepositions would make grammar simpler, it would also obscure some important differences between particles and prepositional structures. Many such differences have been extensively documented in Cappelle (2005a). The following subsection gives a brief overview.

2.2.1 *Differences between particles (and particle phrases) and prepositional phrases*

First, let us compare the syntactic distribution of particles with that of PPs. On the one hand, as the examples in (17) illustrate, it is possible for both categories to follow verbs of movement, to be modified by *right*, to appear in the preposing construction, and to be used in the expletive *X with NP!* construction (cf. Emonds 1972; Jackendoff 1973).

(17)   a.   The boy {came / climbed / ran / rode / walked / went} {[$_{Prt}$ up] / [$_{PP}$ up the hill]}.
       b.   The heel broke right {[$_{Prt}$ off] / [$_{PP}$ off my boot]}.
       c.   {[$_{Prt}$ Out] / [$_{PP}$ Out the door]} it ran.
       d.   {[$_{Prt}$ Down] / [$_{PP}$ Down the hatch]} with the tequila!

These parallelisms have been taken as evidence that particles are in fact not significantly different from 'ordinary' prepositions; that is, just because particles do not take an NP complement, this does not mean we have to introduce a separate category for them. Moreover, as was noted above, if we allow for prepositions that do not take a complement, then PPs conform to X-bar structure in that they no longer have an obligatorily filled complement position.

On the other hand, the sentences in (18) show that particles and PPs behave differently with respect to a number of other constructions. For example, only particles can appear before a direct object NP, directional particles can precede directional PPs but usually not vice versa, PPs but not usually particles can follow the *of*-NP in nominalizations, and PPs but not usually particles can be used in the focus position of special focus constructions:

(18)   a.   The boy pushed {[$_{Prt}$ up] / *[$_{PP}$ up the hill]} a large boulder.
       b.   She walked {[$_{Prt}$ out] [$_{PP}$ through the door] / [$_{Prt}$ through] [$_{PP}$ out the door] / *[$_{PP}$ out the door] [$_{Prt}$ through] / *[$_{PP}$ through the door] [$_{Prt}$ out]}.
       c.   I like the part with the carrying of the piano {?*[$_{Prt}$ down] / [$_{PP}$ down the stairs]}.
       d.   See that high window? There's no way of escape but {*[$_{Prt}$ through] / [$_{PP}$ through it]}.

It should be added here that these differences in behavior do not in themselves necessitate the conclusion that full PPs cannot be included in the extension of the term 'particle phrase'. After all, particle phrases may take other kinds of complements than NPs, as we will see, and such particle phrases may also behave differently from bare particles (e.g., *The boy pushed {[$_{Prt}$ up] / *[$_{PrtP}$ up to the top]} a large boulder*). Furthermore, recall that particles which take a modifier like *right* also have different syntactic distribution from particles not so modified (e.g., *The boy pushed {[$_{Prt}$ up] / *[$_{PrtP}$ right up]} a large boulder*). But full PrtPs, too, differ from PPs in their distribution (e.g., *There's no way of escape but {*[$_{PrtP}$ back through] / [$_{PP}$ back through it]}*). All we can say at this point, then, is that the syntactic environments in which we can find PPs do not entirely coincide with the environments of either bare particles or PrtPs. Therefore, simply saying that particles are in fact a kind of PPs, or that PPs are in fact a kind of PrtPs, may deprive us of the terminological distinctions needed to deal with those distributional differences.

A second reason for maintaining a distinction between particles and PPs headed by their homophonous prepositions is that particles cannot always be analyzed as shortened or reduced PPs, as one could easily but wrongly assume in the light of sentence pairs like (14)–(16) (cf. Fraser 1970: 96–97). Some obvious counterexamples to an NP deletion analysis are *The balloon went up* and *They knelt down*, which we cannot 'reconstruct' as full PPs (*The balloon went* [$_{PP}$ *up something*]; *They knelt* [$_{PP}$ *down something*]). Similarly, we cannot maintain that PrtPs as we define them (i.e., particles heading a phrase but not taking an NP complement) are 'reduced' PPs. For example, *The balloon went* [$_{PrtP}$ *right up*] is not a shortened version of **The balloon went* [$_{PP}$ *right up something*]. Again, we see that PPs and PrtPs are different entities, so that the former cannot be simply included in the latter.

A third reason for considering particles as a class distinct from the class of prepositions is that particles and their prepositional counterparts do not always induce identical event-structural effects (cf. also Cappelle & Declerck 2005). Compare the following pairs of examples:

(19)   a.   We drove across desert plains {for many hours / *in an hour}.
       b.   We drove across {*for many hours / in an hour}.

(20)   a.   I crawled through dense shrubbery {for many hours / *in an hour}.
       b.   I crawled through {*for many hours / in an hour}.

The so-called 'Ground' referred to by the complement of the preposition in (19a) and (20a) lacks clear delineation. Its spatial extendedness is therefore more salient than its spatial boundedness. This renders the motion event atelic, as is evident from the impossibility of adding a temporal adverbial of the '*in* X time' type. By contrast, the corresponding particle in (19b) and (20b) inevitably evokes the crossing of boundaries, however fuzzy these may be. Even when a Ground whose boundaries are not conceptually salient has been mentioned in the preceding context, its referent cannot be omitted without the motion event becoming telic:

(21)   a.   Our journey led to vast desert plains. They looked very daunting, yet we drove across them (for many hours).
       b.   Our journey led to vast desert plains. They looked very daunting, yet we drove across (*for many hours).

This proves that it is an oversimplification to think, as do O'Dowd (1998: 4) and Lee (1999: 50), that a particle can replace a full PP headed by a homophonous preposition whenever the Ground is contextually or otherwise supplied. (Note, incidentally, that (18c) and (18d) confirm my point.)

The difference between the a-examples and the b-examples in (19)–(21) relates to a similar observation made by Svenonius (2004: 25), namely that a locative reading generally requires the presence of an overt Ground (or the presence of a certain type of peripheral premodifier—see Section 4.3). Below are two of his examples:

(22)   a.   What a high fence! A cow could never jump over (it).
       b.   What a high fence! I wonder what is over *(it).

(23)   a.   Listen to the glacier! A chunk is about to break off (it).
       b.   Look at the glacier! I bet all these ice chunks came from off *(it).

In the a-examples above, we are dealing with directional expressions, in which case the spatial elements concerned (*over* and *off*) can be realized either as a particle or as a preposition. In the b-examples, by contrast, the spatial element has to be understood as a locative expression. This is also the case in (23b), in which directional *from* is itself dynamic but selects a locative complement (see also Ayano 2005 for such PPs). Apparently, the locative expressions in these examples resist the use of the spatial element involved as a particle. For another example, consider the following pair:

(24) a. The children jumped in the pool.
      b. The children jumped in.

Sentence (24a) is ambiguous between a directional and a locative reading (cf. Tseng 2005: 170). On the former reading, the preposition *in* can be replaced by *into*, that is, the children were first outside the pool and ended up inside the pool. On the latter reading, the children are conceptualized as already being *in* the pool while jumping (up and down). In (24b), we do not have this ambiguity. Here, the only possible reading is that the children jumped *into* a contextually specified container-like Ground. In sum, prepositions can be used to encode situations referring to either inter-locative ('from-A-to-B') or intra-locative ('within-A') movement, while their corresponding particles may only allow for an inter-locative reading.[7] The same difference can also be found between particle *phrases* and PPs (e.g., *Is the bus stop far away from the bridge?—No, it's* {*[$_{PrtP}$ *right over* / [$_{PP}$ *right over it*]}).

2.2.2 Interim conclusion

To conclude Section 2.2, it might at first sight seem economical to treat PPs as instances of PrtPs. On further consideration, however, we have to conclude that the inclusion of PPs in the class of PrtPs would undermine recognition of the fact that the use of directional elements like *across, in, over, through*, etc. with an overtly expressed Ground can differ quite dramatically from their use as particles, whether or

---

7. The observation that particles convey a 'from-A-to-B' meaning cannot be extended to *about, around* and *along*. In fact, with these particles, we have the converse situation, in that they only allow for a reading that does not evoke the attainment of an inherent end-point, while the corresponding preposition is again compatible with a 'within A' and a 'from-A-to-B' meaning. For example:

(i) a. The island is very popular among nature-loving day-trippers. You can walk around (it) for hours watching the varied fauna and flora. (= 'wander aimlessly in various random directions within the perimeter of the island': 'within A' reading)
     b. The island is very popular among nature-loving day-trippers. You can walk around *(it) in less than half a day and have seen a dozen different kinds of nesting sea birds. (= 'walk in the circumference of the island, with the aim to arrive back at the point where you started out': 'from-A-to-B(=A)' reading)

not these particles head a phrase. This is not to say, as we will see, that there cannot be any material following the particle within the very phrase headed by the particle. However, I categorically do not reckon NPs among the immediate constituents within the PrtP (unless they are measure NPs, more on which in Section 4).

3.   Multiple-particle sequences

3.1   Some extreme examples

While in (2b) we have seen an example of two adjacently positioned particles, the number of particles that can in theory pile up is much higher. Bolinger (1971: 132–133) gives some spectacular made-up examples of particles chaining up into sequences of up to five particles in a row:

(25)   a.   I tried to push báck dówn ín the catchbolt.
     b.   Come on back up over!
     c.   Come on back up through over.
        (Bolinger 1971: 132–133)

In actual fact, though, authentic examples of more than two particles are not so easy to come by. In (26) and (27), I give some lucky finds of three and four sequentially arranged particles, respectively. Such long sequences of particles are often further elaborated by one or more directional PPs. For the sake of easy identification, I have marked the particles with interrupted underlining and following directional PPs, if present, with broken underlining.

(26)   a.   Er I'll be passing back up through about er half past four o'clock.
        (Cobuild corpus)
     b.   "Haw!" He slammed the door, stuck his head back in through through the window, and grinned. (Cobuild corpus)
     c.   I say a few sentences, then go back on away. (www)
     d.   Grasp the ends of the deer hair and pull it back on down over the body. (www)
     e.   You can . . . walk back on up through the rainforest to the visitor center. (www)
     f.   Every now and then the wind would blow so hard that it would take the waterfall and throw it right on back up over the top of the bluff – right up into the trees! (www)
     g.   This was followed a minute or so later by the sound of the helicopter starting up, and flying away on up over the ridge. (www)

(27)   a.   Now, you go on back down home and get well; the darkness is gone from you now. (www)

b.   just driving around, that was all I had in mind, just driving around and circling around and going on back up home. (www)

c.   Does he really think all will be well with black folks when black women quit the feminist plantation and come on back down home to church? (www)

d.   Then, cruse on back over across from the pike to the West to the Hyatt Hotel. (www)

Such long sequences raise two immediate questions. First of all, if we assume that stacked particles form a particle phrase, how can we determine which one of the particles is the head of the phrase? In principle, any particle in the sequence is a possible candidate for headedness. Identifying the head is not always possible, but there can be some clues, as we will see shortly. Secondly, what is the status of a following directional PP: does it belong to the particle phrase as well or does it form a separate constituent, possibly containing the preceding particle as a premodifier to its prepositional head?

In the following sections, we will try to provide an answer to these questions by taking a close look at comparatively more simple sequences. Only then can we try to unravel the internal structure of longer sequences. (For lack of space, we will not discuss the status of a second PP following a particle or string of particles.)

3.2   Finding the head in multiple-particle sequences

Consider the following example, taken from den Dikken (1995: 80, note 49):

(28)   She put the book back down.

Den Dikken considers it "unlikely . . . that this example represents embedding of one particle under another, *back* presumably being a modifier of *down* rather than a head taking *down* as its complement" (den Dikken 1995: 80, note 49). That this is probably the correct analysis is supported by examples like the following:

(29)   a.   My hip was out of joint, but it popped back in. (www)
       b.   I snapped off the tray cover once but it popped back on. (www)
       c.   He smoothed one of the big brown chunks down, but it popped back up. (www)

In all of the examples in (29), the particle following *back* stands in a contrastive relationship to a spatial item in the immediately preceding context: *in* contrasts with *out (of joint), on* with *off,* and *up* with *down.* Given that *out (of), off* and *down* are not dependent on another particle in these preceding clauses, their contrasted particles are most adequately treated as likewise independent. Treating *in, on,* and *up* as heads that have *back* as a premodifier then seems the most plausible option. Of course, *back* need not always modify another particle; it can also be a head itself. This is the case in the following example:

(30)   She even tried putting it through the garbage disposal grinder, but it popped back, cackling with glee. (www)

Back is not the only particle that can premodify a subsequent one. Two more particles that can be seen to function as a premodifier are *on* and, as a less frequently used variant, *along*. Consider the following examples:

(31)   a.   There are now over 1000 photos up there so hop on over and take a look! (www)
       b.   So if you like writing fantasy, hop along over and read about it and join. (www)
(32)   a.   Drop on by and have a look. (www)
       b.   The pub was the Dragon, the keg was not dry / When the Constable happened to drop along by. (www)

Evidence for analyzing *on* as a premodifier rather than a head is furnished by the observation that leaving out the first of the two consecutive particles does not alter the meaning and/or acceptability drastically, as opposed to leaving out the second. Thus, for example, *hop on over* is not that different in meaning from *hop over* but is definitely not semantically equivalent to *hop on*. And while *drop on by* is in essence an embellished version of *drop by*, ?*drop on* is quite nonsensical.

With *along*, these simple tests yield less unequivocal results, since *along* is quite felicitous as the only particle retained in (31b) and (32b), as is illustrated by the following authentic examples:

(33)   a.   please hop along and make your suggestions known on the official forum. (www)
       b.   Why not drop along and check us out? (www)

This means that for (31b) and (32b) we have structural indeterminacy. For example, both of the parses represented by the tree diagrams in (34a, b) can be defended for (31b). (Whether *over* in the analysis shown in (34b) is a modifier (i.e., an adjunct) or a complement is an issue that will be discussed in Section 3.3. Not to complicate matters, I have selected just one labeling here.)[8]

---

8.   I also disregard the possibility that *along* is a part of a complex verb (*hop along*). In that case, *over* can only be a separate constituent.

(34)   a.   b.

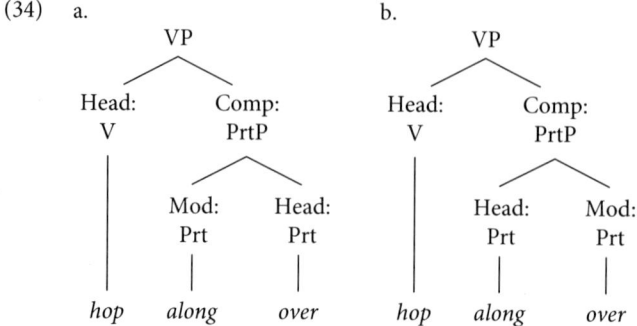

Structural indeterminacy ought to be distinguished from structural ambiguity. Clearly, the difference between the two parsing possibilities shown here is not of the same kind as the difference between the possible parsings of the celebrated sentence *flying planes can be dangerous*. In the case of *hop along over*, the hearer's selection of one parsing rather than another does not have a significant impact on the success of the communication. Both parsings can be simultaneously intended by the speaker, and blend into one another. *Along* and *over* are, in a way, mutually dependent on each other. We could therefore propose the following tree diagram:

(35)

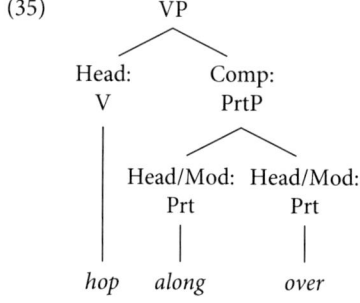

Thus, if *over* is considered to be the head, then *along* functions as a premodifier. If *along* is considered to be the head, then *over* functions as (what I will for now call) a postmodifier. I will elaborate on this latter analysis in the next subsection.

3.3   Element following the particle: adjunct or complement, and of what?

The parse given in diagram (34b) suggests that the particle heading a particle phrase may be followed by another particle functioning as a postmodifier to that head, in other words as an adjunct. However, positing such a structure poses two problems. First, it is hard to find further evidence for its existence, since even expected instances like *fall over down* or *come in through* do not occur. Second, one may doubt whether the second particle is an adjunct, favoring instead an analysis in which it is a complement. In that case, PrtPs conform to general X-bar phrase structure in having a complement position which is optionally filled.

We can best address this second issue by looking at a closely related structure, namely a particle functioning as a head followed by a PP (rather than by a second particle). The following examples, taken from Jackendoff (2002), contain such structures at the front of the sentence:

(36) a. Back from Hollywood comes that star of stage and screen, Groucho!
b. Up to the soldiers marched the sergeant.
c. {Down / Out} {from / to} the darkness crept the lizard.

(Jackendoff 2002a: 93, note 4)

That the particle in these examples should be analyzed as the head of the entire directional phrase and not as a specifier to the preposition is clear from the fact that it is the particle which licenses the inversion. As Jackendoff points out, without the particle, the directional PP headed by *from* or *to* is of somewhat questionable acceptability in this pattern:

(37) a. ?From Hollywood comes that star of stage and screen, Groucho!
b. ?To the soldiers marched the sergeant.
c. ?{From / To} the darkness crept the lizard.

(Jackendoff 2002a: 93, note 4)

What Jackendoff leaves undecided with respect to (36a–c) is whether the PP is an adjunct or a complement of the particle. However, in his discussion of a set of very similar examples, he argues that the PP following the particle is a complement. The examples for which he makes this assertion are given below in (38):

(38) a. Jill grew up into a strong woman.
b. Please look out for Harry.
b. Sam ran away to the city.
d. The secretary sent a schedule out to the stockholders.

(Jackendoff 2002a: 72)

The argument Jackendoff (2002a: 92, note 1) uses to show that the PPs in these examples ought to be analyzed as complements is as follows. If the PPs were adjuncts rather than complements, we should be able to encounter them stranded in a *do-so* conjunct, parallel to the example in (39a). However, the unacceptability or at least seriously reduced acceptability of the examples in (40) – I adopt Jackendoff's judgments – shows that the relevant PPs cannot be analyzed as adjuncts; hence that they must be complements, parallel to the example in (39b). Compare:

(39) a. John ate his lunch on Thursday, and Fred did so on Friday.
(*on Thursday* and *on Friday* are adjuncts)
b. *John put a banana on the table, and Fred did so on the chair.
(*on the table* and *on the chair* are complements)

(40)   a.   *Jill grew up into a strong woman, and Jerry did so into a tall man.
       b.   ??I looked out for Harry, and you did so for Sam.
       c.   *Sam ran away to the city, and Aaron did so to the country.
       d.   *The secretary sent a schedule out to the stockholders, and the boss
             did so to the administration.

The *do-so* test, however, is not suitable for our concerns, in that it is used to di-
agnose the complement/adjunct status of a sister constituent of the verb. The fact
that the particle and a PP may be fronted together suggests that they (can) form
a single constituent (more on which shortly). Thus, the reason why (40)c, in particular, is ungrammatical may not be that *to the city* is a complement of the verb
but rather that it forms an integral part of the spatial phrase *away to the city*. There
is no syntactic test that I know of which enables us to determine its status within
that phrase, that is, which reveals whether it is an adjunct of the particle or a
complement of the particle. On one hand, it makes most sense to analyze the
PPs in (36) as adjuncts (in other words, as postmodifiers), since their analysis
as complements would mean that they are subcategorized for (to use generative
terminology) by the particle, while the optionality of the PPs in question suggests that they are not. On the other hand, complements may also be optionally
selected by heads (as is the case with, for instance, the verb-ite), so the optionality
of the PP is not a sufficient argument against its complementhood. Returning to
Prt-Prt sequences like *along over*, we need to conclude, then, that our analysis of
the second particle in (34)b as a postmodifier is only tentative, and that we should
accept an alternative analysis of the second particle as a complement of the first
particle (beside, of course, an analysis in which *over* is the head of the particle
phrase, as in (34a)).

We have said above that Prt-PP sequences like *away to the city* should be analyzed as single constituents, on the basis of the observation that such sequences
can be fronted as a whole, as in (36)a–c. Now note that the PP may also be stranded after the verb, with the particle being fronted on its own. Compare:

(41)   a.   . . . and <u>away to the corner-flag</u> he ran . . . (www)
       b.   . . . and <u>away</u> he ran <u>to the other side of the field</u> . . . (www)

The discontinuous appearance of the particle and the PP could mean that they
do not always form a single constituent after all. This is confirmed by sentences
which contain an intervening adverb. Given that adverbs cannot be inserted in a
daughter constituent of the VP – see (42a–b) – we must conclude that the particle
and the PP form distinct constituents within the VP in (43a–b):

(42)   a.   *He ran to quickly the other side of the field.
       b.   I let him drive in my fast yellow car. (*fast* can only be an adjective
             here, not an adverb)

(43) a. He ran <u>away</u> quickly <u>to the bicycle racks</u>. (www)

  b. ... push the bar <u>down</u> slowly <u>to the front</u> ... (www)

Den Dikken (1995) gives examples in which the particle is stranded while the PP, which canonically follows it, is fronted:

(44) a. <u>On the shelf</u> were put <u>down</u> some books.

  b. <u>Under the table</u> sat <u>down</u> a big fat cat.

  c. <u>Under the table</u> turned <u>up</u> a big fat cat.   (den Dikken 1995: 37)

Again, this seems to be evidence that the particle and the PP do not make up a single constituent. (A single-constituent analysis is especially implausible for (44)c, where the PP is spatial whilst the particle is not.) den Dikken argues that the PPs in question are predicative complements, because only such constituents are said to be allowed sentence-initially in the locative inversion construction.[9]

Note also that the Prt and the PP may occasionally be split up by a direct object NP, as is the case in (45):

(45) ... he put <u>down</u> the gun <u>on the table outside the inn</u>... (www)

In this case, of course, the particle is not the head of a particle phrase but a part of the complex verb *put down*, as in (11a). Such an analysis may be extended to intransitive V-Prt compounds followed by a PP. Consider (46):

(46) I sat <u>down</u> quickly <u>on another divan</u>... (www)

---

9. This is actually not quite correct. First of all, while it is true that adjuncts cannot generally occur in the locative inversion construction (e.g., *On a leash ran the dog*), they sometimes can:

(i) Two days later came a medical report stating that his death was due to a cerebral hemorrhage. (www)

Second, not all preposed complements in this pattern are *predicative* complements, as is witnessed by the sentences in (ii), where the sentence-initial phrase (in italics) does not predicate anything over the subject.

(ii) a. *On and on* he talked, but Horatio didn't listen anymore. (www)

  b. As a climatological sauna baked the nation's capital, here in our own mini seat of power, the air conditioning had gone kaput. But *away* I typed, skittering ever nearer to finishing each speech, even as I melted into my cheap, gray chair. (www)

We can safely ignore this second complication, since the number of non-predicative preposed complements is limited to a limited number of types, namely (a) *on (and on) (and (ever) on)* and (b) *away*.

The occurrence of an adverb between the particle and the PP already excludes the possibility of them forming a constituent together, and although there are no arguments to prove that *sit down* is a compound verb, there isn't any basis on which such an analysis can be rejected either.

Accepting the possibility that a PP following the particle may be an immediate constituent of the VP all by itself, we can now offer an overview of the different ways in which a Prt-PP sequence can be analyzed. (We ignore, of course, cases in which the PP is an adjunct of the PP, as in *Get up at five o'clock*).[10]

1. The particle is the head of a particle phrase also containing the PP, which is an adjunct of the particle.
2. The particle is the head of a particle phrase also containing the PP, which is a complement of the particle.
3. The particle is the head of a particle phrase but does not contain the PP, which is a separate complement of the VP.
4. The particle is part of a complex V and the PP is a complement of this complex verb.

I would like to stress that, in the absence of indications to the contrary (e.g., possibility of an intervening adverb, possible stranding of the particle or of the PP, etc.), all of these analysis can make sense for a given Prt-PP sequence. Since there

---

10.   Apart from these four analyses, there is also the possibility, not discussed in Section 3.3, of the particle being a specifier to the preposition within a PP, as in (ia–b):

(i)   a.   {Off / over} *(in that room), John usually sits for lunch.
      b.   {Down / back} *(under the ocean), the temperature is pretty constant.

(Jackendoff 2002a: 93)

Jackendoff notes that the particle cannot occur without the following PP in these examples. (This is due to the fact that this preposing pattern without inversion expresses stative situations. Recall from our discussion of (22) and (23) above that an overt Ground is required here.) Since it is the presence of a prepositional phrase which licenses this construction, the particle must be analyzed as a specifier (a premodifier) to the preposition heading that phrase. This is confirmed by the acceptability of leaving out the particle in (ia–b).

In addition, there are sequences like *out of NP, off of NP, away from NP*, etc., where the first and the second item have traditionally been analyzed as compound (two-word) prepositions rather than as a particle followed by a preposition. A compromise between these analyses has been offered in Cappelle (2001; 2005b: Section 4.3.4). The compromise is not altogether dissimilar from what Huddleston and Pullum (2002: 56) call 'fusion', in this case fusion of two head roles: *out* (as in *out of the room*) functioning simultaneously as head of a PrtP and as (co-) head of a PP.

are no semantic differences among them, they constitute a complex case of structural indeterminacy but not of structural ambiguity.

3.4 Back to more complex cases

Now observe that it is possible for two out of three elements of the set of premodifying particles consisting of *back*, *on*, and *along* (cf. Section 3.2) to co-occur as particles preceding a third particle. The order between the two premodifying particles appears to be rather free; at least, each of the three possible combinations (*back + on*; *back + along*; *on + along*) can be encountered in its two potentially available orders, as the examples below jointly illustrate.

(47) a. With a faint sigh, he turns to walk <u>back along home</u>. (www)
      b. Whistlings kept following me as I walked <u>along back home</u>. (www)
      c. Would you come <u>back on up</u> please? (www)
      d. Dr Corday, come <u>on back up</u>. (www)
      e. . . . he was going to move <u>on along up</u> into the higher ranks . . . (www)
      f. Run <u>along on up</u> to his study, now, there's a good lad. (www)

One way of analyzing these sequences is to accord equal status to the first two particles, that is, to consider them both as directly premodifying the third particle. We can then either have a ternary-branching structure, as in (48a), or we can fuse the premodifiers under a single node, as in (48b).

(48) a.   b.

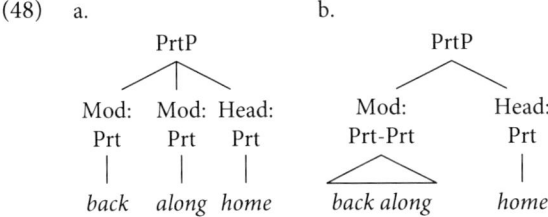

However, there may be some other analyses that suggest themselves. Given that *back*, *along*, and *home* are all possible heads in (47a) (to single out just one exemplary sentence), each of the parses represented in (49) are, in principle, viable alternatives to the ones shown in (48).

In (49a–b), *back* is the head of the three-particle phrase, with *along home* being a complement or an adjunct of it (cf. Section 3.3), the difference between (49a) and (49b) being that *along* is a further embedded head in the former and a modifier in the latter. In (49c–d), *back* is a premodifier to the two-particle phrase *along home*, (49c) and (49d) again differing with respect to which particle is the head (not only of that two-particle phrase but now also of the larger three-particle phrase). In fact, (49d) is a structure that comes close to the structures shown in (48a, b,) in

(49)   a.   b.

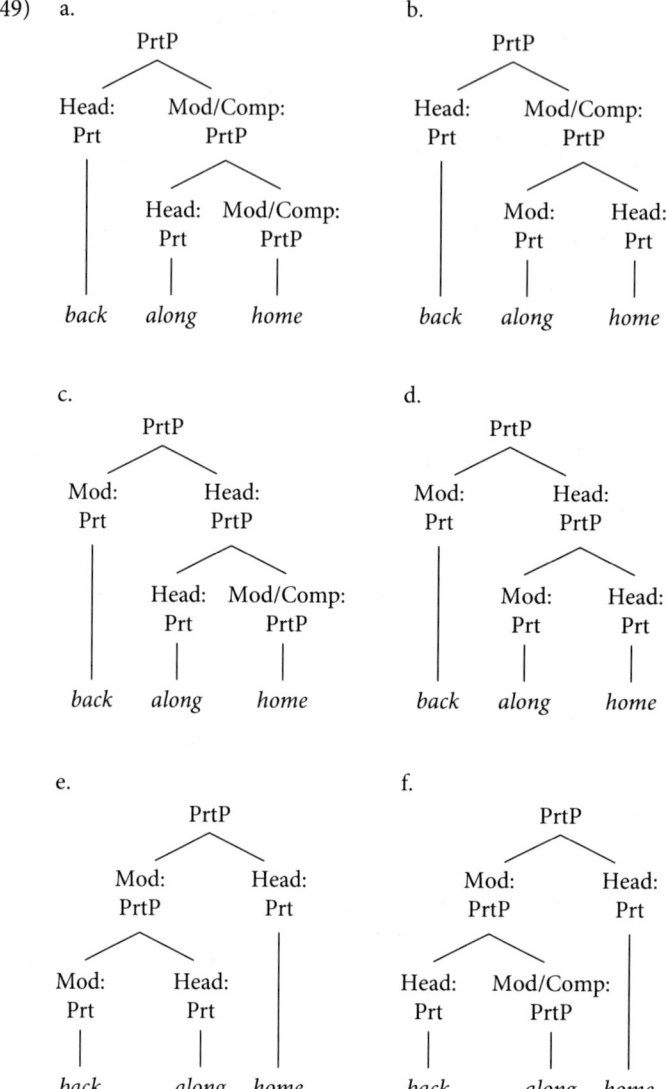

that the first two particles are premodifiers. However, these particles are no longer seen as part of a flat phrase. Instead, the second particle directly premodifies the third particle, with which it forms a phrase, and the first particle then premodifies that phrase (rather than just the third particle). Finally, in (49e–f), *home* is the head, and the two-particle phrase *back along* preceding it premodifies it. Again, these two parses differ with respect to which particle is assigned the status of head in the premodifier phrase.

In fact, there are no grounds on which any of these parses can be excluded, except perhaps the stark semantic difference between (47a) and the version in which *along* is retained as the only particle. So, given that *walk back along home* is clearly nonequivalent to *walk along*, we can probably exclude (49c) as a plausible analysis, but the other analyses do not seem to correspond to straightforward differences in meaning in the way that, for example, the different parses of the textbook example *I saw the man with the binoculars* do. In other words, we might again say that the multiple-particle sequences in (47a–f) display structural vagueness (indeterminacy) but not structural ambiguity.

Let us briefly consider examples (47e, f), where the sequence of three particles is followed by a directional PP. We might consider this PP as a separate constituent (a sister complement of the three-particle phrase) or we might alternatively consider this PP to be a part of the particle phrase containing the three particles. The tree diagram in (50) shows just one plausible phrase for such Prt-Prt-Prt-PP phrases, with the third particle the head of the entire spatial expression, the preceding particle premodifying it and the following PP postmodifying or complementing it (and the first particle premodifying this entire structure).

(50)

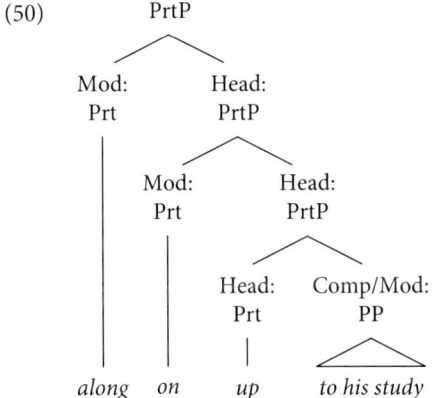

The reason why the third particle is a plausible head is that it is the only particle that could substitute for the entire phrase on its own without causing a drastic change of meaning.

Retaining only the PP leads to an even less drastic loss of meaning. This may be seen as evidence that the head of the entire spatial phrase is the preposition, and that the three particles preceding are premodifiers (cf. footnote 10). In that case, a plausible structure is given in (51):

Thus, although we explicitly rejected the inclusion of prepositional phrases within the class of particle phrases (cf. Section 2.2), the fact that the analysis in (50)

(51)

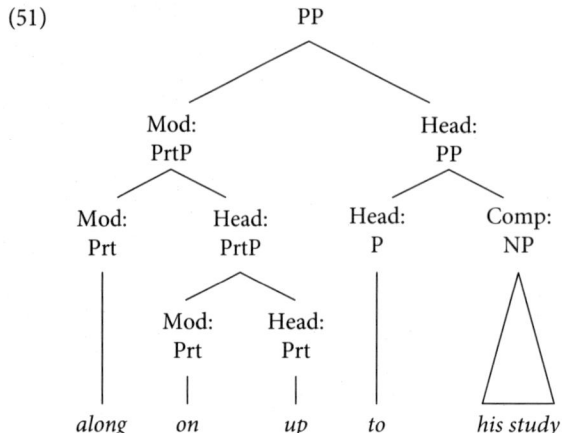

and the one represented in (51) seem both valid options suggests that a certain directional phrase can nevertheless be structurally indeterminate between being a particle phrase and being a prepositional phrase.

3.5   Interim conclusion

We have seen that particles can form stackings of at least up to three particles. Assuming that these multiple-particle sequences form a single phrase, it is not always easy to determine which particle is the head of that phrase. One helpful observation is that the particles *back, on* and *along* often function as premodifiers to another particle, which conveys the more primary spatial information (and which therefore most likely is the head). Occasionally, we find that two premodifying particles form a cluster among themselves, their order being apparently free. It is not clear whether the first particle then directly modifies the third particle or whether it is a modifier of a more deeply embedded phrase consisting of the second particle and the third.

A particle may also postmodify or complement a preceding particle, but such a structure is quite rare. More common is the occurrence of a PP as a postmodifier or complement of a particle, but there are arguments (based on adverb insertion, stranding, etc.) that such a PP may also form an immediate constituent of the VP. Moreover, such a PP may govern a preceding particle, or even a group of preceding particles forming a premodifying particle phrase within the PP.

One of the most striking ideas in the discussion of this section is that multiple-particle sequences (possibly followed by a PP) may be analyzed in a variety of ways and that, more often than not, no single analysis stands out as clearly superior to other possible analyses.

4. Peripheral modifiers

4.1 Some examples

The leftmost position in particle phrases is reserved for what could be called 'peripheral modifiers' (cf. Huddleston & Pullum 2002: 55). If there are any pre-modifying particles (*back, on* and *along*), then these have to follow the peripheral modifiers (see again example (3)). The most frequently encountered peripheral modifier is *right*, but the left-peripheral structural slot can be occupied by a wide range of items, sometimes combining among themselves. The list below gives a flavor of the variety. For a fuller overview, see Cappelle (2005b: 157–174).[11]

(52) a. The roof of the car came <u>clean</u> off, along with the heads of several of the occupants. (www)

b. As I run off the edge I hit a wall and fall <u>smack dab</u> down on the edge and land with a thump. (www)

c. I was wearing bluejeans, heavy waders and still managed to kneel <u>right smack</u> dab down on a piece of broken glass. . . (www)

d. Tack the ledger board in place with 16 penny nails driven <u>only partway</u> in (to allow for easy removal). (www)

e. As a coldpower model, it flew well enough, but never went <u>terribly high</u> up. (www)

f. . . . the two men fell <u>a good twenty feet straight</u> down, then began rolling and tumbling. (www)

4.2 Some constraints

Combinations of peripheral modifiers obey some conventions. For one example, the two-word sequences *slam bang, slap bang,* and *smack dab* are fossilized (and hence often hyphenated), while very similar sequences like *?*bang slam, ?*bang slap, ?*dab smack* and *?*slam smack* do not occur at all. For another example of grammatical convention, intensifiers like *clean, dead, flat, plumb, right, straight,* etc. can neither precede nor follow proportional degree expressions like *partway, halfway* or even *completely* (see (53a–d)). Neither can they precede or follow non-proportional degree expressions like *deep, high, far,* etc. (see (54a–d)).

(53) a. he thrust the weapon completely through (www)

b. he thrust the weapon right through

---

11. The terminology used here departs from that used in Cappelle (2005b), where in a sequence like *come right on through, on* was called a specifier and *right* a prespecifier of *through*. In the present study, I call *on* a premodifier and *right* a (left-)peripheral modifier.

  c.   *he thrust the weapon right completely through
  d.   *he thrust the weapon completely right through

(54) a.   its stock price will shoot high up (www)
      b.   its stock price will shoot straight up
      c.   *its stock price will shoot straight high up
      d.   *its stock price will shoot high straight up

By contrast, an intensifier can combine with a measure NP, as is illustrated by example (52f). However, the measure NP has to precede the intensifier in that case. Thus, we could not reverse the order of the peripheral modifiers in that example. This suggests that we have to reserve a higher place for such measure NPs in the syntactic structure of particle phrases, as shown in (55).

(55)

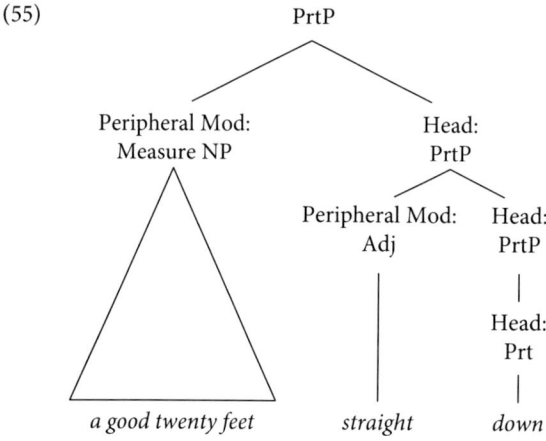

Measure NPs do not combine with degree expressions, even though such combinations do occur with PPs (Cappelle 2005a: 43).[12] This ties in with our claim made

---

12.   A particle on its own can still be used after the stative verb *be*, but its meaning then tends to be idiosyncratic (cf. also Cappelle 2005b: 351–352; McIntyre 2002: 101; 2004: 545–547):

(i)   a.   They were off. (= 1. (with human subject) 'They were off shift'; 2. (with human subject) 'They were mistaken'; (said of sporting events) 'They were cancelled')
      b.   They were down. (= 1. (with human subject) 'they were depressed'; 2. 'they were lying flat'; 3. 'they were (back) on the ground' (and not just 'downstairs'); 4. (said of machines) 'they were not functioning')
      c.   They were up. (= (among other meanings) 1. (with human subject) 'they were out of bed'; 2. (said of grades, prices, etc.) 'they were higher'; 3. 'they were erect', 'they were in a raised position'; 4. (said of machines) 'they were operational')
      d.   They were away. (= (with human subject) 'They were away from home')
      e.   They were out. (= (among other meanings) (with human subject) 'they were out of house' or 'they were out of office'; (said of lights) 'they were extinguished' 3. 'they were no longer fashionable')

above (cf. section 2.2) that PrtPs and PPs should not simply be collapsed into a single category:

(56) a. She ventured five meters deep {into the cave / *in}.
      b. The submarine sank 1000 meters deep {below the surface of the sea / *down}.
      c. This type of ball could be catapulted fifty yards high {into the sky / *up}.

An explanation for why a PP unlike a particle is possible in these sentences may be sought in the fact that we are actually dealing here with stative expressions headed by the inherently locative adverbs *deep* and *high*. This is supported by the following paraphrases:

(57) a. She ventured to a depth of five meters into the cave.
      b. The submarine sank to a depth of 1000 meters below the surface of the sea.
      c. This type of ball could be catapulted to a height of fifty yards into the sky.

Admittedly, the paraphrase makes use of the directional preposition *to*, but the complement of this preposition is an NP expressing a location and as we saw in Section 2.2.1, particles cannot be used in locative contexts. Remarkably, the directionality of *into* does not appear to clash with the locative meaning of *deep/depth* and *high/height*. The sheer presence of a Ground argument (e.g., *the cave, the sky*) may be sufficient to background the inherent directionality of *into*. This directionality, however, still plays a role in the interpretation of the overall spatial expression, as it expresses the path by which the location is reached.

4.3 Quantifying peripheral premodifiers enable a locative reading of particles

Although particles cannot generally be used locatively, as we have repeatedly noted, such a use is nonetheless possible if the particle is preceded by a quantifying peripheral premodifier (cf. Svenonius 2004):

(58) a. They were two centimeters off (the center of the picture).
      b. They were way off (the back).
      c. They were twenty feet down (the drainpipe).
      d. They bounced partway up (the wall).
      e. They were miles away (from the rhinoceros).
      f. They were twenty meters out (of the yard).   (Svenonius 2004: 26)

Quantifying peripheral modifiers can be measure NPs, proportional degree expressions like *halfway* or *completely*, or non-proportional degree expressions like *far* or *way*. Svenonius gives an explanation in terms of scalarity. Basically, for an inherently directional item like *off, down, away, out*, etc. to be admissible in a locative context, it needs to have a scalar structure. This scalar structure can be furnished by an overtly expressed Ground or by (what I call) a quantifying peripheral modifier. Exactly why scalar structure is needed for the conversion of directional to locative meaning is not clear to me, however. Nor is it clear how a Ground argument can introduce scalar structure. For instance, a reference point like *the center of the picture* in (58a) does not have any dimensions in itself, so this type of Ground cannot straightforwardly supply a scalar structure to *off*.

I do not believe that scalarity is what is needed for a spatial item to be used in a locative context. Rather, it suffices that a Ground is expressed, either directly or indirectly. Direct expression of the Ground can be established, of course, by using the spatial item as a preposition and introducing the Ground as its complement. Indirect expression of the Ground can be realized via a quantifying expression, which inevitably evokes the Ground as part of its interpretation. Indeed, you cannot interpret an utterance like *They were two centimeters off* unless you can identify the point in space from which the subject referent was at a distance of two centimers.

4.4   Measure NPs expressing a span of time

Measure NPs used with spatial expressions need not explicitly refer to a distance in space. They can also refer to a distance in time. Some examples are given in (59):

(59)   a.   Yes, I drove the seven or so hours right back home (www)
       b.   After leaving LA, we flew a solid 13 hours over to New Zealand. (www)

Svenonius (2004) also mentions this possibility with respect to directional PPs that are used in stative sentences:

(60)   Fredrik's house is fifteen minutes through those trees.
       (Svenonius 2004: 16)

Not very surprisingly, such temporal measure NPs are like spatial measure NPs in also allowing locative (i.e., stative) uses of particles (cf. Section 4.3), primarily of *away*:

(61)   Nice International Airport is just ten minutes away by car. (www)

Svenonius (2004) accounts for the use of (temporal) measure NPs in stative expressions by inserting covert elements (notably JOURNEY) in the expression's syntactic representation. However, he admits that the requirement to use a plural morpheme on the head noun in the time expression renders his analysis somewhat problematic (compare *a fifteen-minute journey through those trees* versus **fifteen-minute through those trees*). In fact, an analysis in terms of a silent JOURNEY node in the tree is equally problematic for spatial measure NPs, since the plural –*s* on such NPs also has to be explained (compare *a three-hundred mile journey across the country* versus *three-hundred miles across the country*).

I do not think that an account of the use of temporal and spatial measure NPs need involve an intricate accommodation in the syntactic representation of the phrase. What syntax should merely specify is the position any kind of measure NP (whether spatial or temporal) has to occupy within a spatial phrase. The use of time expressions as measure NPs in a spatial phrase can then simply be explained, it seems to me, as the result of a metonymical relation between an extent in space and the time needed to cover that extent. Thus, *Fredrik's house is fifteen minutes through those trees* means that Fredrik's house is (under normal circumstances, and with a contextually defined standard mode of transportation) to be found at *fifteen minutes' worth of distance* as measured from the deictic point on a path through those trees. Similarly, (59a) means that the speaker drove *the distance that took her seven or so hours to cover* right back home and in (59b), *a distance that took the subject referent a solid 13 hours to cover* was flown to reach New Zealand. So, there is nothing mysterious about examples like (59a, b) if we realize that the extent of a path need not be expressed in terms of a length unit like inch, meter, etc., but can just as well be stated in terms of the time it takes to move from its beginning to its end.[13]

Note that we can, conversely, also find a spatial measure NP where we might actually expect a time expression, as in *John slept all the way to Boston*, where *all the way to Boston* represents, say, a three hours' worth of distance. This goes to show that temporal and spatial distance can substitute for each other because of their metonymy relatedness: when you travel someplace, time inevitably goes by, and during a lapse of time, you can travel someplace. (It is precisely this metonymical relationship between spatial and temporal distance that underlies the concept of a *light-year*.)

4.5 Right-peripheral modifiers

A next point to be observed is that peripheral modifiers can usually also occur at the right periphery. The following examples are taken from Bolinger (1971), but see also Jackendoff (2002a: 71):

---

13. We need to set apart examples like the following, which involve a conventionalized metaphorical mapping (temporal distance conceptualized as spatial distance) and in which the distance is still measured in terms of temporal units:

(i) a. The deadline is still several days away.
     b. In the face of global competition every second counts and with CHIRON you'll always be seconds ahead. (www)

No metonymical relation between temporal and spatial distance is invoked in such sentences.

(62)   a.   He stood the pole {straight up / up straight}.
       b.   It blew the handles {clean off / off clean}.
       c.   He took it {completely off / off completely}.
       d.   I pushed the stylus {a couple of inches away / away a couple of inches}.
       e.   He backed {ten feet off / off ten feet} and waited.
       f.   He came {part way down / down part way}.
       g   I left it {partly in / in partly}.
       h.   He hammered the nail {deep in / in deep}.
       i.   They traveled {far away / away far}.   (Bolinger 1971: 136–137)

One can add here the example *Put it {safe away / away safe}*.

However, it is not always possible to put the peripheral modifier in right-hand position (e.g., *I pushed the lever {half down / *down half}*; *He fell {quite down* (archaic) */ *down quite})*. Especially intensifying adjectives that have acquired an almost purely adverbial meaning (*right* and, to a lesser extent, *straight*), the adverb *way*, and intensifiers with an onomatopoeic origin like *plumb, plunk, smack dab*, etc. resist post-particle placement:

(63)   a.   The roof came {right off / *off right}.
       b.   She fell {straight over / *over straight}.
       c.   The temperature went {way down / *down way}.
       d.   He knocked the cap {plumb off / *off plumb}.   (Bolinger 1971: 137)

A left-peripheral and right-peripheral modifier can flank a particle head (and a possibly present premodifier), as in (64a–d):

(64)   a.   He goes way up high and he goes way down low! (www)
       b.   I thought that the show started off great from episodes 1 through 11 then in January it started to dip, but at the start of episode 15 it went straight back up high! (www)
       c.   It was really cool to ring the bell, the rope would take you right on up high. . . probably two feet off the ground! (www)
       d.   . . . you can just grab the paper by the corner and peel it right off clean. (www)

Evidence that the particle and the words clustering around it make up a single phrase is provided by fronting, but this evidence is tentative, because fronting gives mixed results:

(65)   a.   Fireworks cheer: "Way up high it goes. . . Boom! Boom! Boom! Ahhhh!" (www)
       b.   Straight back up high it went!
       c.   Right on up high I went. . . probably two feet off the ground!
       d.   ??I pulled the paper by the corner and right off clean it came.

If the particle head is followed by a modifier/complement (like *to the sky* in the example below), a right-peripheral modifier should in principle follow that modifier/complement:

(66)   Well, they're movin' on up to the sky high. (www)

However, we more commonly encounter elements like *high* and *deep* as premodifiers in a PP following the particle:

(67)   A typical flushing response of a longspur is to fly almost straight up, high into the sky. . . (www)

As is clear from punctuation or prosody, such a PP then typically forms an immediate constituent of the VP, outside the particle phrase (see again possibility 3 mentioned at the end of Section 3.3 above).

4.6   Freezes

A final point of observation is that peripheral modifiers often enter into a fixed and idiomatic combination with a particle. Here are some examples:

(68)   a.   She had expected it *all along*.
       b.   He's an *all-around* athlete.
       c.   I'm afraid you'll think me very outspoken – but that's me *all over*. (www)
       d.   Congratulations! You did a really *bang-up* job on that test.
       e.   *Deep down* I knew I was wrong.
       f.   *How far along* is she, seven months or so?
       g.   This is not some *far-out* Orwellian scenario. (www)
       h.   She's a bit *full-on* for me. She treats me like a sister and I hardly know her. (www)
       i.   Yes, sir. *Right away*, Mr. Congressman, sir. (www)
       j.   Wow! Yeah! *Right on*!
       k.   And like always Claire was *spot on* with her diagnosis of the problem. (www)

Clearly, most of these idioms do not have spatial meanings. That modification is not the prerogative of spatial particles is the topic of the next section.

5.   Modification of non-spatial particles

5.1   Non-peripheral modification of non-spatial particles

It is often assumed that only particles used in their literal (spatial) sense allow modification (Dirven & Radden 1977: 184–186; Gries 2003: 55; Lohse et al. 2004: 257, note 42). This is not true. Consider, first of all, the sentences in (69):

(69)   a.   Switch off the computer. Wait five minutes. Switch the computer *back on*. (www)

b.   Once the lights went *back on*, people immediately wanted to be better prepared if the lights went *back off* again. (www)

While the function of *back* with spatial particles is to convey that the resultant position implied by the following particle is a restoration of an original position (cf. again the examples in (29a–c)), *back* here extends this meaning to any "restoration of an original state" (Bolinger 1971: 137–138), via the common conceptual metaphor STATES ARE LOCATIONS (Lakoff & Johnson 1980).

Note that we are still dealing with semantically independent particles in (69a, b), even though they do not express a spatial meaning. What I mean by this is that the particle does not depend on the verb for its interpretation, so it can occur after *be* (*The computer is on*) or in a small clause (*With the computer on, I can't really hear what they're saying in the room next door*). However, *back* can also be used as a modifier to particles which are semantically dependent that is, which receive their proper interpretation only when considered in relation with the verb, as in (70 a–d).

(70)   a.   I passed out. I remember waking up once, and then *passing back out*. (www)
       b.   It was all locked up, so I opened the side door, and *locked* it *back up* after we had entered. (www)
       c.   Suddenly, her fear turned to anger and she attacked the mirror, using her hand to wipe the condensation off its silvery surface. She recoiled from her reflection then watched as the mirror *clouded back up* again. (www)
       d.   So, this requires that two different, but compatible RNA strands manage to form, and come into contact, with conditions suitable to reproducing, before the strands are *broken back down* by cosmic rays. (www)

The particle *on*, too, can occasionally be found as a premodifier to semantically dependent particles, as the following examples illustrate:[14]

(71)   a.   hey folks, and don't forget to *dress on up* as your favorite Hero or Villain and *party on down* this saturday night 10/28 to benefit The IMC and Studio X (www)
       b.   I wish the book companies would just *hurry on up* and get to the same century everyone else is in. (www)
       c.   Life is a rollercoaster, so *buckle on up* for the ride. (www)
       d.   Pop in disc two and *chill on out*. (www)
       e.   So *cheer on up*, Vash, and grab yourself a donut! (www)

---

14.   Examples of *along* premodifying a non-spatial particle could not be found.

While non-spatial particles do not seem to allow postmodification or complementation by another particle – a possibility that could not be unequivocally shown to exist for spatial particles either – the following sentences arguably provide instances of a PP being used as a postmodifier or complement to a non-spatial particle:

(72) a. *Chop* it *up into pieces.*
      b. Traffic got *slowed down to a standstill.*
      c. The model will be *broken down into its components.*

However, as in the case of PPs following spatial particles, one might again object that the PP does not form part of the PrtP but instead forms a separate constituent of its own. Note, for example, that it can be separated from the particle by an intervening adverbial (see (73)) or that it can (somewhat less easily) be separated from it in a cleft construction (see (74)):

(73)   Chop it up carefully into even-sized pieces.

(74)   It was to a regular standstill that traffic had slowed down.

This illustrates that there is again structural indeterminacy in (72a–c), just as in the case of spatial particles followed by a PP (cf. again Section 3.3).

5.2 *Peripheral modification of non-spatial particles*

There is overwhelming evidence that non-spatial particles are allowed to take a peripheral modifier. Especially *right* can be found (see (75)), but other intensifying peripheral modifiers occasionally occur as well (see (76)).

(75) a. This article just *freaks* me *right out*! (www)
      b. The above problems had *messed* the process *right up* (www)
      c. A pigment can be bright in dry form and *dull right down* when mixed with oil. (www)
      d. So, you did such a good job you *faked* me *right out*!! (www)
      e. You should come over for a burrito, Jack. It'll *straighten* you *right out*. The chopped london broil is now marinating in lime juice, kosher salt, black pepper, garlic, and crushed red pepper flakes. We'll *party* that hangover *right off*! WOOOOOOOOO!!! (www)

(76) a. Sometimes he would *pass plumb out* unconscious and have to be carried home. (www)
      b. At this, my friend hit the floor, *passed dead out*. (www)
      c. She was a screamer, a choker, a biter. She was in midbite when she *fainted dead away*. (John Irving, *The Fourth Hand*, New York: Random House, 2001, p. 220)

d.   It kinda makes me laugh the way he knocks off them banks and *gets clean away*
     with it. (Truman Capote, *Music for Chameleons*. London: Penguin, 2000. p. 47)
e.   Lorna *screwed* her eyes *up tight.*[15] (www)

Non-spatial particles can also be preceded by peripheral modifiers expressing a
degree (cf. Fraser 1976: 26; Lindner 1981: 30):

(77) a.   I've *messed all around* with the Exceed Xconfig and nothing helps. (www)
      b.   They *freaked completely out*! (www)
      c.   There were hundreds of clocks: little and big, carved and plain, some with
           wooden faces and some with porcelain ones–shelf clocks, cuckoo clocks,
           clocks with chimes and clocks without; and they all hung on the walls,
           covering them *quite up.* (www)
      d.   This section also had the loud breaks, the last one was particularly wild,
           before the music *slowed all the way down.* (www)

The following set of sentences, finally, illustrates that non-spatial particles can even
take multiple modifiers, just like spatial ones can.

(78) a.   Suddenly, "DM" hooks a hard louie into hot, foggy electric blues,
           smothering the brutality under passionate, unrequited longing for
           something or other. One might call it honorable. Then, with a "heeey!"
           and a "wow-da – wow – da," "Nothing" *freaks* us *right back out.* (www)
      b.   Let the whole picture come into focus: it's an entire body of joints that
           broke down and were redefined, only to be *broken right back down* again.
           (www)
      c.   Take a peek at them every few hours, but remember to *seal* them *back up*
           tight (duct tape works well for that). (www)

5.3   Discussion

What is important in connection with modification of non-spatial particles is that
all the examples in (70)–(71) and (75)–(78) display a mismatch between what is
modified syntactically and what is modified semantically. Fraser (1976: 26) notes
that *all* in *They cleaned it all up* (on the reading 'They cleaned it up completely')
functions as "some type of verbal modifier". Likewise, Dehé (2002: 45) correctly
observes that *right* added to a non-directional particle seems to modify the entire VP

---

15.   *Up tight,* with the peripheral modifier in post-particle position, is again a combination
which, like the combinations illustrated in (68), has undergone lexicalization (cf. Bolinger 1971:
136). For example:

(i)   For an *uptight* prude, you do a good line in sensual kissing. (BNC) rather than the particle itself. For example, *I'll look it right up* can be paraphrased as *I'll look it up right away*. The modifier(s) cannot directly and exclusively relate to the meaning of the head particle since the head particle does not have an independent meaning in the first place. Nevertheless, it seems as though the grammar of English avoids proliferating syntactic structures and, instead, exploits a single schematic structure for the communication of quite different meanings. This schematic structure is inherited by a number of well-entrenched constructional templates which we might assume to be also stored in the grammar. One such pattern is shown in (79).

(79)

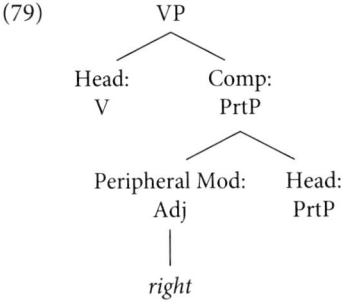

This pattern can then be put to multiple uses. For example, it can be used in cases in which the speaker wants to modify the particle itself, conveying the idea that the independent meaning of the particle "is fully and literally correctly satisfied" (Pullum & Huddleston 2002: 644), or, to borrow Svenonius's (2004: 11) semantic description of *right* in locative expressions and applying it to the construction under study, that the directional path in the event is "archetypal" for the kind of path denoted by the particle. This is the case in example (80) below.

(80)   Then I got hit in the neck and the bullet went *right through.* (www)

Alternatively, the structure in (79) can be used to convey that the event itself "is fully and literally correctly satisfied" (to use the same phrase as above) and/or that it occurred immediately, without delay, adding often also a sense of rapture on the part of the speaker, as in (81).

(81)   Now, we all know this is the song Damian provokes the crowd to sing along to, but this time, he didn't even have to, before he could tell us, we all sang *right along* so loud, he had to stop and laugh. (www)

It should be noted that the distinction between path-modification and event-modification is not clear-cut, as (80) may also be seen as being in part an instance of the latter. The modification of *right* in this example could be seen as a kind of semantic merger: both the path and the event seem to be targeted at the same time. Also, note that the distinction between path-modification and event-modification does not correlate with the distinction between independent and dependent particles. Consider example (82):

(82)   After all of my CG issues, I had my 2nd maiden flight this morning. The plane went *right up* and I got about five minutes of wonderful flight time :) :) (www)

Here, the particle *up* carries an independent, spatial meaning but the modifier *right* nevertheless has wide scope over the entire VP – it is very evident from the context that the upward motion was not in a perfectly vertical direction; rather, what the speaker wants to emphasize is that there was upward motion at all.

What these examples show, in sum, is that a single structure may be endowed with multiple meanings, leaving it to the hearer to find out which meaning is intended. The relevant syntax is identical in all three sentences, despite the fact that the semantics involved is not uniform.

6.   Conclusion

We can distill three main concluding remarks from this paper:

First, particles, defined as (basically) spatial elements which can occur between a verb and an object NP and which do not directly govern this or any other NP, can head full-fledged syntactic phrases which contain a multiplicity of structural positions. In a particle phrase, there is a position for:

(1) one or two pre-modifying particles (*back*, *on* and *along*);

(2) a post-modifier or complement, which is usually a PP;

(3) one or more peripheral modifiers to the left: onomatopoeias like *bang* and *plumb*, intensifying adjectives like *right* and *straight* and, most exterior, quantifying expressions like *completely*, *high*, and *several inches*; some of these peripheral modifiers can also occur to the right.

Second, for any string of multiple particles, especially when this string is followed by a PP, it is usually possible to propose a multiplicity of valid structural analyses which do not correspond to obvious differences in meaning. For example, whether the PP is parsed as being part of the PrtP made up of the particles or as forming a sister constituent to that PrtP on its own does not affect the interpretation of the whole sequence. We have therefore called this phenomenon structural indeterminacy (as opposed to structural ambiguity).

Third, and most relevant to the dominant theme of this volume (i.e., the interface between the syntax and the semantics of spatial items), we have seen that there is also a multiplicity of ways a single structure can be put to communicative use. One such case that we have encountered in the course of our discussion is the use of measure NPs before particles. We have seen that measure NPs can either express a distance in space or a distance in time. We can keep syntax relatively simple if we assume that all it has to do in connection with such NPs is state their position within the particle phrase. Although we might think that spatial phrases with a spatial measure NP are somehow more 'basic' than spatial phrases with a temporal NP, the syntactic component of language remains much leaner if it does not have to handle any derivation from spatial measure NPs to temporal measure NPs. Indeed, syntax should not have to handle this at all, since the inextricable relationship between movement on the one hand and time consumed whilst moving on the other is something that is part of speakers' non-syntactic cognition.

In the previous section, we more explicitly defended the view that the grammar of English may consist of several conventionalized pieces of linguistic organization whose syntax has some degree of autonomy over semantics (broadly defined). For example, it is likely to assume that speakers have direct access to a phrasal pattern containing a slot for a particle which is syntactically modified by *right*, since this is a configuration that has considerable token frequency. For some of these tokens, the word *right* also *semantically* modifies (in accordance with its syntactic position) the item plugged into the particle slot, but for other tokens, it rather modifies the entire VP, or it seems to modify both the particle and the VP at the same time. What is crucial, though, is that whatever is meant to be modified semantically, the same syntactic structure can be used in each case. In other words, we have shown that one structure can map onto multiple meanings, lending support to Jackendoff's (2002a, b), and Culicover and Jackendoff's (2005) claim that a strictly isomorphic syntax-semantic interface has to be abandoned. Rather than inventing new structures for each different communicative purpose, speakers appear to make do with the existing structures they find in their grammatical "toolbox", adopting them for diverse communicative needs.

References

Ayano, S. 2005. The layered internal structure of spatial PPs. In *Adpositions of Movement*, H. Cuyckens, W. De Mulder & T. Mortelmans (eds), 3–27. Amsterdam: John Benjamins.

Bolinger, D. 1971. *The Phrasal Verb in English*. Cambridge MA: Harvard University Press.

Cappelle, B. 2001. Is *out of* always a preposition? *Journal of English Linguistics* 29(4): 315–328.

Cappelle, B. 2005a. The particularity of particles, or why they are not just 'intransitive prepositions'. In *Adpositions of Movement*, H. Cuyckens, W. De Mulder & T. Mortelmans (eds), 29–57. Amsterdam: John Benjamins.

Cappelle, B. 2005b. Particle Patterns in English: A Comprehensive Coverage. PhD Dissertation, K.U. Leuven.

Cappelle, B. 2006. Particle placement and the case for 'allostructions'. In *Constructions All Over: Case Studies and Theoretical Implications* [Special volume of *Constructions*], D. Schönefeld (ed.).

Cappelle, B. To appear. Contextual cues for particle placement: Multiplicity, motivation, modeling. In *Context and Constructions* [Constructional Approaches to Language], A. Bergs & G. Diewald (eds). Amsterdam: John Benjamins.

Cappelle, B. & Declerck R. 2005. Spatial and temporal boundedness in English motion events. *Journal of Pragmatics* 37: 889–917.

Carstairs-McCarthy, A. 2005. Phrases inside compounds: A puzzle for lexicon-free morphology. *Skase Journal of Theoretical Linguistics* 2(3): 34–42.

Culicover, P.W. & Jackendoff, R. 2005. *Simpler Syntax*. Oxford: OUP.

Dehé, N. 2002. *Particle Verbs in English: Syntax, Information Structure, and Intonation* [Linguistik Aktuell/Linguistics Today 59]. Amsterdam: John Benjamins.

den Dikken, M. 1995. *Particles: On the Syntax of Verb-Particle, Triadic, and Causative Constructions* [Oxford Studies in Comparative Syntax]. New York NY: OUP.

den Dikken, M. 2003. When particles won't part. Ms., The City University of New York.

Dirven, R. & Radden, G. 1977. *Semantische Syntax des Englishen*. Wiesbaden: Athenation.

Emonds, J.E. 1970. Root and Structure-Preserving Transformations. PhD Dissertation. MIT.

Emonds, J. 1972. Evidence that indirect object movement is a structure-preserving rule. *Foundations of Language* 8: 546–561.

Farrell, P. 2005. English verb-preposition constructions: Constituency and order. *Language* 81(1): 96–137.

Fraser, B. 1970. Some remarks on the action-nominalization in English. In *Readings in English Transformational Grammar*, R.A. Jacobs & P.S. Rosenbaum (eds), 83–98. Waltham MA: Ginn.

Fraser, B. 1976. *The Verb-Particle Combination in English*. New York NY: Academic Press.

Gries, S.T. 2003. *Multifactorial Analysis in Corpus Linguistics: A Study of Particle Placement* [Open Linguistics Series]. London: Continuum.

Guéron, J. 1990. Particles, prepositions, and verbs. In *Grammar in Progress: Glow Essays for Henk van Riemsdijk* [Studies in Generative Grammar 36], J. Mascaró & M. Nespor (eds), 153–166. Dordrecht: Foris.

Haegeman, L. & Guéron, J. 1999. *English Grammar: A Generative Perspective* [Blackwell Textbooks in Linguistics 14]. Oxford: Blackwell.

Harley, H. & Noyer, R. 1998. Mixed nominalizations, short verb movement and object shift in English. *Proceedings of the 28th Annual Meeting of the North East Linguistic Society*, P.N. Tamanji & K. Kusumoto (eds), 143–157. Amherst MA: GLSA.

Huddleston, R. 2002. The clause: Complements. In *The Cambridge Grammar of the English Language*, R. Huddleston & G.K. Pullum (eds), 213–321. Cambridge: CUP.

Huddleston, R., Payne, J. & Peterson, P. 2002. Coordination and supplementation. In *The Cambridge Grammar of the English Language*, R. Huddleston & G.K. Pullum (eds), 1273–1364. Cambridge: CUP.

Huddleston, R. & Pullum, G.K. 2002. Syntactic overview. In *The Cambridge Grammar of the English Language*, R. Huddleston & G.K. Pullum (eds) 43–69. Cambridge: CUP.

Hudson, R.A. 1982. Incomplete conjuncts. *Linguistic Inquiry* 13: 547–550.

Jackendoff, R. 1973. The base rules for prepositional phrases. *Festschrift for Morris Halle*, S.R. Anderson & P. Kiparsky (eds), 345–356. New York NY: Holt, Rinehart and Winston.

Jackendoff, R. 2002a. English particle constructions, the lexicon, and the autonomy of syntax. In *Verb-Particle Explorations* [Interface explorations 1], N. Dehé, R. Jackendoff, A. McIntyre & S. Urban (eds), 67–94. Berlin: Mouton de Gruyter.

Jackendoff, R. 2002b. *Foundations of Language: Brain, Meaning, Grammar, Evolution*. Oxford: OUP.

Jespersen, O. 1924. *The Philosophy of Grammar*. London: Allen and Unwin.

Lakoff, G. & Johnson, M. 1980. *Metaphors We Live By*. Chicago IL: University of Chicago Press.

Langacker, R.W. 1987. *Foundations of Cognitive Grammar*. Vol. 1: *Theoretical Prerequisites*. Stanford CA: Stanford University Press.

Lee, D. 1999. Intransitive prepositions: Are they viable? In *The Clause in English: In Honour of Rodney Huddleston* [Studies in Language Companion Series 45], P. Collins & D. Lee (eds), 133–147. Amsterdam: John Benjamins.

Lindner, S.J. 1981. A Lexico-Semantic Analysis of English Verb Particle Constructions with *Out* and *Up*. PhD Dissertation, UCSD.

Lohse, B., Hawkins, J.A. & Wasow, T. 2004. Domain minimization in verb-particle constructions. *Language* 80: 238–261.

McIntyre, A. 2002. Idiosyncracy in particle verbs. In *Verb-Particle Explorations* [Interface explorations 1], N. Dehé, R. Jackendoff, A. McIntyre & S. Urban (eds), 95–118. Berlin: Mouton de Gruyter.

McIntyre, A. 2004. Event paths, conflation, argument structure and VP shells. *Linguistics* 42: 523–571.

Nicol, F. 2002. Extended VP-shells and the verb-particle construction. In *Verb-Particle Explorations* [Interface explorations 1], N. Dehé, R. Jackendoff, A. McIntyre & S. Urban (eds), 164–190. Berlin: Mouton de Gruyter.

O'Dowd, E.M. 1998. *Prepositions and Particles in English: A Discourse-Functional Account*. New York NY: OUP.

Pullum, G.K. & Huddleston, R. 2002. Prepositions and preposition phrases. In *The Cambridge Grammar of the English Language*, R. Huddleston & G.K. Pullum (eds), 597–661. Cambridge: CUP.

Ramchand, G. & Svenonius, P. 2002. The lexical syntax and lexical semantics of the verb-particle construction. In *Proceedings of the 21st West Coast Conference on Formal Linguistics* [WCCFL 21], L. Mikkelsen & C. Potts (eds), 387–400. Somerville MA: Cascadilla.

Spencer, A. 1988. Bracketing paradoxes and the English lexicon. *Language* 64: 663–682.

Stillings, J.T. 1975. The formulation of gapping in English as evidence for variable types in syntactic transformations. *Linguistic Analysis* 1: 247–273.

Svenonius, P. 1992. Movement of P^0 in the English verb-particle construction. In *Syntax at Santa Cruz. Volume 1*, A. Black & J. McCloskey (eds), 93–113. Santa Cruz CA: University of California at Santa Cruz.

Svenonius, P. 2004. Spatial P in English. Ms., University of Tromsø.

Talmy, L. 1985. Lexicalization patterns: Semantic structure in lexical forms. In *Language Typology and Syntactic Description*. Vol. 3: *Grammatical Categories and the Lexicon*, T. Shopen (ed.), 57–149. Cambridge: CUP.

Talmy, L. 1991. Path to realization: A typology of event conflation. In *Proceedings of the Seventeenth Annual Meeting of the Berkeley Linguistics Society* [BLS 17] L.A. Sutton, C. Johnson & R. Shields (eds), 480–519. Berkeley CA: Berkeley Linguistics Society.

Tomasello, M. 1998. *The New Psychology of Language: Cognitive and Functional Approaches to Language Structure*. Mahwah NJ: Laurence Erlbaum.

Tseng, J. 2005. Directionality and the complementation of Dutch adpositions. In *Adpositions of Movement*, H. Cuyckens, W. De Mulder & T. Mortelmans (eds), 167–194. Amsterdam: John Benjamins.

Zeller, J. 2002. Particle verbs are heads and phrases. In *Verb-Particle Explorations* [Interface explorations 1], N. Dehé, R. Jackendoff, A. McIntyre & S. Urban (eds), 233–267. Berlin: Mouton de Gruyter.

PART II

Expressions of directionality

The correspondence between directionality and transitivity*

Sander Lestrade
Radboud University Nijmegen, PIONIER Project Case Cross-Linguistically

In this paper I argue that there is a correspondence between the verbal and prepositional domain. Transitivity and Proto-Patient characteristics can straightforwardly be used in the analysis of adpositional phrases. Directional goal and route meaning can thus be analyzed as more transitive-like than locative meaning, and the object of goal and route adpositions as more Proto-Patient-like than the object of source and locative ones.

Next, I argue that accusative case inherently has Proto-Patient meaning and that locative meaning is preferred to directional meaning. With these findings, the adpositional accusative-oblique case alternation is explained, in which locative meaning pairs up with an oblique case form, whereas directional meaning combines with accusative case.

1. Introduction

Adpositions and case marking are two important ways to express spatial meaning. I discuss the way these two systems can be combined. I only consider those instances in which an adposition may take different morphological cases, one of which is accusative. I argue that there is a correspondence between spatial meaning on the one hand and the notions of transitivity (Hopper & Thompson 1980) and Proto-Patient (Dowty 1991) on the other. The same parameters with which the transitivity of an event or the Proto-Patient-likelihood of an object is determined

*   This paper has been presented at the Conference on spatial P and the semantics workshop of Stanford University. I would like to thank the audience of both occasions for valuable comments. Many thanks go to Helen de Hoop, Vivienne Fong, Joost Zwarts, Tatiana Nikitina, Geertje van Bergen, three anonymous reviewers, and the members of the Optimal Communication research group for useful comments on an earlier version of this paper. Also, I gratefully acknowledge the Netherlands Organization for Scientific Research (NWO), grant 220–70–003 PIONIER project Case cross-linguistically, principal investigator Helen de Hoop.

can be used for the analysis of the adpositional domain. With this correspondence established, I account for cross-linguistically attested adpositional accusative-oblique case alternations.

I introduce the adpositional case alternation in Section 2. A structural proposal for this alternation is briefly discussed in Section 3. I introduce a semantic analysis of adpositions in Section 4 in order to establish a correspondence between the verbal and adpositional domain in Section 5. In Section 6, I deal with the question why source adpositions behave differently with respect to case marking. I argue that accusative case has inherent meaning in Section 7. Before coming to conclusions, I propose a bidirectional Optimality Theoretic account to explain the attested patterns.

2.   Case and adpositions

In some languages a particular adposition may combine with several morphological cases in the same linguistic context. This is very similar to so called 'fluid' Differential Object Marking (DOM) in the verbal domain (De Hoop & Malchukov 2006). Consider an example of this latter phenomenon from Finnish:

(1)   a.   Anne rakensi talo-a.
          A.   built   house-PART
          'Anne was building a/the house.'
      b.   Anne rakensi talo-n.
          A.   built   house-ACC
          'Anne built a/the house.'

Accusative case marking of the object correlates with a resultative interpretation in (1b), while the use of partitive case usually combines with an irresultative interpretation as in (1a). Importantly, the *same noun phrase* in the *same linguistic context* can take different case markers, leading to a difference in meaning (De Hoop & Malchukov 2006).

In the adpositional domain too, the meaning of the resulting prepositional phrase (PP) depends on the combination of the preposition and the case of its complement. An example of a case alternating adposition is German *auf*.

(2)   a.   Paul läuft auf der   Blumenwiese.[1]
          P.   walks AUF the.DAT flower.meadow
          'Paul walks on the flower meadow.'

---

1.   Abbreviations used in this paper: 1 first person, 2 second person, 3 third person, ABL ablative case, ABS absolutive case, ACC accusative case, ALL allative case, AOR aorist, AUX auxiliary,

b. Julia läuft   auf   die   Blumenwiese.
J.   walks AUF the.ACC flower.meadow
'Julia walks onto the flower meadow.'

With the complement dative marked as in (2a), the PP conveys a locative meaning, the place in which some event takes place. However, with the accusative case, the PP denotes the goal of a motion event.

In this paper, I will only consider adpositions that exhibit a case alternation in which one of the cases is accusative. (For a more elaborate discussion on these adpositions see Lestrade 2006). I will use the label *oblique* for any non-accusative case, be it genitive, dative, ablative, instrumental, or locative. As I will show, the use of accusative case instead of some oblique case always results in a specific meaning difference.

The next example of such an adposition comes from Latin.

(3) a. Latin (Rotteveel Manseveld & Waleson 1970)
        in urbe   vivere
        IN city.ABL to.live
        'to live in the city'
    b. in aquam   cadere
        IN water.ACC to.fall
        'to fall in the water'

Just like in the German example above, in combination with accusative case a goal reading is obtained; in combination with oblique case a locative one. Also in Sorbian and Polish, we see this same pattern return, as the reader may verify.

(4) Sorbian (Schuster-Šewc 1999)
    a. na dźěło   hić
        NA work.ACC to.go
        'to go to work'
    b. być na dworje
        to.be NA yard.LOC
        'to be in the yard'

AxPart axial part, Cl-I noun class I, Cl-II noun class II, CP complement phrase, DAT dative case, DegP degree phrase, DIR directional (meaning), DirP directional phrase, DP determiner phrase, ERG ergative case, F feminine, FUT future tense, GEN genitive case, ILL illative case, INTR intransitive, K case function, KP case phrase, LOC locative (meaning), LOC locative case, M masculine, MID middle voice, N/A nominative or accusative, NEG negation marker, NOM nominative case, NP noun phrase, PART partitive, PRTC participle, PathP path phrase, PlaceP place phrase, PL plural, PP adpositional phrase, ProtoP proto-patient, PRS present tense, PRT particle, SG singular, TR transitive, VOC vocative case, VP Verb phrase.

(5)   Polish (Bielec 1998)
    a.   Pracuję   na poczcie.
       work:1sg   NA post.office.LOC
       'I work at the post office.'
    b.   Idę   na pocztę.
       go:1sg   NA post.office.ACC
       'I'm going to the post office.'

One might argue that the case alternation in the last three examples could be due to the different verbs in the sentence pairs. However, as we saw in the German example above and in the following Russian example, the case alternation can occur in the very same linguistic context.

(6)   Russian (A. Malchukov, p.c.)
    a.   Ja xodil v magazin.
       I went V shop.ACC
       'I went to the shop.'
    b.   Ja xodil v magazine.
       I went V shop.DAT
       'I was walking in the shop.'

Some other examples of case alternating adpositions that yield this very same meaning difference, i.e., a goal versus a location reading, are Polish *miedzy* '(to) among,' *nad* '(to) above,' *za* '(to) behind,' Sorbian *nad(e)* 'above, over,' *pod(e)* '(to) under,' *před* '(to) in front of,' Russian *na* 'on(to),' *za* '(to) behind,' *pod* '(to) under,' Czech *na* 'on(to),' *o* 'against, leaning on,' *v* 'in(to),' *po* 'up to, (around) in,' Ancient Greek *huper* 'above, over,' *epi* 'on, towards, over,' *pros* 'at, towards,' *ana* 'up (to),' German *an* 'on(to),' *in* 'in(to),' *unter* '(to) under,' and Latin *sub* 'under.'[2]

According to Luraghi (2003) the accusative-oblique case alternation may also express a different meaning distinction. In the next example from Ancient Greek a distinction is made within route meaning.

(7)   a.   di' ōmou   khálkeon   égkhos   ēlten
       DIA shoulder.GEN bronze.N/A spear.N/A go.AOR.3SG
       'the spear of bronze went through his shoulder'
                  (Iliad 4.481–2, taken from Luraghi 2003: 168)
    b.   helixámenos   dià bēssas
       turn.PRTC.AOR.MID.NOM DIA glen.ACC.PL.F
       '[a wild boar] turning around through the glens'
                  (Iliad 17.283, taken from Luraghi 2003: 171)

---

2.   These languages are all Indo-European, as these often have both a case and prepositional system. I leave the extension to non-Indo-European languages for future research.

With genitive case, *dia* is said to mean 'straight through'. In combination with the accusative case, *dia* does not express a straight line, but a more complex, random path inside a ground.[3] Apparently, in the alternation with *dia* different spatial properties become important. When the object of the adposition is covered by the path to a greater extent it gets accusative marking. I will elaborate on this distinction below.

Before I propose my semantic analysis, I will discuss the way Den Dikken (2003) approaches this case alternation in German in the next section.

3.   A structural approach

Jackendoff (1990) decomposes directional adpositions as a path function over a place function to a thing. This can be illustrated by 'into the house', in which the path function TO is added to the place function IN.

(8) $[_{Path}$ TO $([_{Place}$ IN $([_{Thing}$ HOUSE])])]

Directional meaning, in the form of an additional Path level, is thus seen as an elaboration of locative meaning. This idea is pursued in Koopman (1997), Den Dikken (2003), and Svenonius (2006) in their analyses of locative vs. directional adpositions. Den Dikken (2003) discusses the concomitant dative-accusative case alternation in German. He represents the maximal structure of a directional PP as follows:

(9) $[_{CP(Path)}$ [C(PATH) $[_{DegP(Path)}$ DEG(PATH) $[_{PathP}$ [PATH $[_{PP}$ P_{DIR} $[_{CP(PLACE)}$ [C(Place) $[_{DegP(Place)}$ [DEG(PLACE) $[_{PlaceP}$ [PLACE $[_{AgrP}$ [Agr $[_{PP}$ P_{LOC} DP]]]]]]]]]]]]]]]

There are two lexical P-heads in this representation, P_{DIR} and P_{LOC}, each with their own extended projection, the Path domain and Place domain respectively. A PathP cannot take a DP as its direct complement. According to Den Dikken, structural case assignment is dependent on the presence of an aspectual head. For locative Ps, this means that P_{LOC} may check dative case if and only if the aspectual projection Place is present in the structure (Den Dikken 2003: 23). Whenever the maximal structure is projected dative case must be checked due to the presence of Place. Accusative case can only be assigned in a directional PP, if P_{DIR} selects PP_{LOC} directly, instead of the full-fledged CP_{Place} as in (9) above. This means

---

3.   A *ground* is the reference object with respect to which a *figure* is located. Due to space restrictions, I refer to Talmy 2001 for an elaborate discussion of figure and ground.

that accusative case may only be assigned if the structure of the directional PP is as follows:

(10) $[_{CP(Path)} [C(Path) [_{DegP(Path)} Deg(Path) [_{PathP} [Path [_{PP} P_{DIR} [_{PP} P_{LOC} DP]]]]]]]$

In this representation PP_{LOC} is directly selected and, therefore, Place is not present. Only in this case may path assign accusative case. This accounts for the fact that dative case is sometimes assigned in directional PPs. Locative PPs in the complement of a V always have a full-fledged projection, whence their dative case marking; locative PPs in the complement of a directional P however may come in a short or long version (see (10) and (9)), leading to accusative or dative case marking respectively. Thus, in Den Dikken's account of the German adpositional case alternation, the functional Path head assigns accusative case on the prerequisite that the object of PlaceP is not already assigned dative case by the functional Place head. In this view, adpositional case is structural, as it is assigned by virtue of some functional head (viz. Path or Place). A PathP may alternatively take a full-fledged CP_{place} or a PP_{LOC} as its complement, leading to dative or accusative case marking.

There are a number of problems with the account of Den Dikken. Zwarts (2006b), in a discussion of Den Dikken (2003), wonders whether the absence of Place in some directional PPs may not lead to a problem of compositionality. Consider German *in das Zimmer* 'into the.ACC room.' In this sentence, one would expect to have a Place function present, just like the Jackendoffian analysis above would predict. The path function TO applies to the place function IN, to convey the meaning INTO. According to Den Dikken (2003) however, the accusative case marking by definition shows that such a head is not present. Accusative is assigned on the prerequisite that the object of PlaceP is not already assigned dative case by the functional Place head. Also, the motivation of the assignment of accusative case is rather opaque. Directional source meaning in German, and in the other languages of my sample, never combines with accusative case. This would mean that source adpositions by definition select for a full-fledged CP_{PLACE}, whereas directional goal and route adpositions may differ in their choice, sometimes going for a short PP_{LOC} as well. There seems to be no rationale behind this pattern. Den Dikken (2003: 28) claims that there is 'a lexical property of *aus* qua P_{DIR} – it is lexically specified (via its *subcategorisation frame*) to select an extended projection of P_{LOC} (not just a "bare" PP_{LOC}).' In my view, this proposal does not account for my finding that source meaning cross-linguistically virtually never combines with accusative case. Also, the assignment of structural dative case by virtue of the presence of Place does not seem to hold cross-linguistically. Some languages combine different oblique cases with different locative adpositions, only one example being Sorbian, which uses locative case for *na* 'on, at', but instrumental case for *pod(e)* 'under, beneath.'

In order to avoid the various problems that a purely structural approach such as Den Dikken's meets, I will come up with a more semantically motivated account. Before I can do this, however, I will first have to show how spatial adpositions can be analyzed semantically.

4.   An analysis of spatial adpositions

Spatial adpositions can be divided into static (or locative) and dynamic (or directional) adpositions. Within the latter category a further distinction can be made between source, route, and goal adpositions. Zwarts (2005b) shows how directional adpositions can contribute to the aspectual properties of a sentence. In the verbal domain, a distinction can be made between telic and atelic predicates, that is between predicates that have a natural endpoint and those that lack one. A simple test to distinguish between the two that suffices for my present purpose is their ability to combine with certain time adjuncts: telic predicates can combine with an adjunct like *in ten minutes*, atelic predicates with an adjunct like *for ten minutes*. The predicates in the following examples are atelic in isolation (cf. *Alex walked/ drove/ran for an hour*), but combined with different directional PPs a difference in aspect may result.

(11)   a.   Alex walked onto the platform/out of the hotel . . . in/*for ten minutes.
       b.   Alex drove toward the mountains/along the river . . . *in/for a day.
       c.   Alex ran around the lake/through the grass . . . in/for one hour.

In (11a) the prepositions *onto* and *out of* lead to telic aspect (shown by the possibility of combining them with *in ten minutes*, but the impossibility of combining them with *for ten minutes*); in (11b) the prepositions *along* and *toward* lead to an atelic reading, and in (11c) the prepositions *around* and *through* allow both readings. Adpositions conveying a telic reading can be said to be bounded; adpositions conveying an atelic reading unbounded. This distinction can be motivated with the notion of path. Zwarts (2005b) defines a path as a directed stretch of space with a starting point, an end point, and points in between on which the path imposes a non-temporal ordering. A PP can be interpreted as a set of paths, and directional adpositions are functions that map objects to a set of paths. A path by itself is not telic or atelic. It depends on the view taken whether a path is directed *into the kitchen, towards the fridge*, or *along the working top*. Zwarts (2005b: 9) assumes paths are 'continuous functions from the real unit interval $[0,1]$ to positions in some model of space. [. . .] [T]he starting point of a path p is p(0), the end point is p(1) and for any $i \in [0,1]$ p(i) is the corresponding point of the path.' Several paths p can form a new path P by the sum operation *concatenation*. When path p starting from A and having an end point B, is concatenated with path q with starting point B and end point C, by concatenation the path p+q from A to C is formed. (Note that p and q are necessarily sub-paths of p+q). Obviously, concatenation can only be applied when two paths are connected head to tail: the end point of p has to be the starting point of q (i.e., $p(1) = q(0)$).

Whether a PP, i.e., a set of paths, is bounded or not depends on the notion *cumulativity* (Zwarts 2005b).

(12)   A set of paths X is *cumulative* iff
     i.   there are p, q ϵ X such that p+q exist and
     ii. for all p, q ϵ X, if p+q exists, then p+q ϵ X

If two paths are *towards* a ground, their sum is as well, on the prerequisite that the sum exists (that is, if it is possible for the two paths to be connected head to tail). Bounded PPs such as *to the house* are not cumulative, as this set of paths P necessarily includes the path that actually reaches the house. Zwarts concludes:

(13)   a.   A PP is unbounded iff it has cumulative reference.
       b.   A PP is bounded iff it does not have cumulative reference.

The aspect of directional PPs is thus represented in cumulativity properties: Unbounded or atelic PPs are cumulative, bounded or telic PPs are not. With this theoretical background now set, we can establish the correspondence between directional meaning and transitivity in the next section.

5.   The correspondence of directional meaning and transitivity

Hopper & Thompson (1980) note that transitivity in the verbal domain is a gradable notion, which is determined by a combination of factors. Clauses can be characterized as more or less transitive. The higher the transitive properties of a clause, the more transitive it is. They claim that '... transitivity is a crucial relationship in language, having a number of universally predictable consequences in grammar, and ... that the defining properties of Transitivity are discourse determined.' Transitivity has to be understood as an 'activity [that] is "carried-over" or "transferred" from an agent to a patient.' Hopper and Thompson decompose the notion into a number of parameters with which the transitivity of a sentence can be determined. I will not discuss all parameters here, but restrict myself to those parameters of interest for my present purpose. These are precisely those parameters that Malchukov (2006) categorizes as properties of the event and the object, recasting Hopper & Thompson's list into a Transitivity scale from subject via verb to object related properties. Following the original numbering, the parameters of concern are B, C, D, I, and J:

(14)   Parameters of Transitivity

	High	Low
B. KINESIS	action	non-action
C. ASPECT	telic	atelic
D. PUNCTUALITY	punctual	non-punctual
I. AFFECTEDNESS OF O	O totally affected	O not affected
J. INDIVIDUATION OF O	O highly individuated	O non-individuated

The property Kinesis distinguishes actions from states: in the former something can be transferred from one participant to another, in the latter this does not hold. In the first sentence below something actually happens to Sally, but this is not the case in the second sentence:

(15)   Action: I hugged Sally.
Non-action: I like Sally.

This kinesis distinction in the verbal domain obviously has its parallel in the distinction between static and dynamic adpositions. This is illustrated in the following example.

(16)   Action/dynamic: John walks to the shop.
Non-action/static: John is at home.

A dynamic event by definition involves more action than a static one. Both action and non-action are compatible with a static meaning, as every event can be said to take place somewhere, but whereas actions can be combined with a change of state implied by a dynamic adposition (as in 16), non-actions cannot: John could not be *sitting* to the shop.

The distinction in Aspect (C) is between a telic action and an atelic action. The former is viewed from its endpoint, and hence, is more effectively transferred to the patient than an atelic action. This is illustrated in the following examples.

(17)   Telic: I ate it up.
Atelic: I am eating it.

The aspectual distinction between telicity and atelicity clearly corresponds to the distinction between bounded and unbounded in the adpositional domain, discussed above. Bounded adpositions are not cumulative, and hence could be said to have an inherent endpoint, whereas unbounded adpositions are cumulative.

(18)   Telic/bounded: into the house
Atelic/unbounded: towards the house

The third transitivity parameter of concern is punctuality (D). Punctuality is about the difference between on-going actions and those that lack an obvious transitional phase between inception and completion. The latter have a more marked effect on their patients than actions that are inherently ongoing, as is illustrated by the following sentences:

(19) Punctual: I kicked the ball.
       Non-punctual: I carried the ball.

Punctuality could be said to correspond to a combination of the property bound-edness and the opposition dynamic-static in the adpositional domain.

(20) Non-punctual/static: John walks in the shop.
       Non-punctual/dynamic, unbounded: John walks towards the shop.
       Punctual/dynamic, bounded: John walks into the shop.

A non-punctual event can correspond to a static adposition: the spatial setting stays the same and there is no clear distinction between inception and completion. When corresponding to a dynamic, unbounded adposition, the relation between figure and ground changes without a clear transition point. A punctual event corresponds to a bounded, dynamic adposition. There is a clear distinction between the moment at which John is outside of the shop, and the moment he enters it. This can be illustrated by means of the following representation (also used in Fong 1997; Vanden Wyngaerd 2001; Zwarts 2006b):

(21) Representation of 'into':
       $\sim P|P$

The tilde is used to negate some predicate or relation P (x being in y, in the present example). In this paper, the '|' is used to indicate the transition moment from $\sim P$ to P. Static adpositions like *in* and dynamic, unbounded adpositions like *toward* lack such a transition moment. Interestingly, route adpositions like *through* could either have a transitional phase or lack one, making the event punctual or non-punctual respectively.

(22) Representations of 'through'
       a.   P
       b. $\sim P|P|\sim P$

In the unbounded version of *through* in (22a), John, for example, could have been walking through the forest all day (non-punctual); in the bounded version of (22b), John could have walked through the forest in an hour (punctual).

Rehbein & Van Genabith (2006), in this respect, discuss an example from German in which an event of rain soaking the soil is perceived either as punctual (23a) or non-punctual (23b), thereby nicely illustrating the case alternation of my present concern.

(23) a. [Der   Regen] sickert   in   die   Erde ein.
          the.NOM rain   soak.3.SG IN   the.ACC   soil PRT
          'The rain soaks into the soil.'
      b. [Der   Regen] sickert   in   der   Erde ein.
          the.NOM   rain   soak.3.SG IN   the.DAT   soil PRT
          'The rain soaks the soil.'

The difference lies in the fact that in the first sentence, the rain water enters the region of the object (~P|P), whereas in the second sentence, the rain water is already there and soaking through the region (P).

The next two transitivity parameters are affectedness (I) and individuation (J). Affectedness, notoriously a vague notion, concerns the degree to which an action is transferred to a patient. In fact, it may serve as a cover term for all other transitivity parameters, as all distinctions made above could be explained along some dimension of affectedness. Hopper & Thompson connect affectedness to the notion Object Individuation, which is a cover term for a number of properties of the object. It constitutes both the distinctness of the patient from the agent, and the distinctness from its own background. A prototypical individuated object is said to be a proper noun, human, concrete, singular, countable and referential and definite; a non-individuated object is prototypically a common noun, inanimate, abstract, plural, a mass noun and non-referential. The more individuated the object, the more effectively an action can be transferred to it, and hence, the more affected it is. This can be seen in the following example from Hebrew, in which the object *milxama* 'war' is only marked with accusative case when it is definite:

(24) Hebrew (Aissen 2003)
      a. Ha-seret   her?a   et-ha-milxama.
          the-movie   showed ACC-the-war
          'The movie showed the war.'
      b. Ha-seret   her?a   (*et-)milxama.
          the-movie   showed (ACC-)war
          'The movie showed a war.'

The affectedness of the object can be compared to the extent to which the path covers the ground. In this comparison, the ground of a route adposition could be said to be more affected than the ground of a goal, since for the former the whole ground is part of the path, whereas for the object of a goal adposition, the spatial extension of the ground is irrelevant. Within route meaning, the ground can even be further covered. We already saw an example of this for Ancient Greek in Section 2, repeated here in translation only for convenience.

(25) a. The spear of bronze went through his shoulder.
      b. turning around through the glens.

This difference is illustrated by Figure 1 (taken from Luraghi 2003). Clearly in Figure 1 the path covers the ground in the figure on the right more extensively than in the figure on the left. The more complex the path, the greater the part of the ground that is covered by it. If we translate the degree to which a ground is covered into direct object terms, we could say that the ground in (25b) is more affected than in (25a).

Figure 1. Representation of route paths.

Let us now have a closer look at the properties of the adpositional object itself, rather than at the properties of the phrase it appears in. Grammatical subject and object do not always cover the same class of participants in an event. The subject can be, and indeed often is, a real agent, in the sense of a volitional, active causer of the event, but sometimes the subject can be patient-like as well.

(26) a. Suzanne kisses John.
      b. Suzanne underwent an operation.

This mismatch between grammatical and semantic properties has led linguists to distinguish between grammatical and thematic roles. The latter express the semantic role a participant plays in an event. However, the lack of precise definitions and growing lists of thematic roles has led to a sloppy use of this notion. Therefore, Dowty (1991) proposes a new account of thematic roles introducing so-called Proto-Roles. Dowty argues that thematic roles are difficult to define because they are not discrete categories at all, but rather contextually modified instantiations of cluster concepts. Two Proto-Roles suffice to describe the argument selection of verbs, namely Proto-Agent and Proto-Patient. Dowty (1991: 572) 'preliminarily' lists a number of semantically independent contributing properties for both roles. For my present purpose, I will only focus on the Proto-Patient properties. Again, I will only discuss the relevant ones, omitting two properties while maintaining the original numbering.

(27) Contributing properties for the Patient Proto-Role
      A. Undergoes change of state
      B. Incremental theme
      D. Stationary relative to movement of another participant

The first property, Change of state, captures both coming into existence and ceasing to exist, and both 'definite and indefinite' change of state (Dowty 1991: 574).

Although Dowty is not explicit about the distinction between definite and indefinite change of state, this seems to be about the specification of the change. *John paints his house* would then be indefinite; *John paints his house from green to pink* definite. Change of state of course connects with the transitivity parameter affectedness: the more affected the object, the bigger the change of state. The second property, Incremental theme, may need a little bit more explanation. An incremental theme is a new role category Dowty introduces. The aspect of telic predicates depends on their NP arguments. This is captured in the principle that the meaning of a telic predicate is a homomorphism from its structured theme argument denotations into a structured domain of events. A homomorphism in this context is a function from an argument NP to its governing verb, which preserves some structural relation determined for the NP in a similar relation determined for the verb (Dowty 1991: 567). This 'preserved relation' can be illustrated for telic predicates by the part-of-relation. If x is part of y then a telic predicate that maps y to some event e maps x to an event e' which is part of e. The state of the Incremental theme is indicative for the whole of the predicate. The proportion of John's house that is red tells you something about the extent to which the event of John painting his house is finished. An Incremental Theme is an object on which the separate stages of the change caused by the event are actually distinguishable (cf. also Vanden Wyngaerd 2001). The last property (D) basically states that a non-moving argument makes a better patient than a moving one.

The Proto-Roles are of importance for argument selection in the way defined by the 'Argument Selection Principle' (Dowty 1991: 576).

> In predicates with grammatical subject and object, the argument for which
> the predicate entails the greatest number of Proto-Agent properties will be
> lexicalized as the subject of the predicate; the argument having the greatest
> number of Proto-Patient entailments will be lexicalized as the direct object.

An argument that is an incremental theme, that is changed, or stationary relative to another participant is more likely to be marked as the structural direct object. The higher in transitivity a clause is in the definition of Hopper and Thompson (1980), the more Proto properties the verb entails for its arguments in the definition of Dowty (1991), and vice versa. In a highly transitive clause, the two arguments are typically an agent and a patient, rather than a beneficiary and an instrument, for example.

Here too, we can establish a correspondence with the adpositional domain. The constituent of a directional adposition is more patient-like than the constituent of a locative adposition. The former undergoes a change of state (A): it is either reached, entered, or traversed by a figure. The ground in a locative PP, on the other hand, does not change at all. In directional route meanings, the ground is like an Incremental theme (B): the different stages in which something is being 'traversed' can be distinguished, and this corresponds to the extent to which the passing event is completed. However, in locative PPs nothing happens with the ground, rendering it by definition unable to be an Incremental theme. For both directional and locative meaning it holds, by Talmy's (2001) definition, that the adpositional object is stationary (D). But only in case of directional objects could the fact that the object is stationary be formulated with respect to the movement of the other participant.

The idea of a correspondence between transitivity or patienthood and directional goal and route meaning can also be verified in an ergative language like Basque. In Basque, motion and location verbs can give rise to a transitivity alternation (Hualdé & Ortiz de Urbina 2003: 369). In the alternation shown below, transitive structures are produced by changing the auxiliary from intransitive *izan* 'be' to transitive *edun* 'have'. If the subject were expressed, its marking indeed would change from absolute to ergative. According to Hualdé & Ortiz de Urbina (2003: 369), the transitive alternate produces an 'affected' reading, where the whole surface of the movement gets 'used up'.

(28)   Ibai   hartatik   igaro   dira.
       river   that.ABL   pass.by   AUX.INTR
       'They went through that river.'

(29)   Ibai   hura   igaro   dute.
       river   that.ABS   pass.by   AUX.TR
       'They crossed that river.'

The ease with which the PP *ibai hartatik* 'through that river' of the ablative construction in (28), is promoted to a direct object in (29), may serve as support for the similarity of a route object and a transitive object.

Another piece of evidence for the correspondence between directional meaning and transitivity comes from so-called spray-load alternations. These alternations are a well-known phenomenon in transitivity theories (cf. Dowty 1991; Anderson 1971; Baker 1997; Svenonius 2001, 2002). In these constructions an object is sprayed or loaded with some substance. Two alternative constructions can be chosen, that virtually have the same meaning. In the first construction the loaded or sprayed object is the direct object of the spray/load verb whereas the substance sprayed with is expressed in an adpositional phrase, in the other construction this is done the other way around. According to Dowty (1991) and Anderson (1971), the two constructions are not complete paraphrases. In the a-sentences below the total supply of hay or paint would be used, while the b-sentences would suggest that the wall is fully covered with paint, or the truck is completely filled with hay respectively.

(30)   a.   Mary loaded the hay onto the truck.
       b.   Mary loaded the truck with the hay.

(31)   a.   Mary sprayed the paint onto the wall.
       b.   Mary sprayed the wall with the paint.

Whether or not the two constructions differ in meaning does not really matter here. What is important, however, is that the objects of the directional goal adpositions, i.e., the goals, in the a-examples resemble Proto-Patients to such an extent, that they can easily be put in direct object position in the b-constructions.

In her dissertation on transitivity, Rice (1987) discusses the prepositional verb (VPP, verbs to which a preposition has coalesced grammatically and/or semantically) in English. Often, verbs that are intransitive in themselves (like *swing*) become highly transitive with the addition of a preposition (*swing at*). According to Rice, some of these prepositions are highly transitive inherently. The spatial meaning conveyed by prepositions is usually thought of as simple verbal modification. According to Rice, this meaning sometimes can serve as a lexical instantiation of the channel that the action must pass across as its effect is carried from one participant to another. Rice argues that in examples like *the suspect swung at the policeman, the muddy child climbed on the new couch,* and *that flea-bitten dog has slept in this bed again* the prepositional object is more like a full-fledged participant in the action than only a spatial reference point. The prepositional object is not only capable of being affected by the action, but the NP of the PP behaves like a direct object complement with respect to passivization as well. One could very easily passivize the above examples into *the policeman was swung at, the couch was climbed on, the bed was slept in.* However, this cannot be done across the board, as Rice shows. One cannot as easily change *sleep/exercise in the living room* into *the living room was exercised/slept in.* One way or another, the object has to be 'affected' in order to passivize it; a living room apparently is too big to suffer from an exercising or sleeping event. This ability to passivize is not an absolute distinction, according to Rice, but rather a continuum.[4]

In this corpus research, Rice looks at the percentage of VPPs that may passivize. She finds *on, to,* and *at* (qualified as goal oriented, and invoking a terminate path) highly transitivizing. The adpositions are in maximal contrast with non-transitive, source oriented prepositions which invoke an initiative path: *off* and *from,* which very rarely passivize.

(32)   *The bed was fallen off / tumbled off / slipped off / slid off by the child.

---

4.   The view on the passivization distinction as a continuum might explain the questions an anonymous reviewer had with respect to the grammaticality judgments of some of Rice's examples.

Passivization is in particular possible when motion and manner are combined in the event description. In these cases, the object of an adposition can be thought of as a real participant. The verb *go to* in the example below is neutral with respect to manner, hence the ungrammaticality of its passive construction. Transfer, according to Rice, requires both a medium and an address, while pure movement requires neither. The other verbs do combine motion and manner, and passivize without any problems.

> (33)   The narrow footbridge was walked on / trodden on / run on / trampled on / stumbled on / wobbled on / slid on / slipped on / *gone on by the kindergartners.

Also, Rice notes that the properties of the object are of importance. The more diffuse or spacious the endpoint is, the less likely it will serve as a participant of the action and the more likely it will be construed as a setting (cf. the transitivity parameter object individuation above).

> (34)   John /* the countryside was rushed to by Mary.

The effect on the passive participant, marking the successful transfer of something, is considered the essence of transitivity. Rice distinguishes *channels* from *paths*. A path is only a verbal modifier, describing the trajectory of some motion event. Channels, however, are said to be more like full-fledged participants than spatial reference points. Channels, unlike paths, are transitive. The extent to which an arbitrary path becomes a (physical) channel determines the transitivity of the VPP. According to Rice (1987) *on*, *to*, and *at* suggest a channel of transfer, whereas *off* and *from* suggest a path of movement.

In conclusion, Rice (1987), too, notes that adpositions can be analyzed in terms of transitivity. Based on corpus findings she argues that complements of goal oriented adpositions can be passivized, whereas source oriented ones virtually cannot. This means that, indeed, as outlined in the previous sections, there seems to be a correspondence between directional goal and route meaning and transitivity. Also, what has become clear in this discussion, and what I have not discussed so far on purpose, is that source adpositions behave differently from other directional adpositions. But, why would source meaning behave differently from goal meaning?

6.   On source

Source meaning patterns differently from route and goal meaning. This obviously yields a problem. If the directional goal is transitive object-like because of all characteristics mentioned above, then why does the same not hold for source meaning? Consider the following representations:

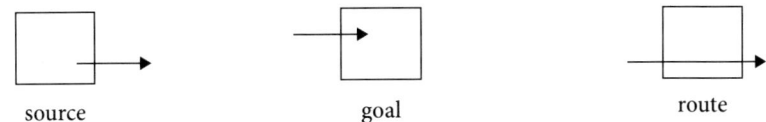

source   goal   route

Figure 2.   Goal vs. source meaning.

All properties that make goal meaning more transitive-like, seem to hold to the same extent for source meaning. That is, the properties Kinesis, Aspect, Punctuality, being stationary with respect to some motion, and a change of state similarly apply to source meaning as well. Still, source meaning is virtually never assigned accusative case.

The explanation lies in the very definition of transitivity. Recall the definition of transitivity of Hopper & Thompson (1980). Transitivity is an activity that is transferred from an agent to a patient. The spatial metaphor says it all: the 'to the patient' is a goal, the 'from an agent' a source. Source meaning is more like the agent than the patient. It is the participant from which the transferring event originates, which causes, or starts the event. Indeed, Dowty (1991) argues that Source and Proto-Agent have a conceptual connection. In some events, like throwing something or handing an object to someone, the agent stays behind, while the object moves away from it. The agent is the starting point for some action. Anderson (1971) too notes the parallels between ergative and ablative case. As an illustration, he mentions the superficially identical representation of the two roles in languages like Latin, in which *a(b)* expresses ablative meaning, as well as the agent in passive constructions. Finally, Rice (1987) claims that the failure to passivize is due to the direction of transfer from agent to patient.

7.   On accusative case

Accusative case is generally thought of as a structural case, i.e., the result of a purely syntactic licensing requirement on noun phrases (cf. a.o. Chomsky 1981), which implies that it lacks inherent semantics. In this section, I will argue that accusative case in fact does have its own meaning (cf. a.o. Luraghi 2003; Malchukov 2006; Vainikka & Maling 1996). Cross-linguistically, the structural use of accusative case denoting the direct object indeed is abundantly attested. However, in languages that exhibit a case alternation in the marking of the direct object, accusative case is quite often used for the objects of highly transitive verbs, whereas some other case (or no case) is used for verbs that are lower in transitivity. Therefore, I claim that accusative case has inherent meaning, namely the meaning of a Proto-Patient. Most of the time, this meaning is overruled by the structural use of accusative case as object marking, but sometimes this inherent meaning may become manifest. Also in the adpositional domain, where no structural constraints of the VP apply, the inherent Proto-Patient meaning of the accusative can emerge as we will see later. First consider the following sentences from Icelandic (Barðdal 2001, quoted in Naess 2004):

(35)   a.   Hann   klóraði   mig.
             he.NOM scratched me.ACC
             'He scratched me.' (painfully)
       b.   Hann   klóraði   mér.
             he.NOM scratched me.DAT
             'He scratched me.' (because my back was itching)

Alternations like these are often explained by assigning the non-accusative construction a special meaning: either the event described by the verb is said to be not finished yet, or the object is less patient-like due to claimed increased prominence. This neglects the fact that in alternations like these, the accusative form consequently marks the more patient-like object. Indeed, according to Naess (2004), (35b) implies that the person being scratched had an itch and is actually benefiting from the event, whereas (35a) denotes an act of violence, causing the patient to feel pain. The accusative, then, denotes a more Proto-Patient-like meaning. This might seem like a trivial way of describing the very same thing in other words, but I think it is not. Instead of disregarding any inherent meaning of the accusative by saying that it is the (default) structural case, whereas the oblique case does have its own meaning, the accusative itself is assigned inherent meaning.[5]

In Russian too, objects of high transitive verbs are assigned accusative case, whereas those of low transitive ones get genitive. This is illustrated in the following examples (A. Malchukov, p.c.):

(36)   Ja bojusj mam-y.
       I   fear   mam-GEN
       'I am afraid of (my) mother.'

(37)   Ja udaril (/obnjal)   mam-u.
       I   hit   (/embraced)   mam-ACC
       'I hit (/embraced) (my) mother.'

---

5.   As an anonymous reviewer correctly pointed out, the disappearance of the accusative case under passivization may be a problem for its inherent status claimed here.

The verbs 'to hit' and 'to embrace' are higher in transitivity than 'to fear', hence the accusative case marking on the object in (37), but not in (36). This case alternation is not the same as the 'split' type discussed by Aissen (2003). Aissen argues that accusative case is used to distinguish the core arguments of a transitive verb. On this account the case alternation is dependent on the properties of the DP. Here, however, the case alternation seems to mark increasing transitivity. If accusative case were used to discriminate between two arguments, there would be no reason for this function to apply in (37) but not in (36) as the prominence relation between the two arguments *I* and *my mother* is the same in both sentences. Although the Russian alternation is not an example of fluid case alternation as the linguistic context changes, we do find the more Proto-Patient-like object marked with accusative case again.

I will account for this case alternation using Optimality Theory (OT). In OT grammar rules are universal and violable constraints, which can be in conflict with each other. Weak constraints can be violated in order to satisfy stronger ones, and every language has its own specific constraint ranking, leading to cross-linguistic variation (Prince & Smolensky 1993/2002). Preferences in interpretation are phrased as violable constraints as well (cf. Hendriks & de Hoop 2001). I propose the following constraint for the meaning of the accusative:

(38)   The Accusative meaning constraint
       ACC/PROTO-P: Accusative case denotes Proto-Patient meaning

The structural use of the accusative mentioned above would be motivated by a high ranked (syntax) constraint like the following:[6]

(39)   The structural use of the accusative constraint
       OBJ/ACC: Mark the object with accusative case

OT evaluation processes are represented in tableaux. In these tableaux, the constraints are ranked in the top row from left to right depending on their importance. Input candidates (which are form-meaning pairs in Bidirectional OT, to be discussed below) are listed in the left column. The violations a candidate yields are marked by an asterisk in the corresponding cell. With the constraints OBJ/ACC and ACC/PROTO-P illustrated in the tableau below, it is clear why ACC/PROTO-P stays hidden in a language that does not allow for case variation on its direct object.

In standard OT, only one candidate is found optimal. As is clear from Table 1, accusative case is selected for any object (indicated by '☞'), independent of the

---

6.   Of course, much more could be, and indeed has been, said about this structural use. I do not want to claim that these two constraints can account for all uses of the accusative case; I only want to show how Acc/Proto-P normally remains invisible.

Table 1. OT syntax: the distribution of the accusative

Input: non Proto-Patient-like object	OBJ /ACC	ACC/PROTO-P
☞ ACC		*
Any non-ACC	*!	
Input: non Proto-Patient-like object		
☞ ACC		
Any non-ACC	*!	

thematic role, or contributing Proto-Role properties, of the argument. Any non-accusative form of the object, be it Proto-Patient-like or not, leads to a violation of Obj/Acc, which is expressed by the asterisk in the corresponding cell. The violation of this constraint is decisive, as the accusative marked object is the only candidate left. This is indicated by the addition of an exclamation mark to the violation. Obj/Acc is decisive for all inputs and Acc/Proto-P cannot become manifest in languages without case alternation in the verbal domain.

Instead of going only either from form to meaning or from meaning to form, Bidirectional Optimality Theory (BiOT) gives a general procedure of optimization of the relation of form and meaning, simultaneously optimizing in both directions, from meaning to form, and from form to meaning. Hence, BiOT evaluates *form-meaning pairs* (Blutner et al. 2006). In bidirectional OT a form-meaning pair is recursively defined as super-optimal if and only if there is no other super-optimal form-meaning pair with a less marked form that expresses the same meaning, and there is no other super-optimal form-meaning pair with a different meaning that is a better interpretation of that same form. This yields two super-optimal form-meaning pairs, namely the unmarked form with the unmarked meaning, and the marked form with the marked meaning. (Due to space restrictions I refer to Blutner et al. 2006 for a discussion of BiOT). Thus, BiOT is ideal for dealing with meaning and form optionality in the same linguistic context in which there is a one-to-one correspondence of meaning and form (de Hoop & Malchukov 2006). If languages allow for fluid case alternation, we find precisely such form and meaning optionality.

In the BiOT analysis, the same constraints as used above account for the patterns of Icelandic and Russian (exx. 35–37).

In BiOT there are two rounds of optimization, in which the second super-optimal pair is determined by means of the first. In the first round of optimization, the combination of the accusative combined with the Proto-Patient meaning is found super-optimal as it does not yield a violation of any constraint. (Note that super-optimal pairs are indicated by the marker '☜'). All other candidates violate

Table 2. biOT: structural fluid case marking

Input: ⟨form, meaning⟩	OBJ /ACC	ACC/PROTO-P
☞ ⟨ACC, Proto-P⟩		
⟨ACC, non-Proto-P⟩		*
⟨OBL, Proto-P⟩	*	
☞ ⟨OBL, non-Proto-P⟩	*	

one or more constraints. In the second round the combination of some oblique case with the less Proto-Patient-like meaning is found super-optimal, as all other candidates are blocked by the first super-optimal pair. The pair ⟨ACC, non-Proto-P⟩ is blocked as the first super-optimal candidate combines this form with the Proto-Patient meaning. The pair ⟨OBL, Proto-P⟩ is blocked as the first super-optimal candidate combines this meaning with the accusative form already. The last form-meaning pair ⟨OBL, non-proto-P⟩ is neither blocked due to its form, nor to its meaning, and therefore becomes the second super-optimal candidate.

8. A BiOT account for adpositional case alternation

Now, let us return to the domain of adpositions. Static adpositions could be said to be less marked qua meaning than dynamic ones. There are a number of reasons to argue for this difference in markedness of meaning. First, directional meaning by definition implies a change in place (cf. Helmantel 1998; Jackendoff 1983). Therefore, the meaning of dynamic adpositions is always an extension of the meaning of locative ones. Also, as was briefly mentioned above, locative PPs can combine with any event (both actions and states), whereas it is only possible for dynamic PPs to combine with actions. Such combinatorial possibilities are indicative for markedness. The difference is also reflected in the order of acquisition of spatial prepositions, as locatives are acquired before directionals (Bowerman & Choi 2001).

If possible, then, a spatial adposition is preferably interpreted as locative rather than directional. Consider example (40).

(40) a. in de goal
          'in the goal'
      b. De bal ligt in de goal.
          'The ball lies in the goal.'
      c. Jan schiet de bal in de   goal.
          'Jan shoots the ball into the goal.'

The preferred meaning of an ambiguous adposition is locative. Indeed, in (40a), where no further context is given, this reading is obtained. A non-action context as in (40b), maintains this reading. A directional reading can be obtained by the right context as in (40c), where the motion verb *schieten* 'to shoot' enforces a goal reading. But even here it is possible to get a locative reading in which the whole shooting event takes place in the goal.

The result of these findings can be stated in the following markedness constraint:

(41)   The complexity constraint
        *COMPLEXITY: avoid a complex interpretation if possible (i.e., interpret as locative rather than directional if possible).

Of course, the complexity constraint can only hold in cases where both a simple and a complex interpretation in principle are possible for a form. For English *into*, by definition only the directional goal reading is allowed, therefore *COMPLEXITY cannot apply. For Dutch prepositional *in*, on the other hand, the constraint does apply, as two readings in principle are possible.

Now, with these constraints established, we can account for all adpositional fluid differential case marking attested in Section 2, as once more illustrated by the following Russian example:

(42)   Russian (Malchukov, p.c.)
        a.   Ja xodil v   magazin.
             I   went   V   shop.ACC
             'I went to the shop.'
        b.   Ja xodil v   magazine.
             I   went   V   shop.DAT
             'I was walking in the shop.'

Consider the following tableau in which this general pattern is illustrated:

Table 3. The general pattern

	OBJ/ACC	ACC/PROTO-P	*COMPLEXITY
☞ ⟨OBL, LOC⟩			
⟨OBL, DIR⟩			*
⟨ACC, LOC⟩		*	
☞ ⟨ACC, DIR⟩			*

The highest ranked constraint OBJ/ACC is vacuously satisfied in this context, as there is no direct object to be structurally marked. In the first round of optimization, the form-meaning pair ⟨OBL, LOC⟩ is found super-optimal as it yields no violations of the constraints whatsoever. As explained above, a locative meaning is less complex than a directional one. The candidates ⟨OBL, DIR⟩ and ⟨ACC, DIR⟩ are out as their directional meaning violates *COMPLEXITY. The candidate ⟨ACC, LOC⟩

violates ACC/PROTO-P as it combines the non-Proto-Patient-like locative mean-ing with the accusative case form. In a second round, both the pairs ⟨OBL, DIR⟩ and ⟨ACC, LOC⟩ are again out, as they are blocked by the first super-optimal pair: the oblique form of the former and the locative meaning of the latter are already combined in the first superoptimal pair. The pair ⟨ACC, DIR⟩ then comes out as the second super-optimal pair. Although it violates *COMPLEXITY, there is no better form for the directional meaning, nor a better interpretation for the accusative form. With one tableau, we have accounted for all adpositional case alternations of Section 2 in which oblique case pairs up with locative meaning and accusative case pairs up with goal meaning.

Also, the more complex *dia* 'through' example from Classical Greek can be accounted for with these constraints. Again consider the alternation from (7) above, only given in translation here.

(43) a. The spear of bronze went through his shoulder.GEN.
       b. turning around through the glens.ACC.

This difference between the two constructions (represented in Figure 1 above) was said to be the extent to which the path covered the ground. Translated into object terms, we could say that the more covered, the more Patient-like an object is, hence the asterisk in the first column for the short route interpretation of the accusative form in Table 4. Also, a short, straight route is less complex than a long, complex one. There-fore, long route meaning yields a violation of the constraint *COMPLEXITY.

Table 4. The route-route distinction

		OBJ /ACC	ACC/PROTO-P	*COMPLEXITY
☞	⟨OBL, short route⟩			
	⟨OBL, long route⟩			*
	⟨ACC, short route⟩		*	
☞	⟨ACC, long route⟩			*

The pair ⟨OBL, short route⟩ is found super-optimal in the first round of optimiza-tion, as it leads to no violation of any constraint. Following bidirectional reasoning, the pairs ⟨OBL, long route⟩ and ⟨ACC, short route⟩ are out of competition, as there is a better interpretation for the oblique form and a better form for the short route meaning that are already combined in the first super-optimal pair. The pair ⟨ACC, long route⟩ is the second super-optimal pair.

One could argue that the adpositional object of (43a) is more like a Proto-Patient than that of (43b), as a shoulder obviously suffers more from the piercing of a spear than glens from a moving event. This likeliness however seems not to be determined on such grounds. A spear transfixing a shield is also expressed with genitive case marking on the ground, as illustrated in the following example:

(44)   Ancient Greek   (Iliad 3.357–358, taken from Luraghi 2003: 168)
       dià mèn aspídos   êlthe   phaeinês   óbrimon   égkhos
       DIA PTC shield.GEN.F   go.AOR.3SG   shining.GEN.F mighty.N/A   spear.N/A
       'The mighty spear went through the bright shield.'

Now, what can we say about the form of the adpositional objects? Oblique cases could be considered the default option for adpositional objects. It is intuitively clear that in order to avoid ambiguity languages should not choose a case, viz. accusative, already in use marking the verbal object as the default for adpositions. A second argument in favor of this is the case preference of newly derived or not completely grammaticalized adpositions. For example, in Greek, improper prepositions always combine with genitive case, and in Sorbian, adpositions derived from adverbs or nouns never take accusative. Another telling argument is that accusative case is used more often in case alternations than as the only option for adpositions. Indeed, Zwarts (2006a) and Bierwisch (1988) note that dative should be regarded as the unmarked case for adpositions in German and not accusative. This is illustrated by the fact that dative case, not accusative, is taking over the use of genitive case in combination with prepositions. Finally, a very notable fact is that if accusative case is used in the adpositional domain in the languages I have considered, it most often expresses directional goal meaning. Within case alternations this even holds almost exclusively. As oblique case has a wider range, it could be said to be less marked. Indeed, in my language sample, there were many more instances of adpositions combining with oblique case than with accusative. (Cf. also Zwarts 2005a & Volk 2003 for German). All these findings imply that in the adpositional domain oblique case is preferred to accusative.

9.   Conclusion

In this paper, I have shown that there is a correspondence between spatial meaning and the notions of transitivity and Proto-Patient. Transitivity and Proto-Patient characteristics can straightforwardly be used in the analysis of adpositional phrases. By doing so, directional goal and route meaning can be analyzed as more transitive-like than locative meaning, and the object of goal and route adpositions as more patient-like than the object of source and locative ones. In context, a transitivity distinction can be made within directional meaning as well.

Furthermore, I have claimed that accusative case inherently has Proto-Patient meaning. This inherent meaning can become manifest when languages allow for case alternation. Also, I have argued that locative meaning is preferred to directional meaning if there is a choice, as locative meaning is less complex and less marked than directional meaning.

With these findings, I have accounted for the adpositional accusative-oblique case alternation using a bidirectional approach. The interaction between the constraints *Complexity and Acc/Proto-P was shown to account for all attested cross-linguistic accusative-oblique case alternation. Locative, or less transitive, meanings consistently pair up with an oblique case form, whereas directional, or more transitive, meanings combine with accusative case.

References

Anderson, J.M. 1971. *The Grammar of Case. Toward a Localistic Theory*. Cambridge: CUP.

Aissen, J. 2003. Differential object marking: Iconicity vs. economy. *Natural Language and Linguistic Theory* 21: 435–483.

Baker, M. 1997. Thematic roles and syntactic structure. In *Elements of Grammar: Handbook of Generative Syntax*, L. Haegeman (ed.), 55–89. Dordrecht: Kluwer.

Barðdal, J. 2001. Case in Icelandic. A Synchronic, Diachronic and Comparative Approach. PhD Dissertation, Department of Scandinavian languages, University of Lund.

Bielec, D. 1998. *Polish. An Essential Grammar*. London: Routledge.

Bierwisch, M. 1988. On the grammar of local prepositions. In *Syntax, Semantik und Lexikon* [Studia Grammatica 19], M. Bierwisch, W. Motsch & I. Zimmermann (eds), 1–66. Berlin: Akademie-Verlag.

Blutner, R., de Hoop, H. & Hendriks, P. 2006. *Optimal Communication* [CSLI Lecture Notes 177]. Stanford CA: CSLI.

Bowerman, M. & Choi, S. 2001. Shaping meanings for language: Universal and language-specific in the acquisition of spatial semantic categories. In *Language Acquisition and Conceptual Development*, M. Bowerman & S.C. Levinson (eds), 475–511. Cambridge: CUP.

Chomsky, N. 1981. *Lectures on Government and Binding*. Dordrecht: Foris.

den Dikken, M. 2003. On the syntax of locative and directional adpositional phrases. Ms., The Graduate Center of the City University of New York.

Dowty, D. 1991. Thematic proto-roles and argument selection. *Language* 76(3): 547–619.

Fong, V. 1997. The Order of Things: What Directional Locatives Denote. PhD Dissertation, University of Stanford.

Helmantel, M. 1998. Simplex adpositions and vector theory. *The Linguistic Review* 15: 361–388.

Hendriks, P. & de Hoop, H. 2001. Optimality theoretic semantics. *Linguistics and Philosophy* 24: 1–32.

de Hoop, H. & Malchukov, A. 2006. Fluid case marking. Ms., Radboud University Nijmegen.

Hopper, P.J. & Thompson, S.A. 1980. Transitivity in grammar and discourse. *Language* 56(2): 251–299.

Hualde, J.I. & Ortiz de Urbina, J. (eds) 2003. *A Grammar of Basque*. Berlin: Mouton de Gruyter.

Jackendoff, R. 1983. *Semantics and Cognition*. Cambridge MA: The MIT Press.

Jackendoff, R. 1990. *Semantic Structures*. Cambridge MA: The MIT Press.

Koopman, H. 1997. Prepositions, postpositions, circumpositions and particles: The structure of Dutch PPs. Ms., UCLA.

Lestrade, S.A.M. 2006. Adpositional Case. MA Dissertation, Radboud University Nijmegen.

Luraghi, S. 2003. *On the Meaning of Prepositions and Cases* [Studies in Language Companion Series]. Amsterdam: John Benjamins.

Malchukov, A. 2006. Transitivity parameters and transitivity alternations: Constraining co-variation. In *Studies on Case, Valency and Transitivity* [Studies in Language Companion Series 77], L. Kulikov A. Malchukov & P. de Swart (eds), Amsterdam: John Benjamins.

Naess, Å. 2004. What markedness marks: The markedness problem with direct objects. *Lingua* 114(9–10): 1186–1212.

Prince, A. & Smolensky, P. 1993/2002. Optimality theory. Constraint interaction in generative grammar. *Rutgers University Center for Cognitive Science Technical Report* 2.

Rehbein, I. & van Genabith J. 2006. German particle verbs and pleonastic prepositions. *Proceedings of the Third ACL-SIGSEM Workshop on Prepositions*. Trento: EACL.

Rice, S.A. 1987. Towards a Cognitive Model of Transitivity. PhD Dissertation, UCSD.

Rotteveel Mansveld, F.G. & Waleson, R. 1970. *Latijnse Leergang. Grammatica.* Groningen: Wolters-Noordhof.

Schuster-Šewc, H. 1999. *Grammar of the Upper Sorbian Language. Phonology and Morphology* [LINCOM studies in Slavic Linguistics 3], Translated by G.H. Toops. Munich: Lincom.

Svenonius, P. 2001. Case and Event Structure. *ZASPIL* 26.

Svenonius, P. 2002. Icelandic case and the structure of events. *Journal of Comparative Germanic Linguistics* 5: 97–225.

Svenonius, P. 2006. The category P. Course handouts, LOT Winter School in Linguistics, Amsterdam, January 9–13, 2006.

Talmy, L. 2001. *Toward a Cognitive Semantics*. Cambridge MA: The MIT Press.

Vainikka, A. & Maling, J. 1996. Is partitive case inherent or structural? In *Partitives: Studies on the Distribution and Meaning of Partitive Expressions*, J. Hoeksema (ed.), 179–208. Berlin: Mouton de Gruyter.

Vanden Wyngaerd, G. 2001. Measuring events. *Language* 77(1): 61–90.

Volk, M. 2003. German prepositions and their kin. A survey with respect to the resolution of P attachment ambiguities. In *Proceedings of the Workshop on The Linguistic Dimensions of Prepositions and their Use in Computational Linguistics Formalisms and Applications*. Toulouse.

Zwarts, J. 2005a. The case of prepositions: Government and compositionality in German PPs. Ms. Radboud Universiteit Nijmegen.

Zwarts, J. 2005b. Prepositional aspect and the algebra of paths *Linguistics and Philosophy* 28: 739–779.

Zwarts, J. 2006a. Case marking directions: The accusative in German PPs. Ms. Radboud Universiteit Nijmegen.

Zwarts, J. 2006b. Aspects of a typology of direction. Ms., Radboud Universiteit Nijmegen.

Pragmatic factors and variation in the expression of spatial goals

The case of *into* vs. *in*

Tatiana Nikitina
Stanford University / ILI RAN, St. Petersburg

Languages often allow for alternative ways of describing the same motion event. This paper investigates the use of *into* vs. directional *in* as alternative strategies for expressing spatial goals in English. Based on results of a corpus study, I discuss factors that favor the use of one or the other strategy. Firstly, *in* tends to be used only when the directional meaning can be inferred from some other element of the sentence. Secondly, the choice of a preposition is influenced by factors that are relevant for the pragmatic construal of a motion event, suggesting that pragmatic notions, such as the relative prominence of different subparts in the conceptualization of a complex event, may affect the morphosyntactic encoding of a locative argument.*

1. Variation in the expression of spatial goals

1.1 Strategies for expressing goals

Languages vary widely with respect to the means by which they encode events of directed motion. Variation in the lexical encoding of spatial goals is particularly well-studied (Talmy 1975, 1985, 1991; Slobin 1996, 2006, inter alia). In an early study of the typology of expressions of directed motion, Talmy (1975, 1985) formulated a distinction between *path languages* and *manner languages*, based on whether directed motion can be encoded by manner of motion verbs with adpositional goal phrases. The two patterns are contrasted in (1a) from Spanish (a path language) and (1b) from English (a manner language). In English, but not in Spanish, verbs of

---

* I am grateful to Beth Levin, Joan Bresnan, and the audience of the *Syntax and Semantics of Spatial P* in Utrecht for their comments on earlier versions of this paper, as well as to the editors and the reviewers for their help and valuable suggestions. Needless to say, I alone am responsible for all errors that remain.

manner of motion combine with prepositional phrases indicating the goal of motion. In Spanish, the manner of motion cannot be expressed in this way. It can only be specified by an adverbial or gerundive phrase, and an additional non-manner verb must be used as the main verb:

> (1)   a.   Entró corriendo/volando/nadando a la cueva.   (Talmy 1985: 111)
>   'He entered the cave running/flying/swimming.'
>   b.   He ran/flew/swam into the cave.   (Talmy 1985: 111)

Talmy explains this contrast by appealing to a difference in *lexicalization patterns* of motion verbs. In English, verbs of motion conflate the fact of motion and the manner of motion, while in Spanish, verbs can only conflate the fact of motion and its path (but not manner).

The distinction between path languages and manner languages roughly corresponds to a difference in the inventory of devices for distinguishing goals from static locations that are available in a given language (Aske 1989; Slobin 1996; Song 1997; Song & Levin 1998; Beavers, Levin & Tham 2006; also Jones 1983 and Cummins 1996 on French prepositions). Only some languages have specialized "satellites", such as particles or adpositions, which can encode the directional meaning (cf. the English preposition *into*). Such languages (defined as "satellite-framed" languages by Talmy 1991) typically behave as manner languages and allow the manner of motion to be expressed with goals of motion. Languages lacking any specialized satellites for the expression of goals tend to rely on the use of specialized verbs that encode the directional meaning, such as *entró* 'entered' in (1a) from Spanish. As a result, in such languages (in Talmy's terminology, "verb-framed" languages) only a subset of motion verbs can be used in expressions of directed motion. This subset of specialized directional verbs typically excludes verbs of manner of motion, which results in the pattern observed in path languages, as in (1a).

I will approach the problem of expressing directional motion from a slightly different perspective, treating the two patterns introduced by Talmy not as language types but rather as descriptions of alternative encoding strategies, which may and often do co-exist within a single language; this approach is compatible with Talmy's original proposal and at the same time accounts for the kinds of data discussed, inter alia, by Aske (1989), Gehrke (2007), Jones (1983), Kopecka (2006). One strategy is to encode the directional meaning in a specialized satellite, when such a satellite is available in the language; a goal expressed in this way can then combine with any verb, including manner verbs. The other strategy, preferred by languages that lack specialized satellites, is to encode the directional meaning in a specialized class of inherently directional verbs (which typically exclude manner verbs). The fact that only some languages have specialized satellites and can rely on the first strategy creates the illusion of a division between path languages and manner languages. The two strategies, however, may be used in a single language as competing options for describing the same event.

Typically, the directional meaning is either encoded by a specialized satellite that distinguishes goals from static locations or expressed through the use of a specialized inherently directional verb. There is, however, a third option of describing directed motion, which is widely used cross-linguistically and which is often ignored in the studies of motion expressions, since apparently no language uses exclusively this strategy. Languages lacking specialized means of encoding directionality outside of the verb (by specialized satellites) do not always restrict expression of directed motion to a subset of inherently directional verbs. This is illustrated by examples (2a-c) from three different languages that are usually classified as path languages and which lack specialized prepositions for expressing spatial goals. In all three examples, manner verbs are used in expressions of directed motion.

(2) a. Max a couru dans sa chambre/au magasin.
         'Max ran into his room/to the store.'   (French; Cummins 1996: 48)
     b. Mi ejercicio consiste en caminar a la biblioteca dos veces al día.
         'My exercise consists of walking to the library twice a day.'
         (Spanish; Aske 1989: 3)[1]
     c. La palla rotolò sotto il tavolo (in un secondo).
         'The ball rolled under the table (in one second).'
         (Italian; Folli 2001: 53)

In the examples above, the directional meaning is neither encoded in a satellite nor contributed by a specialized inherently directional verb. The manner verbs used need not describe motion oriented toward a unique goal and do not have to receive a directional interpretation. Neither of the strategies of lexical encoding of directionality applies to such examples and the directional meaning is not expressed overtly. In this sense, this strategy of expressing directed motion relies on contextual inference rather than lexical encoding. I believe that the use of this "zero" encoding strategy is more common across languages than it is usually assumed (in Nikitina (forthcoming), I discuss it in relation to the distinction between sources and goals).

1.2 Co-existing strategies: the problem of *into* vs. *in*

The problem discussed in this paper is directly related to the use of the "zero"-encoding strategy, leaves the directional meaning lexically unspecified. In many

---

1. Speakers' judgments of this sentence seem to vary. Some speakers of Spanish accept it on the directional reading; others prefer the locational reading ('walking inside the library').

languages, including American English, this strategy is combined with the use of one or both of the major patterns of lexical encoding. Although English has prepositions specialized for overt encoding of goals, such as *into*, the same meaning is often expressed with the non-specialized preposition *in*, which is also used to mark static locations when no motion is involved (as in *The cat is in the box*). For example, the prepositional phrase in a sentence like (3a) can be interpreted in the same way as the *into*-phrase in (3b).

(3) a.   He walked in the room.
     b.   He walked into the room.

Unlike in (3b), where the directional meaning is lexically encoded, in (3a) that meaning has to be inferred from context, since the preposition itself is underspecified with respect to the role of its locative argument, which can be a goal or a location. I present the results of a study of factors involved in the choice between the two competing strategies illustrated in (3a) and (3b) in three corpora of American English. The results provide support for a compositional view of directional meaning, showing that more than one element in the sentence can contribute to the directional interpretation and, furthermore, that the directional meaning need not be overtly encoded by specialized lexical material in order to be inferred (section 3). The study also suggests that the choice of a strategy partly depends on factors that have to do with alternative ways of conceptualizing motion events (section 4).

2.   Database

In this study, I was interested in naturally occurring examples of *into* and directional *in* from spoken and written discourse. I extracted all instances of the use of the two prepositions from three parsed corpora of American English – the Brown corpus of written text (Francis & Kucera 1964; Marcus, Santorini & Marcinkiewicz 1993), the corpus of publications in the *Wall Street Journal* (Marcus, Santorini & Marcinkiewicz 1993), and the parsed portions of the Switchboard corpus of telephone conversations (Godfrey, Holliman & McDaniel 1992). After extracting all directional uses of *into* and *in*, I excluded those that were irrelevant for a study of spatial goals. First of all, excluded were all non-spatial uses, such as temporal and other types of non-literal use illustrated in (4a–d), where the goal phrases do not describe locations in space.

(4) a.   Stock-fund managers, meantime, *went into October* with less cash on
          hand than they held earlier this year.
     b.   Before the law *went into effect* last month, . . .
     c.   I know because, I know when my mother was, you know, *going into
          the work force* there wasn't very many opportunities for her, I guess,

d. Asked about a bid for Quantum, a BP spokesman says, 'We pretty much have a policy of not commenting on rumors, and I think that *falls in that category.*'

Similarly, I excluded examples describing situations that do not involve actual motion, such as examples with various verbs of looking (5a) and other non-motion verbs (5b-d).

(5) a. He *peered* in *the boxes* themselves.

b. She cut the engines and slowly the cruiser swung around on the end of its lines until its bow was *pointing into the wind* and the cockpit faced toward the shore.

c. He parked facing it and left the headlights on, but when he started into the tunnel with the suitcase, he found the illumination *extended no farther than half a dozen feet into the passage.*

d. From a helicopter a thousand feet above Oakland after the second-deadliest earthquake in U.S. history, a scene of devastation emerges: a freeway *crumbled into a concrete sandwich*, hoses pumping water into once-fashionable apartments, abandoned autos.

The uses illustrated above seem to be derived through metaphorical extension from the literal spatial use of *into* and *in* (on relation of paths of vision to paths of motion see Slobin forthcoming). Since metaphorical uses describe a much more variable set of situations than motion events, inclusion of such examples could have resulted in interference of additional factors that are irrelevant for the basic spatial uses of *into* and *in*.[2]

As I was looking for factors that affect the choice of a strategy in cases where in principle both *into* and *in* are possible, I also excluded examples in which only one of the two prepositions was allowed. In particular, I removed from the database all uses of *in* as a particle, as in *I came in*, since they have no equivalent use with *into* (see Cappelle this volume).

Finally, I excluded examples that describe not a transition into a new location, but rather contact with a surface. Such uses are illustrated in (6a,b). The *into*-phrases in such examples do not, strictly speaking, describe a goal of motion, and they are in general not paraphrasable with *in*.

(6) a. Mine hasn't had any trouble except last week a shopping cart *crashed into it.*

b. With the field a blur of white the unfortunate pilot had simply *flown into the hillside.*

---

2. In general, the metaphorical uses of *into* and *in* seemed to depend mostly on the event's aspectual characteristics, *in* being used primarily in descriptions of punctual events. This factor was not as prominent, compared to other factors, in descriptions of motion in space. Further investigation of this difference lies outside the scope of this study.

After all the irrelevant examples had been removed (one other minor type of example that was excluded is discussed in section 4.1), the database consisted of 518 clauses with spatial goals marked by *into* and *in*, both with transitive and intransitive verbs. The goal of motion was marked by *into* in 85% and by *in* in 15% of examples. The database was annotated for a number of factors that I expected to affect the choice of the preposition based on a survey of literature and a previous pilot study. In order to test which factors correlate with the use of *into* or *in*, I used the logistic regression model, which identifies factors that are significant independently of other factors. The analysis of the distribution of *into* and *in* confirmed the significance of two groups of factors, which can be characterized as factors contributing to inferability of directional meaning, and factors related to event construal. I discuss the two groups in more detail in sections 3 and 4. All factors, percentages and the coefficients of the logistic regression model are listed in the Appendix.

3.   Contextual inferability of directional meaning

3.1   Lexical encoding of the directional meaning

The most important difference between the English prepositions *into* and *in* is their association with the meaning of goal and the meaning of static location, respectively. If *into* can be treated as a lexical marker of goals, *in* is ambiguous and can only be used to mark a goal of motion when the meaning of change of location is encoded by some other element in the sentence or, alternatively, if it can be inferred from context. This dependence of the directional interpretation of *in*-phrases on directionality expressed by other elements in the sentence predicts that the verb should play a major role in the choice of the preposition to mark the goal of motion, since the directional interpretation is typically licensed by the use of a motion verb.[3] The statistical analysis revealed a strong correlation between the use of directional *in* and the aspectual type of the motion verb. I divided all verbs into those that tend to describe transitions and those that describe processes. Although both (7a) and (7b) are interpreted as referring to a transition, the verb *slide*, when used without a PP, tends to describe an unbounded process.

---

3.   Unlike inherently directional verbs, which can be described as verbs that *encode* directed motion, manner of motion verbs only *license* the directional interpretation of the PP, since they allow the PP to be interpreted directionally but do not require it, cf. the two readings of *walk in the room.*

(7) a.   And the cat was getting, um, fleas and stuff and *bringing* them in the house.

  b.   Roberta Landis put her hand on her husband 's arm as he *slid* in the driver's seat beside her.

Directional *in* was used in 40 out of 208 clauses with verbs describing transitions (i.e., in 19% of cases), and only in 37 out of 310 clauses with verbs describing processes (i.e., in 12% of cases). This difference is statistically significant (see Appendix) and highly unlikely to be due to chance. It confirms that verbs that tend to describe transitions (such as *get, bring, put, dip*) occur more frequently with directional *in* than verbs that describe inherently unbounded processes (such as *climb, drive, pull, carry*).

The verb, however, is just one element in the sentence that contributes to the directional reading. This meaning can also be inferred from a set of directional particles, as in examples (8a–d).

(8) a.   She climbed *up* into one of those orange streetcars, rode away in it, and never came back.

  b.   If I don't come *back* in the house, Breed's going to . . .

  c.   At the end of the performance, Dave and Max came *out* into the brilliantly lit foyer among a surge of gowned and tuxedoed firs nighters.

  d.   We were coming *down straight* into their canal.

In the above examples the prepositional phrase is introduced by a directional particle, which provides additional information about the path of motion and is unambiguously associated with the directional reading.[4] I coded for the use of such particles, and this factor also proved to be significant. In the absence of a directional particle, *in* was used in 56 out of 428 cases (13%), while in examples with such a particle it was used in 22 out of 90 cases (24%). Since this factor was also shown to be significant independently of other factors in the logistic regression model, we can conclude that the use of directional *in* is more likely when the directional meaning can be inferred from a particle.

The significance of such factors as the aspectual type of the verb and the presence of a directional particle is consistent with the fact that *in* is typically used to mark static locations. The static interpretation is the default reading received by an *in*-phrase when the directional meaning is not provided by context.

---

4.   Other elements, such as *all over* or *around*, may be, in turn, strongly associated with a non-directional reading, as in *He runs around in the backyard*, where the adverb describes the motion as non-directional. Unlike *back* and *straight*, which typically characterize a unique path of directional motion, *all over* and *around* qualify paths that are not oriented toward a single goal. The two types of element should of course be treated separately.

3.2   Overriding the default (static) interpretation

The verb and the particle were the only lexical elements contributing the directional meaning that I looked at in this study. A number of other constraints on
the directional use of *in*, however, can be accounted for by the same principle of
contextual inferability of the meaning that is not encoded overtly. In the rest of this
section I briefly describe how this principle (the directional meaning is inferred
based on the previous context) helps to explain certain correlations between the
interpretation of a PP and its relative position with respect to the verb.

Due to the inherently static meaning of English *in*, the directional interpretation of the *in*-phrase typically has to be licensed by a preceding element in the
sentence or by a preceding context. This could explain the apparent constraints on
the position of the directional *in*-phrase with respect to the verb, illustrated below
by examples from Thomas (2001, 2005).

(9)   a.   ?? In this pool John fell.
     b.   ?? In which pool did John fall?
     c.   ?? The pool in which John fell is extremely deep.

Examples with topicalization (9a), questions (9b), and constructions with rela-
tivization (9c) do not sound, on the directional reading, as grammatical for most
speakers as the corresponding sentence *John fell in the pool*, where the verb precedes
the *in*-phrase. Examples like (9a–c) also did not occur in my database. Thomas
explains this contrast by appealing to a syntactic constraint on adjacency of the
verb and the directional phrase. In light of the preceding discussion of the role of
context in contributing the directional interpretation, the apparent ungrammaticality of such constructions could be explained instead by the relative position of
the PP and the verb.[5] In all three examples the motion verb, which plays a major
role in licensing the directional interpretation of a PP, is preceded by the *in*-phrase
with the intended interpretation of goal of motion. This would predict a stronger
preference for the static interpretation of *in*, hence a stronger preference to use *into*
on the directional reading.

With the standard order of the motion verb and the prepositional phrase the
directional reading is more accessible, as in (10a), or even in (10b), where the
preposition is embedded in a relative clause (cf. 9c).

(10)   a.   John fell in this pool.
      b.   The pool that John fell in is extremely deep.

---

5.   Additional examples of non-adjacent *in*-phrases explained by Thomas (2005: 151–2) in
terms of syntactic adjacency can be accounted for in terms of more general restrictions on explicit mention of path and manner of motion (see section 4).

Sentences like (10b) are attested in the corpus, cf. the following example from Switchboard:

(11)   This cave that we used to go in was small.

Furthermore, it appears that even when the verb follows the directional *in*-phrase, the sentence can still be improved if the directional interpretation is licensed by a preposed directional particle. Examples like (12) are attested widely on the web, which also suggests that the phenomenon under discussion is non-categorical and not due to a purely structural constraint. Rather, the constraint on directional interpretation has to do with the general mechanism of inferring the directional meaning of a PP from the preceding context.

(12)   a.   Back in the water it went.
       b.   I pulled it out the box and thought it felt to much like a toy, so back in the box it went.

A similar restriction on the linear order of a non-static PP is discussed in Birner & Ward (1998: 244–5) for cases of locative preposing. In examples like (13a,b), which do not describe any motion, the PP can appear before the verb.

(13)   a.   My neighbors have a huge back yard. *Across it* runs a string of beautiful Japanese lanterns.
       b.   My neighbors have a huge back yard. *Through it* they've run a string of beautiful Japanese lanterns.

Strikingly, when the sentence requires a dynamic interpretation and the PP specifies not a static location but a path of motion, preposing of the PP is no longer acceptable.

(14)   a.   My neighbors have a huge back yard. #*Across it* runs their German shepherd all the time.
       b.   My neighbors have a huge back yard. #*Through it* my kids like to run.

The restriction on locative preposing of PPs that are interpreted dynamically as path phrases stems from the same general mechanism of licensing the more marked (dynamic) reading: in the absence of an element from which the directed motion can be inferred the PP tends to receive a static interpretation[6]. This restriction is

---

6.   The contrast in markedness is manifested, for example, in the fact that locational PPs are compatible with a wider range of predicates than the directional ones, and any event can be described as having a spatial location while only some events can be described as having a spatial goal. This leads me to conclude that, at least in the absence of a motion predicate, the static interpretation is the default one, and it can even be enforced, in the absence of a preceding motion verb, on prepositions like *across* or *through*, for which the directional reading may be otherwise more frequent.

exactly parallel to the restriction on the position of *in*-phrases: a preposed PP fails to describe goals of motion in the case of *in* in (9a–c), just as it fails to describe paths of motion in the case of *through* and *across* in (14a–b). Unfortunately, the number of examples with preposed PPs in my database was not large enough to take this factor into account in the statistical model; in all of them, however, the preposition was *into*.

Interestingly, the word order constraint on the directional interpretation is not as strong in Dutch as in English. In Dutch, *in*-phrases can receive the directional interpretation even when followed by the verb, e.g., in embedded clauses. This difference is expected, since directional *in*-phrases seem to have a wider distribution in Dutch, where there is no exact lexical equivalent of *into*, than in English, where directional *in* competes with a specialized goal preposition *into* (Tseng 2005: 171). The overall frequency of the use of directional *in* may vary even across English dialects, and it is possible that in some of them the use of *in* is allowed in a wider range of contexts. However, if my explanation is correct, the directional interpretation should be less accessible in preposed PPs than in PPs that follow the verb. In other words, a language may allow both *into* (a specialized satellite, if there is one) and *in* (a non-specialized satellite) to be preposed, it may disallow both, or it may allow only one of them. In the latter case only the specialized satellite (the equivalent of *into*) should be acceptable in the position before the verb. A broader typological study is needed to test this hypothesis.

The main conclusion that can be drawn from this section concerns the use of what can be described as the "zero" encoding pattern, where the directional meaning is not encoded overtly by any one lexical item in the sentence but is inferred from a combination of a motion verb and the broader context. I have argued that the use of the preposition *in* to mark goals of motion is constrained by mechanisms of contextual inference of the directional meaning, i.e., *in* tends to be used in contexts where the directional meaning is licensed by a preceding motion verb or a directional particle.

4. Event construal

4.1 Salience of path vs. process of motion

In the previous section I discussed one type of factor that is responsible for the choice between *into* and *in* as a goal marker. Prominence of such factors is due to the mechanism of contextual inference, rather than lexical encoding, of directional meaning with *in*. This mechanism, however, does not account for all factors, since variation extends to contexts where directional meaning can be inferred and there is, in principle, no need to mark it overtly by *into*. Are the two prepositions used interchangeably in such contexts, or are there additional preferences and re-strictions on their use?

A closer look at the distribution of *into* and *in* reveals that even in cases where inferring the directional meaning is not a concern the two strategies are not in free variation. Most importantly, the use of directional *in* is strongly dispreferred with descriptions that focus on path or manner of motion. First of all, *in* does not occur with explicit mentions of path, when either the source of motion (15a,b) or the path (15c,d) is specified in addition to its goal:

(15)   a.   John walked out of the kitchen and into/??in the living room.
       b.   John walked from the kitchen into/??in the living room.
       c.   John walked through the corridor and into/??in the kitchen.
       d.   John walked down the corridor and into/??in the kitchen.

The tendency to avoid *in* in such examples is surprising, since the directional meaning is not only licensed by a motion verb but it should be further supported by a description of the source or path of motion. Still, directional *in* tends to be avoided in sentences like (15a–d), and this tendency does not seem to depend on the choice of the actual verb. This restriction was categorical in my corpus data, which made me exclude all examples of this sort from the final counts as non-alternating.

Secondly, directional *in* is dispreferred with verbs that describe highly specific manners of motion:

(16)   a.   He crawled into/??in the room.
       b.   They danced into/??in the ballroom.
       c.   The boy biked into/??in the garage.
       d.   The man limped into/??in the house.

Restrictions on combinations of directional *in* with explicit descriptions of paths or highly specific manners of motion suggest that *in* describes the resulting state of a spatial transition and is incompatible with the profiling of the process of motion along a path. This intuition is expressed by Lindstromberg in his book on preposi-tions intended for learners of English as a second language:

> Our prototypical mental image of 'in-ness' is surely that of a Landmark enclos-ing a Subject. Often, a context may make it clear that prior to enclosure there was movement. But use of *in* in such a context stresses 'resultant enclosure' without clear images of the preceding movement <. . .> The meaning of *into*, on the other hand, seems to give movement and result about equal emphasis.
> (Lindstromberg 1997: 29–30).

Somewhat similar to this, Smith (1995: 298) suggests that '*in* tends to emphasize the endpoint of the path, while *into* emphasizes the path itself', and Dirven (1989: 539) writes that '*into* tends to denote a more emphatic action. From a diving-board one would jump <u>into</u> the water, but from a lower point, e.g., the bank, one would jump <u>in</u> the water.'

All these descriptions suggest that the two expressions correspond to two different event conceptualizations and profile different subparts of the motion event: *into* profiles the process of motion along a path, and *in* profiles the resulting state (see also the discussion in Van der Leek 2000: 316–7). This contrast, if confirmed by the usage data, could explain the tendency to avoid *in* with descriptions of path (15a–d), and it is also consistent with the constraint on the use of *in* with verbs of highly specific manners of motion (16a–d).

Unfortunately, factors related to event conceptualization, or conceptual salience, are difficult to assess directly. How can we predict which event in a given context will be conceptualized as involving a prominent path or process of motion, and which will be described from the point of view of the resulting state? As a first attempt at approaching this problem, I used the type of location as a proxy for the likelihood that the event is conceptualized as involving a prominent path. I distinguished between two types of location based on a relatively objective characteristic – the presence or absence of well-defined boundaries. The first type includes locations with well-defined boundaries, such as rooms, buildings, boxes, cars, etc. Due to the presence of a well-defined boundary, goals of this type (I refer to them as "containers") allow for a possibility of a punctual transition that does not involve a prominent path of motion. Examples (17a, b) illustrate the use of *into* and *in* with locations classified as containers.

(17)   a.   He went *into the hotel* and searched till he found the razor.
       b.   I mean, someone walks *in a classroom*.

Locations like water and ground were also classified as containers, since water and ground are delineated in space by a clear boundary and are not surrounded by a transitional zone that is perceived as neither contained by the location nor located outside of it.

The other type comprises locations that lack a well-defined boundary. These are cities, mountains, countries, as well as space, forests, neighborhoods, etc. All such locations (which I refer to as "areas") are typically surrounded by a transitional zone that a theme has to pass in order to travel from outside of an area to its inside. The use of *into* and *in* with areas is illustrated in (18a, b).

(18)   a.   You think you'd, you think you'd, uh, go up *in space* if you had a chance?
       b.   If I walk *into a bad neighborhood* I'm sure I'd want to walk through with you because I'm sure you have above the average instinct for how to use guns and how to use them effectively and everything.

The location type defined in such a way was intended to serve as a predictor of the likelihood that the event is conceptualized as involving a prominent path.[7] The distinction between the two types of location does not by itself constitute a linguistically relevant category; rather, it can be expected to belong to a cluster of correlated properties that are subsumed under such a category (a somewhat similar problem of correlated factors related to topicality and structural complexity is discussed in Bresnan et al. 2007). I expected to find a higher rate of directional *into* with transitions into locations of the second type (the areas), since they are more often associated with a salient path: a trip to the mountains or to a city is more likely to be perceived and described as involving a prominent path of motion than a transition into a room or into a house. The results of the statistical analysis bear out this prediction. With areas, *in* was used in 12 out of 127 examples (9%), while with containers, it was used in 66 out of 391 examples (17%); this difference is significant in the logistic regression model independently of all other factors (e.g., independently of the aspectual type of the verb).[8] The distinction between areas and containers is no doubt a very imprecise measure of the probability that the transition is conceptualized as involving a prominent path, and I hope that further research will yield a more exact definition of this factor.

Apart from differences in the marking of "areas" and "containers" in the corpus, the relevance of the type of spatial goal for the choice of the preposition is confirmed by the relative acceptability judgments of sentences like (19a–b) and (20a–b). The container-type locations (locations with well-defined boundaries) in (19a) and (20a) are more acceptable as the goal of motion than the area-type locations (location without clear boundaries) in (19b) and (20b). The latter tend to be interpreted as the place, rather than goal, of motion.

(19) a. He walked in the room/backyard/store. (locational or directional)
      b. He walked in the city/field/mountains. (locational / ??directional)

---

7. Use of such proxies is a well-established methodology in studies of factors that cannot be assessed directly. Length and syntactic weight are often used as predictors of conceptual complexity in studies of syntactic variation (for an overview, see Wasow 2002). Similarly, fine-grained discourse status categories are sometimes established in empirical studies based on the distance from a previous mention.

8. When the type of location is taken into account, all instances of *in* are covered by the factors discussed so far, i.e., all examples of directional *in* in my corpus involve a verb that describes a transition, a directional particle, or a container-type location. This does not mean, however, that the result is satisfactory or that no other factor is relevant, since we also need to explain why directional *in* was not used in the rest of examples, where *into* was preferred.

(20)   a.   Then we went in the room/backyard/store.
      b.   ??Then he went in the city/field/mountains.

Finally, one additional piece of evidence suggesting that the presence of a salient path affects the acceptability of directional *in* comes from verbs of continuous imparting of force. Verbs of continuous imparting of force, such as *pull* and *push*, are classified by Pesetsky (1995: 139–40) as verbs that impose the locational reading on their *in*-phrase and do not allow it to be interpreted directionally, hence the preference for *into* in (21).

(21)   Mary pushed the heavy box into/??in its proper place.

Interestingly, the directional reading becomes more acceptable with an *in*-phrase when the same verb describes a punctual event that does not involve a prominent path of motion. Such uses are attested; (22a–d) come from the LexisNexis Academic database of news articles. In the examples with directional *in*, the change of location is momentary:

(22)   a.   He *pushed me in the room*. And then the door slammed shut.
      b.   'It will be easy. Just hit her on the head and *push her in the pool*.'
      c.   Brooke bolts after her, grabs her arm and *pulls her back in the room*.
      c.   'When they see me walking down the hall and they have a problem, they *pull me in the room*,' says Terrance Bolton, 12.

Unlike in (21), which describes motion along a path with continuous imparting of force, in all of the above examples the same verbs *push* and *pull* describe punctual events of causing a change of location. Durative events are more readily conceptualized as involving a salient process of motion than punctual events, just as transitions into "areas" are more often conceptualized as involving a prominent path of motion than transitions into "containers" (with "containers", the transition can be punctual and perceived as a momentary change of state). The relevance of such factors points to an additional effect of event construal.

4.2   Event construal and expression of goals in languages other than English

The relevance of the factors discussed in the previous sections for the choice of encoding strategy is independent of the contextual characteristics and suggests that the choice of the preposition can be affected by subtle differences in conceptualization of the motion event. Events that are construed from the point of view of motion along a path are more likely to be described with *into* than events that are construed from the point of view of the resulting location, as not involving a prominent path of motion. This suggests a parallel to variation in the expression of goals in other languages, where the choice of the morphosyntactic encoding of a spatial goal can be influenced, with some verbs, by viewpoint. I can only very cursorily discuss this phenomenon here; its more detailed analysis is a topic of a separate study.

In Russian, goals and locations are distinguished, with some prepositions, by case marking on the argument of the preposition. With the preposition *na* 'on', the accusative case marks goals of motion, and the prepositional (sometimes referred to as the locative) case marks static locations.

(23) a. Ključi ležat na stole   / *na stol
          keys lie   on table.PREP / on table.ACC
          'The keys are lying on the table.' (Place)
      b. Ključi upali na stol   / *na stole
          keys   fell on table. ACC / on table.PREP
          'The keys fell down onto the table.'   (Goal)

In (24), however, the object of the preposition *na* 'on' can be marked either by the accusative or by the prepositional case, i.e., the locative argument of the verb 'put' can be expressed as either static location or goal. In other words, what can only be understood as a spatial goal in this example can receive either the usual goal marking or the marking associated with static locations (in this sense, this variation is analogous to *Put the keys on* vs. *onto the table*).

(24) Položi ključi na stole   / na stol
      put   keys   on table.PREP / on table.ACC
      'Put the keys on/onto the table.'   (Place or Goal marking)

The choice between the two case forms is influenced by a number of factors, including the intended duration of the resulting state and presence or absence of an independent path of motion. In particular, the prepositional marking is more likely to be used when the resulting location is relatively permanent, but only the accusative marking is acceptable when the resulting location is temporary. The event of placing flowers on the table is likely to have a longer-lasting result than the event of setting the table for dinner; hence the contrast between (25a, b).

(25) a. Postav' vazu / cvety   na stol   / na stole
          put   vase / flowers on table-ACC / on table-PREP
          'Put the vase on the table.'   (Goal or Place marking)
      b. Postav' tarelku na stol   / ?na stole
          put   plate   on table-ACC / on table-PREP
          'Put the plate on the table.'   (Goal marking only)

A different factor – the presence of an independent path of motion – defines the lexical restrictions on this variation. Only some verbs allow for the prepositional (static) marking; these are, most importantly, verbs that describe accompanied motion, such as verbs of putting. Verbs of accompanied motion describe events of caused motion where the theme does not move independently of the agent (in the event of putting, the theme only moves insofar as it is contained in the agent's hands). Verbs that describe situations where the theme moves independently along its own path and is not accompanied by the agent (e.g., verbs of throwing) do not allow for the static goal marking, cf. (24) and (26).[9]

(26)   Bros'   ključi   na stol   / #na stole
       throw   keys   on table.ACC / on table.PREP
       'Throw the keys onto the table.'   (Goal marking only)[10]

The variable encoding of goals in Russian is similar to the variation between *into* and *in* in American English in that the choice of case marking depends on subtle differences in the event construal. In English, however, the set of verbs that allow for variable expression of goals is less restricted than in Russian.

Similar variation in case marking of spatial goals is attested in other languages that normally encode goals in a way different from static locations. For example, in Ancient Greek, the distinction between goals and static locations is normally marked by case, the accusative being associated with the directional, and the dative with the locational meaning. The form of the preposition 'in' also varies depending on the role of the locative argument: *eis* with the accusative is used to mark goals, while *en* with the dative is associated with static locations. In some cases, however, the goal of motion can receive the static case marking (*en* + dative) "to anticipate the rest that follows the action of the verb" (Smyth 1920: 368).

(27)   en tô   potamô   épeson
       in the river-DAT fell-AOR3PL
       'they fell in the river (and remained there)'   (Xen. Ages.1.32)

The variable case marking is attested in Ancient Greek with a number of verbs, including the verb 'throw', as illustrated in (28a,b), where the goal of motion is expressed in two different ways – in a way typical of goals (*eis* + accusative), and in a way typical of static locations (*en* + dative).

---

9.   Another notion that might be relevant is the "markedness" of the resulting location, i.e., whether the resulting position of the theme with respect to the Ground is canonical or not (cf. Jones 1983: 181–3). Additional examples and a discussion of some pragmatic features involved in the choice of case marking in Russian can be found in Zaitseva (1994), Israeli (2004). For a discussion of variable case with verbs of placement in Ukrainian see Nedashkivska (2001).

10.   The static marking is acceptable in this example if the verb is interpreted as a synonym of 'leave', and the theme again does not move independently of the agent; when the verb is understood as 'throw', the prepositional marking cannot be used.

(28) a. eís   hála   lúmata   bállon   (Hom. Il.1.314)
            into sea.ACC water.used.in.washing.ACC throw.IMPF.3PL
            'They threw the dirty water into the sea.'   (Goal marking)
      b. kaí tá   mén en purí   bálle   (Hom. Od.14.429)
            and DEF.N.ACC.PL PART in fire.DAT throw.IMPF.3SG
            'And these things he threw in the fire.'   (Place marking)

The difference between the two case marking options is analyzed by Luraghi (2003:
66) in terms of profiling: the accusative profiles the trajectory, while the dative profiles
the endpoint of motion. If this explanation is correct, the use of accusative in (28a)
profiles the dynamicity of action, or the motion itself, and with the dative in (28b) the
focus is on the resulting location of the theme and not on the action of throwing.

Such examples suggest that variation in the expression of goals is not a unique
feature of English. It is not uncommon in other languages, including Slavic languages, Latin, Gothic and some others, although it is typically restricted to only
a small set of motion verbs. The fact that this variation is so widespread suggests
that the variation between *into* and *in* in English is not explained by idiosyncratic
properties of *into* (c.g., by the fact that *in-to* is compositional, cf. Gruber 1965).
Rather, this phenomenon is a more general consequence of competition between
different patterns of goal expression, where the strategy of using specialized goal
marking co-exists with the "zero encoding" strategy, i.e., with the strategy of encoding the directional meaning elsewhere or leaving it lexically unspecified.

5. Additional factors: register and transitivity

There were two additional factors that I coded for in this study and which were
not directly subsumed under the two broad families of factors discussed above.
The fact that my data came from both written (Brown and Wall Street Journal)
and spoken (Switchboard) sources allowed me to test for effects of register on the
choice between *into* and *in*. Register turned out to be a very strong predictor in the
variation, with directional *in*-phrases occurring significantly more often in spoken language (61 out of 171 examples, i.e., 36%) than in writing (17 out of 347
examples, i.e., 5%). The use of directional *in* also appears to be more restricted in
British English than in American English, both in terms of absolute frequency of
directional *in* and in terms of lexical restrictions on its use (I did not, however, use
corpus data to test this observation, since all my examples came from corpora of
American English).[11] Why exactly register is such a significant factor and how it

---

11. For the speakers of British English I consulted, many intransitive inherently directional
verbs, such as *come* and *go*, were only marginally acceptable with directional *in*. A comparative
study of the use of *in* in English dialects remains to be done.

relates to the diachronic developments in the use of directional *in* in English dialects remains to be studied.

Another factor that has some importance is transitivity of the verb: transitive verbs are slightly more likely to be used with *in* than intransitive ones. The examples below illustrate an intransitive and a transitive use of the same verb.

(28)   a.   I just moved into this small community.
       b.   We just, uh, moved my grandfather into, not a nursing home but, you know, a transitional type facility.

With transitive verbs, *in* occurred in 36 out of 174, i.e., in 21% of examples; with intransitive verbs, it occurred only in 42 out of 344, i.e., in 12% of examples. Transitivity is, however, the weakest factor in the model, and its effect should be further investigated. The weak effect of transitivity may be ultimately related to the notion of manner specificity, discussed in section 4.1, i.e., to the tendency to avoid the use of *in* in descriptions that provide detailed information about the manner of motion. Unlike many intransitives, transitive verbs tend to describe the way of causing motion but not highly specific manners of motion. If this is indeed so, the difference between transitive and intransitive verbs could be subsumed by the tendency to avoid *in* with verbs that describe specific manners. The effect of transitivity could then be explained by the tendency to use *into* when the event is conceptualized as involving a salient manner of motion.

6.   Conclusion

In this study I explored the directional use of the preposition *in* in American English as opposed to the alternative strategy of marking the goal of motion by *into*. I discussed two types of significant factors that affect the choice between *into* and *in*: (i) factors contributing to contextual inferability of the directional meaning, and (ii) factors related to event construal. The significance of the former set of factors points to the compositional nature of directional meaning. Even in a language like English, where directionality can be encoded lexically by means of a specialized preposition *into*, the same meaning need not be overtly expressed and can be instead inferred from context, allowing speakers multiple options in describing the same event.

The complex nature of variation in the expression of goals in American English and the importance of contextual information in the encoding of the directional meaning demonstrate that the use of directional *in* can hardly be described in terms of rigid rules and purely structural constraints. The extent to which the directional meaning must be encoded lexically and the extent to which it can be left unspecified may vary with language, dialect (see footnote 11), or register. As a result, the frequency of usage of directional *in* may vary across different corpora; we can expect, however, to find the highest proportion of directional *in* in a predictable set of contexts, where the directional meaning is contributed by a verb of directional motion or by a particle.

The tendency to avoid the use of directional *in* in descriptions that focus on manner or path of motion suggests that the choice between available options is further constrained by pragmatic factors related to conceptualization of the event. In this study I used the type of location as a proxy for the likelihood of the event to be conceptualized as involving a prominent path of motion. The significance of this factor, together with observations of incompatibility of directional *in* with explicit descriptions of manner and path, indicate that event conceptualization may contribute to the choice between *into* and *in* in cases when both options are allowed. Further research is needed to investigate in more detail the nature of this factor and its exact correlates.

Finally, I suggested that variation in the expression of spatial goals is found in languages other than English and that the problem of choosing between *into* and *in* is related to a more general problem of co-existence of alternative strategies of expressing directed motion. I hope that cross-linguistic variation in the factors that are involved in the choice of a strategy will receive more attention in the future studies of spatial expressions.

Appendix: Summary of the data

Table 1 summarizes the frequency of responses for each individual value.

Table 1. Distribution of *into* and *in*

Parameter		Number of *in* responses	Number of *into* responses	Total (100%)
directional particle:	present	22 (**24%**)	68 (76%)	90
	absent	56 (13%)	372 (**87%**)	428
aspectual class:	telic	40 (**19%**)	168 (81%)	208
	process	37 (12%)	273 (**88%**)	310
location type:	container	66 (**17%**)	325 (83%)	391
	area	12 (9%)	115 (**91%**)	127
transitivity:	transitive	36 (**21%**)	138 (79%)	174
	intransitive	42 (12%)	302 (**88%**)	344
register:	spoken	61 (**36%**)	110 (64%)	171
	written	17 (5%)	330 (**95%**)	347

Coefficients of the logistic regression model are listed in Table 2. The columns correspond to the estimates of the regression coefficients for each factor, their standard error, and tests for their significance in the model. The last column lists the p-value for each factor; all factors are significant above a .05 level.

Table 2. Logistic regression coefficients

	Coef	S.E.	Wald Z	P
Intercept	−4.9767	0.5272	−9.44	0.0000
register = spoken	2.9167	0.3407	8.56	0.0000
use = preposition+particle	1.1258	0.3526	3.19	0.0014
aspectual type = telic	1.0448	0.3553	2.94	0.0033
location = container	0.8993	0.3874	2.32	0.0203
transitivity = transitive	0.7455	0.3533	2.11	0.0348

References

Aske, J. 1989. Path predicates in English and Spanish: A closer look. In *Proceedings of the Fifteenth Annual Meeting of the Berkeley Linguistic Society*, 1–14. Berkeley Linguistics Society.

Beavers, J., Levin, B. & Tham, S.W. 2006. The typology of motion events revisited. Paper presented at the 80th Annual Meeting of the Linguistic Society of America, Albuquerque NM.

Birner, B.J. & Ward, G. 1998. *Information Status and Noncanonical Word Order in English*. Amsterdam: John Benjamins.

Bresnan, J., Cueni, A., Nikitina, T. & Baayen, R.H. 2007. Predicting the dative alternation. In *Cognitive Foundations of Interpretation*, G. Bouma, I. Krämer & J. Zwarts (eds), 69–94. Amsterdam: Royal Netherlands Academy of Arts and Sciences.

Cummins, S. 1996. Movement and direction in French and English. *Toronto Working Papers in Linguistics* 15(1): 31–54.

Dirven, R. 1989. Space prepositions. In *A User's Grammar of English: Word, Sentence, Text, Interaction*, R. Dirven (ed.), 519–50. Frankfurt: Peter Lang.

Folli, R. 2001. Two strategies to construct telicity: A comparative analysis of English and Italian. *Oxford University Working Papers in Linguistics, Philology and Phonetics* 6, 47–65. Oxford: OUP.

Francis, W.N. & Kucera, H. 1964. *Brown Corpus Manual: Manual of Information to Accompany a Standard Corpus of Present Day Edited American English*. Providence RI: Brown University.

Gehrke, B. 2007. Putting path in place. In *Proceedings of Sinn und Bedeutung* 11, E. Puig-Waldmüller (ed.), 244–260. Barcelona: Universitat Pompeu Fabra.

Godfrey, J., Holliman, E. & McDaniel, J. 1992. SWITCHBOARD: Telephone speech corpus for research and development. In *Proceedings of ICASSP-92*, 517–520. San Francisco.

Gruber, J. S. 1965. Studies in Lexical Relations. PhD Dissertation, MIT. (Reproduced by Indiana University Linguistics Club, 1970).

Israeli, A. 2004. Case choice in placement verbs in Russian. *Glossos* 5.

Jones, M.A. 1983. Speculations on the expression of movement in French. In *A Festschrift for Peter Wexler* [Occasional Papers No 27 of the Department of Language and Linguistics], J. Durand (ed.), 165–194. Colchester: University of Essex.

Kopecka, A. 2006. The semantic structure of motion verbs in French: Typological perspectives. In *Space in Languages: Linguistic Systems and Cognitive Categories*, M. Hickmann & S. Robert (eds), 83–101. Amsterdam: John Benjamins.

Lindstromberg, S. 1997. *English Prepositions Explained*. Amsterdam: John Benjamins.

Luraghi, S. 2003. *On the Meaning of Prepositions and Cases: The Expression of Semantic Roles in Ancient Greek*. Amsterdam: John Benjamins.

Marcus, M., Santorini, B. & Marcinkiewicz, M. A. 1993. Building a large annotated corpus of English: The Penn Treebank. *Computational Linguistics* 19: 313–330.

Nedashkivska, A. 2001. Whither or where: Case choice and verbs of placement in contemporary Ukrainian. *Journal of Slavic Linguistics* 9(2): 213–251.

Nikitina, T. In press. Subcategorization pattern and lexical meaning of motion verbs: A Study of the Source/Goal ambignity. To appear in *Linguistics*.

Pesetsky, D. 1995. *Zero Syntax: Experiencers and Cascades*. Cambridge MA: The MIT Press.

Slobin, D.I. 1996. Two ways to travel: Verbs of motion in English and Spanish. In *Grammatical Constructions: Their Form and Meaning*, M. Shibatani & S.A. Thompson (eds), 195–220. Oxford: Clarendon Press.

Slobin, D.I. 2006. What makes manner of motion salient? Explorations in linguistic typology, discourse, and cognition. In *Space in Languages: Linguistic Systems and Cognitive Categories*, M. Hickmann & S. Robert (eds), 59–81. Amsterdam: John Benjamins.

Slobin, D.I. Forthcoming. Relations between paths of motion and paths of vision: A cross-linguistic and developmental exploration. In (title to be announced), V. Gathercole (ed.).

Smith, M. 1995. The DAT/ACC constraint with German two-way prepositions. In *Insights in Germanic Linguistics I: Methodology in Transition*, I. Rauch & G. F. Carr (eds), 293–323. Berlin: Mouton de Gruyter.

Smyth, H.W. 1920. *Greek Grammar*. Cambridge MA: Harvard University Press.

Song, G. 1997. Cross-Linguistic Differences in the Expression of Motion Events and Their Implications for Second Language Acquisition. PhD Dissertation, Northwestern University.

Song, G. & Levin, B. 1998. A compositional approach to cross-linguistic differences in motion expressions. Paper presented at the 72nd Annual Meeting of the LSA, New York.

Talmy, L. 1975. Semantics and syntax of motion. In *Syntax and Semantics*, Vol. 4, J. P. Kimball (ed.), 181–238. New York NY: Academic Press.

Talmy, L. 1985. Lexicalization patterns: semantic structure in lexical forms. In *Language Typology and Syntactic Description*, Vol. 3, T. Shopen (ed.), 57–149. Cambridge: CUP.

Talmy, L. 1991. Path to realization: A typology of event integration. *Buffalo Papers in Linguistics* 1: 91–101 & 147–187.

Thomas, E. 2001. On the expression of directional movement in English. *Essex Graduate Papers in Language and Linguistics* 4: 87–104.

Thomas, E. 2005. On 'syntactic' versus 'semantic' telicity: Evidence from In and On. In *Adpositions of Movement*, H. Cuyckens, W. de Mulder & T. Mortelmans (eds), 145–166. Amsterdam: John Benjamins.

Tseng, J. 2005. Directionality and the complementation of Dutch adpositions. In *Adpositions of Movement*, H. Cuyckens, W. de Mulder & T. Mortelmans (eds), 167–194. Amsterdam: John Benjamins.

Van der Leek, F. 2000. Caused-motion and the 'bottom-up' role of grammar. In *Constructions of Cognitive Linguistics*, A. Foolen & F. van der Leer (eds), 301–331.

Wasow, T. 2002. *Postverbal Behavior*. Stanford CA: CSLI.

Zaitseva, V. 1994. The metaphoric nature of coding: Toward a theory of utterance. *Journal of Pragmatics* 22: 103–126.

Complex PPs in Italian

Raffaella Folli

This paper discusses complex prepositional phrases in Italian of the type *dietro a* (behind to), *dentro a* (inside to), *sopra a* (over to), *sotto a* (under to) and their occurrence with verbs of manner of motion. Their occurrence confirms the validity of a proposal by Tortora (2005, 2006 and this volume) about a conceptualisation of PLACE as bounded/unbounded in line with what was already proposed for PATH by Jackendoff (1990, 1991) and the existence of linguistic correlates for such a distinction.

1. Introduction

In this paper I discuss complex prepositional phrases in Italian such as *dietro a* (behind to), *dentro a* (inside to), *sopra a* (over to), *sotto a* (under to). These types of P phrases are formed by two prepositions, one indicating the path of motion and one indicating the end point of motion. The analysis of these prepositional complexes will allow me to draw three conclusions. First, the occurrence of these PPs with a certain class of motion verbs in Italian confirms that the contention according to which Italian, and in general Romance languages, cannot form goal of motion structures without relying on verb-framed strategies is far too strong (Mateu 2002).

Talmy (1985, 1991) argues that if we look at the patterns of lexicalisation of motion across different languages we must distinguish three groups:

i. Chinese and Indo-European languages (except post-Latin Romance), which present a lexicalisation pattern for motion which shows conflation of manner/cause with the verbal root, while the goal of motion is expressed independently by the adjunction of prepositional phrases (namely a verb satellite) (1).

> 1. The rock slid/rolled/bounced down the hill.   (Talmy, 1985: 62)

ii. Semitic, Polynesian and Romance languages, which express at the same time in the verbal root motion along a path and goal, while manner and cause are added separately (2).

2. La botella entró   a   la   cueva (flotando).   (Talmy, 1985: 69)
    the bottle entered to the cave (floating)
    the bottle floated into the cave.

iii. Finally, a third group of languages, among which Atsugewi (a Hokan language of northern California), which present in the conflated verbal root motion plus figure, while path, manner and cause are lexicalized separately.

The descriptive power of this typology according to which English can be defined as a *satellite-framed language* and Italian as a *verb-framed language* can be easily seen in relation to the behaviour of English and Italian in an example like the following. Imagine a situation where *John appears in the room by walking into it*. The typical way in which this situation is described in English is by means of a verb + PP structure such as *John came into the room*. In the same scenario, Italian (and Romance languages more generally) displays a preference for the use of verbs encoding the 'telos' of motion in the verb itself. Accordingly, Italian would express the scenario given above with a sentence such as *Gianni è entrato nella stanza (John entered in the room)*. Of course, English also possesses verbs like *enter*, where the path is encoded in the meaning of the verb itself, but the crucial thing for Talmy is that languages like English prefer to express the path and the goal of motion on prepositional phrases or verbal particles. This is contrary to what happens in Italian where the broad use of verbs like *enter, exit* to express the goal of motion is an indication of the *verb-framed* nature of this language. In this paper I will provide evidence for the need to consider the distinction proposed by Talmy as an indication of a tendency, and not of a sharp and definite clear-cut distinction between these two languages. It will be shown that Italian can resort to a *satellite-framed* strategy to express the goal of motion, though in a much more constrained way.[1]

The second issue I will address is related to Tortora's (2005, 2006) claim that the notion of boundedness and unboundedness applies not only to the category PATH, but also to the category PLACE. We will see that one typical scenario in Italian where a verb of manner of motion in combination with a PP can be used to express the goal of motion is when complex PPs made of two prepositions such as *dietro a* (behind to), *dentro a* (inside to) are used. These complex prepositional phrases involving two PPs are discussed by Tortora (*ibid*) and are claimed to be used to express unbounded PLACES. I will discuss in more depth the formation of goal of motion interpretation with these PP complexes and show that in some

---

1. For discussion of similar issues with respect to French, see Fong and Poulin (1997).

cases, when both PPs are present, the spatial geometry involved might be one that does not imply a clear bound.

Third, the examination of examples of goal of motion structures with complex PPs will allow us to make stronger claims about the strategies the language has at its disposal to form these interpretations. In particular, we will see that while Italian has a strategy to form goal of motion structures of the well-known type, the language is characterised by a need for morphological realisation of aspectual heads. This property is in fact related not only to the ability to form goal of motion interpretations, but also to a difference in the formation of resultative structures discussed in Folli (2001), Folli & Ramchand (2005): Italian allows resultatives with PPs (*Gianni ha rotto il bicchiere in mille pezzi* 'Gianni broke the glass in a thousand pieces'), while adjectival resultatives are banned (**Gianni ha rotto il bicchiere aperto* 'Gianni broke the glass open'). This is due to the fact that while prepositional phrases can fill the aspectual head (Rv) that is responsible for the formation of resultative predication, adjectives cannot and Italian being unable to license empty aspectual heads, resultatives with adjectives are not available. This constraint against unfilled aspectual heads is further confirmed by the need, in certain cases which we will discuss below, of two PPs to fill the aspectual heads that are projected in a goal of motion structure.

2. Prepositions and motion

A vast amount of work in the literature (Talmy 1985, 1991; Bowerman & Choi 2001; Higginbotham 1997, 2000; Folli 2001; Svenonius 2003, 2004; Slobin 2004; among many others) has been devoted to investigating the different strategies that languages use in the linguistic encoding of motion. Let us consider a few examples from Latin, English, Afrikaans and Italian:

(3) a. Ambulabat Caesar in acie.   [*Latin*]
           walk-IMP Caesar in field- ABL
           'Caesar was walking (up and down) the battle field.'

      b. Ambulavit Caesar in aciem.
           Walked Caesar in field- ACC
           'Caesar walked onto the battle field.'

      c. Ambulavit Caesar per aciem.
           Walked Caesar through field- ACC
           'Caesar walked through the battle field.'

(4) a. The bottle floated into the cave in five minutes/*for five minutes   [*English*]
      b. The bottle floated in the cave for five minutes/*in five minutes

    c.   John walked around the fountain in a minute/for a minute

    d.   The boat floated beneath/underneath the bridge *in a minute/for a minute

(5)   a.   Hulle loop in die veld.   [*Afrikaans*]
          They   walk in the bush
          'They walks in the bush.' (locative interpretation only)

    b.   Hulle loop die veld in.
          They   walk the bush in
          'They walk into the bush.'

    c.   Hulle loop in die veld in.
          They   walk in the bush in
          'They walk into the bush.'

(6)   a.   La bottiglia entrò   nella grotta galleggiando.   [*Italian*]
          The bottle   entered in.the cave   floating
          'The bottle floated into the cave.'

    b.   La bottiglia galleggiò nella   grotta per un'ora/*in un'ora.
          The bottle   floated   in.the cave   for an hour/*in an hour
          'The bottle floated (around) in the cave for an hour/*in an hour.'

In the examples in (3) from Latin, the contrast between the locative and directional motion is encoded syntactically on the Ground DP, which is realised in accusative case when motion is directional, and in ablative case when motion is locative. In (3c) we see that in this language directional motion can also be expressed with another unambiguously directional preposition, *per* 'through' which only occurs with Accusative case.

In English, in (4a-b), it is the preposition itself which gives rise to the alternation: a locative preposition such as *in* produces an interpretation of the motion event as locative and atelic, while a complex preposition such as *into* (cf. Pustejovsky 1991, Higginbotham 2000, *accomplishment prepositions*) gives rise to telic/directional motion.[2,3] Example (4)c shows that the combination of a manner of motion verb and a preposition can, in the majority of cases, indicate both locative and directed motion. Example (4)b shows that in English certain prepositions express unequivocally the goal of motion; hence a sentence with a preposition like *to*, *into*, *onto* can never receive a locative interpretation. This is further confirmed by the following set of examples portraying the unavailability of these PPs in simple copular constructions and as complements of stative verbs (7).

---

2.   The fact that certain varieties of English allow a telic interpretation for *in* is not crucial. The important thing for us now is that there are grammars of English that draw a one-to-one distinction between *in* and *into* and atelic and telic readings.

3.   The reason for calling prepositions like *into* and *to* 'complex' will become apparent below.

(7) a. *John is to the woods.
     b. *The ball is into the basket.[4]
     c. *The ball remained/burnt into the basket.

The reason for referring to these PPs as complex is that, arguably, prepositions of this type encode the two sub-events that form an accomplishment predicate, the process sub-event and the result sub-event. It is the complex sub-eventual structure of these prepositions that explains the occurrence of this type of prepositions with *in an hour*, but not with *for an hour* adverbials (Higginbotham 2000). The ordered pair of event positions characterising these accomplishment prepositions is also called by Higginbotham (2000) a *telic pair*. Accomplishment prepositions, in essence, are cases of lexical accomplishments, i.e., the equivalent in the PP domain of verbs like *cross, break* and *build*. English clearly possesses some of these prepositions in its lexical inventory, and an interesting question is whether every time a motion sentence gets a goal of motion interpretation an accomplishment preposition is involved, or whether telic pair formation can take place thanks to an activity verb and a preposition each contributing one event of the pair. These issues are discussed at length in Folli (2001).

As argued in Folli & Ramchand (2005), the complex eventive structure of accomplishment prepositions translates naturally into a complex syntactic structure (see also Koopman 2000; Folli 2001; den Dikken 2003; Svenonius 2003; Tungseth 2005, among others), involving two aspectual heads. In Folli & Ramchand (2005) the structure adopted is the one in (8) below. Since the discussion in the remainder of this paper is going to be crucially related to the notion of PATH and PLACE as building blocks of the syntactic and semantic representations of these prepositions, I chose to represent the complex structure of these PPs as in (9) below.

---

4. Svenonius (p.c.) notices that these prepositions can nevertheless occur in certain derived nominals, as for example in the following examples:

  (i) A blow to the head is dangerous.
  (ii) The backhand toss into the basket was brilliant.

It should be noticed that these examples all require an implied notion of directed movement. Similar examples are discussed by Higginbotham (2000) and by R. Bhatt (p.c.); again they notice that in subject infinitival relatives such as the *(first) man to fall down*, the presence of an ordinal modifier saves the otherwise ungrammatical structure.

We find a similar effect with adjectival resultatives in Italian. These types of resultatives are normally impossible in Italian (*Gianni ha martellato il metallo piatto* 'Gianni hammered the metal flat') but there are cases where the structure can be saved by modifiers (Gianni ha martellato il metallo piatto piatto 'Gianni hammered the metal flat flat'). See Folli and Ramchand (2005) for further discussion of these examples.

(8)

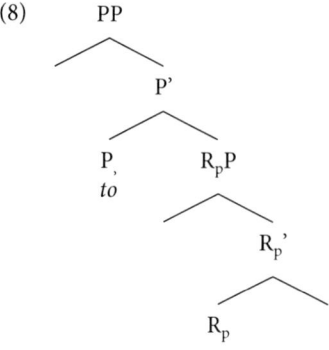

(9)

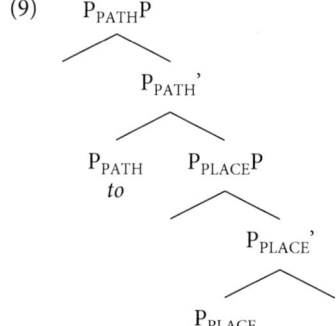

Nothing relevant for the material presented and the analysis proposed in this paper hinges on this choice.

Lastly, example (4)d shows that the combination of a manner of motion verb with the prepositions *beneath* and *underneath* is unambiguously locative. This in turn might imply that in English the availability of a telic interpretation is crucially related to the presence of an accomplishment PP, and that accomplishments cannot be formed via a process of telic pair formation where a verb and a preposition each contributes an event position of the telic pair (see Higginbotham 2000 for discussion). Since *beneath* and *underneath* are truly locative prepositions, the sentence in (4)d is only assigned a locative motion interpretation.[5] Notice that this has further implications. Telic pair formation might in fact turn out to be the strategy adopted by languages lacking lexical items such as *into* and *to*. Again, I will return to this point below once Italian is discussed in more depth.

---

5.   As noted by a reviewer this issue is complicated by the existence in English of cases where a verb like *jump* or *push* can combine with a locative PP such as in and give rise to a goal of motion interpretation as in *jump in the ditch*. See Thomas (2001, 2003), Nikitina (this volume), Tungseth (2006), and Gehrke (2007) for further discussion.

In the examples in (5) from Afrikaans we see that the postpositional and the circumpositional structures are the syntactic configurations that produce a directional meaning, while the prepositional structure is used to express locative motion.[6]

Finally, in Italian the scenario is again different, since in (6) no real alternation is available. The verb of manner of motion combines with the PP to give a locative interpretation, while to obtain a goal of motion interpretation for a motion event, a verb of inherently directed motion needs to be used. This is what Talmy refers to as a *verb-framed* strategy, since it is the verb itself that encodes the path of motion.

The examples in (3)–(5), where one kind of verb can be used to express different types of motion events (namely, a directed versus undirected type of motion) and where an argument can be interpreted in different ways (e.g., as the external argument of an activity verb in (3a), and as the resultee of a change of event where the undergoer 'ends up in the field' as in (3b) are typical examples of what in the literature is referred to as argument structure alternations. In work on the lexicon-syntax interface, the study of verb classes and alternations has been particularly important. In English, for example, we see that verbs display an impressive versatility, often being able to occur in several different argument structures. Yet, the formation of alternation is not complete; not every verb can give rise to as many argument structure types (e.g., *break* can be transitive and intransitive, while *destroy* can only be transitive), making the relation between the syntactic component and the lexical component a very interesting issue to investigate. Vast amount of work on verb classes and alternation (see for example the impressive work in Levin 1993) has allowed for the identification of common syntactic properties of verbs with common semantic characteristics, which in turn seems to suggest that some kinds of generalisations are indeed possible.[7]

Based on the shared agreement on the possibility of making generalisations about verb classes and syntactic structure, different proposals have placed the emphasis on either one of the two components, the lexicon (Chomsky 1970; Chomsky 1981; Levin & Rappaport-Hovav 1995; Jackendoff 1990; Baker 1988; among others) or the computational system (Pustejovsky 1988; Borer 1998, 2005;

---

6. The behaviour of Afrikaans in this respect is very similar to the behaviour of Dutch. For discussion see Koopman (2000); van Riemsdijk (2002); den Dikken (2003); Gehrke (2007) among many others.

7. Fodor (1970 inter alia) and Fodor & Lepore (1997 inter alia) put forward a different view, arguing for a lexical-conceptual atomism, fundamentally opposed to any type of lexical decomposition.

Travis 1994; Kratzer 1996; van Hout 1996; Marantz 1997; Ritter & Rosen 1998; Harley & Noyer 2000; Ramchand 2004; among others). Both lexicalist and constructionalist positions agree in this sense in trying to provide a systematic correlation between the meaning of a verb and the structure it appears in, although the way this correlation is conceived varies quite fundamentally.

Essentially, drawing from this brief discussion, we can say that argument alternations can be studied on two levels:

-on the level of lexical semantics, i.e., trying to understand to what extent argument alternations can be constrained by the identification of certain core aspects of verb meaning which might allow us to predict syntactic behaviour, and

-on the level of syntax, i.e., trying to understand which syntactic properties of language in general and which specific properties of a given language are at work in determining the structure underlying the different types of argument structure a verb can appear in and constraining the types of alternations we see in a language.

This paper will argue that both types of information are crucial in understanding the phenomenon of argument structure alternations, and the study of goal of motion interpretations in Italian can provide evidence for this view.

In particular, from looking at the data in (6), Italian does not seem to have at its disposal the possibility of inserting verbs of manner of motion in different syntactic structures to achieve the locative/goal of motion alternation. But the data set out in (6) is far from providing a complete representation of the way Italian expresses the goal of motion. Like Spanish, Italian lacks prepositions such as *to*, *into* which are necessarily aspectually complex. All its location prepositions are fundamentally locative. This claim is supported by the fact that any PP can occur with a copular verb or a stative verb as we see in the set of examples in (10).

(10)   a.   Gianni è **a** casa di Maria.
            John   is at house of Mary
            'John is at Mary's house.'

        b.   La palla è bruciata **nel** cestino.
            the ball is burnt in.the basket
            'The ball burnt in the basket.'

        c.   La palla è rimasta **sotto** il tavolo.
            the ball is remained under the table
            'The ball remained under the table.'

Nevertheless, even if *accomplishment prepositions* are not available in Italian, a verb of manner of motion can in certain cases give rise to a telic/goal of motion interpretation. This possibility essentially depends on the lexical properties of the verb. I will explain this in more detail below since this is the first point this paper wishes to clarify.

2.1 Italian manner of motion verbs

Italian manner of motion verbs split into two classes with respect to their ability to give rise to goal of motion interpretations with simple prepositions such as *in/a/ sotto* (in/to/under) (see Folli 2001 and Folli & Ramchand 2005 for further discussion). Table 1 shows how verbs of manner of motion split in Italian with respect to the possibility of forming goal of motion interpretations when in construction with simple prepositions.

Table 1.   Italian verbs of manner of motion

Verbs that *allow* a goal of motion reading	Verbs that *disallow* a goal of motion reading
Correre (run)[8]	Galleggiare (float)
Rotolare (roll)	Camminare (walk)
Rimbalzare (bounce)	Galoppare (gallop)
Scivolare (glide, slide)	Danzare (dance)
Gattonare (crawl)	Nuotare (swim)
Saltare (jump)	Sciare (ski)
Volare (fly)	Passeggiare (walk around)
Saltellare (hop)	Vagabondare (wander)

Let us see some examples:

(11)   a.   Gianni   è   corso   a   casa.
           Gianni   is   run   to   home
           'Gianni ran home.'

      b.   Marco   è   scivolato   **nel**   buco.
           Marco   is   slid   in.the   hole
           'Marco slid into the hole.'

      c.   La   palla   è   rimbalzata   **sotto**   il   tavolo.
           the   ball   is   bounced   under   the   table
           'The ball bounced under the table.'

---

8.   The distinction between *run*-type verbs and *walk*-type verbs, for example, is present in Italian, French (Fong & Poulin 1997), but also Greek (Anagnostopoulou 2003) and Afrikaans (Biberauer & Folli 2004). In Afrikaans, while any type of motion verb receives unambiguously a goal of motion interpretation in postpositional and circumpositional structures, but a locative interpretation in prepositional structures, run-type verbs can give rise to goal of motion interpretations also with prepositional structures, presumably by means again of a process of telic pair formation as defined by Higginbotham (2000). Thus, as emphasised by Zubizarreta & Oh (2004), analysing the difference between languages that allow goal of motion interpretation for manner of motion verb+PP combination and languages that do not as a matter of a difference in the availability of a generic strategy of template augmentation (Levin & Rappoport-Hovav 1995) is too simplistic.

    d.   *Gianni è   camminato a   casa.
          Gianni is   walked   to   home
          'Gianni walked home.'

    e.   *Maria è   danzata **nella**   stanza.
          Maria is   danced into the room
          'Maria danced into the room.'

    f.   Gianni è   andato a   casa   (camminando).
          Gianni is   gone   to   home (walking)
          'Gianni walked home.'

The examples in (11) show that while the strategy of combining a verb and a preposition to express the goal of motion is available in Italian, this is only possible with a subclass of manner of motion verbs. In Folli & Ramchand (2005), it is argued that this strategy is in fact available for those verbs that encode in their lexical entry a possibility for resultativity, which in that paper is expressed in terms of an Rv feature being associated with certain verbs in the lexicon (see Folli 2001 for extensive discussion). In an exo-skeletal view of argument structure derivation (e.g., Borer 2005), these verbs/roots can be inserted in a frame with a resultative aspectual head and produce a resultative interpretation. This in turn implies that while the syntactic structure involving a resultative phrase is available in the language, the lexical properties of the items inserted in the derivation are crucial in determining the convergence of the derivation itself.[9]

In Folli & Ramchand (2005), we proposed an analysis of these kinds of constructions based on the idea that event decomposition involves three different subevents, hence three different aspectual projections, one for the causing event (vP), one for the process event (VP) and one for the 'telos' (RvP). An event composition rule allows for two events to combine in a specific way such that the first event is the process/transition of the second event which is interpreted as the result state of that transition, in other words a *telic pair* (see also Parson 1990 and Higginbotham 2000). Although in this paper I do not intend to discuss in further detail the specific implementation offered there for the analysis of verb alternation,[10] it is worth mentioning that the possibility for telic pair formation, or result augmentation, (as we referred to this event composition rule in the paper), was found to be crucially dependent in Italian on the lexical specification of the verb. We argued there that while in English the presence of accomplishment prepositions

---

9. See Folli & Harley (2005) for extensive discussion of the problems of accounting for verb alternation and in particular gaps in verb alternations with a strictly constructionalist/syntax-based approach.

10. See also Ramchand (2004) for a detailed discussion.

ensures that goal of motion structures can always be formed and, in general, results be added, independently of whether the verb itself licenses a result, (hence the possibility for both *arrive* and *walk* to freely combine with a *to-phrase* to give rise to a goal of motion interpretation), in Italian things are dramatically different. In this language, the verbs must specify in the lexicon whether a result projection can be licensed and hence a result augmentation allowed; in other words, while the strategy of forming a telic pair, and allowing a verb and a (point locating) preposition each to contribute an event variable of a telic pair is available in Italian, (also in French[11] and in Spanish though in a more limited way in the latter[12]), such a strategy depends crucially on the information attached to the verb itself: verbs which encode directionality, i.e., verbs that express motion which might be occurring on a PATH can enter the process of *telic pair formation* and give rise to goal of motion readings, while verbs which express undirected motion cannot.

From this initial discussion we can draw the following set of conclusions:

i.   Languages put in place different strategies to form goal of motion interpretations.

ii.   English has at its disposal a set of prepositions which are equivalent to verbal accomplishments of the well-known type. Just as for verbal accomplishments, a set of ordered event positions can be identified for this type of preposition which therefore can never be used to express locative motion.

iii. Italian lacks accomplishment prepositions, but can adopt a *satellite-framed* strategy to form goal of motion constructions.

iv.   This crucially depends on the lexical properties of the verb, namely on the presence among the lexical item features of a directional feature (allowing motion on a PATH) which licenses resultativity.

---

11.   Fong & Poulin (1997) notice that the verb *courir* 'run' in French gives rise to ambiguity between Activity and Accomplishment readings. Accordingly, *la petite fille a couru dans la maison* 'the little girl has run in the house', means both 'the little girl ran within the house' and 'the little girl entered the house running'. The ambiguity could not be related to the preposition *dans*, since the combination of *dans* with a verb such as *nager* 'swim' does not give rise to the same ambiguity. Fong and Poulin's idea is that in the case of MANNER+PATH of motion verbs, the ambiguity and therefore the Accomplishment reading, do not derive from the lexical semantic properties of the preposition, but from the properties of the verbs themselves, which by incorporating a PATH component allows the formation of a telic interpretation. The ambiguity therefore is due to a case of lexical ambiguity of the verb, which for them translates into the existence of different lexical semantic representations for the verbs: *courir* is a MANNER+PATH motion verb, while *nager* is only a MANNER of motion verb.

12.   See Zubizarreta and Oh 2004 for discussion.

Next we consider more closely the examples in (11) and introduce another set of prepositions which also allow the formation of goal of motion interpretation, namely complex prepositions formed with a combination of two locative prepositions.

3.   Goal of motion structures in Italian: simple prepositions

As I briefly outlined above, it is inaccurate to say that Romance languages uniformly form telic interpretations for motion situations encoding the path and the goal of motion on the verb. There are cases where Italian forms telic interpretations in a way that, on a surface level, is very similar to the English examples analysed above. Let us look at a couple of examples again:

(12)   a.   Gianni è   corso a   casa   in un   secondo.
             Gianni is run   to   home   in a   second
             'Gianni ran home in a second.'
       b.   Marco   è   scivolato nel   buco in   un   attimo.
             Marco   is slid   in.the hole in   an   instant
             'Marco slid into the hole in an instant.'

In these examples, we see that a motion verb in Italian can form a goal of motion interpretation with a preposition indicating the end point of motion. As argued at length in Folli (2001), I take this to be evidence that Italian has at its disposal a process of *telic pair formation* where the event position of the activity verb and the event position of the preposition can together form a telic pair, i.e., an ordered pair of events where both a process and a *telos* are present.

The availability of goal motion interpretations in Italian is obviously related to the question as to whether Italian has resultative constructions or not (Napoli 1992; Tortora 1998; Higginbotham 2000; Folli 2001; Folli & Ramchand 2005, among others). The two constructions have very similar syntactic and semantic properties and have therefore traditionally been treated as two of a kind. I have argued elsewhere for the existence of resultatives in Italian, and here I would like to draw attention to a further set of data which seems to confirm the availability in this language of resultatives of the PP type (13).

(13)   a.   Gianni ha   martellato il   chiodo nel   muro.
             Gianni has hammered   the   nail   in.the wall
             'Gianni hammered the nail into the wall.'
       b.   Gianni ha   spinto   la   matita nel   buco.
             Gianni has pushed   the   pencil in.the hole
             'Gianni pushed the pencil into the hole.'

c. Gianni ha spalmato la cera dentro ogni fessura.
Gianni has spread   the wax inside each crack
'Gianni spread the wax into each crack.'

In (13)a–c an activity verb is combined with the PP to form transitive resultatives where the embedded object is the subject of the secondary predicate: as a result of the events described in (13)a–c *the nail is in the wall, the pencil is in the hole* and *the wax is in each crack*. The presence in Italian of resultative structures of this type clearly confirms the capacity of the language to use activity verbs in structures that involve a resultative aspectual head.

Returning to motion verbs, a verb like *correre* 'run' can of course also be used to express a pure activity and in this case there is a switch in the auxiliary (14).[13]

(14) a. Gianni ha corso per un'ora.
Gianni has run   for an hour
'Gianni ran for an hour.'

As with many others (e.g., Hoekstra & Mulder 1990 for Dutch, Anagnostopoulou 2003 for Greek) I would like to argue that the shift in auxiliary selection accompanying the directed-motion interpretation confirms the unaccusative nature of the structures in (12) and the argumental status of the PP.

Notice though that not all prepositions that can give rise to these constructions are alike. Consider the following examples:

(15) a. Gianni è corso a casa/a scuola/al parco/all'ufficio postale
Gianni is run to home/to school/to the park/to the post office
b. ?*Gianni è corso all'ufficio/alla camera/alla cucina
Gianni is run to.the office/to.the room/to.the kitchen

(16) Gianni è corso in ufficio/in camera/in cucina
Gianni is run in office/in room/in kitcken

The examples above show that *a* and *in* combine with different NPs. *A* seems to combine with NPs expressing a Ground which can be interpreted as extended, or unbounded. In other words, in our mental representation, we think of schools, parks or post offices as extended PLACES, which might be signalled by a sign, and

---

13. A reviewer raises an important questions regarding the learnability issue related to the role played by lexical features in determining the different syntactic behaviour of verbs like *correre* 'run' versus *camminare* 'walk'. A crucial difference between these two verbs is that while *camminare* can only occur with *avere* 'have', *correre* can take both auxiliaries, *essere* 'be' when it is used to express a goal of motion intepretation, and *avere* 'have' when it is used to express a locative intepretation. Arguably, the difference in auxiliary selection of these two verbs could play a crucial role in explaining how the child learning the language converges onto a grammar where *correre* can be used to form a goal of motion interpretation, while *correre* cannot.

typically have an entrance and a perimeter. When they are used as complements of *a* in Italian, the motion event (e.g., the running event in the examples above) is seen as a motion <u>towards</u> a location (home, school, the park or the post office), while the end point of motion, that is the reaching of these locations, is left unspecified and is subject to entailment. Accordingly, when *a* is used with a complement which is more confined and giving rise to the expectation that the motion should be more explicitly ending 'inside the Ground', *a* is not felicitous. However, the preposition *in* gives a completely different result. The examples in (16) are all well-formed with *in*. It would therefore seem that while both prepositions can contribute a location (we can call that PLACE, in conformity to many in the literature and in particular Jackendoff 1983) which in combination with the right kind of verb produces a goal of motion, the two prepositions contribute a semantically different type of PLACE, one which is unbounded and one which is more clearly bounded.

Of course, a locative *a*-phrase can appear with copular or stative verbs as a predicate (17).

(17) a. Gianni   è   a   casa.
          Gianni   is   at   home
      b. Gianni   è   rimasto   a   casa.
          Gianni   is   remained   at   home
          'Gianni stayed home.'
      c. Gianni   vive   a   Parigi.
          Gianni   lives   at   Paris
          'Gianni lives in Paris.'

Interestingly, a locative phrase introduced by *a* can be used in Italian in conjunction with DPs referring to cities, villages and small islands (which again in conformity with the discussion above can be identified more clearly as having a sign or a clear perimeter), but not with DPs referring to countries (18).

(18) a. Gianni   vive   a Milano/Skye/*Sardegna
          Gianni   lives   at Milan/Skye/*Sardinia
      b. Gianni   vive   *a Italia/in   Italia
          Gianni   lives   *at Italy/in   Italy

Renzi & Salvi (1988) give the following account of this pattern: 'This rule can be given the following generalization: *a* is required with locations which can be conceived of as 'pointed' in our mental representation of their geographical nature,' (ibid p. 513). This seems to be the opposite of what we saw above in (15)a–b, namely that *a* in conjunction with a directional motion verb expresses a location which is extended in some relevant sense to be further investigated. I will return to this below.

So far we have seen that Italian allows goal of motion interpretation with certain kinds of motion verbs and that this combinatorial possibility is also mirrored in the availability of certain types of resultative constructions. Interestingly though, the conditions on the formation of goal of motion structure with verbs that encode a directionality feature are rather tight and so a verb that allows the formation of a goal of motion structure will not always combine felicitously with a PP. There seems to be a restriction due to the nature of the Ground encoded by the PP. Next I review a proposal by Tortora which supports the idea that PLACE as well as PATH can be interpreted as extended.

4.   Tortora's bounded PLACE

Tortora (2005, 2006, this volume) argues that the Jackendovian (1990, 1991) proposal to conceptualise PATH as bounded and unbounded extends to the other conceptual category of PLACE. This in turn has grammatical consequences which surface in Italian in a number of cases.

First, she notices that the alternating morphemes *qui/qua* for 'here' and *lì/là* for 'there' differ semantically in that *qui/lì* can be used to refer to a 'punctual space' while *qua/là* can be used to refer to an 'uncircumscribed region' (see also Cinque 1971; Vanelli 1995). Accordingly, she identifies cases where the use of the bounded version cannot be used since the event described by the verb requires an unbounded place (19) (examples from Tortora 2005, taken from Cinque 1971).

(19)   a.   I libri erano sparsi qui e lì/ qua e là
             The books were dispersed here and there
        b.   Girava qua e là senza meta/ *girava qui e lì senza meta
             He roamed here and there without any purpose

Second, she notices that this contrast is not limited to these locative forms but extends to other prepositions in Italian, in particular to prepositional minimal pairs of the following type: *dietro/dietro a* 'behind/behind to', *dentro/dentro a* 'inside/inside to'. Here are some of the relevant examples (from Tortora 2005):

(20)   a.   Gianni   era   nascosto   dietro   l'albero
             Gianni   was   hidden   behind   the tree
        b.   Gianni   era   nascosto   dietro   all'albero
             Gianni   was   hidden   behind   to.the tree

The crucial difference is that while (20)a refers to an event involving a 'wider' space, (20)b can only refer to an event taking place in a 'punctual' space. The same pattern is found again in the following pair of examples:

(21)   a.   Ho messo la tovaglia sopra al   tavolo
             I put the table cloth over at.the   table

b.   Ho messo la tovaglia sopra il tavolo
     I put the table cloth over the table

Here the difference in interpretation is very strong: (21)a means that the subject has spread the table cloth across the table (over an unbounded place), while (21)b can only be interpreted to mean that the table cloth was placed on the table, in a specific spot on the table.

The syntactic account of these facts relies on the hypothesis that PPs are headed by an AspP which incorporates a feature for boundedness. When *a* is present, the Asp feature is unspecified, hence leading to the interpretations in (20)b and (21)a discussed above. Conversely, when *a* is not realised in Asp, the feature [bounded] is positively valued and the interpretation of the spatial configuration consequently also bounded.

The crucial idea relevant for this discussion is that the category PLACE, just like the category PATH, can be bounded or unbounded. The details of Tortora's syntactic proposal, on the other hand, are in fact crucially opposed to the ones proposed in this paper. Notice that all the examples above involve stative predications and not goal of motion structures. As we will see in the next sections, when the preposition *a* is used in complex PPs to form goal of motion interpretations, its role is to identify the aspectual head that encodes resultativity.

5.   Complex PPs with *a* and aspectual heads identification

Thus far, our discussion has brought evidence for the availability in Italian of goal of motion interpretations with manner of motion verbs. In this section I show that this is in fact possible not only with simple prepositional phrases such as *a* (at/to), *in* (in), *sopra* (over), *sotto* (under)[14], but also with complex prepositional phrases composed of two prepositions such as *sotto a* (under to), *dentro a* (inside to), *dietro a* (behind to), *accanto a* (beside to), *fino a* (until at) etc. Some examples are given in (22).

(22)   a.   Gianni corse dentro al parco.
            Gianni ran inside to.the park
       b.   La palla rotolò dietro al muro.
            The ball rolled behind to.the wall

---

14.   In Folli (2001) I referred to those as point locating prepositions (in contrast to *path locating prepositions* which identify extended locations) given their ability to define a specific point in space and suitability in certain contexts to indicate the endpoint of motion. Based on the previous discussion and Tortora's analysis of structures with *a*, this classification would need to be revised.

    c.   Maria gattonò fino alla cucina.
           Maria crawled until to.the kitchen

Folli (2001) and Folli & Ramchand (2005) propose, together with many others in the literature (e.g., Koopman 2000; Den Dikken 2003; Svenonius 2003); that these prepositional phrases have a complex functional structure and that in particular they encode a path or process component, and location or result component. It is precisely because of their complex lexical functional structure that verbs which normally in Italian cannot be used to depict directional motion can, in conjunction with one of these phrases, do so (23).[15]

(23) a. Gianni camminò fino a   casa in poco più di   dieci minuti.
          Gianni walked   until to home in little more than ten   minutes
     b. *Gianni camminò a   casa in poco più di   dieci minuti.
          Gianni walked   to home in little more than ten   minutes
     c. La barca galleggiò dentro alla   grotta in un attimo.
          the boat   floated inside to.the cave in a   moment
     d. *La barca galleggiò alla   grotta in un attimo.
          the boat   floated to.the cave in a   moment
     e. La barca galleggiò dentro lagrotta *in un attimo /per un attimo.
          the boat   floated inside the cave in a moment /for a moment
     f. Gianni nuotò dietro a Maria senza che lei se ne accorgesse.
          Gianni swam behind to Maria without her noticing it
     e. *Gianni   nuotò   dietro Maria senza che lei se ne accorgesse.
          Gianni   swam   behind Maria without her noticing it
     g. *Gianni   nuotò   a Maria senza che lei se ne accorgesse.
          Gianni   swam   to Maria without her noticing it

The examples in (23) show that three verbs, which normally can only express locative motion, can form goal of motion structures as long as the complex prepositional phrases *fino a* (until to), *dentro a* (inside to), and *dietro a* (behind to) are used. Crucially, (23)b shows that *a* alone cannot be combined with the verb *camminare* (walk) and an *in X* adverbial. (23)d shows the same for *galleggiare* (float), while (23)e is grammatical with a *for X* adverbial only, as we would expect. Finally, we have the verb *nuotare* (swim) failing to receive a goal of motion interpretation with the preposition *dietro* (behind) in (23)e or with the preposition *a* (to) in (23) g, in contrast with (23)f where *dietro a* (behind to) permits the formation of a goal of motion interpretation.

From the examples in (23), we can draw the following preliminary conclusions: first, verbs like *galleggiare* (float) or *camminare* (walk), which are not

---

15. A reviewer points to the existence of speaker variation with respect to this data.

inherently directional, can be inserted into a syntactic structure that is able to deliver a telic interpretation for the event. Second, it seems that the two prepositions are indeed necessary for a directional interpretation to be possible, and that in fact the telicity of the event is produced by the complex PP itself.

The next question then is how this relates to Tortora's discussion of these complex PPs and, more importantly, to her hypothesis regarding the unboundedness of PLACE and the crucial role played by *a* in delivering an interpretation where PLACE is unbounded.

Let us compare the following examples:

(24) a. Rimasi   dietro   al   / dietro   il   muro   ad aspettarla.
          remained   behind   (to.the) / behind   the   wall   to wait for her
          'I remained behind the wall waiting for her.'
      b. Corsi   dietro   al   / dietro   il   muro ad aspettarla.[16]
          ran   behind   (to.the) / behind   the wall   to wait for her
          'I ran behind the wall to wait for her.'
      c. La barca è   galleggiata sotto   al   ponte   in un   secondo.
          the boat is floated   under   to.the bridge in a   second
          'The boat floated under the bridge in a second.'
      d. * La   barca è   galleggiata sotto   il   ponte   in un   secondo.
          the   boat   is floated   under   the   bridge in a   second
          'The boat floated under the bridge in a second.'

(24)a is locative and in this case *a* can be used or omitted without causing a change in grammaticality. When it is present it further specifies the location. The crucial contrast is the one we see in (24)b–d. In (24)b the verb is *correre* 'run' and the sentence is grammatical in its goal of motion interpretation both with the single preposition *sotto* 'under' or with the complex PP *sotto a* 'under to'. Conversely,

---

16. Interestingly the sentences in (24)b–c are marginally better if the NP is a not a pronoun. Here is another minimal pair:

(i)   a. Gianni   corse   dietro   a   Maria /??dietro Maria.
          Gianni   ran   behind   to   Maria /behind   Maria
      b. ??Gianni corse dietro   Maria.
          Gianni   ran   behind   Maria
(ii) a. Gianni   corse   dietro   a   lei.
          Gianni   ran   behind   to   her
      b. *Gianni corse   dietro   lei.
          Gianni   ran   behind   her

In the judgement of several speakers, the ungrammaticality of (ii)b is definitely more severe than that of (i)b. I leave the investigation of this problem to future research.

examples (24)c–d show that with the verb *galleggiare* 'float' both PPs are necessary to give rise to a goal of motion interpretation.

Further, the following minimal pair allows us to see how the locative/directional interpretations pan out for sentences like the following:[17]

(25) a. Gianni corse dentro al   parco.   [directional]
          Gianni ran   inside to.the park
      b. Gianni corse dentro il   parco.   [locative/directional]
          Gianni ran   inside the   park

In (25)a *correre* (run) is interpreted as encoding directional motion, hence implying that Gianni ends up inside the park, while (25)b can be interpreted both as implying a run by Gianni inside the perimeter of the park, or a run towards the park.

How does this set of facts fit with Tortora's examples in (19)–(21)?

The hypothesis I would like to argue for assumes the proposal made by Folli (2001) and Folli & Ramchand (2005) whereby Italian is characterised by a ban on empty aspectual heads, which is crucial in accounting for other properties of the language such as the lack of double object constructions, of adjectival resultatives and of zero derived deadjectival and denominal verbs (see Folli 2001 and Folli & Ramchand 2005 for discussion). In general, it seems that this language forms structures that express resultativity when the verb is one that encodes in its lexical entry an Rv feature. This allows the projection of a syntactic structure with a resultative aspectual head which the verb can identify. With verbs that do not encode this feature and hence cannot be merged into a structure with a resultative aspectual head, the formation of goal of motion is more restricted. Since empty aspectual heads are not possible in Italian and since some verbs cannot identify an Rv head, only complex PPs can produce goal of motion interpretations because complex PPs have two prepositions and each preposition can identify a component of a goal of motion event, the path component and the location component (see tree in (9)). This is precisely what happens in the grammatical examples in (23). In particular, in those examples the role of the first preposition of the complex PP is to identify the Path component, while the preposition *a* 'to' identifies the Location component. Conversely, when the verb is locative as Tortora's examples in (19)–(21) above, *a* is not identifying the result of motion. Semantically it seems to contribute a further specification of PLACE as pointed in the words of Renzi and Salvi (1988) or bounded as proposed by Tortora.

---

17. Notice that *corse dentro al parco* (ran inside to.the park) could also have a locative interpretation since the two PPs could both be adjuncts, *dentro* modifying the event and *a* modifying *dentro*.

Next, in light of everything we have said so far, I elucidate in more explicit terms the two ways in which Italian gives rise to goal of motion interpretations.

5.1   The first case

We saw above that a verb like *correre* (run) allows a directional interpretation. This is due to the availability of two different derivations: one where the verb itself identifies the path of motion and the preposition gives the final location; one where each one of the prepositions making up the complex PP identifies a portion of motion. For this reason, *correre* 'run' can in the example (24)b above compose with both the simple PP *sotto* 'under' or the complex PP *sotto a* 'under to' and give rise to a goal of motion interpretation. We see examples of each case in (26) and (27).

(26)

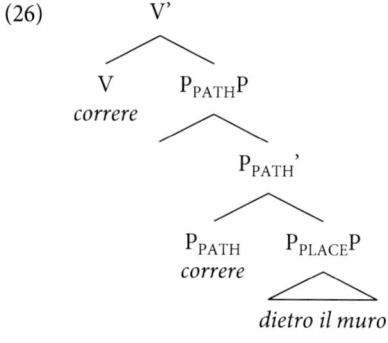

(27)

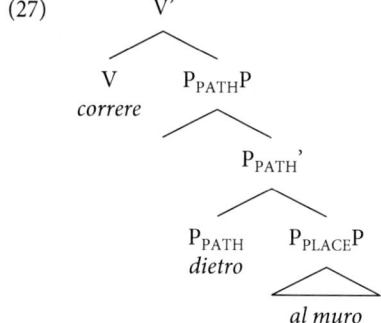

5.2   The second case

As discussed above, in Italian, verbs of manner of motion split into two classes: one class of verbs which may encode directional motion along a path, and one class which does not. *Galleggiare* 'float' and *camminare* 'walk' belong to the second class. The type of motion they express is non-directional, hence when combined with a preposition like *a* 'to', *in* 'in', and *dentro* 'inside', they always only return a locative interpretation. Nevertheless, in examples (23)a, c, f above we saw that *galleggiare* 'float', *camminare* 'walk' and *nuotare* 'swim' can produce a goal of motion interpretation if they are combined with a complex PP encoding PATH and PLACE such as phrases like *fino a* 'until to', *dentro a* 'inside to', and *dietro a* 'behind to'. Crucially the examples in (23)b,d,e,g were ungrammatical, confirming the need for the aspectual head to be filled. Also in (24)c–d above we saw that *galleggiare* 'float' can give rise to a goal of motion structure if both PPs *sotto a* 'under to' are present (28).

(28)

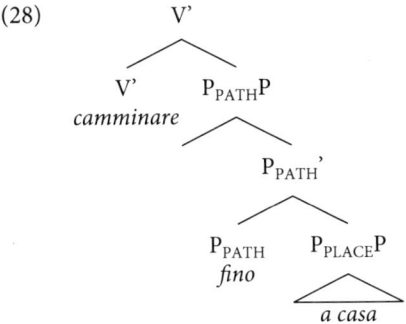

5.3   Unbounded grounds, filled aspectual heads, and concluding remarks

We are now in the position to return to some of the data presented above. In line with Tortora's analysis, it seems that it is correct to extend the notion of boundedness to the category PLACE. This is not just visible in cases where the verb is locative and *a* is used in combination with another PP as discussed in Tortora (2005 and 2006), but also in the examples above in (18) repeated in (29).

(29)   a.   Gianni vive a Milano/Skye/*Sardegna
             Gianni lives at Milan/Skye/*Sardinia
       b.   Gianni vive *a Italia/in Italia
             Gianni lives *at Italy/in Italy

Here, the contrast must be due to the property of PLACE.

Things are radically different when we consider constructions involving manner of motion verbs and in particular the formation of directional interpretations. Italian, can indeed form goal of motion interpretations with manner of motion verbs, but the grammatical constraint of Italian against unfilled aspectual heads forces the presence of *a* when the verb is one that cannot identify by itself a resultative aspectual head. In those cases, the complex PPs that have been the focus of this paper are crucially involved in the formation of such interpretations. These PPs are composed of two prepositions, and each preposition fills an aspectual head. In this sense, the analysis proposed here is essentially opposed to the one made by Tortora since for us the presence of *a* is crucially related to the licensing and identification of an aspectual head.

In conclusion we have seen that while non-directional motion is typically realised in Italian with a locative PP, namely via a simple (i.e., single P-containing) prepositional structure, directed motion involves a complex P-structure which involves (at least) two heads, one for the PATH of motion, and one for PLACE. We have discussed how in Italian the formation of goal of motion structures with lexically simple PPs is limited to a subclass of verbs bearing a directional feature in their lexical specification which allows them to combine with a LOCATION PP and give rise to directed motion reading. More generally, we have seen that the availability of goal of motion interpretations can result from the complex interplay of various components involved in the formation of these structures: the lexical meaning of the verb, the syntactic composition of heads and the lexical meaning of the Ground (see Svenonius 2004 for a detailed discussion of this last point).

The general thrust behind this discussion has been that, even though structure is what determines interpretation, and therefore argument structure alternations are due to the availability of different structures made available by principles of syntax in general (Hale & Keyser 1993), combined with the parametric choices of individual languages, crucial elements of meaning attached to verbs cannot be discounted in explaining what is a possible alternation or not. The identification of clear patterns makes resorting to encyclopaedic knowledge too vague and ultimately less explanatory. On the other hand, a structural account of argument alternations is not incompatible with the identification of semantic restrictions because the integration of structure and semantically acceptable scenarios is obviously at the basis of grammatical, but unacceptable sentences such as *Tiredness murdered Mary*. The important question, we think, is whether the restrictions we identify are systematic and if they turn out to be so, whether they can be related to well-known building blocks of conceptual structures. The answer to both questions seems positive as very often the restrictions that are at work in constraining alternations are related to notions such as path or direction which several decades of work in lexical semantics have shown to be at the basis of the conceptual structure.

References

Anagnostopoulou, E. 2003. *The Syntax of Ditransitives. Evidence from Clitics*. Berlin: Mouton deGruyter.
Baker, M. 1988. *Incorporation: A Theory of Grammatical Function Changing*. Chicago IL: University of Chicago Press.
Biberauer, T. & Folli, R. 2004. Constructing directional motion in Afrikaans. Paper presented at LAGB 2004.
Borer, H. 1998. Deriving passives without theta-grids. In *Morphology and its Relations to Phonology and Syntax*, S. Lapointe, D. Brentary & D. Farrell (eds), 60–99. Stanford CA: CSLI.

Borer, H. 2005. *Structuring Sense*. Oxford: OUP.

Bowerman, M. & Choi, S. 2001. Shaping meanings for language: Universal and language-specific in the acquisition of spatial semantic categories. In *Language Acquisition and Conceptual Development*, M. Bowerman & S. Levinson (eds), 475–511. Cambridge: CUP.

Cinque, G. 1971. Analisi Semantica Della Deissi in Italiano. Tesi di laurea, University of Padova.

Chomsky, N. 1970. Remarks on nominalization. In *Readings in English Transformational Grammar*, R. Jacobs & P. Rosenbaum (eds), 184–221. Waltham MA: Ginn.

Chomsky, N. 1981. *Lectures on Government and Binding*. Dordrecht: Foris.

den Dikken, M. 2003. On the syntax of locative and directional adpositional phrases. Ms., CUNY.

Fodor, J. 1970. Three reasons for not deriving 'kill' from 'cause to die'. *Linguistic Inquiry* 1: 29–38.

Fodor, J. & Lepore, E. 1997. Morphemes matter: The continuing case against lexical decomposition. Ms., Center for Cognitive Science, Rutgers University.

Folli, R. 2001. Constructing Telicity in English and Italian. PhD Dissertation, University of Oxford.

Folli, R & Harley, H. 2005. Flavors of v: Consuming results in Italian and English. In *Aspectual Enquiries*, P. Kempchinsky & R. Slabakova (eds), 95–120. Dordrecht: Springer.

Folli, R. & Ramchand, G. 2005. Prepositions and results in Italian and English: An analysis from event decomposition. In *Perspectives on Aspect*, H. Verkuyl, A. van Hout & H. de Swart (eds), 1–20. Dordrecht: Springer.

Fong, V. & Poulin, C. 1997. Verb classes and argument structure in French and English. Ms., Stanford University.

Gehrke, B. 2007. On directional readings of locative prepositions. In *Proceedings of ConSOLE XIV*, S. Blaho, L. Vicente & E. Schoorlemmer (eds), 99–120.

Harley, H. & Noyer, R. 2000. Formal vs. encyclopaedic properties of vocabulary: Evidence from nominalizations. In *The Lexicon-Encyclopedia Interface*, B. Peeters (ed.), 349–374. Amsterdam: Elsevier.

Higginbotham, J. 1997. Location and causation. Ms., University of Oxford.

Higginbotham, J. 2000. Accomplishments. In *Nazan Glow Proceedings*.

Hoekstra, T. & Mulder, R. 1990. Unergatives as copular verbs. *The Linguistic Review* 7: 1–79.

van Hout, A. 1996. *Event Semantics of Verb Frame Alternations* [TILDIL Dissertation Series]. Tilburg: Tilburg University.

Jackendoff, R. 1983. *Semantics and Cognition*. Cambridge MA: The MIT Press.

Jackendoff, R. 1990. *Semantic Structures*. Cambridge: The MIT Press.

Jackendoff, R. 1991. Parts and boundaries. *Cognition* 41: 9–45.

Koopman, H. 2000. Preposition, postpositions, circumpositions and particles. In *The Syntax of Specifiers and Heads*, H. Koopman (ed.), 204–260. London: Routledge.

Kratzer, A. 1996. Severing the external argument from its verb. In *Phrase Structure and the Lexicon*, J. Rooryck & L. Zaring (eds), 109–137. Dordrecht: Kluwer.

Levin, B. 1993. *Verb Classes and Alternations: A Preliminary Investigation*. Chicago IL: The University of Chicago Press.

Levin, B. & Rappaport-Hovav, M. 1995. *Unaccusativity: At the Syntax-Lexical Semantics Interface*. Cambridge MA: The MIT Press.

Marantz, A. 1997. No escape from syntax: Don't try morphological analysis in the privacy of your own lexicon. In *University of Pennsylvania Working Papers in Linguistics* 4(2), A. Dimitriadis & L. Siegel (eds), 201–225.

Mateu, J. 2002. Argument Structure. Relational Construal at the Syntax-Semantics Interface. PhD Dissertation, UAB, Bellaterra.

Napoli, D.J. 1992. Secondary resultative predicates in Italian. *Journal of Linguistics* 28: 53–90.

Parson, T. 1990. *Events in the Semantics of English*. Cambridge MA: The MIT Press

Pustejovsky, J. 1988. The geometry of events. In *Studies in Generative Approaches to Aspect*, C. Tenny (ed.), 34–62. Centre for Cognitive Science, MIT.

Pustejvosky, J. 1991. The syntax of event structure. *Cognition* 41: 47–81.

Ramchand, G. 2004. Verb meaning and the lexicon. Ms., University of Tromsø.

Renzi, L. & Salvi, G. 1991. *Grande Grammatical Italiana di Consultazione*, Volume II. Bologna: Il mulino.

van Riemsdijk, H. 2002. The unbearable lightness of Going: The projection parameter as a pure parameter governing the distribution of elliptic motion verbs in Germanic. *Journal of Comparative Germanic Linguistics* 5: 197–225.

Ritter, E. & Rosen, T.S. 1998. Delimiting events in syntax. In *The Projection of Arguments*, M. Butt & W. Geuder (eds), 135–164. Stanford CA: CSLI.

Slobin, D. 2004. The many ways to search for a frog: Linguistic typology and the expression of motion events. In *Relating Events in Narrative II*, S. Strömqvist & L. Verhoeven (eds), 219–257. Mahwah NJ: LEA.

Svenonius, P. 2003. Limits on P: Filling in holes vs. falling in holes. *Nordlyd* 31(2): 431–445

Svenonius, P. 2004. Spatial P in English. Ms., Tromsø University.

Talmy, L. 1985. Lexicalization patterns: Semantic structure in lexical forms. In *Language Typology and Syntactic Description* III: *Grammatical Categories and the Lexicon*, T. Shopen (ed.), 57–149. Cambridge: CUP.

Talmy, L. 1991. Path to realisation: A typology of event integration. *Buffalo Papers in Linguistics* 91: 147–187.

Thomas, E. 2001. On the expression of directional movement in English. *Essex Graduate Student Papers in Language and Linguistics* 4: 87–104.

Thomas, E. 2003. Manner-specificity as a factor in the acceptance of *in* an *on* in directional contexts. *Essex Graduate Student Papers in Language and Linguistics* 5: 117–146.

Tortora, C. 1998. Verbs of inherently directed motion are compatible with resultative phrases. *Linguistics Inquiry* 29(2): 338–345.

Tortora, C. 2005. The preposition's preposition in Italian: Evidence for boundedness of space. In *Theoretical and Experimental Approaches to Romance Linguistics*, R. Gess & E. Rubin (eds), 307–327. Amsterdam: John Benjamins.

Tortora, C. 2006. Aspect and the internal structure of Romance PLACE PPs. Paper presented at the 36th Meeting of the Linguistic Symposium on Romance Languages (LSRL36), Rutgers University.

Travis, L. 1994. Event phrase and a theory of functional categories. In *1994 Proceedings of the Canadian Linguistic Association*, 559–570.

Tungseth, M. 2006. Verbal Prepositions in Norwegian: Paths, Places and Possession. Phd Dissertation, University of Tromsø.

Vannelli, L. 1995. La deissi spaziale. In *Grande Grammatica Italiana di Consultazione* [volume III], L. Renzi, G. Salvi & A. Cardinaletti (eds), 269–183. Bologna: Il mulino.

Zubizarreta, M.L. & Oh, E. 2004. The lexicon-syntax interface: The case of motion verbs. Ms., USC.

On the l-syntax of directionality/resultativity

The case of Germanic preverbs*

Jaume Mateu
Universitat Autònoma de Barcelona (UAB)

This paper offers a l(exical)-syntactic explanation of some challenging patterns of Germanic complex verbs that have been argued to cause non-trivial problems to Hale & Keyser's (1993, 1997a) theory of argument structure. I tackle the task of dealing with all of them in two important ways: on the one hand, drawing on Hale & Keyser's (2000) insight concerning 'P as a cognate complement' in English complex verbs of the type *heat up*, I provide the relevant l-syntactic analyses for some German complex location verbs and complex deadjectival verbs. On the other hand, following McIntyre's (2004) and Zubizarreta & Oh's (2007) recent adaptations of Mateu's (2001a, 2002) 'plug-in' theory of Manner conflation, I show that Hale & Keyser's (1997b) and Mateu's (2000, 2001b) original syntactic analyses of so-called 'lexical subordination processes' are on the right track.

1. Introduction

Given the abundant literature on Germanic verb-particle constructions,[1] I would like to start this paper by making it clear that my present goal is quite specific: i.e., to provide a l(exical)-syntactic account of those Germanic preverb constructions that have been argued to cause serious problems to Hale & Keyser's (henceforth: H&K) syntactic approach to argument structure. In a sense, this paper can then

* This research has been supported by the grants BFF2003-08364-C02-02, HUM2006-13295-C02-02 (Spanish Ministerio de Educación y Ciencia), and 2005-SGR-00753 (Catalan Direcció General de Recerca). For comments and suggestions, I would like to thank Víctor Acedo, Susanna Padrosa, Gemma Rigau, and the participants of the *Spatial P* Conference, in particular, Andrew McIntyre and Peter Svenonius. I especially acknowledge gratitude to two anonymous reviewers for their helpful observations and positive comments. Needless to say, all the shortcomings of this paper are mine alone.

1. See Dehé et al. (2002) and Booij & Marle (2003) for two recent compendia.

be taken as an extensive reply to Stiebels's (1998) criticism of their syntactic approach. In particular, she claims that the list of German complex verbs that cannot be explained by H&K includes complex location verbs of the type *einrahmen* ('in-frame'), complex denominal verbs of the type *verslumen* ('become a slum'), complex locatum verbs of the type *überdachen* ('roof over'), complex denominal verbs of the type *versanden* ('sand up'), and complex denominal verbs of the type *vergärtnern* ('garden away').

As is well-known, most of generative linguists dealing with verb-particle constructions are divided between those who argue for a Complex Predicate analysis and those who argue for a Small Clause analysis. Following H&K (2002: chap. 8) and Ramchand & Svenonius (2002), among others, I will be arguing for a particular version of the SC account but without assuming the existence of a truly clausal complement (cf. Kayne 1985; Hoekstra 1988; Mulder 1992; Den Dikken 1995, among others). Unlike the proponents of a CP account (cf. Johnson 1991; Neeleman 1994; Zeller 2001, among others), I posit that the internal DP argument is merged with the predicative particle/preverb before that substructure is merged with the verb.

The organization of the present article is as follows: in Section 2 I review the basics of H&K's (1997a, 1998, 2000, 2002) theory of argument structure, on which I will ground my l-syntactic analyses of Germanic complex verbs. Due to my present concerns, I pay special attention to their claim that P heads a cognate complement in English complex verbs of the type *heat up*. In Section 3, I put forward an l-syntactic analysis for different types of German complex verbs, showing also why my present account based on H&K's (1997b, 2002) theory of l-syntax is to be preferred to Stiebels's (1998) semantic one based on Wunderlich's (1997) Lexical Decomposition Grammar (LDG). In Section 4 I show how the present account of Germanic preverbs can be integrated into Mateu's (2002) l-syntactic approach to Talmy's (1991, 2000) descriptive typology of satellite- vs. verb-framed languages. Section 5 contains some concluding remarks.

2. The basic elements of argument structure

Argument structure is conceived of by H&K as the syntactic configuration projected by a lexical item, i.e., argument structure is the system of structural relations holding between heads (nuclei) and the arguments linked to them, as part of their entries in the lexicon. Although a lexical entry is much more than this, of course, argument structure in the sense intended by H&K is precisely this and nothing more. Their main assumptions can be expressed informally as follows: argument structure is defined in reference to two possible relations between a head and its arguments, namely, the head-complement relation and the head-specifier relation. According to H&K (1998: 82), a given head (i.e., x in 1) may enter into the following structural combinations in 1: these are its argument structure properties, and its syntactic behavior is determined by these properties.[2]

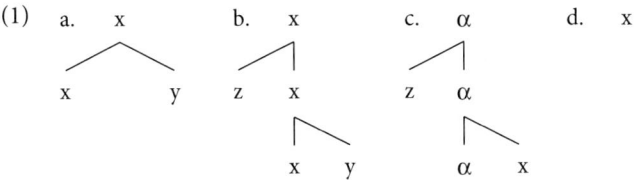

Figure 1. Head (x); complement (y of x), predicate (x of z).

The main empirical domain on which H&K's hypotheses have been tested includes denominal verbs (unergative verbs like *dance* in 2a, location verbs like *shelve* in 2b, or locatum verbs like *saddle* in 2c) and deadjectival verbs like *clear* in 2d.

(2) a. John danced.
     b. John shelved the book.
     c. John saddled the horse.
     d. John cleared the screen / The screen cleared.

Unergative verbs are argued to be transitive since they involve merging a non-relational element (typically, a noun) with a verbal head (see 3a); both location verbs (e.g., *shelve*) and locatum verbs (e.g., *saddle*) involve merging the structural combination in 1b into the one of 1a: see 3b. Finally, unaccusative deadjectival verbs involve the structural combination in 1c, the transitive or causative one involving two structural combinations, i.e., the one depicted in 1c is merged into the one in 1a: see 3c.[3]

---

2.   According to H&K, the prototypical or unmarked morphosyntactic realizations in English of the syntactic heads in 1 (i.e., the x's) are the following ones: V in 1a, P in 1b, *Adj* in 1c, and N in 1d.

3.   Uriagereka (1998) has argued that adopting H&K's conservative argument for the existence of phrasal projection inside lexical entries runs into problems with Chomsky's (1995) minimalist program. In order to solve them, Uriagereka (1998) argues that those structures given in 3 are not lexical representations, but syntactic structures corresponding to lexical representations, after they are selected from the numeration. For example, Uriagereka (1998: 438) points out that i. is to be regarded as the actual lexical representation of the denominal verb *saddle* that determines the syntactic argument structure in 3b (NB: the abbreviations in (ia) are used by Uriagereka (1998: 434–438) to mean the following: F-P = feature-P (i.e., "a-Prep-incorporates-into-me"), v-F = v-feature (i.e., "I-incorporate-into-v"), F-N = feature-N (i.e., "a-Noun-incorporates-into-me"), and P-F = P-feature (i.e., "I-incorporate-into-P").

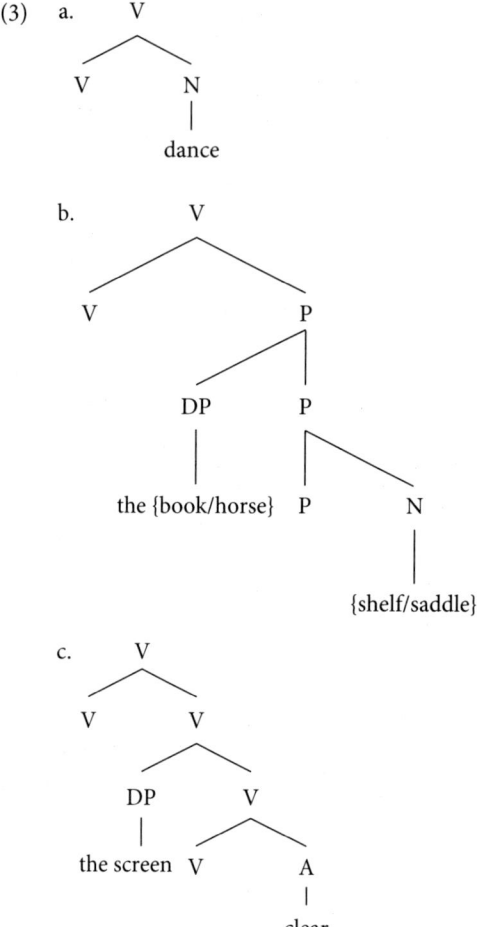

(3)   a.   V

b.   V

c.   V

Figure 2. L(exical)-syntactic analyses of unergative verbs (3a), location/locatum verbs (3b), and deadjectival verbs (3c).

i.   a.   [-N, +V, F-P...] + [-N, -V, v-F, F-N] + [+N, -V, P-F]
     b.   v   +   P   +   saddle

According to Uriagereka, the features in (ia) are purely combinatorial markings, uninterpretable formal features of words like *saddle* and *shelve* that are idiosyncratic to each of these verbs. Be this as it may, since the analyses to be presented in the present paper do not crucially hinge on assuming Uriagereka's feature-based refinements such as those in (i) to derive argument structures like the one in 3b, I will omit such a discussion here. As far as I can tell, my present proposal can be regarded as compatible with both H&K's 'conservative' and Uriagereka's minimalist ways of constructing syntactic argument structures.

The external argument of transitive constructions (unergatives included) is argued by H&K to be truly external to the argument structure configurations: for example, they typically appeal to this proposal when accounting for why unaccusative structures can be transitivized (cf. 2d),[4] while unergatives ones cannot (*Mary danced John). The external argument can be said to occupy the specifier position of a functional projection in s(entential)-syntax.[5] Alternatively, as argued by H&K themselves, following Koopman & Sportiche (1991), this argument is structurally an adjunct to the VP and, moreover, a 'distinguished adjunct' coindexed with the VP.

According to H&K (1998), all verbs in 2 implicate a process of conflation, i.e., a specific kind of incorporation that conforms to an especially strict version of the Head Movement Constraint (Travis 1984; Baker 1988), an operation that copies a full phonological matrix into an empty one, this operation being carried out in a strictly local configuration: i.e., in a head-complement one. This guarantees locality and precludes conflation of a specifier: e.g., 4a and 4b are ruled out since the specifier of P is not selected by the verbal head in 3b.[6]

(4)   a.   *John booked the shelf (on the reading *John put a book on the shelf*)
      b.   *John horsed the saddle (on the reading *John provided the horse with a saddle*)

Applying then the conflation operation to 3a involves copying the full phonological matrix of the noun *laugh* into the empty one corresponding to the verb. Applying it to 3b involves two steps: the full phonological matrix of the noun {*shelf/saddle*} is first copied into the empty one corresponding to the preposition; since the phonological matrix corresponding to the verb is also empty, the conflation applies again from the saturated phonological matrix of the preposition to the unsaturated matrix of the verb. Finally, applying the conflation process to 3c involves two steps as well: the full phonological matrix of the adjective *clear* is first copied

---

4.   See H&K (2002: chap. 6) on why unaccusatives of the *arrive* type do not causativize.

5.   According to H&K, the term 'sentential syntax' is used to refer to the syntactic structure assigned to a phrase or sentence involving both the lexical item and its arguments and also its 'extended projection' (Grimshaw 1991) and including, therefore, the full range of functional categories and projections implicated in the formation of a sentence interpretable at PF and LF.

6.   In contrast to conflation, incorporation in s(entential)-syntax is argued to be constrained by government. Since a head governs the specifier of its complement, there is no barrier to incorporating from that position (see Baker (1988) and H&K (1993, 1998, 2002) for further discussion).

into the empty one corresponding to the internal verb; since the phonological matrix corresponding to the external verb is also empty, the conflation applies again from the saturated phonological matrix of the inner verb to the unsaturated matrix of the external verb.

It is however important to point out that H&K's definition of 'conflation' has recently changed: e.g., conflation is no longer viewed by H&K (2002: chap. 3) as an operation akin to Baker's (1988) incorporation, but rather is said to be subsumed by Selection. Indeed, the existence of hyponymous and cognate constructions like those in 5 has been essential to their arguing for such a theoretical move:

(5)   a.   John danced a polka.
      b.   John shelved the book onto the top shelf.

On the one hand, H&K (1997a) argue that a full DP can be inserted in the argumental position corresponding to the complement of the verb in 3a/5a or to the complement of the preposition in 3b/5b. It is crucial for that analysis that the trace of the raised N is not a 'referential' trace of the sort defined by DP movement, for example. On the other hand, H&K (2002: chap. 3) assume that the verbs *dance* and *shelve* are not to be derived in the way intended by their corresponding argument structures in 3, but are entered as such in the lexicon. The idea would be that the full verbs *dance* and *shelve* in 2a and 2b would be 'rich enough' (*sic*) in semantic features to license the nominal categories involved in their corresponding argument structures. According to H&K (2002: 103), conflation is merely the binding relation that holds between the semantic features of a verb (phonologically overt now) and features of the nominal head. For example, an overt verb (e.g., *dance*) could be said to be directly provided with hyperonymic semantic features corresponding to the activity of *dancing*. These superordinate features assigned to the verb could then impose strong restrictions on the semantic nature of the nominal complement, which would be provided with more specific or subordinate (i.e., hyponymic) content: e.g., *a polka* is to be understood to refer to something belonging to the class of dances.

However, I am not sympathetic to H&K's (2002: chap. 3) recent proposal of (re)defining conflation on the basis of constructions like 5: as emphasized by Mateu (2005a), verbal heads in 3 cannot be directly associated with encyclopedic semantic features because of their merely relational eventive character (e.g., cf. Harley & Noyer's (2000: 358f) flavors of *v*: BECOME, CAUSE, etc.). So for example in 3a all the encyclopedic features should be directly associated to the complement position, i.e., the hyperonymic ones to the nominal root √DANCE, and the hyponymic ones to the root of the DP inserted later. My claim is then that their semantic compatibility is to be established out of the computational system, i.e., in the encyclopedia component (Marantz 1997; Harley & Noyer 2000). For my present purposes, I will then continue assuming H&K's (1997a) theory of cognate object constructions.[7]

2.1 Some remarks on the l-syntax of English verb-particle constructions

Verb-particle constructions like those exemplified in 6 are discussed by H&K (2002: chap. 8), their main concern there being the manner in which the specifier is introduced into syntactic argument structures. H&K argue that particles do not in and of themselves require specifiers (cf. den Dikken 1995), and they are said to function only synergetically with their overt complements in the projection of specifiers. Accordingly, they point out that *the books* in 6a and *her saddle* in 6b occupy the specifier position of the complex predicative structure formed by *down on the shelf* and *up on the fence*, respectively: see 7.

(6) a. They put the books down on the shelf.
　　 b. She put her saddle up on the fence.

(7)

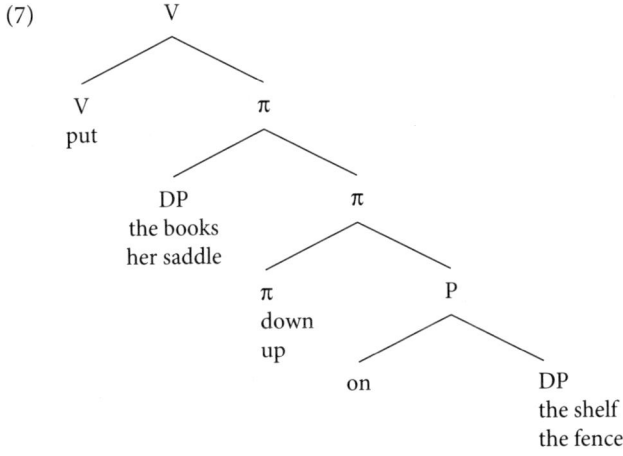

Figure 3. L(exical)-syntactic analysis of (6).

---

7. An anonymous reviewer points out that a formal representation of the encyclopedia component should be provided rather than "pushing the problems at hand into another module." I partly agree with that criticism but my claim is simply that the syntactic component (H&K's l-syntax included) should not be made responsible for explaining the contrast between *John danced a polka* vs. *#John danced a table.* Indeed, the real (and not trivial!) problem here is not that one,

H&K (2002: 232) point out that 8a,b are ruled out because of economical reasons: in their words, the 'delayed gratification' involved in 6a, b (defined wrt the introduction of the specifier into the complex π+P structure in 7) is said to preempt the 'immediate gratification' involved in 8a, b. Notice also that the interesting contrast between 8a, b and 8d has to do with the fact that the PP is a complement in the former examples but not in the latter, where it is an adjunct (but see Den Dikken (1995) for another view).

(8)   a.   *They put down the books on the shelf.   (cf. 6a)
      b.   *She put up her saddle on the fence.   (cf. 6b)
      c.   They put decorations up in the kids' room.
      d.   They put up decorations in the kids' room.

Consider now H&K's (2000: 39) examples in 9, which are more relevant for our present purposes.

(9)   a.   We heated the soup.
      b.   We heated the soup up.
      c.   The soup heated (slowly).
      d.   The soup heated up (finally).

H&K (2000: 39–49) put forward the interesting proposal that the examples in 9b, d involve a cognation process similar to the one found in 5: in particular, they assume that the prepositional particle that appears in 9b, d can be analyzed like those hyponymous and cognate objects in 5. Moreover, this prepositional element is said to have the following semantics: "it is the component of an adjectival expression which refers to the 'degree' or 'intensity' at which the quality denoted by the adjective is realized (. . .) If it is indeed correct, then we have a source for the particles *up, off, down*, and the like, as they occur in association with deadjectival verbs" (p. 40). Notice that this non-trivial modification leads them to replace the l-syntactic analysis of deadjectival verbs in 3c by the one in 10.

---

but rather the following one mentioned by the same reviewer: my accepting H&K's (1997a) theory of cognate objects "leads to a lot of controversies, about cyclicity, about different kinds of syntax in and out of the lexicon, etc." I agree that all these matters should be in the agenda of all those linguists who accept H&K's non-trivial distinction between l-syntax and s-syntax. For the time being, my personal view is that those technical problems concerning cyclicity should wait their turn since our present priority is "to determine the extent to which the possible predicate argument structures are a function of the elementary properties of the linguistic elements which are *necessarily* involved in defining them –i.e., the lexical categories and the fundamental relations of complementation and predication" (H&K 1997a: 62).

(10)

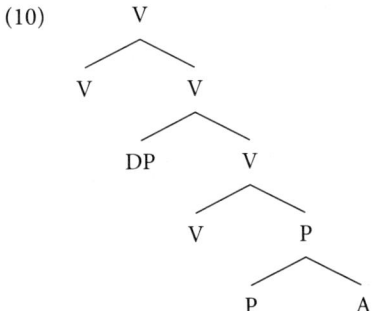

Figure 4. L(exical)-syntactic analysis of (complex) deadjectival verbs.

According to H&K, in 9b the overt particle *up* is inserted in place of the empty P in 10, i.e., in the position corresponding to the 'trace' left by incorporation of P into V. In 10 "P does not head a separate, autonomous predicate. Instead, it is as if A and P jointly head one and the same predicate. And this, like any adjectival predicate, finds its subject external to its own projection" (H&K 2000: 45–46).[8]

2.2 Generalizing the P(ath) structure

As emphasized by H&K (2000: 40f), the analysis in (10) is not only posited for complex deadjectival verbs but, more generally, for 'simple' deadjectival verbs. Although I am fully sympathetic to the generalized replacement of 3c by 10, I think that the semantic description H&K associate to the P in 10 is not the correct one (cf. supra).[9] Rather it seems to me that the relational semantics of P in 10 is not so different from the one associated to π in 7: i.e., my claim is that both denote a Path relation, which in turn subcategorizes for a P(lace) relation in 7 and a State (i.e., an abstract Place) encoded by A in 10. As a result, notice that my arguing that π in 7 and P in 10 are the very same P(ath) element strenghtens a parallelism which

---

8. As noted by H&K (2000: 46; fn. 23), "it is unlikely that there is a synchronically real phonological derivation here; the relationship ⟨between *hot* and *heat*: JM⟩ is essentially suppletive, but in many other cases, e.g., *warm, cool*, the adjective and the derived verb are homophonous, and in many, the relation involves affixal morphology, as in *redden, widen, darken*." See also H&K (1998) for further discussion on similar cases.

9. My proposal is that semantic notions like 'degree' or 'intensity' should not be associated to the l(exical)-syntax of argument structure. Rather they should be associated to a non-lexical category which is usually referred to as DegreeP, i.e., the extended/functional projection of the lexical category Adjective.

is not captured by the previous analyses of change of location verbs like *shelve* (cf. 3b) and change of state verbs like *clear* (cf. 3c).

Indeed, as is well-known, H&K do not posit a direct association of the Path and Place functions with the prepositional(like) elements of l-syntax. Rather they prefer using the notions of terminal and central coincidence relations (Hale 1986; H&K 2000).[10] Be this as it may, I think that there is an emerging consensus concerning the semantics associated to the prepositional(like) elements, the notions of Path and Place being the most relevant ones (see Svenonius (this volume) for an excellent review). In this sense, I think that H&K's syntactic project can provide configurational approaches with an important insight: H&K (2000, 2002) argue that the distinction between terminal coincidence relation and central coincidence one can in fact be derived or read off from the *mere* l-syntactic structure: i.e., the terminal coincidence meaning is derived from a configuration containing two P's, while the central coincidence one is derived from a configuration containing only one P.[11] Indeed, *mutatis mutandis*, the same parallelism could be adopted for reading Path and Place functions from syntactic structure, i.e., a P(ath) structure would always contain two P's -or one P(ath) particle + Adjective as in 10- and a P(lace) structure would always contain only one P (or A).[12] In short, the structures in 3b and 3c should both be replaced by those in 7 and 10, respectively, the P(ath) generalization commented on above applying to superficially 'complex' verbs (e.g., *bottle up* or *clear up*) and, less trivially, to superficially 'simple' verbs (e.g., *bottle* or *clear*) as well.

---

10.   Roughly, a terminal coincidence relation (e.g., cf. *to, out of, from*, etc.) involves a coincidence between one edge or *terminus* of the theme's path and the place, while a central relation (e.g., cf. *with, at, on*, etc.) involves a coincidence between the center of the theme and the center of the place. See Hale (1986) for further discussion.

11.   Accordingly, in spite of the fact that examples like ia and ib are superficially identical, H&K (2000, 2002) posit that the former involves a complex P structure (i.e., *to* = the terminal coincidence relation *to* plus an abstract central coincidence relation: e.g., *at*), while the latter involves a simple P structure, the one headed by *in*. See H&K (2002: 221–224) for more discussion.

    i.   a.   Leecil went to Tucson.
         b.   Leecil stayed in Tucson.

12.   See Mateu (2002, 2005b) for a radical approach which prevents the category A from having primitive status in grammatical theory (contra Baker (2003) and H&K (1993f)). In particular, it is argued that adjectives can be further decomposed into a relational (prepositional-like) element plus a non-relational (nominal-like) element. See Mateu (2002: chap. 1; 2005b) for theoretical and empirical arguments in favor of such a reduction.

3. Stiebels's (1998) challenging patterns of German complex verbs revisited

With the previous theoretical background in mind, we are ready to tackle the task of refuting the main objections raised by Stiebels (1998) against H&K's syntactic theory of argument structure. I will deal with all those alleged challenging patterns that are said to cause serious problems to H&K's approach. As will be seen below, most of her criticisms are mainly based on the idea that their approach is too restrictive and empirically inadequate since it cannot deal with those complex verbs that are said to involve 'adjunct incorporation' of the preverb (cf. sections 3.1, 3.3, 3.4, and 3.6). Here I argue that the formation of complex verbs in German can be explained by appealing to two different l-syntactic analyses: (i) a P 'cognation' analysis in H&K's (2000) sense is claimed to be involved in those complex verbs where the Ground is conflated in the verb (cf. sections 3.1 to 3.3), and (ii) a root-V compound analysis (cf. McIntyre 2004; Zubizarreta & Oh 2007) is shown to be involved in the rest of complex verbs (cf. sections 3.4 to 3.6).

3.1 Complex denominal verbs of the type *einrahmen*

Consider the following examples from Stiebels (1998: 290):

(11) a. Sie rahmte das Foto ein.
          she framed the photo in
      b. Sie bahrten den Leichnam auf.
          she biered the corpse on

Stiebels (1998: 296) points out that these complex verbs "should not occur according to H&K because they violate the Head Movement Constraint". My reply is as follows: indeed, the examples in 11 would be ungrammatical on the analysis where the N *Rahmen* 'frame' jumps the intervening P element by incorporating directly into the verb. However, as shown in section 2.1 above, this is not the analysis I want to posit for the examples in 11. Rather my explanation of the data in 11 is to be based on my considering the directional particle *ein* 'in' as a cognate complement of the verb in a similar way as *onto the top shelf* can be argued to be a cognate complement of the denominal verb *shelve* (on the relevant, i.e., non-adjunct reading) in 5b *John shelved the book onto the top shelf*: see 12. Crucially, notice that it is not the case that the nominal root *Rahmen* incorporates into the particle *ein*: rather my claim is that this prepositional element is inserted into the P(ath) head *after* the ('simple') denominal verb has been formed. The relevant derivational steps would be the following ones: (i) the root *Rahmen* is inserted into the nominal head, (ii) it conflates with the null complex P, (iii) the complex P+N conflates with the null verb giving the simple denominal verb *rahmen*, and finally (iv) the specific particle *ein* is inserted into the

P(ath) head via P-cognation.[13] Similarly, *onto the top shelf* is inserted as a full P(ath) constituent after the denominal verb *shelve* has been formed or, for that matter, the DP *the polka* is inserted into the complement position of the unergative verb after the denominal verb *dance* has been formed: cf. 5a *John danced a polka*).

(12)

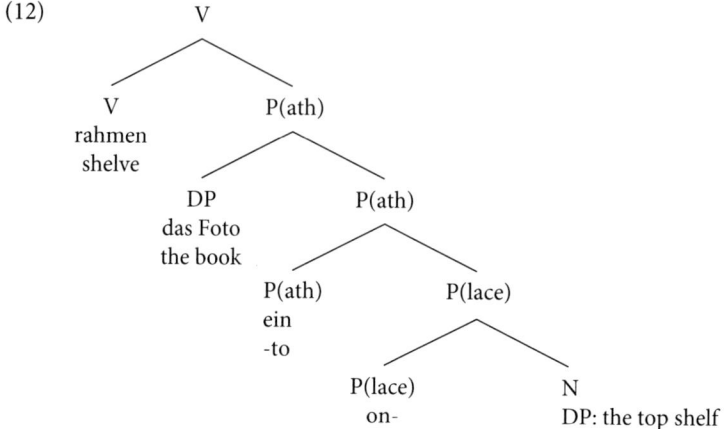

Figure 5. L(exical)-syntactic analysis of complex location verbs.

To a certain extent, my l-syntactic analysis of the 'cognation' process involved in 11 is not so different from the redundant lexical entry that Stiebels (1998: 290–291) assigns to complex location verbs like *einrahmen*. According to her, "an analysis which starts with the denominal base *rahmen* should be preferred (. . .) the preverb redundantly specifies what may be conceptually inferred from the simple denominal verb." The (final) semantic derivation posited by Stiebels (1998: ex. 48d) is depicted in 13, which can be paraphrased as follows: 'x causes that y becomes located in a frame & y becomes located inside the frame.'

(13)   [ein [rahmen]$_V$] $_V$: λy λx λs [CAUSE (x, BECOME(LOC(y, R$_{prox}$ [FRAME]))) (s) & BECOME(LOC(y, INT [FRAME])) (s)

Indeed, I believe that one important advantage of H&K's syntactic approach over Stiebels's semantic one is that the (syntactically relevant) semantics is not acting freely but is read off or determined by syntax: as far as I can tell, it is not clear which principled device contrains the 'adjunct incorporation' operation in Stiebels's LDG framework.

---

13.   An anonymous reviewer wonders whether a motivation could be provided for the present derivational analysis which crucially requires that the preverb element be inserted after the conflation of the nominal root has taken place. My reply is that the derivation I have proposed for 12 is valid if and only if we agree that we are dealing with a cognate object construction. Otherwise, the only alternative derivation possible within the present framework would involve analyzing the type *einrahmen* via the root-V compound strategy (cf. the complex denominal verbs analyzed in sections 3.4 to 3.6).

In contrast, it is clear why syntax constrains the apparent addition of 'extra material' into argument structures: e.g., see H&K (2000: 34f) for a principled explanation of why examples like *We overheated the soup up are ruled out, this being based on the general uniqueness restriction: to put it in our present terms, over- and up compete for the very same (syntactic!) P(ath) position.[14]

3.2 Complex denominal verbs of the type verslumen

Consider the following examples from Stiebels (1998: 293):

(14)   a.   Dieses   Stadtviertel ver-slum-t   immer mehr.
             this   quarter   ver-slum-3sg   more and more
             'This quarter is becoming more and more like a slum.'
      b.   Diese   Firma   ver-schrott-et   täglich   20 Autos.
             this   company   ver-scrap_metal-3sg   daily   20 cars
             'This company scraps 20 cars a day.'

Assuming as correct Stiebels's (1998: 293) claim that the prefix ver- in 14 "does not contribute any specific meaning", the more plausible l-syntactic analysis would be to consider it as part of the phonological matrix of the verb (e.g., similar to the verbal suffix –en). Alternatively, assuming as correct the claim that the prefix ver- does have a semantic contribution in 14,[15] it could be regarded as an instantiation of the P(ath) head. Given the latter analysis, as in the einrahmen type above, I do not want to argue for the proposal that the nominal root Slum incorporates into the prefix ver-; rather my claim would be that this preverb is inserted into the P(ath) head after the denominal verb has been formed. See 15 for the l-syntactic analysis of 14a, where the curly brackets are intended to indicate that the prefix can be regarded as a verbal prefix or a prepositional-like one. For the time being, I remain undecided wrt choicing the more adequate analysis of the prefix ver- in

---

14.   See H&K (2000: 35) for some reasons why Keyser & Roeper's (1992) 'abstract clitic hypothesis' is to be abandoned in favor of their new analysis. As shown by H&K's (2000: 35) examples in ia, b, two prefixes like re- and over- are not incompatible provided that they occupy different syntactic positions (see Svenonius (2004) for an elegant syntactic distinction between 'lexical' prefixes and 'superlexical' ones). See also McIntyre (2003) for insightful semantic analyses of prefixes like re- and over-.

    i.   a.   rereheat the soup
        b.   reoverheat the soup

15.   According to one anonymous reviewer, "the prefix ver-, contrary to Stiebels's claim, does have a constant lexical semantic contribution, namely the sense of disintegration of the internal argument, of its seizing to exist in the form that it had before the event (i.e., losing one of its distinctive properties, leaving the relevant place, disappearing); cf. the English away, or the Slavic prefix raz-."

14: be this as it may, what is important for me is to have shown that examples like 14 do not cause problems to H&K's syntactic approach.

(15)

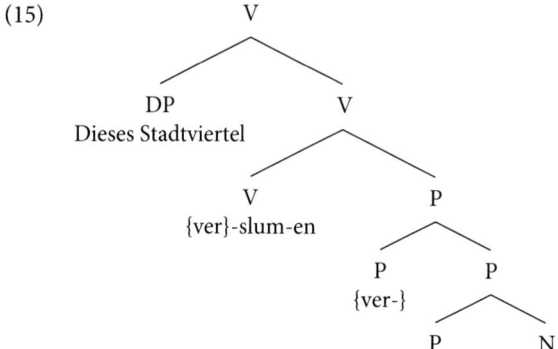

Figure 6. L(exical)-syntactic analysis of *verslumen*.

3.3   Complex deadjectival verbs of the type *eindeutschen*

Consider the following examples from Stiebels (1998: 280):

(16)   a. ein_{pt}-deutsch-en 'germanize'
       b. auf_{pt}-heiter-n 'cheer up'

These complex verbs could be said to be analyzed within H&K's syntactic approach as follows: (i) the adjective root is conflated with the preverb and (ii) this complex predicative head (P+A) is then conflated with the null verb, providing it with phonological content. Again this is not the analysis I want to argue for the examples in 16: as in the *einrahmen* denominal type above, my claim is that the directional/ resultative preverbs in 16 are inserted into the P(ath) head after the deadjectival verb has been formed. Accordingly, I argue that the appropriate analysis for the complex deadjectival verbs in 16 is the same one H&K (2000) posit for examples like *We heated the soup up/The soup heated up*, i.e., the l-syntactic analysis in 10, repeated below in 17 (cf. section 2.1 for its original motivation).

(17)

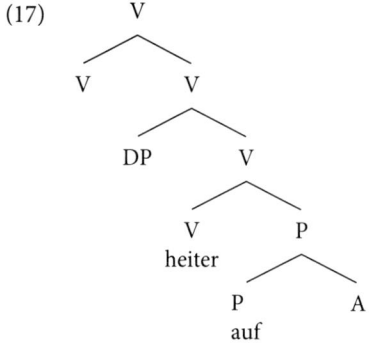

Figure 7. L(exical)-syntactic analysis of complex deadjectival verbs.

As noted in section 2.2, it is important to bear in mind that, unlike H&K (2000), I do not assume that the P in 10/17 refers to the degree or intensity at which the quality denoted by the adjective is realized. Rather I argue that P in 17 encodes the very same Path meaning found in complex location verbs. Indeed, the so-called 'Localist Hypothesis' provides us with the right results since the German examples in 16 are quite transparent in this sense:[16] e.g., *ein* projects the spatial 'go *into* X' schema onto that of becoming German(ized), while *auf* delineates the upper path typically associated with positive emotions (see Lakoff & Johnson (1980) for interesting discussion on so-called 'orientational metaphors'). Notice then that the 'cognation' analysis allows us to capture the typical hyponymic vs. hyperonymic contrast involved: i.e., the preverb specifies and/or elaborates on the abstract trajectory associated to the change of state encoded by the deadjectival verb.

So far I have provided an l-syntactic analysis for those complex verbs that conflate a Ground element (as noted above, the adjectival base in 16 can also be interpreted as Ground: cf. Gruber's (1965) or Jackendoff's (1990) Localist Hypothesis). Most of times I have made use of H&K's (2000) P-cognation analysis in order to explain why a preverb can co-occur with a Ground element conflated in the verb. From now on I will deal with more complex cases, i.e., cases that involve what has often been referred to in the literature as *lexical subordination processes* (Levin & Rapoport 1988; Spencer & Zaretskaya 1998; Mateu 2000, 2002, 2005b; McIntyre 2004, among others).

3.4 Complex denominal verbs of the type *vergärtnern*

Stiebels (1998: 285–286) points out that H&K's syntactic approach cannot explain the formation of complex denominal verbs like those in 18. Once again her main criticism is based on the fact that complex verbs with an alleged integrated adjunct (e.g., the prefixes *ver-* and *er-* in 18a and 18b) should not occur according to H&K.

(18)   a.   Er ver-gärtner-te   sein gesamtes Vermögen.
             he ver(away)-gardener-ed his whole   fortune
             'In gardening, he used up all his fortune.'
       b.   Sie er-schreiner-te   sich den   Ehrenpreis der Handwerkskammer.
             she er(poss)-carpenter-ed herself$_{DAT}$ the prize   of-the trade-corporation
             'She got the prize of the trade corporation by doing carpentry.'

Stiebels claims that these prefixes, the 'consumptive' *ver-* in 18a and the possessive *er-* in 18b, are lexical adjuncts that turn out to affect the argument structure of the

---

16.   See Mateu (2002, 2005b) for the localist claim that the P(ath) element involved in directional PP's and resultative AP's is the very same one (see Gruber (1965) and Jackendoff (1990) for relevant discussion on the Localist Hypothesis).

base denominal verb: the first one adds one argument ('the consumed object' *(u)* in 19a), whereas the second one adds two arguments (the object *(v)* and its possessor *(u)* in 19b).

(19)   a.   [ver [gärtner]$_V$]$_V$ $\lambda u\ \lambda x\ \lambda s$ [GARDENER (x) (s) & CONSUME (u) (s)]
       b.   [er [schreiner]$_V$]$_V$ $\lambda v\ \lambda u\ \lambda x\ \lambda s$ [CARPENTER (x) (s) & BECOME (POSS ((u,v)) (s)]

However, as argued by Mateu (2001b, 2003), Stiebels's (1998: 285) requirement that the verbal prefixes in 18a-b be 'lexical adjuncts' is not to be taken for granted. According to the 'lexical subordination approach' (cf. Levin & Rapoport 1988; Spencer & Zaretskaya 1998), it is precisely the preverb element (e.g., *ver-* in 19a and *er-* in 19b) that must be considered as part of the main thematic structure, the surface head element (e.g., *[gärtner]$_V$* in 19a and *[schreiner]$_V$* in 19b) being a subordinate predicate. The point of departure of Mateu's (2001b, 2003) analysis of those Germanic preverb constructions that involve l-syntactic subordination is to be found in Spencer & Zaretskaya's (1998) insightful semantic description of verb prefixation in Russian: they argue that some verb prefixation constructions in this language (e.g., 20a) can be given the same L(exical) C(onceptual) S(tructure) analysis as that assigned by Levin & Rapoport (1988) to English resultative constructions like *They drank the pub dry*. Both constructions are explained by making use of a 'lexical subordination operation' to be introduced by the semantic operator *BY* (cf. 20b)). Spencer & Zaretskaya (1998: 17–18) interpret 20a "to mean that the pen became 'exhausted' (in some sense that is defined in part semantically and in part pragmatically) by virtue of writing activity. This is then completely parallel to the analysis given for *They drank the pub dry*."[17]

(20)   a.   Ona is-pisala   svoju ručku   (Russian)
            she iz(out)-write her   pen.ACC
            'Her pen has run out of ink' (lit. She has written her pen out (of ink))
       b.   [[CAUSE [ACT (she)], IZ (pen)], BY [WRITE (she)]]

According to Spencer & Zaretskaya, the core predicate (i.e., the semantically primary predicate) corresponds to the preverb (e.g., *iz-*), or to the resultative phrase (e.g., *dry*), while the subordinate predicate (i.e., the semantically secondary predicate) corresponds to the verb (e.g., {*write/drink*}). Mateu (2001a, b; 2003) pointed out that one of the most important advantages that can be attributed to the lexical subordination analysis is that it can provide an elegant explanation of so-called

---

17. This English resultative construction is assigned the following LCS by Spencer and Zaretskaya (1998: 7): [[CAUSE [ACT (they))], BECOME [DRY (pub)]], BY [DRINK (they)]], i.e., 'they caused the pub to become dry by drinking.'

'unselected object constructions'.[18] For example, the unselected kind of direct object in 20a is due to the fact that it is only with the prefix *iz-* ('out') that the basic verb *pisat'* ('to write') can take such an object. As Spencer & Zaretskaya (1998: 17) correctly observe, "the best way of regarding this case is to take the *iz-* prefix as the core predicator in a complex predicate, with the activity verb *pisat'* as a subordinate predicator."[19]

As pointed out by Mateu (2001b, 2003), Spencer & Zaretskaya's (1998) lexical subordination analysis of verb prefixation can be extended naturally to account for the German complex denominal verbs in 18, which are also examples of unselected object constructions: quite roughly, the complex verbs in 18 could be said to be assigned the LCS analyses in 21.[20]

(21) a. [[CAUSE [ACT (he)], *VER* (all his fortune)], BY [GARDEN (he)]]
          (i.e., 'he caused all his fortune to go away by gardening') (cf. 20b)
      b. [[CAUSE [ACT (she)], *ER* (herself, the prize)], BY [DO-CARPENTRY (she)]] (i.e., 'she caused herself to get the price by doing carpentry')

This notwithstanding, the major point of Mateu's (2001b, 2003) is to claim that Spencer & Zaretskaya's (1998) analysis of verb prefixation as lexical subordination is not to be grounded in a non-syntactic LCS, but rather in H&K's l-syntax, the latter being regarded as the locus of parameterization of morphosyntactic facts affecting argument structure. As emphasized by Mateu (2001b, 2003), there seems

---

18. See Goldberg (1995), Wunderlich (1997), Spencer & Zaretskaya (1998), Mateu (2001a, 2005b), McIntyre (2003, 2004), Svenonius (2004), among others.

19. Given this, notice that a unified analysis of unselected object constructions such as those in i appears to be possible: indeed, as shown by Levin & Rapoport (1988), it is precisely this unification what the lexical subordination analysis can account for in an elegant way (the Russian examples in id, e are taken from Spencer & Zaretskaya (1998: ex. 74, 83)).

i. a. They drank the pub dry.
    b. They danced the night away.
    c. Daniel slept his way to the top.
    d. On pro-pil   vsju svoju zarplatu   (Russian)
        he pro-drank all   his   wages
        'He's drunk his way through all his wages.'
    e. Rebënok do-kričal-sja   do xripoty
        baby   do-cried-sja(itself)   to hoarseness
        'The baby cried itself hoarse.'

20. See Rappaport Hovav & Levin (1998) for a more precise distinction between the 'structural' vs. 'idiosyncratic' components of lexical meaning.

to be strong empirical evidence pointing to the fact that the kind of lexical-syntactic variation involved in Talmy's (1991, 2000) well-known typology between verb- and satellite-framed languages plays a crucial role in accounting for the formation of the data in 18 or 20a: to the extent that this kind of linguistic variation cannot be explained in *purely* lexical-conceptual terms, it is natural to transfer the responsibility of the formation of these complex predicates to the realm of syntax (see section 4 below for further discussion of Talmy's typology).

According to Mateu (2003), the l-syntactic analysis of complex verbs like 18a involves the syntactic composition of two l-syntactic structures: the 'main' one is a transitive structure that expresses a caused change of location and the 'subordinate' one is an unergative one. Mateu (2003) argued that complex denominal verbs like 18a can be analyzed by means of a 'generalized transformation' (H&K 1997b: 228–229; Mateu 2001b; pace Chomsky 1995), whereby the subordinate unergative verb is to be conflated with the main null transitive verb: see 22.[21]

(22)

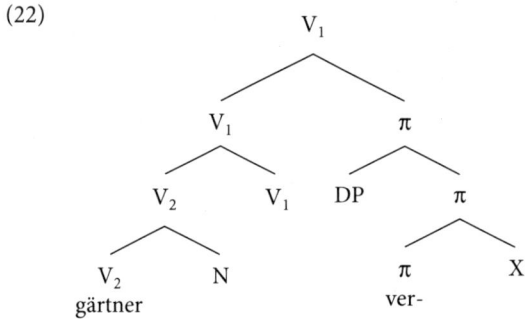

Figure 8. Mateu's (2003) l-syntactic analysis of *vergärtnern*.

Accordingly, the semantic intepretation involved in the so-called 'lexical subordination process' could be argued to be read off from the complex l-syntactic structure in 22, roughly:

(23)   [(he) [[DO-garden]-CAUSE] [all his fortune away]] (i.e., 'he caused all his fortune to go away by doing gardening')

Following McIntyre's (2004) and Zubizarreta & Oh's (2007) insightful adaptations of Mateu's (2001a, 2002) syntactic 'plug-in' theory of 'lexical subordination

---

21.   The resultative prefix (e.g., *ver-*) is the head of the inner SC projection (i.e., *P*), which turns out to be adjoined to the superior complex verbal head because of its affixal status. Moreover, following H&K (2002: chap. 8) and Svenonius's (1996) original idea, the proposal that bare particles incorporate their Ground complement was also assumed. See also Svenonius (2004: 243) for an alternative syntactic analysis of 20a.

processes' via generalized transformations, here I want to provide a slightly modified analysis of the relevant conflation process depicted in 22.[22] Basically, I want
to adopt from McIntyre's (2004) and Zubizarreta & Oh's (2007) analyses the idea
that the relevant conflation involved in 22 is not carried out via subordinating a
full-fledged unergative verb (V+N) to a null transitive verb, but rather only a root
to this null light verb: cf. 24. I recognize that there is no empirical evidence for
one to posit that a complex bieventive verbal head like the one depicted in (22) is
involved in the l-syntactic formation of the German verb *vergärtnern* (as noted by
Zubizarreta & Oh (2007: 56), Germanic is not a S(erial)-V(erb) C(onstruction)
language). Given this, notice that the simpler analysis in 24 is more appropriate
than my (2003) analysis in 22, which is in fact identical to the one argued by Mateu
(2001b: 44). For sake of simplicity, the decomposition of π into a complex P(ath)-
P(lace) constituent is omitted here: see sections 2.1 and 2.2 above.

(24)

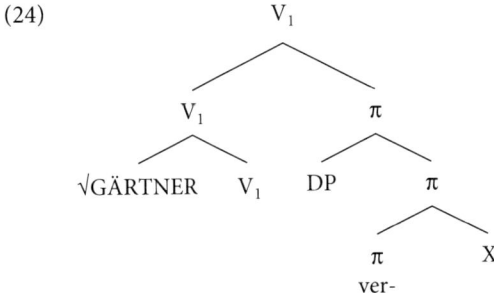

Figure 9. L-syntactic analysis of *vergärtnern* revisited.

An anonymous reviewer points out that the complex l-syntactic analysis depicted
in 24 is not predicted by H&K's basic theory of argument structure, which could
be considered a step back with respect to their restrictive proposals summarized in

---

22.   McIntyre's (2004) and Zubizarreta & Oh's (2007) also agree with Mateu's (2000, 2001b,
2002) proposal that the formation of Germanic complex resultative(-like) constructions (those
ones in 18 included) is not to be carried out in a semantic level but rather in a syntactic one
(*contra* Wunderlich 1997; Stiebels 1998; Spencer & Zaretskaya 1998). However, concerning the
relevant linguistic/parametric variation involved, the former appear to be more sympathetic to
Snyder's (2001) relating the formation of resultative constructions to his 'compounding parameter', whereas I think that it is Talmy's (1991, 2000) well-known typology what is stake here. We
postpone this issue until section 4, where I show why Snyder's 'compounding parameter' is not
empirically well-grounded; moreover, in this section, I will review my previous l-syntactic explanation of Talmy's (1991, 2000) descriptive typology between verb-framed vs. satellite-framed
languages by paying special attention to important differences between some Germanic vs.
Romance Path constructions.

section 2. At the risk of losing explanatory power, Hale & Keyser (1997b: 228–229) and Mateu (2001b: 44) decided to take such an extension as necessary in order to provide an account of how an independent manner component is allowed to enter into a path of motion construction. For a more detailed empirical justification for such a move within a Hale-Keyserian framework, see also Zubizarreta & Oh (2007), which is clearly based on our previous proposals.

Furthermore, one could argue that the structural or configurational semantics associated to the subordinated unergative verb in 22 (i.e., V_2 N: *DO-gardening*) is lost in 24. However, following Hale & Keyser (1997b: 228–229) and Mateu (2001b: 43–44), I argue that that two familiar interpretations can still be argued to be derived from the complex l-syntactic structure in 24: on the one hand, the $V_1+\pi$ configuration provides us with the typical change of location meaning (cf. 3b); on the other, the V_1+root configuration provides us with the creation meaning typically associated to monadic structures of the V+N type, i.e., the one associated to unergative verbs.

3.5 Complex denominal verbs of the type *versanden*

Consider the following examples from Stiebels (1998: 291):

(25)   a.   Die Bücher ver-staub-en.
        the books ver-dust-3pl
        'The books get dusty.'
    b.   Die Bucht ver-sand-et.
        the bay   ver-sand-3sg
        'The bay gets full of sand.'

After positing an LDG-based semantic analysis for 25, which I will not review here for reasons of space, Stiebels (1998: 296) points out that the verbs in 25 should be analyzed by H&K as follows: "the base noun, being the internal argument of P, is moved to the overt P, and then this complex is moved to V. This derivation, however, violates the fact that the prefix does not attach to nouns."

Contra Stiebels's suggestion above, I want to argue that the appropriate l-syntactic analysis of the examples in 25 does *not* involve any relation between the prefix *ver-* and a noun. Rather my proposal is that these examples involve an l-syntactic subordination process like the one I have argued for the *vergärtnern* type above. In 25 the resultative prefix *ver-* specifies that the surface of the subject DP is fully affected: indeed, *ver-* is the SC predicate (see Mulder 1992),[23] which, in my system, means that it is the prepositional-like head of a subpredicative structure

---

23.   See also Mulder (1992) for an insightful SC analysis of the polysemic prefix *ver-* in Dutch, which is, to our view, more explanatory than Lieber & Baayen's (1992) descriptive semantic account.

merged with the upper verb (cf. sections 2.1 and 2.2 above). Following my previous revision of l-syntactic subordination processes, I claim that the introduction of *Sand* into the complex verb in 26 is via a root-verb compounding (McIntyre 2004; Zubizarreta & Oh 2007).

(26)

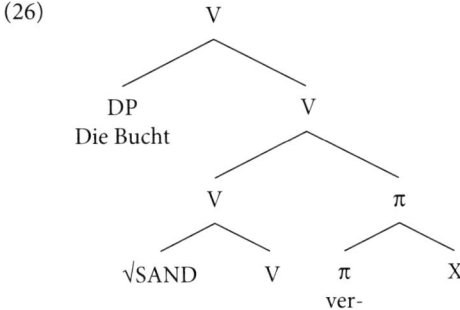

Figure 10. L(exical)-syntactic analysis of *versanden*.

3.6 Complex locatum verbs of the type *unterkellern*

Consider the following examples from Stiebels (1998: 288):

(27) a. Sie unter-keller-ten das Haus
they under-cellar-ed the house
'They put a cellar under the house.'
b. Sie über-dach-ten den Vorgarten
they over-roof-ed the front yard
'They roofed (over) the front yard.'

Stiebels points out that an adequate paraphrase of the meaning of the verb in 27a is not a locative one ('to cause that a cellar becomes located under the house'), but rather a possessive one ('to cause that the house gets a cellar, which becomes located under the house'). Its final semantic derivation is formalized in 28, where the preverb is said to serve to specify the spatial relation.

(28) [unter [keller]$_V$]$_V$ $\lambda y \, \lambda x \, \lambda s$ [CAUSE (x, BECOME(POSS(y, CELLAR)))(s)
& BECOME (LOC (CELLAR, UNDER [y])) (s)

As pointed out by Stiebels, there is no way for H&K to deal with this adjunct analysis. This notwithstanding, assuming the prefix *unter* is not an adjunct but the SC predicate, I would like to argue for an alternative l-syntactic analysis based on or inspired by the one put forward by Svenonius (2004) when dealing with what he calls 'unaccusative particle constructions' like *fill in the form* (vs. *fill in the information*): cf. 29a. According to Svenonius (2004: 223), "what distinguishes unaccusative particle constructions is the absence of a Figure-introducing *p* head, parallel to the Agent-introducing *v* of much recent work. (. . .) In ⟨29a: JM⟩ no internal case is available, as in the classic Burzio's Generalization cases, so the complement of P must get case from the verb, and does not surface as a prepositional complement." The corresponding analysis of 27a expressed in Svenonius's (2004) and Ramchand & Svenonius's (2002) terminology is given in 29b, 29c being its proper translation into my present l-syntactic terms.

(29)   a.

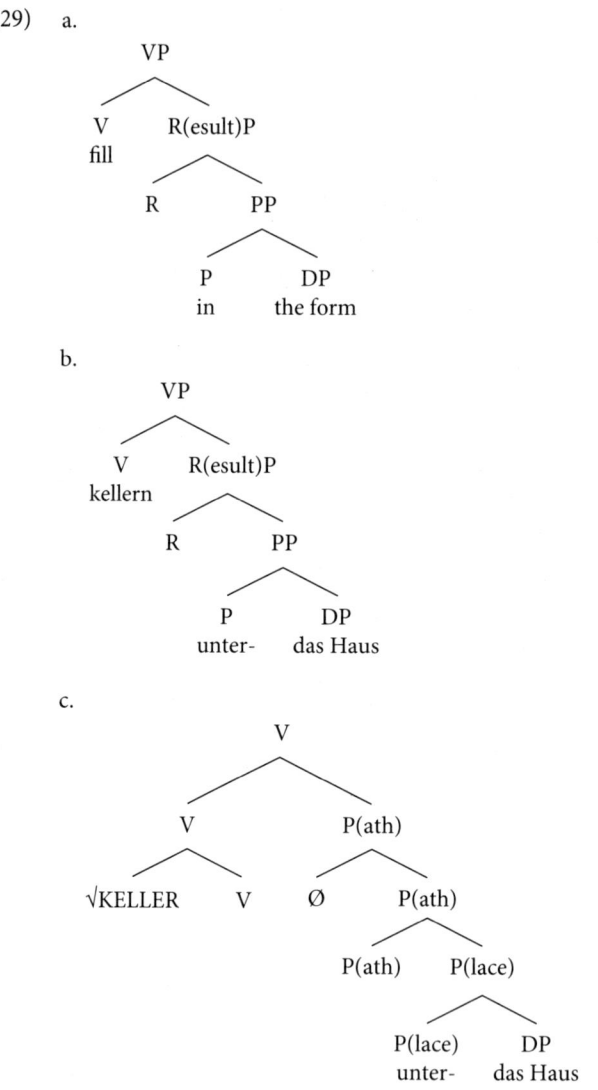

Figure 11. L(exical)-syntactic analyses of 'unaccusative particle constructions'.

Interestingly, notice that in these locatum constructions the Figure/Theme argument can be expressed via a *with/mit* adjunct: e.g., *fill in the form with relevant information*; similarly, *mit einem Kohlenkeller* (i.e., 'with a coal cellar') can also be added to 27a.[24] It seems then that there is a correlation between promoting the Ground argument to an affected direct argument position and demoting the Figure/Theme argument out of the complex predicative PP headed by the preverb. In a sense, notice that such a demoting process is similar to the one found in the passive construction, a well-known example of unaccusative construction. This said, I must recognize that I have no account for the (in)direct relation between the absence of internal subject and the root-verb compound involved in complex locatum verbs. Notice then that there is a non-trivial step involved in the derivation of 29c: i.e., assuming that encyclopedic roots cannot typically be directly associated to V (as noted above, due to their relational nature, verbal heads can only be directly associated with so-called 'light' stuff: cf. 'light verbs'), I posit that the nominal root in 27 is introduced via a root-V compound strategy (cf. section 3.4 above). As will be shown immediately below, the assumption that verbal heads and, more generally, relational heads cannot be directly associated with potentially open-ended encyclopedic stuff is not only based on theoretical grounds (Mateu 2005a) but on empirical ones as well: next I will show how this assumption relates to my l-syntactic conception of Talmy's (1991, 2000) typological difference between satellite- and verb-framedness.

4. Talmy's (1991, 2000) typology of satellite- vs. verb-framed languages revisited: Path constructions in Germanic vs. Romance

In this section, after briefly reviewing Mateu's (2000) l-syntactic explanation of Talmy's well-known descriptive typology, I will deal with some apparent counterexamples to his typology (e.g., the existence of directional preverbs in Romance).[25]

First of all, it will be useful to introduce some relevant background on his typological work. Consider some paradigmatic examples of his typology in 30: while English can typically be taken as an example of satellite-framed language, Catalan can typically be regarded as an example of verb-framed language (Mateu & Rigau 2002; Mateu 2002). To put it in Talmy's (1985) terms, 30a involves conflation of Motion with Manner, or alternatively, in Talmy's (1991) terms, 30a involves conflation of AGENTIVEMOVE with [EVENT]SUPPORTING. In contrast, the corresponding counterpart of 30a in a Romance language like Catalan (cf. 30b) typically involves a different

---

24. An anonymous reviewer points out how the possessive interpretation (cf. *Poss* in 28) is derived in my l-syntactic account. My reply is that the possessive relation involved in complex locatum verbs is not represented in the argument structure in 29c (see Harley (2005: 58) for a similar claim) but rather by means of the PP adjunct headed by *with/mit* (see Hale (1986) for how this semantic notion can be associated to the so-called 'central coincidence relation', whose prototypical instantiation in English is the preposition *with*).

25. For some relevant parameterizable morphosyntactic facts involved in Talmy's typology, see also Klipple (1997), Mateu (2000), and Mateu & Rigau (2002).

lexicalization pattern, i.e., conflation of Motion with Path, the Manner component (or the Co-event) being expressed as adjunct.

(30) a. The boy danced into the room.
      b. El   noi   entrà   a l'habitació   ballant.   (Catalan)
          the boy went-into/entered loc.prep the room dancing

The 'satellite-framedness' of Germanic languages is to be related to the fact that, for example, the P(ath) element *into* in 30a is not conflated in the verb, this null verb being then allowed to be conflated with the so-called {'Manner constituent'/ [EVENT]$_{SUPPORTING}$}. To put it in Mateu's (2000) terms, an 'l-syntactic subordination' process is involved in 30a, which H&K's theory allows us to express in the following morphosyntactic terms: the non-conflating (i.e., 'satellite') nature of *into* allows the phonologically null unaccusative verb to be merged with the root √DANCE (cf. 31a). In contrast, the conflating nature of this Path element in Catalan gives a directional verb (*entrar* 'enter'), the adjunct *ballant* ('dancing') being merged outside the main argument structure: cf. 31b.

(31) a.

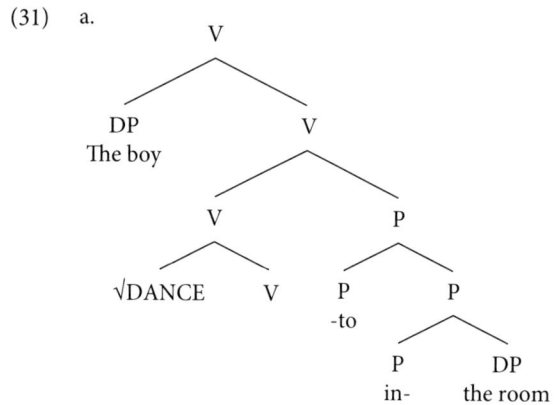

      b.

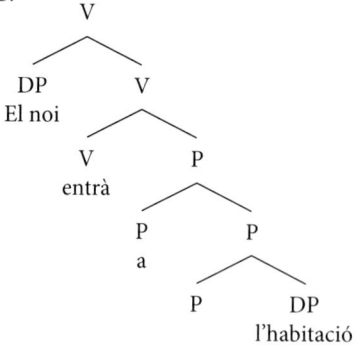

Figure 12. L(exical)-syntactic analyses of *The boy danced into the room* and Cat. *El noi entrà a l'habitació*.

As emphasized by Mateu (2003), Talmy's (1991, 2000) typology accounts for why Romance languages (and, more generally, 'verb-framed languages') typically lack both complex path of motion constructions like 30a and resultative preverb constructions like those ones in 18a,b and 20a. Basically, my explanation of this descriptive fact is that verb-framed languages typically lack the l-syntactic pattern in 31a since in these languages it is the Path (and not an independent root) what typically provides the relevant null motion verb with phonological content: cf. 31b.[26]

This notwithstanding, there appear to be some counterexamples to Talmy's typology. Indeed, there is a variety of directional constructions in Romance languages that could be taken as problematic for his typology since they appear to involve 'satellite-framed' constructions, i.e., constructions where a directional P is apparently not conflated in the verb: e.g., cf. (a) Italian verb-particle constructions; (b) *correre*-verbs in unaccusative contexts or (c) directional prefixes in Romance.[27]

(32) a. It. mettere *giù* 'put down'; buttare *via* 'throw down'; saltare *dentro* 'jump in'
      b. It. Gianni è corso *a* casa (lit. 'Gianni is run to home', 'Gianni ran home')
      c. It. *im*bottigliare; Cat. *em*botellar; Fr. *em*bouteiller: *IN*bottle, 'to bottle' (cf. 'to put *IN*to a bottle')
      c'. It. *a*llargare; Cat. *a*llargar; Sp. *a*largar: *TO*large, 'to enlarge' (cf. 'to cause X to go *TO* the state of ⟨large⟩)

My present proposal is that the formation of the examples in 32 does not involve an l-syntactic pattern like the one in 31a but rather they are all cases of P-cognation,

---

26. As noted above, the parametric differences between English and Catalan I am discussing in the context of Talmy's typology could also be related to Snyder's (2001) alternative explanation, which is based on the connection between productive compounding (like N-N compounds) and complex predicates (like resultatives). Indeed, Snyder's approach appears to make the correct predictions for languages like English and Catalan (i.e., while the former shows both productive N-N compounding and complex resultative constructions, the latter lacks both). However, his predictions are not borne out when considering other language families: for example, on the one hand, Slavic languages do have resultative constructions like the one in 20a (cf. Spencer & Zaretskaya (1998); Mateu (2002); Svenonius (2004); *contra* Snyder (2001: 329)), but lack productive N-N compounding. On the other hand, Basque lacks resultative constructions but has productive N-N compounding. Given this fact, I do not consider Snyder's alternative explanation as correct and, for my present purposes, will limit myself to basing my l-syntactic analysis on Talmy's (1991, 2000) empirically well-grounded typology.

27. Although the literature on directional constructions in Romance is not so extensive as the one on Germanic preverbs, here are some recent references: for Italian verb-particle constructions, see Masini (2005), among others; for *correre* verbs in directional contexts, see Folli & Ramchand (2005) and Zubizarreta & Oh (2007), among others; for Romance directional prefixes, see Di Sciullo (1997), Padrosa (2005), and Acedo-Matellán (2006, in press), among others.

i.e., cases where the prepositional(like) element specifies the P(ath) element that has already been conflated in the verb.[28] Accordingly, the constructions in 32 are 'verb-framed' in the sense that P(ath) is already conflated in the verb: concerning 32a, b, notice that the verb itself encodes a directional meaning which is further specified through a directional P, i.e., a particle in 32a and a directional preposition in 32b.[29]

Concerning the directional prefixation cases in 32c-c', my claim is that their corresponding l-syntactic analyses involve the P-cognation process I have put forward for the denominal type *einrahmen* (cf. section 3.1) and the deadjectival type *eindeutschen* (cf. section 3.3), respectively.[30] Accordingly, my claim is that the derivational steps involved in 32c-c' are the following ones:

(33)   a.   the simple {denominal/deadjectival} verb is formed:
       (ai)   the root {*bottiglia/larg(o)*} is inserted into the {nominal/ adjectival} head;
       (aii) the root conflates with a null P;

---

28.   Indeed, notice that this is precisely the case of 30b/31b as well, where the preposition *a* 'to' specifies the Path that has been conflated in the verb (see Mateu & Rigau 2002: 224).

29.   Unsurprisingly, the list of *correre*-verbs that can enter into an unaccusative construction is quite reduced, which includes *correre* 'run', *saltare* 'jump', *volare* 'fly', and a few more (see Folli & Ramchand (2005) and Zubizarreta & Oh (2007)). For me it is crucial to point out that *all* of them encode a directional component which is to be l-syntactically related to P(ath): if so, the directional preposition/particle co-occuring with the '*correre*-verb' could be analyzed as a case of P-cognation. Clearly, such an analysis is not possible for the Italian counterpart of 34b *John danced into the room* (cf. It. *Gianni è ballato alla stanza*), since manner of motion verbs that do not lexically involve a directional component are excluded from the unaccusative context. In striking contrast to that, in Germanic languages manner of motion verbs systematically enter into the unaccusative context.

Similar qualifications hold for Italian verb-particle constructions: it is important to realize that the list of Italian verbs that enter into these constructions is reduced to directional verbs as well. In contrast, as shown by the example in 34a *John worked the night away*, this restriction does not hold in Germanic.

All in all, I think that the existence of both verb-particle constructions and unaccusative constructions containing *correre*-verbs in a verb-framed language like Italian cannot be taken as a serious counterexample to Talmy's typological generalizations concerning Romance, since both constructions do involve verbs that already encode a directional meaning, which is further specified, I argue, by P(ath).

30.   Alternatively, one could argue that the P(ath) cognation strategy is typically valid for Romance (or, more generally, for verb-framed languages) and that the formation of German verbs like *einrahmen* 'to frame' or *eindeutschen* 'to germanize' involves an l-syntactic subordination process like the one depicted in 24. Accordingly, for example, *einrahmen* could roughly be paraphrased as 'to put X into a space in a framing manner'. However, in this paper, I have argued for extending H&K's (2000) P-cognation analysis of English complex verbs like *heat up* or *warm up*

(aiii) the complex P+{N/A} conflates with a null verb giving the simple
verb {*bottigliare/largare*};

b. the prefix (e.g., It. *in-* 'in'; *a-* 'to')) is then inserted into P(ath) via
P-cognation;

c. finally, the prefix is incorporated onto the upper verb, giving the final
complex verb {*imbottigliare/allargare*}.

On the other hand, as predicted by Talmy's typology, examples like those in 34
are not found in Romance: this is not surprising at all since in these cases the verb
does *not* lexically involve a directional meaning. Indeed, the constructions in 34
do not involve a P cognation analysis; rather they involve an l-syntactic structure
where the phonological matrix of the relevant null verb has been saturated by an
independent root: for example, see 31a for 34b.

(34) a. John worked the night away.
b. The boy danced into the room / The truck rumbled into the yard.
c. Pat outplayed Peter in the final.
d. John talked us into a stupor.
e. The dog barked the chickens awake.
f. He slept his way into a wonderful world.

For reasons of space, I must leave this admittedly sketchy discussion here. At least
I hope to have shown that those apparent counterexamples in 32 should not be
taken as involving serious problems to Talmy's typology (as I understand it). In
contrast, it should be clear that to find cases like those ones in 34 in verb-framed
languages would indeed contribute to refuting his typology. As far as I can tell,
such cases are not easy to find, which leads me to conclude that Talmy's typological
patterns are quite robust.

5.   Concluding remarks

As noted above, the goal of the present paper was quite specific: i.e., to provide a
l(exical)-syntactic explanation of some challenging patterns of Germanic complex

---

to those German complex verbs involving a very similar semantics, i.e., those that have an (abstract) Ground conflated in the verb: e.g., *einrahmen* 'to frame' or *eindeutschen* 'to germanize'. Of
course, H&K's (2000) and my P-cognation analyses for these Germanic verbs could be wrong as
well as the associated strong intuition that they conflate a final location or state, an l-syntactic
subordination analysis being then more appropriate for these cases. I leave it for further research
to determine which of these two competing analyses is more viable for those verbs that (appear
to) have a Ground conflated.

verbs that were taken by Stiebels (1998) to cause non-trivial problems to H&K's (1993, 1997a) syntactic theory of argument structure. I have reached a very different conclusion from Stiebels's: i.e., semantic approaches to the formation of complex verbs like *cool off*, *gamble away* or *outdrink* can be descriptively adequate, but cannot provide a principled explanation of why so-called 'verb-framed languages' typically lack them. This fact led me to pursue an l-syntactic explanation of Talmy's (1991, 2000) typology within H&K's (2002) theory of argument structure (Mateu 2002, 2005b, i.a.). To my view, the difficulty of finding (clear) counterexamples to Talmy's typology (as I understand it) leads me to claim that it is empirically well-grounded and that its associated descriptive generalizations are quite robust. Additionally, I hope that the l-syntactic explanations I have provided for them will contribute to show the explanatory power of H&K's (1998, 2000, 2002) syntactic approach to argument structure.

References

Acedo-Matellán, V. 2006. Prefixes in Latin and Romance and the satellite-/verb-framed distinction. Ms. Universitat de Barcelona.

Acedo-Matellán, V. In press. Una aproximació sintàctica als verbs prefixats en català. *Estudis Catalans*.

Baker, M. 1988. *Incorporation: A Theory of Grammatical Function Changing*. Chicago IL: University of Chicago Press.

Baker, M. 2003. *Lexical Categories. Verbs, Nouns, and Adjectives*. Cambridge: CUP.

Booij, G. & van Marle, J. 2003. *Yearbook of Morphology*. Dordrecht: Kluwer.

Chomsky, N. 1995. *The Minimalist Program*. Cambridge MA: The MIT Press.

Dehé, N., Jackendoff, R., McIntyre, A. & Urban, S. (eds). 2002. *Verb Particle Explorations*. Berlin: Mouton de Gruyter.

Di Sciullo, A.-M. 1997. Prefixed verbs and adjunct identification. In *Projections and Interface Conditions*, A.-M. Di Sciullo (ed.), 52–73. New York NY: OUP.

den Dikken, M. 1995. *Particles. On the Syntax of Verb-Particle, Triadic, and Causative Constructions*. Oxford: OUP.

Folli, R. & Ramchand, G. 2005. Prepositions and results in Italian and English: An analysis from event decomposition. In *Perspectives on Aspect*, H.J. Verkuyl & H. de Swart (eds), 81–105. Dordrecht: Kluwer.

Goldberg, A. 1995. *Constructions. A Construction Grammar Approach to Argument Structure*. Chicago IL: University of Chicago Press.

Grimshaw, J. 1991. Extended Projection. Ms., Brandeis University.

Gruber, J. 1965. Studies in Lexical Relations. PhD Dissertation, MIT.

Hale, K. 1986. Notes on world view and semantic categories: some Warlpiri examples. In *Features and Projections*, P. Muysken & H. van Riemsdijk (eds), 233–254. Dordrecht: Foris.

Hale, K. & Keyser, S.J. 1993. On argument structure and the lexical expression of syntactic relations. In *The View from Building 20: Essays in Linguistics in Honor of Sylvain Bromberger*, K. Hale & S.J. Keyser (eds), 53–109. Cambridge MA: The MIT Press.

Hale, K. & Keyser, S.J. 1997a. On the complex nature of simple predicators. In *Complex Predicates*, A. Alsina et al. (eds), 29–65. Stanford CA: CSLI.

Hale, K. & Keyser, S.J. 1997b. The limits of argument structure. In *Theoretical Issues at the Morphology-Syntax Interface*, A. Mendikoetxea & M. Uribe-Etxebarria (eds), 203–230. Bizkaia: UPV.

Hale, K. & Keyser, S.J. 1998. The basic elements of argument structure. *MIT Working Papers in Linguistics* 32: 73–118.

Hale, K. & Keyser, S.J. 2000. Aspect and the Syntax of Argument Structure. Ms. MIT.

Hale, K. & Keyser, S.J. 2002. *Prolegomenon to a Theory of Argument Structure*. Cambridge MA: The MIT Press.

Harley, H. 2005. How do verbs get their names? Denominal verbs, manner incorporation, and the ontology of verb roots in English. In *The Syntax of Aspect. Deriving Thematic and Aspectual Interpretation*, N. Erteschik-Shir & T. Rapoport (eds), 42–64. Oxford: OUP.

Harley, H. & Noyer, R. 2000. Formal versus encyclopedic properties of vocabulary: Evidence from nominalisations. In *The Lexicon-Encyclopedia Interface*, B. Peeters (ed.), 349–374. Amsterdam: Elsevier.

Hoekstra, T. 1988. Small clause results. *Lingua* 74: 101–139.

Hoekstra, T. 1992. Aspect and theta-theory. In *Thematic Structure: Its Role in Grammar*, I.M. Roca (ed.), 145–174. Dordrecht: Foris.

Jackendoff, R. 1990. *Semantic Structures*. Cambridge MA: The MIT Press.

Johnson, K. 1991. Object positions. *Natural Language and Linguistic Theory* 9: 577–636.

Kayne, R.S. 1985. Principles of particle constructions. In *Grammatical Representation*, J. Guéron et al. (eds), 101–140. Dordrecht: Foris.

Keyser, S.J. & Roeper, T. 1992. Re: the abstract clitic hypothesis. *Linguistic Inquiry* 23: 89–125.

Klipple, E. 1997. Prepositions and variation. In *Projections and Interface Conditions*, A.-M. Di Sciullo (ed.), 74–108. New York: OUP.

Koopman, H. & Sportiche, D. 1991. The position of subjects. *Lingua* 85: 211–259.

Lakoff, G. & Johnson, M. 1980. *Metaphors We Live By*. Chicago IL: University of Chicago Press.

Levin, B. & Rapoport, T. 1988. Lexical subordination. *Chicago Linguistics Society* 24: 275–289.

Lieber, R. & Baayen, H. 1992. Verbal prefixes in Dutch: A study in lexical conceptual structure. In *Yearbook of Morphology 1992*, G. Booij & J. van Marle (eds), 51–78. Dordrecht: Kluwer.

Marantz, A. 1997. No escape from syntax: Don't try morphological analysis in the privacy of your own lexicon. *University of Pennsylvania Working Papers in Linguistics* 4: 201–225.

Masini, F. 2005. Multi-word expressions between syntax and the lexicon: The case of Italian verb-particle constructions. *SKY Journal of Linguistics*. 18: 145–173.

Mateu, J. 2000. Why can't we wipe the slate clean? A lexical-syntactic approach to resultative constructions. *Catalan Working Papers in Linguistics*. 8: 71–95.

Mateu, J. 2001a. Unselected objects. In *Structural Aspects of Semantically Complex Verbs*, N. Dehé & A. Wanner (eds), 83–104. Frankfurt: Peter Lang.

Mateu, J. 2001b. Preverbs in complex denominal verbs: lexical adjuncts or core predicates? *Catalan Working Papers in Linguistics* 9: 37–51.

Mateu, J. 2002. Argument Structure. Relational Construal at the Syntax-Semantics Interface. PhD Dissertation, Universitat Autònoma de Barcelona.

Mateu, J. 2003. Complex denominal verbs and parametric variation: A lexical-syntactic approach. In *Topics in Morphology: Selected Papers from the 3rd MMM*, G. Booij et al. (eds), 267–284. Barcelona: IULA Publications.

Mateu, J. 2005a. Impossible Primitives. In *The Compositionality of Meaning and Content: Foundational Issues*, M. Werning et al. (eds), 213–229. Frankfurt: Ontos.

Mateu, J. 2005b. Arguing our way to the DOR on English resultatives. *Journal of Comparative Germanic Linguistics* 8: 55–82.

Mateu, J. & Rigau, G. 2002. A minimalist account of conflation processes: Parametric variation at the lexicon-syntax interface. In *Theoretical Approaches to Universals*, A. Alexiadou (ed.), 211–236. Amsterdam: John Benjamins.

McIntyre, A. 2003. Preverbs, argument linking, and verb semantics: German prefixes and particles. In *Yearbook of Morphology 2003*, G. Booij & J. van Marle (eds), 119–144. Dordrecht: Kluwer.

McIntyre, A. 2004. Event paths, conflation, argument structure, and VP shells. *Linguistics* 42: 523–571.

Mulder, R. 1992. The Aspectual Nature of Syntactic Complementation. PhD Dissertation, Leiden University.

Neeleman, A. 1994. Complex Predicates. PhD Dissertation, Utrecht University.

Padrosa, S. 2005. Argument Structure and Morphology: The Case of en- prefixation in English and Catalan. MA Thesis, Universitat Autònoma de Barcelona.

Ramchand, G. & Svenonius, P. 2002. The lexical syntax and lexical semantics of the verb-particle construction. *WCCFL* 21: 101–114.

Rappaport Hovav, M. & Levin, B. 1998. Building Verb Meanings. In *The Projection of Arguments. Lexical and Compositional Factors*, M. Butt & W. Geuder (eds), 97–134. Stanford: CSLI.

Snyder, W. 2001. On the nature of syntactic variation: Evidence from complex predicates and complex word-formation. *Language* 77: 324–342.

Spencer, A. & Zaretskaya, M. 1998. Verb prefixation in Russian as lexical subordination. *Linguistics* 36: 1–39.

Stiebels, B. 1998. Complex denominal verbs in German and the morphology-semantics interface. In *Yearbook of Morphology 1997*, G. Booij & J. van Marle (eds), 265–302. Dordrecht: Kluwer.

Svenonius, P. 1996. The verb-particle alternation in English and Scandinavian. Ms. University of Tromsø.

Svenonius, P. 2004. Slavic prefixes inside and outside VP. *Nordlyd* 32: 205–253.

Talmy, L. 1985. Lexicalization patterns: Semantic structure in lexical forms. In *Language Typology and Syntactic Description*, Vol. 3, T. Shopen (ed.), 57–149. Cambridge: CUP.

Talmy, L. 1991. Path to realization: A typology of event conflation. *Berkeley Linguistics Society* 17: 480–519.

Talmy, L. 2000. *Toward a Cognitive Semantics*. Cambridge MA: The MIT Press.

Travis, L. 1984. Parameters and Effect of Word Order Variation. PhD Dissertation, MIT.

Uriagereka, J. 1998. *Rhyme and Reason*. Cambridge MA: The MIT Press.

Wunderlich, D. 1997. Argument extension by lexical adjunction. *Journal of Semantics* 14: 95–142.

Zeller, J. 2001. *Particle Verbs and Local Domains*. Amsterdam: John Benjamins.

Zubizarreta, M.L. & Oh, E. 2007. *On the Syntactic Composition of Manner and Motion*. Cambridge MA: The MIT Press.

PART III

Locative PPs

The distribution and interpretation of adjunct locative PPs

Naoko Tomioka
Université du Quebéc à Montréal

This paper presents previously unknown properties of adjunct locative post-positional phrases in Japanese. Unlike their English counterparts, these adjunct locatives can only take the Davidsonian event as their figure argument. Based on this observation, I explore the core assumption of the mediated modification hypothesis: Davidsonian event modifiers combine with a functional projection above VP. Specifically, I hypothesize that adjunct locatives in Japanese can only adjoin to voice P. To test this hypothesis, I examine the behaviour of adjunct locatives with various types of complex sentences, such as lexical causatives, syntactic causatives and restructuring. The investigation provides support for the mediated modification hypothesis over an account of modification based on the morphology/syntax division of the grammar.

1. Introduction

Recent explorations of the syntax and semantics of spatial prepositions have advanced our knowledge of various properties of these elements (e.g., Zwarts & Winter 2000; Svenonius 2004). Within expressions of location, the puzzle which attracted most attention is the emergence of the direction/path reading and the variations of syntactic properties relating to it (e.g., Talmy 1975; Svenonius 2004; Tungseth 2006), and hence most research focuses on the expressions of directional spatial PPs. The syntactic properties of non-directional locative expressions, in contrast, have received little attention, (see however, Nam 1995; Kracht 2002; and Maienborn 2003 for discussion on the semantics of simple adjunct locatives and Schweikert 2005 for the syntax of adjunct locatives), and the cross-linguistic variation of the syntax of non-directed adjunct locative has remained unknown. In this paper, I present a previously unnoticed pattern of Japanese locative PPs, highlighting how these expressions contrast with their English counterparts. The empirical discovery I report has important theoretical implications for our understanding of both the syntax and semantics of adjuncts in general and the structure of VPs.

Adjunct locative PPs in Japanese, at first glance, appear rather similar to their counterparts in other well-studied languages, such as English. English adjunct locative prepositional phrases can be translated with adjunct locative post-positional phrases in Japanese in many contexts. However, a closer examination reveals that adjunct locative PPs in Japanese are subject to stricter interpretive restrictions. English adjunct locatives are ambiguous as to what part of the sentence they modify. Japanese adjunct locatives, in contrast, do not show this ambiguity. I attribute this interpretive restriction to their syntactic distribution (i.e., where they can be licensed). Namely, adjunct locatives in Japanese need to combine with voice P, which denotes an event. The exploration of the distribution of the adjunct locatives leads to our second goal, which is couched in a larger project concerning event modification which hypothesizes that there is a functional element (in our case, voice) that licenses the presence of event-modifying adverbials. I show that certain complex event expressions do not allow the internal reading of the locative adjuncts in Japanese. I attribute this interpretive restriction to the absence of the functional category, which in turn, supports the mediated event modification hypothesis.

1.1 English locatives

Adjunct locative PPs in English exhibit flexibility in what figure argument they may take. The figure argument is an individual when a locative is used as a nominal modifier, as in (1a), the object (1b) or the subject and the object (1c). Nam (1995) and Kracht (2002), who report on the variation present in the type of figure argument, term this property orientation. Hence, the spatial PP in (1b) is said to be object-oriented while the locative in (1c) is subject-object oriented.

(1) a. The chef washed the potatoes in the bag but not the ones in the box.
    b. The chef washed the potatoes in the sink.
    c. The chef washed the potatoes in the kitchen.

Before proceeding with the discussion, I should make clear the points on which I depart from the previous accounts of locative expressions. Nam (1995) and Kracht (2002) examine the orientation of spatial PP in relation to the classification of verbs – some verbs induce the object orientation, while others induce subject orientation. The current paper departs from their discussion in focus and terminology. I focus on verbs that allow ambiguous orientation in English, as shown in (1), since this class of verb allows us to observe the clearest contrast between English and Japanese. Secondly, I describe the figure argument of the locative in terms of events, rather than in terms of subject or object. I believe that in treating the event, rather than the individual argument (i.e., subject or object) as Nam (1995) does, as the figure argument of the locative expression, we are able to provide a more accurate description of the Japanese locative phenomena. For the sake of consistency, I describe English locative expressions as event modifiers as well.

Returning to the examples, in (1a), the locative *in the bag* expresses that the potatoes in question have the properties of being in the bag at some circumstantially determined time. We should note that this use of PP, in which the PP is a nominal modifier, does not make reference to the event that the main predicate expresses, and hence, this use of spatial PPs falls out of the scope of this paper. Meanwhile, in (1b), the spatial PP *in the sink* expresses the location of the object at the time of washing, hence the locative here must make reference to some sort of event (or a time reference). In (1c), in contrast, the most natural interpretation of this sentence is that both the chef and the potatoes were in the kitchen when he washed the potatoes. The difference between the two locatives in (1b) and (1c) can be attributed to what kind of figure argument the locative combines with. Namely, in (1b), the figure argument of the locative is a sub-event and in (1c), the figure argument is what I call the Davidsonian event. This distinction becomes crucial in understanding the difference between English and Japanese adjunct locative PPs. Thus, I briefly discuss this distinction between sub-events and the Davidsonian event and how they are mapped onto syntactic structures in the next section, before we investigate the properties of Japanese locative PPs.

1.2   Two types of event arguments

There are two types of "events" in linguistics, classified as such based on the type of phenomena these notions are derived from. On one hand, there is what I call the Davidsonian event argument, which is associated with an entire clause. The support for postulating the Davidsonian event argument comes from the behaviour of adverbial elements which express the properties of this event (Davidson 1967; Higginbotham 1985). The Davidsonian event argument is associated with the syntactic node voice, and hence I follow the general assumption that one of the functions of voice is to introduce the Davidsonian event argument (Travis 1994; Harley 1995; Kratzer 1996). In other words, this syntactic node is necessary in the licensing of the Davidsonian event modifiers. The other notion of event, which I call sub-event, emerges in the studies on causative expressions (see e.g., Lewis 1973; Dowty 1979; Parsons 1990). A causative predicate expresses that there are two events, one of which causes the unfolding of the other. As Shibatani (1973) and Pylkkänen (2002) point out, a lexical causative predicate is associated with a single Davidsonian event, but at the same time, with two sub-events – the causing event and the caused event. In English, an adjunct spatial PP may modify either one of the sub-events (in case the expression contains causative meaning) or the Davidsonian event. This flexibility in the distribution makes adjunct locative PPs different from adverbs, which generally appear in a fixed position (but see e.g., Morzycki 2005 for a discussion on the various locations of these adverbs, and von Stechow 1996 for discussion on *wieder* 'again', a type of adverb that shows a wider range of combinatorial patterns than regular adverbs).

Returning to the examples with spatial expressions, we are now able to express the difference between (1b) and (1c) in the following way. In (1b), the figure argument of the locative is the caused sub-event: the potatoes being washed. In (1c), the figure argument is the Davidsonian event: the chef washing the potatoes. This pattern of modification is represented in (2).

(2) a. in_the_kitchen (e)   (the salient interpretation of (1c))
     b. in_the_sink (e$_{sub}$)   (the salient interpretation of (1b))

As we see in the next section, (2b) is the only available interpretation for an adjunct locative PP in Japanese, and this has a consequence for its distribution, which differs from the distribution of adjunct locative expressions in English.

2. Japanese locatives

In this section, I describe how adjunct locative PPs in Japanese are interpreted. I summarize the main generalization in section 2.1. The examples in 2.1 provide the crucial patterns most clearly and with little inter-speaker variation. In section 2.2, I pay special attention to other examples, which are met with various judgments. At first glance, these examples appear to pose questions concerning the validity of the generalization made in section 2.1. However, a closer examination reveals that once we understand the subtleties that are involved in interpreting spatial expressions, these examples do follow the simple pattern discussed in 2.1.

2.1 The interpretation of adjunct locatives

In Japanese, adjunctive locative PPs do not exhibit the various combinatorial possibilities seen in English. Instead, Japanese adjunct locatives always express the location of both the subject and the object.

(3) a. Kotaro-ga daidokoro-no naka-de buta-o   arat-ta.
         K.-NOM   kitchen-GEN   in-LOC   pig-ACC wash-PAST
         'Kotaro washed the pig in the kitchen.'
         (Both Kotaro and the pig were in the kitchen)
     b. ?Kotaro-ga o:bun-no naka-de   imo-o   yai-ta.[1]
         K.-NOM   oven-GEN in-LOC   potatoes-ACC bake-PAST

---

1. The judgment on this sentence varies from "odd, because if he is in the oven, he cannot really be doing the baking," to "bad, because if he is in the oven, he is not doing the baking."

'Kotaro baked the potatoes in the oven.'
(Both Kotaro and the potatoes were in the oven) (cf. English locative in (1b))

c. Ansatsusha-ga butai-no   ue-de   yakusha-o ut-ta.
    Assassin-NOM stage-GEN top-LOC actor-ACC shoot-PAST
    'The assassin shot the actor on the stage.'
    (Both the assassin and the actor were on the stage.)

The locative PP in (3a) expresses the location of the subject and the object at the time of the baking. The interpretation of this sentence, thus, mirrors the salient interpretation of the English locative example in (1c). This example illustrates that some Japanese locative adjuncts appear uninterestingly similar to their English counterparts, aside from the minor difference that Japanese locatives are headed by post-positions, rather than prepositions. What is interesting is the PP in example (3b), which expresses the location of both the subject (Kotaro) and the object (the potatoes) at the time of baking. This interpretation of the locative in (3b) contrasts with its English counterpart seen in (1b), which only expresses the location of the object. Although the English-like interpretation is more plausible, Japanese speakers are unable to have such an interpretation of the sentence in (3b). This interpretive fact, thus, indicates that it is the syntax of Japanese that does not allow the locative PP to combine with the VP, which would yield the more pragmatically plausible interpretation.

The example in (3c) shows that even with a different locative (*no-ue de* 'on'), we observe the same restriction on the interpretation of the locative adjunct. The sentence in (3c) contains the verb *ut* 'shoot'. Conceptually, it is easy, and possibly more natural, to imagine that an assassin be off the stage when he/she shot the actor. When Japanese speakers hear the sentence in (3c), however, the interpretation they have is that both the assassin and the actor were on the stage. Again, I take this to mean that it is the grammatical properties of Japanese language that forces this interpretation despite the pragmatic considerations.

As I mentioned in the previous section, locative adjuncts express the location of subjects and objects when their figure argument is the Davidsonian event. The pattern we observe in Japanese, in which the locative adjunct necessarily includes the location of the subject, indicates that Japanese locative adjuncts do not combine with sub-events, but only with the Davidsonian event. In a framework in which event modification is associated with a particular phrase structure, we are able to make certain predictions about the distribution of elements that exclusively combine with Davidsonian events. In particular, the Davidsonian event argument is associated with the syntactic node voice. If Japanese locative adjuncts only combine with the Davidsonian event, the distribution of these spatial PPs mirrors the presence of the voice node. In the following section, we see that this prediction is born out, confirming that Japanese locative PPs are predicates of

Davidsonian events, and moreover, this exploration, in turn, provides new support for the structure-based account of event modification.

As an aside, we should note that in Japanese, nominal modifiers are morphologically distinct from verbal modifiers. The third reading of the locative phrase, in which it modifies the nominal, is available in Japanese, but the locative phrase in this context appears with a genitive case marker -*no*, rather than the adjunct marker -*de*, as shown in (4).

> (4)   Kotaro-ga nabe-no naka-**no**   imo-o   arat-ta.
>   K.-NOM   pot-GEN inside-GEN potato-ACC wash-PAST
>   'Kotaro washed the potatoes that are in the pot.'

For the purpose of this paper, I focus on the verbal modification of spatial expressions and leave aside the use of these spatial expressions in the nominal context.

To summarize, the pattern we observe in this section is that locative PPs in Japanese modify the Davidsonian event, expressing the location of both the subject and the object of the sentence. The sub-event interpretation is unavailable even when such interpretation would be more pragmatically plausible. This unavailability of the sub-event interpretation makes Japanese different from English. Before I investigate the implication of this difference in section 3, I turn to more complicated examples in the next section to ensure that the empirical pattern I describe in this section holds generally with different types of verbs.

2.2   The subtleties of locative expressions

In this section, I would like to shift our attention to other examples of adjunct locatives which require more careful examination. The following examples, at first glance, appear to contradict the claim made in the previous section, that Japanese locatives have a simple, restricted interpretation. However, once we take into consideration the contextual and pragmatic effects involved in interpreting these locatives, we are able to conclude that the grammatical principle postulated in the previous section holds of these expressions as well.

The first set of puzzling facts involves expressions involving physically small locations. At first, it appears that some Japanese speakers allow for an English-like interpretation of the spatial PP in the following sentences, in which the locatives express the location of the object but not the subject.

> (5)   a.   Kotaro-wa nagasi-no naka-de   buta-o   arat-ta.
>   K.-TOP   sink-GEN inside-LOC pig-ACC wash-PAST
>   'Kotaro washed the pig in the sink.'
>   b.   Kotaro-wa nabe-no naka-de   udon-o   yude-ta.
>   K.-TOP   pot-GEN inside-LOC noodle-ACC boil-PAST
>   'Kotaro boiled the noodles in the pot.'

These speakers accept these sentences as true when the subject is not in the sink (in 5a) or in the pot (in 5b). This interpretation seems to suggest that locative PPs express the location of the caused sub-event (the pig being washed in (5a), and the noodle being boiled in (5b)), rather than the Davidsonian event of Kotaro's washing of the pig (in 5a) or Kotaro's boiling of the noodle (in 5b). If this were true, these examples undermine the claim made in the previous section. However, a close examination of these speakers' interpretive mechanism reveals that this is not the case. The speakers who allow an English-like interpretation of (5), find the following sentences in (6) odd. These sentences are interpreted as odd because the locative PPs here can only be taken to be modifiers of the Davidsonian event, expressing the location of both the subject and object.

(6) a. ?Kotaro-wa   sentakki-no naka-de   buta-o   arat-ta.
         K.-TOP   w.m.-GEN   inside-LOC pig-ACC   wash-PAST
         'Kotaro washed the pig in the washing machine.'
     b. */?Kotaro-wa nabe-no naka-de   gohan-o tai-ta.
         K.-TOP   pot-GEN inside-LOC rice-ACC cook-PAST
         'Kotaro cooked the rice in the pot.'

The key difference between the sentences in (5) and (6) is pragmatic / conceptual in nature. In (5), the locative PPs describe an open space, while in (6), they describe a closed space, in a sense that when one boils noodles, the lid is off the pot while when one cooks rice, the lid must be on, closing the space described as 'in the pot'. Moreover, the interpretation of the sentences in (5) suggests that a part of the agent's body (or its extension) must be in the space the spatial expressions specify. In (5a), we see that in washing the pig, Kotaro's hands are in the sink, and in boiling the noodles, he is likely to insert chop sticks to stir them. In contrast, according to our world knowledge, we close the lid when we use a washing machine and also when we cook rice, which makes it unlikely for a part of the agent's body to be in the specified space. In these contexts, the English-like interpretations of the spatial PPs are excluded. The key property of Japanese locatives, hence, is that part of the causer (agent) and the object must be in the location the PP specifies. The following example illustrates this key point clearly.

(7) Ansatsusha-ga shacho-o kuruma-no naka-de   ut-ta.
     Assassin-NOM CEO-ACC car-GEN   inside-LOC shoot-PAST
     'The assassin shot the CEO in the car.'

Some Japanese speakers interpret this sentence to mean that both the assassin and the CEO were in the car when the assassin shot the CEO. Others accept this sentence as being true, when the assassin is standing outside of the car. Crucially, however, for this second group of speakers, the sentence implies that at least the tip of the gun was in the car (through the open window, for example). This example, thus, clearly shows that the interpretation of adjunct locative PPs in Japanese is different from the interpretation of their English counterparts, in that Japanese locative PPs always assert the location of both the subject and the object.

The subtle nuances of the locative expressions shown in this section leads us back to the choice of terminology I mentioned in section 1.1. As previously mentioned, I chose to refer to the figure arguments of the adjunct locatives as the Davidsonian event or sub-event, rather than subject-oriented or object-oriented as Nam (1995) does. My choice is based on the indirect way that the locative restricts the location of the agent argument in (7). That is, in (7), the locative expresses that the event of the assassin shooting the CEO took place in the car and for this statement to be true, part of the causing event (i.e., the tip of the gun) must be in the car. It is not the case that Japanese locatives are inherently loose in associating the figure argument to the specified location – in a sentence that simply states the location of individuals (as exemplified in (8)), the said individual must be in the location expressed, not just part of the individual.

(8)   Ansatsusha-wa   kuruma-no   naka   da.
      Assassin-TOP   car-GEN   inside   copular.PRES
      'The assassin is in the car.'

Hence the sentence in (8) would be false if the assassin were standing outside of the car with the tip of his gun in the car. The contrast between (7) and (8), which is the difference in the exact relation between the position of the individual argument (the assassin) and the location the PP expresses, arises from the difference in the type of figure argument these locatives take. In (7), the figure argument of the locative is an event, and hence the relation between the exact location of the agent (i.e., a participant of the event) and the location the PP expresses is somewhat indirectly connected. In contrast, in (8), the figure argument of the locative is the individual argument of the sentence, the sentence being a locative expression, and hence the relation between the location of the individual and the location the PP expresses is direct.

The second feature of locatives I would like to point out is the difference between the Japanese locative –no naka-de and the English locative inside.[2] The English locative inside tends to resist combining with the sub-event; a number of native speakers of English interpret the following sentence to mean that both the assassin and the CEO were in the bedroom at the time of shooting.

(9)   The assassin shot the CEO inside the bedroom.

---

2.   I would like to thank the reviewer for pointing out this possibility.

The properties of *inside* for these speakers seem to pattern with that of the Japanese locative, *-no naka-de* 'inside'. However, I discovered the following puzzling fact: Pragmatic considerations can override this tendency of *inside* in English, but not of its Japanese locative *-no naka-de*. The following examples illustrate this contrast.

(10) These poor bunnies! Someone shot them inside their cage!

(11) Dareka-ga   ori-no   naka-de   usagi-o   ut-ta.
     Someone-NOM cage-GEN inside-LOC bunny-ACC shoot-PAST
     'Someone shot the bunnies in the cage.'

With the Japanese sentence in (11), we observe the two patterns mentioned previously: For some speakers, (11) means that someone was inside the cage with the bunnies when he/she shot them. For other speakers, that heartless someone could be outside of the cage, but their interpretation still requires that the tip of the gun was inserted in the cage. For English speakers (those who require the assassin to be in the bedroom in (9)), (10) provides a puzzling contrast, for they feel that this sentence can be true without the shooter, or any part of the gun, in the cage. Hence, I leave this discussion with a cautionary comment that we shall not jump to the conclusion that Japanese locatives, such as *no naka-de* are simply the same as a complex locative expression observed in English (e.g., *inside*).

The discussion here points out that an investigation of the interpretive properties of locative expressions is not a simple matter. The observed inter-speaker variation is due to their sensitivity (or the lack thereof) to conceptual features such as closed/open distinction as the examples in (6) reveal. That is, unlike some Japanese speakers who reject the English-like interpretations (and hence the sentences in (6)), other speakers allow a "loose" reading of what it means for an event to be in the space specified by the locative expression. By introducing the parameter of "complete closedness", we see that it is indeed this conceptual feature that allowed for an English-like interpretation in sentence (6), rather than the formal, grammatical feature of the locative. The distinction between adjunct locatives in Japanese, even with the speakers who accepted (6), is clearly seen in the examples with expressions of larger space in (9) to (11). We can thus conclude that formally, spatial locative PPs modify events in the sense of Davidson (1967), and unlike English locative expressions, cannot modify sub-events.

3.   The distribution of predicates of *e*

As we briefly saw in Section 1.3, the notion of Davidsonian event arguments plays a crucial role in formalizing the adverbial modification facts (e.g., Davidson 1967; Higginbotham 1985). Davidson postulates that what a verb of activity expresses is the assertion that there is an event of some kind (e.g., running, eating, etc.). He notes that a number of adverbial elements can be treated as predicates of this event and that the combination of these adverbial elements and the main verb can be treated conjunctively. Hence, the sentence (12a) can receive the semantic representation of (12b).

(12)   a.   The chef buttered the toast slowly.
       b.   butter (c, t, e) & slowly (e)

We will see in the following sections that these elements that can be seen as predicates of the Davidsonian event are subject to certain distributional restrictions. Some researchers provide detailed classifications within modifiers of events (e.g., Cinque 1999), but for the purpose of the current investigation, we simply postulate that there is (at least) a node above the lexical verbal projection that is responsible for the licensing of Davidsonian event modifiers. This claim, in spirit, follows the accounts provided in Harley (1995); Kratzer (1996); and Travis (1994), among many others, who argue that the syntactic head voice is associated with event-ness.

Although the current claim follows Cinque's (1999) mediated modification hypothesis in spirit, we must note that Japanese spatial expressions contradict one of the peripheral claims made in Cinque (1999). Cinque notes that English adjunct locative PPs are different from adverbs in being able to appear in various positions, and hence we observe the varied interpretation of the locatives in (1).[3] However, Japanese locative PPs do not exhibit the same varied interpretation, which leads us to wonder whether their distribution is as restricted as so called "small" modifiers. This term "small modifiers" is adopted from Cinque (1999) and it refers to adverbials that appear in the functional domain above VP. In particular, we are interested in the type of "small" modifiers that take Davidsonian event arguments. In this section, we will indeed see that Davidsonian event predicates and spatial PPs are subject to the same distributional restrictions in Japanese.

The difference between Japanese and English on these facts reflects a more general difference between the two languages. I will show in section 5 that other adverbial elements also fail to combine with sub-events in Japanese.

---

3.   There are a few adverbials that show the same type of interpretive flexibility as locative expressions in English. *Again* is one of them. Von Stechow (1996) examines the various interpretations of the German counterpart of *again* (*wieder*) and provides a structure-based account of it. He claims that *wieder*, unlike other adverbials, is able to appear inside the lexical verbal projection and that is how it can receive the restitutive reading.

3.1 Lexical vs. syntactic causatives

The distinction between Davidsonian events and sub-events becomes most apparent when we compare the lexical causative construction and the syntactic causative construction. In the syntactic causative construction, the argument of the causative predicate is associated with the Davidsonian event argument. The argument of the causative predicate in the lexical causative construction, on the other hand, is simply a sub-event. Hence, predicates of the Davidsonian event (henceforth e_D), such as manner adverbs, may modify the caused event of the syntactic causative construction, but not the caused event of the lexical causative construction (Tomioka 2006a, b). We should note that the distinction between the lexical causative construction and the syntactic causative construction is a syntactic one, but this difference has semantic consequences (see Shibatani 1973 for details).

The distinction between the lexical causative construction and the syntactic causative construction is defined syntactically, as shown in (13).

(13) a.   [causeP cause [voice P]]   Syntactic Causative
      b.   [causeP cause [VP]]   Lexical Causative

We should also note that voice is a functional category that introduces the Davidsonian event (e.g., Kratzer 1996; Harley 1995; Travis 1994, 2000). By combining these two assumptions, we can form a new hypothesis that the caused event of the lexical causative construction, which has the structure of VP, is associated with a sub-event, but that the caused event of the syntactic causative construction, which has the structure of voice P, is associated with a Davidsonian event. Hence, we predict that predicates of Davidsonian events may apply to the caused event of the syntactic causative construction, but not to the caused event of the lexical causative construction. The following examples show that this prediction is borne out.

Shibatani (1973) shows that adverbial elements such as *damatte* 'being quiet, quietly' may express the state of the causee argument of the syntactic causative (14a). Since modification in the main clause is also possible, the sentence is ambiguous: in one reading, it was Kotaro who was quiet in making Jiro put on his clothes. In the other reading, it was Jiro who was quiet when Kotaro made him put on his clothes. The lexical causative construction, on the other hand, does not show this ambiguity. In (14b), the adverbial element *damatte* can only be treated as the modifier of the main predicate (the causative predicate) and the sentence unambiguously asserts that Kotaro was quiet when he put clothes on Jiro.

(14) a.   *Syntactic causative*
           Kotaro-ga Jiro-ni damatte   huku-o   ki-sase-ta.
           K.-NOM   J.-DAT   being.quiet clothes-ACC   wear-cause-PAST
           'Kotaro made Jiro put on his clothes silently.'

b.   *Lexical causative*
    Kotaro-ga Jiro-ni damatte   huku-o   ki-se-ta.
    K.-NOM   J.-DAT being.quiet clothes-ACC wear-cause-PAST
    'Kotaro silently put clothes on Jiro.'

Another adverbial element, *hitoride* 'by oneself' exhibits the same pattern. In (15a), the adverbial appears in the syntactic causative construction and provides two possible interpretations. In one reading, it was the causer (Kotaro) who was without anyone's help when he made Jiro put on his clothes. Crucially, in the second reading, the adverbial modifies the action of the causee. In this reading, the sentence asserts that Jiro did not receive anyone's help when Kotaro made him put his clothes on. When the same adverbial element is used in the lexical causative construction, the first reading is available, but not the second one.

(15) a.   *Syntactic Causative*
        Kotaro-ga Jiro-ni hitori-de   huku-o   ki-sase-ta.
        K.-NOM   J.-DAT by.himself clothes-ACC wear-cause-PAST
        'Kotaro made Jiro put on his clothes by himself.'
        (No one helped Jiro, or no one helped Kotaro.)
    b.   *Lexical causative*
        Kotaro-ga Jiro-ni hitori-de   huku-o   ki-se-ta.
        K.-NOM   J.-DAT by.himself clothes-ACC wear-cause-PAST
        'Kotaro put clothes on Jiro by himself.'
        (No one helped Kotaro, NOT no one helped Jiro.)

These examples show that there are elements that can modify the caused event of the syntactic causative construction, but not the caused event of the lexical causative construction. These elements are predicates of Davidsonian events, and hence, their inability to combine with the caused event of the lexical causative construction is attributed to the fact that the caused event of the lexical causative construction is a sub-event, rather than a Davidsonian event.

Having seen the behaviour of Davidsonian event predicates, we are now ready to compare them with locative PPs. The following examples show that adjunct locatives in Japanese behave exactly the same as Davidsonian event predicates. In (16) the locative phrase, *kuruma no naka de* 'in the car' is used in the syntactic causative construction (the verb *ne* 'sleep' is suffixed with the syntactic causative morpheme *sase*). The locative in this sentence can be interpreted as modifying the location of the causer (Kotaro) or the causee (Jiro). In the latter interpretation, the sentence does not specify where Kotaro was at the time of the event. Similarly, the locative PP *sinsitu-no naka-de* 'in the bedroom' in (16b) is used in a syntactic causative construction and provides two interpretations. Again, if the spatial expression is taken to modify the caused event, the sentence does not specify where the causer was.

(16) *Syntactic causative and locative PP*
 a. Kotaro-ga Jiro-o **kuruma-no naka-de** ne-sase-ta.
   K.-NOM J.-ACC car-GEN inside-LOC sleep-cause-PAST
   'Kotaro made Jiro sleep in the car.'
   (Jiro was in the car, but Kotaro need not have been there)
 b. Kotaro-ga Jiro-ni **sinsitu-no**   **naka-de** huku-o
   K.-NOM J.-DAT bedroom-GEN inside-LOC clothes-ACC
   ki-sase-ta.
   wear-cause-PAST
   'Kotaro made Jiro put on his clothes in the bedroom.'
   (Jiro was in the bedroom, but Kotaro need not have been there.)

Now, we see that the ambiguity that arises in the syntactic causative construction is absent in the lexical causative construction. In (17a), the same spatial PP is used in a lexical causative construction. In this sentence, however, the interpretation of the locative phrase is unambiguous. It specifies the location of the causer, Kotaro. The same pattern is observed in (17b).

(17) *Lexical causative and locative PP*
 a. Kotaro-ga buta-o **nagasi-no naka-de** kirei-ni si-ta.
   K.-NOM pig-ACC sink-GEN inside-LOC clean do-PAST
   'Kotaro cleaned the pig in the sink.'
   (Kotaro was in the sink)
 b. Kotaro-ga Jiro-ni **sinsitu-no**   **naka-de** huku-o ki-se-ta.
   K.-NOM J.-DAT bedroom-GEN inside-LOC clothes-ACC wear-cause-PAST
   'Kotaro put clothes on Jiro in the bedroom.' (Kotaro was in the bedroom)

These examples show that an adjunct locative PP may modify the caused event of the syntactic causative construction, but not the caused event of the lexical causative construction. This is exactly the pattern we observed with Davidsonian event predicates. Hence, we conclude that in Japanese, locative phrases are predicates of Davidsonian events.

3.2 Restructuring

The current proposal is that event modification involves a projection above VP (i.e., voice), and that the distribution of adjunct locative PPs in Japanese is subject to the presence of this projection. In order to strengthen our argument, we shall examine another context in which the VP, but not the voice P node, is present. This phenomenon is referred to as restructuring. It has been argued that the embedded clause in the restructuring context lacks the functional category that licenses and determines the case of the object DP (Wurmbrand & Bobaljik 2004). I have shown elsewhere that in fact, the embedded clause in the restructuring context even lacks the voice node, which introduces the Davidsonian event argument that the embedded verb describes (Tomioka 2006b). The consequence of the absence of a voice node is that the modification of the embedded verb is impossible. This is exactly what we see in the following examples.

In (18), we see the contrast between the restructuring context and the non-restructuring context in the interpretation of the modifier *mata* 'again'.[4] In a non-restructuring context, where the embedded clause is a full clause, the adverb *mata* 'again' can take scope below the matrix verb *wasure* 'forget'. Hence, Japanese speakers who hear this sentence presuppose that previously Taro had called Jiro, but that he forgot to call him this time. The adverb *mata* in (18a) can take scope over the main verb *wasure* 'forget', too, but the crucial point of (18a) is that the lower interpretation of *mata* 'again' is present. In the restructuring context in (18b), in contrast, the adverb must take scope over the matrix verb *wasure* 'forget' and the speakers must presuppose that Taro had forgotten to call Jiro previously and again he had forgotten to do so. Hence, in a context in which Taro had previously called Jiro, the sentence in (18a) can be true but not the sentence in (18b).

(18) a. *Non-restructuring*
       Taro-wa Jiro-ni **mata** denwa-o   su-ru-no-o   wasure-ta.
       T.-TOP   J.-DAT again   phone-ACC do-PRES-COMP-ACC forget-PAST
       'Taro forgot to call Jiro again (he had previously called Jiro)'
       'Taro again forgot to call Jiro'

    b. *Restructuring*
       Taro-wa Jiro-ni **mata** denwa-o   si-wasure-ta
       T.-TOP   J.-DAT again   phone-ACC do-forget-PAST
       'Taro again forgot to call Jiro (he had previously forgotten to call Jiro)'

These examples show that the lexical causative construction was not unique in disallowing the modification of the embedded clause. In the restructuring context too, we see that the predicate of a Davidsonian event, such as the adverb *mata* 'again', may not modify the embedded clause. The discussion in the previous section leads us to expect that locative phrases should show the same sensitivity to restructuring as the adverb *mata* 'again', and the following examples confirm our hypothesis.

---

4. I am aware that the English counterpart of *mata, again* may combine with the caused sub-event, as discussed in von Stechow (1996). It has been argued that *mata*, like *again*, may pick out the caused sub-event in certain contexts (see Beck 2005). However, the sub-event reading does not arise with the examples I show here, and I leave this minor puzzle of why this variety arises in the examples Beck (2005) observed for a future research.

In (19), again, we see two sentences containing the same matrix verb *wasure* 'forget', and the same embedded verb phrase *shasin-o tor* 'taking of the picture'. The sentence in (19a), however, contains a full CP as an embedded clause while the sentence (19b) contains a reduced clause, i.e., it is a restructuring sentence. As we expect, the locative in (19a) may be interpreted as expressing the location of the embedded event (Jiro's taking of the picture) or the main event (Jiro's forgetting to take the picture). Given the availability of the lower interpretation of the locative (the interpretation (i.), the sentence is true even if Jiro did not go to the museum.

(19) a. *Non-restructuring*[5]
Jiro-ga shasin-o **bijutukan-no naka-de** to-ru-no-o
J.-NOM picture-ACC museum-GEN inside-LOC take-PRES-COMP-ACC
wasure-ta.
forget-PAST
'Jiro forgot to take the picture in the museum.'
i. What Jiro forgot was to take the picture in the museum.
ii. Jiro's forgetting of picture-taking took place in the museum.
b. *Restructuring*
Jiro-ga shasin-o **bijutukan-no naka-de** tori-wasure-ta.
J.-NOM picture-ACC museum-GEN inside-LOC take-forget-PAST
'Jiro forgot to take the picture in the museum. '
(The forgetting event took place at the museum)

In the restructuring context, however, the locative phrase cannot be interpreted as modifying the embedded event. Rather, it must modify the main event (forgetting). Hence, the sentence is false if Jiro did not go to the museum.

These examples show that the distribution of adjunct locative PPs in Japanese is highly restricted. To be more precise, the use of these spatial PPs requires the presence of the element called voice. Restructuring provides the second context (after the lexical causative construction) in which the embedded clause is lacking the voice projection. In this context, adjunct locative PPs, as well as so-called "small" modifier element such as *mata* 'again', fail to modify the embedded clause.

To conclude, we see in this section that adjunct spatial PPs in Japanese have the same distributional properties as adverbial elements such as *hitoride* 'alone'. So the restriction on the behaviour of these adverbials is not surprising. According to Cinque (1999), "small" modifiers are subject to stricter distributional constraints than "large" modifiers. However, the data containing the spatial PPs indicate that

---

5. The sentences in (9) are given with the following story: One day, Jiro planned to do a number of bad things: smoke in the bus, pee in the pool, eat in the library, and take a picture in the museum. When he got home from doing most of these bad things, he realized that he did not go to the museum. Therefore . . . (the sentences in (9) are given here).

in Japanese, locative PPs, which are considered "large" according to Cinque (1999), pattern with these "small" modifiers. The evidence indicates that Cinque's (1999) notion of "small" and "large" cannot be correct in its simple form. I leave open the question of whether Japanese spatial PPs are an exception to a robust cross-linguistic generalization, or whether the small-large classification does not hold once we include lesser-known languages. This paper provides a description of problematic data in attempt to start a rhetoric on this topic of small-large modifiers, which is often taken for granted.

4. Against the complex predicate analysis

In this section, I consider an alternative explanation that may be provided for the distribution of adjunct locative PPs. The particular hypothesis I critique involves the idea that head-movement (or incorporation) creates a unit that is often referred to as a "complex predicate". By refuting this hypothesis, I will conclude that the current explanation, which relies on the notion of the Davidsonian event and its introduction by the voice node, provides a superior explanation.

4.1 Head Movement does not create a complex predicate.

There is a line of thought that postulates that head movement (i.e., incorporation) creates a logical unit called a "complex predicate". Various forms of this idea surface throughout the literature (e.g., Saito 2000; Tada 1992; Lakoff & Ross 1972; Rapp & von Stechow 1999). Even though each researcher mentioned above employs different theoretical tools, their work shares the basic assumption that when two predicates are realized as one word, the internal make-up of the word is invisible to syntactic relations such as modification. In this section, I show that this hypothesis is false. As we saw in Section 3.1, the adverbial elements that fail to modify the embedded predicate of the lexical causative construction are able to modify the embedded predicate of the syntactic causative construction. We should recall that adjunct locative PPs exhibit the same pattern, as repeated in (20) below. In (20), the locative phrase, *nagasi-no naka de* 'in the sink' can modify the embedded event, and in this interpretation, the locative specifies the location of Jiro's sleeping, without making any assertion about Kotaro's location.

> (20) Kotaro-wa nagasi-no naka-de Jiro-o ne-sase-ta.
> K.-TOP sink-GEN inside-LOC Jiro-ACC sleep-cause-PAST
> 'Kotaro made Jiro sleep in the sink'

In all of these constructions (lexical causative, restructuring, syntactic causative) the main verb and the embedded verb form a morphologically complex word in Japanese. That is, the morphological form of the predicate does not distinguish the syntactic causative constructions from the lexical causative construction or from restructuring verbs. We thus have reason to assume that head movement does not automatically create a "complex predicate".

The second critique of the complex predicate hypothesis is that we can find a context in which the adverbial modification of an embedded predicate is disallowed, even when the embedded predicate is morphologically free. In Èdó resultative serial verb constructions, the two verbs of the construction appear separately. Still, an adverbial element cannot modify just one member of the predicate, as shown in (21).

> (21) Òzó hòó ùkpòn fàfà ègìégìé.   (Baker & Stewart 1999: 23)
>   Ozo wash dress fade quickly
>   'Ozo quickly washed the dress so it faded.'
>   (NOT 'Ozo washed the dress such that it faded quickly.')

Some researchers assume that the two verbs in serial verb constructions undergo covert head movement and that these verbs do form a compound at LF (e.g., Collins 1997, 2002; Nishiyama 1998). However, we have already seen that head movement does not automatically create a "complex predicate" effect. Given the failure of this first assumption, attributing the modification fact of Èdó (shown in (21)) to LF incorporation is undesirable.

In the current account, both syntactic causative constructions and resultative serial verb constructions can be understood without additional stipulations. In a syntactic causative construction, the embedded clause contains a voice projection, and hence the adverbials and adjunct locative can modify the embedded clause. In resultative serial verb constructions, the embedded verb lacks a voice projection (as assumed in Baker & Stewart 1999; Stewart 2000; and Tomioka 2006a), and hence the modification of the event this verb expresses is impossible. I thus conclude that the hypothesis involving Davidsonian event arguments and the node provides a better understanding of the modification facts than the complex predicate hypothesis.

5. Beyond adjunct locatives

So far, we have seen how Japanese adjunct locatives differ from their English counterparts. The question one must eventually address is what this difference means to the grammar in general. The complete answer to this question remains speculative at this point, but I show in this section that the observed difference between the two languages reflects a more general pattern which encompasses all the "functional" adverbials. Functional adverbials (this term is introduced in von Stechow 1996) are different from the typical adverbs that are discussed in Cinque (1999). Functional adverbs appear in a lower, lexical domain, where regular adverbs may not appear. In other words, functional adverbs/modifiers combine with sub-events. Examples of these adverbials are shown in (22–23).

(22) a.   The chef spun the knife twice.
           → He acted on the knife twice.   (Davidsonian event modification)
      b.   The chef spun the knife two and a half times.
           → The knife spun two and a half times.   (sub-event modification)

(23) a.   The chef put the cake in the oven for five minutes.
           → He spent five minutes putting the cake in the oven. (Davidsonian event)
           → The cake remained in the oven for five minutes.   (sub-event)

These adjunct phrases have roughly the same variation in their interpretation as the adjunct locative PPs. They can be interpreted as the Davidsonian event modifier, or the sub-event modifier. We should note that (22b) would be taken as pragmatically odd if the modifier *two and a half times* were taken to be modifying the Davidsonian event. Similarly, the example in (23) feels coerced with the first interpretation and the second interpretation (where the modifier *for five minutes* is taken to modify the sub-event) feels more natural. With the following examples, we see that their counterparts in Japanese, like the adjunct locatives, fail to modify the sub-event.

(24) a.   Ryourichoo-ga hoochoo-o nikai mawasi-ta.
           Chef-NOM   knife-ACC twice spin-PAST
           'The chef spun the knife twice.'
      b.   ?Ryourichoo-ga hoochoo-o nikai-han   mawasi-ta.
            Chef-NOM   knife-ACC twice-half spin-PAST
            'The chef spun the knife two and a half times.'

(25) ?Ryourichoo-ga keeki-o   oobun-no naka-ni   gohun   ire-ta.
        Chef-NOM   cake-ACC   oven-GEN inside-DAT five.minutes put.in-PAST
        'The chef put the cake in the oven for five minutes.'

Both the sentences in (24b) and (25) feel odd because the adverbial *nikai-han* 'two and half times' and *gohun* 'for five minutes' fail to modify the sub-events, and they yield odd interpretations when they are taken as modifying the Davidsonian event. The oddity of the two sentences (19b and 20) indicates that these adverbials, too, are restricted to combining with the Davidsonian event.

There are two possible accounts of this observed pattern. One is that the mechanism that is available in English for licensing the combination of functional adverbials with sub-events is unavailable in Japanese. The other is that the structure of Japanese verb phrases is fundamentally different from that of English. The latter account, in spirit, follows the proposal in Sabbagh (to appear). I leave these options open and leave this puzzle as the topic of future research.

6. Conclusion

In this paper, I have shown that adjunct locative PPs in Japanese have a more restricted interpretation than their English counterparts. I have argued that this restriction is due to the fact that Japanese locative PPs are predicates of Davidsonian events. I thus compared other predicates of Davidsonian events and locative PPs in the context of syntactic causative constructions, lexical causative constructions and restructuring. Indeed, these examples show that when the voice node (the element that introduces the Davidsonian event argument) is absent in a clause, the modification of that clause is impossible, either by a "small" modifier or by the locative PP.

References

Baker, M. & Stewart, O.T. 1999. On double-headedness and the anatomy of the clause. Ms., Rutgers University.

Beck, S. 2005. There and back again: A semantic analysis. *Journal of Semantics* 22: 3–51.

Cinque, G. 1999. *Adverbs and Functional Heads: A Cross-Linguistic Perspective*. New York NY: OUP.

Collins, C. 1997. Argument sharing in serial verb constructions. *Linguistic Inquiry* 28: 461–497.

Collins, C. 2002. Multiple verb movement in Hoan. *Linguistic Inquiry* 33: 1–29.

Davidson, D. 1967. The logical form of action sentences. In *The Logic of Decision and Action*, N. Roscher (ed.), 81–95. Pittsburgh PA: University of Pittsburgh Press.

Dowty, D. 1979. *Word Meaning and Montague Grammar: The Semantics of Verbs and Times in Generative Semantics and Montague's PTQ*. Dordrecht: Reidel.

Harley, Heidi. 1995. Subjects, events and licensing. PhD Dissertation. MIT.

Higginbotham, J. 1985. On semantics. *Linguistic Inquiry* 16: 547–593.

Higginbotham, J. 2000. On accomplishments. In *Proceedings of GLOW Asia*. Nanzan University.

Kracht, M. 2002. On the semantics of locatives. *Linguistics and Philosophy* 25: 157–232.

Kratzer, A. 1996. Severing the external argument from its verb. In *Phrase Structure and the Lexicon*, J. Rooryck & L. Zaring (eds), 109–137. Dordrecht: Kluwer.

Lakoff, G. & Ross, J. 1972. A note on anaphoric islands and causatives. *Linguistic Inquiry* 3: 121–125.

Lewis, D. 1973. Causation. *Journal of Philosophy* 70: 556–567.

Maienborn, C. 2003. Event-internal modifiers: Semantic underspecification and conceptual interpretation. In *Modifying Adjuncts*, E. Lang, C. Maienborn & C. Fabricius-Hansen (eds), 475–510. Berlin: Mouton de Gruyter.

Morzycki, M. 2005. Mediated Modification: Functional Structure and the Interpretation of Modifier Position. PhD Dissertation. University of Massachusetts at Amherst.

Nam, S. 1995. Semantics of Locative Prepositional Phrases in English. PhD Dissertation, UCLA.

Nishiyama, K. 1998. V-V compounds as serialization. *Journal of East Asian Linguistics* 7: 175–217.

Parsons, T. 1990. *Events in the Semantics of English: A Study in Subatomic Semantics.* Cambridge MA: The MIT Press.

Pylkkänen, L. 2002. Introducing Arguments. PhD Dissertation, MIT.

Rapp, I. & von Stechow, A. 1999. Fast 'almost' and the visibility parameter for functional adverbs. *Journal of Semantics* 16: 149–204.

Sabbagh, J. to appear. Adjectival passives and the structure of VP in Tagalog. Lingua.

Saito, M. 2000. Predicate raising and theta relations. Ms., Nanzan University.

Shibatani, M. 1973. Semantics of Japanese causativization. *Foundations of Language* 9: 327–373.

von Stechow, A. 1996. The different readings of wieder 'again': A structural account. *Journal of Semantics* 13: 87–138.

Stewart, O.T. 2001. *The Serial Verb Construction Parameter.* New York NY: Garland.

Svenonius, P. 2004. Spatial P in English. Ms., University of Tromsø.

Schweikert, W. 2005. *The Order of Prepositional Phrases in the Structure of the Clause.* Amsterdam: John Benjamins.

Tada, H. 1992. Nominative objects in Japanese. *Journal of Japanese Linguistics* 14: 91–108.

Talmy, L. 1975. Semantics and syntax of motion. In *Syntax and Semantics* 4, J. P. Kimball (ed.), 181–238.

Tomioka, N. 2006a. Resultative Constructions: Cross-Linguistic Variations and the Syntax-Semantic Interface. PhD Dissertation, McGill University.

Tomioka, N. 2006b. The interaction between restructuring and causative morphology in Japanese. Paper presented at the 2006 annual meeting of the Canadian Linguistics Association, York University.

Travis, L. 1994. Event phrase and a theory of functional categories. In *Proceedings of Canadian Linguistics Association Meeting.*

Travis, L. 2000. Event structure in syntax. In *Events as Grammatical Objects*, C. Tenny & J. Pustejovsky (eds), 145–185. Stanford CA: CSLI.

Tungseth, M. 2006. Verbal Prepositions in Norwegian: Path, Places and Possession. PhD Dissertation. University of Tromsø.

Wurmbrand, S. & Bobaljik, J. 2004. Anti-reconstruction effects are anti-reconstruction Effects. In *Proceedings of the 2003 Annual Meeting of the CLA.*

Zwarts, J. & Winter, Y. 2000. Vector space semantics: a model-theoretic analysis of locative prepositions. *Journal of Logic, Language and Information* 9: 169–211.

Aspect inside PLACE PPs*

Christina Tortora
City University of New York (College of Staten Island
and The Graduate Center)

Spanish and Italian (and other Romance languages) exhibit minimal pairs of
place PPs (to be distinguished from path, or directional, PPs), where one member
of the pair can be characterized as "complex," and the other as "simplex." The
complex PP involves a lexical preposition in combination with the grammatical
preposition *a* (e.g., Italian: *dietro all'albero* 'behind a the tree'), while the simplex
counterpart occurs without *a* (e.g., Italian: *dietro l'albero* 'behind the tree'). This
paper examines a number of different (locative) lexical Ps that can appear in
these complex/simplex pairs in both Spanish and Italian, and shows that there is
a systematic semantic and syntactic difference between the complex type and the
simplex type, which suggests a unified cross-linguistic analysis, despite the fact
that Italian seems to differ in certain respects from Spanish. Abstracting away
from the differences (which are attributed to, among other things, the different
nature of the grammatical preposition *a* in the two languages), the generalization
is the following: while the complex PP denotes a space that is unbounded, the
simplex PP denotes a space that is bounded (or 'punctual'). The data and analysis
support the view that place PPs, like VPs (and NPs), have their own functional
structure, which contains an Aspectual Phrase (the head of which encodes the
boundedness feature, instantiated by *a* when the feature has no value). Beyond
the syntactic analogy between locative prepositions and nouns and verbs, we also
find a semantic analogy, whereby (non-linear, two- and three-dimensional) space
is linguistically conceptualized as either bounded or unbounded, much in the way
entities (count vs. mass) and events (delimited vs. undelimited) are.

---

*   I am indebted to so many wonderful people for taking the time to discuss Italian, Spanish,
Portuguese, French, and Catalan data with me, including Paola Benincà, José Camacho, Ivano
Caponigro, Anna Cardinaletti, Guglielmo Cinque, Federico Damonte, Raffaella Folli, Federico
Ghegin, Mary Kato, Roberta Maschi, Jaume Mateu Fontanals, Jairo Nunes, Rafael Nuñez-Cedeño,
Francisco Ordóñez, Andrea Padovan, Nicoletta Penello, Acrisio Pires, Jean-Yves Pollock, Cecilia
Poletto, Liliana Sanchez, Cristina Schmitt, Laura Sgarioto, Marina Tortora, and Raffaella Zanut-
tini. I should note that some of the Italian data do not reflect all speakers' judgments. I report the
judgments nevertheless, in the spirit of working towards a description of a possible grammar, and
I hope that future work will lead to a better understanding of variation in judgments. Future work
will also include a discussion of the relevant Portuguese, French, and Catalan facts shared with
me by some of the colleagues listed above.

1. Introduction

Based on a subtle interpretive difference between semantically related pairs of locative prepositional phrases in Romance, I argue that space, much like entities and
events, are linguistically conceptualizable as either bounded or unbounded, and
that this difference has a syntactic reflex.

As an introduction to the problem, let's consider the fact that Spanish and Italian (and other Romance languages) exhibit minimal pairs of PLACE PPs (to be distinguished from PATH, or directional, PPs), where one member of the pair can be
characterized as "complex," and the other as "simplex." The complex PP, which can
be seen in (1a) for Spanish and in (2a) for Italian, involves a lexical preposition in
combination with the grammatical preposition *a*. The simplex counterparts ((1b)
and (2b)) occur without *a*:

(1)   a.   *Juan se había escondido [bosque adentro].*   SPANISH
           Juan se had   hidden   [forest   a.inside]
     b.   *Juan se había escondido[dentro del bosque].*

(2)   a.   *Gianni era nascosto [dietro   a ll'albero].*   ITALIAN
           G.   was hidden   [behind   a the.tree]
     b.   *Gianni era nascosto[dietro l'albero].*

In this paper, I examine a number of different (locative) lexical Ps that can appear
in these complex/simplex pairs in both Spanish and Italian, and show that there is a
systematic semantic and syntactic difference between the complex type (1a/2a) and
the simplex type (1b/2b), which suggests a unified cross-linguistic analysis, despite
the fact that Italian seems to differ in certain respects from Spanish. Abstracting away
from the differences (also to be discussed, and to be attributed to, the different nature
of the grammatical preposition *a* in the two languages), the generalization is the following: while the complex PP (1a/2a) denotes a space that is unbounded, the simplex
PP (1b/2b) denotes a space that is bounded (or "punctual"). The data and analysis I
discuss support the view that PLACE PPs, like VPs (and NPs), have their own functional structure, which contains an Aspectual Phrase (the head of which encodes
the boundedness feature, instantiated by *a*). Beyond the syntactic analogy between

I would also like to thank Paola Benincà and Marcel den Dikken for reading and (very help-
fully) commenting on previous versions of this work, as well as the two anonymous reviewers,
and Berit Gehrke, Andrew McIntyre, Peter Svenonius, and the other participants at the Utrecht
Conference on the Syntax and Semantics of Spatial P, for exciting discussion. This article, which
follows up on Tortora (2005), is a development of Tortora (2006) (which was published as a
working paper). This work was supported by two grants from the City University of New York
PSC-CUNY Research Award Program (Grants #67317-0036 and #68496-0037).

locative prepositions and nouns and verbs, we also find a semantic analogy, whereby (non-linear, two- and three-dimensional) space is linguistically conceptualized as either bounded or unbounded, much in the way entities (count vs. mass) and events (delimited vs. undelimited) are.

The paper is organized as follows: in section 1, I give a brief overview of the Jackendovian conceptual categories PATH and PLACE (as subcategories of the supercategory SPACE), the notion of (un)boundedness of PATH, and the idea that (un)boundedness is also relevant to the category PLACE. In section 2 I give an overview of PP data from Italian, examined in Tortora (2005), which confirm that PLACE (which represents regions of any dimensionality (including 2D and 3D)), much like PATH (1D), is linguistically conceptualizable as either bounded or unbounded, and that this aspect of PLACE is encoded syntactically. In this part, I sketch a possible syntactic analysis for the data under investigation. Then, in section 3, I consider similar PP data from Spanish, where we find that the "ground" in the presence of *a* gets a "mass" interpretation (which I claim is connected to the unbounded interpretation of the space); I also discuss semantic and syntactic similarities and differences with Italian, and in section 4 I investigate Italian PPs with mass/plural arguments. In section 5 I conclude.

2.   Bounded PATH, bounded PLACE

Here I review the idea that PATH is linguistically conceptualizable as bounded or unbounded (Jackendoff 1983). Given this possibility for PATH, I introduce the question of whether boundedness is also relevant to the category PLACE (despite the fact that it differs from PATH in that the latter represents linear space, while the former represents two- or three-dimensional space). Preliminary linguistic data from Italian suggests that PLACE is in fact conceptualizable as such.

To put the discussion in context, consider Jackendoff's proposal that the conceptual categories PATH and PLACE underlie locative PPs (where (3a) contains both PATH and PLACE categories, while (3b) contains the PLACE category (examples from Jackendoff)):

(3)   a.   *The mouse ran into the room.*
          $[_{Path}$ TO $([_{Place}$ IN $([_{Thing}$ ROOM$])\,]\,)\,]$
      b.   *The mouse is under the table.*
          $[_{Place}$ UNDER $([_{Thing}$ TABLE$])\,]$

The idea that PATH and PLACE are two different categories has most recently been pursued (and executed in elaborate syntactic structures) by Koopman (1997) and den Dikken (2003), who argue that the syntax of locative PPs in Dutch can only be understood if such PPs involve PATH and/or PLACE as projecting syntactic categories (see section 2).

Now, for the present purposes, we must consider Jackendoff's (1983) observation that the representation of PATH does not necessarily involve motion, or "traversal" of the path. Contrast, for example, (4a) with (4b) (from Jackendoff 1983: 168).

(4)   a.   *John ran into the house.*
      b.   *The highway extends from Denver to Indianapolis.*

While both (4a) and (4b) involve a path, only the former denotes an eventuality that involves any temporal succession (i.e., (4b) is a state, and not an event, in Bach's 1986 terms). Crucially, however, it is important to note that paths which participate in states (i.e., non-motion eventualities) are still conceptualized as either bounded or unbounded. Compare the stative sentence in (4b), which contains a bounded path, with the stative example in (5b), which involves an unbounded path (much like the event example in (5a); examples from Jackendoff):

(5)   a.   *The train rambled along the river (for an hour).*
      b.   *The sidewalk goes around the tree.*

Sentences such as those in (4b) and (5b) thus illustrate that the linguistic concept of *path*, which is a kind of space, does not have to be associated with any temporal succession. These examples further illustrate, though, that even such non-temporally organized paths are treated as either bounded or unbounded (regardless of the fact that they denote states). Note for example that (5b) can be followed by "...for a piece, and then continues in a straight line" (see footnote 7 in Tortora 2005). Thus, we have evidence that PATH, a kind of space, is conceptualized as bounded or unbounded (independent of whether the eventuality that it is a part of is stative or not).

A question which arises, then, is whether the category PLACE (which is the other type of linguistic space) is likewise conceptualizable as bounded or unbounded. If so, this would mean that any PLACE specified in a stative eventuality (such as (3b), for example) is either bounded or unbounded, much like PATH (which is bounded in (4b) and unbounded in (5b)). If this idea is on the right track, what we would find is that boundedness is relevant not only to *entities* (mass vs. count) and *events* (undelimited/delimited), but to a third category, *space* (in the spirit of Jackendoff 1991), which encompasses both PATH and PLACE. Before I discuss PP data from Italian (and Spanish) which indicate this idea is right, I would like to briefly introduce some Italian data from Cinque (1971) (and subsequently found in Vanelli 1995) which already point in this direction.

As Cinque (1971) notes, Italian has two morphemes for 'here' (and two for 'there'): *qui* and *qua* 'here' (and *lì* and *là* 'there'). For the most part, *qui* and *qua* can be used in the same environment (the same holds for *lì* and *là*). So, if one wishes to express something like 'Put the book here,' either morpheme (*qui* or *qua*) would be appropriate:

(6) a. *Metti il libro qui.*
      b. *Metti il libro qua.*

Despite the grammaticality of both (6a) and (6b), however, Cinque notes that *qui* (like *lì*) denotes a space which is "punctual," while *qua* (like *là*) denotes a general, "uncircumscribed" region. As such, there are certain circumstances where use of *qui* (and *lì*) will yield ungrammaticality, as in (7b) (data from Cinque 1971):

(7) a. *Girava   **qua** e **là** senza meta.*
         they roamed **qua** and **là** without any purpose
      b. **Girava **qui** e **lì** senza meta.*

The sentence in (7b) is unacceptable because roaming around requires open-ended (uncircumscribed) space, something which the morphemes *qui* and *lì* do not denote. And as mentioned above, while there are circumstances under which either (set of) morpheme(s) can be used, the choice of one (*qua / là*) over the other (*qui / lì*) yields entirely different spatial (aspectual) interpretations. Consider in this regard another example from Cinque (1971):

(8) a. *I libri   erano sparsi   **qua** e **là**.*
         the books were dispersed **qua** and **là**
      b. *I libri   erano sparsi   **qui** e **lì**.*
         the books were dispersed **qui** and **lì**

Specifically, the sentence in (8a) denotes that books were strewn all over the place, while the sentence in (8b) denotes that there were books in two defined, distinct points (e.g., two piles of books).

The data from Cinque (1971) thus show us that language does encode two kinds of two- and three-dimensional (i.e., non-linear) space: one which we can characterize as punctual (or bounded), and another which we can encode as non-punctual (or unbounded).

In the following section, I will show that language does not restrict this distinction to single lexical items (so, the distinction is not merely encoded in the lexicon). Rather, this distinction shows up in PP syntax, suggesting that aspect (i.e., (un)boundedness) is found among the extended projections of lexical prepositions as well.

3. Prepositions in Italian

As observed by Rizzi (1988), there are certain (what I will term here "lexical") prepositions in Italian (e.g., *dietro* 'behind' or *dentro* 'inside') that may occur with or without the grammatical preposition *a*. This can be seen in (9a) vs. (9b), respectively (examples from Rizzi 1988: 522):

(9) a. *Gianni era nascosto **dietro** **all'** albero.*
         G.   was hidden   **behind** a.the   tree
     b. *Gianni era nascosto **dietro** **l'** albero.*
         G.   was hidden   **behind** the   tree

I have deliberately chosen stative examples, to make it clear that the relevant type of space under discussion is PLACE (and not PATH).

I have not provided glosses for this set of examples, because their subtle difference in meaning requires some discussion, which I engage in to some extent here (for issues not touched upon here, including a discussion of the question of which lexical prepositions may occur optionally with the grammatical preposition *a*, see Tortora 2005). P. Benincà notes (p.c.) that (9a) can refer to an event that takes place in a "wider" space, while (9b) can only refer to an event taking place in a "punctual" space. In what follows, I present and discuss various pairs of examples with different lexical prepositions which allow us to isolate this semantic difference more precisely.

3.1   The lexical preposition *dietro*

The examples in (10) isolate the semantic difference between (9a) and (9b) more precisely (note that although these are not stative eventualities, *giocare* 'play' is an activity verb, and the PP adjunct 'behind the tree' is interpreted as a location (PLACE), not a path):

(10) a. *Vai   a giocare **dietro** **a** quell' albero.*
          go.2SG   a play   **behind** **a** that   tree
          'Go play behind that tree.'
      b. **Vai   a giocare **dietro** quell' albero.*
          go.2SG   a play   **behind** that   tree

The ungrammaticality of (10b) can be readily understood in light of the semantic difference noted for (9a) and (9b). That is, predicates such as 'play' and 'run' denote activities that require a wide, open-ended, unbounded space, which is something that the structure in (10a), with the grammatical preposition *a*, denotes. The *a*-less prepositional phrase in (10b), on the other hand, denotes a bounded (or punctual) space, and as such is incompatible with such predicates. Of course, the predicate in (9) ('be hidden') denotes a state that is compatible either with a wide or a punctual space, which is why both prepositional phrases (with and without *a*) are possible.

Understanding the semantic difference between the two possibilities allows us to grasp another set of examples provided by Rizzi (1988: 522) (the interpretation of which he does not discuss):[1]

(11) a. *Vai   **dietro** al   postino, che è appena passato.*
            go.2SG **behind** a.the postman, that is just   passed
            'Go after the postman, he just passed by.'
    b. **Vai   **dietro** il postino, che è appena passato.*
            go.2SG **behind** the postman, that is just   passed

As can be seen by the translation, the salient interpretation of (11a) is that the hearer should pursue the postman; this is highlighted by the phrase 'he just passed by' (which explicitly suggests that the postman is moving along). It is precisely the presence of *a*, which denotes an unbounded space (i.e., a space that is allowed to flexibly expand and change shape, size, or dimension), that suggests the postman's onward movement. The example in (11b), on the other hand, cannot be interpreted as 'follow the postman'; that is, the absence of *a* forces an interpretation in which the space behind the postman is bounded (and hence not allowed to expand or change shape or size). This is why adjunction of the phrase 'he just passed by' is nonsensical, yielding ungrammaticality.

In this regard, it is worth considering the grammaticality of the *a*-less PP in (11b) without adjunction of the phrase 'he just passed by':

(12) *Vai   **dietro** il postino.*
      go.2SG **behind** the postman
      'Go behind the postman'

The sentence in (12) is interpretable (and grammatical) in, say, a picture-taking event, where the hearer is being asked to place himself directly behind the postman in the photo line-up. Again, here we see that the *a*-less PP is compatible with an event (or state) that takes place in a bounded (circumscribed) space.

To conclude this section on *dietro*: we have seen that the presence of *a* in the PP headed by *dietro* yields an unbounded interpretation, much like we saw with the morphemes *qua* and *là*. This is confirmed by the following contrast, where we

---

1. The reader may notice that this and some subsequent examples involve motion verbs, so that a path might also be involved in the interpretation of the locative PP; nevertheless, it is the interpretation of the embedded PLACE constituent that is at issue; if we separate PATH from PLACE in the structure (as Jackendoff 1983 and den Dikken 2003 do), then the nature of the PLACE (bounded or unbounded) holds, independently of the nature of the PATH. See also section 3.3 and note 5 below.

find that *qua* (the proform denoting unbounded space) is not compatible with the *a*-less PP (which denotes a punctual space); see (13b):

(13) a. *Gianni era nascosto **qua, dietro** all'albero.*
G. was hidden **qua, behind** a the.tree
b. ??*Gianni era nascosto **qua, dietro** l'albero.*
G. was hidden **qua, behind** the.tree
c. *Gianni era nascosto **qui, dietro** l'albero.*
d. *Gianni era nascosto **qui, dietro** all'albero.*

The compatibility between *qui* and both the simplex and the the complex PP in (13c) and (13d) is expected (for (13d), this is because the complex PP can also denote a punctual space).[2]

Thus, unboundedness of space not only has a lexical realization, but a syntactic reflex as well. As we will see in the following subsection, this phenomenon is not restricted to the lexical preposition *dietro*.

3.2 The lexical preposition *dentro*

The semantic difference between (14a) and (14b) is subtle but discernable:

(14) a. *Vai **dentro alla** stanza.*
go.2SG **inside at.the** room
'Go inside the room.'
b. *Vai **dentro la** stanza.*
go.2SG **inside the** room
'Go inside the room.'

The use of *a* with *dentro* 'inside' is preferred if one wishes to refer to the entire internal space of the container (considering all points of the contained space); (14b) is preferred in describing an event in which there is a simple passage from the outside to the inside of the room, without any reference to the internal space of the room (this intuition on the part of the speaker is replicated with similar Spanish data; see section 4 below, discussion of example (35b)).

---

2. The fact that *qua* and *là* (the proforms that denote unbounded space) end in *-a* makes it tempting to imagine that these forms are bi-morphemic, and that the *-a* is none other than the morpheme *a* we find in the complex PPs (something also suggested by an anonymous reviewer). However, there are two facts that deter me from this conclusion: first, some speakers who have both the forms *qui* and *qua* (and *lì* and *là*) do not exhibit any distinction between the simplex and complex PPs (see note 4 below). Second, while the complex PP can denote both a bounded and unbounded space, this is not the case for *qua* (and *là*); these proforms only denote and unbounded space.

Let us consider some more examples involving *dentro* which highlight which kind of circumstance calls for the presence of *a*, and which kind of circumstance calls for its absence:

(15) a. *Mettilo*   **dentro** *la*   *scatola.*
        put.2SG.it   **inside** the box
        'Put it inside the box.'

     b. *Guarda*   *bene* **dentro** *alla*   *scatola.*
        look.2SG   well   **inside** a.the box
        'Take a good look inside the box.' ('. . .maybe you'll find it in there.')

     c. **Dentro** *alla*   *mia stanza ci*   *sono delle*   *piante.*
        inside a.the my   room   there are   of.the plants
        'Inside my room there are plants around.'

Consider (15b) and its translation. Here we have a situation in which the hearer is being asked to consider the box's entire inner area (which may be obstructed by other objects in it), as the object being looked for could be in any part of that space. In this case, the lexical preposition requires presence of *a* (which allows us to flexibly consider all the space inside the box). This is similar to the case in (15c), where the room is being described as having plants all around in it; thus, the entire inner area of the room is being considered (hence the use of *a*).[3] This contrasts with the example in (15a), which does not contain *a*; here instead we have a situation in which the hearer, being asked to place an object inside a box, will naturally have to choose a specific, 'punctual' spot inside the box's inner area.

Before moving on, I would like to consider one final set of examples with *dentro* not considered in Tortora (2005) (and which I owe to C. Poletto, p.c.). Note that the verb *correre* 'run' can occur with a PP, yielding either a goal of motion interpretation, or a location of motion interpretation. Here I would like to consider both, beginning with the former. In this regard, consider the examples in (16):

GOAL OF MOTION:

(16) a. *Corri*   **dentro** *al*   *parco.*
        run.2SG   **inside**   at.the park
        'Get into the park'   [NO SPECIFIC POINT IS CONCEPTUALIZED]

     b. *Corri*   **dentro** *il*   *parco.*
        run.2SG   **inside**   at.the park
        'Get into the park'   [TO A SPECIFIC POINT, EITHER TO THE MIDDLE OF IT OR JUST INSIDE, CLOSE TO THE ENTRANCE]

What is noteworthy here is the following: while both (16a) and (16b) denote 'Run into the park', the former (with *a*) is interpreted with no specific point in mind.

---

3. See section 5.1 for further discussion of this type of example.

In contrast, (16b) (without *a*) is interpreted with a specific point in mind (e.g., either the running has to culminate in the middle of the park, or perhaps at a point close to the entrance). Once again, the absence of *a* forces the conceptualization of a point in space, while the presence of *a* allows for an interpretation of the space as uncircumscribed.[4] Note that this distinction is replicated even when this sentence has a location of motion interpretation. In this regard, consider (17):

LOCATED MOTION:

(17) a. *Corri **dentro** al parco.*
'Engage in the activity of running inside the park'
[WHEREVER YOU WANT]

  b. *Corri **dentro** il parco.*
'Engage in the activity of running inside the park'
[BUT IN A SPECIFIC PLACE, LIKE A TRACK, OR ALONG THE PARK'S PERIMETER]

Thus, while *corri dentro il/al parco* can also mean 'engage in the activity of running around inside the park', (17a) (with *a*) is again interpreted with no specific point in mind (the listener can run around wherever she likes). In contrast, (17b) (without *a*) is interpreted with a specific point in mind (e.g., a track, or along the park's perimeter). Here we again see the absence of *a* forcing the conceptualization of punctual space, where the presence of *a* allows for an interpretation of the space as uncircumscribed.

In section 4, after a discussion of data from Spanish, I discuss Italian examples with plural/mass arguments, which further illustrate the semantic effect of the presence (or absence) of the grammatical preposition *a*. For the moment, however, I would like to turn to a syntactic analysis of these PPs.

3.3   A syntactic analysis

The data examined until now suggest that the aspectual concept of *boundedness* be extended to the spatial domain. In this section, I provide an analysis (developed in Tortora 2005) which instantiates this idea syntactically, and which allows us to account for the data in sections 3.1–3.2.

In particular, I adopt the idea, developed by Koopman (1997) and den Dikken (2003) (following work by van Riemsdijk 1990) that locative prepositions, like

---

4.   I thank Ivano Caponigro and Raffaella Folli for noting (p.c.) that the judgment for this particular set of examples is not shared by all speakers. While a discussion of (and an account for) the varying judgments for these examples is beyond the scope of this work, it is important to ultimately pursue an understanding of the different grammars that speakers may form with respect to PPs with and without *a* (in this regard, I should note that some speakers in fact find no difference in interpretation between (9a) and (9b), even though they exhibit the difference between *qui* and *qua*).

verbs, nouns, and adjectives, are dominated by a series of functional projections. As argued by these authors, whose goal is to explain the complex semantic and syntactic behaviors of prepositions, postpositions, and circumpositions in Dutch, these extended projections of the preposition parallel (at least loosely) the functional structure of DP and CP.[5]

Following these authors, I propose for Italian that it is the lexical preposition that projects the (PLACE) PP, while the grammatical preposition, when present, heads an AspP which is among the extended projections of the PP. This is sketched in (18), which is the underlying structure for the place PP *dietro all'albero* in (9a):[6]

(18)

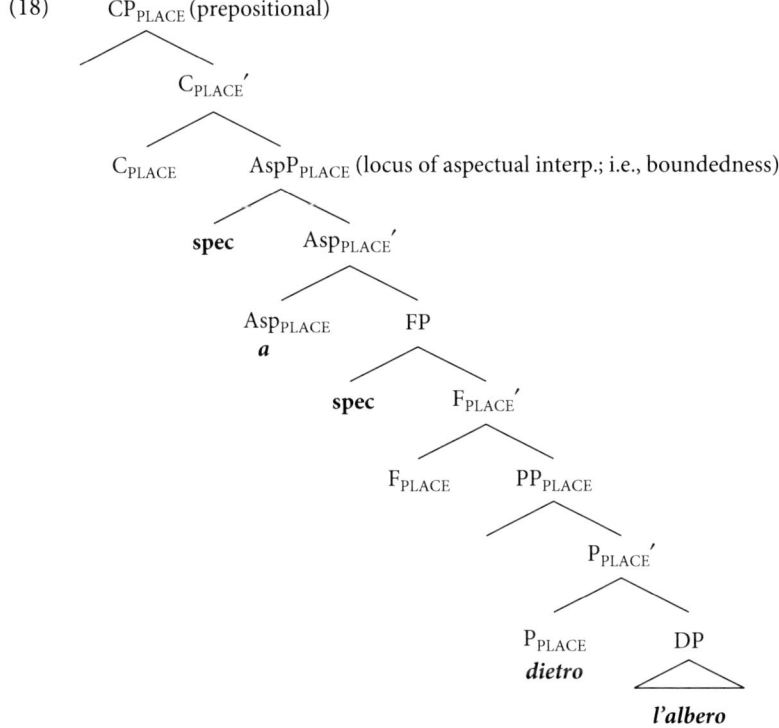

5.   In what follows, I simplify their proposals a great deal for the sake of argument. The structures den Dikken (2003) proposes for directional PPs, for example, are highly articulated and involve two types of preposition, P_{LOC} and P_{DIR}, each projecting its own functional architecture (ending in CP_{PLACE} and CP_{PATH}, respectively; in this regard, his proposal is an extension of Jackendoff's 1983 idea that PATH embeds PLACE in directional PPs).

6.   Note that this structure would be embedded under a PATH PP if we were dealing with a PP that denoted a path (as in (16a) or (3a)). The PATH PP would contain its own series of functional projections, which of course could also include an AspP.

I would like to suggest that the Aspectual Phrase is the locus of the aspectual feature [bounded]. To account for the data discussed in sections 3.1–3.2, I propose
that the presence of *a* reflects the presence of the underspecified feature [bound-
ed], which, when applied to a lexical preposition that denotes place (such as *dietro*
'behind'), yields the interpretation of the location (in e.g., (9a)) either as spatially
unbounded or bounded. The absence of *a*, however, reflects the presence of the
(positively valued) [+bounded] feature; this, in turn, accounts for the interpretation of the location (in e.g., (9b)) as necessarily spatially bounded.

It is worth noting that this previously unexplored semantic difference between
pairs like (9a) and (9b) reveals that the grammatical preposition *a* is arguably
merged to the left of the lexical preposition, despite surface indications to the
contrary (the proposal offered here is reminiscent of Kayne's (1999, 2001) recent
interpretation of *a* (and *di*) as an infinitival complementizer; see Tortora 2005).
A question which arises of course is how the surface order exhibited in (9a) is
derived.

Given that the configuration proposed for the grammatical preposition in (18)
is similar to the proposal offered by Kayne (1999, 2001) for grammatical prepositional complementizers, it would not be unreasonable to pursue a derivation for
the surface word order found with the lexical PP (*dietro all'albero*) that is similar
to the remnant movement derivation Kayne proposes for his prepositional complementizer cases. In particular, I propose that first, the DP *l'albero* moves to the
specifier of the FP in (18) (perhaps for reasons of Case), leaving t_k in (19). Then,
subsequent movement of the remnant PP (headed by *dietro*) to the specifier of
AspP obtains, leaving t_i. Thus, the surface order *dietro all'albero* is derived:

(19)   CP$_{PLACE}$ (prepositional)

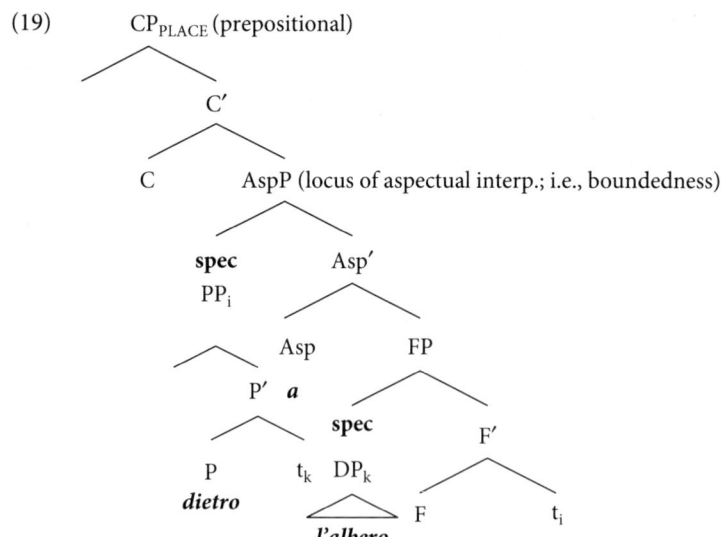

Perhaps PP movement obtains for interpretive reasons; i.e., the locative PP receives the unbounded interpretation by virtue of landing in the specifier of the
aspectual head.

Note that the proposal offered here is reminiscent of Kayne's (1999) recent
interpretation of the so-called infinitival complementizers *a* and *di* (which are not
taken to be complementizers *per se*, but rather to instante heads inside the functional structure projected by the verb). In what immediately follows, then, I say
a few words in support of the idea that grammatical prepositions do not project
their own PPs, but rather reside as heads of functional projections.

3.3.1 The "complementizers" *a* and *di*

It is well known that in Italian (as well as other Romance languages), grammatical
prepositions appear in places other than prepositional phrases. In particular, depending on the matrix verb, they may or may not introduce embedded infinitivals.
Some infinitival-embedding verbs, i.e., modal verbs, do not occur with a grammatical preposition at all. These can be seen in (20):

(20) *dovere, volere*
      must, want
      (*Gianni deve mangiare.* 'Gianni must eat.')

However, some verbs that take infinitival complements obligatorily appear with
the grammatical preposition *di*; these can be seen in (21):

(21) *sperare, tentare, dimenticare, cercare...*
      hope,   try,   forget,   seek
      (*Gianni spera di cantare.* 'Gianni hopes to sing.')

Still other verbs which take infinitival complements obligatorily appear with the
grammatical preposition *a*; these can be seen in (22):

(22) *venire, andare, continuare, cominciare, provare...*
      come,   go,   continue,   begin,   try
      (*Gianni prova a cantare.* 'Gianni is trying to sing.')

If we look at the three groups of verbs in (20), (21), and (22), we see a parallel
with the three groups of lexical prepositions discussed in Tortora (2005). That is,
Italian employs Ø, *di*, or *a* with embedded infinitivals, just as it does with lexical
prepositions.[7] Given this parallel, we can hypothesize that *a* and *di* are structurally
similar in both domains.

---

7. This is something also noted by Starke (1993), who takes the grammatical prepositions that
occur with lexical prepositions to be Complementizers within the DP complement of the lexical
preposition.

Independent support for the idea that *a/di* are similar types of creature in both cases comes from an observation made by Manzini (1991). She notes that certain verbs that take infinitival complements, such as *convincere* 'convince' and *persuadere* 'persuade', select either *a* or *di*. She further reports that the choice of grammatical preposition (*a* or *di*) determines the temporal interpretation of the embedded infinitive; in particular, when these verbs take *a*, the embedded infinitive is interpreted as future. Compare (23) and (24):

(23) *Ho   convinto / convincerò   Gianni ad andarsene.*
      have.1SG convinced / convince.FUT.1SG Gianni a   go.SE.NE
      'I convinced / I will convince Gianni to leave.'
      (convince = induce a decision to do something)

(24) *Ho   convinto Gianni di essermene andato.*
      have.1SG convinced Gianni di be.ME.NE   gone
      'I convinced Gianni that I had left.'
      (convince = induce a belief in the existence of an event)

(25) **Ho   convinto / convincerò   Gianni di andarsene.*
      have.1SG convinced / convince.FUT.1SG Gianni di go.SE.NE

Both (23) and (24) contain the verb 'convince' with an embedded infinitival. Only the infinitival preceded by *a*, however, can be interpreted as a future (this is confirmed by the ungrammaticality of (25), with *di*, which can only mean that "I convinced (or will convince) Gianni that he left" (which is strange, since Gianni should know whether he left or not).

Given the hypothesis that tense (like aspect) is instantiated by a functional head, it is not unreasonable to conclude that *a* instantiates a temporal functional head. The facts in (23–25) thus suggest that *a* has a similar function in both the extended projections of the verb and the extended projections of the (lexical) preposition. It also suggests that Kayne's (1999) proposal that such "complementizers" are morpho-syntactic instantiations of functional heads in the extended projection of the verb is on the right track.[8]

Another piece of evidence that *a* has a similar function in both the extended projections of the verb and the lexical preposition derives from an observation made in Penello (2003) regarding the Northern Italian dialect spoken in Carmignano di Brenta. Specifically, Penello notes that in contrast with Italian,

---

8. R. Kayne observes (p.c.) that French lacks the possibility of *a* both with the equivalent of *convincere/ persuadere* and with the equivalent of *dietro*, further suggesting that *a* in Italian has the same status in both the lexical PP and in the verbal domain.

Carmignano does not have a "complementizer" (in Kayne's sense); this can be seen in (26a) and (26b):

(26) a. *Vao (*a) casa.*
          I-go   home
          'I'm going home.'   (Ital.: *Vado **a** casa*)

      b. *A   setimana che   vien   ndemo (*a) catar Mario.*
          the week   that comes we.go   meet Mario
          Next week we're going to see Mario.   (Ital: *andiamo **a** trovare Mario*)

Penello notes that this is consistent with the fact that *a* is strongly dispreferred with PPs; that is, in contrast with Italian, Carmignano does not have complex PPs with *a*:

(26) c. *sotto (??a) la tola*   (Ital: *sotto **alla** tavola*)
          under   the table

Penello's generalization can be understood in light of the proposal made here: *a* instantiates a particular kind of head inside the functional structure projected by both PPs and VPs (so if a variety does not instantiate the head in the VP domain, it will also be absent in the PP domain).

4.   PLACE PPs in Spanish

The proposal that *a* is merged to the left of the lexical preposition (and that it is the reflex of the unspecified feature [bounded] in Asp) may find support from Spanish, an idea that I pursue in this section.

Plann (1988) discusses sets of Spanish examples which to me seem to exhibit a pattern whereby a monomorphemic lexical preposition (e.g., *dentro*) corresponds to a bimorphemic lexical postposition which contains the grammatical preposition *a* (e.g., *adentro*):

(27) a. *trás, atrás (detrás)* 'back; behind'
      b. *bajo, abajo (debajo)* 'below'
      c. *(en), dentro, adentro* 'in(side)'
      d. *fuera, afuera* 'outside'
      e. *delante, adelante* 'ahead; in front'

For Spanish there is of course the question of how productive these pairs are. Both Plann (1988) and Pavón (1999) discuss many examples of the complex version (i.e., the P with *a*) which seem to have fixed, idiomatic, meanings; consider for example the following:

(28) a. *La piedra rodó montaña abajo.*
          the stone rolled mountain a.down
          'The stone rolled down the mountain'

    b.   *Los niños estaban bajo la cama.*
        the kids   were   under the bed

(29) a.   *El ejército marchó tierra adentro.*
        the army   marched land a.inside
        'The army marched inland'

    b.   *El bolígrafo estaba dentro la bolsa.*
        the pen   was   inside the bag

(30)   *Hay que seguir camino adelante.*
       have to   go on way   a.front
       'You have to keep going'

(31)   *Es difícil correr cuesta arriba.*
       it's hard to run uphill
       'It's hard to run uphill'

(32)   *El novio vivía rio abajo.*
       the boyfriend lived river a.down
       'Her boyfriend lived downstream.'

Note for (31), for example, there is no corresponding form *riba*. Nevertheless, I would like to show that it is possible to construct less idiomatic pairs, which I discuss shortly. I would like to suggest that the bimorphemic cases (i.e., the "complex" PP) could simply be taken to be cases where the grammatical preposition *a* precedes the lexical preposition (as in the d-structure for Italian *dentro a* 'inside', which is *a dentro*). Interestingly, in the case of Spanish, the lexical prepositions with *a* are syntactically <u>postpositions</u> (although see example (40a) below), with the complement necessarily a bare noun; consider in this regard the following example:

(33)   *Los cazadores cazaban monte adentro.*
       the hunters hunted wilderness a.inside
       'The hunters hunted inside the wilderness.'

Thus, if we consider the structure in (18), it seems that in Spanish, the (bare) NP moves to the left of *a* (in the specifier of AspP), in contrast with Italian (where it is the (remnant) PP that moves; perhaps it is the bare nature of the Spanish NP that requires it to move to Asp, instead of the PP). The PP remains in situ (in contrast with Italian), yielding the order grammaticalP+lexicalP; see derivation in (34).

    Of course, this analysis would only make sense if it turned out to be the case that Spanish PPs with and without *a* semantically differed in the same way that the Italian complex and simplex PPs differ. In what follows, I will discuss a number of pairs of Spanish examples which indicate that there are some striking similarities with the pairs of Italian examples discussed in section 3.[9]

---

9. As we will see in a moment, there are also some notable differences between Spanish and Italian. One similarity between the two however is that like Italian, Spanish has pairs of proforms

(34)   Structure for Spanish **monte adentro** (cf. (33)):

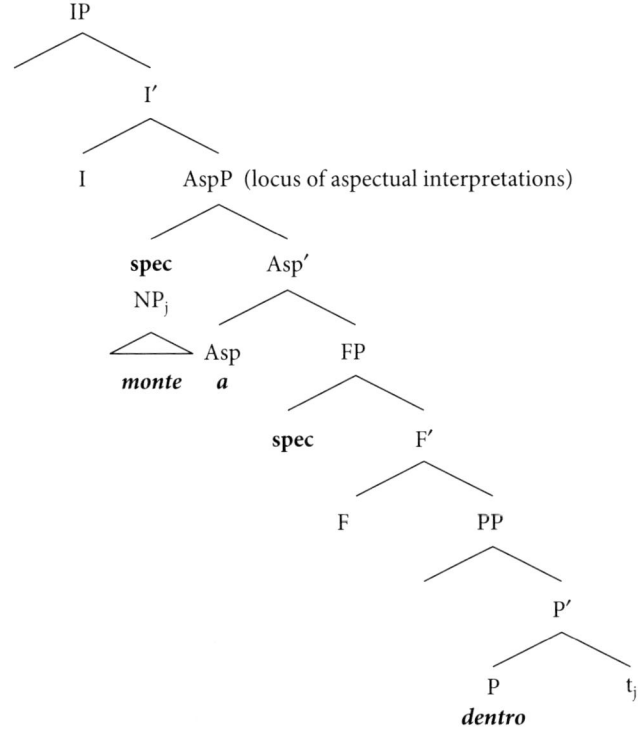

which denote 'here' (*aquí, acá*) and 'there' (*allí, allá*). According to Sacks (1954), the *-á* version of
each pair (*acá* and *allá*) is compatible with motion verbs (such as *venir* 'come'), while the *-í* version (*aquí* and *allí*) is compatible with stative verbs. However, I believe it is necessary to pursue
a study of the grammars of individual speakers, because a preliminary investigation reveals that
some speakers find the distinction between *aquí* and *acá* (and *allí* and *allá*) to be strictly analagous to that found in Italian for *qui* and *qua* (and *lì* and *là*). That is, *acá* and *allá* denote what
Sacks and Pavón would call a "vague" space (our "unbounded" space), while *aquí* and *allí* denote
what they would call a "specific" space (our "punctual" space). L. Sánchez (p.c.), for example,
reports this distinction for her grammar (and also reports an additional semantic dimension for
allá, namely, denoting a place that is "more distant than *allí*" – perhaps akin to non-standard
yonder (further away) vs. *there*). Thus, Sánchez reports the following minimal pair, which is
entirely analgous to the Italian pair in (8) in section 2 above:

    i.   *Los libros estaban dispersos por* **acá** *y*   *por* **allá**.
          the books were   scattered for **acá** and for **allá**
          [books all over the place]

    ii. *Los libros estaban dispersos por* **aquí** *y*   *por* **allí**.
          the books were   scattered for **aquí** and for **allí**
          [books in two specific points]

Let us first (re-)consider the complex PP in (33) (with *a*), repeated here as (35a), together with its simplex counterpart (without *a*) in (35b):

(35)　a.　*Los cazadores cazaban monte adentro.*
　　　　　the hunters　hunted　wilderness　a.inside
　　　　　'The hunters hunted inside the wilderness.'
　　　　　[THE BOUNDARIES/PERIMETER OF THE WILDERNESS ARE NOT
　　　　　CONCEPTUALIZED IN SPEAKER'S MIND; THE HUNTERS ARE TOWARD
　　　　　THE CENTER OF THE WILDERNESS]
　　　b.　*Los cazadores cazaban dentro del monte.*
　　　　　the hunters　hunted　inside　of.the wilderness
　　　　　'The hunters hunted inside the wilderness.'
　　　　　[THE BOUNDARIES/PERIMETER OF THE WILDERNESS ARE CONCEPTUALIZED
　　　　　IN SPEAKER'S MIND; SIMPLE OPPOSITION TO 'OUTSIDE']

As can be seen by the translations, both (35a) (with *adentro*) and (35b) (with *dentro*) denote 'The hunters hunted inside the wilderness'. However, there is a difference in the interpretation of the space. Specifically, in (35a) (with *a*), the speaker conceptualizes the hunters as being far inside the wilderness, with the boundaries or the perimeter of the wilderness not conceptualized. In contrast, with (35b) the speaker conceptualizes the boundaries or the perimeter of the wilderness, and the hunters could be taken to be close to the perimeter. Some speakers spontaneously report that (35b) can be used simply to indicate that the hunters are hunting inside the wilderness, as opposed to outside. This simple 'opposition' interpretation is reminiscent of that reported spontaneously by Italian speakers for example (14b) – without *a* (*Vai dentro la stanza* 'Go inside the room'). The difference in interpretation between (35a) and (35b) is replicated with the following two sets of examples in (36) and (37):

(36)　a.　*Se había escondido bosque adentro.*
　　　　　se had　hidden　forest　a.inside
　　　　　'He hid inside the forest.'
　　　　　[FROM THE SPEAKER'S PERSPECTIVE, HE IS HIDING AWAY
　　　　　TOWARDS THE CENTER]

A datum from Pavón (1999: 609) confirms this bounded vs. punctual difference between the pair in *-á* vs. the pair in *-í*; as can be seen, the former can be modified by *más* (indicating that the space is flexible), while the latter cannot (indicating the punctual nature of the space):

iii.　*Colócalo unos centímetros más **acá**.*　　　　　* aquí
　　　Put it　some centimeters more **here**
iv.　*Llévatelo unos pasos más **allá**.*　　　　　*allí
　　　Take it　some steps more **there**

b. *Se había escondido dentro del bosque.*
se had hidden inside of.the forest
'He hid inside the forest.'
[THE BOUNDARIES OF THE FOREST ARE SALIENT IN SPEAKER'S MIND]

(37) a. *Los barcos están mar adentro.*
the boats are sea a.inside
'The boats were inside the sea.'
[FAR AWAY FROM THE SHORE, WHERE YOU DON'T SEE ANY LAND; THE
BOUNDARIES OF THE SEA ARE NOT CONCEPTUALIZED IN SPEAKER'S MIND]

b. *Los barcos están dentro el mar.*
the boats are inside the sea
'The boats were inside the sea.'
[CAN SEE LAND; IN THE SEA, AS OPPOSED TO BEING OUTSIDE OF THE SEA]

There are two properties exhibited by all three sets of examples above (35–37) that are worth discussing, especially since these properties do not seem to be exhibited in the Italian sets of complex/simplex examples. First, most Spanish speakers report that examples with *a* require a space that is sufficiently large. So, the lexical postposition (in this case *adentro*) is most felicitously used with a space like the sea, or the wilderness, or a forest; some speakers report a resistance to examples where the object of the complex preposition represents a smaller space, like a park, for example, so that sentences such as that in (38a) are not accepted by all speakers:

(38) a. %*Los niños jugaban parque adentro.*
the kids played park a.inside
'The kids played inside the park.'
[FROM THE SPEAKER'S PERSPECTIVE, THEY ARE PLAYING
TOWARDS THE CENTER]

b. *Los niños jugaban dentro del parque.*
the kids played inside of.the park
[THE BOUNDARIES OF THE PARK ARE CONCEPTUALIZED;
THE LIMITS OF THE PARK ARE SALIENT]

J. Camacho notes (p.c.) that the issue is not necessarily the size of the space so much as the ability to interpret it as both large and homogeneous. Thus, while a city may be large, *ciudad* is not possible in this configuration for some speakers, given the fact that a city (unlike a sea or the wilderness) is conceptualized as having distinct sub-parts:

(38) c. %*Ellos caminaban ciudad adentro.*
they walked city a.inside

Other speakers, however, report (38c) as grammatical, but imagine the city as an undifferentiated "jungle-like" space. Note that speakers who reject (38a) (or (38c)) have no trouble accepting (38b) (thus, this requirement on the size of the space – and its homogeneity – only holds when *a* is present in the structure). This restriction does not exist in Italian (as can be seen, for example, by the grammaticality of (17a), *Corri dentro al parco* 'Run around inside the park').

Second, in contrast with the Italian examples with *a*, the Spanish examples with *a* in (35–37) involve an interpretation whereby the 'figure' is to be found someplace along a trajectory towards the inside of the 'ground' (from the speaker's point of view). This is not the case with the (b) examples (without *a*). In other words, in the Spanish complex PPs in (35–37), the presence of *a* forces the speaker to conceptualize a trajectory away from himself and toward the center of the 'ground'.

Concerning this later property (not exhibited in Italian), I conjecture that this is related to the fact that Spanish (in contrast with Italian) does not use the preposition *a* statively (see, e.g., Torrego 2002):

(39) a. *Estamos en / *a Paris.*   SPANISH
      b. Siamo a Parigi.   ITALIAN

It could be, then, that the restriction responsible for the ungrammaticality of *a* in (39a) is the same restriction that disallows a "purely" stative reading of the (a) examples in (36–37); that is, although (36) and (37) are clearly stative, given the "grammar of *a*" in Spanish, the speaker is forced to conceptualize a trajectory in these examples.

Concerning the former property (namely, that Spanish speakers require sufficiently large and homogeneous spaces – such as seas, or forests, or the wilderness – in order to be able to use the PP with *a*): I will leave this issue open for future research but I would like to suggest that this property of the Spanish PPs with *a* is related to the requirement that the NP be bare (which is of course something that in itself must be understood); that is, the bare nature of the NP yields a mass-like interpretation of the space (I return to the issue of mass NPs and Italian shortly).[10]

Despite these differences between Spanish and Italian (which of course need to be better understood), it is important to note that there are striking similarities between the two languages: both have a subset of lexical prepositions which may occur (optionally) with the grammatical preposition *a*, and the presence of *a* in both languages yields a semantic interpretation of the space denoted by the PP that

---

10. A (perhaps related) problem is that in Italian, the presence of *a* does not *require* that the space be interpreted as unbounded. So, (9a) for example can indicate either a bounded (punctual) or unbounded (non-punctual) space. In Spanish, on the other hand, the presence of *a* only yields one interpretation (unbounded). Another (again, perhaps related) problem is that in Italian, the boundedness of the space can be characterized in terms of 'punctuality' (so that in many of the examples discussed in section 3, the space in the examples without *a* is conceptualized as punctual (point-like)). It is not clear that this is the case for the Spanish examples.

is aspectually distinct from the semantic interpretation of the space denoted by the *a*-less PP. As such, we will tentatively maintain that the PPs with these particular lexical Ps in both languages have similar underlying structures (as in (18)), with different derivations ((19) vs. (34)) yielding different surface word orders.

I would like to make one final observation here regarding the Spanish data, before returning to Italian, and a discussion of some novel facts. Given that the presence of *a* seems to correlate with the post-positioning of the lexical preposition (and with the presence of a bare NP), one might wonder whether it is in fact the syntactic position of the postposition (or the presence of a bare NP, for that matter) which is responsible for the particular interpretation of the space (and not, as we have been asserting, the presence of *a* itself). In this regard, I would like to consider the following example, allowed by some speakers:

(40) a. %*Los niños corrían afuera   del   parque.*
        the kids ran   a.outside of.the park
        'The kids ran around outside the park.'
        [WHERE THE BOUNDARIES OF THE PARK ARE NOT CONCEPTUALIZED IN THE SPEAKER'S MIND; THE RUNNING IS OUTSIDE THE PARK SOMEPLACE, BUT DOES NOT HAVE TO BE NEAR]

    b. *Los niños corrían fuera   del   parque.*
        the kids ran   outside of.the park
        'The kids ran around outside the park.'
        [PERIMETER OF PARK CONCEPTUALIZED IN THE SPEAKER'S MIND; CLOSE TO THE SURROUNDINGS OF THE PARK; RELATED TO THE PARK IN SOME WAY]

Not all speakers allow *afuera* 'outside' (with *a*) to be used as a *pre*-position (with a full DP complement). However, those who do allow (40a) also spontaneously report a clear semantic distinction between (40a) and (40b) (without *a*). Specifically, (40a) is taken to denote that the running is outside the park someplace, but that the location is not necessarily related to the park (so that the boundaries of the park are not conceptualized).[11] In contrast, (40b) is taken to denote that the running is taking place in a location close to the surroundings of the park, so that the space is taken to be related to the park in some way, with the perimeter of the park conceptualized as part of the space.

What these data show us is that it is the presence of *a* (and not the position of the preposition, or the presence of a bare NP) that is responsible for the unbounded interpretation of the space. Of course, the fact that some speakers allow the form with *a* to be used *pre*-positionally (and with a full DP) suggests that the

---

11. This interpretation of *afuera* correlates with the fact that *afuera* (but not *fuera*) can be modified by *más* 'more'; see note 9, p.290, above.

form *afuera* for these speakers is itself ambiguous between a bimorphemic and monomorphemic form (so that *a+fuera* is analyzed either as two distinct syntactic entities, or as a lexicalized form). I raise this possibility, because for the speakers who allow (40a), the post-positional configuration (with the bare NP) is also possible:

(40) c. %*Corrían parque afuera.*
         ran   park   a.outside
        'They ran around in the outskirts of the park.'
        [FROM THE SPEAKER'S PERSPECTIVE, WHICH IS TOWARDS
        THE CENTER OF THE PARK]
        'They ran towards the outskirts of the park'
        [FROM THE SPEAKER'S PERSPECTIVE, WHICH IS TOWARDS
        THE CENTER OF THE PARK]

However, although (40c) is also possible for the speakers who allow (40a), the above example is interpreted as involving a trajectory (both with the activity reading and with the directed motion reading of 'run'; see translations and bracketed qualifications above). This is in contrast with (40a), where no such trajectory is necessarily conceptualized. Thus, when *afuera* is analyzed by the speaker as bimorphemic (and appears as a post-position), the morpheme *a* contributes the concept of trajectory; however, when *afuera* is analyzed by the speaker as monomorphemic (and appears as a pre-position), there is no separate morpheme *a*, so no trajectory interpretation is entailed.

5. Back to Italian (and some notes on English): mass, plural, and geometrically complex 'figures'

As we just saw, the presence of *a* in Spanish generally requires that the argument of the locative P be a bare NP (and that it appear to the left of the *a+lexicalP* complex). While this is not the case for Italian, I would like to discuss the fact that the nature of the argument (and whether it is interpretable as a mass or plural argument) is relevant to whether or not a simplex or complex PP is used. In the discussion, we will thus see another way in which lexical Ps are analagous to Vs. That is, it is well known that with events, the nature of the argument affects the aspectual interpretation of the event, so that mass or plural objects give rise to events that are interpreted as undelimited:

(41) a. John drank **the beer** in one hour.   Count Noun object
     b. John drank **beer** for hours.   Mass Noun object
     c. John ate **grapes** for hours.   Bare Plural object

In this regard, let us first consider the lexical prepositions *dentro* and *dietro* in Italian, and consider how the nature of the argument affects the aspectual interpretation of the PLACE PP.

5.1   *dentro; dietro* (INSIDE; BEHIND)

Consider the following two pairs of examples with *dentro* 'inside', in which the "figure" (in the sense of Talmy 1983) is a plural:

(42)   a.   ***Dentro** alla   mia stanza ci   sono <u>delle   piante.</u>*
             inside a.the my room   there are   <u>of.the plants</u>
             'Inside my room there are plants around.' or
             'There are plants all inside my room.'

       b.   ***Dentro** la   mia stanza, ci   sono delle   piante.*
             inside the my room   there are   of.the plants
             'Inside my room there are some plants (in one spot)'

(43)   a.   *Ci   sono <u>delle   penne</u> **dentro** al   cassetto.*
             there are   <u>of.the pens</u> **inside** a.the drawer
             'There are pens all inside the drawer.'

       b.   *Ci   sono <u>delle   penne</u> **dentro** il   cassetto.*
             there are   <u>of.the pens</u> **inside** the drawer
             'There is a bunch of pens inside the drawer.'

In both sets of examples, the figure ('some plants' in (42) and 'some pens' in (43)) can be interpreted either as being distributed throughout the space denoted by the PP ((42a) and (43a)), or it can be interpreted as being point-like, located in a specific spot within the space denoted by the PP.[12] What is noteworthy is that the distributed interpretation (which I have translated with a PP modified by *all*) obtains with the complex PP (i.e., in the presence of *a*), while the point-like interpretation obtains with the simplex PP. Thus, if the object is to be conceptualized as a mass, a PP with *a* is required, while if it is to be conceptualized as a discrete point (or as a count entity), a PP without *a* is required.

The same can phenomenon can be found for DPs that refer to entities which are conceptualizable as aggregates. As can be seen in (44) with the preposition *dietro* 'behind', the first example contains a PP with *a* (hence, one that denotes an unbounded space), and as such allows for a distributed interpretation of the object (again in this case, the figure 'the bees'); the second example (44b), without *a*, however, yields a point-like interpretation of 'the bees', so that they are conceptualized as conisting of a bounded entity.

---

12.   When understood from this perspective, the concept of unbounded space becomes reminiscent of Jackendoff's (1990: 104) "distributed" (vs. "ordinary") location.

(44) a. *Ci   sono delle api dietro all' albero.*
           there are   of.the bees **behind** a.the tree
           [BEES ARE SPREAD OUT IN A WIDE SPACE, PERHAPS FLYING AROUND]
     b. *Ci   sono delle api dietro l' albero.*
           there are   of.the bees **behind** the tree
           [BEES ARE IN ONE SPOT TOGETHER, PERHAPS SITTING ON THE TREE]

Likewise, inherently mass nouns such as 'mold' can get a mass or count interpretation, depending on whether the "ground" they are related to (i.e., the space denoted by the PP) is linguistically marked as unbounded or bounded. So, the sentence in (45a) (with *a*) can be used to describe a situation in which a box has mold (mass) covering all of its interior, while the sentence in (45b) (with a simplex PP) describes a situation in which the mold is in one spot (for example, in a microbiology laboratory setting in which someone is indicating that a discrete sample of mold (count) is sitting in a particular box).

(45) a. *Cè   della muffa dentro alla scatola.*
           there's of.the mold **inside** a.the box
           'There's mold all inside the box.'
     b. *Cè   della muffa dentro la scatola.*
           there's of.the mold **inside** the box
           'There's mold (right) inside the box.'

To summarize, it appears that plural and mass NPs get a bounded (count) interpretation with the simplex PPs. This is something we expect if the PP without *a* indeed denotes a punctual (bounded) place.

5.1.1 A note on English

Note (e.g., (45)) that the English translations of the unbounded PLACE PPs can be rendered with modification by *all* (45a), while the bounded (puntual) PLACE PP can be rendered in English with modification by *right* (45b). What is worth mentioning is that not all prepositions in English allow modification of *all* in this way. So while *inside*, *under(neath)*, *along*, *through(out)*, and *around* (as PLACE prepositions; see (46a–f)) all allow modification by *all* (thus yielding an unbounded interpretation), the prepositions *near*, *behind*, and *next to* do not allow modification by *all* (see (46f)):[13]

(46) a. all inside the box
     b. all under(neath) the table

---

13. It is worth noting that although *along* denotes a linear location, it is arguably not fundamentally a PATH preposition, but rather a PLACE preposition which happens to denote a space that is linear. Note, for example, that it does not not necessarily entail directionality (or a trajectory):

  (i)   Mary ran back and forth along the tracks.

    c.   all along the ledge   Talmy (1983)
    d.   all through(out) the aquarium   "
    e.   all around the house
    f.   There were flies *all near / *all behind / *all next to the house

This suggests that the lexical preposition has its own aspectual determination, so that the preposition itself plays a role in determining what kind of AspP it projects. That is, certain prepositions (e.g., those in (46f)), are not compatible with an unbounded AspP. The same can also be said for the bounded interpretation. As can be seen in (47a–e), *inside*, *under(neath)*, *near*, *behind*, and *next to* allow for modification of *right* (compatible with punctual, or bounded space), while *throug(out)* and *around* are incompatible with this point-denoting modifier:

(47)   a.   right inside the box
       b.   right under(neath) the table
       c.   right near the house.
       d.   right behind the house.
       e.   right next to the house.
       f.   There were flies *right through(out) / *right around the house.

If certain lexical prepositions can only denote a place that is bounded, while others can only denote an unbounded place, that means that the prepositions themselves are lexically specified with their own "aspect." It is difficult at this stage to draw an obvious analogy between the aspectual type associated with these PLACE Ps and the aspectual types found in the realm of verbs (achievement, state/activity), but as a first pass we might think of the Ps in (46a–e) (which can denote an unbounded space) as analogous to state or activity verbs, while we might think of the Ps which only allow for a punctual interpretaion (46f) as analogous to achievement or punctual verbs.

As a matter for future research, we might take the preposition's own lexical semantics to explain why, in Italian for example, certain locative prepositions do

---

This suggests that the defining characteristic of a PATH is not linearity, but rather directionality (i.e., that there is a trajectory). As such, *through* in contrast would denote a true PATH:

(ii)   *Mary ran back and forth through the tunnel.

While Jackendoff (1991) suggests that 1-dimensional spaces are necessarily paths, the observation here suggests that places can also be 1-dimensional. This should be unsurprising, given that it would be arbitrary (and inexplicable) for PLACE to involve regions of any dimensionality except for the first dimension.

not allow for the presence of *a*, while others obligatorily appear with *a* (see Tortora 2005 for a brief overview of these two groups). It might turn out to be the case that the fomer group is such that their lexical semantics are "punctual," while the latter group is lexically specified as unbounded.[14]

5.2   *sopra* (OVER/ABOVE/ON)

Before I conclude, I would like to make one final observation concerning structures which involve a so-called "geometrically complex" figure, in the sense of Talmy (1983). As Talmy notes, the "figure" (in contrast with the "ground") is commonly represented or conceptualized as point-like. This can be seen for example in (48), where *the bike* is taken to be a point, while the garage is geometrically complex:

(48)   The bike is *near / behind / inside* the garage.

However, Talmy observes that certain PP expressions can highlight the linear or planar geometry of the figure. This can be seen in (49a), where the figure (the board) is linear, and in (49b), where the figure (the tablecloth) is planar:

(49)   a.   The board lay *across* the railway bed.   figure is linear
       b.   The tablecloth lay *over* the table.   figure is planar

Why do I raise these types of cases here? Because in Italian, the choice of the simplex vs. complex PP bears on the question of whether or not a figure (or the ground, as we will see momentarily) is interpreted as geometrically complex or not. Specifically, we find that the presence vs. absence of *a* with *sopra* 'over' forces or suppresses (respectively) the complex geometry of the figure. Consider in this regard the examples in (50):

(50)   a.   *Ho messo   la   tovaglia   **sopra** al   tavolo.*
            I put   the   tablecloth **on**   a.the   table
            [THE TABLECLOTH IS SPREAD OUT OVER THE TABLE]
            English: The tablecloth lay over the table
                           The tablecloth is on the table.   (ambiguous in English)
       b.   *Ho messo   la   tovaglia   **sopra** il   tavolo.*
            I put   the   tablecloth **on**   the   table
            [THE TABLECLOTH IS FOLDED UP ON THE TABLE]
            English: The tablecloth is right on the table.   (unambiguously point-like)

As can be seen in (50a), the presence of *a* inside the PP yields an interpretation of the tablecloth (the figure) as planar (i.e., the tablecloth is spread out). Given that

---

14.   This might be similar to the fact that certain abstract nouns are (arbitrarily) lexically specified as being either mass or count, despite the fact that there is nothing concrete that would determined this classification (cf. mass *advice* (*advices*) vs. count *threat* (*threats*)).

the presence of *a* in all other cases yields an unbounded interpretation of the space denoted by the PP, it is reasonable to conclude that the interpretation of the figure as geometrically complex is a manifestation of the unboundedness of the space denoted by the PP. In (50b), on the other hand, we see that the absence of *a* inside the PP yields an interpretation of the tablecloth as point-like. Given that the absence of *a* in all other cases yields a punctual conceptualization of the space denoted by the PP, it is equally reasonable to conclude that that the interpretation of the figure as point-like is a corollary of the punctuality of the space denoted by the *a*-less PP. Thus, without *a* the planar nature of the figure is supressed, and we are forced to conceptualize the figure as point-like. This is analagous to the variable status of plural and mass NPs, which may be conceptualized as point-like, as we saw above.

What is interesting to note is that in English, the modifier *right* (which, as we saw in section 5.1.1, only modifies punctual space), like the absence of *a* in Italian, (expectedly) yields the unambiguous intepreation of the tablecloth as point-like (*the tablecloth is right on the table* can only mean that the tablecloth is all folded up; this is in contrast with *the tablecloth is on the table* (without *right*), which is ambiguous between the tablecloth being spread out on the table and being folded up).[15] Once again, then, it seems that *right* serves the same function as the absence of *a* does in Italian (namely, to denote a point-like space).

Thus, it seems that planar figures are treated like mass/plural NPs. This is reminiscent of an issue discussed in Tenny (1994) in the realm of the VP. In particular, Tenny notes that a sentence such as *Mary painted the wall* involves, for some speakers, a delimited reading, while for other speakers it involves a non-delimited reading. This ambiguity seems to be due to the fact that a wall is conceptualizable either as geometrically complex (i.e., planar, and therefore unbounded), or as point-like (i.e., bounded).

5.3   *sotto* (UNDER)

Note that the question of geometrical complexity (or not) arises with respect to the ground as well. In this regard, consider the following examples with the lexical preposition *sotto* 'under' in Italian:

(51)   a.   *Ho messo   il   tovagliolo **sotto** alla   tovaglia.*
             I put   the napkin   **under** a.the tablecloth
             [SPEAKER CONCEPTUALIZES THE TABLECLOTH AS SPREAD OUT
             ON THE TABLE]

---

15.   It might help to imagine the sentences in (i) and (ii) as answers to the question "I want to get the dining room ready for dinner; where's the tablecloth?"

(i)   The tablecloth is on the table. (ambiguous between spread out and folded up)
(ii)   The tablecloth is right on the table. (must be folded up)

b. *Ho messo il tovagliolo **sotto** la tovaglia.*
I put   the napkin   **under** the tablecloth
[SPEAKER CONCEPTUALIZES THE NAPKIN AS FOLDED UP UNDER A FOLDED
UP TABLECLOTH (IN A PILE)]

Note that the presence of *a* entails the geometrical complexity of the tablecloth, which this time is the ground in (51a). In contrast, the absence of *a* yields an interpretation of the tablecloth as point-like (so the eventuality in (51b) is interpreted with a folded-up tablecloth). So here again we see that in the context of an object which is potentially conceptualizable as geometrically complex (planar), the unboundedness feature lines up with planar conceptualization.

6. Conclusion

To summarize the discussion in this paper: The PP data from Italian suggest that PLACE, like PATH, can be conceptualized as bounded or unbounded, and that this has a reflex in the grammar. This extension of the 'boundedness' feature to PLACE allows for the more general claim that SPACE (the supercategory that subsumes PATH and PLACE; Jackendoff 1991) can be conceptualized as bounded or unbounded. This in turn reveals that boundedness is relevant not only to *events* and *entities*, but to *space* as well, suggesting that these three super-categories themselves are all potentially treatable, in the abstract, in a similar way (whatever the general linguistic and specific syntactic analyses of boundedness ultimately ends up being). This itself is consistent with the tradition, initiated by Bach (1986) (among others), and expanded upon by Jackendoff (1991), of unifying major linguistic categories under one abstract semantic system.

Furthermore, the particular details regarding the behavior of the Italian PPs (i.e., presence vs. absence of the grammatical preposition *a*) suggest that PPs are unified with NPs and VPs in terms of clausal architecture (i.e., functional syntax). That is, the data discussed in this paper supports the claim (proposed by e.g., van Riemsdijk 1990) that Ps are syntactically like Vs and Ns (projecting similar types of functional categories). This similarity across categories is further corroborated by the discussion in section 5, where we see that the nature of the argument (e.g., plural vs. singular) can affect the aspectual interpretation of the entire PP. And finally, this view opens a line of thought regarding the proper syntactic (and semantic) treatment of PPs that apparently contain a grammatical P in Spanish. Although there are a number of differences between Italian PPs with *a* and Spanish PPs with *a*, the similarities between the two languages warrant exploring a unified analysis.

References

Bach, E. 1986. The algebra of events. *Linguistics and Philosophy* 9: 5–16.

Cinque, G. 1971. Analisi Semantica della Deissi in Italiano. Tesi di Laurea, Università di Padova.

den Dikken, M. 2003. On the syntax of locative and directional adpositional phrases. Ms., CUNY Graduate Center.

Jackendoff, R. 1983. *Semantics and Cognition*. Cambridge MA: The MIT Press.

Jackendoff, R. 1990. *Semantic Structures*. Cambridge MA: The MIT Press.

Jackendoff, R. 1991. Parts and boundaries. *Cognition* 41: 9–45.

Kayne, R. 1999. Prepositional complementizers as attractors. *Probus* 11: 39–73.

Kayne, R. 2001. Prepositions as probes. Ms., NYU.

Koopman, H. 1997. Prepositions, postpositions, circumpositions and particles. Ms., UCLA.

Manzini, R. 1991. Il soggetto delle frasi argomentali all'infinito. In *Grande Grammatica Italiana di Consultazione*, Vol. 2, L. Renzi & G. Salvi (eds), pp. 485–497. Bologna: Il Mulino.

Pavón Lucero, M.V. 1999. Clases de partículas: preposición, conjunción y adverbio. In *Gramática Descriptiva de la Lengua Española: Sintaxis Básica de las Clases de Palabras* Vol. 1, I. Bosque & V. Demonte (eds), 565–655. Madrid: Espasa Calpe.

Penello, N. 2003. Capitoli di Morfologia e Sintassi del Dialetto di Carmignano di Brenta. Tesi di Dottorato, Università di Padova.

Plann, S. 1988. Prepositions, postpositions, and substantives. *Hispania* 71: 920–926.

van Riemsdijk, H. 1990. Functional prepositions. In *Unity in Diversity*, H. Pinkster & I. Genee (eds), 229–241. Dordrecht: Foris.

Rizzi, L.1988. Il sintagma preposizionale. In *Grande Grammatica Italiana di Consultazione* Vol. 1, L.Renzi (ed.), 508–531. Bologna: Il Mulino.

Sacks, N.P. 1954. Aquí, acá, allí, allá. *Hispania* 37(3): 263–266.

Starke, M. 1993. Notes on Prepositions and Clause Structure. Ms., University of Geneva.

Talmy, L. 1983. How language structures space. In *Spatial Orientation: Theory, Research, and Application*, H. Pick & L. Acredolo (eds), 225–282. New York NY: Plenum Press.

Tenny, C. 1994. *Aspectual Roles and the Syntax-Semantics Interface*. Dordrecht: Kluwer.

Torrego, E. 2002. Aspect in the prepositional system of Romance. In *Current Issues in Romance Languages*, T. Satterfield, C. Tortora & D. Cresti (eds), 337–357. Amsterdam: John Benjamins.

Tortora, C. 2005. The preposition's preposition in Italian: Evidence for boundedness of space. In *Theoretical and Experimental Approaches to Romance Linguistics*, R. Gess & E. Rubin (eds), 307–327. Amsterdam: John Benjamins.

Tortora, C. 2006. On the aspect of space: The case of PLACE in Italian and Spanish. In *Atti dell'undicesima giornata di dialettologia* [Quaderni di lavoro ASIS 5], N. Penello & D. Pescarini (eds), 50–69. Padova: CNR.

Vanelli, L. 1995. La deissi spaziale. In *Grande grammatica italiana di consultazione* Vol. 3, L. Renzi, G. Salvi & Anna Cardinaletti (eds), 269–283. Bologna: Il Mulino.

PART IV

Silent Ps

The place of PLACE in Persian

Marina Pantcheva*
CASTL, University of Tromsø

In this paper I briefly present the prepositional system in Persian, focussing on the noun-like behaviour of Class 2 prepositions. Considering silent PLACE hypotheses suggested for Greek and Hebrew locatives, I suggest that a null PLACE element in the prepositional phrase can account for several nominal properties of the Class 2 Ps. I argue that Class 2 Ps are distinct from true nouns, the only property they share with nouns being that they can modify nouns, including the silent PLACE element. Finally, I show how the entire structure can capture various phenomena characterizing this prepositional class.

1. Introduction

The Persian spatial prepositional system can be said to consist of two types of prepositions. The first type is "well-behaved" true prepositions. The categorial status of the second type, however, is highly controversial. Because of the nominal properties they exhibit, the literature on Persian prepositions has been long preoccupied by the question whether they should be assigned the status of true nouns (Ghomeshi 1996; Larson & Yamakido 2005; Karimi & Brame 1986) or they should be regarded as prepositional elements, though with a noun-like behaviour (Samiian 1994; Pantcheva 2006). In this paper, I defend their non-nominal syntactic status. I argue that their nominal properties can be explained by assuming the presence of a silent noun PLACE in the prepositional syntactic structure and I will base my assumption on already existing hypotheses about silent PLACE elements in the syntactic structure for locative adverbs in English (Katz & Postal 1964; Kayne 2004) and prepositional phrases in Greek (Terzi 2006) and Hebrew (Botwinik-Rotem, this volume).

The paper is organized as follows. In section 2, I give an overview of existing hypotheses in the linguistic literature which make use of the idea of a silent

* I thank the audience of the P conference held in Utrecht, 2–4 June 2006, for the useful comments and suggestions. Thanks also to Peter Svenonius for fruitful discussion and advices and to two anonymous reviewers for their remarks.

noun PLACE in the syntactic structure of certain adverbials and PPs, paying special attention to the null PLACE hypotheses for Greek and Hebrew locatives. In section 3, I present the data from Persian, setting the scene for the proposal about a non-phonologically realized noun PLACE present in Persian prepositional phrases. In section 4, I will lay out and develop the proposal and show which syntactic phenomena it can account for and which problems still remain to be explained. Section 5 concludes the paper.

2. Silent PLACE now and before

2.1 Katz & Postal (1964)

The notion of a silent PLACE element was introduced by Katz & Postal (1964). They claim that the structure of English adverbial phrases contains a head noun which can be either covert (in a *pro-form*) or overt (in a *non-pro-form*). In the former case the adverb will occur as a single-word variant like *where, when*, etc. Katz & Postal observe that for some single-word adverbs with a pro-form there exist corresponding identical adverbials with a non-pro-form where the head noun of the adverbial is overtly represented in the syntax. The non-pro-forms reveal the underlying structure consisting of a preposition and a noun phrase. In other words, the single-word adverbial expressions are reduced instances of complex adverbial phrases, the only difference being that the head noun in the former is silent, whereas in the structure of the latter it is overt. Thus they associate adverbials with silent nouns with adverbial expressions consisting of the same noun plus a preposition and a definite/indefinite element or a wh-word, depending on the meaning. The correspondence between some single-word adverbials and a prepositional phrase will be then like the one shown in (1) and (2) for adverbials containing the pro-forms PLACE and TIME.

(1) PLACE
    a. *where* – at what place
    b. *here* – at this place

(2) TIME
    a. *when* – at what time
    b. *now* – at this time

The decomposition presented in (1b) bears on some issues connected to the interpretation of demonstratives in Persian prepositional phrases, as will be discussed in Section 4.1. Therefore, it is relevant to present the syntactic structure underlying the adverbials *here* and *there*.

(3)

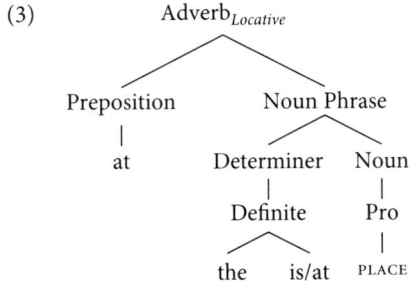

Figure 1. Katz & Postal's (1964) decomposition of *here* and *there*.

As can be seen from the structure in (3), the adverbials *here* and *there* are decomposed into *at this place* and *at that place*, respectively. The syntactic structure consists of a null preposition AT which takes a noun phrase as a complement. The noun phrase is headed by a silent pronominal element, PLACE in this case, which, in its turn, is preceded by a demonstrative. On Katz & Postal's analysis the demonstratives *this* and *that* are complex, consisting of a determiner plus a proximal or a distal element, respectively. More specifically, *this* = *the* + *is*, and *that* = *the* + *at*.

It is worth noting that the underlying structure proposed by Katz & Postal for *here* and *there* resembles their surface structure in some languages, for example, Korean and Persian. Korean locative *here*, *there* and *yonder* are in fact a combination of a demonstrative and the bound morpheme *-eki*, which historically is a noun meaning *place*. An example is provided in(4).[1]

(4) Ku sangca-lul ecey   pwunmyenghi
     the box-ACC *yesterday certainly*
     yeki/keki/ceki(-ey)   twu-ess-ta.
     this/that/yonder.place-LOC *put.on*-PAST-DC
     '(I) certainly put the box here/there/over there yesterday.'[2]

2.2 Kayne (2004)

Kayne further develops Katz & Postal's idea about a silent PLACE element as a component in the syntactic structure of the locative adverbs *here* and *there*. Based on the similar semantic and syntactic behaviour of *here/there* and the dialectal phrases *this here place/that there place*, he suggests that there is an unpronounced

---

1. Glosses in the paper are as follows: ACC - Accusative, CL - Clitic, DC - Declarative, EZ - Ezafe linker, GEN - Genitive, OM - Object Marker, PAST - Past Tense, PL - Plural, SG - Singular.

2. Data provided by Minjeong Son, p.c.

demonstrative THIS/THAT and an unpronounced PLACE element. In other words, he argues that the locative *here/there* are instances of the demonstrative *here/there* simply being embedded in a larger structure with unpronounced demonstrative and noun. Thus, the locative interpretation is due to the presence of the silent PLACE.

The underlying structure of *here/there* is as shown in (5) with the complete derivation of *(John) is from here* presented in (6).

(5)　a.　*here* - THIS here PLACE
　　　b.　*there* - THIS there PLACE

(6)

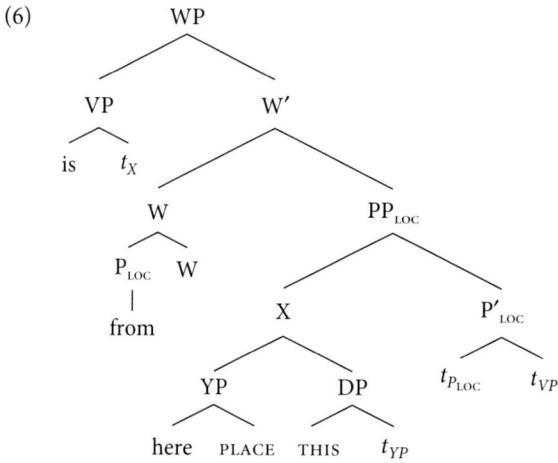

Figure 2. Derivation of *(John) is from here* (Kayne 2004).

The initial step in the derivation presented above is the merge of first the verb with XP and then with the adposition *from*. Then, *here*+PLACE raises past the silent demonstrative followed by raising of the entire adverbial phrase X to the Specifier of the prepositional phrase. Afterwards, the preposition *from* moves up and adjoins to the W(ord order) head of the WP. Eventually, the remnant verb phrase moves to the Specifier of WP.

The idea about a null PLACE has been adopted by Terzi (2006) whose hypothesis about a silent PLACE element in Greek prepositional phrases will be examined in the next section.

2.3　Terzi (2006)

Terzi draws on Kayne's idea and, investigating the properties of Greek locative PPs, finds empirical support for the existence of a silent PLACE element in their syntactic structure. Reasoning from the observation that Greek locative prepositions have a "nominal flavour", she accounts for this fact by suggesting that they are modifiers of a non-phonologically realized noun, PLACE. The silent PLACE is, in its turn, licensed by a functional head P_{LOC}. Assuming both a noun element and a functional preposition in the extended P projection, Terzi is able to explain the dual behaviour of Greek locatives. On the one hand, PLACE is responsible for their nominal properties; on the other hand, the presence of a phonetically null functional locative preposition, P_{LOC}, explains the syntactic distribution of the phrase as a whole.

Since in the sections to come I will draw a parallel between the structure of Greek and Persian PPs, it is worth paying more attention to the proposal put forth by Terzi.

Greek locative prepositions participate in two syntactic structures, which Terzi calls Frame A and Frame B. Frame A consists of a locative P with nominal properties followed by a "light" preposition (*apo* or *se*) and a DP_{GROUND} in accusative case. Frame B consists of a locative P directly followed by a genitive-marked DP, which, in fact, can surface only as a genitive clitic.

(7) Frame A: Locative P – "light" P – DP_{ACC}
      Kathisa piso   apo ti Maria.
      *sat.*1SG *behind apo the Mary.*ACC
      'I sat behind Mary.'   (Terzi 2006: 11, ex. (25))

(8) Frame B: Locative P – clitic (DP_{GEN})
      Kathisa piso   tis   /*tis Maria.
      *sat.*1SG *behind she.*CL.GEN */the Mary*
      'I sat behind her/Mary.'   (Terzi 2006: 11, ex. (26))

The prepositions *apo* and *se* can occur on their own giving rise to a more general interpretation of location compared to the case when they are preceded by a locative P. Interestingly, the same distinction is at play in Persian, as will be shown in Section 3.1.

(9) a. To vivlio ine sto   trapezi.
          *the book is se.the table.*ACC
          'The book is on the table.'   (Terzi 2006: 11, ex. (28a))
      b. To vivlio ine epano sto   trapezi.
          *the book is on   se.the table.*ACC
          'The book is on (top of the) table.'   (Terzi 2006: 11, ex. (29a))

In (9a) the location of the book is not specified with respect to the parts of the table, for instance, the book might be in a drawer in the table. In (9b), on the contrary, the book has to be on the top surface of the table.

On Terzi's analysis in both frames the locative **modifies** a silent noun PLACE, the latter being preceded by an empty determiner. The object of the locative, that is, the DP_{ACC} or the genitive clitic, is in fact the **possessor** of the silent noun. The structure for Greek locatives is presented in (10), conflated for the two frames.

(10)   Greek locative PP structure (Terzi 2006)

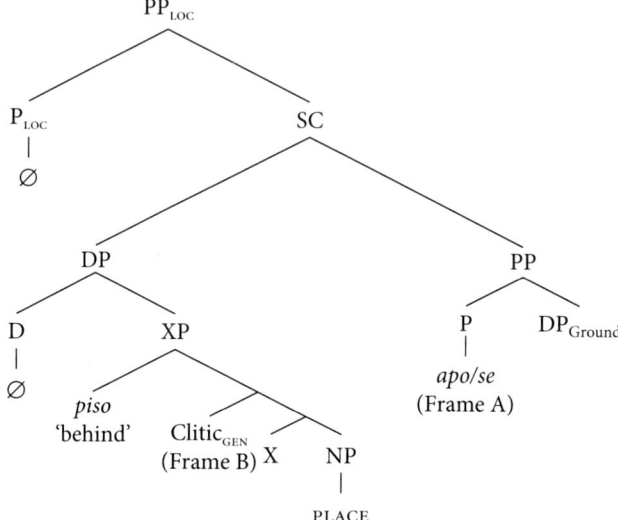

In the structure above both *se* and *apo* can optionally occur in the null P position taking the small clause as a complement. The presence of the latter in the structure is justified by the fact that possession in Greek nominals is associated with small clauses, for which Terzi cites Alexiadou & Stavrou (2000). Terzi points out the parallelism between the structure in (10) and the one proposed by them for nominal possession in the presence of an adjective. For a more detailed account I refer the reader to her paper and turn now to the very similar structure proposed by Botwinik-Rotem (this volume) for Hebrew locatives.

2.4   Botwinik-Rotem (this volume)

Botwinik-Rotem (this volume) points out that Hebrew locative prepositions differ from non-locative ones in that the former can be full-fledged predicates, suggesting a richer structure, whereas the latter cannot, i.e., they are purely functional elements. She argues that the representatives of the category P are uniformly functional and accounts for the lexical behavior of the locative ones by suggesting that they originate in the functional projection of a silent noun PLACE.

Hebrew spatial prepositions can be divided in two types. Adopting the terminology in Botwinik-Rotem's article, I will refer to the first type of prepositions as *basic* prepositions. These are actually represented by two directional and two locative prepositions, listed in (11).

(11)   Hebrew "basic" prepositions

	Directional	Locative
	mi 'from'	*al* 'on'
	el/le 'to'	*be* 'in'

The directional and locative basic prepositions are in complementary distribution and for that reason Botwinik-Rotem assumes that they occupy the same position in the P projection. Furthermore, a basic preposition can precede a preposition belonging to the second type, namely a "lexical" preposition, thereby expressing GOAL and SOURCE Path, for the directional ones, and location, for the two locative ones.

Botwinik-Rotem suggests that the structure for Greek locatives proposed by Terzi (2006) can be applied to Hebrew locative PPs, with some modifications, as shown in (12). Thus, she accounts for the possibility of locative PPs to be independent predicates (i.e., to assign an external semantic role) by suggesting that the source for the external semantic role is a phonetically null noun PLACE heading the projection of locative PPs. Besides the external referential slot, the noun PLACE defines two more semantic slots – a "possessor" slot, satisfied by the DP_GROUND complement, and a spatial relation slot, satisfied by a lexical preposition.

(12)   The syntactic structure of Hebrew PPs

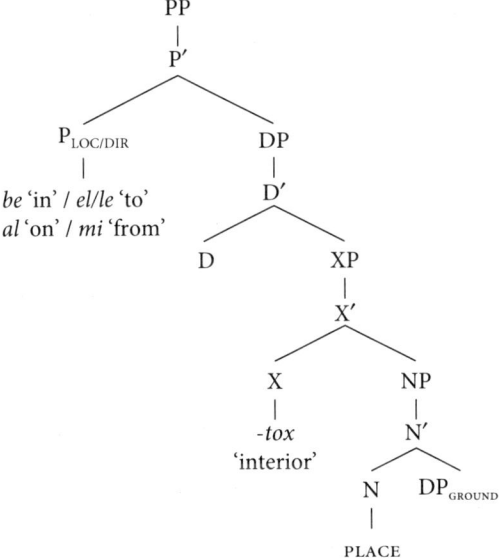

The main difference between the structure proposed by Terzi for Greek and the Hebrew structure is that Botwinik-Rotem suggests that the locative lexical prepositions are hosted by the X head, whereas in Greek, Terzi argues, they are phrasal modifiers found in the Specifier of the XP. Still, in both languages the relation between the silent noun and the Ground DP is that of possession.

To summarize, based on the literature overview above, the idea of the presence of a silent PLACE element in locative adverbs and in spatial prepositional phrases has been in the air for more than four decades. It is therefore interesting to try applying it to Persian spatial PPs and for that reason in the next section I will start out with a presentation of the prepositional system in Persian.

3.   The Persian data

3.1   General overview and Class 1 Ps

The Persian spatial prepositional system is, in fact, quite similar to the Hebrew one. Just like Hebrew prepositions, the Persian ones are divided into two main types, which I will call Class 1 and Class 2 prepositions, abbreviated as C1 Ps and C2 Ps, respectively (for a more extensive discussion of Persian prepositional classes see Pantcheva 2006). Class 1 Prepositions form a closed class containing a few monomorphemic prepositions in complementary distribution which are almost synonymous to the Hebrew basic prepositions. Consider (13) and compare with (11).

(13)   Persian Class 1 Ps

Directional	Locative
æz 'from'	*bær* 'on'
be 'to'	*dær* 'in, at'
ta 'up to'	

Class 2 prepositions, on the other hand, is a larger class. Most of its members exhibit some nominal properties and for this reason they have been classified as real nouns by Karimi & Brame (1986), Ghomeshi (1997) & Larson & Yamakido (2005), among others.

However, they do not pattern like nouns in all respects and this has been the reason for classifying them as functional elements with some lexical properties. For example, Samiian (1994) accounts for their dual syntactic behaviour by assuming a [+N] feature neutralization.

The syntactic status of Class 1 prepositions is uncontroversial. They are assumed to be pure functional elements which radically differ in their syntactic behaviour from the lexical Class 2 Ps. For example, C1 Ps have to be followed by a DP complement (14b), whereas C2 Ps are allowed to occur on their own (15b), just like Greek locatives (16).

(14)   Class 1 P *dær* 'in, at'
    a.   Zæn   dær xane   montæzer bud.
        woman in   house anticipant was
        'The woman was waiting in the house.'

b. *Zæn   dær montæzer bud.
    woman in anticipant was

(15) Class 2 P *posht* 'behind'
    a. Zæn   posht-e   xane montæzer bud.
        woman behind-EZ house anticipant was
        'The woman was waiting behind the house.'
    b. Zæn   posht montæzer bud.
        woman behind anticipant was
        'The woman was waiting in the back.'

(16) I   Maria kathise piso.
      the Mary sat.3SG behind
      'Mary sat in the back/behind.'   (Terzi 2006: 3, ex. (3a))

Persian C1 Ps can be combined with C2 Ps thereby specifying the Path or location expressed by the C2 P. When expressing location, GOAL Path and VIA Path, the C1 preposition can be omitted leaving the context to disambiguate the meaning of the C2 P. For SOURCE Path the preposition *æz* is obligatory.

(17) a. (dær) posht-e   xane
          at   behind-EZ house
          'behind the house'   Location
      b. (be) posht-e   xane
          to   behind-EZ house
          'to the place behind the house'   Goal
      c. æz   posht-e   xane
          from behind-EZ house
          'from behind the house'   Source

Compare (17) with the Hebrew data in (18).[3]

(18) a. be-tox   ha-bayit
          in-inside the-house
          'inside the house'   Location
      b. el tox   ha-bayit
          to inside the-house
          'into the house'   Goal
      c. mi-tox   ha-bayit
          from-inside the-house
          'out of the house'   Source

---

3. It should be noted, though, that Hebrew basic preposition can be used on their own, having exactly the same meaning as the corresponding complex ones. The same is true for Persian in cases where the context is rich enough as to allow the Class 2 P to be inferred.

Semantically, the locative Class 1 Ps differ from Class 2 Ps, too, in a way highly similar to Greek *se* and Hebrew basic prepositions. Just like Greek *se* and Hebrew *al* 'on' and *be* 'in', Persian *dær* 'at, in' and *bær* 'on' express location which is more general and vague than the one expressed by the corresponding C2 Ps. Consider the following examples.

(19)   Greek (repeated from (9))
    a.   To vivlio ine sto   trapezi.
       *the book is se.the table.*ACC
       'The book is on the table.'   (Terzi 2006: 11, ex. (28a))
    b.   To vivlio ine epano sto   trapezi.
       *the book is on   se.the table.*ACC
       'The book is on (top of the) table.'   (Terzi 2006: 11, ex. (29a))

(20)   Hebrew (Botwinik-Rotem, this volume)
    a.   Dan be-bet-sefer.
       Dan in-house-book
       'Dan is at school.'
    b.   Dan be-tox   bet-sefer.
       Dan in-inside house-book
       'Dan is inside the school.'

(21)   Persian
    a.   Reza dær mædræse æst.
       Reza at   school   is
       'Reza is at school.'
    b.   Reza (dær) tu-ye mædræse æst.
       *Reza at   in-*EZ *school   is*
       'Reza is inside the school.'

Comparing the data in (20b) and (21b), it seems that in Hebrew it is the "lexical" preposition that can be omitted and the functional one is obligatory. In Persian, on the contrary, it is the functional C1 preposition which can be omitted in the presence of a C2 P. It is also noteworthy that Persian locative C1 P *dær* 'at' and the directional C1 P *be* 'to' can be omitted even when there is no C2 P following. This is allowed, though, only when the DP complement of the preposition is a proper place name, an institution, or any other kind of conventionalized location (e.g., *Iran, Utrecht, store, department, yard, etc.*). Thus, the example provided in (21a) is grammatical, and in fact preferred, without the occurrence of any prepositions (see (22a)). (22b) illustrates that the directional C1 preposition can be omitted, too.

(22)   a.   Reza mædræse æst.
       Reza school   is
       'Reza is at school.'

b. Reza ræft   mædræse.
   Reza   went   school
   'Reza went to school.'

In the subsections to follow I will present the data about the ambivalent Persian Class 2 prepositions, by making a division between the cases when they behave more or less like nouns (Section 3.2) and the cases when they appear to be functional (Section 3.3).

3.2   Similarities between Class 2 Ps and nouns

In this section I'm going to provide some data showing that Persian Class 2 prepositions have a certain "nominal flavour" in that they exhibit properties typically ascribed to nouns. It should be borne in mind that the syntactic phenomena I discuss here cannot be uniformly applied to **all** prepositions belonging to this class. There will be exceptions in every case but I will specifically mention only those cases when the deviation is considerable or potentially relevant for the analysis.

3.2.1   *The Ezafe linker*
Probably the most striking similarity between Class 2 prepositions and nominals is the availability of the Ezafe linker for C2 Ps. *Ezafe* is a linking morpheme phonologically realized as /e/ after a consonant and /je/ after a vowel. The Ezafe appears between the elements within noun phrases and adjectival phrases, that is, phrases headed by [+N] elements. Phonologically it forms a unit with the preceding element. For the purpose of this paper, it is worth paying some more attention to this phenomenon because of its central role in the ongoing discussion about the syntactic status of Persian Class 2 prepositions (see Karimi & Brame 1986; Samiian 1994; Ghomeshi 1997, among others). I focus on Ezafe within the noun phrase, since phrases headed by adjectives are not relevant to the issue.

Ezafe attaches to nouns when they are followed by a modifier, be it an adjective (23a), a noun (23b), or a C2 preposition (23c).

(23)   a.   gol-e   sorx
            *flower-*ez *red*
            'red flower'

       b.   kif-e   chærm
            *bag-*ez   *leather*
            'leather bag'

       c.   tæbæqe-ye   bala
            *floor-*ez *above*
            'the floor above/the upper floor'

If the noun is modified by more that one element, each modifier, except the last one, bears Ezafe. Put in other words, each modified constituent is affixed with an Ezafe.

(24)   [kif-e   chærm]-e   sorx
        bag-EZ   *leather*-EZ   *red*
        'red leather bag'

In possessive constructions, Ezafe is affixed to the possessee.

(25)   [kif-e   sorx]-e   daneshdju
        bag-EZ   *red*-EZ   *student*
        'the red bag of the student'

The first Ezafe vowel in (25) attaches to the noun *kif* 'bag' because of the following modifying adjective *sorx* 'red'. The appearance of the second Ezafe linker, which attaches to the phrase [*kif-e sorx*] 'red bag', is triggered by the presence of the possessor *daneshdju* 'student'. The tree structure for the example in (25) is presented below. To anticipate my proposal, which I develop in Section 4, I give the structure of the phrase in (25) with a preceding demonstrative.

(26)

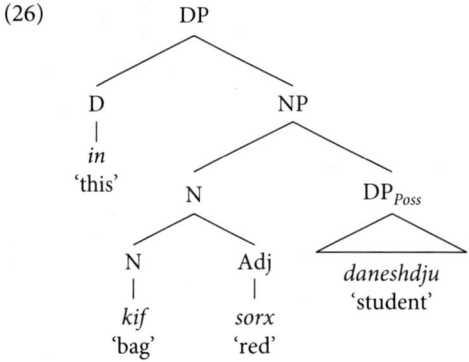

Figure 7. Possession construction — *this red bag of the student.*

Although in a sequence of nouns, such as the one in (25), Ezafe appears both in front of modifying nouns and before possessors, there is one important difference between the two cases. Only possessors can be full DPs, (27a). Nouns used as modifiers of other nouns cannot be DPs but bare N heads or NPs, (27b) (cf. Ghomeshi 1997).

(27)   a.   kif-e   in   daneshdju
              bag-EZ   *this*   *student*
              'the bag of this student'

b. *kif-e   in   chærm
    bag-EZ this leather

Interestingly, all C2 prepositions take the Ezafe linker when followed by their DP complement (28). It should be mentioned, though, that a small number of C2 Ps have the option of taking a DP complement without Ezafe (29). I will refer to these preposition as Class 2a following Pantcheva (2006).

(28) a. kenar-e   dærya
          next.to-EZ sea
          'at the sea'

      b. dour-e   mæn
          around-EZ   I
          'around me'

(29) a. tu(-ye)   eshkaf
          inside(-EZ) cupboard
          'in the cupboard'

      b. pæhlu(-ye) to
          beside(-EZ) you
          'beside you'

The availability of Ezafe for C2 Ps has been an important argument for classifying them as true nouns (see, for example, Ghomeshi 1996; Larson & Yamakido 2005).

3.2.2 *Demonstratives*

Some, but not all, Class 2 Ps can be preceded by a demonstrative. Crucially, the semantic interpretation of the demonstrative in such cases is not one of definiteness, but of the adverbs *here* and *there* for the proximal and distal demonstrative, respectively.

(30) a. in   tu-ye   kif
          this inside–EZ bag
          'here in the bag'

      b. un   zir-e   miz
          that under-EZ table
          'there under the table'

Considering Katz & Postal's (1964) decomposition of *here* and *there*, presented in Section 2.1, as well as Kayne's (2005) analysis, discussed in Section 2.2, the interpretation of the demonstrative in Persian C2 PPs strongly suggests the existence of a silent PLACE element in the syntactic structure.

When preceded by a demonstrative, C2 Ps can take plural morphology as illustrated in (31).

(31)   Æks-ha   in   zir-ha-ye   kaqæz budænd.
       photo-PL *this* *under*-PL-EZ *paper* *were*
       'The photos were all over under the paper(s).'

With respect to the semantics, the plural morpheme in (31) has a distributive reading.

3.2.3   *Pronominal clitics*

According to the traditional grammars Persian pronominal clitics have three functions, listed in (32) (Mahootian 1997; Mace 2003).

(32)   Persian pronominal clitics can:

1.   indicate a definite direct object when attached to a verb.

(33)   Xund-æm-esh.
       read.PAST-1SG-3SG.CL
       'I have read it.'

2.   express the possessor in possessive constructions when attached to the possessed NP.

(34)   Mashin-esh did-æm.
       car-3SG.CL   *saw*-1P.SG
       'I saw his/her car.'

3.   attach to a C2 P and express its Ground DP complement.

(35)   a.   Mush pærid   tu(-ye)   quti.
            mouse jumped inside(-EZ) *box*
            'The mouse jumped into the box.'
       b.   Mush pærid   tu-sh.
            mouse jumped inside-3SG.CL
            'The mouse jumped into it.'

In Section 4.4, I will unify the second and the third function thus reducing the number of the relations expressed by Persian clitics to two. For the time being, it is important to note that all Class 2 prepositions can take pronominal clitics, with no exceptions.

(36)   a.   Gorbe posht-e   deræxt pærid.
            cat   behind-EZ *tree*   *jumped*
            'The cat jumped behind the tree.'
       b.   Gorbe posht-esh   pærid.
            cat   behind–3SG.CL *jumped*
            'The cat jumped behind it/her/him.'

The structure in (36b) is reminiscent of Frame B of Greek locative PPs where, as Terzi (2006) argues, the genitive clitic expresses the possessor of a silent noun

PLACE. However, unlike the Greek ones, Persian clitics are not subject to animacy restrictions, as can be seen from the translation of (36b) where the clitic can stand for the Ground DP *the tree*.

3.2.4 Modifiers

Finally, a property shared by all C2 P(P)s is their ability to modify nouns, as already hinted in example (23c) above, repeated as (37b) below. Noun modification by a C2 P is possible both when the preposition is followed by a complement, (37a), and when it appears on its own, (37b).

(37) a. tæbæqe-ye bala-ye   mæqæze
          *floor-*EZ   *above-*EZ *shop*
          'the floor above the shop'
      b. tæbæqe-ye bala
          *floor-*EZ   *above*
          'the floor above/the upper floor'

Although noun modification is a general property of locative PPs in many languages, this is not the case with Persian. While C2 Ps can modify nouns, prepositional phrases headed by a Class 1 preposition are strikingly ungrammatical as modifiers, no matter whether with, (38a), or without a complement, (38b).

(38) a. *ketab-e   dær quti
          *book-*EZ   *in   box*
          ('the book in the box')
      b. **ketab-e dær
          *book-*EZ   *on*
          intended meaning: 'the book in(side)'

The examples in (38) can be rescued by exchanging the Class 1 P *dær* 'in, (at)' by the almost synonymous C2 preposition *tu* 'in, inside'.

Going back to the Persian C2 Ps counterparts in Greek, there is one important observation to be made. While Greek locatives modify a silent noun PLACE (Terzi 2006), Persian C2 Ps are much less restricted as to what kind of noun they can modify. They can directly adjoin to any NP/DP thus giving rise to modification structure.

3.3 Differences between Class 2 Ps and nouns

Although they appear to pattern like nominal elements, Persian C2 Ps differ from nouns in some important aspects. In this section, I will focus on some properties which distinguish them from true nouns.

3.3.1 Class 2 PPs in a subject position

According to Samiian (1994) and Ghomeshi (1996), C2 PPs can occupy argument positions in the clause. An example is provided in (39).

(39)   Zir-e   miz kæsif-e.
       *under-*EZ *table dirty-is*
      'The space under the table is dirty.'

Nevertheless, I will argue that the position the C2 PP occupies in (39) is not that of a subject. Assuming that the C2 PP is not a subject, we are left with a sentence with no overt subject. This, however, does not pose a problem, since Persian generally makes use of null subjects, especially in impersonal constructions, such as, for example, the one in (40).

(40)   Qafi-e.
       enough-is
       'It's enough.'

Further indication that the C2 PP in (39) is not necessarily an argument comes from the following data. Here, first, there is a clear contrast in the meaning of the lexical item *posht* meaning both 'behind', as a preposition, and 'back', as a noun. Second, the two uses of *posht* 'back' differ also with respect to the possibility of being referred back to by a pronoun.

(41) a.   Posht-e xane   tarik bud, næ-tunestæm bebinæm-esh.
           *back-*EZ *house dark was *NEG-*could.1*SG *see-3*SG.*CL
           'It was dark behind the house, I couldn't see it.'
           (it = the house)
    b.   Posht-e gorbe siya   bud, næ-tunestæm bebinæm-esh.
           *back-*EZ *cat   black was *NEG-*could.1*SG *see-3*SG.*CL
           'The cat's back was black, I couldn't see it.'
           (it = the back or the cat)

The two examples are significantly different, both with respect to their semantics and to their underlying syntactic structure. In (41b) *posht* is a relational noun which refers to a body part. In (41a), however, *posht* denotes a location which is calculated by projecting vectors from the Ground DP complement *house* of the C2 P *behind* in the sense of Zwarts (2005) and Svenonius (2006). In addition, the pronoun test suggests that 'behind the house' in (41a) is not an argument, since it cannot be referred back to (unlike 'back of the cat' in (41b)). Therefore, it cannot be a subject.

Additional support comes from the fact that coordinate Class 2 prepositional phrases occuring in what seems like a subject position do not trigger plural agreement on the verb (42).

(42)   Hæm ru-ye miz   hæm zir-e   miz kæsif æst.
       also   on-EZ table also under-EZ table dirty is
       'It is dirty both under the table and on the table.'

Coordinated DPs, however, do trigger plural agreement on the verb, as illustrated in (43).

(43)   Hæm reza   hæm   mina   xæste hæstænd.
       also   Reza   also   Mina   tired   are
       'Both Reza and Mina are tired.'

To summarize, there seem to be no compelling reasons to view C2 PPs as the subject in examples like (39).

3.3.2   *Complement of directed motion verbs*

As mentioned in Section 3.1, the locative C1 P *dær* 'at, in' and the goal-directional C1 P *be* 'to' can be optionally omitted when their noun complement is a conventionalized place.

The following minimal pair contains the word *posht* which can function either as a body part noun meaning 'back' or as a C2 P meaning 'behind'. Since it is clear that *the cat's back* cannot denote a conventional location, it is not surprising that in (44a) the phrase has to be preceded by an overt C1 preposition. However, in (44b) the homophonous C2 P can occur with no preceding overt preposition.

(44)   a.   Pærid   *(be) posht-e gorbe.
            jumped   to   back-EZ cat
            'She/he/it jumped to the cat's back.'
       b.   Pærid   posht-e deræxt.
            jumped   back-EZ tree
            'She/he/it jumped behind the tree.'

This data set clearly suggests that it is not unproblematic to ascribe the same properties to the Class 2 preposition in the phrase *posht-e deræxt* 'behind the tree' and to the body part noun in the NP *posht-e gorbe* 'the cat's back', since they behave differently with respect to the possibility of appearing with or without a preposition in (44). Now, given that we know that the directional C1 P is optional with conventionalized places, but obligatory with non-conventional ones, it is expected that there be a C1 P in (44a). The fact that it can be omitted in (44b) suggest two things: either this sequence is not nominal, or, to anticipate my solution which I will present in Section 4.2, there is a silent element in the structure which encodes the notion of a conventionalized place.

3.3.3   *Adjectival modification and quantifiers*

Class 2 prepositions generally reject adjectival modification, as shown in (45).

(45) *tu-ye tarik-e gænje
  inside-EZ *dark*-EZ *closet*
  'the dark inside of the closet'

The same holds for modification by quantifiers.

(46) *hær zir-e miz
  every *under*-EZ *table*
  'every space under the table'

The unavailability of adjectives and quantifiers shows once again that Class 2 Ps do not behave like true nouns.

3.4 Summary

I will start the summary of the section by first making the distinction between Class 1 and Class 2 Ps clearer. Apart from the availability of the Ezafe linker, C2 Ps manifest a range of other distinctions compared to C1 Ps in that they [i] occur without a complement, [ii] follow a demonstrative, [iii] take plural morphology, [iv] host pronominal clitics, [v] occupy what appears to be an argument position and, finally, [vi] can be NP modifiers. C1 Ps, in their turn, can precede any C2 PP to specify a GOAL Path, a SOURCE Path and location, depending on which C1 P is used.

When it comes to the nominal behaviour of C2 Ps, they pattern like nouns, as can be seen from [i]-[vi] in the preceding paragraph. However, they differ from true nouns in that they [a] do not trigger plural agreement on the verb when in "subject position", [b] can be the complement of motion verbs without the support of a directional preposition, [c] do not allow adjectival modification and [d] do not allow quantifiers either.

It is therefore very tempting to apply the hypothesis about a silent PLACE element in the Persian PPs in order to account both for their noun-like properties and for their P-like properties.

4. Silent place in Persian PPs

Considering all properties exhibited by Persian Class 1 and Class 2 prepositions, and crucially the fact that C2 Ps can be NP modifiers, I propose that the syntactic structure of Persian PPs contains a silent noun PLACE selected by a Class 1 preposition.

Abstracting from the DP and NP nodes in (47), the structure I propose is based on the one suggested by Svenonius (2006). He proposes a PP consisting of a Path head, a Place head, and a head for locative elements which he calls Axial Parts (abbreviated AxParts).[4] The Class 1 prepositions are hosted by the two highest functional heads. The directional C1 Ps are Path heads expressing TO, FROM and VIA Path. The two locative C1 Ps are under the Place head. The AxPart label, introduced by Svenonius (2006), stands for elements that are used instead of adpositions to express spatial relations. Generally, AxParts are noun-like elements similar to relational nouns which, however, do not refer to a certain part of an object but to a space specified with reference to that object. On the basis of a cross-linguistic survey of AxPart elements, Svenonius (2006) argues that they are to be regarded as a separate syntactic category, distinct from both nouns and prepositions. As a matter of fact, in some languages AxParts exhibit some adjectival properties (for instance in Japanese, see Takamine 2006).

(47)

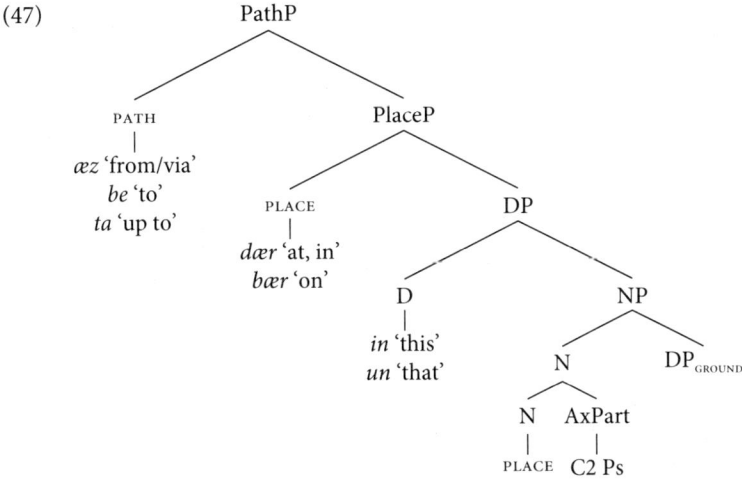

Figure 8. Syntactic structure of Persian C2 PPs.

In actuality, since the directional and the locative C1 Ps are in complementary distribution, it is arguable whether they should be hosted by two distinct heads in the projection. The top part of the tree structure is nevertheless not significant for the purpose of the present paper and, furthermore, keeping it as it is gives rise to desired cross-linguistic generalizations. For that reason, I will not dwell on this issue but will proceed to discussing the silent PLACE element I propose.

The crucial difference between (47) and the PP structure suggested by Svenonius is that in the latter a Class 1 preposition directly licenses an Axial Part element, whereas in the former the functional preposition first selects a DP containing a null PLACE which, in its turn, is modified by a Class 2 preposition, i.e., by an AxPart. Here following Botwinik-Rotem (this volume), I assume that the noun

---

4. In the structure proposed by Svenonius (2006) there is an additional projection KP for case immediately above the DP$_{GROUND}$. I do not include it here, but if we adopt the hypothesis put forward in Samiian (1994) that the Ezafe morpheme is a case-assigner, KP will be a plausible host.

PLACE is such that it defines a spatial relation slot which has to be satisfied by an AxPart. This will ensure the presence of a Class 2 preposition whenever there is a silent PLACE in the structure.

Persian, in fact, has the possibility of overtly expressing all the elements in (47), although the presence of an overt noun *place* makes the expression slightly clumsy. Below, I present the structure for an example with a null PLACE. If PLACE were phonetically realized, it would occupy the same position.

(48)   a.   Ketab-ra gozæsht (be) in   PLACE tu-ye   quti.
            book-OM put   to   this PLACE inside-EZ box
            'She/he put the book here in the box.'

b.

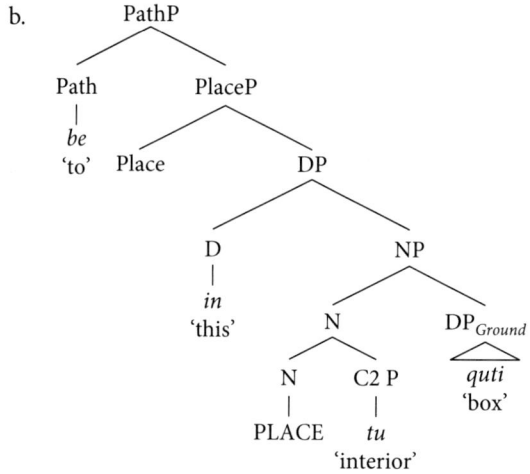

Figure 9. Structure for the PP in *She/he put the book here in the box.*

The presence of a null PLACE can account for several facts which I will discuss in the following subsections.

4.1   Demonstratives and plural morphology

The vital indication for the presence of a silent PLACE element in Persianpreposi-tional phrases comes from the semantic interpretation of the demonstratives in the PP.

Recall Katz & Postal's (1964) decomposition of *here* and *there* presented in Section 2.1. They decompose the words *here* and *there* into *at this place* and *at that place*, respectively. Interestingly, the Persian words for 'here' and 'there' consist of exactly the demonstrative *in* 'this' and *un* 'that', respectively, and the noun *dja* 'place'.

(49)   Persian *here* and *there*:

    a.   *indja* 'here' = proximal demonstrative *in* 'this' + *dja* 'place'

    b.   *undja* 'there' = distal demonstrative *un* 'that' + *dja* 'place'

Bearing this in mind, consider again the structure in (47). If a demonstrative is hosted by the D head, at Spell-out it will appear to directly precede the C2 PP, still the interpretation of *here* and *there* will remain thanks to the null PLACE in the structure.

Furthermore, the silent PLACE might account for the availability of plural morphology. As suggested by M. den Dikken (p.c.), the plural ending will attach to the Class 2 preposition because it needs a phonologically realized host to attach to.

However, it still remains unexplained why the plural morphology is available only in the presence of a demonstrative. Besides, it is not clear why not all Class 2 Ps can be preceded by a demonstrative.

Finally, I want to address the question of noun modification by Class 2 PPs and their interaction with demonstratives. As already discussed in Section 3.2.4, nouns, while disallowing modification by a Class 1 PP, can be modified by Class 2 PP. However, if the C2 PP is preceded by a demonstrative, the structure is ungrammatical. This is illustrated in the data set below.

(50)   a.   *tæbæqe-ye   un   bala-ye   mæqæze
         *floor-*EZ   *that   above-*EZ *shop*
         ('the floor there above the shop')

    b.   tæbæqe-ye   bala-ye   mæqæze
         *floor-*EZ   *above-*EZ *shop*
         'the floor above the shop'

The structures I propose for the data in (50) are based on (47) and presented in (51a) (for (50a)) and (51b) (for (50b)).

(51)

    a.

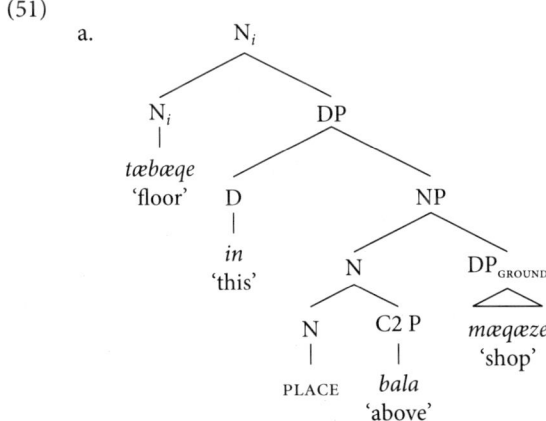

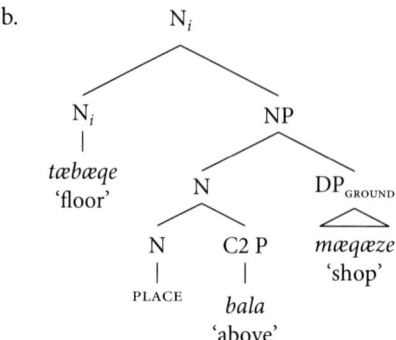

b.

Now, recall from Section 3.2.1 that nouns can be modified only by NPs or bare nouns but, crucially, never by full DPs. If the tree structures in (51) are indeed the correct ones, the ungrammaticality of (50a) will automatically fall out.[5]

4.2   Optionality of Class 1 Ps

The Class 1 preposition can, of course, be omitted because the silent PLACE doubtlessly denotes a conventional location and this straightforwardly explains the optionality of *dær* 'at' and *be* 'to' in (17), repeated below.[6]

(52)   a.   (dær) posht-e   xane
             at   *behind-ez house*
             'behind the house'

        b.   (be) posht-e   xane
             to   *behind-ez house*
             'to the place behind the house'

I will, however, suggest a different treatment of the data in in (52) in Section 4.5.

---

5.   Here, the question arises what the structure is in the cases when a noun is modified by a C2 P without a DP$_{GROUND}$ complement. I assume that it is not the same as in (51b) (with the DP$_{GROUND}$ simply being omitted). I rather propose that it is the same structure that we have in noun phrases where the modifier is an adjective or another noun. In other words, the structure for *tæbæqe-ye bala* 'the floor above' does not contain a null PLACE but the C2 P *above* directly modifies the noun *floor*. I base my claim on the relative order of noun modifiers in Persian and the fact that a noun-modifying C2 P with a Ground DP has to obligatorily be the very last modifier of the head noun, whereas noun-modifying sole C2 Ps can be both preceded and followed by an adjectival modifiers of the same noun and, in general, behave as "lighter" elements.

6.   On the assumption that the presence of a silent PLACE in the PP structure is universal, the question arises whether other languages with attested P-drop will pattern like Persian. I suggest that the lack of a "light" preposition in FrameB locative PPs in Greek, which is a P-drop language, is support for my claim. Hebrew basic prepositions will not be omitted, though, since P-drop in Hebrew is generally restricted only to the noun *home*.

Regarding C1 Ps, a legitimate question is whether the DP of PLACE is present in the structure in PPs containing only a Class 1 P. I assume not and suggest that the functional Class 1 prepositions have the option of directly selecting their DP$_{Ground}$ complement and in doing so the truncated structure will bear only core spatial meanings (i.e., GOAL, VIA and SOURCE Paths and general location). The structure would be then as in (53).

(53)

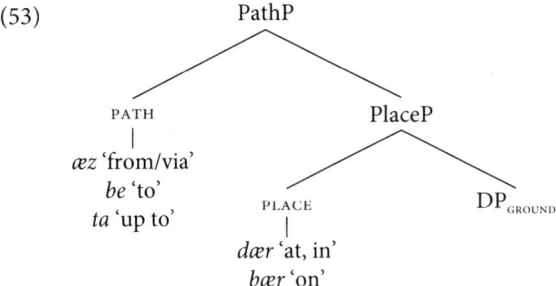

Figure 12. Persian Class 1 PPs.

4.3 Optionality of Ezafe

Recall from Section 3.2.1 that there are a small number of so called C2a prepositions that take the Ezafe linker optionally before an overt Ground complement (see (29)).[7] Now, we can turn back to them and account for some aspects of their behavior. First thing to observe is that the Ezafe, although optional in general, becomes obligatory in certain contexts. Ezafe has to be suffixed on a C2a P when there is an overt Class 1 P present in the structure (see (54)).

(54)   a.   tu(-ye)   quti
              inside-EZ *box*

        b.   dær   tu*(-ye)   quti
              at   *inside*-EZ *box*
              'inside the box'

Ezafe is also obligatory when there is a demonstrative preceding a Class 2a P.

(55)   a.   tu(-ye)   quti
              inside-EZ *box*

        b.   in   tu*(-ye)   quti
              this   *inside*-EZ *box*
              'here inside the box'

---

7. These prepositions are *tu* 'inside', *ru* 'on', *pæhlu* 'beside somebody, at somebody's place', *jelow* 'in front of' and, for some speakers, *kenar* 'beside'.

I propose that Class 2a prepositions have a dual syntactic status. They are able to function both as an AxPart and as a functional preposition. In other words, in a C2a P+Ground DP sequence, the C2a preposition can can occupy the Place head in (53) and then no Ezafe will be necessary. Another option is that the C2a P is hosted by the AxPart in (47). In this case the presence of the NP headed by PLACE will trigger the insertion of Ezafe. The optionality of Ezafe is the direct consequence of these two possibilities for C2a Ps. Now, consider the case when the Place head is occupied by a Class 1 preposition, as in (54b), then the Class 2a preposition will have no other option but to be under the AxPart. The Ezafe will become obligatory because of the PLACE-NP in the structure. The same line of reasoning can explain the obligatoriness of Ezafe in (55b). The presence of a demonstrative before a C2a P is a clear indication of the presence of the NP headed by PLACE. Again the noun PLACE will trigger the occurence of Ezafe.

The structure in (53) makes some other true predictions with respect to the unavailability of pronominal clitics for C1 Ps which will be discussed in the next section.

4.4   Clitics and intransitive C2 Ps

In the proposed structure, the Ground DP complement is the 'possessor' of the space specified by PLACE and the C2 P which requires an Ezafe linker to attach to the last element of the constituent expressing the possessee, that is, to the C2 P. This provides us with a way to unify two of the functions Persian pronominal clitics have (according to the traditional description of the facts). Namely, I suggest unifying the cases when they attach to nouns to express possessors and the cases when they attach to C2 prepositions to express their complement. More specifically, I claim that in both cases the clitic attaches to a phrase headed by a noun and expresses the possessor. Thus, in the structure in (47) the clitic, in actuality, attaches to the last element in the constituent headed by PLACE, i.e., to the C2 P. In other words, the reason clitics are available with C2 Ps is that there is possessive relationship between the DP$_{GROUND}$, which they replace, and the phrase headed by PLACE. Notice the parallel structures in (56) and (57).

(56)   [mashin-e   abi]-sh
       car-EZ   blue-3SG.CL
       'his/her blue car.'

(57)   [PLACE   tu]-sh
       PLACE   inside-3SG.CL
       'in it'

Moreover, when the possessor is omitted this would leave the C2 preposition to appear without a DP$_{GROUND}$ complement, as in (15b), repeated in (58b) with an added demonstrative so as to show that it is available in this context too.

(58) a. Zæn un posht-e xane montæzer bud.
           woman that behind-EZ house anticipant was
           'The woman was waiting there behind the house.'
     b. Zæn un posht montæzer bud.
           woman that behind anticipant was
           'The woman was waiting there in the back.'

The structure for C1 PPs I proposed in (53) shows why clitics cannot attach to C1 Ps. The reason is that the DP_{GROUND} complement of a C1 P is not a possessor because of the lack of NP headed by silent PLACE and, therefore, the lack of a possessive relation since the possessee is missing. Assuming that Persian clitics can express two relations – i. possessors and ii. direct object of verbs – neither of them fits in a C1 P phrase.

4.5 Remaining problems

Assuming a silent PLACE is an attractive explanation of the nominal properties of Persian Class 1 Ps. However, if there is a DP in the P projection, examples like (42), repeated in (59), will be surprising, since one would expect two null PLACE nouns to trigger plural agreement on the verb.

(59) Hæm ru-ye miz hæm zir-e miz kæsif æst.
           also on-EZ table also under-EZ table dirty is
           'It is dirty both under the table and on the table.'

In order to provide an explanation, I must reanalyze the cases with an optional C1 preposition and postulate a silent one. In such cases, every prepositional phrase in Persian will be headed by a Class 1 preposition, crucially even when the only visible P element is a C2 P. This entails that the "optional" C1 Ps in (17) are always present in the structure and their optionality boils down to whether they are phonologically realized or not.

     Furthermore, the unavailability of quantifiers remains unaccounted for. As to the adjectival modification, it can be said that PLACE, being a special kind of noun, cannot be modified by anything but an AxPart (cf. Botwinik-Rotem, this volume).

5. Conclusion

In this paper I briefly presented the Persian prepositional system, focusing on the similarities it has with the Greek and Hebrew prepositional systems. In all three languages, there is a class of spatial elements with a controversial status swinging between functional and lexical. I suggested that there is a null noun PLACE in the P projection, which accounts for the nominal properties of the aforementioned elements.

This hypothesis has the virtue of unifying to a certain approximation the account for Persian PPs with the one provided by Terzi (2006) for Greek locative phrases and the one presented by Botwinik-Rotem (this volume) for Hebrew locatives.

The structure I propose still allows us to maintain the distinction between Axial Parts and nouns making the former even less nominal by assuming that the only property they share with nouns is that they can be noun modifiers. Since, as Svenonius (2006) shows, AxParts are cross-linguistically widely represented, it is highly interesting to attempt to apply the silent PLACE hypothesis to other languages.[8]

References

Alexiadou, A. & Stavrou, M. 2000. Adjective-clitic combinations in the Greek DP. In *Clitics in Phonology, Morphology and Syntax*, B. Gerlach & J. Grijzenhhout (eds), 63–84. Amsterdam: John Benjamins.

Ghomeshi, J. 1996. Projection and Inflection: A Study of Persian Phrase Structure. PhD Dissertation, University of Toronto.

Ghomeshi, J. 1997. Non-projecting nouns and the Ezafe construction in Persian. *Natural Language and Linguistic Theory* 15(4): 729–788.

Karimi, S. & Brame, M. 1986. A generalization concerning the EZAFE construction in Persian. Ms., University of Washington & University of Arizona.

Katz, J.J. & Postal, P.M. 1964. *An Integrated Theory of Linguistic Descriptions*. Cambridge MA: MIT Press,

Kayne, R.S. 2004. Here and there. In *Lexique, Syntaxe et Lexique-Grammaire/Syntax, Lexis & Lexicon-Grammar: Papers in Honor of Maurice Gross*, C. Leclère, E. Laporte, M. Piot & M. Silberztein (eds), 253–275. Amsterdam: John Benjamins.

Larson, R.K. & Yamakido, H. 2005. Ezafe and the position of nominal modifiers. Ms., Stony Brook University.

Mace, J. 2003. *Persian Grammar for Reference and Revision*. London: Routledge Curzon.

Mahootian, S. 1997. *Persian*. London: Routledge.

Pantcheva, M. 2006. Persian Preposition Classes. In *Nordlyd: Tromsø Working Papers in Linguistics*, 33.1, P. Svenonius (ed.), 1–25. Tromsø: Tromsø University.

Samiian, V. 1994. The Ezafe construction: some implications for the theory of x-bar syntax. In *Persian Studies in North America*, Mehdi Marashi (ed.), 17–41. Bethesda, MD: Iranbook.

Svenonius, P. 2006. The emergence of axial parts. In *Nordlyd: Tromsø Working Papers in Linguistics*, 33.1, P. Svenonius (ed.), 50–77. Tromsø: Tromsø University.

Takamine, K. 2006. The axial part phrase in Japanese. In *Nordlyd: Tromsø Working Papers in Linguistics, 33.1*, P. Svenonius (ed.), 72–91. Tromsø: Tromsø University.

Terzi, A. 2006. The misleading status of locative prepositions. Ms., Technological Educational Institute of Patras.

Zwarts, J. 2005. Prepositional aspect and the algebra of paths. *Linguistics and Philosophy* 739–779.

---

8.   Axial Parts are to be found in Japanese, Kîitharaka, Finnish, and other unrelated languages. Presumably also Hebrew and Greek locatives can be assigned to this syntactic category.

Why are they different? An exploration of Hebrew locative PPs*

Irena Botwinik-Rotem

This paper focuses on a specific aspect that distinguishes (Hebrew) locative PPs from their non-locative counterparts, namely their ability to function as full-fledged predicates, assigning an external semantic role. Assuming a uniformly functional classification of P, I argue that the external role of locative PPs originates in the phonetically null noun PLACE that heads the extended (nominal) projection of a locative PP. Building on the analysis of Greek locative PPs developed in Terzi (2005 a, b, c, 2006), I examine various types of evidence that Hebrew offers, arguing that (most) Hebrew locatives, like their Greek counterparts, originate in the functional projection of NP-PLACE, distinct from the locative PP. An additional variety of evidence involving complex and basic locatives and their interaction with (deictic) directionals motivates the claim that Hebrew basic locatives and directionals are merged in the same structural position, namely in P selecting a DP which encloses PLACE.

1. Introduction

In the past four decades the classification of the category P along the lexical/functional dimension ranged from uniformly lexical (Jackendoff 1977; Chomsky 1981), through semi-lexical (Emonds 1985; van Riemsdijk 1990, 1998) to uniformly functional (Grimshaw 2000; Baker 2003; Botwinik-Rotem 2004). This is probably because a uniform classification of P along the functional/lexical axis does not extend naturally to all members of the class P. For instance, subcategorized Ps (1) do not fit well with the lexical classification of P; arguably, they are not theta-assigners, but rather case-related functional heads (cf. Hestvik 1991, Botwinik-Rotem 2004; Kayne 2005).

* Earlier version of this work has been presented at the *Syntax and Semantics of Spatial P Conference* (UiL OTS, Utrecht University, June 2006). I would like to thank the audiences of this event for their comments and suggestions. For written comments I am deeply grateful to Marcel den Dikken, Idan Landau, Aya Meltzer, Omer Preminger, Tali Siloni, Arhonto Terzi, and two anonymous reviewers. The remaining errors are mine and mine alone.

(1)   Dan relies on Mary.

The uniformly functional classification of P, which I assume here, is compromised by locative Ps, whose 'lexical flavor' is difficult to deny. Compared to other Ps, the variety of locative Ps is much larger, e.g., *in, on, near, above, behind,* etc. (as noted in Marantz 1984), and their distribution freer and more diverse. Being less restricted by the subcategorization frame or the lexical semantics of the associated lexical head, locative PPs can modify almost any nominal or verbal phrase, as shown in the Hebrew examples (2a) and (3a), which is not possible for non-locative PPs ((2b, c), (3b, c)). In contrast to non-locative PPs, locative PPs are not necessarily modifiers or complements, they can also be subjects (4).[1]

(2)   a.   dan axal / diber / xalam / rac   ba-gina   Vs and locative PP
            Dan ate / talked / dreamt / ran in+the-garden

      b.   dan *axal / *diber / *xalam / rac   la-gina   Vs and non-locative PP
            Dan   ate / talked / dreamt / ran   to+the-garden

      c.   dan *axal / diber / xalam / *rac   al   ahava
            Dan   ate / talked / dreamt / ran   about love

(3)   a.   ha-yeladim/ha-tiyulim/ha-diyunim   be-hodu hayu meragšim
                                                                          Ns and locative PP
            the-children/the-trips/the-discussions   in-India were exciting

      b.   *ha-yeladim/ha-tiyulim/*ha-diyunim   le-hodu hayu meragšim
                                                                          Ns and non-loc PP
            the-children/the-trips/the-discussions   to-India were exciting

      c.   *ha-yeladim/*ha-tiyulim/ha-diyunim   al   ahava hayu   meragšim
            the-children/the-trips/the-discussions about love   were   exciting

---

1.   Two remarks are in order. First, the term "locative" is restricted in this work to locational (not directional) Ps. In this respect, note that the directional PP headed by *le-* ('to'), (2b), (3b), indeed patterns with the non-locative PPs. Second, I use the term "modifier" as a general cover term to refer to constituents whose relation to the head is not mediated by theta-assignment, in the sense of Grimshaw 1990. Specifically, both locative PPs, whose addition to the nominal is free (3a), and also non-locative PPs whose combination with the nominal is limited by the lexical semantics of the appropriate Ns (3b, c), are referred to as "modifiers", because the nominals under consideration are simple, rather than event-nominals, and hence are not associated with a theta-grid. In Grimshaw's 1990 terminology, only locative PPs would be referred to as "modifiers", while non-locative PPs would be defined as "complements" (as opposed to "arguments"). The simplification of Grimshaw's terminology is not meant to deny the differences between these PPs. Rather, its purpose is mainly presentational; to distinguish between phrases licensed within the maximal projection of the relevant head (e.g., N), as opposed to phrases functioning as cross-copular predicates (this issue will become more concrete in section 2.2).

(4) a. Under the table is a good hiding place.   (from Stowell 1981)

Compare: b. *About love is an interesting topic.

Moreover, various aspects of their internal and external syntax have led to analyses according to which locative PPs are associated with rich functional structure, schematized in (5) (cf. Koopman 2000 and den Dikken 2006), which is taken to suggest that locative Ps are lexical heads, heading their own extended projection, in the sense of Grimshaw 2000.

(5) ...$[_{CP}$ C $[_{DegP}$ Deg $[_{PlaceP}$ Place $[_{PP}$ P$_{LOC}$ DP]]]]

In this paper I will focus on a particular aspect of the lexical flavor of locative PPs, namely their behavior as genuine predicates, and argue that it is fully reconcilable with the uniformly functional classification of P, and should be attributed to a nominal structure with which locative PPs are associated.

The paper is structured as follows. In section 2 I introduce and discuss three properties which show that locative PPs, unlike other PPs, are indeed genuine predicates, assigning an external semantic role. Given our working hypothesis that members of the category P are uniformly functional, combined with the traditional assumption (cf. Chomsky 1981) that only lexical heads engage in theta-assignment, this behavior of locative PPs appears problematic. It is accounted for in section 3, where the locative relation is proposed to be instantiated in an extended nominal projection, headed by a phonetically null N PLACE (cf. Terzi 2005 a, b, c). It is argued further that locative expressions participating in this projection saturate one of the argument positions in the N-PLACE. Consequently, what appears to be the external semantic role of a locative PP is, in fact, the external semantic argument R of the N-PLACE. Section 4 explores the implementation of the nominal extendeded projection to Hebrew locative PPs. Building on the analysis of Greek locative PPs developed in Terzi (2005 a, b, c, 2006), I examine various types of evidence that Hebrew offers, and which suggest that (most) Hebrew locatives, like their Greek counterparts originate in the functional projection of NP-PLACE, distinct from the locative PP. This examination sheds light on the nature of the heads participating in the nominal locative projection and on the variety of elements realizing the P head. Section 5 summarizes the main claims of the analysis of Hebrew locative PPs, as well as its possible benefits.

2.   The unique properties of the Hebrew locatives

Apart from the aforementioned general differences between locative and non-locative P(P)s, in what follows I present specific syntactic phenomena in which the attested differences between (Hebrew) locative and non-locative PPs point to the same conclusion; only locative PPs can be considered full-fledged predicates, assigning an external semantic role to an argument.

2.1   Binding

As is well-known, locative Ps behave differently from other Ps with respect to Binding (Hestvik 1991; Reinhart & Reuland 1993). Consider (6), which shows that while a pronominal clitic –*o* ('him') within a locative PP can be co-indexed with the subject (6a), the same is ungrammatical if the clitic –*av* ('him') is part of a non-locative PP (6b):[2]

(6)   a.   bart$_i$ sam et   ha-sukarya leyad-o$_i$/*leyad acmo$_i$ locative
             Bart put   ACC the-candy   near-him/near himself
        b.   dan$_i$ diber   *al-av$_i$/al acmo$_i$
             Dan talked   about-him/about himself   non-locative

In the framework of "Reflexivity" (Reinhart & Reuland 1993), the grammaticality of the pronoun co-indexed with the subject in (6a) indicates that the subject (*Bart*) and the pronoun (*him*) are not co-arguments, namely they are not arguments of the same predicate, which in this case would be the verb (*sam* 'put'). Rather, the pronoun embedded in the locative PP is the argument of a distinct predicate, presumably the locative preposition *leyad* ('near'), and therefore it is grammatical despite being co-indexed with the subject. In contrast, the impossibility of the pronoun embedded in a non-locative PP to be co-indexed with the subject, (6b), suggests that there is no additional predicate in the sentence, apart from the verb.

Note that although in the "Reflexivity" framework the contrast in (6) is accounted for via the notion of 'predicate', this notion refers to predicates in the lexical sense. That is, a predicate is a lexical V/P/N/A-head (rather than its maximal projection), the assigner of the thematic roles. This conception of a 'predicate', and my claim that Ps, including the locative ones, are functional (see Botwinik-Rotem 2004), and therefore not theta-assigners, are incompatible. It should be clear then, that although I believe the contrast in (6) to be related to the predicatehood of

---

2.   The form of the pronominal clitic, -*o*/-*av*, is dictated by the preposition. In this relation, it is worth mentioning that the binding pattern exemplified in (6a) can change to some extent, depending on the preposition. Specifically, it seems to be the case that the small P *be-* ('in') in a context similar to (6a) requires a reflexive, rather than a pronominal clitic (i). I have no explanation for this fact.

(i)   be-xalom, bart taka   et   ha-sakin *b-o/be-acmo
        in-dream, Bart stuck ACC the-knife in-him/in himself
        'In a dream, Bart stuck the knife in himself.'

locative PPs, the exact sense of this notion with respect to locatives under the present assumptions remains to be determined (see ahead, section 3.2).

2.2   Cross-copular predication

Hebrew present tense copular constructions do not include a verb, but may include the so-called 'pronominal copula' termed *Pron* by Doron (1983) (7). Greenberg (1994), following the insight of Rubinstein (1968) and Ben-David (1971), argues that the absence or presence of *Pron* correlates with a semantic distinction which can be described in terms of stage-level vs. individual-level predicates (Carlson 1977). Thus in (7a), which does not include *Pron, nexmad* 'nice' is a stage-level predicate (a predicate denoting a temporary property), and therefore it can be modified by a temporal adverb *hayom* 'today'. In the minimally different (7b), the addition of the temporal adverb is infelicitous, because the occurrence of *Pron* renders *nexmad* 'nice' an individual-level predicate (i.e., a predicate denoting a permanent property), disfavoring temporal modification.

(7)   a.   bart nexmad (hayom)
           Bart nice   today
           Bart is nice (today).   (stage-level)
      b.   bart hu   nexmad (#hayom)
           Bart *Pron* nice   today
           Bart is <u>generally</u> nice./Bart is a nice person.   (individual-level)

In light of this, consider Hebrew cross-copular predication with non-locative and locative PPs exemplified in (8). Since *Pron* occurs with individual-level predicates, it is not surprising that it is rather marginal with locative predicates (8a), which denote stage-level properties.[3] In contrast, with non-locative PPs *Pron* cannot be omitted ((8b, c) vs. (8a)), which might suggest that this is so, because these are individual-level predicates. Note, however, that although the occurrence of *Pron* in sentences with with non-locative PPs has a major effect on their grammaticality (i.e., without it they would be completely ungrammatical), it does not render these sentences fully grammatical (compare with (7b) above). In other words, even if the obligatory occurrence of *Pron* in (8b, c) is due to the individual-level status

---

3.   If, based on our world knowledge, we identify the locative PP as a permanent location of the subject (i.e., an individual-level property), *Pron* is obligatory:

(i)   migdal eifel   *(hu)   be-pariz
      tower   Eifel   *Pron* in-Paris
      'The Eifel tower is in Paris.'

of the non-locative PPs, this, in itself, does not explain why the sentences remain marginal, when *Pron* is present.

(8) a. ha-sefer   (?hu) al ha-šulxan   locative PP
         the-book *Pron* on the-table
         'The book is on the table.'
     b. ha-diyun   *(?hu) al   ahava   non-locative PPs
         the-discussion *Pron* about love
         'The discussion is about love.'
     c. ha-tiyul *(?hu) la-ya'ar
         the-trip *Pron* to+the-forest
         'The trip is to the forest.'

Taking the stage/individual-level distinction out of the equation, it is reasonable to explore the possibility that the contrast between the locative and non-locative PPs in (8), in particular, the ability of the former, as opposed to the inability of the latter to form fully grammatical sentences (even with *Pron*) derives from the predicate/modifier distinction. Specifically, if only locative PPs are genuine predicates, whereas other PPs can only be modifiers, the latter would arguably fail to form fully grammatical sentences without their modifyee, as is, presumably, the case in (8b, c), and should give rise to fully grammatical sentences if the appropriate modifyee is present. In contrast, such addition should not be suitable for the locative PPs, if, as assumed, they are genuine predicates.

Consider, thus, the examples in (9), where an appropriate noun (the modifyee) is added in front of the PPs. This addition, as expected, renders the construction with the locative PP ungrammatical (9a), and the ones with the non-locative PPs fully grammatical (9b, c):

(9) a. *ha-sefer   hu   sefer al ha-šulxan   locative PP
         the-book *Pron* book   on the-table
     b. ha-diyun   hu   diyun   al   ahava   non-locative PPs
         the-discussion *Pron* discussion about love
         'The discussion is a discussion about love.'
     c. ha-tiyul hu   tiyul la-ya'ar
         the-trip *Pron* trip   to+the-forest
         'The trip is a trip to the forest.'

The contrast in (9) supports the assumption that the two kinds of PPs behave differently, and this is what underlies the contrast attested in (8); (8b, c), featuring the non-locative PPs, are not instances of cross-copular predication to begin with, but rather instances of elliptic modification (or complementation, see note 1), which might be the reason for their marginality, whereas in (8a) the locative PP is a genuine cross-copular predicate.

2.3 Clausal modification

Finally, unlike any other PP, locative PPs can form clausal modifiers (i.e., relative clauses) via the complementizer *še-/ašer* ('that') (10a):

(10) a. ha-ec   (še-/ašer) ba-ya'ar   karas   locative
       the-tree   that   in+the-forest   fell down
       'The tree (that is) in the forest fell down.'

      b. ha-sefer (*še-/*ašer) al   ahava azal   non-locative
       the-book   that   about   love   [was] sold out
       'The book about love was sold out.'

      c. ha-tiyul (*še-/*ašer) la-ya'ar   nidxa
       the-trip   that   to+the-forest [was]   postponed
       'The trip to the forest was postponed.'

Following Botwinik-Rotem 2004 (where the traditional analysis of relative clauses is assumed), clausal PP-modifiers (10a) have the structure schematized in (11):[4,5]

(11)   ha-ec [$_{C_p}$ Op$_i$ še- [$_{TP}$ t$_i$ T$_{[present]}$ [$_{PP}$ t$_i$ ba-ya'ar]]] . . .
      the-tree   that-   in+the-forest

Taking PPs, in general, to be able to function as modifiers of nouns (3), (10), the inability of non-locative PPs to modify via a relative clause (10b, c) is, in fact, expected. Abstracting away from the details, modification is a local relation, taking place under sisterhood between the (PP-)modifier and the modified NP, and involving the external slot of the modifier and the external argument of the modified NP (cf. Higginbotham 1985, but see section 3.3 for a more elaborate proposal). This would be impossible if the PP were associated with clausal structure, namely buried within the NP's CP-sister, as in (11). In such cases the PP has to function as a predicate, assigning its external semantic role to the null operator (Op).

The fact that only locative PPs have the ability to modify via a relative clause further supports their unique status as independent predicates.

Before we proceed with the main issue, namely the predicate-hood of the locatives, a brief remark regarding modification by locative PPs is in order. It is

---

4. The postulation of T$_{[present]}$ is motivated in Botwinik-Rotem 2004 by empirical and theoretical reasons. Its empirical motivation is based on the distribution of the adverb *mamaš* (roughly, 'right', literally, 'really'), which requires licensing by T (or V). On the theoretical side, it is based on Siloni (1997), who argues that the difference between the functional heads C and D is that D combines with a projection lacking tense, while C necessarily combines with a T-projection.

5. I follow the common assumption (originating with Milsark 1974; Stowell 1978) that a locative PP is a predicate of a locative small clause (SC). The exact structure(s) of the locative SC will not concern us in this paper. For some discussion of the issue, see Botwinik-Rotem 2004, chapter 4.

commonly assumed that locative PPs can modify both VPs and NPs. This, however, appears somewhat inaccurate. Modification of a VP is indeed fully acceptable (12a), and it is presumably achieved via the *e*(vent) variable of the locative P (Parsons 1990).[6] But simple modification of an NP, at least in Hebrew, is somewhat degraded (12b), and it improves when the locative PP is preceded by the complementizer (12c), forming a relative CP, in which the locative PP functions as a predicate, assigning its external semantic role to the Op (see (11)), rather than as a simple PP-modifier.

(12)   a.   dan   axal   ba-gina   locative PP as VP-modifier
             Dan   ate   in+the-garden
             'Dan   ate   in the garden.'
       b.   ?ha-ec   ba-ya'ar   karas   locative PP as NP-modifier
             the-tree   in+the-forest   collapsed
             'The tree in the forest collapsed.'
       c.   ha-ec   še-/ašer   ba-ya'ar   karas
             the-tree   that   in+the-forest   collapsed
             'The tree which is in the forest collapsed.'

Based on this, it seems to be the case that locative PPs function naturally as modifiers of eventualities. The question whether modification of an NP by a locative PP is on a par with modification by a non-locative PP (e.g., *the book about love*), or rather should be viewed as elided (CP) modification, will be left open for the time being.[7]

To recap, based on various syntactic phenomena, I demonstrated in this section that locative PPs, unlike other PPs, are capable to function as full-fledged predicates, assigning an external semantic role. This behavior of the locatives is not readily expected on the background assumption of this paper, namely that P is a uniformly functional category.

---

6.   Throughout this paper I am abstracting away from the *e* variable of locatives.

7.   Admittedly, and as pointed out by two anonymous reviewers, the Hebrew facts regarding cross-copular predication by locative vs. non-locative PPs, as well as clausal and simple modification do not seem to hold in English: the English counterpart of the marginal Hebrew (8b) is fully grammatical (i), a non-locative PP in English is perfect with or without the relative layer (ii) (cf. (10b)), and English locative PPs appear to make quite good NP modifiers (iii) (cf. (12b).

       i.   The book is about love.
       ii.   The book (that is) about love was sold out.
       iii. The tree in the forest fell down.

These (but probably additional) contrasts between Hebrew and English clearly deserve close examination, which is beyond the scope of this paper. A direction which comes to mind and seems plausible would be to focus on the difference attested in the present tense auxiliary system of the two languages, namely on the fact that the present tense copula in Hebrew is not verbal but nominal (*Pron*).

Alternatively put, on the traditional view (cf. Chomsky 1981), functional categories, unlike the lexical ones, do not assign theta-roles. If P is a functional category, as is assumed here, the fact that some of its members (i.e., locative Ps), may have the status of a predicate, namely an entity assigning an external semantic role, is, at best, puzzling.

Let us see then, how the aforementioned discrepancy can be reconciled, and the behavior of locatives be made less surprising.

3. The proposal

Maintaining the uniformly functional classification of P (cf. Grimshaw 2000, Botwinik-Rotem 2004), I propose that the existence of the external semantic role of locative P(P)s follows from their participation in an (extended) nominal projection. Specifically, following Terzi (2005 b, c, 2006) and Botwinik-Rotem and Terzi (to appear) I hold that the locative relation, commonly ascribed directly to a locative P, is actually instantiated via the combination of P with a nominal projection headed by a phonetically null N, which I mark PLACE (cf. Kayne 2004 regarding *here* and *there* in English). Thus, the DP usually referred to as the complement of P is merged not with P, but rather with N-*Place*, as schematized in (13). I take the relation of the DP embedded in the NP to the head-N (PLACE) to be some sort of possession (cf. Terzi 2005a,b,c, 2006). Accordingly, the structural position of this DP is that of a non-thematic complement of PLACE.[8]

(13) $[_{PP_{LOC}} P_{LOC} [_{DP} D [_{NP} PLACE\ DP]]]$

The structure of a locative PP in (13), which I will make more concrete in section 4, will suffice to address the issue of the predicate-hood of locatives. But before that, some support for its nominal core is in order.

3.1 Nominal structure: initial support and necessary clarifications

The existence of the nominal head in the structure of locatives is suggested by certain facts attested in a variety of languages. In Greek, for instance, the pronominal clitic of locatives is genitive, which is the case associated exclusively with complements of nominals in the language (14):[9]

---

8. Two additional positions which might have been appropriate are spec-NP or spec-DP. However, spec-NP is assumed to be the position of the Agent argument of event-denoting Ns (Ritter 1991; Siloni 1997, among others), but PLACE is clearly not such a noun. Spec-DP is argued in Landau 1999 to be the base-generated position of the so-called dative possessors. The latter, however, require a certain verbal projection for their licensing, which is absent in (13).

(14)   epano   tou
       on   he-cl.Gen.
       'on him'

Furthermore, the clitic of locatives in Greek is subject to animacy restrictions (15a), on a par with the possessive clitic, following the adjectival modifier and preceding the nominal head in the regular nominal domain (15b) (for more details, see Terzi 2005c, 2006):

(15)   a.   *I Eleni   perimene   brosta   apo tin   eklisia   ke   i Maria [$_{PP}$
            the E.   was-waiting in front of   the   church   and   the Mary
            mesa   tis$_i$ [$_{NP}$ PLACE t$_i$]]
            inside she-cl.Gen
            'Eleni was waiting in front of the church and Mary inside her.'
       b.   [$_{DP}$ O   trelos   tou   [$_{NP}$ odigos]]
            the crazy he-cl.Gen driver
            'His crazy driver' (i.e., the driver of Mr. X but *not* the driver of the car)

                                                                    (Terzi 2006)

In Persian, some of the so-called class 2 locative prepositions can be preceded by a demonstrative (related exclusively to Ns), and even bear plural morphology (16) (Pantcheva 2006, this volume):

(16)   in   zir(-ha)
       this under (-pl.)
       'down here' (distributive reading)

In some languages, like Chichewa, locative phrases are DPs, rather than PPs (Bresnan 1994). The locative interpretation is achieved via an appropriate classifier, namely a determiner-like element, presumably residing in D of N-PLACE, in the structure of locatives proposed here (13), with the PP-layer missing all together.

Finally, Aboh (2006) argues that locative adpositions in some West African Kwa languages, like Gbe, are not Ns, and yet, locative phrases are similar to possessive constructions, which are typically nominal.

A word of clarification is in order at this point (to be developed in section 4). In the current proposal the locative relation is claimed to involve a projection headed by N-PLACE. Crucially, however, the locative expressions themselves (e.g., *near, on*) are not viewed as the lexicalization of this noun, as is implied in some alternative proposals (cf. Noonan 2005), and therefore nominal properties are not expected to be attested with all locative Ps in all languages. In a language like Hebrew, viewing the locatives as the lexicalization of N-PLACE is especially tempting.

---

9.   In Modern Greek genitive and dative clitics are homophonous. However, Terzi (2005a) provides evidence showing that the clitic following the locative is genitive, rather than dative.

Most Hebrew locatives indeed resemble nouns, or include a nominal part, probably because they developed diachronically from the corresponding nouns (e.g., *leyad* literally: to-hand, meaning: 'near'). However, this, in itself, should not lead to their synchronic analysis as Ns, primarily because they do not behave like nouns in a number of ways.

For instance, one of the well-known properties of nouns across languages is that they can occur with or without a complement (modulo event nominals, Grimshaw 1990). The behavior of locatives with respect to occurrence with an overt complement is not systematic within a given language and across languages.[10] In some languages (e.g., Greek), almost any locative can occur with or without a complement, whereas in others (e.g., Russian), almost none of the locatives can occur without an overt complement, and between these two extremes lie languages like Hebrew or English where some locatives can occur without a complement, but some cannot. There is no such variation in the nominal domain, however.[11]

Defining the factors that determine the occurrence of locatives with or without an overt complement in a given language and across languages is a task worth pursuing. Whatever its results will be, the phenomenon is clearly not on a par with its counterpart in the nominal domain.

I believe this, in itself, can be viewed as an argument against considering locatives to be the lexicalization of the noun PLACE. Combined with the aforementioned nominal properties attested in locative phrases in a variety of languages, it can be taken to support the claim that an independent nominal head, N-*Place*, is part of the structure of locative phrases.

---

10.   For additional, languages-specific diagnostics, identifying adpositions as distinct from nouns in a variety of unrelated languages, see Svenonius (to appear), where locatives are taken to constitute a distinct syntactic category termed "Place".

11.   In principle, if locatives belong to the functional category P, we do not expect them to be able to occur without a complement. The fact that in a language like Greek they do is attributed in Botwinik-Rotem and Terzi (to appear) to their phrasal status, which leads to their phonological parsing as a prosodic word (PWd) (i) Along similar lines, Botwinik-Rotem and Terzi (to appear) account for the fact that only a particular subset of Hebrew locatives (those prefixed with *mi-*, like *mitaxat* 'under') can occur without an overt complement, because they are complex, and therefore free, phonologically independent heads, parsed as a PWd on their own (iia), rather than construct heads (iib) (see also section 4.2).

(i)   epano]$_{PWd}$ (sto Niko)]$_{PWd}$ Greek
        on   *se*-the Nick

(ii)   a.   mitaxat]$_{PWd}$ (le-ecim)]$_{PWd}$ Hebrew
            *mi*under   *le* trees

Compare: b.   leyad   *(ecim)]$_{PWd}$
              near   trees

With the above in mind, let us turn to the issue raised at the end of section 2, namely the predicate-hood of locative PPs.

3.2   Deriving the predicate-hood of locative PPs

As already mentioned, one of the consequences of viewing P as a uniformly functional category, is that it cannot be assumed that P assigns thematic roles. Therefore, even though a phrase like *leyad ha-yam* 'near the sea' is clearly a predicate, namely it denotes a property of individuals (or events), this cannot be because the locative P *leyad* 'near', in itself, is a two-place predicate, as is commonly assumed (cf. Svenonius to appear and references cited therein, Zwarts & Winter 2000, among others).

I assume instead, that the noun PLACE heading the projection of the locative PP (see (13)) defines the following semantic slots: a 'possessor' slot (satisfied by 'the sea' in 'near the sea'), a spatial relation slot, and an external referential slot (referred to as *R* in the works of Williams 1981, Higginbotham 1985, di Sciullo & Williams 1987). The atomic interpretation of PLACE, thus, is as given in (17a).[12] Further, I take locative expressions like *leyad* 'near', *meaxorey* 'behind', *mitaxat* 'under' etc. to satisfy the spatial relation slot (L) in the denotation of PLACE, and generate the set of individuals (or events) standing in the particular spatial relation to the location of an individual. Their interpretation is illustrated in (17b) for *near* (note that, in itself, the interpretation of such a spatial relation does not include an external slot for individuals):[13, 14]

(17)   <u>Atomic semantic interpretations</u>
    a. $[\![\text{PLACE}]\!] = \lambda y.\lambda L.\lambda x.x \in L(loc(y))$

(A function from individuals (y) and spatial relations (L) to a property of individuals that stand in the spatial relation L to the location of y.)

---

12.   As pointed out by one of the reviewers, the claim that PLACE is relational, namely a noun occurring obligatorily with a complement, might undermine the argument put forward in the previous section regarding the status of locatives as distinct from nouns. Specifically, if N-PLACE is a noun for which complementation is obligatory, unlike nouns in general, why couldn't the locatives occurring with a complement be considered as belonging to the same class of nouns as PLACE? Despite of the arguable existence of the relational N-PLACE, I believe the locatives still should not be collapsed either with nouns in general or even with a particular group of (relational) nouns, because the set of locatives occurring obligatorily with a complement varies across languages, whereas the claim that PLACE is relational is arguably universal.

13.   I am deeply grateful to Omer Preminger, without whom the crystallization of my preliminary intuitions regarding the semantics of Ps in general and locatives in particular, could not have been achieved.

14.   In principle, the semantics of a set is equivalent to a two-place relation: $\lambda x.\lambda l..x$ is near l. This in itself, however, is not of great significance. Many semantic operators take a set as their argument.

b. $[\![near]\!]$ = λl.{the set of things that are near l} l would be the location of y in (17a)

The compositional semantics of $[_{P'}$ *leyad ha-yam*] 'near the sea' is illustrated in (18):

(18) $[\![_{P'LOC}$ leyad$[_{DP}$ D$[_{NP}$ PLACE ha-yam]]]$]\!]$ = $[\![[_{NP}$ PLACE ha-yam]$]\!]$($[\![$leyad$]\!]$) = $\lambda x.x$
       $\in$ {the set of things that are near loc ($[\![$ha-yam$]\!]$)}

In the first line of (18) the denotation of [PLACE ha-yam 'PLACE the sea'] takes the denotation of *leyad* 'near' as a semantic argument (L). Notice that the last line of (18) is exactly what we wanted; P' ('near the sea') is a property of individuals (i.e., a semantic object of type $\langle e, t\rangle$). Moreover, note that the open (i.e., unassigned) individual slot (x) of P' originates in the open slot (x) in the interpretation of PLACE, rather than in the interpretation of *leyad* 'near'.[15]

The above points will become even clearer, once I spell out the semantics of modification by non-locative PPs immediately below.

3.3   Modification by non-locative PPs

Similarly to locative Ps, I assume that non-locative Ps like *about,* do not denote relations (in contrast to canonical modifiers such as A(P)s). But while locative PPs come to denote a property (through N-*Place*) (see 3.2), non-locative PPs do not.

Intuitively speaking, the external slot of non-locative PPs defines the kind of Ns it can combine with by virtue of their denotation (e.g., *about* is appropriate with Ns like *book, story, movie,* etc. that have a 'content' slot in their lexical semantics, termed here as 'theme'). Put differently, the external slot of P relates the appropriate slot of the noun to its denotation, specified by the complement of P. Accordingly, the atomic interpretation of a non-locative P like *about,* is as in (19):

Some of them leave the external slot of the set open, whereas others do not. Since *near* is the argument of PLACE, what is important here is the semantics of PLACE, namely that it has an external slot, rather than whether *near* has one as well.

15.   I assume that: i. When the locative PP functions as a VP-modifier, its *e* variable is identified with the *e* argument of the verb and saturated by the tense operator. ii. The individual slot of a P' functioning as a VP-modifier is either realized as controlled PRO (in spec-PP), or undergoes existential closure (cf. Reinhart & Reuland 1993; Beit Arie 1994) (but see Svenonius, to appear, for a different view).

(19)   The interpretation of *about*
       ⟦about⟧ = $\lambda c.\lambda P.\lambda x.P(x) \wedge c \in$ {the set of themes which x is about}

(A function from 'themes' and properties to a new property, which is the set of individuals with the original (given) property, and whose set of themes includes the given theme.)

The compositional semantics of, for instance, [$_N$' *book about love*], is given in (20a) and (20b):

(20)   Compositional semantics
   a. ⟦[$_{PP}$ about [$_{DP}$ love]]⟧ = ⟦about⟧ (⟦love⟧) = $\lambda P.\lambda x.P(x) \wedge$ ⟦love⟧ ∈ {the set of themes which x is about}

(A function from predicates to properties of individuals, such that both the predicate holds of the individual, and also 'love' belongs to the set of themes of the individual.)

   b. ⟦[$_{NP/N'}$ book[$_{PP}$ about [$_{DP}$ love]]]⟧ = ⟦[$_{PP}$ about [$_{DP}$ love]]⟧ (⟦ book⟧) = $\lambda x.book$ $(x) \wedge$ ⟦love⟧ ∈ {the set of themes which x is about}

(A property of individuals that are 'books', and 'love' is in the set of themes the individual is about.)

Notice that here we only reach the semantic type 'predicate' after *book* is introduced. This is the same kind of predicate as *book* when it appears without a determiner. Indeed, the interpretation in the last line of (20b) is of the same type as $\lambda x.book(x)$, which is desirable given that the distribution of *book* and that of *book about love* is the same, i.e., both can be selected by the various determiners (e.g., *a/the/every*). Moreover, in (20) there is never a constituent with the interpretation, $\lambda x.about(x, ⟦love⟧)$ or $\lambda x.x \in$ {the set of things that are about love}. This is consistent with the intuition that while there is a group {the set of things that are near l}, and therefore this is part of the denotation of the locative P *leyad* 'near' (17b), it is quite difficult to conceive of {the set of things that are about love}.

If non-locative PP-modifiers are necessarily of the type $\langle\langle e, t\rangle, \langle e, t\rangle\rangle$, i.e., functions to be saturated by property denoting elements, rather than by individuals, they would not be able to function as genuine predicates (e.g., in cross-copular constructions), in contrast to their locative counterparts.

In light of the above, an interesting consequence (to be further examined in the future) seems to emerge: If modification of an NP by a PP (as opposed to say, by an AP) is necessarily as proposed above, namely the PP-modifier has to be of the type $\langle\langle e,t \rangle, \langle e, t\rangle\rangle$ (20a), this might be the reason for the fact noted in sub-section 2.3 that simple modification of a nominal by a locative PP is degraded, at least in Hebrew (see (12b)). Specifically, for a locative PP to function as a modifier of an NP, its semantic type has to be 'raised' from $\langle e, t \rangle$ (see (18)), to $\langle\langle e, t \rangle$, $\langle e, t \rangle\rangle$, which might be cumbersome semantically and/or syntactically.[16]

In this connection it should be pointed out that the semantics of locative PPs proposed here is probably equivalent to their more conventional variant, where the locative expression itself is viewed as a two-place relation (cf. Svenonius to appear). The present proposal might prove superior, if indeed the aforementioned fact bearing on the modification of a nominal by a locative PP can be shown to derive from their semantics, as suggested above.

To summarize this section, I have proposed that the source of the predicate-hood of locative PPs, namely of their ability to assign an external semantic role, is the nominal PLACE which heads the locative (extended) projection; while the locative expression saturates the spatial relation slot in the denotation of PLACE, the external referential slot of PLACE (R) is left open, and is eventually saturated via assignment to an appropriate individual argument.

Since the locative phrase (P') has an external semantic role, it can function as a full-fledged predicate, namely assign this role to an external argument, be it the subject of a cross-copular construction (see 2.2, (8a)), or an Op in spec-TP of a locative relative clause (see 2.3, (10a)). A pronoun embedded in a locative phrase can corefer with the external argument of the verb (see 2.1 (6a)), because the former is indeed an argument of a distinct predicate, PLACE (rather than of the locative expression).

If on the right track, the compositional semantics of locatives, based on the nominal structure of locatives assumed here (see (13)), allows us to maintain the uniformly functional classification of the category P within the standard lexical/functional divide, as concerning theta-role assignment.

In principle, the semantics of locative phrases should not differ dramatically across languages. This, however, still leaves some room for variation in their syntax (as long as it fits the compositional semantics of locative phrases, namely includes the N PLACE, and its arguments). In the following section, thus, I will discuss the

---

16. A question arises as to why there are languages in which modification by a locative PP is not as cumbersome. Assuming the proposed semantic analysis, two options come to mind: i. Some languages have a syntactic device facilitating the 'raising' of the semantic type of the locative; ii. modification by locatives involves a reduced relative (i.e., it is not modification, but rather predication). A possible example for the former might be Brazilian Portuguese where locatives include a 'there'-like element (Avelar 2006). English might be an instantiation of the latter, since it can be shown independently that it has reduced relatives where both C and T are not realized (e.g., *The boat floating on the river will sink.*). At this point, this is merely a specula-tion, awaiting cross-linguistic evaluation.

implementation of the nominal locative structure, as pertaining to Hebrew locative PPs.

4. The structure of Hebrew locatives: an exploration

The schematic structure of locative phrases proposed in (13) (repeated in (21)) seems to accommodate Hebrew locative PPs quite well, as illustrated in (22a) for the locative PP *meaxorey ha-šulxan* 'behind the table'; the locative expression *meaxorey* 'behind' occupies the head position P_{LOC}, and the DP *ha-šulxan* 'the-table' is the complement of N-PLACE. This is consistent with the observation that in Hebrew locatives are heads. In fact, following Botwinik-Rotem & Terzi (to appear), Hebrew prepositions, by and large, are construct heads, i.e., heads endowed with the genitive feature (Siloni 2002). They form a Construct State (CS) with the phonetically realized DP that immediately follows them (the complement of *Place* in (22a)). The CS is argued in Siloni (2002) to constitute a single Prosodic Word (PWd), defining a phonological domain in which genitive case is checked at PF (22b).

(21)   Schematic structure of locative PPs
       . . . [$_{PPLOC}$ P_{LOC} [$_{DP}$ [$_{NP}$ PLACE DP]]]

(22)   a.   Hebrew locative structure (preliminary)
            . . . [$_{PPLOC}$ [$_{PLOC}$ *meaxorey*] [$_{DP}$ [$_{NP}$ *Place* [$_{DP}$ *ha-šulxan*]]]]
                              behind   the-table
       b.   Prosodic structure
            . . .[$_{PP}$ *meaxorey ha-šulxan*]$_{PWd}$]
            'behind the table'

Despite its intuitive appeal, I believe there are conceptual as well as empirical reasons to doubt the syntactic analysis of Hebrew locative PPs in (22a). These are elaborated in the following sub-sections.[17]

4.1   Setting the stage

The term 'locative expression', on a par with terms like 'demonstrative' or 'pronominal suffix', is a descriptive term, implying very little as to the syntactic behavior and structural position of the elements it describes. For instance, English

---

17.   Importantly, as will be clear in the following subsections, the revision of the structure in (22a) has no bearing on the claim that Hebrew locative PPs form a CS, because, regardless of the structural revision, the locative and the following DP remain phonetically adjacent.

demonstratives are analyzed as D-elements, but in Hebrew they behave on a par with adjectival modifiers.

In the same vein, it appears to be the case that locatives across languages do not have the same syntactic status, namely, they are not necessarily heads. Terzi (2005b,c 2006) argues that Greek locatives are phrasal modifiers of the N-*Place*, base-generated in the specifier of the functional projection of *Place,* symbolized as XP, while Ploc is phonetically null in Greek (in most cases). Accordingly, the structure of Greek locatives can be schematized as in (23) (abstracting away from certain details), using the locative *epano* 'on' for illustration:[18]

(23)   Greek locative structure
$$\ldots [_{\text{PPLOC}} \, P_{\text{LOC}} \, [_{\text{DP}} \, D \, [_{\text{XP}} \, [\text{epano}] \, X \, [_{\text{NP}} \, \text{PLACE DP} \,]]]]$$
$$\phantom{\ldots [_{\text{PPLOC}} \, P_{\text{LOC}} \, [_{\text{DP}} \, D \, [_{\text{XP}} \, [}\text{on}$$

Greek offers good empirical evidence for the structure in (23); both for the phrasal status of the locatives but, more importantly, for their structural (base) position below P_{LOC}. Now, if a functional projection above NP-PLACE, XP, plays such a central role in the structure of locative PPs in one language (e.g., Greek), it may be taken to suggest that this projection is typical of locative PPs, rather than being a language specific property. Based on this line of reasoning alone, it is worth examining whether such projection exists in other languages, more precisely, whether this projection, rather than the PP, is the base position of locatives in a given language (Hebrew, in our case).

With this in mind, and given that Hebrew locatives are heads (unlike their Greek counterparts), let us revise the Hebrew locative structure sketched in (22a), namely merge the Hebrew locative at the X-head, as shown in (24), (rather than in P_{LOC}, compare with (22a)):

(24)   Hebrew locative structure (revised)
$$\ldots [_{\text{PPLOC}} \, P_{\text{LOC}} \, [_{\text{DP}} \, D \, [_{\text{XP}} \, [_{\text{X}} \, \textit{meaxorey}] \, [_{\text{NP}} \, \text{PLACE} \, [_{\text{DP}} \, \textit{ha-šulxan} \,]]]]]$$
$$\phantom{\ldots [_{\text{PPLOC}} \, P_{\text{LOC}} \, [_{\text{DP}} \, D \, [_{\text{XP}} \, [_{\text{X}} \, }\text{behind} \text{the-table}$$

From a theory-internal perspective, generalizing the structure of locatives across languages, in our case Greek and Hebrew is, of course, desirable. The question is whether it can be justified on independent grounds. I believe the following can be viewed as initial support for taking this path (additional empirical evidence bearing on the question will be discussed in the following sub-section).

---

18.   Recall that in the semantic analysis of locatives proposed here, a locative expression is an argument of PLACE, rather than its modifier. In this connection, it is worth mentioning that given a variety of semantic analyses involving adverbials and quantifiers, in which either syntactic heads or syntactic phrases may correspond to semantic arguments, the head/phrase distinction has no bearing on the semantic analysis of locatives proposed in section 3.2.

Let me note first that although the schematic structure of locative PPs, which does not include the XP, appears quite accommodating for Hebrew locative phrases (22a), there are phenomena involving locatives for which it is not satisfactory.

For instance, in colloquial Hebrew some locative expressions can be prefixed by the definite article (*ha-* 'the') and take a nominal complement introduced by *šel* ('of'), as illustrated in (25). In this case, the locative actually forms a full-fledged DP, rather than a PP. Base-generating Hebrew locatives below D enclosing the NP headed by PLACE, as in (24), allows a straightforward account of this phenomenon; presumably, *ha-mitaxat* 'the-under', similarly to regular Hebrew nouns (e.g., *ha-sefer* 'the-book'), raises to D to check its definiteness feature realized by *ha-* (cf. Siloni 1997).[19] In contrast, if the locative is necessarily merged in P_{LOC} above D (22a), it would be difficult to explain how its definiteness is checked.

(25) $[_{DP}$ (kol) $[_{XP}$ ha-mitaxat $[_{NP}$ PLACE šel ha-oto]]] haya meluxlax
       all   the-under   of the-car was dirty
     The whole underneath/bottom of the car was dirty.

Further, under the natural assumption, Hebrew locative pronouns *šam* 'there', and *po/kan* 'here', on a par with personal pronouns, are D-heads, occurring without a complement, and selected by P_{LOC}, as shown in (26) (for arguments that locative pronouns are PPs, see Kayne 1984). The fact that they cannot co-occur with locative expressions (e.g., **leyad/*al/*meaxorey šam* 'near/on/behind there') follows straightforwardly from the structure of locative PPs in (24); by assumption, the merge position of locatives (XP), being the complement of D, is missing in (26). If, on the other hand, locative expressions are base-generated in P_{LOC}, this has to be stipulated (see also section 4.3 for an additional argument against base-generating the locative pronouns in P_{LOC}).

(26) $[_{PPLOC} P_{LOC} [_{DP}$ šam]]
             there

Moreover, the proposal made in Botwinik-Rotem and Terzi (to appear) regarding the possibility to phonetically realize PLACE in Greek (27a), and the impossibility to do so in Hebrew (27b) can be viewed as additional support for the base position of Hebrew locatives immediately above NP-PLACE:

(27)   a.   To   kato   meros
          the under place

---

19.   Note that the occurrence with the definite article, in itself, does not entail that locatives are nouns; Hebrew *ha-* is an agreeing prefix of nominal modifiers, which attaches to a variety of elements (*ha-yeled ha-lo mukar* 'the-boy *the-not* known', *ha-yeled ha-me'od ayef* 'the-boy *the-very* tired', *ba-pa'am ha-ani lo yodaat kama* 'in+the-time *the-I* don't know how many', meaning roughly: I don't know how many times [I have to tell you this]).

    b.   *ha-mitaxat   (ha)-makom/*mitaxat (ha)-makom
           the-under   (the)-place/under (the)-place

The proposal is based on the assumption that the abstract noun PLACE is formally licensed via incorporation into a c-commanding head (similarly to the proposals of den Dikken (1995) and Kayne (2000) following Freeze (1992) with respect to the abstract dative TO in English). If the incorporating (the hosting) head is X, which is occupied by the locative in Hebrew (24), but (phonetically) vacant in Greek (23) by virtue of the fact that the locative is not a head but a phrase in spec-XP, the contrast in (27) can be accounted for in the following way: it may be the case that when the hosting head is phonetically realized, PLACE must remain silent, as is the case in Hebrew (27b), but when the incorporating head is (phonetically) vacant, phonetic realization of PLACE, as in Greek (27a), is possible.

    Finally, it is important to note that given the compositional semantics of locative phrases in section 3.2, in particular the claim that the locative is an argument of PLACE, the base position of the locative should be 'closer' to N-PLACE than it is in (22a). A couple of reasonable options would be: (i) inside the NP of PLACE, presumably in its specifier (Tali Siloni, Marcel den Dikken p.c.), but given the claim that Hebrew locatives are heads, this option seems less likely (but not excluded), or (ii) in a functional projection immediately dominating NP-PLACE. On the assumption that the DP enclosing NP-PLACE is not a candidate, being reserved for the external referential argument of PLACE, such a projection, namely XP, is ready available in (24), but absent from the more minimal (22a).

    Given this preliminary support for analyzing Hebrew locative PPs on a par with their Greek counterparts, let us now explore the nature of P enclosing DP of PLACE in Hebrew.

4.2   P in the Hebrew locative structure

Assuming the revised structure of Hebrew locative PPs in (24) (repeated below as (28a)), a question arises as to the syntactic function of P_{LOC} in this structure, and in particular, its relation to the locatives. For instance, do locatives, possibly together with the incorporated PLACE, move to P_{LOC}, as shown in (28b)?

(28)   a. $\ldots$ [$_{PPLOC}$ P_{LOC} [$_{DP}$ [$_{XP}$ [$_X$ *meaxorey* [$_{NP}$ PLACE DP]]]]]
                             behind

       b. $\ldots$ [$_{PPLOC}$ [$_{PLOC}$ *meaxorey* (+ *Place*) [$_{DP}$ t [$_{XP}$ [$_X$ t [$_{NP}$ (PLACE) DP]]]]]]
                     behind

Based on the observation that in the familiar variety of languages (e.g., Hebrew, English, Greek, Russian, etc.) location is realized as a PP, P_{LOC} is the functional head that syntactically represents location, serving as the locus for semantic computation that involves other elements, on a par with C in the clausal domain. Formally, one can posit that P has the feature [LOC] which has to be checked against an appropriate element (head or phrase). Consequently, on the assumption that locatives are base-generated in X, they will be attracted to P_{LOC}, on a par with, say T moving into C in main clauses in V2 languages, or in interrogatives in even a wider variety of languages.[20] This movement will be unnecessary, and therefore should not occur, if the feature [LOC] is realized by an element originating in the P-head.

This, of course, raises the following question: What can be base-generated in P selecting a DP which encloses PLACE in Hebrew?

Terzi (2006) argues that the light P *se,* which is used alongside the light P *apo* in Greek locative PPs to introduce the DP following the locative modifier (29a), realizes P_{LOC} when it is used without the locative modifier (29b). (The sentences in (29) have similar, but not identical meanings.) With this in mind, in what follows I will focus on Hebrew basic locatives *be-* 'in', and *al* 'on', and argue that, unlike other Hebrew locatives, they originate in P_{LOC}, rather than in X.

(29) a. To vivlio ine epano sto   grafio.
          the book   is   on   *se*-the desk
      b. To vivlio ine sto   grafio.
          the book   is   *se*-the desk
          'The book is on the desk.'

Hebrew basic locatives *be-* 'in', and *al* 'on' differ from the rest of Hebrew locatives in not having a fixed semantic interpretation. As a result, their distribution is wider; they occur in locative contexts admitting the corresponding complex locatives with a highly specific interpretation, as well as in contexts in which their locative interpretation is less specific, and even in contexts where they are arguably devoid of any locative interpretation (e.g., *somex al* 'relies on'), and therefore irrelevant for the present discussion.

The idea that Hebrew basic locatives originate in P, rather than in X, is motivated in the following subsection, examining the instances of basic locatives in which their meaning overlaps with the corresponding complex ones.

---

20. Like T-to-C movement, the movement into P_{LOC} does not necessarily have to be overt. As far as Hebrew is concerned, I will assume overt movement. Unfortunately, since Hebrew locatives cannot be separated from the following DP, under no circumstances, this movement cannot be established using word-order manipulations; the locative will always immediately precede the DP, and be preceded by all other material (e.g., degree modifiers).

4.2.1   Hebrew basic locatives and their complex counterparts

In some cases Hebrew basic locatives *be-* 'in', and *al* 'on' are simply the abbreviated forms of their complex counterparts: *be-tox* literally, 'in interior', meaning, 'inside', and *al pney* literally, 'on (sur)face', meaning, 'on', respectively. That is, in these cases every instance of the complex locative (e.g., *be-tox* 'inside') can be replaced by the corresponding simple one (e.g., *be-*'in'), with no change in meaning. As shown in (30a), we can use either *be-* 'in' or *be-tox* 'inside' with 'the drawer', as it has interior, but not with 'the table', which, in itself, does not have interior space. The same holds for *al* 'on' and *al pney* 'on the surface' (30b); both can be used with 'the table', as it has a surface, but not with 'the drawer', which has mainly the interior:[21]

(30) a.   ha-et   ba-megira/be-tox ha-megira/*ba-šulxan
           the-pen   in+the-drawer/inside the-drawer/in+the-table
           'The pen is in the drawer/inside the drawer/*in the table.'

      b.   ha-etim   hitpazru al ha-šulxan /al pney ha-šulxan/*al ha-megira
           the-pens scattered on the-table/on surface the-table/on the-drawer
           'The pens scattered on the table/on the surface of the table/*on the drawer.'

For simplicity of presentation, I will focus on *be-tox* 'inside'. Given its clearly bi-morphemic structure (comprising of *be-* and *-tox*), and the fact that *be-* can be used independently (30a), it is reasonable to analyze *be-tox* as in (31a), with *tox* originating in X, and *be-* in P_{LOC}. Naturally, then, the instances of the locative *be-* 'in' which are interchangeable with *be-tox* 'inside', namely the abbreviated version of *be-tox*, has essentially the same representation, with the only difference that the locative morpheme merged in X (*tox* in (31a)) is phonetically null, symbolized as TOX (31b):

(31) a.   . . . [$_{PPLOC}$ [$_{PLOC}$ *be-* [$_{DP}$ [$_{XP}$ [$_X$ *tox* [$_{NP}$ PLACE   *ha-megira*]]]]]]
                          in   interior   the-drawer

      b.   . . . [$_{PPLOC}$ [$_{PLOC}$ *be-* [$_{DP}$ [$_{XP}$ [$_X$ *tox* [$_{NP}$ PLACE *ha- megira*]]]]]]
                          in   'interior'   the-drawer
           'inside/in the drawer'

Note that in the complex locative *be-tox* 'inside', the head *tox* satisfies the spatial relation slot of *Place*, and the contribution of *be-* 'in' is trivial, entailed by the meaning of *tox*.

The analysis of the complex locative *be-tox* (31a) as involving amalgamation of morphemes realizing two syntactic heads, P and X, is plausible (cf. Terzi 2006 for certain English locatives). Importantly, Hebrew provides a quite compelling empirical

---

21.   Note also that the rather popular example used to illustrate the semantic difference between 'in' and 'inside' in say, English (but also in other languages) (i.e., one can be 'inside' a box only if he/she is properly contained by the box) is not replicated in Hebrew. That is, *be-tox* 'inside' can be used in both cases – properly or partially contained.

evidence supporting this analysis; it can be shown that the complex locative *be-tox* 'inside' cannot be analyzed as a single complex head (formed in the lexicon), originating in X, supporting the idea that Hebrew basic locatives are merged in P enclosing DP of PLACE, rather than in X. We turn to such evidence directly below, and will complete the picture in (31), namely discuss the representation of basic locatives whose locative meaning does not overlap with the complex ones, after that.

In addition to the aforementioned complex locatives, *be-tox* 'inside' and *al pney* 'on', Hebrew has a somewhat different group of complex, bi-morphemic locatives, all of which are prefixed with *mi/me-*: e.g., *mitaxat, meal, mimul* ('under', 'above', 'across').[22]

Recall that Hebrew Ps, by and large are construct heads forming a single Prosodic Word (PWd) with the following phonetically realized DP, whose case is checked at PF by virtue of being part of the CS. A typical property of construct heads is that they are phonologically weak. Therefore, phonologically complex, bi-morphemic heads are not likely to be construct heads. Indeed, it has been observed that construct heads are necessarily simplex (see Botwinik-Rotem & Terzi 2006 for this effect in nominal constructs, and Siloni 2002 for adjectival constructs). Consequently, complex locatives prefixed by *mi-* are argued in Botwinik-Rotem & Terzi (to appear) to be parsed by the phonological component as independent prosodic words, forming a Free State (FS) with the following DP ('the house' in (32)) whose case is checked by the dative *le-* (rather than in a CS):

(32)   hu   haya [$_{PP}$ mitaxat]$_{PWd}$ la-bayit]$_{PWd}$]
       he/it was   *mi*under   *le*+the-house
       'It/he was under the house.'

Now, clearly, this is not the case with *be-tox* 'inside', which does not allow its complement to be introduced by the dative *le-* (33), indicating that it does form a construct with the following DP:

(33)   hu   haya be-tox *la-bayit/ha-bayit
       he   was inside *le*+the-house/the-house
       'He was inside the house.'

Since, as mentioned above, construct heads are necessarily simplex, we can conclude that *be-tox*, unlike *mitaxat*, is not a single complex head. Rather, each of its

---

22.   This instance of *mi-*, although homophonous with the directional *mi-* 'from', is semantically vacuous. This is particularly clear in (i), where both the directional *el* 'to' and the prefixal *mi-* occur, and the sentence is not contradictory in any sense; it is completely natural and fully grammatical.

(i)   hu hitgalgel el   mitaxat la-bayit
       he rolled   to   *mi*under *le*+the-house
       'It/he rolled under the house.'

parts occupies a different head-position; *tox* is the locative merged in X, and *be-* is in P, as suggested in (31a) above.

Given this, we can maintain the analysis in (31b), in which Hebrew basic locatives used as the abbreviated forms of their complex counterparts originate in P enclosing the DP of PLACE.

4.2.2   *Additional instances of basic locatives*

Needless to say, not all instances of the basic locative *be-* 'in' (or *al* 'on') are interchangeable with the complex *be-tox* 'inside' (or *al pney* 'on surface'). For instance, (34a) does not entail (34b). Moreover, there are, of course, locations which do not have an interior (e.g., air, Paris), and therefore cannot combine with *be-tox* 'inside' (34c), but only with *be-* 'in' (34d):

(34)   a.   dan   be-bet-sefer
            Dan in-house-book (house-book = 'school')
            'Dan is at school.'
       b.   dan   be-tox   bet-sefer
            Dan in-side   house-book
            'Dan is inside the school.'
       c.   *dan   be-tox   Pariz/avir
            Dan   inside   Paris/air
       d.   dan   be-Pariz/avir
            Dan in-Paris/air
            'Dan is in Paris/the air.'

Keeping in line with the analysis of basic locatives in (31b) (repeated as (35a)), and taking into account that the meaning of these other instances of basic locatives is less specific than of their abbreviated counterparts, it is reasonable to assume that the representation of the former is as shown in (35b); *be-* 'in' (or *al* 'on') is base-generated in P_{LOC} while X is realized by an abstract locative expression corresponding to AT:[23]

(35)   a.   ... [$_{PPLOC}$ [$_{PLOC}$ *be-* [$_{DP}$ [$_{XP}$ [$_X$ *TOX* [$_{NP}$ PLACE *ha- megira*]]]]]]
                          in   'interior'   the-drawer
            'inside/in the drawer'

---

[23]. Keeping the presence of the XP projection constant, as deriving from the semantics of locatives, there are two logically possible alternatives: i. *be-* 'in' (or *al* 'on') originates in X, like other locatives, contributing non-trivially to the compositional semantics of the locative phrase (Idan Landau p.c.); ii. *be-* 'in' is base-generated in D of PLACE, and X is realized by AT. Anticipating the following discussion regarding the interaction between basic locatives and directionals in Hebrew (section 4.3), these analyses will force us to posit obligatory movement of the basic locatives to P_{LOC}, in order to account for their inability to co-occur with the directionals. This is not ruled out on general grounds, and therefore should be kept in mind.

b. … [$_{PPLOC}$ [$_{PLOC}$ *be-* [$_{DP}$ [$_{XP}$ [$_X$ *AT* [$_{NP}$ PLACE *bet-sefer*]]]]]]
             in   school
    'at school'

At this stage, (35b) is a reasonable suggestion, which will gain more support in the following section, where I examine the interaction between Hebrew (basic) locatives and directionals such as *el* 'to' and *mi-* 'from'.

Before we conclude this part of the discussion, I would like to draw our attention to the fact mentioned earlier, regarding the inability of Hebrew locative pronouns (e.g., *šam* 'there') to occur with locatives, basic or non-basic alike, (36):

(36)   a.   hu gar (*be-) šam
              he   lives in-there
              'He lives there.'
       b.   hu gar (*leyad) šam
              he   lives near   there

Recall that I assume that Hebrew locative pronouns are D-heads occurring without a complement, embedded in the PP-shell (37). The facts in (36) were originally invoked to support the base-generation of Hebrew locatives below D, namely attributing the impossibility of the combinations in (36) to the unavailability of the structural position in (37) to merge the locatives (i.e., XP). Despite the distinction we have drawn between basic and non-basic locatives, especially the claim that the former are merged in P, which is present in (37), the facts in (36) are accounted for. Locatives, according to the analysis advocated here, are related directly or indirectly to the presence of the XP projection; non-basic locatives are base-generated in X, while with the basic ones, X is realized by an abstract locative element (TOX, AT, see (35)). The XP, however, is a functional projection of N-PLACE that is missing in the structure of locative pronouns (37). Hence, we do not expect any kind of locatives, basic or non-basic, to occur with locative pronouns.

(37)   [$_{PP}$ P [$_{DP}$ *šam*]]
               there

Building on the analysis of Hebrew locatives developed so far, in the following section I examine additional data, involving directional Ps, which, I believe, is instrumental to clarifying the variety of function carried out by P enclosing the DP of PLACE.

4.3   The function(s) of P enclosing DP of Place

According to the analysis of Hebrew locative PPs developed so far, P enclosing the DP of PLACE can be phonetically null, associated with the feature [LOC], and triggering movement of the locative from X to P. Alternatively, based on the discussion in the previous section, it can be occupied by the basic locatives, *be-* 'in', *al* 'on', realizing this feature, in which case movement of the locative into P does not occur.

Under widely held views, directional Ps occupy a head position above the locative PP, taking either a DP or a locative PP as their complement (Koopman 2000; van Riemsdijk & Huybregts 2001; den Dikken 2006; Svenonius 2007; to appear, Noonan 2005). This is illustrated in (38) and (39), using Hebrew directional Ps, *el/le-* 'to', and *mi-* 'from', to which the following discussion is limited.[24, 25] However, certain Hebrew facts challenge this view, suggesting that (at least) in Hebrew, basic locatives and directionals occupy the same structural position, namely P enclosing the DP of PLACE.

(38)   a.   hu   hitgalgel   el   ha-šulxan
             he   rolled   to   the-table
             'It/he rolled to the table.'

---

24.   In the directional context, *le-* and *el* 'to' are almost completely interchangeable (ia). However, unlike *el* which is clearly directional, *le-* is ambiguous, used also as the dative marker (ib). Moreover, unlike *el*, (directional) *le-* is quite marginal with a locative PP (ic). This might be related to its morpho-synatctic status as a D-clitic, suggested in Botwinik-Rotem 2004.

(i)   a.   hu   nasa   le/el -dina
            he   went   *le/el*-Dina
            'He went to Dina.'

      b.   hu   natan   et   ha-sefer   le-dina/*el-dina
            he   gave   ACC. the-book   *le*-Dina/*el*-Dina
            'He gave the book to Dina.'

      c.   hu   hitgalgel   le-(??meaxorey)   šulxan
            he   rolled   to   behind   table
            'It/he rolled to the table.'

25.   On the semantic side, directional PPs including a locative phrase ((39a) repeated in (ia)) differ from those without such a phrase ((38a) repeated in (ib)), as shown in (iia) and (iib), respectively (recall that L is the spatial relation slot in the denotation of *Place*):

(i)   a.   hu hitgalgel   el   mitaxat ha-šulxan
            he rolled   to   under   the-table
            'It/he rolled under the table.'

      b.   hu   hitgalgel   el   ha-šulxan
            he   rolled   to   the-table
            'It/he rolled to the table.'

(ii)   a.   L gets $\lambda l.$\{the set of things that are under l\} l = the location of the table
      b.   L gets $\lambda l.$\{l\} (i.e., the set of locations which are the location of the table; a one-member set)

    b.   hu   yaca   mi-ha-aron
         he   exited from-the-closet
         'It/he went out from the closet.'

(39) a.   hu   hitgalgel el   mitaxat/meaxorey ha-šulxan
         he   rolled   to   under/behind   the-table
         'It/he rolled under/behind the table.'
    b.   hu   yaca   mi-mitaxat/meaxorey ha-aron
         he   exited from under/behind   the-closet
         'It/he went out from under/behind the closet.'

Following standard views regarding the position of directionals outside the locative PP, and integrating them with the analysis of Hebrew locative PPs developed here, the combination of a directional P with a locative PP (e.g., (39a)) would be represented as in (40). The complex locative (e.g., *mitaxat* 'under') originates in X (it is a complex head, see the discussion in section 4.2), and moves into P_{LOC}, checking the latter's feature:

(40) ...$[_{PPDIR}$ el $[_{PPLOC}$ mitaxat$_i$ $[_{DP}$ $[_{XP}$ t$_i$ $[_{NP}$ PLACE ha-šulxan$]]]]]$
           to   under   the-table

As we have seen in the previous section, complex locatives such as *be-tox* 'inside' and *al pney* 'on', have a different morpho-syntactic structure, involving two syntactic heads, P and X. But given the standard position of the directional outside the locative PP, there should be no problem with combining the directional with these locatives as well. Surprisingly, however, there is. The examples in (41), where the directionals are combined with *be-tox* and *al pney* ('inside', 'on') are completely ungrammatical.

(41) a. *hu hitkarev   el al   pney   ha-šulxan
         he came closer to on surface the-table
    b. *hu   nixnas   el be-tox   ha-bayit
         he   entered to in-interior the-house
    c. *ha-xalalit   himri'a mi-be-tox   ha-bayit
         the-spaceship took off from-in-interior the-house
    d. *ha-xalalit   hitraxaka mi-al   pney   ha-yare'ax[26]
         the-spaceship went away from-on surface the-moon

---

26. For some speakers (41d) might have a grammatical reading, which is irrelevant for the present discussion:

(i) ha-xalalit   hitraxaka meal [pney   ha-yare'ax]
    the-spaceship went away above surface the-moon
    Intended meaning (?): The spaceship made its way above the face of the moon.

From the syntactic point of view, this is quite unexpected; there are enough head-positions to accommodate the combinations in (41), as schematized in (42):

(42)   ...[$_{PPDIR}$ *el/mi-* [$_{PPLOC}$ *be/al* [$_{DP}$ [$_{XP}$ *tox/pney*   [$_{NP}$ PLACE *ha-bayit/ha-yare'ax*]]]]]
           to/from   in/on   interior/surface   the-house/the-moon

One might attempt a semantically based approach to account for the facts in (41). But this is clearly untenable in our case. Intuitively speaking, there is no semantic clash between the meanings of the directionals (to, from) and the meanings of the locatives in (41); motion towards or outwards the interior or exterior of an object is conceivable. More importantly, the examples in (41) become fully grammatical, if we just remove the basic locatives:

(43)   a.   hu   hitkarev   el   pney   ha-šulxan
           he   came closer to   surface the-table
           'He came closer to (the surface of) the table.'
     b.   hu   nixnas   el   tox   ha-bayit
           he   entered to   interior the-house
           'He entered inside the house.'
     c.   ha-xalalit   himri'a   mi-tox   ha-bayit
           the-spaceship   took off from-interior the-house
           'The spaceship took off from inside the house.'
     d.   ha-xalalit   hitraxaka mi-pney   ha-yare'ax
           the-spaceship   went away   from-surface the-moon
           'The spaceship made its way from the moon.'

Note also that removing the non-basic locatives (*tox, pney*), and leaving the basic ones (*be-, al*), does not have the same ameliorating effect, resulting in ungrammatical sentences again:

(44)   a.   *hu hitkarev   el   al   ha-šulxan
            he came closer to   on   the-table
     b.   *hu nixnas   el   ba-bayit
            he entered   to   in+the-house
     c.   *ha-xalalit   himri'a   mi-ba-bayit
           the-spaceship   took off from-in+the-house
     d.   *ha-xalalit   hitraxaka mi-al   ha-yare'ax
           the-spaceship   went away   from-on the-moon

Summarizing the facts observed so far, directionals can combine with complex locative heads, originating in X (e.g., *mitaxat* 'under') (39). They can also combine with complex locatives involving two syntactic heads, P and X (e.g., *be-tox* 'inside'), but only if the P-part (e.g., *be-* 'in') is missing (43), and they cannot combine with basic locatives (44).

All these facts can be accounted for, if we assume that basic locatives and directionals 'compete' for the same structural position. According to this line of reasoning, and given the position of basic locatives established in the previous section, namely P enclosing the DP of PLACE, we conclude, thus, that this same position is also the position of Hebrew directionals, as schematized in (45).[27]

(45) a. $\ldots[_{PPLOC} [_{PLOC} be\text{-}/al] [_{DP} [_{XP} [_X [_{NP} \text{PLACE DP}]]]]]$ locative PP
in/on

  b. $\ldots[_{PPDIR} [_{PDIR} mi//el/le\text{-}] [_{DP} [_{(XP)} [_{(X)} [_{NP} \text{PLACE DP}]]]]]$ directional PP
from//to

According to the structures in (45), P enclosing DP of PLACE can be occupied by a basic locative or directional, each realizing the appropriate feature, [LOC] and [DIR], respectively. In this case, if the DP of PLACE includes a locative merged in X, this locative will, of course, stay in situ, as the feature of P is realized by the elements originating there. Consequently, directionals can combine with complex locative heads like *mitaxat* 'under', leaving them intact (i.e., without truncating the prefix *mi-*), because *mi-* is part of the X-head, rather than P (46a). In contrast, *be-* of a complex locative like *be-tox* 'inside' occupies P enclosing the DP of PLACE (46b). Since, by hypothesis, this is also the position of directionals, when a directional combines with *be-tox,* there is no P position left for *be-* of *be-tox,* and it is omitted (46c). By the same rationale, basic locatives and directionals cannot possibly co-occur (44), because both originate in the same structural position, P enclosing the DP of PLACE.

(46) a. $\ldots[_{PPDIR} [_{PDIR} mi//el] [_{DP} [_{XP} [_X mitaxat] [_{NP} \text{PLACE } ha\text{-}bayit]]]]$
from//to   under   the-house

  b. $\ldots [_{PPLOC} [_{PLOC} be\text{-}] [_{DP} [_{XP} [_X tox] [_{NP} \text{PLACE } ha\text{-}bayit]]]]$
in   interior   the-house

  c. $\ldots[_{PPDIR} [_{PDIR} mi//el] [_{DP} [_{XP} [_X tox] [_{NP} \text{PLACE } ha\text{-}bayit]]]]$ $be\text{-} \to \emptyset$
from//to   interior   the-house

Notice that locative pronouns (e.g., *šam* 'there'), which were shown in the previous sections to not co-occur with locatives (e.g., **leayd šam* 'near there'), do occur with directional Ps in Hebrew (47). This is fully consistent with the analysis of directionals proposed above (45b), which embodies the claim that directionals are generated in P selecting DP-PLACE.

---

27. I take the obligatory presence of XP with P_{LOC} to be dictated by the compositional semantics of locative PPs in accordance with their structure in (24). For the optionality of the XP with P_{DIR}, see note 25.

(47)   hu gilgel oto   mi-kan/le-kan[28]
       he rolled it-ACC from-here/to-here
       'He rolled it from here/here.'

Recall that locatives are related (directly or indirectly) to the XP projection (see 4.2.2), which is missing in the structure of locative pronouns ((repeated in (48)). In contrast, such a relation is not assumed for directionals; they can combine with the DP of PLACE including an XP inhibited by a locative expression, or without it (see also note25). Therefore, nothing prevents the directionals from occupying the P-head in the structure of a locative pronoun (48), namely occurring with locative pronouns, in accordance with the facts in (47).

(48) $[_{PP} P [_{DP} šam]]$
                    there

To summarize this section so far, based on conceptual as well as empirical evidence, I have explored the idea that the (extended nominal) structure of Hebrew locative PPs is richer than the schematic structure we have started with, closely resembling the structure of Greek locative PPs argued for in the work of Terzi (2005a,b,c, 2006). In particular, I have examined the base-position of Hebrew locative expressions and showed that most of them (modulo the basic ones)

---

28.   The directional preposition *el*, unlike *le-*, cannot combine with locative pronouns (ia). Interestingly, *el*, but not *le-*, is also ungrammatical with geographic names (ib,c):

(i)   a.   hu nasa   *el/le-šam
           he went   to there
           'He went there.'
      b.   hu   nasa   el ha-ir/*el   pariz
           he   went   to the-city/to Paris
Compare: c.   hu   nasa   la-ir/le-pariz
           he   went   to+the-city/to-Paris
           'He went to the city/to Paris.'

Geographic names are, in some sense, like proper names; the former are proper names of places, and the latter are proper names of individuals. Although I have no principled explanation as to why *el* is limited in this particular way, I find the phenomenon reminiscent of the phenomenon attested in the nominal domain in a variety of languages, among them Hebrew, where a definite article cannot combine with proper names and pronouns.

It is worth noting that the sensitivity of geographic names to the directional Ps is not limited to Hebrew. In German, for instance, the directional P *zu* 'to' cannot introduce geographic names and *nach* 'to' is used instead (Noonan 2006). Interestingly, though, the noted sensitivity seems to go in a different direction in German as compared to Hebrew. While in Hebrew the 'pure' directional *el* is replaced by the ambiguous (dative/directional) *le-* (ic), in German it is the other way around – the ambiguous *zu* (dative/directional) is replaced by the more specific *nach*.

originate in a functional projection XP, whose exact identity is yet to be clarified, but which is positioned right above the NP headed by the nominal head of the locative projection, PLACE. I have also addressed the role of the P-head in the structure of Hebrew locative PPs, and suggested that it should be viewed on a par with the role of a functional head like C, in the sense that it might be associated with an appropriate feature, [LOC], triggering movement of the locatives, or be occupied by basic locatives or directionals, realizing the feature of P.

The upshot of the analysis of Hebrew locative (and directional) PPs advocated here is that the notion of location associated with these PPs is contributed by the nominal head PLACE, whose extended projection includes the locative expressions, as well as the functional head P, resulting in what we call a locative PP.

The centrality of the extended projection in the present analysis of locative PPs is reminiscent of the analyses of Dutch and German locative PPs in Koopman 2000; and den Dikken 2006. Abstracting away from the details, the analyses differ, however, as to the nature of the extended projection of locative PPs – nominal vs. prepositional. This calls into question the plausibility of the nominal, as compared to the prepositional core of the extended projection of locative PPs.

4.4 The head of the extended locative projection: N-Place vs. P

As mentioned at the very beginning of this paper, in some analyses of Dutch and German locatives, a locative P is argued to be lexical, rather than functional, because it is able to support additional functional heads such as PLACE, DEG and C (49a) (cf. Koopman 2000; den Dikken 2006), namely to head an extended projection, in the sense of Grimshaw 2000.[29] The notion of the extended locative projection is quite central in the current proposal as well, but it is a nominal extended projection, which includes P_{LOC} as a functional head, rather than being headed by it (49b).

(49)   a. $\ldots[_{CP} \text{C} [_{DegP} \text{Deg} [_{PlaceP} \text{PLACE} [_{PP} \text{P DP}]]]]$
        b. $\ldots[_{PPLOC} P_{LOC} [_{DP} \text{D} [_{XP} \text{X} [_{NP} \text{PLACE DP}]]]]$

Whether it is possible to accommodate the variety of phenomena attested in German and Dutch by the structure of locative PPs argued for here is an important question, the answer to which lies beyond the scope of this paper. Here I merely wish to point out that as far as the nature of the extended projection in each of the proposals is concerned, the nominal core in the current proposal (49b) is, at least, as justified as its prepositional rival (49a).

---

29. The structure in (49a) is highly schematic, conveying only the general idea behind the proposals mentioned in the text. For a much more detailed proposal, whose theoretical as well as empirical argumentation is compelling, see den Dikken 2006.

Note first that the mere existence of additional functional structure does not necessarily lead to the conclusion that P is lexical (and therefore heads the projection). A lexical head denoting location (N-PLACE) in the structure argued for here (49b) is (and probably must be) able to support the functional projections related to its denotation; minimally, X and P_{LOC}, but possibly also Deg.

In this relation, consider a possible alternative for degree phrases like *two meters*, which are typically related to locative PPs as their modifiers. In principle, modifiers can be accommodated as adjuncts of locative PPs, not necessarily as additional functional projections. Moreover, the empirical evidence motivating the postulation of DegP, namely the relative order between these modifiers and *r*-pronouns in Dutch, i.e., whether the modifier precedes the *r*-pronoun or rather follows it, might be accounted for if we assume some flexibility regarding the relative placement of specifiers and adjuncts.[30] Specifically, the *r*-pronoun will precede the modifier, if the latter is adjoined below spec-PP, but follow it, if adjunction is above spec-PP. Since spec-PP in our analysis is not a thematic specifier, there seems to be no compelling theoretical reasons to believe that such variable placement of specifiers and adjuncts should be ruled out (Marcel den Dikken p.c.)

Finally, regarding the mere occurrence of the *r*-pronouns in Dutch, I believe the analysis developed here might have a certain advantage. Following van Riemsdijk (1978:25), *r*-pronouns in Dutch are a property of the category P, in the sense that they co-occur with any P, locative and non-locative alike (see note 30), and only with them. In Koopman 2000, and den Dikken's 2006 analyses of locative PPs, *r*-pronouns are assumed to obligatory raise to spec-Place, above the PP, for their licensing. Consequently, the occurrence of these pronouns in non-locative contexts, which presumably lack Place, is rather surprising (e.g., *Ik had er op gerekend*, literally: I had there on counted, meaning: 'I had counted on it'). Under the present assumptions, locative and non-locative P is essentially the same; it is a functional head in the nominal extended projection. Specifically, PP is the outer shell of a DP like 'love' in 'about love', or of a DP like 'PLACE the table' in

---

30. In Dutch [-human] pronominal complements of Ps, regardless of the function of the corresponding prepositions, are systematically replaced with special pronouns preceding the P(i). These pronouns are usually called *r*-pronouns (following van Riemsdijk 1978), as they have the *r*-sound in their phonological form (e.g., *er/daar,* 'there'):

(i)   a.   Ik   had   *op het/ er op   gerekend
           I   had   on it/ there on   counted
      b.   Hij   gaat   *voor het/er voor   altijd   golfen
           He   goes   before it/there before   always   play-golf
      c.   Hij   zat   *achter   het/daar   achter
           He   sits   behind   it/there   behind

'under the table'. On a reasonable assumption that r-pronouns are, in fact, licensed in spec-PP, though they may originate in spec-PLACE, their occurrence with any P is expected.

5. Summary

In this paper I have focused on a specific aspect that distinguishes locative PPs from their non-locative counterparts, namely their ability to function as full-fledged predicates, assigning an external semantic role.

Assuming a uniformly functional classification of P, I have argued that the external role of locative PPs originates in the phonetically null noun PLACE that heads the extended (nominal) projection of a locative PP. I explored the possibility to analyze Hebrew locative PPs on a par with their Greek counterparts, arguing that Hebrew locatives are base-generated lower than P_{LOC}, and raise to this position, when it is free. A variety of evidence involving complex and basic locatives and their interaction with directionals led to the surprising conclusion that basic locatives and directionals are base-generated in the same structural position, namely in P selecting a DP which encloses PLACE.

If on the right track, the proposed analysis is appealing because it reconciles the uniformly functional classification of P with the lexical flavor of locative PPs, and specifically, with their ability to function as predicates, without ruling out the possibility that in some languages locatives are associated with additional functional structure, namely they are part of a bigger extended projection of N-PLACE (rather than of P_{LOC}). It also quite naturally allows for languages where locatives are full-fledged DPs, rather than PPs, including a locative classifier, presumably base-generated in D of PLACE, or languages whose locatives exhibit nominal properties.

References

Aboh, E.O. 2006. Possession and predication in complex spatial phrases. Paper presented at the Syntax and Semantics of Spatial P Conference, OTS, Utrecht University.

Avelar, J. 2006. The edge of locative PPs in Brazilian Portuguese. Paper presented at the Edges in Syntax Conference, Nicosia, Cyprus.

Baker, M. 2003. *Lexical Categories: Verbs, Nouns, and Adjectives* [Cambridge Studies in Linguistics]. Cambridge: CUP.

Beit-Arie, O. 1994. Anaphora within Locative Prepositional Phrases. MA Thesis, Tel Aviv University.

Ben-David, A. 1971. *Lashon mikra velashon chachamim* (Language of the Bible and language of scholars). Tel Aviv: Dvir.

Botwinik-Rotem, I. 2004. The Category P: Features Projections, Interpretation. PhD Dissertation, Tel Aviv University.

Botwinik-Rotem, I. & Terzi, A. To appear. The structure of Greek and Hebrew locative PPs: A unified case-driven account. *Lingua*.

Bresnan, J. 1994. Locative inversion and the architecture of universal grammar. *Language* 70: 72–131.

Carlson, G. 1977. Reference to Kinds in English. PhD Dissertation, University of Massachusetts, Amherst.

Chomsky, N. 1981. *Lectures on Government and Binding*. Dordrecht: Foris.

den Dikken, M. 1995. *Particles: On the Syntax of Verb-Particle, Triadic, and Causative Constructions*. Oxford: OUP.

den Dikken, M. 2006. On the syntax of locative and directional adpositional phrases. Ms., CUNY Graduate Center.

Di Sciullo, A.M. & Williams, E. 1987. *On the Definition of Word*. Cambridge MA: The MIT Press.

Doron, E. 1983. Verbless Predicates in Hebrew. PhD Dissertation, University of Texas, Austin.

Emonds, J. 1985. *A Unified Theory of Syntactic Categories*. Dordrecht: Foris.

Freeze, R. 1992. Existentials and other locatives. *Language* 68: 553–595.

Greenberg, Y. 1994. Hebrew Nominal Sentences and the Nature of the Stage-Individual Level Distinction. MA Thesis, Bar-Ilan University.

Grimshaw, J. 1990. *Argument Structure*. Cambridge MA: The MIT Press.

Grimshaw, J. 2000. Extended projection and locality. In *Lexical Specification and Insertion*, P. Coompans, M. Everaert & J. Grimshaw (eds), 115–133. Amsterdam: John Benjamins.

Hestvik, A. 1991. Subjectless binding domains. *Natural Language and Linguistic Theory* 9: 455–497.

Higginbotham, J. 1985. On semantics. *Linguistic Inquiry* 16: 547–593.

Jackendoff, R. 1977. *X'-Syntax: A Study of Phrase Structure*. Cambridge MA: The MIT Press.

Kayne, R. 1984. *Connectedness and Binary Branching*. Dordrecht: Foris.

Kayne, R. 2000. *Parameters and Universals*. Oxford: OUP.

Kayne, R. 2004. Here and there. In *Syntax, Lexis and Lexicon-Grammar. Papers in Honour of Maurice Gross*, C. Leclère, E. Laporte, M. Piot & M. Silberztein (eds), 253–273. Amsterdam: John Benjamins.

Kayne, R. 2005. Prepositions as probes. In *Movement and Silence*. Oxford: OUP.

Koopman, H. 2000. Prepositions, postpositions, circumpositions, and particles. In *The Syntax of Specifiers and Heads*, H. Koopman (ed.), 204–260. London: Routledge.

Landau, I. 1999. Possessor raising and the structure of VP. *Lingua* 107: 1–37.

Marantz, A. 1984. *On the Nature of Grammatical Relations*. Cambridge MA: The MIT Press.

Milsark, G.L. 1974. Existential Sentences in English. PhD Dissertation, MIT.

Noonan, M. 2005. R-particles. Paper presented at the GLOW colloquium, Geneva Switzerland.

Noonan, M. 2006. The path along the edge. Paper presented at the Edges in Syntax Conference, Nicosia, Cyprus.

Pantcheva, M. 2006. Persian preposition classes. In *Nordlyd, University of Tromsø Working Papers in Language & Linguistics* 33.1, P. Svenonius & M. Pantcheva (eds), 1–25. Tromsø: Tromsø University.

Parsons, T. 1990. *Events in the Semantics of English. A Study in Subatomic Semantics* [Current Studies in Linguistics Series]. Cambridge MA: The MIT Press.

Reinhart, T. & Reuland, E. 1993. Reflexivity. *Linguistic Inquiry* 24: 657–720.

van Riemsdijk, H.C. 1978. *A Case Study in Syntactic Markedness: The Binding Nature of Prepositional Phrases*. Lisse: The Peter de Ridder Press.

van Riemsdijk, H.C. 1990. Functional prepositions. In *Unity in Diversity: Papers presented to Simon C. Dik on His 50th Birthday*, H. Pinkster & I. Genee (eds). Dordrecht: Foris.

van Riemsdijk, H.C. 1998. Categorial feature magnetism: The endocentricity and distribution of projections. *Journal of Comparative Germanic Linguistics* 2: 1–48.

van Riemsdijk, H.C. & Huybregts, R. 2001. Location and locality. Ms., Tilburg University.

Ritter, E. 1991. Two functional categories in noun phrases: Evidence from modern Hebrew. In *Perspectives on Phrase Structure: Heads and Licensing, Syntax and Semantics 25*, S. Rothstein (ed.), 37–62. San Diego CA: Academic Press.

Rubinstein, E. 1968. *Hamishpat hashemani* (The nominal clause). Tel Aviv: Hakibbutz Hameuchad.

Siloni, T. 1997. *Noun Phrases and Nominalizations: The Syntax of DPs*. Dordrecht: Kluwer.

Siloni, T. 2002. Construct States at the PF-Interface. In *The Year Book of Language Variations 1*, P. Pica & J. Rooryck (eds), 229–266.

Stowell, T. 1978. What was there before *there* was there? In *Proceedings of the 13th Regional Meeting of the Chicago Linguistics Society*, D. Farkas et al. (eds), 458–471. Chicago IL.: Chicago Linguistics Society.

Stowell, T. 1981. Origins of Phrase Structure. PhD Dissertation, MIT.

Svenonius, P. To appear. Spatial P in English. In *The Cartography of Syntactic Structures*, vol. 6, Cinque & L. Rizzi (eds). Oxford University Press.

Svenonius, P. 2007. Adpositions, particles, and the arguments they introduce. In *Argument Structure*, E. Reuland, T. Bhattacharya & G. Spathas (eds). Amsterdam: John Benjamins.

Terzi, A. 2005a. Locative prepositions as possessums. In *Proceedings of the 16th International Symposium on Theoretical and Applied Linguistics*, M. Mattheoudakis & A. Psaltou-Joycey (eds), 133–144. Thessaloniki: University of Thessaloniki.

Terzi, A. 2005b. Locative prepositions, predicate inversion and full interpretation. In *Proceedings of the 16th International Symposium on Theoretical and Applied Linguistics*, M. Mattheoudakis & A. Psaltou-Joycey (eds). Thessaloniki: University of Thessaloniki.

Terzi, A. 2005c. The misleading lexical status of locative prepositions. Ms., Technological Educational Institute of Patras.

Terzi, A. 2006. Locative prepositions and *place*. In *The Cartography of PPs*, G. Cinque & W. Schweikert (eds). Oxford: OUP.

Williams, E. 1981. Argument structure and morphology. *The Linguistic Review* 1: 81–114.

Zwarts, J. & Winter, Y. 2000. Vector space semantics: A model-theoretic analysis of locative prepositions. *Journal of Logic, Language and Information* 9: 169–211.

Silent prepositions: Evidence from free relatives[*]

Ivano Caponigro
Department of Linguistics, University of California, San Diego
Lisa Pearl
Department of Cognitive Sciences, University of California, Irvine

Silent prepositions are hypothesized to be prepositions that are phonologically null, but syntactically and semantically contentful. Their existence in the grammar has been argued for on the basis of the behavior of expressions like *there*, *now*, and *that way*, which look like nominals but can (or must) behave as prepositional phrases. We bring further evidence in favor of silent prepositions by studying the syntactic and semantic behavior of free relative clauses introduced by the wh-words *where*, *when*, and *how*. We propose a fully compositional syntactic/semantics analysis for these free relatives that accounts for their puzzling nominal/prepositional distributional and interpretative properties. This analysis is crucially based on silent prepositions. We also briefly discuss how our proposal can be extended to interrogative clauses introduced by the same wh-words, as well as what the licensing conditions and semantic properties of silent prepositions are.

1. Introduction: silent prepositions

As noticed by Emonds (1976, 1987), there are a restricted number of phrases in English that look like NPs, but have the same distribution and interpretation as either NPs or PPs. Larson (1985) labels these phrases *bare NP-adverbs*, while McCawley (1988) calls them *adverbial NPs*. An example is the string *few places that I cared for*, which appears to simply be a (complex) NP. In (1)a, it occurs in a position in which only NPs usually occur (i.e., the subject position of a predicate like *be beautiful*), receiving the usual interpretation of an NP subject (i.e., an individual or a generalized quantifier). However, in (1)b the very same string occurs

[*] We are very grateful to Grant Goodall, Richard Larson, Howard Lasnik, Carson Schütze, and the participants at the Syntax and Semantics of Spatial P Workshop at the University of Utrecht for their very helpful comments and suggestions. Any remaining errors are, of course, our own.

in the same position as the bracketed locative PP adjunct in (1)c and has the same interpretation as that PP.

(1)   a.   [Few places that I cared for] are really beautiful.   *NP-like*
      b.   You have lived [few places that I cared for].   *PP-like*
      c.   You have lived [PP in [few places that I cared for]].

Adverbial NPs are restricted to three semantic areas: spatial expressions (2), temporal expressions (3), and manner expressions (4).[1]

(2)   *Spatial adverbial NPs*

         a.   You have lived [there].   *PP-like*
         b.   [There] is really beautiful.   *NP-like*
         c.   I went [home].   *PP-like*
         d.   [Home] never changes.   *NP-like*

(3)   *Temporal adverbial NPs*

         a.   John arrived [that day]/[Sunday]/[yesterday].   *PP-like*
         b.   [That day]/[Sunday]/[Yesterday] was fantastic.   *NP-like*

(4)   *Manner adverbial NPs*

         a.   You pronounced my name [that way]/[every way one
              could imagine].   *PP-like*
         b.   [That way]/[Every way one could imagine] was not feasible.   *NP-like*

NPs from other semantic areas do not exhibit the same behavior; they can only behave like NPs and not like PPs (5).

(5)   a.   *Jack came [her]/[Lily]/[the person he is in love with].   **PP-like*
              (cf. Jack came for/with/after [her]/[Lily]/[the person he is in love with].)
      b.   [She]/[Lily]/[the person he is love with] does not really like him.   *NP-like*

Larson (1985) argues that adverbial NPs are syntactically NPs with the (lexical) property of self-assigning Case, but Emonds (1987) and McCawley (1988) convincingly show that Larson's proposal is empirically and theoretically problematic. Emonds (1976, 1987) and McCawley (1988) argue that adverbial NPs are NPs that can occur in positions to which no Case is assigned and behave like PPs in virtue of a *silent* preposition that takes the NP as its complement (6).

(6)

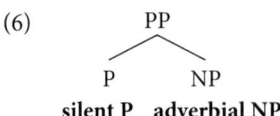

_____

1.   Examples (2)a, (3)a, and (4)a from Larson (1985).

In this paper, we bring further support for silent prepositions in the grammar by looking at the syntactic and semantic behavior of embedded non-interrogative wh-clauses known as *free relatives* (FRs). The bracketed FR in (7)a has the same distribution and roughly the same interpretation as the NP in (7)a'. Yet, in (7)b what looks like the very same FR now occurs in the same position as the PP in (7) b' and receives a similar interpretation.

(7) a.   [Where you used to live] was really great.   *NP-like*
     a'. [$_{NP}$ The little town you used to live in] was really great.
     b.   I live [where you used to live].   *PP-like*
     b'. I live [$_{PP}$ in [the town you used to live in]].

We will argue that this and another puzzling property of FRs can receive a straightforward account if silent Ps are available in the grammar and the same structure as in (6) is assumed. The only difference is that the silent P takes a FR as its complement rather than an adverbial NP (8).[2]

(8)

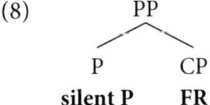

PP
P   CP
silent P **FR**

The paper is organized as follows. First, we will discuss two puzzles about FRs (§2), and present a proposal that accounts for them (§3). Then, we will bring further independent evidence to support the proposal (§4), and discuss potential alternatives and their associated problems (§5). Finally, we will briefly mention some open issues and conclude (§6).

2.   Two puzzles about free relatives

We focus on two puzzles (among many) which FRs raise that have not received much attention previously. We argue that they can be accounted for by means of silent Ps.

2.1   Puzzle I: Are FRs like NPs or PPs?

Some FRs can have the same distribution and interpretation as NPs or PPs. These are the FRs that are introduced by the wh-words *where* (place), *when* (time), and *how* (manner) (henceforth, **w/w/h FRs**). The examples from (9)–(11) illustrate this

---

2.   We will discuss later why we assume that a FR is syntactically a CP.

point. (9)a shows that a w/w/h FR introduced by the spatial wh-word *where* can behave like an NP, since it can be replaced and paraphrased with the complex NP *the place that this very tree grows* (9)a'. On the other hand, (9)b shows that what looks like the very same w/w/h FR can syntactically and semantically behave like the complex PP *in the place that this very tree grows* (9)b'. The same is true for w/w/h FRs introduced by the temporal wh-word *when* (10) and the manner wh-word *how* (11).

(9) a. Lily adores [$_{FR}$ *where* this very tree grows [$_{PP}$ __]].
    a'. Lily adores [$_{NP}$ *the place* that this very tree grows [$_{PP}$ __]].
    b. Lily napped [$_{FR}$ *where* this very tree grows [$_{PP}$ __]].
    b'. Lily napped [$_{pp}$ *in the place* that this very tree grows [$_{PP}$ __]].

(10) a. Lily dreaded [$_{FR}$ *when* Jack had to go [$_{PP}$ __]].
    a'. Lily dreaded [$_{NP}$ *the time/moment* that Jack had to go [$_{PP}$ __]].
    b. Lily cried [$_{FR}$ *when* Jack had to go [$_{PP}$ __]].
    b'. Lily cried [$_{pp}$ *at the time* that Jack had to go [$_{PP}$ __]].

(11) a. Lily loathes [$_{FR}$ *how* all thieves work [$_{PP}$ __]] – secretly.
    a'. Lily loathes [$_{NP}$ *the way* that all thieves work [$_{PP}$ __]] – secretly.
    b. Jack works [$_{FR}$ *how* all thieves work [$_{PP}$ __]] – secretly.
    b'. Jack works [$_{pp}$ *in the way* that all thieves work [$_{PP}$ __]] – secretly.

Bresnan and Grimshaw (1978: §5) were the first to notice this distribution of w/w/h FRs, though they only discuss examples of FRs introduced by *where* and *when*, without mentioning FRs introduced by *how*.

So, we see that w/w/h FRs exhibit the same puzzling behavior as adverbial NPs: they can have the same distribution and interpretation as either NPs or PPs.

2.2   Puzzle II: An NP or a PP gap?

The second puzzle concerns the nature of the gap within w/w/h FRs. To the best of our knowledge, this has not been noticed before. Similar to other wh-clauses like interrogatives and headed relative clauses, FRs are characterized by a gap in argument or adjunct position. In (9)–(11) above, we marked and labeled the gaps in the w/w/h FRs and the corresponding headed relatives. All the gaps are PP gaps, and this is not by chance. It does not matter whether the whole w/w/h FR behaves like an NP or a PP – only a PP gap is licensed within the w/w/h FR. Even if the predicate in the w/w/h FR selects for an NP, w/w/h FRs can not yet license an NP gap – and it does not matter if the whole w/w/h FR behaves like a PP (12)a or an NP (13)a. Notice that the corresponding headed relatives can license an NP gap, independently from the properties of their heads (cf. (12)a vs.(12)b and (13)a vs. (13)b).

(12) a. ?*Lily always naps [$_{FR}$ *where/when/how* Jack despises [$_{NP}$ __]].
    b. Lily always naps [$_{pp}$ {*in the place*}/{*at the time*}/{*in the way*} that Jack despises

$[_{NP}$ __ $]]$.

(13) a. ?*Lily adores $[_{FR}$ *where/when/how* Jack despises $[_{NP}$ __ $]]$.

  b. Lily adores $[_{NP}$ {*the place*}/{*the time*}/{*the way*} that Jack despises $[_{NP}$ __ $]]$.

There is an important exception, though. An NP gap can be licensed as the complement of an overt P in a w/w/h FR that is introduced by *where*, whether the whole FR behaves like an NP or a PP (in §4.1, we will discuss similar examples with FRs introduced by the wh-word *when*). For example, the w/w/h FR introduced by *where* in (14)a allows for an NP gap in the complement position of the P *past*. Since *past* can only take NP complements, we can be sure that we are dealing with an NP gap. The whole FR behaves like an NP. In fact, it can be replaced and paraphrased with the bracketed complex NP in (14)b. Similarly, the w/w/h FR in (15)a licenses an NP in the complement position of the preposition *through*, though it behaves like a PP, as shown in (15)b.

(14) a. Jack disliked $[_{FR}$ *where* we just ran $[_{PP}$ $[_P$ past$]$ $[_{NP}$ __ $]]]$ – it smelled funny.

  b. Jack disliked $[_{NP}$ the place we just ran $[_{PP}$ $[_P$ past$]$ $[_{NP}$ __ $]]]$ – it smelled funny.

(15) a. Lily lives $[_{FR}$ *where* we have to fly $[_{PP}$ $[_p$ through$]$ $[_{NP}$ __ $]]$ on our way to Vancouver$]$.

  b. Lily lives $[_{PP}$ in the area we have to fly $[_{PP}$ $[_p$ through$]$ $[_{NP}$ __ $]]$ on our way to Vancouver$]$.

To sum up, the second puzzle about w/w/h FRs we will address is that only a PP gap seems to be licensed inside w/w/h FRs, unless an overt P occurs, which then triggers the licensing of an NP gap as its complement T.

3. Proposal

The two puzzles just discussed can be solved by giving a syntactic and semantic analysis of w/w/h FRs that relies on silent Ps. Let us start with a preliminary syntactic assumption: FRs introduced by bare phrasal[3] wh-words (*who, what, where, when, how*) are plain CPs with a moved wh-phrase in their specifiers. This is just for the sake of simplicity, since the syntax of FRs is an open issue that goes largely beyond the purposes of this paper.[4] Nonetheless, nothing crucial in our

---

3. "Bare" excludes FRs introduced by wh-*ever* (*whoever, whatever, wherever, whenever*), "phrasal" excludes FRs introduced by wh(-*ever*) + XP (e.g., *I'll drink what(ever) beer you drink*).

4. See Grosu (2003) and van Riemsdijk (2005) for an overview of the open issues of the syntax of FRs, the proposals have been made, and their problems.

proposal hinges on this assumption. Any analysis in which the wh-word in a FR is base-generated in the gap position and moved to a higher position will suffice.

Our proposal then can be articulated in two main claims. First, a whole w/w/h FR (i.e., a CP) can occur as the complement of a silent P. When the w/w/h FR is the complement of a silent P, the whole w/w/h FR looks as if it is a PP. Note that this is because the w/w/h FR is embedded within an actual PP, whose head is silent (16)a. When the w/w/h FR is not the complement of a silent P, then it behaves like an NP, just as all other FRs introduced by bare phrasal wh-words do (16)b. This accounts for the first puzzle, where w/w/h FRs behave sometimes as NPs and sometimes as PPs.

(16)   a.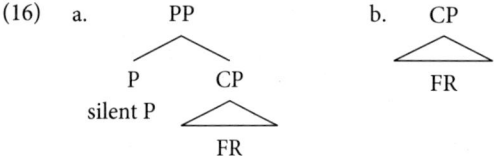

Our second claim is that the wh-words *where*, *when*, and *how*, which introduce w/w/h FRs, are syntactically and semantically NPs that can only be base-generated as the complement of a possibly silent P (17).

(17)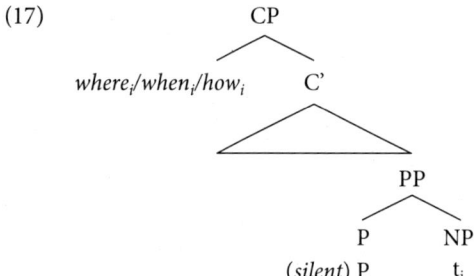

The wh-word that is base-generated as the sister of P moves to the Spec of CP for independent reasons, specifically whatever the reasons for wh-movement in English are. The wh-word leaves behind an NP trace, which is an NP gap. Note that this NP gap is perceptually identical to a PP gap when the P is silent. If the P is overt as in (14) and (15) above, it becomes clear that at least *where* is an NP. Also, according to our analysis, silent Ps are always stranded. This is due to independent semantic reasons that will be discussed below. This accounts for the second puzzle, in which FRs seem to license PP gaps and NP gaps.

Let us now look at the detailed syntactic derivations of two of the previous examples in order to make concrete how our proposal works. The syntactic tree in (18)b includes the CP of a w/w/h FR that behaves like an NP, since it occurs in the complement position of a predicate like *adores* (which selects for an NP complement). The w/w/h FR contains a PP with a silent P and a wh-trace as its complement, resulting from the wh-movement of *where* to the Spec of CP of the w/w/h FR. Notice that the fact that P is silent makes the NP gap perceptually indistinguishable from a true PP gap like in the wh-interrogative clause *In which areas does this tree grow* [$_{PP}$]?

(18) a. Lily adores [$_{FR}$ where this very tree grows].

  b.

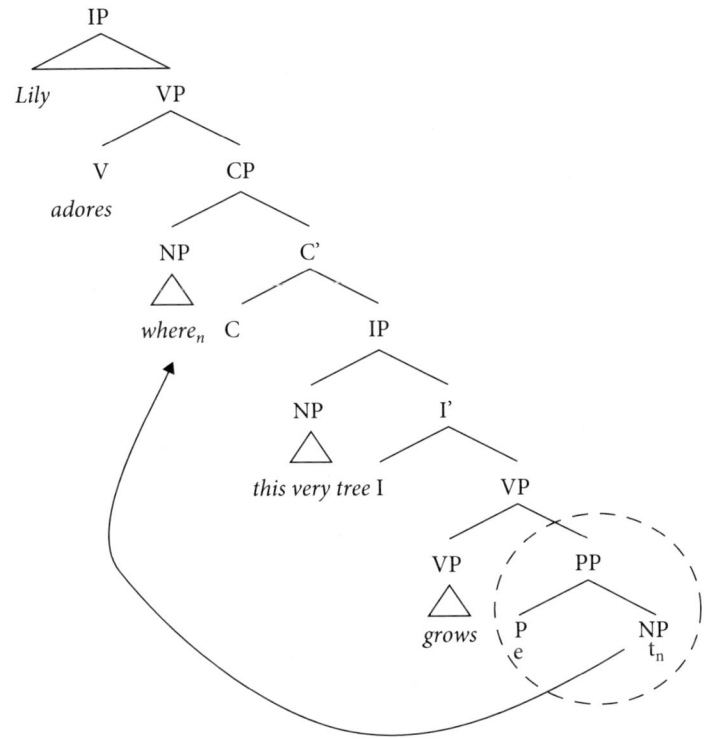

The next example (19)a contains the same w/w/h FR as in (18), but this time the w/w/h FR specifically behaves like a PP. In fact, the FR looks as if it was occurring where a PP, but not an NP, can occur, that is as an adjunct of the predicate *napped*. But our tree in (19)b shows that this apparent puzzling behavior can once again be accounted for as a perceptual illusion. The CP of the w/w/h FR occurs in the complement position of a silent preposition P$_2$. Therefore, the whole w/w/h FR still behaves like an NP, as in (18)b . However, PP$_2$, which is made of its head P$_2$ and the CP of the w/w/h FR as its complement, is perceptually indistinguishable from just the CP of the w/w/h FR, since P$_2$ is silent. The internal structure of the w/w/h FR with the silent preposition P$_1$ in (19)b is identical to (18)b above.

(19)   a.   Lily napped [_FR where this very tree grows].

b.

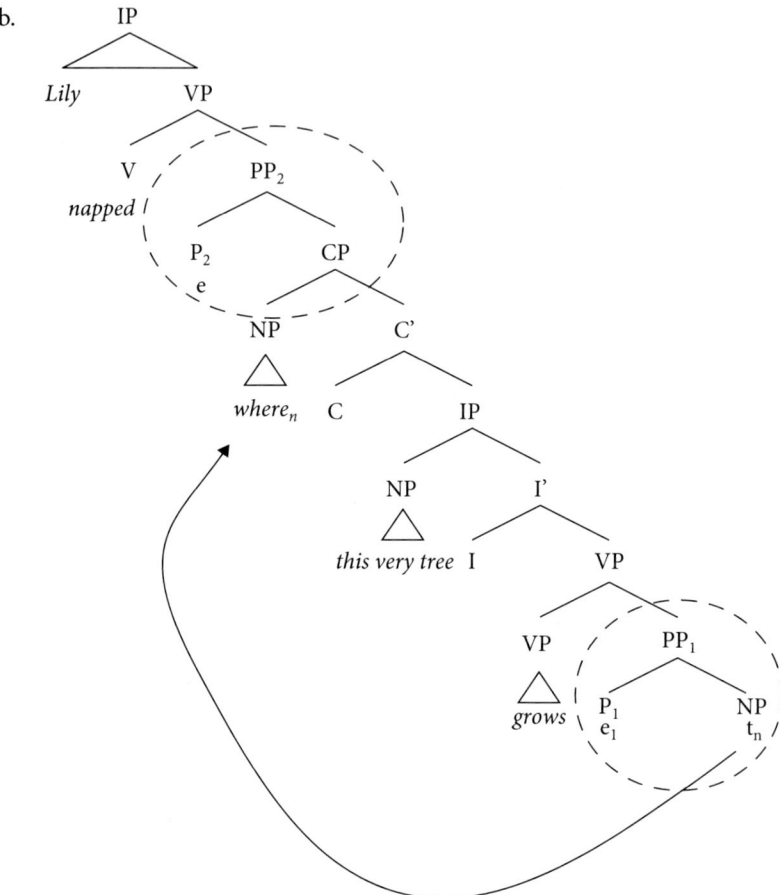

Let us now move to the semantics of w/w/h FRs. This is relevant for our purposes for at least two reasons. First, we want to make sure that the syntactic analysis just suggested is compatible with a semantic analysis that captures the semantic
intuitions we discussed earlier: w/w/h FRs should be semantically equivalent to
either NPs or PPs. Second, we need a detailed semantics for w/w/h FRs, since our
argument to support obligatory stranding of silent Ps is crucially based on the
semantic derivation.

Following the semantic analysis for FRs in Caponigro (2004), we pursue the
idea that w/w/h FRs denote an individual, like non-quantified NPs. How do w/w/h
FRs end up denoting an individual? Let us go step by step from the bottom up, following the schema in (20).

(20)

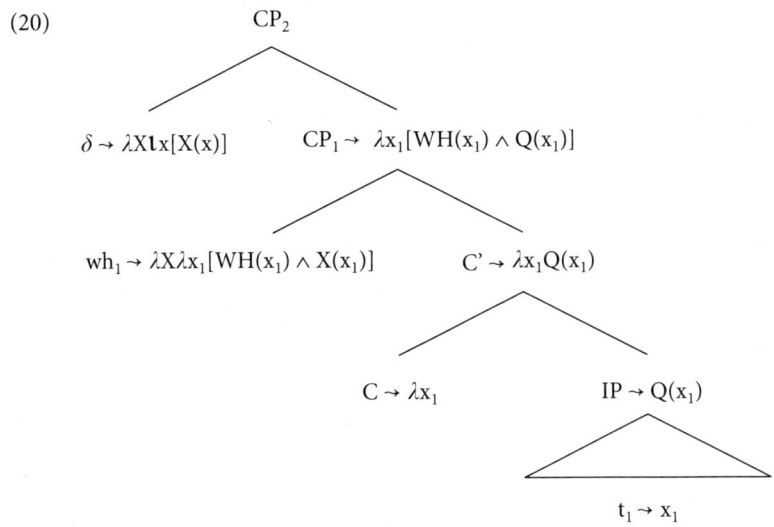

The wh-trace within IP translates into a variable that is bound at by the set-formation operator, the lambda operator (which we assuming to be under C just for the sake of simplicity). Therefore, C' denotes the set of individuals that have the property Q (i.e., the set $\lambda x_1 Q(x_1)$) or, equivalently, the set of individuals that make the proposition Q(x) expressed by the IP true.

The next step is to combine this set with the semantic contribution of the wh-word. But what is the semantic contribution of *where, when,* or *how*? These words behave like set restrictors: they apply to a set of individuals and return a subset. In particular, *where* applies to a set of individuals and returns all and only the individuals that are locations, *when* all and only instants or situations, and *how* all and only manners. When one of these wh-words applies to the set of individuals $\lambda x_1 Q(x_1)$, it returns the subset $\lambda x_1 [WH(x_1) \wedge Q(x_1)]$, i.e., the set of individuals that have both the property Q and the property WH, the restriction conveyed by the wh-word (see Caponigro 2004 for further details and arguments).

So at the level of CP_1, w/w/h FRs denote the set of locations, instants/situations, or manners that satisfy the property Q. But, according to our syntactic analysis, w/w/h FRs, which so far denote sets of individuals (semantic type: $\langle e,t \rangle$), occur in the argument positions of heads (verbs or preposition) that select for an individual-denoting expressions (semantic type: $\langle e \rangle$). It appears we have a so-called type mismatch. Partee (1986), Chierchia (1998), and Dayal (2004) have argued that type-shifting rules are made available by the grammar to fix type-mismatches. Among those, *iota* (ι) applies to a set P and returns its maximal individual (21).

(21)   iota (ι): P → $\iota x P(x)$ ($\langle e,t \rangle$ → $\langle e \rangle$)

The empirical evidence for a type-shifting rule like *iota* originally comes from the crosslinguistic behavior of nominals, in particular bare plurals and bare singulars (Chierchia 1998; Dayal 2004). Caponigro (2004) – developing a suggestions in Jacobson (1995) – adds further support coming from FRs. He syntactically encodes *iota* by means of a silent operator δ, adjoined to CP of FRs. We did the same in (20). The set of individuals denoted by CP_1 in (20) type-shifts to its maximal (plural) individual when it combines with δ at the level of the adjoined CP_2.

In (22) and (23) below, we repeat the syntactic trees in (18) and (19) respectively and add their logical translations in accordance to the analysis we just proposed. PPs are treated as extra arguments of the predicate they modify for sake of simplicity. Also, no detailed semantic analysis is given for PPs, since it is not relevant for our purposes. Any semantics for Ps would suffice as long as Ps select for an individual-denoting complement. Finally, we ignore the deictic nature of nominal *this very tree* for the sake of simplicity and we translate it as the simple individual-denoting expression *tvt*.

(22)

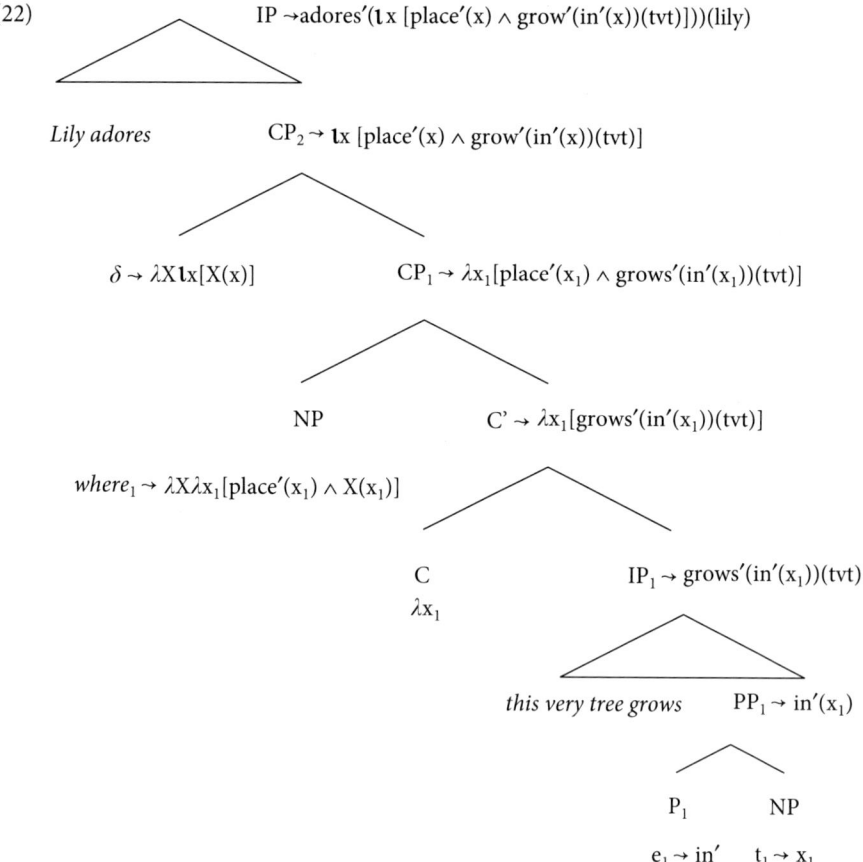

(23)

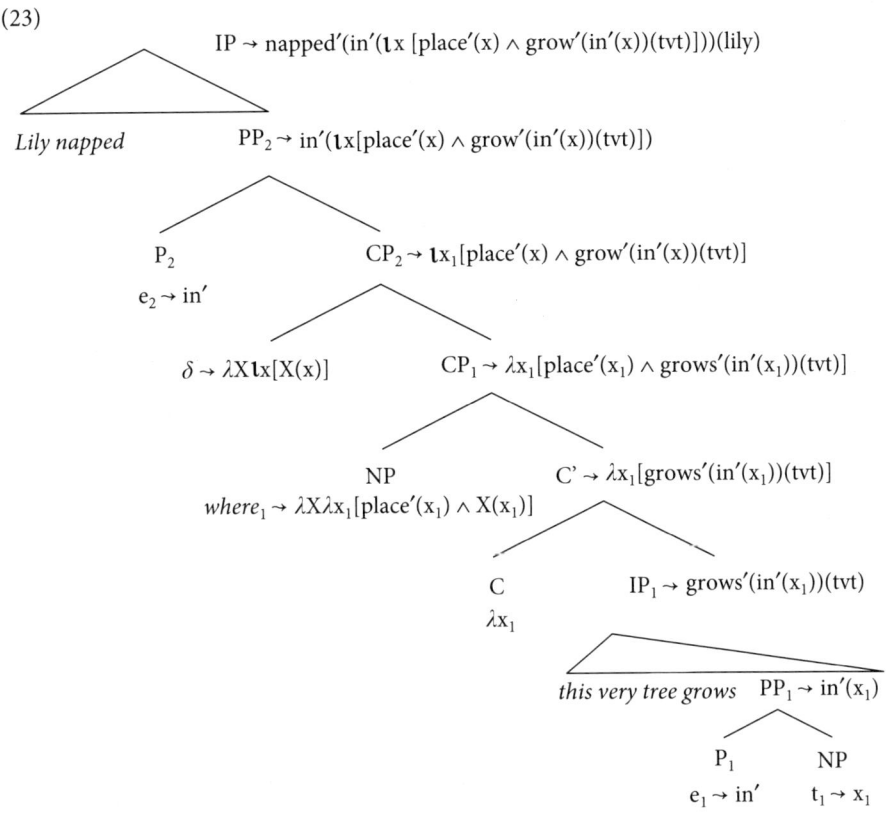

To sum up, we have argued that w/w/h FRs are very similar both syntactically and semantically to the FRs introduced by the bare phrasal wh-words *who* and *what*. Syntactically, they are wh-CPs (or any other phrasal structure that would better account for the property of FRs); semantically, they denote an individual. The crucial difference is the structure of the wh-words that introduce w/w/h FRs: *where*, *when*, and *how* are always base-generated as the complement of a possibly silent P. In addition, whenever the w/w/h FR behaves as if it was a PP, the whole w/w/h FR itself is the complement of another silent P.

4. Further evidence

In this section, we present further evidence in favor of our analysis. We show that silent Ps – either within a w/w/h FR or as its sister – can be replaced with overtly realized Ps in some cases (§4.1). We give further support to our proposal that *where*, *when*, and *how* are NPs, rather than PPs, by showing that Ps usually take an NP as their complement, rather than a PP (§4.2). We then show that our proposal about the syntactic and semantic nature of w/w/h FRs has larger empirical coverage by extending it to wh-interrogatives that are introduced by *where, when* or *how* (§4.3). Finally, we show that the same kinds of restrictions on licensing silent Ps that we noticed for adverbial NPs earlier (§1) are found with w/w/h FRs as well (§4.4), which supports the claim that these two constructions are similar and should receive a similar analysis.

4.1   Overt Ps

We have argued that the wh-trace within a w/w/h FR is always the complement of a possibly silent P and that the whole w/w/h FR is the complement of another silent P whenever the w/w/h FR behaves as if it was a PP. Though these two Ps are silent most of the time, there are cases where one or both of them are overt. In (24), we see that the P that takes the wh-trace of *where* as its complement can be overtly realized, in this case as the P *past*. In (25), we see that the P that takes the whole w/w/h FR introduced by *where* as its complement can be overtly realized, in this case as the P *near*. In (26), both the P sister to the wh-trace and the P sister to the w/w/h FR are overtly realized as *through* and *near*, respectively.

(24)   Jack disliked [$_{FR}$ where$_m$ we just ran [$_{PP}$ [$_P$ **past**] [$_{NP}$ t$_m$]]] – it smelled funny.

(25)   Lily lives [$_{PP1}$ [$_{P1}$ **near**] [$_{FR}$ where$_m$ we had dinner [$_{PP2}$ [$_{P2}$ e] [$_{NP}$ t$_m$]]] last night]].

(26)   Lily lives [$_{PP1}$ [$_{P1}$ **near**] [$_{FR}$ where$_m$ we have to fly [$_{PP2}$ [$_{P2}$ **through**] [$_{NP}$ t$_m$]]] on our way to Vancouver]].

In (27), we see that w/w/h FRs introduced by the wh-word *when* can also occur as the complement of over Ps like *from* or *to*, while (28) shows that the trace of the wh-word *when* can be the complement of an overt P as *by*.

(27)   Lily was sick [$_{PP1}$ [$_{P1}$ **from**] [$_{FR}$ when$_m$ Jack arrived [$_{PP}$ [$_{P2}$ e] [$_{NP}$ t$_m$]]]] [$_{PP3}$ [$_{P3}$ **to**] [$_{FR}$ when$_p$ he left [$_{PP4}$ [$_{P4}$ e] [NP t$_p$]]]].

(28)   Lily's schedule can't accommodate [when$_m$ Jack needs the car [$_{PP}$ [$_p$ **by** [$_{NP}$ t$_m$]]]].

Finally, (29) shows that a whole FR introduced by the wh-word *how* can occur as the complement of an overt preposition like *on*.[5]

---

5.   We have not been able to find any example in which the trace of *how* can occur as the sister of an overt preposition. Although we do not have an account for this asymmetry of *how* with respect to *where* and *when*, we note two possibly related facts. First, a headed relative clause with the nominal *way* as its head, which is the most natural paraphrase for a FR introduced by *how*, can be optionally followed by the complementizer *that* or, crucially, by the relative pronoun *which* preceded by the preposition *in*. No other preposition can occur between *way* and *which*.

(29)   Lily knew that Jack was about to get upset based $[_{PP1} [_{P1}$ on] [**how**$_m$ he was look-ing at her $[_{PP2} [_{P2}$ e] $[_{NP}$ t$_m$]]]]

We take these cases where the P is overt as further evidence in favor of the existence of the two distinct P heads we are arguing for, even when these P heads are not phonologically realized.

4.2   Complements of P must be NPs

We just saw that *where*, *when*, and *how* can be base-generated as complement of Ps like *past*, *through*, or *near*. These Ps can take an NP complement, but not a PP one, as shown in (30)–(32).

(30)   a.   past $[_{NP}$ the house]
       b.   *past $[_{PP}$ **at** the house]

(31)   a.   through [NP the grass]
       b.   *through $[_{PP}$ **on** the grass]

(32)   a.   near $[_{NP}$ the store]
       b.   *near $[_{PP}$ **in** the store]

Since *where*, *when*, and *how* can be base-generated as the complement of Ps like *past*, *through*, or *near* it follows that they must be NPs, rather than PPs. We take this as independent evidence in favor of our conclusions that the categorical status of *where*, *when*, and *how* is NP, rather than PP.

4.3   Wh-interrogative clauses

Our claim that *where*, *when*, and *how* are always base-generated as the comple-ment of a P would look suspiciously restricted if it was true just for w/w/h FRs rather than for any wh-clause introduced by those wh-words. Wh-interrogatives introduced by *where* behave exactly like the w/w/h FRs we saw in §4.1 (33)–(34). Their wh-word is base-generated as the complement of a P that can also be overt. Huang (1982:536) makes a similar point.

(33)   Where$_m$ did we just run $[_{PP} [_p$ **past**] $[_{NP}$ t$_m$]]?

(34)   Where$_m$ do we have to fly $[_{PP} [_p$ **through**] $[_{NP}$ t$_m$]] on our way to Vancouver?

---

i.   Lily knew that Jack was about to get upset based [[on] [the way [(that)/(in/*by/*with which) he was looking at her]]].

Second, the P *in* can never occur as the sister of the trace of *where*, *when*, and *how*. If for whatever reason *in* is the <u>only</u> overt preposition in English that is compatible with very general manner expressions like *way*, but at the same time is incompatible with *where*, *when* and *how*, it follows that no overt preposition can ever take the trace of *how* as its complement.

Also, if no overt P is present, wh-interrogatives introduced by *where, when,* and *how* only license what looks like a PP gap on the surface (35). This is the same behavior that we observed in w/w/h FRs (§2.2).

(35)   a.   *Where/when/how did Lily despise [$_{NP}$ __]?
       b.   Where/when/how did Lily sleep [$_{PP}$ __]?

4.4   Semantic restrictions on silent P licensing and adverbial NPs

At the very beginning of this paper (§1), we mentioned that adverbial NPs in English look like NPs, but can behave like NPs or PPs. We also noticed adverbial NPs are restricted to three semantic areas: spatial expressions (36), temporal expressions (37), or manner expressions (38). NPs from other semantic areas do not exhibit the same pattern (39).

(36)   *Spatial adverbial NPs*

    a.   You have lived [there].   *PP-like*
    b.   [There] is really beautiful.   *NP-like*
    c.   I went [home].   *PP-like*
    d.   [Home] never changes.   *NP-like*

(37)   *Temporal adverbial NPs*

    a.   John arrived [that day]/[Sunday]/[yesterday].   *PP-like*
    b.   [That day]/[Sunday]/[Yesterday] was fantastic.   *NP-like*

(38)   *Manner adverbial NPs*

    a.   You pronounced my name [that way]/[every way one could imagine].   *PP-like*
    b.   [That way]/[Every way one could imagine] was not feasible.   *NP-like*

(39)   a.   *Jack came [her]/[Lily]/[the person he is in love with].   **PP-like*
       (cf. Jack came for/with/after [her]/[Lily]/[the person he is in love with].)
       b.   [She]/[Lily]/[the person he is love with] does not really like him.   *NP-like*

W/w/h FRs show interesting similarities with adverbial PPs. As we have seen, w/w/h FRs can also behave like NPs or PPs. In addition, w/w/h FRs are introduced by wh-words that carry the same semantic feature as adverbial NPs: location/space (*where*), time/situation (*when*), or manner (*how*). This contrasts with FRs introduced by other bare phrasal wh-words like *who* (animate) and *what* (inanimate) that do not behave like adverbial NPs. In particular, they can occur where NPs can occur, but cannot occur where PPs can occur. As an example, (40)a shows that a FR introduced by *what* can occur as the complement of a predicate like *adore*, which selects for an NP complement, as shown (40)a'. However, if the very same FR occurs as the adjunct of an intransitive predicate like *work* in which only PPs are allowed, as shown in (40)b', then the result is unacceptable, as shown in (40)b. The examples in (41) make a similar point for FRs introduced by *who*.

(40) a. Lily adores [$_{FR}$ *what* Jack despises].   *NP-like*
       a'. Lily adores [$_{NP}$ the things Jack despises].
       b. *Lily works [$_{FR}$ *what* Jack despises].   **PP-like*
       b'. Lily works [$_{PP}$ [$_{P}$ on] [$_{NP}$ the things Jack despises]].

(41) a. Lily won't marry [$_{FR}$ *who* the king chooses].   *NP-like*
       a'. Lily won't marry [$_{NP}$ the person the king chooses].
       b. *Lily will dance [$_{FR}$ *who* the king chooses].   **PP-like*
       b'. Lily will dance [$_{PP}$ [$_{P}$ with] [$_{NP}$ the person the king chooses]].

We take these similarities between w/w/h FRs and adverbial NPs as an indication that a similar syntactic and semantic analysis for both constructions is justified. As we briefly mentioned in §1, an analysis based on silent Ps has been convincingly put forth for adverbial NPs (Emonds 1976, 1987; McCawley 1988). We take this to further support our analysis of w/w/h FRs based on silent Ps. In particular, FRs introduced by *who* and *what* lack any spatial, temporal, or manner feature; therefore, they cannot occur as the complement of a silent P.

The reason that FRs introduced by *who* and *what* lack the relevant features is because the wh-words that introduce them and act as a set restrictor lack them as well. This makes the prediction that *who* and *what* should never be base-generated as the complement position of a silent P or, equivalently, FRs introduced by *who* or *what* should never license a PP gap. This prediction is borne out. A FR introduced by *who* or *what* can license an NP gap in the complement of the P *to* (42)a, but cannot license a PP gap within what looks like the same FR except for the omitted P (42)b. As expected, a FR introduced by *where* can easily license a PP gap in the very same environment (42)c.

(42) a. Lily doesn't like [$_{FR}$ *who/what* Jack goes to [$_{NP}$ __] every Friday night].
       b. *Lily doesn't like [$_{FR}$ *who/what* Jack goes [$_{PP}$ __] every Friday night].
       c. Lily doesn't like [$_{FR}$ *where* Jack goes [$_{PP}$ __] every Friday night].

5. Problems with alternative accounts

In this section, we discuss potentially alternatives to our proposal and where they are problematic.

5.1 Against an ambiguity account

A simple alternative to our proposal could be to assume that *where, when,* and *how* are syntactically ambiguous: they are listed in the lexicon as both NPs and PPs. There are two issues with this approach, however. First, we would not be dealing with the idiosyncratic behavior of just one word, but with three lexical items that are members of the same class (wh-words) and exhibit very similar syntactic behaviors (introduce wh-clauses, license both NPs and PP gaps, etc.). Also, we have observed the same pattern in other languages with w/w/h FRs like Italian (although a careful crosslinguistic investigation is needed). This kind of (crosslinguistic) systematic ambiguity appears more like restating the generalization than an actual explanation.

Second, an ambiguity approach would end up making at least two incorrect predictions in this specific case. If *where, when,* and *how* were listed in the lexicon as both NPs and PPs, then they should be able to license either NP or PP gaps in the clause they introduce. But this is not the case, since they license only PP gaps (§2.2). Also, obligatory matching between the syntactic category of the gap and the whole FR would be expected. In particular, if a PP gap is licensed within a w/w/h FR, then the whole w/w/h FR should always behave like a PP. This is also not the case. While *where, when,* or *how* only license a PP-gap within w/w/h FRs, the whole w/w/h FR can behave either like an NP or PP, depending on the matrix predicate (43).

(43) a. Lily adores [$_{FR}$ [where/when/how] Jack sleeps [$_{PP}$ __]].   *NP-like FR*
       b. Lily sleeps [$_{FR}$ [where/when/how] Jack sleeps [$_{PP}$ __]].   *PP-like FR*

5.2 Against a pied-piping analysis

Another alternative approach could be based on optional pipe-piping of silent Ps. Like ours, it would assume that *where, when,* and *how* are always base-generated as the NP complement of a possibly silent P. Unlike ours, it would also assume that whenever the whole w/w/h FR behaves like a PP, this is due to the entire wh-PP moving to the Spec of CP, rather than just the wh-word. In other words, this approach would replace the stranding of the silent P in the w/w/h FRs with its pied-piping. There would be no need to postulate another silent P, which, according to our proposal, takes the whole w/w/h FR as its complement. In (44), we see the syntactic derivation of the example we discussed in (19) according to the pied-piping approach: it is the whole wh-PP [e *where*]$_m$ that moves to Spec of CP, leaving behind the PP trace t$_m$.

(44)   a.   Lily napped [$_{FR}$ where this very tree grows].

   b.

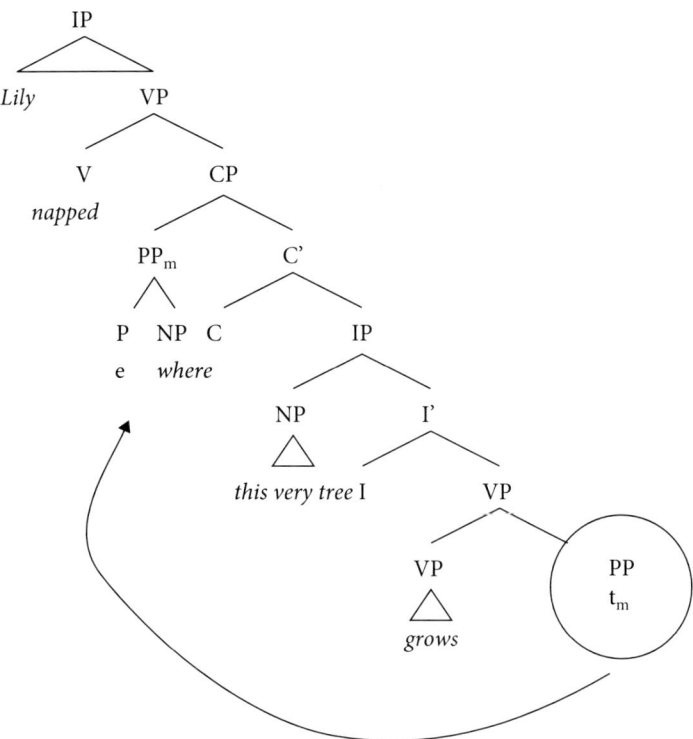

This approach faces at least two major problems. First, it would predict that the silent PP within the w/w/h FR and the whole w/w/h FR should always be interpreted as the same kind of PP, since their interpretation would depend on the very same silent P. This prediction is not borne out. The w/w/h FR in (45)a is interpreted as basically equivalent to the bracketed complex NP in (45)b, the only relevant difference being that all Ps are overt in (45)b. In particular, the PP gap in (45)b results from the movement of the PP *at which*, which is headed by the overt P *at*. Yet, the whole complex NP occurs as the complement of a PP that is headed by a different P: *to*. Crucially, the two Ps are not identical and cannot be interpreted equivalently. If we try to interpret the clauses this way, *at* would also precede the whole complex NP and the result would be semantically different from the intended meaning of (45)a – as well as unacceptable, as shown by (45)c. Thus, a pied-piping approach with only one silent P as in (45)d fails. In contrast, our approach can easily handle these facts, since two independent silent Ps would be present in the syntactic/semantic representation, as shown in (45)e.

(45)   a.   Lily just went [$_{FR}$ where Jack stayed last year on vacation].
   b.   Lily just went [$_{PP}$ to [$_{NP}$ the place [$_{PP}$ at which] Jack stayed [$_{PP}$ t$_j$] last year on vacation]].

c.   *Lily just went [$_{PP}$ **at** [$_{NP}$ the place [$_{PP}$ **at** which] Jack stayed [$_{PP}$ t$_j$]] last year on vacation]].

d.   Lily just went [$_{FR}$ [$_{PP}$[$_p$ e] [where]]$_j$ Jack stayed [$_{PP}$ t$_j$]] last year on vacation]].

e.   Lily just went [$_{PP}$ [$_p$ e$_1$] [$_{FR}$ [$_{NP}$ where]$_j$ Jack stayed [$_{PP}$ [$_p$ e$_2$] [$_{NP}$ t$_j$]]] last year on vacation]].

A similar point can be made with overt Ps. In (46)a, we see a w/w/h FR with a stranded overt P *to*. Notice that *to* cannot be pied-piped (46)b (at least not overtly) which is already unexpected under a pied-piping approach. Besides that, the w/w/h FR can be paraphrased with a complex NP whose internal P is *to* but whose sister is a different P: *in/at* (46)c. The interpretation that the pied-piping approach would predict is once again unacceptable (46)d and the reason is again the lack of a second P as a sister of the whole w/w/h FR (46)b. This contrasts with our analysis (46)e.

(46)   a.   Lily lives [$_{FR}$ where$_m$ Jack is about to go [$_{PP}$ **to** [$_{NP}$ t$_m$]]].
       b.   *Lily lives [$_{FR}$ [$_{PP}$ **to** where]$_j$ Jack is about to go [$_{PP}$ t$_j$]]].
       c.   Lily lives [$_{PP}$ **in/at** [$_{NP}$ the place where$_m$ Jack is about to go [$_{PP}$ **to** [$_{NP}$ t$_m$]]]].
       d.   *Lily lives [$_{PP}$ **to** [$_{NP}$ the place where$_m$ Jack is about to go [$_{PP}$ **to** [$_{NP}$ t$_m$]]]].
       e.   Lily lives [$_{PP}$ [$_p$ e] [$_{FR}$ [NP where]$_j$ Jack is about to go [$_{PP}$ [$_p$ **to**] [$_{NP}$ t$_j$]]]].

Finally, even when the w/w/h FR is preceded by an overt P, the overt P is never pied-piped with the wh-word from within the FR. It is always part of the matrix clause taking the w/w/h FR as its complement. The sentence in (47)a can only have the bracketing in (47)b, according to which *near* is base-generated in the matrix clause and does not form a constituent with *where*. This is the only bracketing that is compatible with the interpretation the sentence receives, which we tried to paraphrase in (47)c. If *near* had been pied-piped with *where* (47)d, then we would expect the interpretation of the sentence to be like (47)e, which is not the case.

(47)   a.   Jack lives **near** *where* we had dinner last night.
       b.   Jack lives [**near** [$_{FR}$ *where* we had dinner last night]].
       c.   Jack lives [**near** [the place at which we had dinner last night]].
       d.   Jack lives [$_{FR}$ [**near** *where*] we had dinner last night]].
       e.   Jack lives [**near** [the place near which we had dinner last night]].

The second incorrect prediction of the pied-piping analysis concerns the semantic derivation that this approach would require. The wh-PP would move to Spec of CP and leave a PP trace in the gap position within the w/w/h FR, rather than an NP trace. As we saw in §3, an NP-trace is translated into a variable whose value ranges over individuals (semantic objects of type $\langle e \rangle$). When the set-formation operation over that variable (λ abstraction) applies, it returns a set of individuals (type $\langle e,t \rangle$). On the other hand, a PP-trace translates into a variable whose value ranges over more complex semantic objects, functions whose semantic type we call $\langle f \rangle$ for convenience. When the set-formation operation over a variable of type $\langle f \rangle$ applies, it returns a set of PP-functions of type $\langle f,t \rangle$. *Iota*, the crucial type-shifting operation that turns a set of individuals into its maximal individual (21), cannot apply this time since there is no set of individuals to begin with. Therefore, the whole w/w/h FR would be left denoting a set of PP-functions, while the matrix clause would require an expression denoting what a PP denote, i.e., just a single PP-function. In conclusion, the FR would be expected *not* to have the same interpretation as a PP and, therefore not even the same distribution. This is contrary to what the data show.

We have argued that silent Ps are always stranded. This is not particularly problematic for a language like English that allows for preposition stranding extensively. But what about those languages (actually, the majority) that have w/w/h FRs but do not allow for preposition stranding (for instance, Italian)? Unfortunately, we are still far from a deep understanding of preposition stranding and why it is so rare across languages. Until then, preposition stranding cannot be used to make a point against or in favor of our proposal. For instance, suppose that the ban on preposition stranding turns out to phonological in nature (maybe due to the clitic-like nature of Ps in many languages). Then, it would not be surprising that silent Ps are always stranded, since they lack any phonological content by definition.[6]

6.   Some open issues and conclusions

There are a few open issues that we believe are particularly relevant and deserve further investigation. First, we saw that silent Ps are licensed only as sisters of phrases that carry spatial, temporal, or manner semantic features (adverbial NPs, wh-words, or FRs). It would be interesting to better understand the nature of this restriction and give it a principled explanation.

It may turn out that this open issue is related to another: the semantic content of silent Ps. More specifically, the semantic contribution of silent Ps is "minimal": they are always interpreted as semantically equivalent to Ps like *to, in, at,* or *on* whose semantic contribution is often fully recoverable from the semantic contribution of the predicate and the complement. Yet, semantic "lightness" and recoverability are necessary but *not* sufficient conditions for the licensing of silent Ps. For instance, the semantic contribution of the silent Ps in the w/w/h FRs in (48)a and (49)a, and in the wh-interrogative in (50)a is fully recoverable: something very

---

6.   Thanks to Richard Larson for pointing out the issue of obligatory stranding.

close to the P *from*, as shown in (48)b, (49)b, and (50)b.[7] While *from* seems semantically "light", none of those silent Ps in these examples is licensed.

(48) a. *Lily really does not like [$_{FR}$ where Jack is coming e].
      b. Lily really does not like [$_{FR}$ where Jack is coming **from**].

(49) a. *Lily is coming [$_{PP}$ e [$_{FR}$ where Jack is coming **from**]].
      b. Lily is coming [$_{PP}$ **from** [$_{FR}$ where Jack is coming **from**]].

(50) a. *Lily wonders [$_{INT}$ where Jack is coming e]?
      b. Lily wonders [$_{INT}$ where Jack is coming **from**]?

To conclude, we have argued in this paper that if silent Ps are assumed in the grammar, we can account not only for adverbial NPs – which had already been suggested – but also for the puzzling syntactic/semantic behavior of a subclass of FRs. In particular, we have argued that a silent P can take a FR introduced by *where*, *when*, or *how* as its complement and that *where*, *when*, and *how* are always base-generated as the complement of a possibly silent P. Silent Ps have allowed us to account for two puzzling properties of these FRs: their NP/PP-like behavior and the restrictions of the internal gap they license. In addition, silent Ps have allowed us to account for unexpected similarities between these FRs and adverbial NPs. We believe there is strong evidence and good reason to assume silent Ps as a component of the grammar. Continued investigation, especially crosslinguistic, would further illuminate their syntactic and semantic properties.

References

Bresnan, J. & Grimshaw, J. 1978. The syntax of free relatives in English. *Linguistic Inquiry* 9: 331–391.

Caponigro, I. 2004. The semantic contribution of wh-words and type shifts: Evidence from free relatives crosslinguistically. *Proceedings of Semantics and Linguistic Theory (SALT) XIV*, R. Young (ed.), 38–55. Ithaca NY: CLC Publications, Cornell University.

Chierchia, G. 1998. Reference to kinds across languages. *Natural Language Semantics* 6: 339–405.

Dayal, V. 2004. Number marking and (in)definiteness in kind terms. *Linguistics and Philosophy* 27: 393–450.

Emonds, J. 1976. *A Transformational Approach to English Syntax*. New York NY: Academic Press.

Emonds, J. 1987. The invisible category principle. *Linguistic Inquiry* 18: 613–632.

Grosu, A. 2003. A unified theory of 'standard' and 'transparent' free relatives. *Natural Language and Linguistic Theory* 21: 247–331.

---

7. Thanks to Grant Goodall for suggesting this kind of example.

Huang, J. 1982. Logical Relations in Chinese and the Theory of Grammar. PhD Dissertation, Massachusetts Institute of Technology, Boston.

Jacobson, P. 1995. On the quantificational force of English free relatives. *Quantification in Natural Languages*, E. Bach, E. Jelinek, A. Kratzer & B. Partee (eds), 451–486. Dordrecht: Kluwer.

Larson, R. 1985. Bare-NP adverbs. *Linguistic Inquiry* 16: 595–621.

McCawley, J. 1988. Adverbial NPs: Bare or clad in see-through garb? *Language* 64: 583–590.

Partee, B. 1986. Noun Phrase interpretation and type-shifting principles. *Studies in Discourse Representation Theory and the Theory of Generalized Quantifiers*, J. Groenendijk, D. de Jongh, & M. Stokhof (eds). 115–143. Dordrecht: Foris.

van Riemsdijk, H. 2005. Free relatives: A syntactic case study. *The Blackwell Companion of Syntax*, M. Everaert & H. van Riemsdijk (eds). Oxford, UK: Blackwell.

PART V

Grammaticalisation

The grammaticalization of prepositional markers in Igbo*

The example of the verb root -*nyé* 'give'

Chinedu Uchechukwu
Institut für deutsche Philologie LMU München

Although prepositions have not been a subject of much research in Igbo linguistics, the few comments on the subject describe the language as lacking in prepositions. This paper argues that the language simply uses different structures to express 'prepositional meanings.' These structures, to be designated 'prepositional markers,' typically arise from the grammaticalization (Heine; Claudi & Hünnemeyer 1991; Lehmann 1995, 2004) and category change of the second verb in a compound verb structure, from a Verb$_1$+Verb$_2$ construction to a Verb+Suffix construction. The verb -*nyé* 'give' is used to illustrate this process and also buttress the fact that the Igbo language does not suffer from a 'poverty of prepositions.' Instead, the tendency is that the verbs with a spatio-temporal meaning grammaticalize into prepositional markers through a persistence of mainly their spatial meaning in a V$_2$ position.

1. Introduction

Although prepositions have not been the subject of much research in Igbo linguistics, one could still recognize a gradual increase in the number of the forms identified as such within the last century. Schön (1861: 74), Green & Igwe (1963: 45) and Emenanjọ (1978: 83) recognized one preposition *nà* 'in, on, at, during, without,' to which Nwachukwu (1987: 23) later added *màkà* 'because.' This was increased to four by Ụwalaka (1997: 69) through her recognition of *n'íhì* 'on account of' and *màkà íhì* 'because of.' In spite of this increase in number, the 'poverty of prepositions' still remains an unaddressed issue. This section introduces

---

* I am indebted to Nolue Emenanjọ (p.c.) for suggesting the title 'Prepositional Markers' and to Christian Lehman and the two anonymous reviewers for their comments and suggestions. However, I bear full responsibility for any shortcomings or inadequacies.

the understanding of 'preposition' and 'prepositional meaning' in Igbo language studies, as well as the particular environment for the structures identified here as 'prepositional markers.'

First of all, the above named works follow the well known method of characterizing a preposition by structurally making "inherent reference to their participation in the prepositional phrase" (Langacker 1991: 153). Thus, Green & Igwe (1963: 45–46) identify three groups of prepositional phrases, made up of nominals, interrogatives and nomino-verbal infinitives, all of which are preceded by the one preposition nà. Emenanjọ (1978: 83–85) characterizes the same preposition as *preceding* nominals and verbals. Finally, Nwachukwu and Ụwalaka simply added the additional forms identified by them, but without any further characterization. However, the discrepancy between the few Igbo prepositions and the numerous English prepositions has not remained unobserved. Emenanjọ for example, speaks in this regard of the additional 'prepositional ideas' that could not be expressed by the few Igbo prepositions, and concludes that "prepositional ideas may be expressed in Igbo through the use of extensional suffixes" (Emenanjọ 1978: 84). The extensional suffixes refer to the suffix components of Verb+Suffix structures, with the suffixes expressing these prepositional ideas. The author does not elaborate on 'prepositional ideas,' but the semantics of these suffixes usually involves such relational meanings as Greenbaum & Quirk describe as the typical *prepositional meanings*, which are "either spatial or figuratively derived from notions of physical space" (Greenbaum & Quirk 1990: 191), and which in English involve such prepositions as *into, out of, towards* and so on. The structures used to express such 'prepositional meanings' in Igbo are mainly verb compounds of either a $Verb_1+Verb_2$ or a Verb+Suffix construction.

The $Verb_1+Verb_2$ compound is usually understood as one event that has an internal *action-result* or *action-goal* meaning (Lord 1975: 29). The first verb expresses the action while the second expresses the result or goal of the action. Two examples in this regard are the combination of the simple verbs -kụ́ 'hit' with -dà 'fall' (-kụ́dà, lit. 'hit fall' → 'hit/knock down') and -bú 'carry' with -bà 'enter,' (-búbà 'carry enter (a destination) → 'carry into'):

(1)   Óbì kụ́-dà-rà   òròmá.
       Obi hit-fall-rv(PAST)[1]   orange.
       'Obi knocked down an orange.'

---

1.   The *-rV-suffix* is also realized as -lV-suffix in the northern Ìgbúzọ̀ dialect. It expresses a good number of grammatical functions. It is marked in this paper as *-rV(PAST)* or *-lV(PAST)* to make explicit which function is meant in the gloss.

(2) *Úchè* **bú-bà-rà**   *ìtè* *ébé* *à.*
     Uche carry-enter-rV(PAST) pot place DET
     'Uche carried a pot into this place.'

Sentence (1) has the typical *action-result* meaning, while the second example has an *action-goal* meaning. Although the second components of the compound verbs in both sentences involve some prepositional meanings in their English translations, these meanings do not seem to diverge a great deal from their meanings as full verbs. In addition, the two verbs -*dà* 'fall' and -*bà* 'enter' are low tone verbs that do not change their tones when used as the Verb$_2$ component of a compound verb. This lack of divergence from their meanings as main verbs, as well as the lack of tonal changes in the compound verb environment, are the two main reasons why the second components of such compound verbs are described as main verbs, leading to the analysis of the whole structure as a Verb$_1$+Verb$_2$ construction.

Verb+Suffix formations on the other hand, evince more tonal variability, although they have the same action-result or action-goal meaning as the Verb$_1$+Verb$_2$ compounds. Sometimes some of the suffixes do not have an inherent lexical tone: instead, they adopt the tone of the initial verb they are combined with. In addition, they also obey the vowel harmony rule, which involves the selection of the vowels of a word from the same harmony group. For example, the eight vowels of the language are divided into two harmony groups, distinguished on the basis of the Advanced Tongue Root (ATR) phenomenon. The two harmony groups are presented in Table 1 below.

Table 1. The two vowel harmony groups

–ATR	ị (I)	ụ (ʊ)	a (a)	ọ (?)
+ATR	i (i)	u (u)	e (e)	o (o)

Many a time when a particular grammatical concept is realized in the language as a suffix, the suffix is realized in two different forms. The vowel of each form is selected from one of the two harmony groups, depending on the vowel of the verb root it is combined with. For example, the suffix to express 'motion towards/to/on' has two forms, _*ta* and _*te*;[2] but in line with the harmony rule, only _*ta* can combine with the verb root -*kụ* 'hit' to yield -*kụtá* 'hit on,' while _*te* can combine with the verb root -*bú* 'carry' to yield -*búté* 'carry to.' This is illustrated in (3) and (4) below where a switch over of the suffixes, as in (3b) and (4b), is unacceptable.

---

2. In the rest of the paper the suffixes are rendered with an initial underscore as in _*ta* and _*te*, and the verbs with an initial hyphen, as in -*nye*.

(3) a.   *Óbì kụ̀-tà-rà*   *m̀ áká.*
          Obi hit-on-rV(PAST) I   hand.
          'Obi hit me with his hand.'
     b.   **Óbì kụ̀-tè̱-rà*   *m̀ áká.*

(4) a.   *Úchè bù-tè̱-rè̱*   *ìtè áhụ̀.*
          Uche carry-to-rV(PAST) pot DET
          lit. 'Uche carried the pot (in the direction of the speaker).'
          'Uche delivered that pot.'
     b.   **Úchè bù-tà-rè̱ ìtè áhụ̀.*

The division between Verb₁+Verb₂ and Verb+Suffix compounds is, however, not often as clear cut as the above presentation. The consequence is some uncertainty with regard to establishing a formal difference between the two. Green & Igwe (1963: 53) and Lord (1975: 33) suspect a verbal origin for some suffixes in a Verb+Suffix environment. Green sees the distinction between verb and suffix as "largely semantic" (Green 1964: 94), but still uses the vowel harmony factor to identify _ta/_te, as in examples (3a) and (4a) above, as a suffix. Similarly, Emenanjọ (1978) admits a possible verbal origin of some of the suffixes in the language, but is more exacting in demanding a tonal, morphological and semantic resemblance to a known verb as the criteria for identifying any second component of a verb compound structure as a verb. Consequently, he sees any deviation from any one of these three qualities, especially the tonal pattern, as qualifying the component as a suffix (Emenanjọ 1978: 99; 1979; 1982).

The above views are further complicated by the fact that the suffixes that function as the second components of compound verbs are generally called 'extensional suffixes' because they "only add something extra to the meaning of the elements with which they are used" (Emenanjọ 1982: 140). However, an examination of the literature seems to reveal that 'extensional suffixes' is a collective term for a group of lexical items of the language that do extend the meanings of the verbs they are attached to, but whose grammatical functions have not yet been fully explored. For example, the extensional suffix _rịrị/_riri has similar deontic and epistemic modal meanings of 'compulsion/obligation/prediction' associated with the English modal verb *must* (Nwigwe 2003: 134–135), and should consequently be identified as a 'modal suffix'; but it has simply been categorized as an 'extensional suffix' (Emenanjọ 1978: 120). The same applies also to a suffix pair like _ta/_te, whose primary function of expressing prepositional meanings in a Verb+Suffix construction is suppressed by including it in the group of extensional suffixes. It is specifically such suffixes like _ta/_te that are being categorized here as 'prepositional markers.'

The above overview highlights the need to make more explicit the semantic aspects and the possible diachronic connections between the Verb₁+Verb₂ and Verb+Suffix compounds in the formation of prepositional markers in the language. In the sections below, I shall use the verb -nyé 'give' to explore the semantic and tonal changes involved in the Igbo Verb$_1$+Verb$_2$ → Verb+Suffix grammaticalization path.

The rest of the paper is organized as follows. Section 2 first introduces the Igbo structures formed with *-nyé* and the issues connected with them. Section 3 examines the spatial aspects of the prepositional markers, while section 4 is on the grammaticalization of *-nyé*. Section 5 forms the conclusion.

2.   The semantics of *-nyé* 'give'

The Igbo verb *-nyé* is like the GIVE verb in any other language that typically involves an act "whereby a person (the GIVER) passes with the hands control over an object (THING) to another person (the RECIPIENT)" (Newman 1996: 1). According to Newman, this scenario involves the spatio-temporal domain, the control domain, the force dynamic domain, and the domain of human interest, all of which are present in the meaning of GIVE (Newman 1996). The spatio-temporal domain involves a physical transfer of THING from the GIVER to the RECIPIENT, while in the control domain, a THING is moved from within the control of GIVER into the 'sphere of influence' of the RECIPIENT. For the force dynamic domain, the initial impulse originates from the GIVER and terminates with the RECIPIENT; within the domain of human interest, the factor of being an advantaged or disadvantaged participant is involved. These four domains play some roles in the uses of *-nyé*. This section first presents the GIVE configuration involved in its literal meaning, before looking at the figurative extensions, both of which form the basis for the grammaticalization of this verb.

2.1   The literal -nyé

The literal aspect of *-nyé* involves the three components of a typical GIVE scenario: a GIVER, a THING and a RECIPIENT.

(5)   *Úchè, nyé m̃ óché áhù̀.*
      Uche give me chair that
      'Uche, give me that chair.'

(6)   *Àdá nyè-rè   Úchè àkpà m̃.*
      Ada give-rv(PAST) Uche bag I
      'Ada gave Uche my bag.'

(7)   *Úchè gà-è-nyé   m̃ àkpá Àdá.*
      Uche AUX-INFL[3]-give I bag Ada
      'Uche shall give me Ada's bag.'

---

3.   This is an inflectional prefix that is realized as *e* or *a*, depending on the rule of vowel harmony.

(8)   Úchè è-*nyé*-lá   m̀ àkpá Ādá.
      Uche INFL-give-PERF   I   bag Ada
      'Uche has given me Ada's bag.'

The additional inflectional morphemes, the prefix *è* and the suffix *lá* in sentences
(6) to (8), neither contribute to nor alter the GIVE scenario expressed with -*nyé*.
Hence, the verb's literal meaning is maintained in all of the above sentences, as it
does not require an additional morpheme to express the typical GIVE scenario.

2.2   -nyé as the first component of a compound verb

The same physical movement of THING to RECIPIENT is involved in the formation
of compound verbs with -*nyé* as V_1, but with some additional meanings sometimes realized as full verb equivalents in other languages.

(9)   Combination of -*nyé* with the verb -*rú* 'reach'
      Ó   nyè-rù-rù   àkpá Ādá.
      he give-reach–rv(PAST) bag Ada
      'He delivered Ada's bag.'

(10) Combination of -*nyé* with the suffix _*cha* 'completely'
      Úchè gà-è-nyé-chá   m̄ há.
      Uche AUX-INFL-give-completely I they
      'Uche shall give them all to me.'

2.3   -nyé as an Inherent Complement Verb

The *Inherent Complement Verb*, also known as a *verbal complex*, is a predominant
structure within the Igbo verb system. It involves the combination of a verb root
with a noun or prepositional phrase to form the equivalent of a simple verb in an
average European language, for example: -*gbá ọ́sọ́* 'run,' -*gbá égwú* 'dance,' -*kpá
nkàtá* 'converse,' and so on. The structure has been compared with the English
phrasal verb (Nwachukwu 1987) and the German *Funktionsverbgefüge* (Uchechukwu
2006). It is especially in the use of -*nyé* to form such verbs that some of the figurative senses and the specific domains of application of the GIVE scenario become
apparent. Sentences (11) to (14) below involve the combination of -*nyé* 'give' with
the nouns *úrù* 'profit or gain,' *ùgwù* 'respect or honour,' *ḿkpé* 'excommunication or
penance,' and *árá* 'madness,' to form the following *inherent complement verbs*: -*nyé
úrù* 'yield profit/be profitable,' -*nyé ùgwù* 'respect or honour someone,' -*nyé ḿkpé*
'excommunicate someone,' and -*nyé árá* 'make someone mad/cause to go mad.'

(11) Òbòdò nyè-rè   hà ḿkpē.
      town give-rv(PAST) they excommunication
      'The town excommunicated them.'

(12)   *Írē   ǹrí   nà-è-nyé   úrù.*
       to.sell   food   AUX-Inf-give   profit
       lit. 'To sell food gives profit.'
       'Food selling is profitable.'

(13)   *Ó   nyè-rè   yà   árá.*
       he   give-rv(PAST)   he   madness
       'He made him mad.'

(14)   *Bíkō,   nyé   yā   ùgwù   yá.*
       please   give   him   respect   his
       lit. 'Please give him his respect.'
       'Please, give him his due respect.'

The different domains of application of the GIVE scenario in the above sentences are made explicit through the noun complements (also known as the *inherent complements*). In sentence (11) for example, no physical object within the spatio-temporal domain is actually passed over to the recipient; instead, the 'town' figuratively acts as the GIVER, that is, the controller and source of a moral force (THING) that, when exercised, is to the disadvantage of the RECIPIENT. The excommunication is the effect of the exerted force 'on' the RECIPIENT. An implicit use of the components of a GIVE scenario is also evident in the other sentences. For example, in sentences (9) and (12) the RECIPIENT in the GIVE scenario is not made morphologically explicit, although it is part of the conventional/general knowledge for understanding the semantics of *-nyé* in the compound verb *nyérú* 'deliver' in sentence (9), and the *inherent complement verb, -nyé úrù* 'give/yield profit or gain,' in sentence (12).

Finally, there is also a slight difference in the nature of the complement to the verb root *-nyé*, either as a full verb, as V_1 of a compound verb, or as the verbal component of an *inherent complement verb* construction. For example, *-nyé* in sentences (5) to (8) can have any entity as its direct object complement (i.e., THING). The same applies also to any compound verb with *-nyé* as its V_1, as in sentences (9) and (10). Its object complements as a full verb or a compound verb can be any entity that can meaningfully be used as the direct or indirect object of the verbs in the language. The *inherent complement verb* construction, on the other hand, is a fixed expression. For example, the verb+noun constructions already highlighted in sentences (11) to (14) above are all fixed expressions, and any change of the complement would either result in another *inherent complement verb* construction or the complement would simply function as the direct object complement. The important point here is that even in an *inherent complement verb* construction, a component of the GIVE scenario, especially the object (i.e., THING, which is also the verb's *inherent complement*), plays a slightly different role. It simultaneously functions as the THING given, as well as the specifier of the domain for the application of the GIVE scenario. For example, although *-nyé úrù* 'yield profit/be profitable' is a fixed expression, the noun *úrù* 'profit' not only functions as the object, i.e., THING component of the GIVE scenario in the construction, it also specifies the domain as the commerce domain.

The next section presents the changes in the meaning of the verb root as the second component of a compound verb structure.

2.4   -nyé as a second component of a compound verb

The most remarkable semantic and phonological changes the verb undergoes are apparent in its occurrence as the second component of a compound verb structure.

2.4.1   *Semantic change*
Here *-nyé* is combined with the verbs *-dé* 'write' and *-bú* 'carry':

(15)   *Dè-nyé   nwókē à   ákwúkwó   íkíké.*
       write-give man   DET book/paper permission
       'Write a permit *for* this man.'

(16)   *Èméká bù-nyè-rè   Íjèómá ìtè.*
       Emeka carry-give-rv(PAST) Ijeoma pot
       'Emeka carried the pot *to* Ijeoma.'

In the above sentences, the verb *-nyé* has mainly 'prepositional meanings' that do not seem to diverge a great deal from its literal meaning involving the movement of THING from GIVER to RECIPIENT. However, a little semantic change can still be detected when seen in the light of the already identified *action-result/goal* meaning of an Igbo compound verb, where the first components of the compound verbs, (in sentences (15) and (16)), express the initial actions, while *-nyé*, as the second component, expresses the *goal* alone in the form of the prepositional equivalents 'for, into, and to.' This semantic modification is further confirmed by the fact that *-nyé* cannot express any of these meanings alone, or as a V_1 of a V_1+V_2 construction, for it always retains its full meaning as a simple verb in both cases.

2.4.2   *Phonological change*
The phonological change has already been shown for the suffix _te/_ta in sentences (3) and (4) above, where in combination with the verb *-kú* 'hit' it is realized as *-kútá*, while in combination with the verb *-bú* 'carry' from the second harmony group, it is realized as *-búté*. Some of the suffixes that harmonize in a similar manner include _gha/_ghe 'durative,' _le/_la 'perfective,' _wa/_we 'inceptive/inchoative.' The verb *-nyé* also forms such a harmony pair in Ìgbúzò, an *Énùànì* dialect of Igbo within the Niger-Igbo region of South-Eastern Nigeria. In a compound structure with a verb like *-gbá* 'eject, let out substance/motion,' which comes from the

first harmony group, *-nyé* is realized in this dialect as *nya*, as in *-gbányá* 'pour in/into,' but with a verb like *-kú* 'scoop (with a concave instrument),' from the second harmony group, it is realized as *-nyé*, as in *-kúnyé* 'scoop, dish out (to someone).'

(17) *Gbà-nyá nḿílī n' ìtè.*
     pour-in water in pot
     'Pour in some water *into* the pot.'

(18) *ọ́ gbà-nyà-lù   ḿmílī n' ìtè.*
     he pour-in-lV(PAST) water in pot
     'He poured in some water *into* the pot.'

(19) *Èméká kù-nyè-lù   Íjèọ́má ōfé.*
     Emeka scoop-give-lV(PAST) Ijeoma soup
     'Emeka dished out soup to Ijeoma.'

In such contexts as sentences (17) to (19), the contrastive pair is *_nya/_nye*, which is similar to any of the other suffix pairs like *_gha/_ghe* 'progressive,' *_we/_wa*, 'inceptive/inchoative,' *_cha/_che* 'completely,' and so on. The consistency of this phonological change can be illustrated by comparing some sentences from the Ìgbúzọ̀ dialect with their realization in Standard Igbo where such a phonological change has not taken place with regard to *nye*. The Ìgbúzọ̀ sentences are the (a) sentences, while their (b) counterparts are their realizations in Standard Igbo. The compound verbs involved are: *-bànyá* 'enter into' (standard Igbo: *bànyé*), *-zúnyá* 'buy for' (standard Igbo: *-zúnyé*), *-bènyè* 'cut out for someone' (standard Igbo: *-bènyè*), and *-kúnyé* 'scoop i.e., dish out for someone' (standard Igbo: *-kúnyé*).

(20) a. *Bà-nyá   n' únọ̀.*   b. *Bà-nyé   n' úlọ̀.*
        enter-into in house   enter-into in house
        'Enter into the house!'   'Enter into the house!'

(21) a. *ọ́ zù-nyà-lù   ṁ ífé.*
        he buy-for-lV(PAST) me something
        'He bought me something.'

      b. *ọ́ zù-nyè-rè   ṁ íhé.*
        he buy-for-rV(PAST) me something
        'He bought me something.'

(22) a. *ó bè-nyè-lù   ṁ ánụ́.*
        he cut-for-lV(PAST) me meat
        'He cut me (a piece of) meat.'

      b. *ó bè-nyè-rè   ṁ ánụ́.*
        he cut-for-rV(PAST) me meat
        'He cut me (a piece of) meat.'

(23) a. *ó kù-nyè-lù   ṁ ófé.*
        he scoop.out-for-lV(PAST) me plate
        'He dished out soup for me.'

b. ó kù-nyè-rè   m̀ ófé.
    he scoop.out-for-rV(PAST) me plate
    'He dished out soup for me.'

In all of the (a) sentences from the Ìgbúzọ̀ dialect, the vowel of the first verb determines whether the suffix is realized as _nye or _nya, but there is no such change in the Standard Igbo sentences.

A further confirmation of the consistency of this phonological change is through the inflectional suffixes. For example, the vowels of the two verbs in sentences (21) and (22), -zụ́ 'buy' and -bè 'cut/slice,' are from the two harmony groups. Within the (a) sentences, i.e., in the Ìgbúzọ̀ examples, this not only determines whether the form should be _nye or _nya, but also whether the following inflectional suffix should be _lụ or _lu. Standard Igbo, on the other hand, is not that consistent, for it uses only the vowel /e/ from the second harmony group, even for the inflectional suffix, regardless of whether the verb's vowel belongs to that group or not.

The (a) and (b) sentences can also not be exchanged within the specific dialect. For example, while (20a) would be unacceptable in Standard Igbo, (20b) would be unacceptable in Ìgbúzọ̀. The same applies to all the other sentences. The acceptance of the (b) sentences to an Ìgbúzọ indigene depends on his exposure to the standard; the reverse is also the case with someone acquainted with either only the standard or with other more central dialects that behave like the standard in this regard. Thus, the phonological change leading to the formation of the suffix pair _nya/_nye is consistent in the Ìgbúzọ̀ dialect; it is yet to be realized in Standard Igbo.

Finally, there are other verbs that also semantically serve as prepositional markers in a V_2 position of a compound verb, but without any phonological change, because they retain their vowels when used as full verbs or as a V_2. Consequently, they do not obey the harmony rule. Some of them are presented in Table 2 below.

Table 2. Verbs with 'prepositional meanings' in a verb$_2$ position of a compound verb structure

Verb$_2$	Verb$_1$(-gbá 'run')+Verb$_2$	Prepositional Meanings of Verb$_2$
-bà 'enter'	-gbábà 'run into'	into
-dà 'fall'	-gbádà 'run down(wards)'	down(wards)
-fè 'go by/ over/across'	-gbáfè 'run over/across'	over; across
-gá 'go'	-gbágá 'run to (a location)'	to(wards)
-rú 'reach'	-gbárú 'run up to'	up to
-sò 'follow'	-gbásò 'run after'	after
-fụ̀/-pụ̀ 'exit'	-gbáfụ̀ 'run out'	out

A common characteristic of all these verbs is a spatio-temporal aspect of their meanings that involves a movement in a specific direction. They are similar to *-nyé* in a V₂ position because, in the light of the identified *action-result/goal* meaning of an Igbo compound verb, they also express the *goal* alone in the form of different prepositional equivalents.

3. The spatial aspects of the prepositional markers

In other to get an insight into the spatial nature of the prepositional markers, it is necessary to examine them in the light of spatial conceptualization, especially as this relates to the typical Igbo spatial preposition *nà*.

Of all the Igbo prepositions, *nà* has a predominantly spatial meaning. As a localizing expression, it is used to establish spatial relations between located objects and reference objects or between the place of a located object and the place occupied by a reference object. These relationships make up the dependencies between located objects and reference objects (Frawley 1992: 251). The dependencies expressed through *nà* are conceptualized as a spatial orientation that involves the inclusion/position of the located object within the space of the reference object, as in the sentences below. The preposition is realized in its full form in (24a), but its vowel is dropped in (24b) as is usually the case when the preposition is combined with a noun that begins with a vowel.

(24) a. *Óbì bì   nà   Légọ́s.*
          Obi live PREP Lagos
          'Obi lives in Lagoes.'
      b. *Èméká nọ̀ n'   ụ́lọ̀.*
          Emeka be PREP house/home
          'Emeka is at home.'

The reference objects, *Legos* and *ụ́lọ̀* 'house/home,' are like containers within which the located objects, *Óbì* and *Èméká*, are positioned. This relationship belongs to the 'prepositional ideas' Emenanjọ sees as being expressed in Igbo through the use of extensional suffixes (Emenanjọ 1978: 84).

A similar relationship between a located object and a reference object can also be confirmed for the suffix pair _ta/_te, whose meaning involves 'motion towards/ to/on,' as in sentences (3a) and (4a), repeated below as (25a) and (25b).

(25) a. *Óbì kụ̀-tà-rà   m̀ áká.*
          Obi hit-on-rV(PAST) I hand.
          'Obi hit me with his hand.'

b. *Úchè* ***bù-tè-rè*** *ìtè áhụ̀.*
Uche carry-to-rV(PAST) pot DET
lit. 'Uche carried the pot (to the direction of the speaker).'
'Uche delivered that pot.'

In both sentences the located objects, *Óbì* and *Úchè*, are not positioned 'in/within' the reference object: instead, there is a spatial relation of surface contact (25a) and direction (25b). The suffix pair _*nyé*/_*nyá*, on the other hand, involves being located or positioned/placed 'within' a container.

Finally, the spatial relationship between the reference and located objects for the different prepositional markers in Table 2 are presented in the last two columns of Table 3 below.

Table 3. The spatial aspects of prepositional markers

Verb₂	Verb₁(-*gbá* 'run')+Verb₂	Meanings as Verb₂	Spatial orientation of located object	Spatial orientation of the reference object
–*bà* 'enter'	-*gbábà* 'run into'	into	within the reference object	contains the located object
–*dà* 'fall'	-*gbádà* 'run down(wards)'	–downwards down	on a higher plane than the reference object	on a lower plane than located object
–*fè* 'go by or over/across'	*gbáfè* 'run -over/across'	over; across	over the surface of the reference object	under the located object
–*gá* 'go'	-*gbágá* 'run to (a location)'	to(wards)	forward – in the direction of reference object	end-point direction of located object
–*rú* 'reach'	-*gbárú* 'run up to'	up to	forward – in the direction of reference object	end-point direction of located object
–*sò* 'follow'	-*gbásò* 'run after'	after	located before the reference object	comes after the located object
–*fụ̀*/-*pụ̀* 'exit'	-*gbáfụ̀* 'run out'	out	outside the reference object	does not contain the located object

The prepositional markers express the same spatial relationships that hold between a reference object and a located object in a locative expression involving a preposition and two nouns, but with the difference that they cannot fully express these relationships as simple verbs or as V_1 of a compound verb, but mainly in a V_2 position as prepositional markers. The differences between a spatial preposition like *nà* and the prepositional markers like -*nyé* are summarized in Table 4 below.

Table 4. The Prepositions and the Prepositional Markers

Preposition	Prepositional Markers
(1) inherent reference to the participation in prepositional phrase	(1) no participation in a prepositional phrase structure
(2) precedes nominals and nomino-verbals in a prepositional phrase structure	(2) does not precede nominals or verbals, but is bound to the V2 position of a V1 + V2 structure
(3) the relational meaning could be either spatial or figuratively derived from notions of physical space	(3) relational meaning could be either spatial or figurative
(4) explicit relationship between the reference object and the located object is expressed in a *locative expression* (Herskovits 1986: 7) that involves two nouns, one before and the other after the preposition.	(4) expresses mainly the spatial relationship between the reference and the located objects in the V2 position
(5) no phonological change	(5) can involve the vowel harmony

The next section examines the grammaticalization issues arising from the above presentation of *-nyé*.

4. The grammaticalization of *–nyé*

The facts of the previous sections necessitate a re-examination of the verb-or-suffix problem of Igbo linguistics (Williamson 1972; Lord 1975; Emenanjọ 1978) in the light of the grammaticalization process (Heine et al1991; Lehmann 1995, 2004).

The grammaticalization process has been identified as involving an "increase of the range of a morpheme advancing from a lexical to a grammatical or from a less grammatical to a more grammatical status" (Kurylowicz 1965: 69). In addition, it also leads to a loss "in autonomy by becoming more subject to constraints of the linguistic system" (Lehmann 2004: 155). The loss in autonomy is especially apparent when the linguistic sign is examined in the light of the 'parameters of grammaticalization,' which actually do not identify the grammaticalization as such but the degree to which a sign is grammaticalized (Lehmann 1995: 127). The degree of autonomy of a linguistic sign can be measured from the *weight, cohesion,* and *variability* of the sign at both the paradigmatic and the syntagmatic angles. The different aspects of these three parameters are presented in Table 5 below.

Paradigmatically, *weight* refers to the *integrity* of a sign as a whole; *cohesion* applies to the degree to which the sign enters a paradigm, while *paradigmatic variability* refers to the possibility of either replacing the sign with other signs or simply dropping it altogether, i.e., the extent to which the sign has become obligatory in the system.

Table 5. The grammaticalization parameters.

	Paradigmatic	Syntagmatic
Weight	integrity	structural scopes
Cohesion	paradigmaticity	bondedness
Variability	paradigmatic variability	syntagmatic variability

Syntagmatically, the weight of a linguistic sign refers to the *structural scope*, i.e., the extent of the constructions it helps to form, while the cohesion would refer to its *bondedness*, i.e., the extent to which it depends on or attaches to other signs. Finally, the syntagmatic variability refers to the possibility of shifting it around in its construction.

4.1   The paradigmatic aspects

The verb *-nyé* has its greatest paradigmatic weight in sentences (5) to (8) above, where its phonological and semantic integrity as a full or main verb are made explicit in the *literal* usage. The same phonological and semantic integrity is maintained in sentences (9) and (10) where it functions as the first component of a compound verb. Even in sentences with *-nyé* based *inherent complement verbs*, as in (11) to (14), the components of a typical GIVE scenario are part of this meaning. But there is a reduction in the semantic integrity of *-nyé* when it functions as the second component of a compound verb. This can be observed in sentences (15) and (16), reproduced below as (26) and (27).

(26)   *Dè-nyé   nwókē   à   ákwúkwó   íkíké.*
       write-give   man   DET   book/paper   permission
       'Write a permit *for* this man.'

(27)   *Èméká   bù-nyè-rè   Íjèómá ìtè.*
       Emeka   carry-give-rV(PAST)   Ijeoma pot
       'Emeka carried the pot *to* Ijeoma.'

Here *-nyé* semantically diminishes by relating more to the *goal* and expressing mainly the 'prepositional meaning' of 'for' and 'to.' Its reduction in phonological integrity can be confirmed in sentences (19) and (21a), reproduced below as (28) and (29).

(28)   *Èméká   kù-nyè-lù   Íjèómá ōfé.*
       Emeka   scoop-give-lV(PAST)   Ijeoma soup
       'Emeka dished out soup to Ijeoma.'

(29)   *ó   zù-nyà-lù   m̀   ífé.*
       he   buy-for-lV(PAST)   me   something
       'He bought me something.'

In combination with the two verb roots *-zụ́* 'buy' and *-kụ́* 'scoop (with a concave instrument)' from the two harmony groups, it now obeys the harmony rule and can consequently be seen as forming the suffix pair *_nya/_nye*.

The paradigmatic cohesion involves formal and semantic integration within a paradigm with some semantic basis. The form *-nyé*, for example, is used to express this 'prepositional meaning' mainly as the second component of a compound verb structure. The same applies also to all the other verbs given in Table 2, even though they do not obey the vowel harmony rule. Thus their formal homogeneity is in their occurrence as the second component of a compound verb formation, while their semantic homogeneity is in their expression of prepositional meanings in such environments.

The paradigmatic variability refers to the language user's freedom of choice with regard to a linguistic sign. To the extent that the language user cannot leave out a structure in a particular context, it becomes obligatory, i.e., relevant in the particular language system, and as such does represent a certain grammatical category. Thus, the verbs shown in Table 2, in being obligatorily used in the V_2 position of a compound verb to express prepositional meanings, belong to the group of 'prepositional markers' that has some relevance within the system of the Igbo language.

4.2   The syntagmatic aspects

The syntagmatic weight or the structural scope of a linguistic sign refers to the structural size of the constructions it can help to form. The structural size decreases with increasing grammaticalization. As a simple verb, *-nyé* has the full structural scope of a main verb at the syntagmatic level. It has the whole sentence as its structural scope, while its structural scope as the second component of a compound verb is narrowed to the VP. Thus, *-nyé* starts as a main verb that functions at the clausal level (see sentences (5) to (14)), but narrows to the VP level in its function as the second component of a compound verb structure (e.g., sentences (26) and (27)). For example, in the sentences below, *-nye* is a full verb in (30), with the whole sentence as its structural scope, but in (31) it is bound as a suffix to its V_1, *-dé* 'write,' where it functions as a prepositional marker.

(30)   *Nyè   nwókē   à   ákwụ́kwọ́   íkíké.*
       give   man   DET   book/paper permission
       'Give this man a paper permit.'

(31)   *Dè-nyé   nwókē   à   ákwụ́kwọ́   íkíké.*
       write-for man   DET   book/paper permission
       'Write a permit *for* this man.'

Syntagmatic cohesion or bondedness refers to the closeness of a structure to another structure with which it bears a syntagmatic relation. This could vary from simple juxtaposition to merger. With an increase in bondedness the sign loses its ability to meaningfully stand alone, and increasingly occurs in combination with another linguistic sign. With regard to -nyé, for example, it can stand alone as a full verb, but is structurally bound as a prepositional marker. The additional phonological change in line with vowel harmony is also a symptom of its bondedness. It is a formal integration within the group of prepositional markers. Even the other verbs of the language illustrated in Table 2, which do not undergo vowel harmony, are also bound to the second position of a compound verb structure for the expression of prepositional meanings in the language.

The syntagmatic variability refers to the ease with which a sign can be shifted around with respect to those constituents with which it forms a construction. There is a reduction in this quality with increasing grammaticalization. As a main verb, -nyé has a greater freedom of movement within a sentence (as far as this is allowed by the language's SVO sentence structure), than in its occurrence as a suffix pair. It can occur as the initial word of an imperative sentence (14), and as the main verb of a simple sentence (6), but can also be modified by auxiliary verbs ((7), (10), (12)). Its fixed position as a prepositional marker ((15) to (23)) does not allow for such variability.

5.　Summary and conclusion

The parameters of grammaticalization indicate that at both the syntagmatic and the paradigmatic levels, there is a loss in the weight and variability of the structure -nyé, but a gain in cohesion.

As the second component of a compound verb formation, -nyé loses in paradigmatic integrity and structural scope and can no longer function as a full verb in this context; instead, it becomes obligatory in the identified V_2 context. In addition, its structural scope narrows to a VP instead of its clausal level structural scope as a main verb. However, these losses in weight and variability are counterbalanced by a gain in paradigmatic and syntagmatic cohesion. Paradigmatically, there is a formal and semantic integration of nyé within a group of 'prepositional markers,' whose syntagmatic quality is being bound to the identified V_2 context for the expression of prepositional meanings.

The development of these prepositional markers from specific verbs also seems to have led to the conclusion that "Igbo prepositions are verb forms" (Nwachukwu 1983: 1). The present state of research, however, seems to point to the conclusion that it is mainly some of the suffixes of the language like _té/_tá that obey the vowel harmony rule, as well as the transparent structures presented in Table 2 above, that together make up the group of 'prepositional markers' in the language.

The problem associated with these structures in Igbo linguistics has always been whether to categorize them as verbs or suffixes, but the insight from the grammaticalization approach is that such a rigidity is unnecessary, because the grammaticalization process is 'gradual' both with regard to the changes the particular lexical item undergoes, as well as with regard to its spread within the language community as a whole.

> a form may be in the process of being reassigned to a different category; some of its tokens exhibit the old properties, others exhibit the new properties (...)(...) An innovative form does not normally emerge all of a sudden throughout the language community. It may be more common in some areas than in others, more common with some speakers than with others.   (Lichtenberk 1991: 39)

The form *-nye* for example, is completely (i.e., semantically and phonologically) integrated within the group of prepositional markers in the Ìgbúzò dialect region, where it exhibits the property of a suffix pair *_nye* and *_nya*; but this is not yet the case in its realization in Standard Igbo, as well as within the Igbo language community in general.

Finally, the recognition of this group of prepositional markers in the language can also be used to address the issue of the kind of categorical shift connected with such structures. It has been argued for example, that a verb like *-fù/-pù* 'exit; go out,' which also functions like other 'prepositional markers' in Table 2, "is a lexical P realized as a verb in Igbo" (Hale; Ihionu & Manfredi 1995: 103). There is no doubt that the verbs used as the second component of a compound verb to express prepositional meanings do include, in their literal meanings as main verbs, some schematic movement in space. Such schematic movements, which have been confirmed for GIVE verbs in different languages (Shibatani 1996), do "persist" (Hopper 1991: 28–30) for the Igbo structures in their function as prepositional markers and in their final realization as suffix pairs that obey the rule of vowel harmony. Their grammaticalization path, in both the Ìgbúzò dialect and Standard Igbo, can be summarily illustrated as in Figure 1 below.

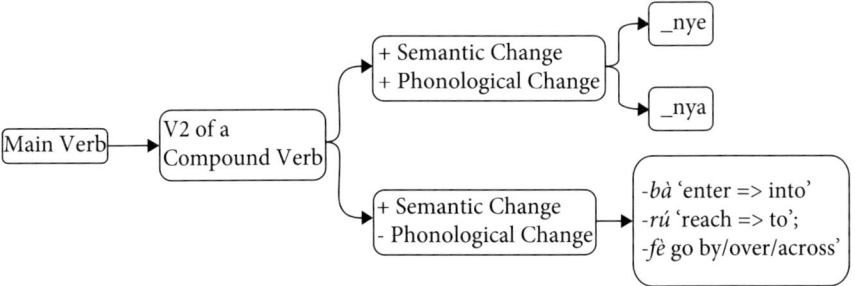

Figure 1. The grammaticalization path of prepositional markers.

The identified grammaticalization path seems to indicate that the diachronic course for Igbo prepositional markers can start with only a semantic change in a V_2 position (as in Standard Igbo), but can also be accompanied by a phonological change (as in the Ìgbúzò dialect). The grammaticalization path is therefore from a lexical verb to a suffix pair, and not from "a lexical P to a verb." Finally, Tables 2 to 4 indicate a tendency for verbs with a spatio-temporal meaning to develop into prepositional markers through the persistence of their spatial meaning in a V_2 position.

References

Emenanjọ, E.N. 1978. *Elements of Modern Igbo Grammar*. Ibadan: OUP.

Emenanjọ, E.N. 1979. On the diachronic aspects of Igbo suffixes. *African Notes* 7(1): 15–19.

Emenanjọ, E.N. 1982. Suffixes and enclitics in Igbo. In *Igbo World* Vol. 1, F.C. Ogbalu & E.N. Emenanjọ (eds), 132–167. Ibadan: University Press Limited.

Frawley, W. 1992. *Linguistic Semanticss*. Hillsdale NJ: Lawrence Erlbaum Associates.

Green, M.M. 1964. Suffixes in Igbo. *African Language Studies* 5: 92–114.

Green, M.M. & Igwe, G.E. 1963. *A Descriptive Grammar of Igbo*. Berlin: Akademie-Verlag.

Greenbaum, S. & Quirk, R. 1990. *A Student's Grammar of the English Language*. England: Longman.

Hale, K., Ihionu, U.P. & Manfredi, V. 1995. Igbo bipositional verbs in a syntactic theory of argument structure. In *Theoretical Approaches to African Linguistics*, Akinbiyi Akinlabi (ed.), 83–108. Trenton NJ: Africa World Press Inc.

Heine, B., Claudi, U. & Hünnemeyer, F. 1991. *Grammaticalization: A Conceptual Framework*. Chicago IL: University of Chicago Press.

Herskovits, A. 1986. *Language and Spatial Cognition*. Cambridge: CUP.

Hopper, P.J. 1991. On some principles of grammaticalization. In *Approaches to Grammaticalization* I, E. Traugott & B. Heine (eds), 15–36. Amsterdam: John Benjamins.

Kurylowicz, J. 1965. The evolution of grammatical categories. *Diogenes* 51: 55–71.

Langacker, R.W. 1991. *Foundations of Cognitive Grammar* 1. Stanford CA: Stanford University Press.

Lehmann, C. 1995. *Thoughts on Grammaticalization*. München: Lincom.

Lehmann, C. 2004. Theory and method in grammaticalization. *Zeitschrift für Germanistische Linguistik* 32(2): 152–187.

Lichtenberk, F. 1991. On the gradualness of grammaticalization. *Approaches to Grammaticalization* 1, E. Traugott & B. Heine (eds), 37–80. Amsterdam: John Benjamins.

Lord, C. 1975. Igbo verb compounds and the lexicon. *Studies in African Linguistics* 6(1): 23–48.

Newman, J. 1996. *Give: A Cognitive Linguistic Study*. Berlin: Mouton de Gruyter.

Nwachukwu, A.P. 1983. Introduction. In *Readings on the Igbo Verb*, A.P. Nwachukwu (ed.), 1–5. Onitsha: Africana-Fep Publishers.

Nwachukwu, A.P. 1987. *The Argument Structure of Igbo Verbs* [Lexicon Project Working Papers 18]. Cambridge MA: The Center for Cognitive Science, MIT.

Nwigwe, V.N. 2003. Mood and Modality in Ngwa Igbo. PhD Dissertation, University of Portharcourt, Nigeria.

Shibatani, M. 1996. Applicatives and benefactives: A cognitive account. In *Grammatical Constructions: Their Form and Meaning*, M. Shabatani & S. Thompson (eds), 157–194. Oxford: OUP.

Schön, J.F. 1861. *Oku Ibo. Grammatical Elements of the Ibo Language*. London: W.M. Watts.

Uchechukwu, C. 2006. Was verrät uns das Image-Schema der Igbo-Verbwurzeln über die deutschen Funkstionsverbgefüge? *Sprachwissenschaft* 31(3): 293–326.

Ụwalaka, M.A.A.N. 1997. *Igbo Grammar*. Ibadan: The Pen Services.

Williamson, K. 1972. *Igbo English Dictionary*. Benin: Ethiope Publishing Corporation.

Index of languages, dialects, and language families

Index of authors

Index of subjects

Linguistik Aktuell/Linguistics Today

A complete list of titles in this series can be found on the publishers' website, *www.benjamins.com*

100 **SCHWABE, Kerstin and Susanne WINKLER (eds.):** On Information Structure, Meaning and Form. Generalizations across languages. 2007. vii, 570 pp.

99   **MARTÍNEZ-GIL, Fernando and Sonia COLINA (eds.):** Optimality-Theoretic Studies in Spanish Phonology. 2007. viii, 564 pp.

98   **PIRES, Acrisio:** The Minimalist Syntax of Defective Domains. Gerunds and infinitives. 2006. xiv, 188 pp.

97   **HARTMANN, Jutta M. and László MOLNÁRFI (eds.):** Comparative Studies in Germanic Syntax. From Afrikaans to Zurich German. 2006. vi, 332 pp.

96   **LYNGFELT, Benjamin and Torgrim SOLSTAD (eds.):** Demoting the Agent. Passive, middle and other voice phenomena. 2006. x, 333 pp.

95   **VOGELEER, Svetlana and Liliane TASMOWSKI (eds.):** Non-definiteness and Plurality. 2006. vi, 358 pp.

94   **ARCHE, María J.:** Individuals in Time. Tense, aspect and the individual/stage distinction. 2006. xiv, 281 pp.

93   **PROGOVAC, Ljiljana, Kate PAESANI, Eugenia CASIELLES and Ellen BARTON (eds.):** The Syntax of Nonsententials. Multidisciplinary perspectives. 2006. x, 372 pp.

92   **BOECKX, Cedric (ed.):** Agreement Systems. 2006. ix, 346 pp.

91   **BOECKX, Cedric (ed.):** Minimalist Essays. 2006. xvi, 399 pp.

90   **DALMI, Gréte:** The Role of Agreement in Non-Finite Predication. 2005. xvi, 222 pp.

89   **VELDE, John R. te:** Deriving Coordinate Symmetries. A phase-based approach integrating Select, Merge, Copy and Match. 2006. x, 385 pp.

88   **MOHR, Sabine:** Clausal Architecture and Subject Positions. Impersonal constructions in the Germanic languages. 2005. viii, 207 pp.

87   **JULIEN, Marit:** Nominal Phrases from a Scandinavian Perspective. 2005. xvi, 348 pp.

86   **COSTA, João and Maria Cristina FIGUEIREDO SILVA (eds.):** Studies on Agreement. 2006. vi, 285 pp.

85   **MIKKELSEN, Line:** Copular Clauses. Specification, predication and equation. 2005. viii, 210 pp.

84   **PAFEL, Jürgen:** Quantifier Scope in German. 2006. xvi, 312 pp.

83   **SCHWEIKERT, Walter:** The Order of Prepositional Phrases in the Structure of the Clause. 2005. xii, 338 pp.

82   **QUINN, Heidi:** The Distribution of Pronoun Case Forms in English. 2005. xii, 409 pp.

81   **FUSS, Eric:** The Rise of Agreement. A formal approach to the syntax and grammaticalization of verbal inflection. 2005. xii, 336 pp.

80   **BURKHARDT, Petra:** The Syntax–Discourse Interface. Representing and interpreting dependency. 2005. xii, 259 pp.

79   **SCHMID, Tanja:** Infinitival Syntax. Infinitivus Pro Participio as a repair strategy. 2005. xiv, 251 pp.

78   **DIKKEN, Marcel den and Christina M. TORTORA (eds.):** The Function of Function Words and Functional Categories. 2005. vii, 292 pp.

77   **ÖZTÜRK, Balkız:** Case, Referentiality and Phrase Structure. 2005. x, 268 pp.

76   **STAVROU, Melita and Arhonto TERZI (eds.):** Advances in Greek Generative Syntax. In honor of Dimitra Theophanopoulou-Kontou. 2005. viii, 366 pp.

75   **DI SCIULLO, Anna Maria (ed.):** UG and External Systems. Language, brain and computation. 2005. xviii, 398 pp.

74   **HEGGIE, Lorie and Francisco ORDÓÑEZ (eds.):** Clitic and Affix Combinations. Theoretical perspectives. 2005. viii, 390 pp.

73   **CARNIE, Andrew, Heidi HARLEY and Sheila Ann DOOLEY (eds.):** Verb First. On the syntax of verb-initial languages. 2005. xiv, 434 pp.

72   **FUSS, Eric and Carola TRIPS (eds.):** Diachronic Clues to Synchronic Grammar. 2004. viii, 228 pp.

71   **GELDEREN, Elly van:** Grammaticalization as Economy. 2004. xvi, 320 pp.

70   **AUSTIN, Jennifer R., Stefan ENGELBERG and Gisa RAUH (eds.):** Adverbials. The interplay between meaning, context, and syntactic structure. 2004. x, 346 pp.

69   **KISS, Katalin É. and Henk van RIEMSDIJK (eds.):** Verb Clusters. A study of Hungarian, German and Dutch. 2004. vi, 514 pp.

68   **BREUL, Carsten:** Focus Structure in Generative Grammar. An integrated syntactic, semantic and intonational approach. 2004. x, 432 pp.

67   **MIŠESKA TOMIĆ, Olga (ed.):** Balkan Syntax and Semantics. 2004. xvi, 499 pp.

66   **GROHMANN, Kleanthes K.:** Prolific Domains. On the Anti-Locality of movement dependencies. 2003. xvi, 372 pp.